Cisco® Router Networking

Paul Ammann

Tata McGraw-Hill Publishing Company Limited

NEW DELHI

McGraw-Hill Offices

New Delhi New York St Louis San Francisco Auckland Bogotá
Caracas Lisbon London Madrid Mexico City Milan Montreal
San Juan Singapore Sydney Tokyo Toronto

Tata McGraw-Hill
A Division of The McGraw·Hill Companies

Tata McGraw-Hill Edition 2000

Reprinted in India by arrangement with The McGraw-Hill Companies, Inc., New York

For Sale in India Only

ISBN 0-07-041299-5

Published by Tata McGraw-Hill Publishing Company Limited, 7 West Patel Nagar, New Delhi 110 008, and printed at Sai Printo Pack, New Delhi 110 044

Dedication

This book is dedicated to my wife, Eve, who has been a tremendous source of motivation.

And also in memory of our fathers, Louis A. Ammann and Edward Altvater.

Contents

Chapter 1   Internetworking Overview 1

The Evolution of Networks 2
    Centralized Processing 2
    Networks.. 3
    Internetworks 4
    Global Internetworking 6
Network Types and Devices............................. 8
    Local Area Networks (LANs) 8
    Wide Area Networks (WANs) 11
    Enterprise Networks.............................. 16

Chapter 2   The OSI Model 21

Open Systems Interconnection (OSI)................... 22
    Peer-to-Peer Communications..................... 24
    OSI Connection-Oriented/Connectionless Modes ... 26
    OSI Adjacent Layer Communication 28
    OSI Profiles...................................... 30
    OSI Summary 30
Physical Layer and Data-link Sublayers 31
    Logical Link Control 32
    Media Access Control 33
Network Layer... 34
Transport Layer....................................... 36
Session Layer... 39
Presentation Layer.................................... 40
Application Layer...................................... 40

Chapter 3   The Network Infrastructure 41

Technology 43
    The Basics 43
    LAN Technologies 45
    WAN Technologies 55
    Asynchronous Transfer Mode (ATM) 74
The Connecting Devices 78
    Hub 78
    Bridge 80

Router 82
Switch 84
LAN Switches 87
ATM vs. Switched High-Speed LAN 90
Factors that Affect a Network Design 91
Size 91
Geography 92
Politics 92
Types of Application 92
Need for Fault Tolerance 92
To Switch or Not to Switch 92
Strategy 93
Cost Constraints 93
Standards 93

Chapter 4   Cisco Router Configuration Basics 95
Router Basics I 96
Configuration Components 96
Router Initialization and Command Modes . . . 98
Router Basics II 103
Logging in to a Cisco Router 103
On-line Help 105
Router Examination 110
Router Configuration 120
Initial Configuration 120
Working with Configuration Files 127
Configuration Control 133
Accessing Configuration 138
Cisco Discovery Protocol 138
Virtual Terminal Connections 141
Basic Connectivity Testing 144

Chapter 5   TCP/IP Addressing 149
Address Management 150
IP Addresses and Address Classes 150
Special Case Addresses 152
Subnets 154
IP Address Registration 160
IP Address Exhaustion 161
Classless Inter-Domain Routing (CIDR) 163

The Next Generation of the Internet Address—IPv6, IPng 166
Address Management Design Considerations 167

Chapter 6   TCP/IP Routing Protocols 171

Basic IP Routing 172
  Routing Processes 174
  Autonomous Systems 175
Routing Algorithms 175
  Static Routing 175
  Distance Vector Routing 177
  Link-State Routing 182
Interior Gateway Protocols (IGP) 184
  Routing Information Protocol (RIP) 184
  Routing Information Protocol Version 2 (RIP-2) 187
  RIPng for IPv6 189
  Open Shortest Path First (OSPF) 191
Exterior Routing Protocols 215
  Exterior Gateway Protocol (EGP) 215
  Border Gateway Protocol (BGP-4) 216
References 228

Chapter 7   Implementing IP-Enhanced IGRP 231

Enhanced IGRP Concepts 232
  Overview 232
  Enhanced IGRP Packet Types 235
  Discovery Methods 236
  Network Routing Table Updates 238
Configuring IP-Enhanced IGRP 239
  IP-Enhanced IGRP Configuration 239
  Enhanced IGRP for IP Integration 241
Routing and Monitoring 242
  Minimizing Routing Updates 242
  Enhanced IGRP Route Summarization 246

Chapter 8   Implementing BGP and
            Route Redistribution 249

Understanding and Configuring BGP 250
  BGP Fundamentals 250
  Configuring and Monitoring BGP 252

Static Routes and Default Networks 258
Route Filtering 260
    Transit Policies 261
    Access Lists and Distribute Lists 262
    AS Path Access Lists 264
    Route Maps 266
Route Redistribution 269
    Understanding Redistribution 270
    Enhanced IGRP and IGRP Redistribution 272
    RIP and OSPF Redistribution 278

Chapter 9   Managing Traffic 285
Managing Complex Internetworks 286
    Internetworking Growth and Hierarchical Design 286
    Introducing Complex Internetworks 287
    Filters and Queues 289
Implementing Traffic Filters 291
    IP Access Lists 291
    Standard Access List Configuration 292
Advanced Traffic Filters 298
    Extended Access List Configuration 298
Queue Configuration 305
    Queuing Overview 306
    Priority Queuing 307
    Custom Queuing 309
    Weighted Fair Queuing 312
Broadcast Management 315
    Managing Broadcasts 315
    IP Helper Address 319

Chapter 10   IPX Overview and Addressing 323
Introduction to Novell IPX 324
    Novell/IPX Protocol Stack 324
    Novell IPX Features 325
    NetWare Media Access 327
IPX Addressing 328
    IPX Address 328
    IPX Encapsulation Types 329

IPX Packet Format 331
Assigning IPX Network Addresses 332
NetWare Transport and Upper Layers 334
IPX SAP and GNS Overview 334
NetWare Transport Layer 336
NetWare Upper Layer Protocols and Services 337

Chapter 11   Implementing NLSP and IPXWAN 341
NLSP and IPXWAN Operation 342
NLSP Benefits 342
NLSP Features 343
NLSP and IPXWAN 346
NLSP Configuration 348
IPXWAN Configuration 354
NLSP Route Aggregation 359
Route Aggregation Overview 360
Route Aggregation NLSP 1.1 Areas 361
Aggregation Configuration of NLSP 1.1 Areas 364
Mixed-Area Route Aggregation 367
Route Aggregation and Mixed NLSP Areas 367
NLSP 1.1 and Enhanced IGRP/RIP Areas 368

Chapter 12   Managing IPX Traffic 375
Managing Complex Networks 376
An Overview of Complex Networks 376
Traffic Congestion on IPX Networks 378
Access Lists and Filters 380
IPX Access Lists 380
IPX Filters 385
SAP/GNS and IP Tunneling 396
SAP and GNS Filters 397
IP Tunneling 404

Chapter 13   AppleTalk Overview and Addressing 411
AppleTalk Overview 412
Understanding AppleTalk 412
AppleTalk's Physical and Data-link Layers 414
AppleTalk's Network and Transport Layers 415
AppleTalk's Upper Layers 418
Network Entities 419

AppleTalk Nodes and Sockets 419
AppleTalk Networks 420
AppleTalk Zones 421
AppleTalk Addressing 423
Network Addresses 423
AppleTalk Address Acquistion 424
Manually Configuring AppleTalk Interfaces 424
Dynamic Configuration with Discovery Mode 429

Chapter 14   Implementing Routing for AppleTalk 433
AppleTalk Routing 434
Datagram Delivery Protocol 434
Routing Table Maintenance Protocol 436
AppleTalk Update-Based Routing Protocol 438
Configuring AppleTalk for Routing 440
AppleTalk Routing Configuration 440
Configuring AppleTalk for Tunneling 443
AURP Configuration 444

Chapter 15   Implementing AppleTalk Enhanced IGRP . 455
Introduction to Enhanced IGRP . . . . : 456
Overview 456
Enhanced IGRP Packet Types 458
Using Routing Tables in Enhanced IGRP 460
Routing Table Updates 462
Configuring AppleTalk Enhanced IGRP 465

Chapter 16   Managing AppleTalk Traffic 475
Managing Complex Networks 476
Overview 476
Traffic Congestion on Networks 477
Queue Configuration 479
Overview 479
Priority Queuing 480
Custom Queuing 481
Weighted Fair Queuing 484
Access Lists and Filters 485
AppleTalk Access Lists 485
AppleTalk Filters 491

AppleTalk Access List and Filter Configuration 494
Setting Network and Cable-Range Filters 500

Chapter 17   WAN Connections 505

Introduction to WAN Services 506
Overview of WAN Service Providers 506
Interfacing WAN Service Providers 507
WAN Services with Routers 508
Introduction to the Point-to-Point Protocol (PPP) 509
Overview of PPP 509
Introduction to Dial-on-Demand Routing (DDR) 510
Overview of DDR 510

Chapter 18   WAN Scalability 513

Scalability Features for WANs 514
Network Connection Considerations 514
Connection Services 515
Packet-switched Services 516
Serial Encapsulation Protocols 520
HDLC, PPP, and LAPB 520
Serial Compression and Channelized T1/E1 522
Serial Compression Techniques 523
Channelized T1/E1 Overview 524

Chapter 19   X.25 Configuration 527

Introduction to X.25 528
X.25 Overview 528
X.25 Encapsulation 534
Configuring X.25 537
X.25 Configuration Tasks 537
Setting the Router as a Switch 544
Configuring and Monitoring X.25 547
X.25 Configuration 552
X.25 Scalability 555
X.25 Throughput v. Bandwidth 555
Call User Facilities 556
Regular Expressions 559
OSPF Using X.25 560

Chapter 20   Frame Relay Configuration 563

Introduction to Frame Relay 564
   Overview of Frame Relay 564
   Frame Relay DLCI Assignment 566
   Cisco LMI Support 569
Frame Relay Configuration 571
   Overview 571
   Configuring and Monitoring Frame Relay 573
   Configure and Monitor Frame Relay 576
Frame Relay Options 579
   Non-broadcast Multiaccess 580
   Frame Relay with Subinterfaces 581
   Subinterface Configuration 585
   Assigning Priorities to DLCI Traffic 586
   Frame Relay Switching 590
Broadcast Issues for Frame Relay 592
   Configuration for Broadcast Traffic 592
   OSPF over Frame Relay 593

Chapter 21   PPP Configuration 597

Introduction to PPP 598
   Overview 598
   PPP LCP Configuration 599
Multilink PPP 601
   Introduction to Multilink PPP 601
   Multilink PPP Configuration 602
PPP Callback 609
   Introduction to PPP Callback 609
   PPP Callback Configuration 610
   Configuring PPP Callback 616
NetBEUI over PPP 618
   Introduction to NetBEUI over PPP 618
   NetBEUI over PPP Configuration 619

Chapter 22   ISDN Configuration 625

Introduction to ISDN 626
   ISDN Services 626
   Functions and Reference Points 628
   ISDN Operation 629

Cisco ISDN Features 631
The Basic Rate Interface 634
   BRI Basic Configuration Tasks 634
   Advanced Configuration Tasks 638
   BRI Configuration on Cisco Routers 641
The Primary Rate Interface 646
   PRI Configuration Tasks 646
   PRI Configuration 649

Chapter 23   **SMDS and ATM Configuration** 651
SMDS Overview 652
   SMDS Networking 652
   SMDS Addressing 654
   SMDS Interface Protocol 655
SMDS Configuration 657
   SMDS Configuration Tasks 657
Introduction to ATM 660
   ATM Overview 660
   ATM Layers 662
   LAN Emulation 664
ATM Configuration 670
   ATM Configuration Tasks 670
   ATM AIP Configuration 673

Chapter 24   **Bandwidth on Demand** 677
Dial-on-demand Routing (DDR) 678
   Overview 678
   DDR Traffic Filters and Authentication 681
DDR and Dial Backup 685
   DDR Using a Rotary Group 685
   Dial Backup 689
   Configuring Dial Backup 691
Configuring DDR Protocol Support 694
   Protocols and Transparent Bridge Routing with DDR 694

Chapter 25   **Transparent and Source-Router
                 Bridging** 701
Bridging Techniques 702
   Bridging Overview 702
   Router/Bridge Operation 705

Bridging Different Media 709
Transparent Bridging 711
Transparent Bridging Overview 711
Learning, Forwarding, and Filtering 712
Spanning-tree and Loop Avoidance 713
Transparent Bridging Configuration 717
Source-route Bridging 721
Overview 721
Multiport SRB Configuration 723

**Chapter 26   Concurrent Routing and Bridging and
Advanced Bridging Options** 729

Concurrent Routing and Bridging 730
Transparent Bridging with CRB 730
CRB Configuration 732
Source-route Transparent Bridging 736
Source-route and SRT Bridging 736
SRT Configuration 738
Source-route Translational Bridging 741
SR/TLB Overview 741
SR/TLB Configuration 743
Remote Source-route Bridging 747
Remote Source-route Bridging Overview 747
RSRB Configuration 748
Data-Link Switching 750
DLSw+ Overview 750
DLSw+ Configuration 754

Index 757

About the Author

Paul T. Ammann is an independent consultant specializing in stalling and configuring Novell, Windows NT, and UNIX servers, configuring and troubleshooting Cisco routers, diagnosing server and client hardware problems, solving network infrastructure (LAN/WAN) problems, and analyzing network performance.

About the Technical Reviewers

As the leading publisher of technical books for more than 100 years, McGraw-Hill prides itself on bringing you the most authoritative and up-to-date information available. To ensure that our books meet the highest standards of accuracy, we have asked a number of top professionals and technical experts to review the accuracy of the material you are about to read.

We take great pleasure in thanking the following technical reviewers for their insights:

Erik J. Freeland, CCNP,CCDA,CNX & MCSE is currently a Network Architect for 20th Century Insurance where he manages the day to day operations of a Cisco based network in a mixed-Frame Relay and ATM configuration running EIGRP. He has over 10 years experience in the networking field and previously served as a Network Manager for Harman International Industries and as a Network Technician for the United States Navy.

Tony Heskitt is a Systems Administrator with 10 years of UNIX and networking experience. He has a B.Sc. in electrical and electronic engineering.

Peter R. Martinez, CCDA,CCNA, MCNE,MCSE, CNE, A+ is currently a Network Engineer with CB Richard Ellis, Inc. where he works as an interface between individual departments on projects related to network infrastructure, server deployment and hardware baselining. In his current position he is also responsible for optimizing the usage of WAN bandwidth and control of NT and IPX broadcast traffic.

Paul Wilkins currently works at Access Systems as a contractor, where he is developing architecture for the maintenance of multiple development environments over distributed server base, employing NIS+, bootp, and Sun's automountd.

Internetworking Overview

This chapter introduces concepts that enable us to move from local to global internetworks. It serves as an introduction to the communication process seen in local, national, and international/global LANs and WANs.

The Evolution of Networks

Centralized Processing

The traditional computer communications environment in the 1960s and early 1970s centered around a host computer, for example a mainframe. In this centralized computing environment unintelligent terminals used low-speed access lines to communicate with the centralized host IBM's computers. Systems Network Architecture (SNA) networks using multidrop lines, and X.25 public data networks are typical examples of this type of networking environment.

SNA, first introduced in 1974, was IBM's scheme for connecting its 3270 family of products (Figure 1.1). SNA was designed in the days when large numbers of nonprogrammable terminals connected to IBM host systems. SNA provided static routing between interconnected hosts so that a user working at one of the terminals could access any of the interconnected hosts.

While SNA was designed for centralized IBM-only mainframe computing environments, it was inadequate in peer-to-peer, client/server, multivendor, and multiprotocol network environments. IBM introduced solutions such as Advanced Program-to-Program Communications (APPC) and Advanced Peer-to-Peer Networking (APPN), which altered the mainframe-centric approach and allowed large and small systems to interoperate as peers.

Accessing resources, running programs, and copying files are relatively straightforward tasks on a single computer or nonprogrammable terminal. The computer identifies the requesting user and the desired destination device or program and coordinates access between them. In this scenario, the single computer is the master of all resources and thus can easily manage and coordinate them.

Coordinating resources becomes much more complex in a network of even two computers. Transferring information requires tasks such as

- **Addressing**—Data structure or logical convention used to identify a unique entity, such as a particular process or network device.
- **Error detection**—Send only enough extra information to detect an error, then request a retransmission from the source. This is called *automatic repeat request (ARQ)*.

- **Error correction**—Send enough additional information to correct problems at the destination. This is called *forward error correction (FEC)*.
- **Synchronization**—Establishment of common timing between sender and receiver.
- **Transmission coordination**—Technique for ensuring that a transmitting entity, such as a modem, does not overwhelm a receiving entity with data. When the buffers on the receiving device are full, a message is sent to the sending device to suspend the transmission until the data in the buffers have been processed. In IBM networks, this technique is called *pacing*.

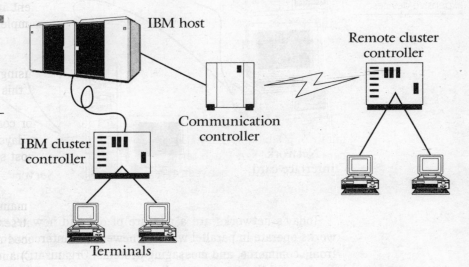

FIGURE 1.1
SNA was designed for centralized IBM-only mainframe computing environments.

IBM host

Remote cluster controller

Communication controller

IBM cluster controller

Terminals

Networks

The introduction of the PC revolutionized traditional communications and computer networks. As businesses realized the flexibility and power of these devices, their use increased. Initially PCs were standalone devices, each requiring its own resources such as disk space and printers. Local area networks (LANs) evolved to connect PCs together and allow the sharing of such expensive devices (Figure 1.2). Early LANs were isolated but organizations quickly realized the strategic importance of interconnecting them. These internetworks provided the basis for enterprise-wide applications such as e-mail and file transfer.

In the 1970s and 1980s minicomputers and shared Wide Area Networks (WANs) evolved. Minicomputers were often located away from the central data center. Their processing power allowed for the emergence of distributed data processing. The Digital Equipment Corporation (DEC) VAX systems and

DECnet networking are typical of this era. In general, however, applications remained separate and independent, and different communications protocols were developed.

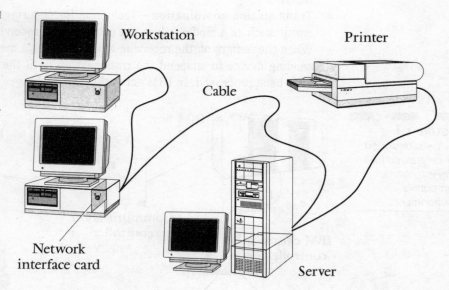

FIGURE 1.2
LANs evolved to connect P.Cs together and thus allow the sharing of such expensive devices.

Today's networks are a mixture of old and new technologies. IBM networks operate in parallel with the newer LAN interconnected networks, electronic commerce, and messaging systems. Organizations have used local networks, public data networks, leased lines, and high-speed mainframe channels on an opportunistic basis, with little regard for overall integration and consistency. Moving applications from central hosts to distributed servers has generated new networking requirements and changing traffic patterns.

The approach to computer communications in most organizations is changing rapidly in response to new technologies, evolving business requirements, and the need for "instant" knowledge transfer. To meet these requirements, the internetwork must be flexible, scalable, and adaptable to suit any organizational level.

Internetworks

Networks have become a fundamental, if not the most important, part of today's information systems. They form the backbone for information sharing in enterprises, governments, and scientific groups. That information can take several forms. It can be notes and documents, data to be processed by another computer, files sent to colleagues, and even more exotic forms of data.

Most of these networks were installed in the late 60s and 70s, when network design was the "state-of-the-art" topic of computer research and sophisticated implementers. It resulted in multiple networking models such as packet-switching technology, collision-detection local area networks, hierarchical enterprise networks, and many other excellent technologies.

From the early 70s on, another aspect of networking became important: protocol layering, which allows applications to communicate with each other. A complete range of architectural models was proposed and implemented by various research teams and computer manufacturers.

The result of all this know-how is that today any group of users can find a physical network and an architectural model suitable for specific needs. These range from cheap asynchronous lines with no other error recovery than a bit-per-bit parity function, through full-function wide area networks (public or private) with reliable protocols such as public packet-switching networks or private SNA networks, to high-speed but limited-distance local area networks.

The down side of this exploding information sharing is the rather painful situation when one group of users wants to extend its information system to another group of users with a different network technology and different network protocols. As a result, even if they could agree on a type of network technology to physically interconnect the two locations, their applications (such as mailing systems) still would not be able to communicate with each other because of the different protocols.

This situation was recognized rather early (beginning of the 70s) by a group of researchers in the U.S. who came up with a new principle: *internetworking* (Figure 1.3). Official organizations involved in this area of interconnecting networks, were the International Telecommunication Union Telecommunication Standardization (ITU-T) (formerly the Committee for International Telegraph and Telephone [CCITT]) and the International Organization for Standardization (ISO). All were trying to define a set of protocols, layered in a well-defined suite, so that applications would be able to talk to other applications, regardless of the underlying network technology and the operating systems where those applications run.

Internetworks tie LANs and WANs, computer systems, software, and related devices together to form the corporate communications infrastructure. An internetwork moves information anywhere within a corporation and to external suppliers and customers. By serving as the organization's *information highway*, the internetwork has become a key strategic asset and a competitive advantage.

FIGURE 1.3
An internetwork.

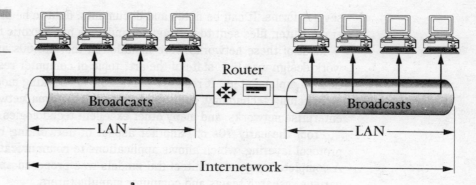

NOTE

An internetwork *is sometimes referred to as an internet, intranet, and extranet.*

An internet *is short for internetwork and should not be confused with the Internet itself.*

An intranet *is an internal network that implements Internet and Web technologies.*

An extranet *is an intranet that has been extended outside the company to a business partner, with transmissions going over the Internet or across private lines.*

Global Internetworking

Today's sophisticated users are placing more and more demands on networks, which must deal with more graphics and imaging, larger files and programs, client server computing, and bursty network traffic. Users nowadays are demanding more bandwidth, bandwidth on demand, low delays and the integration of voice, data, and video.

Future global internetworks will provide even greater bandwidth for new emerging applications. Many of these applications have multimedia requirements of high definition imaging, full motion video, and digitized audio.

Modern network administrators demand the following features from internetworks:

- **Scalability**—A well-designed network should be scalable, so as to grow with increasing requirements. Introduction of new hosts, servers, or networks to the network should not require a complete redesign of the network topology. The topology chosen should be able to accommodate expansion due to business requirements.
- **Open Standards**—The entire design and the components that build the network should be based on open standards. Open standards imply flexibility, as there may be a need to interconnect different devices from different vendors. Proprietary features may be suitable to meet a short-term

requirement but in the long run, they will limit choices, as it will be difficult to find a common technology.

- **Availability/Reliability**—Business requirements demand availability and reliability of the network. A stock trading system based on a network that guarantees transaction response times of three seconds is meaningless if the network is down three out of seven days a week.

    The mean time between failures (MTBF) of the components must be considered when designing the network, as must the mean time to repair (MTTR). Designing logical redundancy in the network is as important as physical redundancy. It is too late and costly to consider redundancy and reliability of a network when you are already halfway through the implementation stage.

- **Security**—The security of an organization's network is an important aspect in a design, especially when the network is going to interface with the Internet. Considering security risks and taking care of them in the design stage of the IP network is essential for complete certitude in the network. Considering security at a later stage leaves the network open to attack until all security holes are closed, a reactive rather than proactive approach that is sometimes very costly. Although new security holes may be found as the hackers get smarter, the basic known security problems can easily be attacked during the design stage.

- **Network Management**—Network management should not be an afterthought of building a network. It is important because it provides a way to monitor the health of the network, to ascertain operating conditions, to isolate faults, and configure devices to effect changes. Implementing a management framework should be integrated into the design of the network from the beginning. Designing and implementing a network and then trying to "fit" a management framework to the network may cause unnecessary problems. A little forethought in the design stage can lead to a much easier implementation of management resources.

- **Performance**—Two types of performance measures should be considered for the network. One is *throughput requirement* and the other is *response time*. Throughput is how much data can be sent in the shortest time possible, while response time is how long a user must wait before a result is returned from the system. Both of these factors need to be considered when designing the network. It is not acceptable to design a network only to fail to meet the organization's requirements in response times. The scalability of the network with respect to the performance requirements must also be considered, as mentioned above.

- **Cost of Ownership**—A network design that meets all the requirements of the organization but is 200% of the budget may need to be reviewed. Balancing cost and meeting requirements are perhaps the most difficult aspects of a good network design. The essence is in the word *compromise*. One may need to trade off some fancy features to meet the cost, while still meeting the basic requirements.

The internetwork must be able to connect many separate, and usually different, networks in order to serve the organization depending on it. It must be able to do this regardless of the range of media attachments, transmission speeds, and other technical details.

The internetwork must be reliable. The organization depends on internetwork tools that include operator interface, the ability to distribute network software updates, utilities to log and monitor performance, and the functions to secure access to resources.

An organization must be able to effectively manage its internetwork. The administrators need to be able to control how the critical resources, such as color printers, are allocated. They also need to be able to straightforwardly perform troubleshooting tasks.

Expanding internetworks demand flexible administrators. Expansion and consolidation efforts may mean overcoming physical or geographic boundaries.

Network Types and Devices

Local Area Networks (LANs)

A LAN is a shared communications system to which many computers are attached (Figure 1.4). As its name implies, it is limited to a local area. This has to do more with the electrical characteristics of the medium than the fact that many early LANs were designed for departments, although the latter accurately describes a LAN as well.

LANs began to appear in the early 1970s They grew from earlier point-to-point connections where a single wire connected two systems. Often the wire was quite long. Why not let multiple computers share the same cable? This required an arbitration mechanism to ensure that only one computer transmitted at a time on the cable. Arbitration methods are called *medium access controls*. Some methods have each workstation determine whether the cable is in use. Other methods use a central controller that gives each station access in turn.

LANs have different topologies, the most common being the *linear bus* and the *star configuration*. (Figure 1.5) In the former, a cable snakes through a building from one workstation to another. In the star configuration, each workstation is connected to a central hub with its own cable. Each has its advantages and disadvantages. Interestingly, the most popular network, *Ethernet*, can take advantage of both topologies.

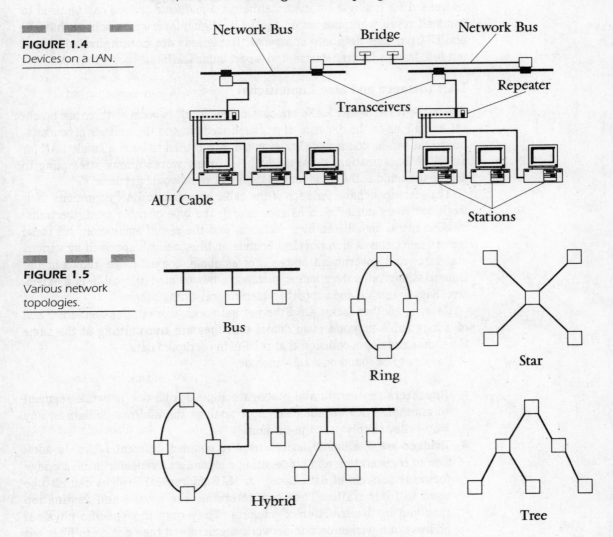

FIGURE 1.4
Devices on a LAN.

FIGURE 1.5
Various network topologies.

A LAN is a connectionless networking scheme, meaning that once a workstation is ready to transmit and has access to the shared medium, it simply puts the packets on the network and hopes that the recipient receives them. There is no connection setup phase in this scheme.

Data is packaged into *frames* for transmission on the LAN. At the hardware level, each frame is transmitted as a bit stream on the wire. Even though all the computers on the network listen to the transmission, only the designated recipient actually receives the frame. A frame is usually addressed for a single computer, although a *multicast address* can be used to transmit to all workstations on the LAN. Higher-layer protocols such as IP and IPX package data into *datagrams*. Datagrams are in turn divided up and put into frames for transmission to a particular LAN.

LAN Distance and Size Limitations

One of the reasons why LANs are considered "local" is because there are practical limitations to the distance of a shared medium and the number of workstations that can be connected. For example, if you tried to build a single LAN for an entire organization, there might be so many workstations attempting to access the cable at the same time that no real work would get done.

The electrical characteristics of the cable also dictate LAN limitations. Network designers must find a balance among the type of cable used, the transmission rates, signal loss over distance, and the signal emanation. All these factors must stay within physical bounds and restrictions specified by various standards and government bodies. For example, coaxial cable allows higher transmissions rates over longer distances, but twisted-pair cable is inexpensive, easy to install, and supports a hierarchical wiring scheme.

Delay is another factor. On Ethernet networks, workstations on either end of a long cable may not even detect that they are transmitting at the same time, thus causing a collision that results in corrupted data.

Devices to be found on a LAN include:

- **Repeaters** regenerate and propagate signals from one network segment to another. They do not change or analyze the address or data in any way—they simply pass the data on.
- **Bridges** are intelligent devices used to connect different LANs. In addition to regenerating and propagating a signal, as a repeater does, a bridge forwards packets of data based on MAC addresses. Bridges can also be used to filter traffic. They can determine the source and destination involved in the transfer of packets. They read the specific physical address of a packet on one network segment and then decide to filter out the packet or forward it to another network segment.
- **Hubs** make it possible to concentrate LAN connections. The devices can be connected to the hub using twisted-pair copper media.
- **Ethernet** and **token ring** switches offer full-duplex dedicated bandwidth to LAN segments or desktops.

- **Routers** are concerned with the routing of packets across a network. They can perform all the functions of bridges as well as much more complex tasks. Routers open up the data packet and make routing decisions based on the contents of the packet.
- **ATM** switches provide high-speed cell switching. They use a cell-relay technology which combines the advantages of conventional circuit- and packet-based systems.

Wide Area Networks (WANs)

The traditional enterprise network has been defined with a hierarchy of network topologies. Internal networks are constructed with LANs, while local and regional networks are constructed with campus backbones and metropolitan area networks (MANs). WANs link geographically dispersed offices. Just about any long distance communication medium can serve as a WAN link, including switched and permanent telephone circuits, terrestrial radio systems, and satellite systems.

NOTE

A MAN is a backbone network that spans a metropolitan area and may be regulated by local or state authorities. The telephone company, cable service, and other suppliers provide MAN services to companies that need to build networks that span public rights-of-way in metropolitan areas. The IEEE 802.6 DQDB (Distributed Queue Dual Bus) is based on QPSX (Queued Packet Synchoronous Exchange), which was developed in 1985 at the University of Western Australia. (Figure 1.6) Complete information on QPSX and DQDB from the Australian point of view can be found at the University of Sydney Web site at **http://www.arch.su.edu.au/~ng_mo/dqdb1.htm**.

WANs are notorious for their high costs and slow data rates, especially if long distance leased lines are required. The slow data rate is due to the nature of the lines that must be used to create WANs and the fact that costs can get exorbitant as data rates increase. A T1 leased line (1.544 Mbits/sec) between two remote offices may cost many thousands of dollars per month, depending on distance. One alternative to a long distance leased line is a satellite link, although the costs and data rates must be compared.

Today, many connections are used to create WANs, as shown in Figure 1.7. Remote offices are interconnected with virtual circuits through packet-switched, frame-relay, or cell-relay (ATM) networks that are more economical than private leased-line networks. In addition, the Internet can provide inexpensive long distance connections between remote offices, or between remote or mobile users at the cost of monthly fees paid to ISPs (Internet service providers).

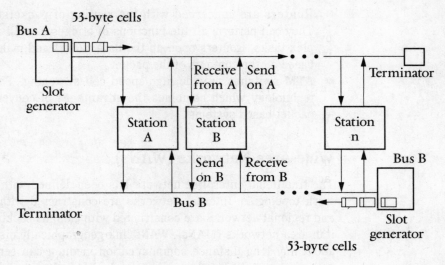

FIGURE 1.6
The IEEE-802.6 (DQDB) metropolitan area network.

FIGURE 1.7
There are many ways to build WANs.

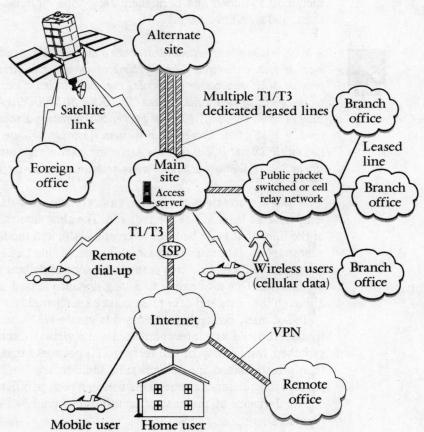

Business-to-business relationships are set up over *extranets*, extensions over the Internet of one company's internal network to another company's internal network. Such connections require authentication and encryption. The inside network must be secured against attacks from the outside with firewalls and other protective measures.

WAN Technologies

At its basic level, a WAN is meant to simultaneously transport the traffic of many users across a transmission medium. Unlike shared LANs, in which access to the network is mediated so that only one transmission can take place at a time, WAN links must accommodate all the users that need to use it although prioritization of some traffic can also be done. That means some technique such as TDM (time division multiplexing), packet switching, or cell relay is required to transport data from many users at the same time.

Routers are also an essential part of the WAN interconnection. They ensure that only WAN traffic is delivered across WAN connections. Routers provide the traffic control that delivers packets to the right destination.

WAN devices include:

- **Routers** that offer many services, including internetworking and WAN interface controls.
- **Switches** that connect to WAN bandwidth for X.25, frame relay, and voice, data, and video communications. These WAN switches can share bandwidth among allocated service priorities, recover from outages, and provide network design and management systems.
- **Modems** that interface voice-grade services; channel service units/digital service units (CSU/DSU) that interface T1/E1 services; and Terminal Adapters/Network Termination 1 (TA/NT1) that interface Integrated Services Digital Network (ISDN) services.
- **Access servers** that concentrate analog (or modem) dial-in and dial-out user communication and provide other services, such as protocol translation between Telnet and X.25 protocol assembler (PAD).
- **Multiplexers** that share a WAN facility among several demand channels.
- **ATM switches** that provide high-speed cell switching.

The technologies for building WANs are:

- Dial-up private networks
- Switched digital services
- Leased-line private networks
- Packet-switching, frame relay, and cell relay services

- Switched Multimegabit Data Service (SMDS)
- Internet (a public packet-switched network)

These communication techniques are briefly outlined in the following subsections.

Dial-up and Modems

A dial-up line can provide an economical WAN connection in a number of scenarios. For example, a dial-up line can be used to provide additional bandwidth when an existing dedicated leased-line WAN link becomes overburdened. A dial-up line may also be used to handle on-again, off-again traffic between corporate sites where little traffic is exchanged. The modem may connect and disconnect continuously throughout the day to handle fluctuations in network traffic, such as e-mail delivery or an occasional user connection. In some cases, it may be more economical to leave a dial-up line on all the time rather than lease a dedicated line from a carrier.

Dedicated (Private Leased Line) Services

A leased line is a communication circuit set up on a permanent basis for an organization by a public service provider such as an local exchange carrier (LEC), a long-distance interexchange carrier (IXC), or both. Because an organization pays a fixed rate for the lines under contract, the lines are often called *leased lines*.

An organization uses leased lines to build *private networks* that interconnect its remote sites or the sites of business partners. The lines are called private because the organization controls transmissions and no one else competes for bandwidth on the line, as with packet-switching networks such as frame relay (although guaranteed bandwidth is available with frame relay). They are also more secure than using open networks like the Internet for wide area connections.

Bridges or routers are set up to direct traffic across the links. Because a fully meshed private network requires a dedicated leased line between each site pair, operating costs increase with the number of sites and the distance between them. For example, to fully interconnect four sites in different cities, you will need six leased lines (one line from each site to every other site).

DSL Services

Digital Subscriber Line (DSL) services are the new kids on the block. The carriers are just starting to make these services available, although they are based on technology that carriers have used for T1 circuits. They provide very efficient throughput on existing lines and customers can use the services in the same way that dedicated leased lines are used, or they can use them to make short-haul connections into packet-switched networks. There are various types of DSL service, ranging in speed from 16 Kbits/sec to 52 Mbits/sec. The most important thing is that DSL services operate over the twisted-pair wiring that exists in the *local loop*, the phone network that is wired to homes and offices throughout the country.

Switched Digital Services (ISDN)

Switched digital services provide many of the same benefits as do dedicated digital lines, including expandable bandwidth. You only pay when the service is connected. Integrated Services Digital Network (ISDN) is the most obvious service. Basic-rate ISDN starts out as two 64-Kbit/sec lines that can be combined to create a 128-Kbit/sec line. Primary-rate ISDN is for companies that need switchable bandwidth in increments of 64 Kbits/sec all the way up to mutlimegabit rates. As bandwidth is required, additional circuits are added and bonded together if necessary.

Packet-Switching, Frame Relay, and Cell Relay Services

These services are grouped together because they provide similar end results, which are any-to-any connections over shared mesh networks that allow variable data rates. The services put data to be delivered into packets (X.25 and the Internet), cells (ATM), or frames (frame relay) that are delivered across a network composed of many point-to-point links. The network has many endpoints and potentially many paths that lead to endpoints, thus providing redundancy and load balancing.

Bandwidth is shared by packets/cells/frames (hereafter called packets) from all the carrier's customers, and assuming the bandwidth is not overbooked, customers can exceed the allotted bandwidth requirements to accommodate surges in traffic at an additional charge from the carrier. The carrier usually defines *virtual circuits* through the network that provide the same guaranteed bandwidth and efficient delivery as a dedicated leased line.

Frame relay is one the most cost-effective WAN technologies available. It allows great flexibility in designing a WAN with a variety of endpoints over wide areas and allows managers to easily change the topology as the organization changes.

Carrier-based ATM networks provide the same benefits with the added features of Quality of Service (QoS), which is useful for prioritizing network traffic, such as real-time audio and video. Another service in this category is Switched Multimegabit Data Services (SMDS).

Remote Access and Wireless Connections

Remote access covers a range of techniques that let home users, mobile users, and remote-office users access remote resources on a corporate network. The usual connection method is through a dial-up modem, although remote access may also be through permanently connected leased lines or even across the Internet. The latter option is discussed next.

The Internet

The Internet is providing a new basis for building wide area networks that span the globe and reduce telecommunication cost. A flat monthly fee to an ISP pays for connection a network that lets you deliver data to any location in the world at no extra charge. The only problem is that the Internet is a shared public network with little security and no way to guarantee bandwidth. If you need guaranteed service, then look into leased lines or carrier-based services such as frame relay. Also, any time you connect an internal network to the Internet, you are essentially opening your network to attack, so firewalls are required.

Still, the Internet provides a low-cost way for mobile and remote users to dial in to corporate networks. Companies can also build virtual private networks (VPNs) over the Internet, which are basically encrypted tunnels through the Internet for delivering packets from one site to another.

Enterprise Networks

During the 1980s and early 1990s, organizations began to install local area networks to connect computers in departments and workgroups. Department-level managers usually made decisions about what type of computers and networks they wanted to install.

Eventually, organizations saw benefits in building enterprise networks that would let people throughout the organization exchange e-mail and work together using collaborative software. An enterprise network connects all the isolated departmental or workgroup networks into an intracompany network with the potential of allowing all computer users in a company to access data or computing resource. It provides interoperability among autonomous and heterogeneous systems and has the eventual goal of reducing the number of communication protocols in use. Toward this goal, industry organizations were formed to create open standards, and vendors developed their own strategies.

The latest trend is to build *intranets* using TCP/IP protocols and Web technologies. While intranet technologies have emerged only recently, they take an approach to consolidating networks different from the traditional enterprise computing strategy. In some respects, the intranet model has achieved better results at less cost and with fewer configuration problems than the traditional enterprise model.

The Traditional Enterprise Network

An enterprise network is both local and wide area in scope. It integrates all the systems within an organization, whether they be DOS-based computers, Apple Macintoshes, UNIX workstations, minicomputers, or mainframes.

Many people thought that a network should be a "plug and play" platform for connecting all sorts of devices, as shown in Figure 1.8. In this platform scenario, no user or group is an island. All systems can potentially communicate with all other systems while maintaining reasonable performance, security, and reliability.

FIGURE 1.8
An enterprise network as a "plug-and-play" platform.

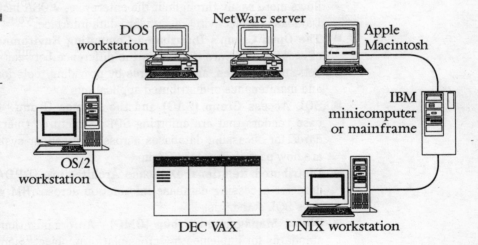

The trick to achieving these "blue sky" objectives is to follow one of two scenarios:

- Create a network platform with underlying standards that allows multivendor hardware and software products to work together
- Create operating systems and applications that support multiple standards.

Over the last few years, both strategies have been implemented. Operating systems vendors included support for almost every network protocol. Driver support was added to clients to access resources on almost any other operating system. It is not uncommon to find a network that simultaneously uses Internetworking Packet Exchange (IPX), TCP/IP, and Systems Network Architecture (SNA) protocols to allow communication with a variety of systems.

However, this strategy has limitations. Just because a Windows NT system supports TCP/IP does not mean that a UNIX station can seamlessly access resources on that system. A higher level of interoperability is necessary, and this is where the enterprise strategies began to show their shortcomings. One solution was to develop client/server computing and middleware strategies that could hide the difference between systems. Here is a sampling of some of the vendor strategies or industry consortium strategies for integrating systems:

- **Microsoft's Windows Open Services Architecture (WOSA)**—A strategy to build middleware directly into its operating systems so that information flows more easily throughout the enterprise. WOSA includes ODBC (Open Database Connectivity), a standard data interface.
- **The Open Group's Distributed Computing Environment (DCE)**—A set of *enabling* software that hides the difference between multivendor products, technologies, and standards by providing tools for the development and maintenance of distributed applications.
- **SQL Access Group (SAG) and the X/Open Group**—Consortia of database vendors that are enforcing SQL (Structured Query Language) standards for accessing databases across multivendor systems. Both groups are now part of The Open Group.
- **Distributed Relational Database Architecture (DRDA)**—An IBM standard for accessing database information across IBM platforms that follows SQL standards.
- **Object Management Group (OMG)**—An organization that is providing standards for implementing cross-platform, object-oriented environments. Common Object Request Broker Architecture (CORBA) is part of OMG's Object Management Architecture (OMA).

The New Enterprise Computing Model

The *enterprise computing strategy* began to take root as more and more organizations adopted TCP/IP. TCP/IP makes internetworking easy. However, a typical enterprise network has a diversity of operating systems, applications, and data formats that restrict the free flow of information. People wanted to collaborate without the need for translating, reformatting, and recompiling their programs and data.

In 1994, people started to notice that the Web provided the heterogeneous environment that people had wanted all along, and that it was practically free. You could use a single interface (the Web browser) to access information on any system running Web server software. In fact, when you access a server on the Web, the server's operating system and hardware platform are unimportant. In this respect, Web browsers are like universal client interfaces.

By the end of 1995, it was clear to many in the industry that at least until something better came along, setting up internal Web servers might be a good way to disseminate information throughout an organization. After all, almost everybody who has access to the Internet has a Web browser. Why not use to access information on back-end database systems and IBM mainframe computer systems?

This new *intranet* strategy brought a lot of things into focus. Why write several different versions of a program to access database servers and mainframe systems when you can write one Web-based application that Macintosh, PC, and UNIX users can access with a Web browser? Web development tools benefit developers, Web site administrators, and users. They merge traditional programming languages and document processing (markup) languages, making it much easier to develop applications with custom user interfaces.

Getting information off database servers and legacy systems is easier because you only need to write a link between the Web server and the back-end system. Users access the Web server and the Web server accesses back-end systems. This is often called a *multitiered approach*. Java applets, ActiveX, and component software technology take advantage of this model.

So intranets are the new enterprise network. This technology has grown without control, for our benefit in most cases. In fact, I sometimes wonder whether we are getting too locked into this technology. At some point, its deficiencies will start to make themselves known. We will then search for new technology to overcome those deficiencies, just as the enterprise network was supposed to overcome the confusion caused by the proliferation of departmental LANs.

The OSI Model

Network communication systems adhere to layered architectures that provide a way for vendors to design software and hardware that are interoperable with other vendors' products. Without open, standardized protocols, you would need to obtain all your networking equipment from one vendor. The OSI protocol stack is the most commonly referenced layered architecture.

Layering is a design approach that specifies different functions and services at different levels in a "protocol stack." The lowest layer defines physical hardware specifications, while the highest layers define user-level application interfaces. Middle layers define network methods. Generally, each layer has a specific set of *services* that it provides to upper layers. Ideally, hardware and software developers only need to be concerned with protocols in a specific layer related to the product they are developing, with a focus on making sure that upper-layer software can interface with it.

Open Systems Interconnection (OSI)

Although we discussed the OSI Reference Model (Figure 2.1) in the first chapter, it is discussed again in this chapter, because of the importance it plays in both network interconnections and internetworking of applications. What should be highlighted is that:

- Each layer performs a unique, generic, and well-defined function.
- Layer boundaries are designed so that the amount of information flowing between any two adjacent layers is minimized. This is accomplished by having each layer within an open system use the services provided by the layer below. Conversely, each layer provides a sufficient number of services to the layer immediately above it.

Below is a brief description of each of the layers:

- **Physical Layer** (Layer 1)—The physical layer describes the electromechanical characteristics for attachment of the open system to the physical medium. These include, for example, the definition of plugs and sockets, definitions of voltage levels and signaling rates, and the mechanism or technique for encoding of data.
- **Data-link Layer** (Layer 2)—The data-link layer is responsible for data transfer between adjacent systems. It detects and possibly corrects errors that may occur in the physical layer. It may also provide flow control function.

FIGURE 2.1
The OSI reference
model.

Layer 7	Application
Layer 6	Presentation
Layer 5	Session
Layer 4	Transport
Layer 3	Network
Layer 2	Data-Link
Layer 1	Physical

■ **Network Layer** (Layer 3)—The network layer provides the addressing, routing, and relay information required to control the data flow between source and destination end systems, and/or among multiple intermediate systems. Controlling the data flow involves establishing, maintaining, and terminating connections between these systems. Services that keep the transport layer independent of the data transmission technology are included. Multiplexing, segmenting, and blocking may also be involved. The network layer also provides internetworking for concatenated subnetworks, such as LANs, X.25 subnetworks, and ISDN subnetworks.

■ **Transport Layer** (Layer 4)—The transport layer provides the end-to-end control of data exchanged between two open systems, which includes:
- Establishing and releasing connections between two end systems.
- Receiving quality-of-service requirements from the session and negotiating them with the network layer.
- Deciding whether to multiplex several connections on a single transport connection.
- Providing end-to-end flow control.
- Arranging the use of expedited data units.
- Establishing the optimum data unit size.
- Segmenting single data units into multiple data units and the reverse.
- Optionally concatenating several data units into a single data unit.
- Providing end-to-end sequencing, error detection and error recovery.

Depending on user needs and the lower layers' capabilities, it provides the required level of reliability of the underlying transmission subsystem. It is this layer that controls the size, sequence, and flow of transport packets and the mapping of transport and network addresses. In addition, it enciphers data if security is needed.

While the session layer is mainly under the control of the application, the transport layer primarily exchanges flows, signals, and operations with the transport facilities beneath.

■ **Session Layer** (Layer 5)—The session layer coordinates the dialog between applications on two open systems by providing functions for negotiating, establishing, controlling, and releasing sessions between these applications. It provides mappings of session-to-transport and session-to-application connections between two cooperating applications.

■ **Presentation Layer** (Layer 6)—The presentation layer provides a common representation or format to be used between application entities. This relieves application entities of any concern with the problem of "common" representation of information, that is, it provides them with syntax independence. It performs encoding and decoding between abstract syntax, which is written in ASN.1 (Abstract Syntax Notation One), and transfer syntax, which is encoded by means of the basic encoding rule for ASN.1. This is necessary because different vendors' systems use various methods for the internal representation of data.

■ **Application Layer** (Layer 7)—The application layer provides services to the actual applications to accomplish information transfer. This involves supporting and managing the communication between end-users on connected open systems, which includes not only exchanges of data but also security checks and requesting other specific application services.

In reality, many implementations of OSI do not include a full seven-layer stack. Instead, a "short stack" of the lower three layers is used to avoid the cost of implementing and using the upper layers. For example, routers use only the lower three layers.

Peer-to-Peer Communications

The OSI Reference Model describes a completely peer-to-peer communications environment. A layer entity of one open system communicates through a set of protocols with its peer entity in the corresponding open system. A layer entity represents one of the seven layers within a given open system.

A given layer entity of Open System 1 communicates with its corresponding entity in the same layer of Open System 2. Both entities use the services of the layers below. This is illustrated in Figure 2.2.

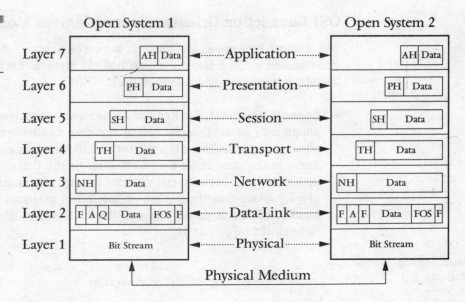

FIGURE 2.2
The OSI peer-to-peer communication.

To accomplish this logical peer-to-peer communication, each layer within an open system uses the services provided by the layer below, and then in turn, provides services to the layer above. The layer providing the services to the layer above is called the *service provider*, and the layer using the services of the layer below it is called the *service user*.

Each layer accomplishes its function:

■ By adding a header to the received data from the upper layer, or
■ By providing data received from another open system to the above layer after handling it according to the protocol information in the header.

As illustrated in Figure 2.2, each lower layer adds or removes the header information depending on the direction of data flow. The header contains the layer-dependent protocol to communicate with another open system using the same protocol.

For example, let's assume that an application entity in Open System 1 wants to communicate with its peer entity, an application entity in Open System 2. To do this, it uses the services of its presentation layer entity (its service provider) for negotiating and defining the kind of presentation. The presentation-layer entity, in turn, uses the services provided by its session-layer entity. This process, referred to as *adjacent-layer communications*, continues down through all layers in the open system.

OSI Connection-Oriented/Connectionless Modes

Two distinct techniques are used on networks to transfer data: the connection-oriented method and the connectionless method. Each has its own philosophy, advantages, and disadvantages.

- **Connection-oriented**—Requires a session connection (analogous to a phone call) be established before any data can be sent. This method is often called a *reliable* network service. It can guarantee that data will arrive in the same order they were sent. Connection-oriented services set up virtual links between end systems through a network as shown in Figure 2.3. Note that the packet on the left is assigned the virtual circuit number 01. As it moves through the network, routers quickly send it through virtual circuit 01.

FIGURE 2.3
A connection-oriented virtual circuit.

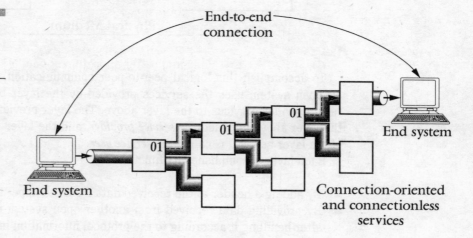

End-to-end connection

End system

01

01

01

End system

Connection-oriented and connectionless services

- **Connectionless**—Does not require a session connection between sender and receiver. The sender simply starts sending packets (called datagrams) to the destination. This service does not have the reliability of the connection-oriented method, but is useful for periodic-burst transfers.

These methods may be implemented in the data-link layers and/or the transport layers of the protocol stack, depending on the physical connections in place and the services required by the systems that are communicating. Transmission Control Protocol (TCP) is a connection-oriented transport protocol, while Internet Protocol (IP) is a connectionless network protocol.

Connection-oriented Service Features

- These features require that a connection be established before data can be transferred. Some setup time is involved.
- The connection that is established is called a *virtual path* or *virtual circuit*.
- Routers along the circuit don't need to make routing decisions because the direction of flow has already been established.
- Packets (segments in TCP) have less overhead and more data because the header only needs the circuit number, not the IP address.
- These features use acknowledgments so that higher-layer protocols are guaranteed that data will be delivered to the destination.
- They are good for long, steady transmission as opposed to short bursts of traffic.
- Because a connection-oriented service guarantees data delivery, upper layer applications can communicate with one another over a network without any need to know about or monitor the activities of the underlying networks.
- Connection-oriented features are implemented by carrier services because they provide easy billing and better allocation of network bandwidth.

Connectionless Transport Service Features

- A datagram service analogous to a letter delivery system.
- Each datagram packet must be addressed individually, adding to the overhead, which means less data is delivered per packet.
- A store-and-forward process moves packets from one router to the next, and each router along the way must make an independent routing decision for each packet.
- Packets may arrive at the destination out of sequence. The destination must spend time organizing such packets.
- There is no setup time involved. A host can send data immediately without the need to go through a session setup process.
- These features do not use acknowledges, which reduces network traffic but requires that higher-layer protocols check for packet delivery.
- These features are good for traffic that is sent in bursts, rather than long steady traffic patterns.

The physical-, data-link-, and network-layer protocols have been used to implement guaranteed data delivery. For example, X.25 packet-switching networks perform extensive error checking and packet acknowledgment because the services were originally implemented on poor-quality telephone connections. Today, networks are more reliable It is generally believed that the underlying network should do what it does best, which is deliver data bits as quickly as possible. Therefore, connection-oriented services are now primarily handled in the transport layer. This allows lower-layer networks to be optimized for speed.

LANs provide connectionless services. A computer attached to a network can start transmitting frames as soon as it has access to the network. It does not need to set up a connect with the destination system ahead of time. However, this activity takes place at the data-link and network level. A computer may still use transport-level TCP to set up a connection-oriented session when necessary.

The Internet is one big connectionless packet network in which all packet deliveries are handled by connectionless IP. However, TCP adds connection-oriented services on top of the IP. Basically, TCP segments are inserted into IP datagrams for delivery across the network. TCP provides all the upper level connection-oriented session requirements to ensure that data are delivered properly.

A WAN service that uses the connection-oriented model is *frame relay*. The service provider sets up permanent virtual connections through the network as requirements or as requested by the customer. Connection-oriented SVCs (switched virtual circuits) are also possible, but many carriers do not yet offer them. ATM is another networking technology that uses the connection-oriented approach.

Generally, network application developers decide which type of service their applications will use. For example, a management application that monitors remote systems for relatively long periods should use connection-oriented services.

OSI Adjacent Layer Communication

Figure 2.4 shows the series of interactions between adjacent layers. The service user in Open System 1 requests a service _1_ from a specific service provider by using a service access point (SAP). A particular layer can provide more than one service to different service users. The service access point, which is a unique interface between two adjacent layers, allows the correct service user to be selected. The service user, in turn, is able to find the corresponding service provider. The service provider entities communicate and exchange data causing the service provider in Open System 2 to indicate _2_ to the desired service user in Open System 2 that a service has been initiated.

Depending on the type of service, the service user in Open System 2 may send a response _3_ indicating that an action has been taken on the information in the indication. The service providers again communicate and the service provider in Open System 1 will confirm _4_ to its service user the action taken on the initial request.

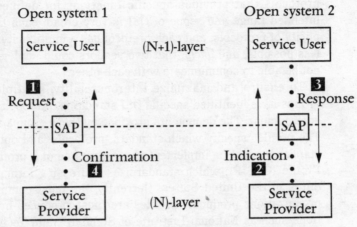

FIGURE 2.4
The OSI adjacent-
layer communication.

for example: (n+1)-layer = Application Layer
(n)-layer = Presentation Layer
SAP: Service Access Point

Layer N uses the services of layer N-1 to communicate with its peer. This continues on down through the layers. At the lowest level, the physical-layer entity in Open System 1 sends the data to its peer, the physical-layer entity in Open System 2. When the data are received by the physical-layer entity in Open System 2, it passes them to the data link-layer entity. This continues up through the layers in Open System 2 until the application-layer entity receives the data.

As previously mentioned, adjacent layer communications use the service access point (SAP) to exchange data and to find the correct service user. A SAP is an internal address that identifies where a service is made available to a user. Each SAP has a *service access point identifier* (*SAP-ID*). Every connection references a unique SAP, which allows multiple communication paths between adjacent layers to exist in parallel. Multiple simultaneous connections may also be established on the same SAP. These different connections are identified by their connection IDs.

SAPs are prefaced with the first letter of the service provider, for example, NSAP for the network layer, and TSAP for the transport layer. The presentation service access point (PSAP) is the point at which the services of the presentation entity are provided to the application layer using the presentation services.

OSI Profiles

Each layer in the OSI Reference Model has a name, a number, and a set of protocols that provides specific functions for defined services. Since the intended range and scope of OSI is very broad, each layer contains a multiplicity of protocols, and each protocol has a multiplicity of options. Therefore, it is possible, and *likely*, that two vendors could implement OSI protocols yet not be able to communicate with each other.

To ensure and maximize interoperability, multiple standards-oriented groups have identified specific OSI standards, protocols, and options for their environment. The documents provided by these groups are called OSI *profiles*. The profiles specify which standard, protocols, and options within the set of standards must be implemented. An example of a profile is Government OSI Profile (GOSIP), which standardizes addressing formats and routing procedures in the United States. Currently, the most common instances of user organizations producing profiles are those produced by government IT functions such as National Institute of Standards and Technology (NIST), which is part of the U.S. Department of Commerce, and Government Centre for Information Systems (GCTA) in the UK.

OSI Summary

OSI has been somewhat slow in gaining acceptance. Standards have taken years to reach full maturity and many areas still require extensive work. Many customers have made large investments in other technologies and continue to generate a high demand for compatible and familiar technologies.

One of the major reasons why customers are not moving to OSI is that OSI requires new and expensive development work. This means that there are not many available products. Not many vendors are willing to undertake an expensive development project unless they are convinced that there will be a huge demand and that the pricing of the product will provide adequate returns.

Another reason, cited earlier, is that many of the standards are complicated and very difficult to implement. A related reason is that many existing non-OSI systems have substantial investments in hardware that cannot adequately support the newer, more powerful OSI implementations. Still other users question whether it is really necessary to go through all seven layers, which could result in poor performance.

Whatever the reason, customers are generally not moving to OSI in one seven-layer cutover. Instead, they express interest in:

- Running OSI higher-layer services, such as X.400, FTAM, or RDA over other networking protocols. For example, X/Open has seen a requirement to run RDA over TCP.
- Replacing other networking protocols with OSI layers 1 through 4, and continuing to run existing applications as well as new OSI applications.

Physical Layer and Data-link Sublayers

Let's look at the two lowest layers of the OSI model, the physical layer and the data-link layer.

At the physical layer, the transmission of data between devices is defined. The definition includes cables and connectors, connector pinouts, voltage levels that represent digital logic levels, bit timing, and the actual network interface device, called a *transceiver* (transmitter/receiver). The IEEE 802 model divides the physical layer into four sub-layers: Physical Layer Signaling (PLS), Attachment Unit Interface (AUI), Physical Medium Attachment (PMA), and Medium Dependent Interface (MDI).

- **Physical Layer Signaling (PLS)**—Defines the signaling and the interface to the transceiver cable.
- **Attachment Unit Interface (AUI)**—Defines the transceiver cable specifications.
- **Physical Medium Attachment (PMA)**—Defines the transceiver operation and specifications.
- **Medium Dependent Interface (MDI)**—Defines the specifications for the portion of the transceiver that connects to specific cable types such as 10BASE5 coaxial cable.

Layer two of the OSI reference model is the data-link layer. This layer is responsible for providing reliable transit of data across a physical link. It is involved with transmission, error detection, and flow control of the data. The major function of the data-link layer is to act as a shield for the higher layers of the network model, controlling the actual transmission and reception process. Error detection and control of the physical layer are the primary functions of this layer, assuring the upper layers that any data received from the network are error free. The IEEE 802 model divides the data link-layer into two sublayers: Logical Link Control (LLC) and Media Access Control (MAC).

Logical Link Control

The LLC is part of the data-link layer in a protocol stack. The data-link layer controls access to the network medium and defines how upper-layer data in the form of packets or datagrams are inserted into *frames* for delivery on a particular network. The underlying physical layer then transmits the framed data as a stream of bits on the network medium.

The IEEE 802.2 standard defines the LLC protocol, which is positioned in the protocol stack as shown in Figure 2.5. Note that LLC resides on the upper half of the data-link layer. The MAC sublayer is where individual shared LAN technologies such as Ethernet are defined. Early on, the data link layer contained only LLC-like protocols, but when shared LANs came along, the IEEE positioned the MAC sublayer into the lower half of the data-link layer.

FIGURE 2.5
Location of LLC in the protocol stack.

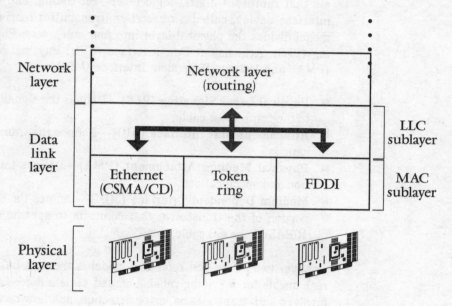

Basically, LLC provides a common interface, reliability, and flow control features. It is a subclass of High-level Data Link Control (HDLC), which is used on wide area links. LLC can provide both connection-oriented and connectionless services.

When LLC receives information from the network layer, it frames the information for an appropriate port (service access point) on the destination system. That port is basically the receiving point for a specific process that runs on the destination system. The MAC layer is responsible for appending the actual physical address of the destination computer to the frame. The physical address is the hardwired address on the network interface card for the destination.

Media Access Control

In the IEEE 802 protocols for shared LANs, the data-link layer is divided into two sublayers, as shown in Figure 2.6. The upper LLC layer provides a way to address a station on a LAN and exchange information with it. The lower MAC layer provides the interface between the LLC and the particular network medium that is in use (Ethernet, token ring, etc.).

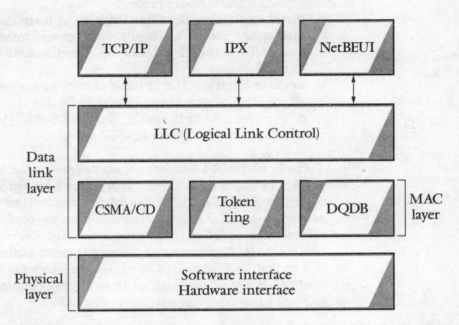

FIGURE 2.6
The MAC sublayer.

The MAC layer frames data for transmission over the network, then passes the frame to the physical layer interface where it is transmitted as a stream of bits. Framing is important because it packages information into distinct units that are transmitted one at a time on the network. If one frame is corrupted during transmission, only it needs to be resent, not the entire transmission.

The other job of the MAC layer is to arbitrate access to the medium shared by all the computers attached to the LAN. On shared networks, two stations cannot transmit on the cable at the same time without corrupting information. The different access methods are described here:

- **Carrier Sense Multiple Access/Collision Detection (CSMA/CD)**—a random access method that is used in Ethenet. Each station attached to the shared network contends for the medium.
- **Token bus**—A distributed technology in which each station gets access to the network in round-robin fashion. A token is passed around the network and held by each station for a period of time. During that time, the station can transmit. The network topology is ring and bus. This access method is used in Manufacturing Automation Protocol (MAP), a factory floor networking scheme.
- **Token ring**—technique similar to token bus except that the topology is ring and star. IEEE 802.5 and Fiber Distributed Data Interface (FDDI) implement this method of access.
- **Distributed Queue Dual Bus (DQDB)**—A reservation protocol in which each station obtains a slot in a synchronous stream of slots divided by time. DQDB is used in the IEEE 802.6 metropolitan area network (MAN) standard.
- **Request priority**—A centralized control access method in which each station is polled serially by a central device. If a station needs to transmit, it is given access to the cable. The IEEE 802.12 standard specifies this technique, and it is used in 100VG-AnyLAN.

Finally, individual LAN addresses are assigned in the MAC layer. A network interface card such as an Ethernet adapter has a hardwired address assigned at the factory. This address follows an industry standard that ensures that no other adapter has a similar address. Therefore, when you connect workstations to an IEEE network, each workstation has a unique MAC address. Workstations on the LAN use the MAC address to forward packets to one another.

Note that LANs connected by routers are internetworks and use a higher-level addressing scheme such as IP to identify each individually connected LAN and a host computer attached to that LAN.

Network Layer

Layer three of the OSI model is the network layer. The network layer sends packets from source network to destination network. It provides consistent end-to-end packet delivery services to its user, the transport layer.

The network layer accepts data from the transport layer and adds the appropriate information to the packet to provide proper network routing and some level of error control. Data is formatted for the appropriate communications method such as local area network, wide area network such as T1, or packet-switched technology such as X.25. A popular protocol that uses the network layer is the IP used by TCP/IP, as explained in the example above.

In wide area networking a substantial geographic distance and many networks can separate two end systems that wish to communicate. Between the two end systems the data may have to be passed through a series of widely distributed intermediary nodes. These intermediary nodes are normally routers. The network layer is the domain of routing.

Routing protocols select optimal paths through the series of interconnected networks. Network-layer protocols then move information along these paths.

One of the functions of the network layer is *path determination*, which enables the router to evaluate all available paths to a destination and determine which to use. It can also establish the preferred way to handle a packet.

After the router determines which path to use it can proceed with switching the packet. It takes the packet it has accepted on one interface and forwards it to another interface or port that reflects the best path to the packet's destination.

When evaluating different paths through a network, routing services use internetwork topology information. This information can be configured by the network administrator or collected through dynamic processes running on the internetwork.

Routers use *routing algorithms* to determine an optimal path to a destination. To aid the process of path determination, routing algorithms initialize and maintain *routing tables*. Routing algorithms fill routing tables with a variety of types of information. This information varies depending on the routing algorithm used. For example, a routing table might hold destination/next-hop associations. When the router receives an incoming packet, it checks the destination address and looks up its routing table. The destination/next-hop associations tell the router that the particular destination can be reached optimally by sending the packet to a particular router. This router represents the "next hop" on the way to the final destination.

Let's look at how routers use network layer to transmitting data. Only a few years ago, bridges were essential devices in corporate networks. Today, routers are more often selected because they provide a better way to connect the individual networks an organization may have installed over the years. Internetworking is all about joining networks with routers. Routers provide the following benefits:

- Limitation of broadcast traffic between networks and intelligent forwarding of packets between networks.
- A security barrier between networks (i.e., routers can filter traffic based on IP address, application, etc.).

- A way to build a network with redundant paths, as shown in Figure 2.7.

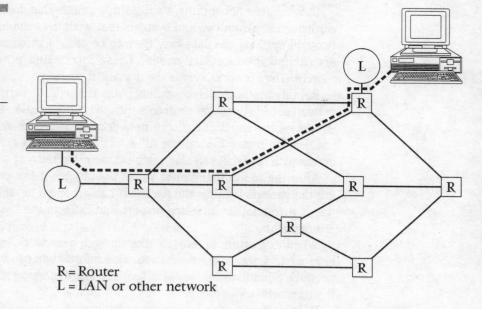

R = Router
L = LAN or other network

Routers join the autonomous networks of the Internet. Each individual network has its own network address as defined by the IP. What IP offers is a higher-level internetwork addressing scheme similar to the way the U.S. ZIP codes provide a way to identify individual cities throughout the nation. In this analogy, each individual network attached to the Internet is like a city or town. Routers examine the IP address and determine the port on which to forward the packet.

To understand the role of routers, it may be useful to consider how the Internet joins the autonomous networks of organizations throughout the globe. The TCP/IP addressing scheme is an important part of the Internet because it provides a way to assign a unique address to all the networks and hosts attached to it. Keep in mind that individual networks already have a MAC-layer addressing scheme that identifies individual nodes on that network. IP identifies individual networks in an internetwork.

Transport Layer

The transport layer deals with the optimization of data transfer from source to destination by managing network data flow and implementing the quality of service requested by the session layer. The transport layer determines the packet size requirements based on the amount of data to be sent and the maximum packet size allowed on the communications media. If the data to be sent are larger than the maximum packet size allowed on the network, the transport layer is responsible for dividing the data into acceptable sizes and sequencing each packet for transmission. During the dividing and sequencing process, this layer adds information such as sequence number and error-control information to the data portion of the packet.

When receiving data from the network layer, the transport layer ensures that the data are received in order and checks for duplicate and lost frames. If data are received out of order, which is possible in a larger, routed network, the transport layer correctly orders the data and passes them up to the session layer for additional processing. A popular protocol that uses the transport layer is Transmission Control Protocol (TCP) used in TCP/IP.

The transport layer provides mechanisms for multiplexing upper layer applications, the establishment, maintenance, and orderly termination of virtual circuits, information flow control, and transport fault detection and recovery. It uses a technique called *multiplexing* to segment and reassemble data from several upper-layer applications onto the same transport-layer data stream.

FIGURE 2.8
The transport layer can engage in end-to-end "conversations" across internetworks.

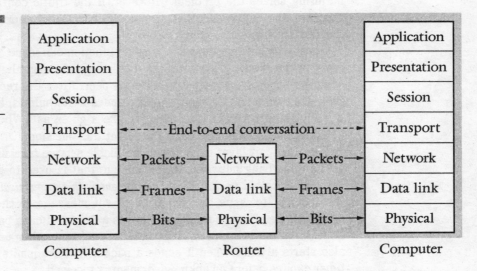

When data are being sent, the source machine includes extra bits with the data that encode the message type, originating application, and protocols used. The destination machine demultiplexes the data stream and reassembles the data for passing up to the destination peer application. The transport layer data stream provides end-to-end transport services. It constitutes a logical connection between the endpoints of an internetwork, that is, the originating host and the destination host.

Before data transfer can begin, both the sending and receiving applications inform their respective operating systems that a connection is going to be initiated. In essence, one machine places a call that must be accepted by the other. Protocol software modules in the two operating systems communicate by sending messages across the network to verify that the transfer is authorized and that both sides are ready.

After all the synchronization has occurred, a connection is said to be established and data transfer can begin. During a transfer using TCP, the two machines continue to communicate with their protocol software to verify that data are received correctly.

Once data transfer is in progress, congestion can occur for two reasons. First, the sending device might be able to generate traffic faster than the network can transfer it. Second, if multiple devices need to send data through the same gateway, or to the same destination, the gateway or destination may experience congestion.

When datagrams arrive too quickly for a device to process, they are temporarily stored in memory. If the datagrams are part of a small burst, this buffering solves the problem. However, if the traffic continues to arrive at this rate, the device eventually exhausts its memory and must discard additional datagrams that arrive.

Instead of losing data, the transport function can issue a "not ready" indicator to the sender. This acts like a stop sign and signals the sender to discontinue sending segment traffic to its peer. After the receiving device has processed sufficient segments to free space in its buffers, the receiver sends a ready transport indicator, which is like a go signal. When it receives this indicator, the sender can resume segment transmission.

The transport layer may provide a reliable service regardless of the quality of the underlying network. One technique that is used to guarantee reliable delivery is called *positive acknowledgment with retransmission*. This requires the receiver to issue an acknowledgment message to the sender when it receives data. The sending device keeps a record of each packet it sends and it waits for an acknowledgment before sending another packet. The sender also starts a timer when it sends a packet. It retransmits the packet if the timer expires before an acknowledgment is received.

Acknowledging every data segment, however, has its drawbacks. If the sender has to wait for an acknowledgment of each data segment, the throughput will be very low. A technique called *windowing* is used to increase the throughput. Time is available after the sender finishes transmitting the data segment, but before the sender finishes processing any received acknowledgment. This is used for transmitting more data. The number of data elements the sender is allowed to have outstanding is known as the *window*. For example, with a window size of three the sender can transmit three data segments before expecting an acknowledgment.

Session Layer

The session layer manages the communication dialogue (the "session") between two communicating devices. The session layer establishes rules for initiating and terminating communications between devices and provides error recovery as well. If an error or communications failure is detected, the session layer retransmits data to complete the communications process. The session layer requests a certain level of service from the transport layer, such as one-way transmission that doesn't require a reply, or a two-way conversation that requires a lot of monitoring and feedback.

Dialogs can be:

- **Simplex (one-way)**—Capability for transmission in only one direction between a sending station and a receiving station. Broadcast television is an example of a simplex technology.
- **Half-duplex (alternate)**—Capability for data transmission in only one direction at a time between a sending station and a receiving station. BSC is an example of a half-duplex protocol.
- **Full-duplex (bidirectional)**—Capability for simultaneous data transmission between a sending station and a receiving station.

NOTE

Binary Synchronous Communication. *Character-oriented data-link layer protocol for half-duplex application. Often referred to simply as* bisync.

Simplex conversations are rare on networks. Half-duplex conversations require a good deal of session-layer control, because the start and end of each transmission need to be monitored. Most networks are capable of full-duplex transmission, but in fact many conversations are in practice half-duplex.

Examples of session-layer protocols and interfaces are Network File System (NFS), concurrent database access, X Windows System, AppleTalk Session Protocol (ASP), and Digital Network Architecture Session Control Protocol (DNA SCP).

Presentation Layer

The presentation layer is layer 6 in the protocol stack, just below the top-level application layer and above the session layer. The presentation layer provides translation of data, defines data formatting, and provides syntax. The presentation layer prepares incoming data for the application layer, where the user views the data. For outgoing data, the presentation layer translates data from the application layer into a form suitable for transfer over the network. There are various encoding rules built into the presentation layer protocols that handle all the data translations. For example, the presentation layer is responsible for syntax conversion between systems that have differing text and data character representations, such as EBCDIC and ASCII.

Application Layer

The application layer is the user's interface with the network. This layer directly interacts with user application programs to provide access to the network. All other layers exist to support the requirements of this layer. The application layer is usually involved with tasks such as electronic mail and file transfer.

The application layer identifies and establishes the availability of the intended communication partner, synchronizes the sending and receiving applications, establishes agreement on procedures for error recovery and control of data integrity, and determines whether sufficient resources for the intended communications exist. Many computer applications include a communications element. For example, a word processor might incorporate a file transfer component.

The World Wide Web links thousands of servers using a variety of formats including text, graphics, video, and sound. This allows millions of users to communicate and use applications such as browsers, search engines, e-mail programs, newsgroup and chat programs, transaction services, and audio/video conferencing

The Network Infrastructure

The network infrastructure is an important component in all network design, simply because, at the end of the day, it is those wires that carry the information. A well-thought-out network infrastructure not only provides reliable and fast delivery of that information, but is also able to adapt to changes, and grow as business expands.

Building a network infrastructure is a complex task, requiring information gathering, planning, designing, and modeling. Though it deals mainly with bits and bytes, it is more of an art than a science, because there are no hard and fast rules for building one. When you build a network infrastructure, you look more at the lower three layers of the OSI model, although many other factors need to be considered. There are many technologies available that you can use to build a network, and the challenge a network manager faces is to choose the correct one and the tool that comes with it. It is important to know the implications of selecting a particular technology, because the network manager ultimately decides what equipment is required. When selecting a piece of networking equipment, it is important to know at which layer of the OSI model the device functions. The functionality of the equipment is important because the equipment must conform to certain standards, it has to live up to the expectation of the application, and it has to perform tasks required by the blueprint—the network architecture.

The implementation of IP over different protocols depends on the mechanism used for mapping the IP addresses to the hardware addresses, or MAC address, at the data-link layer of the OSI model. Important aspects to consider when using IP over any data-link protocol are:

- **Address mapping**—Different data-link layer protocols have different ways of mapping the IP address to the hardware address. In the TCP/IP protocol suite, the Address Resolution Protocol (ARP) is used for this purpose, and it works only in a broadcast network.
- **Encapsulation and overheads**—The encapsulation of the IP packets into the data link layer packet and the overheads incurred should be evaluated. Because different data-link layer protocols transport information differently, one may be more suitable than another.
- **Routing**—Routing is the process of transporting the IP packets from network to network, and is an important component in an IP network. Many protocols are available to provide intelligence in the routing of the IP protocol, some with sophisticated capabilities. The introduction of switching and some other data-link layer protocols has introduced the possibility of building switched paths in the network that can bypass the routing process. This saves network resources and reduces network delay by eliminating the slower process of routing that relies on software rather than on hardware or microcode switching mechanisms.

■ **Maximum Transmission Unit (MTU)**—Another parameter that should be considered in the IP implementation over different data-link layer protocols is the maximum transmission unit (MTU) size. This refers to the size of the data frame (in bytes) that has to be transmitted to the destination through the network. A bigger MTU size means one can send more information within a frame, thus requiring a lower total number of packets to transmit a piece of information.

Different data-link layers have different MTU sizes for the operation of the network. If you connect two networks with different MTU sizes, then a process called *fragmentation* takes place and must be performed by an external device, such as a router. Fragmentation takes a larger packet and breaks it up into smaller ones so that it can be sent onto the network with a smaller MTU size. Fragmentation slows down the traffic flow and should be avoided as much as possible.

Technology

Besides having wires to connect all the devices together, you need to decide the way these devices connect, the protocol in which the devices should talk to each other. Various technologies are available, with differing standards and implementation.

In this section, a few popular technologies are covered and their characteristics are highlighted. These technologies cover LAN, WAN, as well as remote access area.

The Basics

It is important to understand the fundamentals of how data are transmitted in an IP network, so that the difference in how the various technologies work can be better understood. Each workstation connects to the network through a network interface card (NIC) that has a unique hardware address. At the physical layer, these workstations communicate with each other through the hardware addresses. IP, being a higher-level protocol in the OSI model, communicates through a logical address, which in this case is the IP address. When one workstation with an IP address of 10.1.1.1 wishes to communicate with another with the address 10.1.1.2, the NIC does not understand these logical addresses. Some mechanism must be implemented to translate the destination address 10.1.1.2 to a hardware address that the NIC can understand.

Broadcast versus Non-Broadcast Network

Generally, all networks can be grouped into two categories: broadcast and non-broadcast. The mechanism for mapping the logical address to the hardware address is different for these two groups of networks. The best way of describing a broadcast network is to imagine a teacher teaching a class. The teacher talks and every student listens. An example of a non-broadcast network would be a mail correspondence—at any time, only the sender and receiver of the mail know what the conversation is about, the rest of the people don't. Examples of broadcast networks are Ethernet, token ring, and FDDI, while examples of non-broadcast networks are frame relay and ATM.

It is important to differentiate the behavior of both broadcast and non-broadcast networks, so that the usage and limitation can both be taken into consideration in the design of an IP network.

Address Resolution Protocol (ARP)

In a broadcast network, the ARP is used to translate the IP address to the hardware address of the destination host. Every workstation that runs the TCP/IP protocol keeps a table, called an *ARP cache*, containing the mapping of the IP address to the hardware address of the hosts with which it is communicating. When a destination entry is not found in the ARP cache, a broadcast, called *ARP broadcast*, is sent out to the network. All workstations located within the same network will receive this request and check the IP address entry in the request. If one of the workstations recognizes its own IP address in this request, it will proceed to respond with an ARP reply, indicating its hardware address. The originating workstation then stores this information and commences to send data through the newly learned hardware address.

ARP provides a simple and effective mechanism for mapping an IP address to a hardware address. However, in a large network, especially in a bridged environment, a phenomenon known as a *broadcast storm* can occur if workstations misbehave, assuming hundreds of workstations are connected to a LAN, and ARP is used to resolve the address mapping issue. If the workstation's ARP cache is too small, it means the workstation has to send more broadcasts to find out the hardware address of the destination. Having hundreds of workstations continuously sending out ARP broadcasts would soon render the LAN useless because nobody could send any data.

Proxy ARP

The standard ARP protocol does not allow the mapping of hardware addresses between two physically separated networks that are interconnected by a router. In this situation, where there is a combination of new workstations and older workstations that do not support the implementation of subnetting, ARP will not work.

Proxy ARP or RFC 1027, is used to solve this problem by having the router reply to an ARP request with its own MAC address on behalf of the workstations located on the other side of the router. It is useful in situations when multiple LAN segments are required to share the same network number but are connected by a router. This can happen when there is a need to reduce broadcast domains but the workstation's IP address cannot be changed. In fact, some old workstations may still be running an old implementation of TCP/IP that does not understand subnetting.

A potential problem can arise though, when the proxy ARP function is turned on in a router by mistake. This problem manifests itself when displays of the ARP cache on the workstations show multiple IP addresses all sharing the same MAC addresses.

Reverse Address Resolution Protocol (RARP)

Some workstations, especially diskless workstations, do not know their IP address when they are initialized. A RARP server in the network has to inform the workstation of its IP address when an RARP request is sent by the workstation. RARP will not work in a non-broadcast network. Typically in a non-broadcast network, workstations communicate in a one-to-one manner. There is no need to map a logical address to a hardware address because the workstations are statically defined. Most of the WAN protocols can be considered as non-broadcast.

LAN Technologies

There are a few LAN technologies widely implemented today. Although they may have been invented many years ago, they have all proved reliable and stood the test of time.

NOTE

Although different in specifications, the Ethernet, IEEE 802.3, Fast Ethernet, and Gigabit Ethernet LANs will be collectively known as the Ethernet LAN in this book.

Ethernet/IEEE 802.3

Today, Ethernet LAN is the most popular type of network in the world because it is easy to implement and the cost of ownership is relatively lower than that of other technologies. It is also easy to manage and Ethernet products are readily available.

The technology was invented by Xerox in the 1970s and known as Ethernet V1. It was later modified by a consortium made up of Digital, Intel, and Xerox, and the new standard became Ethernet (DIX) V2. This was later rectified by the IEEE, to be accepted as an international standard, with slight modification, and hence, IEEE 802.3 was introduced.

The Ethernet LAN is an example of a carrier sense multiple access with collision detection (CSMA/CD) network. That is, members of the same LAN transmit information at random and retransmit when collision occurs. The CSMA/CD network is a classic example of a broadcast network because all workstations "see" all information transmitted on the network.

FIGURE 3.1
The Ethernet LAN as an example of a CSMA/CD network.

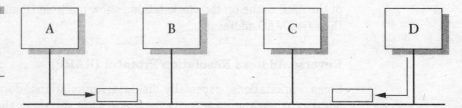

In Figure 3.1, when workstation A wants to transmit data on the network, it first listens to see if somebody else is transmitting on the network. If the network is busy, it waits for the transmission to stop before sending out its data in units called frames. Because the network is of a certain length and takes some time for the frame from A to reach D, D may think that nobody is using the network and proceed to transmit its data. In this case, a collision occurs and is detected by all stations. When this happens, both transmitting workstations must stop their transmission and use a random backoff algorithm to wait for a certain time before they retransmit their data.

As we can see, the chance of a collision depends on the following:

- The number of workstations on the network—the more workstations, the more likely collisions will occur.
- The length of the network—the longer the network, the greater the chance for collisions to occur.
- The length of the data packet, the MTU size—a larger packet length takes a longer time to transmit, which increases the chance of a collision. The size of the frame in an Ethernet network ranges from 64 to 1,516 bytes.

One important aspect of Ethernet LAN design is to ensure an adequate number of workstations per network segment, so that the length of the network does not exceed what the standard specifies, and that the correct frame size is used. While a larger frame means that a smaller number of frames is required to transmit a single piece of information, it can mean that there is a greater chance of collisions. On the other hand, a smaller frame reduces the chance of a collision, but it then takes more frames to transmit the same piece of information.

We mentioned earlier that the Ethernet and IEEE 802.3 standards are not the same. The difference lies in the frame format (Figure 3.2), which means workstations configured with Ethernet will not be able to communicate with workstations that have been configured with IEEE 802.3.

We discuss the difference in frame format below.

FIGURE 3.2
Ethernet frame versus
IEEE 802.3 frame.

Ethernet	Preamble	Start Frame Delimiter	Destination Address	Source Address	Length	Data	Frame Check Sequence
	1010...1010	1010...1010					
	62 Bits	2 Bits	6 Bytes	6 Bytes	2 Bytes	46-1500 Bytes	4 Bytes

IEEE BO2.3	Preamble	Sync	Destination Address	Source Address	Type	Data	Frame Check Sequence
	1010...1010	11					
	56 Bits	8 Bits	6 Bytes	6 Bytes	2 Bytes	46-1500 Bytes	4 Bytes

To implement Ethernet, network managers need to follow certain rules, which can be closely allied to the type of cables being used. Ethernet can be implemented using coaxial (10Base5 or 10Base2), fiber optic (10BaseF), or UTP Category 3 cables (10BaseT). These different cabling types impose different restrictions and it is important to know the difference. Also, Ethernet generally follows the 5-4-3 rule. That is, in a single collision domain, there can be only five physical segments, connected by four repeaters. No two communicating workstations can be separated by more than three segments. The other two segments must be link segments, that is, with no workstations attached to them.

Although it was once thought that Ethernet would not scale and thus would be replaced by other better technologies, vendors have made modifications and improvements to its delivery capabilities to make it more efficient. The Ethernet technology has evolved from the traditional 10-Mbps network to the 100-Mbps network or Fast Ethernet, and now to the 1 Gbps network, or better known as Gigabit Ethernet.

TABLE 3.1
Comparing Ethernet
technologies.

	10Base5	10Base2	10BaseT
Topology	Bus	Bus	Star
Cabling type	Coaxial	Coaxial	UTP
Maximum cable length	500m	185m	100m
Topology limitation	5-4-3 rule	5-4-3 rule	5-4-3 rule
Maximum number of workstations on a single segment	100	30	1 (requires the workstation to be connected to a hub)

The Fast Ethernet, or the IEEE 802.3u, standard is 10 times faster than the 10-Mbps Ethernet. The cabling used for Fast Ethernet is 100BaseTx, 100BaseT4, and 100BaseFx. The framing used in Fast Ethernet is the same as that used in Ethernet. Therefore it is very easy for network managers to upgrade from Ethernet to Fast Ethernet. Since the framing and size are the same as in Ethernet, and yet the speed has been increased 10 times, the length of the network now has to be greatly reduced, or else the collision would not be detected and would cause problems to the network.

The Gigabit Ethernet, or IEEE 802.3z, standard is 10 times faster than Fast Ethernet. The framing used is still the same as that of Ethernet, and thus reduces the network distance by a tremendous amount as compared to the Ethernet. Gigabit Ethernet is usually connected using short wavelength (1000BaseSx) or long wavelength (1000BaseLx) fiber optic cables, although the standard for the UTP (1000BaseT) is available now. The distance limitation has been resolved with the new fiber optic technologies.

Gigabit Ethernet is mainly used for creating high-speed backbones, a simple and logical choice for upgrading current Fast Ethernet backbones. Many switches with 100BaseT ports are beginning to offer a Gigabit Ethernet port as an uplink port, so that more bandwidth can be provided for connections to the higher level of network for access to servers.

NOTE

It is generally agreed that the maximum "usable" bandwidth for Ethernet LAN is about 40%, after which the effect of collision is so bad that efficiency begins to drop.

Besides raw speed improvement, new devices such as switches now provide duplex mode operation, which allows workstations to send and receive data at the same time, effectively doubling the bandwidth for the connection. Duplex mode operation requires a Category-5 UTP cable, with two pairs of wire used for transmitting and receiving data. Therefore, the operation of duplex mode may not work on old networks because they usually run on Category-3 UTP cables.

Most of the early Ethernet workstations are connected to the LAN at 10 Mbps because they were implemented quite some time ago. The 10-Mbps connection is still popular as the network interface card and 10 Mbps hubs are very affordable. At this point, it is important to note that in network planning and design, more bandwidth or a faster network does not mean that the user will benefit from the speed. Due to the development of higher-speed networks such as Fast Ethernet and Gigabit Ethernet, a 10-Mbps network seems to have become less popular. It can still carry a lot of information and a user may not be able to handle the information if there is anymore available. With the introduction of switches that provide dedicated 10-Mbps connection to each user, this has become even more true. Table 3.2 shows the information a 10-Mbps connection can carry.

TABLE 3.2
Application bandwidth requirements.

Applications	Mbps Bandwidth Occupied
Network applications (read e-mail, save some spreadsheets)	2
Voice	0.064
Watching MPEG-1 training video (small window)	0.6
Videoconferencing	0.384
Total bandwidth	<4

The question now is: Can a user clear his/her e-mail inbox, save some spreadsheet data to the server, talk to his/her colleague through the telephony software, watch a training video produced by the finance department, and participate in a videoconferencing meeting, all at the same time?

Giving a user a 100-Mbps connection may not mean it would be utilized adequately. A 10-Mbps connection is still a good solution to use for its cost effectiveness and may be a good option to meet certain budget constraints, while keeping an upgrade option open for the future.

Nowadays, with card vendors manufacturing mostly 10/100-Mbps Ethernet cards, more and more workstations have the option of connecting to the network at 100-Mbps. Gigabit Ethernet is a new technology and is positioned to be a backbone technology rather than being used to connect to end-users. As standards evolve, Gigabit Ethernet will be widely used in the data center and most of the servers that connect to the network at 100-Mbps today will eventually move to Gigabit Ethernet.

Ethernet is a good technology to deploy for a low-volume network or application that does not demand high bandwidth. Because it does not have complicated access control to the network, it is simple and can provide better efficiency in delivery of data. Due to the indeterministic nature of collision, response time in an Ethernet cannot be determined and hence, another technology has to be deployed in the event this is needed.

Although Ethernet technology has been around for quite a time, it will be deployed for many years to come because it is simple and economical. Its plug-and-play nature allows it to be positioned as a consumer product and users require very little training to se up an Ethernet LAN. With the explosion of Internet usage and e-commerce, more companies, especially the small ones and the small, home office (SoHo) establishment, will continue to drive the demand for Ethernet products.

Token Ring/IEEE 802.5

NOTE

Although different in specifications, both the IBM Token Ring and IEEE 802.5 LANs will be collectively known as the token ring LAN in this book.

The token ring technology was invented by IBM in the 1970s and is the second most popular LAN architecture. It supports speeds of 1, 4, or 16 Mbps. There is a new technology, called the High-Speed Token Ring being developed by the IEEE and it will run at 100 Mbps.

The token-ring LAN is an example of a token-passing network; that is, members of the LAN transmit information only when they get hold of the token. Since the transmission of data is decided by the control of the token, a token-ring LAN has no collision.

As Figure 3.3 shows, all workstations are connected to the network in a logical ring manner, and access to the ring is controlled by a circulating token frame. When station A with data to transmit to D receives the token, it changes the content of the token frame, appends data to the frame and retransmits the frame. As the frame passes station B, B checks to see if the frame is meant for it. Since the data are meant for D, B then retransmits the frame; this action is repeated through C and finally to D. When D receives the frame, it copies the information in the frame, sees the frame copied and address recognition bits and retransmits the modified frame in the network. Eventually, A receives the frame, strips the information from it, and releases a new token into the ring so that other workstations may use it. Figure 3.4 shows the frame formats for data and token frames.

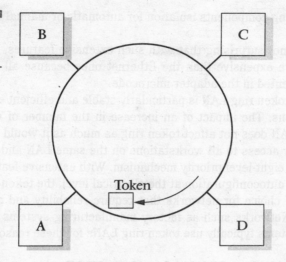

FIGURE 3.3
Passing of token in a token-ring LAN.

Token Frame

FIGURE 3.4
Token-ring frame formats.

Start Delimiter	Access Control	End Delimiter	
1	1	1	Byte Length

Data Frame

Start Delimiter	Access Control	Frame Control	Destination Address	Source Address	Data	Frame Check Sequence	End Delimiter	
1	1	1	6	6	710	4	1	Byte Length

As described, the token passing technique is different from Ethernet's random manner of access. This important feature makes a token-ring LAN deterministic and allows delays to be determined. Besides this difference, token ring also offers extensive network diagnostics and self-recovery features such as:

- Power-on and ring insertion diagnostics
- Lobe-insertion testing and online lobe fault detection
- Signal loss detection, beacon support for automatic test and removal
- Active and standby ring monitor functions
- Ring transmission errors detection and reporting

■ Failing components isolation for automatic or manual recovery

It is not surprising that with such extensive features, token-ring adapters are more expensive than the Ethernet ones because all these functions are implemented in the adapter microcode.

The token-ring LAN is particularly stable and efficient even under high-load conditions. The impact of an increase in the number of workstations on the same LAN does not affect token ring as much as it would Ethernet. It guarantees fair access to all workstations on the same LAN and is further enhanced with an eight-level priority mechanism. With extensive features like self-recovery and autoconfiguration at the electrical level, the token-ring LAN is the network of choice for networks that require reliability and predictable response times. Networks such as factory manufacturing systems and airline reservation systems typically use token-ring LANs for these reasons.

Fiber Distributed Digital Interface (FDDI)

FDDI was developed in the early 1980s for high-speed host connections but it soon became a popular choice for building LAN backbones. Much as in the token-ring LAN, FDDI uses a token-passing method to operate but it uses two rings, one primary and one secondary, running at 100 Mbps. Under normal conditions, the primary ring is used while the secondary is in a standby mode. FDDI provides flexibility in its connectivity and redundancy and offers a few ways of connecting the workstations, one of which is called the *dual attachment station ring*.

In a dual attachment station ring, workstations are called Dual Attachment Stations (DAS). All of them have two ports (A and B) available for connection to the network as shown in Figure 3.5.

In the figure, the network consists of a primary ring and a secondary ring in which data flows in opposite directions. Under normal conditions, data flows in the primary ring and the secondary merely functions as a backup. In the event of a DAS or cable failure, the two adjacent DASs would "wrap" their respective ports that are connected to the failed DAS. The network now becomes a single ring and continues to operate as shown in Figure 3.6.

It is easy to note the robustness of FDDI and appreciate its use in a high-availability network. Since it is similar in nature to token ring, FDDI offers capabilities such as self-recovery and security. Because it mostly runs on fiber, it is not affected by electromagnetic interference. Due to its robustness and high speed, FDDI was being touted as the backbone of choice. But with the development of 100-Mbps Ethernet technology, network managers who are going for bandwidth rather than reliability have chosen to implement 100-Mbps

Ethernet rather than FDDI. Though it may not be as popular as Ethernet or token ring, one can still find many networks operating on FDDI technology.

FIGURE 3.5
FDDI dual
attachment rings.

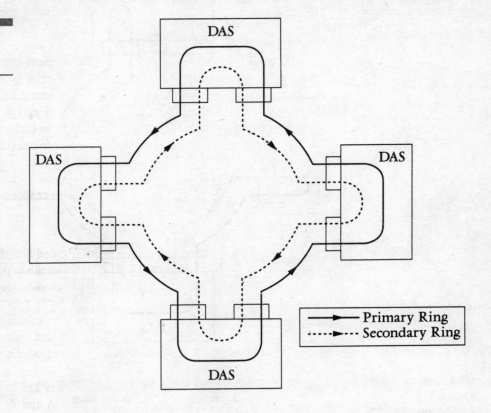

The Ethernet, token-ring, and FDDI technologies are generally referred to as the legacy LANs, as opposed to new technology like ATM.

NOTE

Comparison of LAN Technologies

It is appropriate, at this point, to compare the various LAN technologies we have discussed. These technologies are the most popular ones deployed, and each tends to be dominant in certain particular working environments.

FIGURE 3.6
FDDI redundancy.

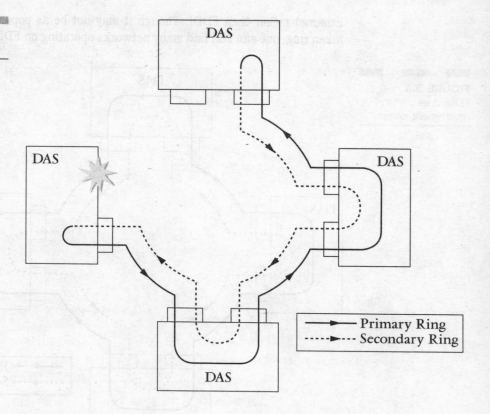

Primary Ring
Secondary Ring

TABLE 3.3
Comparing LAN technologies.

	Ethernet	Token-Ring	FDDI
Topology	Bus	Ring	Dual Rings
Access Method	CSMA/CD	Token Passing	Token Passing
Speed (in Mbps)	10/100/1000	1/4/16/100	100
Broadcast/ Non-Broadcast	Broadcast	Broadcast	Broadcast
Packet Size (Bytes)	64–1516	32–15K	32–4400
Self Recovery	No	Yes	No
Data Path Redundancy	No	No	Yes
Predictable Response Times	No	Yes	Yes
Priority Classes	No	Yes	Yes

continued on next page

TABLE 3.3 continued	Ethernet	Token-Ring	FDDI
Maximum Cable Length	Yes	Yes	Yes
Cost of Deployment (relative to each other)	Cheap	Moderate	Expensive
Typical Deployment Environment	Small offices, SoHo, educational institutes, most corporate offices, e-commerce	Airline, manufacturing floor, banking, most mission-critical networks	Backbone technology for medium and large networks

Table 3.3 shows the difference in characteristics of each of the technologies. Comparison reveals that each of these technologies is more suitable than the rest for certain operating requirements.

The Ethernet technology tends to be deployed in networks where network response time is not critical to the functions of the applications. It is commonly found in educational institutes, mainly for its cost effectiveness, and e-commerce, for its simplicity in technical requirements. Token ring is most suitable for networks that require predictable network response time. Airline reservation systems, manufacturing systems, as well as some banking and financial applications, have stringent network response time requirements. These networks tend to be token ring, although there may be few exceptions. FDDI is commonly deployed as a backbone network in a medium-to-large networks. It can be found in both Ethernet and token-ring environments. As mentioned, with the growing popularity of the Internet and the number of e-commerce setups increasing at an enormous pace, Ethernet is the popular choice for building an IP network.

In deciding on which technology is most suitable for deployment, a network manager needs to ascertain requirements carefully and make the correct decision based on the type of environment he/she operates in, the type of applications to be supported, and the overall expectations of the end-users.

WAN Technologies

WAN technologies are mainly used to connect networks that are geographically separated, for example, a remote branch office located in city A connecting to the central office in city B. Routers are usually used in WAN connectivity although switches may be deployed.

The requirements and choices of WAN technologies are different from those of LAN technologies. The main reason is that WAN technologies are usually a subscribed service offered by carriers, and are very costly. WAN also differs from LAN technologies in the area of speed. While LAN technologies are running at megabits per second, the WANs are usually in kilobits per second. Also, WAN connections tend to be point-to-point in nature, while LAN is multiaccess.

Table 3.4 describes the differences between LAN and WAN technologies.

TABLE 3.4
Comparing LAN and WAN technologies.

	LAN	WAN
Subscribed Service	No	Yes
Speed	4, 10, 16, 100, 155, 622 Mbps, 1 Gbps	9.6, 14.4, 28.8, 56, 64, 128, 256, 512 kbps; 1.5, 2, 45, 155, 622 Mbps
Cost per kbps (relative to each other)	Cheap	Very expensive
Performance of major decision criteria	Yes	No
Cost of major desicion criteria	Maybe	Yes
Cost of redundancy (as opposed to each)	May be expensive	Very expensive
Need specially trained personnel	May not	Definitely

It would seem obvious that the criteria for choosing a suitable WAN technology are different from those for a LAN. They are dependent on the choice of service offered by the carrier, the tariffs, the service quality of the carrier, and availability of expertise.

Leased Lines

Leased lines are the most common way of connecting remote offices to the head office. These are basically permanent circuits leased from the carrier and connected in a point-to-point manner.

Leased line technology has been around for quite some time and many network managers are familiar with it. With speed ranging from 64 kbps to as high as 45 Mbps, it usually runs protocol such as IP and IPX over a point-to-point protocol (PPP).

Routers are usually deployed to connect to leased lines to connect remote offices to a central site. A device called a data service unit/channel service unit (DSU/CSU) connects the router to the leased line, and for every leased line connection, a pair of DSU/CSU is required.

Because of cost and the introduction of many other WAN technologies, network managers have begun to replace leased lines with other technologies.

X.25

X.25 was developed by carriers in the early 1970s and allows the transport of data over a public data network service. The body that oversee its development is the International Telecommunication Union (ITU). Since ITU is made up of most of the telephone companies, this makes X.25 a truly international standard. X.25 is a classic example of a WAN protocol and a non-broadcast network. The components that make up an X.25 network are:

- **Data terminal equipment (DTE)**—DTEs are the communication devices located at an end-user's premises. Examples of DTEs are routers or hosts.
- **Packet assembler/disassembler (PAD)**—A PAD connects the DTE to the DCE and acts as a translator.
- **Data circuit-terminating equipment (DCE)**—DCEs are the devices that connect the DTEs to the main network. An example of a DCE is the modem.
- **Packet switching exchange (PSE)**—PSEs are the switches located in the carrier's facilities. The PSEs form the backbone of the X.25 network.

X.25 end devices communicate just as we use a telephone network. To initiate a communication path, called a virtual circuit, one workstation calls another and upon successful connection of the call, data begin to be transmitted. As opposed to the broadcast network, there is no facility such as ARP to map an IP address to an X.25 address. Instead, mappings are done statically and there is no broadcast required. In an X.25 network, there are two types of virtual circuit:

- **Permanent virtual circuit (PVC)**—PVCs are established for busy networks that always require the service of a virtual circuit. Rather than making repetitive calls, the virtual circuit is made permanent.
- **Switched virtual circuit (SVC)**—SVCs are for seldom-used data transfers. They are set up on demand and taken down when transmission ends.

The X.25 specification maps to the first three layers of the OSI model, as shown in the Figure 3.7.

X.25	OSI
	Network
LAPB	Data-link
Physical	Physical

The encapsulation of IP over X.25 networks is described in RFC 1356. The RFC proposes larger X.25 maximum data packet size and the mechanism for encapsulating longer IP packets over the original draft.

When data are sent to an X.25 data communication equipment, one or more virtual circuits are opened in the network to transmit it to the final destination. The IP datagrams are the protocol data units (PDUs) when the IP over X.25 encapsulation occurs. The PDUs are sent as X.25 complete packet sequences across the network. That is, PDUs begin on X.25 data packet boundaries and the M bit (more data) is used to fragment PDUs that are larger than one X.25 data packet.

There have been many discussions about performance in an X.25 network. The RFC 1356 specifies that every system must be able to receive and transmit PDUs up to 1,600 bytes. To accomplish the interoperability with the original draft, RFC 877, the default value for IP datagrams should be 1,500 bytes, and configurable in the range from 576 to 1,600 bytes. This standard approach has been used to accomplish the default value of 1,500-byte IP packets used in LAN and WAN environments so that one can avoid the router fragmentation process.

Typically, X.25 public data networks make use of low-speed data links and a certain number of routes are incurred before data are transmitted to a destination. The way X.25 switches store the complete packet before sending it on the output link causes a longer delay with longer X.25 packets. If a small end-to-end window size is used, it also decreases the end-to-end throughput of the X.25 circuit. Fragmenting large IP packets in smaller X.25 packets can improve the throughput, allowing a greater pipeline on the X.25 switches. Large X.25 packets combined over low-speed links can also introduce higher packet latency. Thus, the use of larger X.25 packets will not increase the network performance but often decreases it and some care should be taken in choosing the packet size. Some switches in the X.25 network will further fragment packets, so the performance of a link is also decided by the characteristics of the carrier's network.

A different approach for increasing performance relies on opening multiple virtual channels, but this increases the delivery costs over the public data networks. However, this method can overcome problems introduced by the limitation of a small X.25 window size increasing the used shares of the available bandwidth.

The low-speed performance of X.25 can sometimes pose problems for some TCP/IP applications that time out easily. In this case, other connecting protocols would have to be deployed in place of X.25. With the advent of multiprotocol routers, it is possible to find TCP/IP running on some WAN protocols while X.25 is used for other protocols. In fact, with the proliferation of TCP/IP networks, a new way of transporting connections has started to emerge: that of transporting X.25 networks across a TCP/IP network.

Some routers may provide support for the X.25 Transport Protocol (XTP), which works as a protocol forwarder, transferring the incoming X.25 packets to the final X.25 connection destination using the TCP/IP network. A common situation is depicted in the Figure 3.8.

Integrated Services Digital Network (ISDN)

ISDN is a subscribed service offered by phone companies. It makes use of digital technology to transport various information, including data, voice, and video, by using phone lines.

There are two types of ISDN interfaces: the basic rate interface (BRI) and the primary rate interface (PRI). The BRI provides 2 x 64 kbps for data transmission (called B channel) and 1 x 16 kbps for control transmission (called the D channel). B channels are used as HDLC frame-delimited 64-kbps pipes, while the D channel can also be used for X.25 traffic. The PRI provides T1 or E1 support. For T1, it supports 23 x 64 kbps B channels and a 64-kbps D channel. The E1 supports 30 x 64 kbps for data and a 64-kbps channel for control transmissions.

ISDN provides a "dial-on-demand" service that means a circuit is only connected when there is a requirement for it. The charging scheme of a fixed rate plus charges based on connections makes ISDN ideal for situations where a permanent connection is not necessary. It is especially attractive in situations where remote branches need to connect to the main office only for a batch update of records.

Chapter 3

Another useful way of deploying ISDN is to act as a backup for a primary link. For example, a remote office may be connected to the central office through a leased line, with an ISDN link used as a backup. Under normal operation, traffic flows through the leased line and the ISDN link is idle. In the event of a leased-line failure, the router at the remote site can use the ISDN connection to dial to the central office for connection.

FIGURE 3.8
X.25 over IP (XTP).

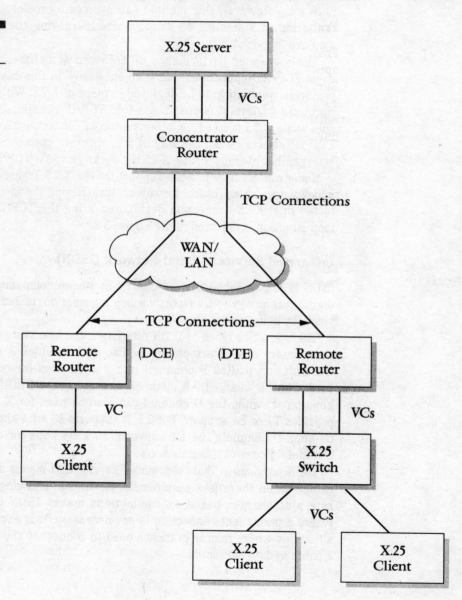

X.31- SUPPORTS OF X.25 OVER ISDN

The ITU standard X.31 is for transmitting X.25 packets over ISDN. This standard provides support for X.25 with unconditional notification on the ISDN BRI-D channel. X.31 is available from service providers in many countries. It gives the router a 9,600 bps X.25 circuit. Since the D channel is always present, this condition can be an X.25 PVC or SVC.

Frame Relay

Frame relay is a fast switching technique that can combine the use of fiber optic technologies (1.544 Mbps in the United States and 2.048 Mbps in Europe) with the benefits of port-sharing characteristics typical of networks such as X.25. The design point of frame relay is that networks are now very reliable; error checking is left to the DTE. Thus, frame relay does not perform link-level error checks and enjoys higher performance levels than X.25.

The frame relay network consists of switches provided by the carrier and responsible for directing the traffic within the network to the final destination. Routers are connected to the frame relay network as terminal equipment, and connections are provided by standard-based interfaces.

The frame relay standards describe both the interface between the terminal equipment (router) and the frame relay network, called *user-to-network interface* (UNI), and the interface between adjacent frame relay networks, called *network-to-network interface* (NNI) (Figure 3.9).

There are three important concepts in frame relay that you need to know:

- **Data link connection identifier (DLCI)**—The DLCI is just like the MAC address equivalent in a LAN environment. Data are encapsulated by the router in the frame relay frames and delivered through the network based on the DLCI, which can have a local or a global significance. Both uniquely identify a communication channel.

  Traffic destined for or originating from each of the partnering endstations is multiplexed, carrying different DLCIs, on the same user-network interface. The DLCI is used by the network to associate a frame with a specific virtual circuit. The address field is either two, three, or four octets long. The default frame relay address field used by most implementations is a two-octet field. The DLCI is a multiple-bit field of the address field whose length depends on the address field length.

- **Permanent virtual circuits (PVC)**—PVCs are predefined paths through the frame relay network that connect two end systems to each other. They are logical paths in the network identified locally by the DLCIs. As part of a subscription option, the bandwidth for PVCs is preallocated and a charge is imposed regardless of traffic volume.

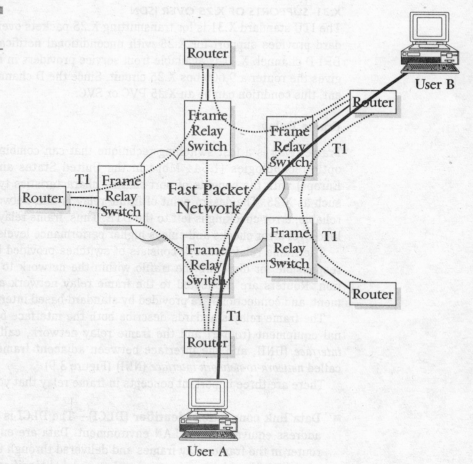

FIGURE 3.9
Frame relay network.

- **Switched virtual circuits (SVC)**—Unlike the PVCs, SVCs are not permanently defined in the frame relay network. The connected terminal equipment may request a call setup when there is a requirement to transmit data. A few options, related to the transmission, are specified during the setup of the connection. The SVCs are activated by the terminal equipment, such as routers connected to the frame relay networks, and the charges applied by a public frame relay carrier are based upon the circuit activities and are different from those of PVCs.

It is interesting to note that although regarded as a non-broadcast network, frame relay supports the ARP protocol as well as the rest of TCP/IP routing protocols.

NOTE

FRAME RELAY CONGESTION MANAGEMENT

Frame relay provides a mechanism to control and avoid congestion within the network. Basic concepts that need to be described include:

- **Forward Explicit Congestion Notification (FECN)**—This is a 1-bit field that notifies the user that the network is experiencing congestion in the direction the frame was sent. The user will take action to relieve the congestion.
- **Backward Explicit Congestion Notification (BECN)**—This is a 1-bit field that notifies the user that the network is experiencing congestion in the direction opposite to that of the frame. The user can slow down the rate of delivering packets through the network to relieve the congestion.
- **Discard Eligibility (DE)**—This is a 1-bit field indicating whether or not this frame should be discarded by the network in preference to other frames if there are congested nodes in the network. The use of DE requires that everyone in the network "play the game." In networks such as public frame relay networks, DTEs never set a DE bit because in the event of a congestion, its operation will be the first one affected.

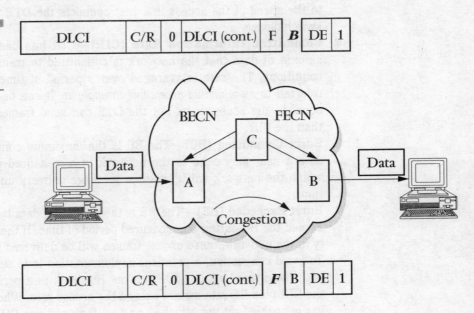

FIGURE 3.10
Frame relay
congestion
management.

The congestion control mechanism ensures that no stations can monopolize the network at the expense of others. It includes both congestion avoidance and congestion recovery.

The frame relay network does not guarantee data delivery and relies on a higher-level protocol for error recovery. When experiencing congestion, network resources will inform users to take appropriate corrective actions. FECN/BECN bits will be set during mild congestion, while the network is still able to transfer frames. In the event of severe congestion, frames are discarded. The mechanism to prioritize the discarding process of frames relies on the discard eligibility (DE) bit in the address field of the frame header. The network will start to discard frames with the DE field set first. To keep severe congestion from happening, a technique called *traffic shaping* is deployed by end-user systems.

TRAFFIC MANAGEMENT

For each PVC and SVC, a set of parameters can be specified to indicate bandwidth requirement and to manage burst and peak traffic values. This mechanism relies on:

- **Access Rate**—The access rate is the maximum rate that the terminal equipment can use to send data into the frame relay network. It is related to the speed of the access link that connects the DTE to the frame relay switch device.
- **Committed Information Rate (CIR)**—CIR has been defined as the amount of data that the network is committed to transfer under normal conditions. The rate is averaged over a period of time. The CIR is also referred to as *minimum acceptable throughput*. It can be set lower than or equal to the access rate, but the DTE can send frames at a higher rate than the CIR.
- **Burst Committed (BC)**—The BC is the maximum committed amount of data a user may send to the network in a measured period of time for which the network will guarantee message delivery under normal conditions.
- **Burst Exceeded (BE)**—The BE is the amount of data by which a user can exceed the BC during the measured period of time. If there is spare capacity in the network, these excess frames will be delivered to the destination. To avoid congestion, a practical implementation is to set all these frames with the discard eligible (DE) bit on. However, in a period of one second, the CIR plus BE rate cannot exceed the access rate. When circuit monitoring is enabled on the attached routers they can use CIR and BE parameters to send traffic at the proper rate to the frame relay network.
- **Local Management Interface (LMI) Extension**—The LMI is a set of procedures and messages that will be exchanged between the routers and the frame relay switch on the health of the network through:

- Status of the link between the connected router and switch
- Notification of added and deleted PVCs and SVCs
- Status messages of the circuit's availability.

Some features in LMI are standard implementations while others may be treated as options. Besides the status checking for the circuits, the LMI can have optional features such as multicasting, allows the network to deliver multiple copies of information to multiple destinations in a network. This is a useful feature, especially for running protocols that use broadcast, for example ARP. Routers can also provide features such as protocol broadcast which, when turned on, allows protocols such as RIP to function across the frame relay network.

IP ENCAPSULATION IN FRAME RELAY

The specifications for multiprotocol encapsulation in frame relay is described in RFC 2427. This RFC supplants the widely implemented RFC 1490. Changes have been made in the formalization of the SNAP and Network Level Protocol ID (NLPID) support, in the removed fragmentation process, address resolution in the SVC environment, source routing BPDUs support, and security enhancements.

The NLPID field is administered by ISO and the ITU. It contains values for many different protocols including IP, CLNP, and IEEE Subnetwork Access Protocol (SNAP). This field tells the receiver what encapsulation or what protocol follows in a transmission.

IP datagrams are sent over a frame relay network in encapsulated format. Within this context, IP can be encapsulated in two different ways: NLPID value indicating IP, or NLPID value indicating SNAP. Although both these encapsulations are supported under the given definitions, it is advantageous to select only one method as the appropriate mechanism for encapsulating IP data. Therefore, IP data should be encapsulated using the NLPID value of 0xCC indicating an IP packet. This option is more efficient because it transmits 48 fewer bits without the SNAP header and is consistent with the encapsulation of IP in an X.25 network.

The use of the NLPID and SNAP network-layer identifier enables multiprotocol transport over the frame relay network, thus avoiding other encapsulation techniques either for bridged or routed datagrams. This goal was achieved with the RFC 1490 specifications. Multiplexing of various protocols over a single circuit saves cost and looks attractive to network managers. However, care must to be taken so that mission-critical data are not affected by other less-important data traffic. Some implementations use a separate circuit to carry mission-critical applications but a better approach is to use a single PVC for all traffic and manage prioritization by a relatively sophisticated queuing system such as BRS.

MTU SIZE IN FRAME RELAY NETWORKS

Frame relay stations may choose to support the exchange identification (XID) specified in Appendix III of Q.922. This XID exchange allows the following parameters to be negotiated at the initialization of a frame relay circuit: maximum frame size, retransmission timer, and the maximum number of outstanding information (I) frames. If this exchange is not used, these values must be statically configured by mutual agreement of data link connection (DLC) endpoints, or must be defaulted to the values specified in Q.922.

There is no commonly implemented minimum or maximum frame size for frame relay networks. Generally, the maximum will be greater than or equal to 1600 octets, but each frame relay provider will specify an appropriate value for its network. Frame relay data terminal equipment (DTE), therefore, must allow the maximum acceptable frame size to be configurable.

INVERSE ARP

There are situations in which a frame relay station may wish to dynamically resolve a protocol address over a PVC. This may be accomplished using the standard ARP encapsulated within a SNAP-encoded frame relay packet. Because of the inefficiencies of emulating broadcasts in a frame relay environment, a new address resolution variation was developed, called Inverse ARP. It describes a method for resolving a protocol address when the hardware address is already known. In a frame relay network, the known hardware address is the DLCI. Support for inverse ARP function is not required, but it has proved useful for frame relay interface autoconfiguration.

At times, stations must be able to map more than one IP address in the same IP subnet to a particular DLCI on a frame relay interface. This need arises in situations involving remote access, where servers must act as ARP proxies for many dial-in clients, each assigned a unique IP address but sharing the bandwidth on the same DLC. The dynamic nature of such applications results in frequent address association changes with no effect on the DLC's status.

As with any other interface that utilizes ARP, stations may learn the associations between IP addresses and DLCIs by processing unsolicited ARP requests that arrive on the DLC. If one station wishes to inform its peer station on the other end of a frame-relay DLC of a new association between an IP address and that PVC, it should send an unsolicited ARP request with the source IP address equal to the destination IP address, and both set to the new IP address being used on the DLC. This allows a station to "announce" new client connections on a particular DLCI. The receiving station must store the new association and remove any existing association, if necessary, from any other DLCI on the interface.

IP ROUTING IN FRAME RELAY NETWORKS

It is common for network managers to run an IP network across a frame relay network and there may be a need to deploy protocols that rely on a broadcast mechanism to work. In this case, some configuration is required so that these protocols continue to function across the frame relay network.

OSPF OVER PVCS When using a dynamic routing protocol such as Open Shortest Path First (OSPF) over a frame relay network, the OSPF protocol must be told about the non-broadcast multiaccess (NBMA) network's understanding of frame relay. Although OSPF is usually deployed in a broadcast network, it does work in a non-broadcast network with some configuration changes. In a non-broadcast network, network managers must provide a router with static information such as the designated router and all the neighbors. Generally, you need to perform the following tasks:

- Define the frame relay interface as non-broadcast.
- Configure the IP addresses of the OSPF neighbors on the frame relay network.
- Set up the router with the highest priority to become the designated router.

In most frame relay implementations, the topology is typically a star (Figure 3.11), or "hub and spoke." The router at the central site has all the branches connected to it with PVCs. Some products provide added features to simplify the configuration for OSPF in this setup. In the Cisco router family, you can use the OSPF point-to-multipoint frame relay enhancement. Network managers need only configure a single IP subnet for the entire frame relay network, instead of multiple subnets for every PVC connection. The central router is configured to have the highest router priority so that it is always chosen as the designated router.

IP ROUTING WITH SVCS

The use of SVCs in a frame relay network offers more flexibility and features such as dial-on-demand and data path cut-through. With SVCs, network design can be simplified and performance can be improved.

Bandwidth and cost have always been at odds when it comes to network design. It is important to strike a balance, so that an acceptable performance is made available within a budget. In some cases, having permanent connectivity is a waste of resources because information exchange takes place only at a certain time of day. Having the ability to "dial on demand" when the connectivity is required saves cost. The IP address of the destination is associated with a DLCI and a call setup request is initiated when a connection to that IP address is required. When the originating workstation has sent its data, the circuit is taken down after a certain timeout period.

FIGURE 3.11
Star topology in a
frame relay network.

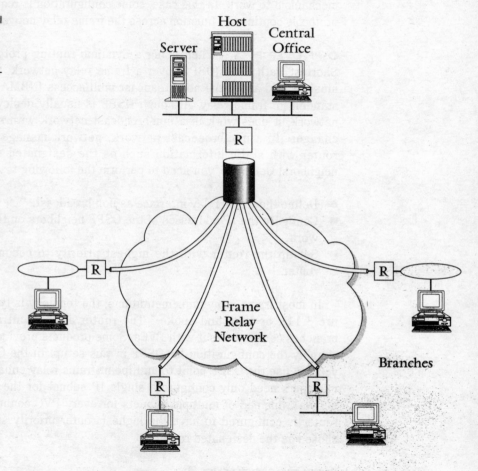

Usually, remote branches are connected to the central site and there is little requirement for them to have interconnection. Building a mesh topology using PVCs is costly and not practical. SVCs are more suitable here because they help to conserve network bandwidth, as well as reduce bandwidth cost. Moreover, in a star-topology configuration, interbranch communication has to go through the central site router, which increases the number of hops to reach the destination.

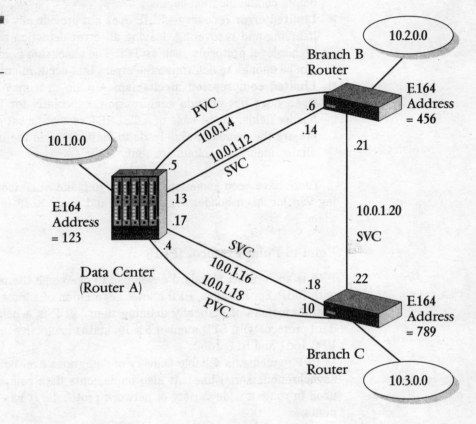

FIGURE 3.12
SVCs in a frame relay network.

With SVCs, the following protocols can be implemented across the frame relay network: IP, RIP, OSPF, and BGP-4.

Serial Line IP (SLIP)

Point-to-point connections have been the mainstay of data communication for many years. In the history of TCP/IP, the Serial Line IP (SLIP) protocol has been the de facto standard for connecting remote devices and it is still implemented. SLIP provides the ability for two endstations to communicate across a serial line interface and is usually used across a low-bandwidth link.

SLIP is a very simple framing protocol that describes the format of packets over serial line interfaces and has the following characteristics:

- **IP data only**—As its name implies, SLIP transports only the IP protocol and the configuration of the destination IP address is defined statically before communication begins.
- **Limited error recovery**—SLIP does not provide any mechanism for error handling and recovering, leaving all error detection responsibility to the higher-level protocols such as TCP. The checksum field of these protocols can be enough to determine the errors that occur in noisy lines.
- **Limited compression mechanism**—Ironic as it may seem, the protocol itself does not provide compression, especially for frequently used IP header fields. In the case of a TELNET session, most of the packet headers are the same and this leads to inefficiency in the link when too many almost-identical packets are sent.

There have been some modifications to make SLIP more efficient, including Van Jacobson header compression, and many SLIP implementations use them.

Point-to-Point Protocol (PPP)

PPP is an Internet standard developed to overcome the problems associated with SLIP. For instance, PPP allows negotiation of addresses across the connection instead of statically defining them. PPP is a network-specific standard protocol with STD number 51. Its status is elective and it is described in RFC 1661 and RFC 1662.

PPP implements reliable delivery of datagrams over both synchronous and asynchronous serial lines. It also implements data compression and can be used to route a wide variety of network protocols. It has three main components:

- A method for encapsulating datagrams over serial links
- A Link Control Protocol (LCP) for establishing, configuring, and testing the data-link connection
- A family of Network Control Protocols (NCPs) for establishing and configuring different network-layer protocols. PPP is designed to allow the simultaneous use of multiple network-layer protocols.

The format of the PPP frame is similar to that of the HDLC. PPP provides a byte-oriented connection exchanging information and message packets in a single format frame. The PPP Link Control Protocol (LCP) is used to establish, configure, maintain, and terminate the connection and goes through the following phases to establish a connection:

- **Link establishment and configuration negotiation**—The connection for PPP is opened only when a set of LCP packets is exchanged between the endstations' PPP processes. Among the information exchanged is the maximum packet size that can be carried over the link and use of authentication. A successful negotiation leads the LCP to the Open state.
- **Link quality determination**—The optional phase does not specify the policy for quality of the link but instead provides tools such as echo request and reply.
- **Authentication**—The next step is going through the authentication process. Each of the end systems is required to use the authentication protocol as agreed upon in the link establishment stage to identify the remote peer. If the authentication process fails, the link goes to the Down state.
- **Network control protocol negotiation**—Once the link is open, endstations negotiate the use of various Layer 3 protocols (for example, IP, IPX, DECnet, Banyan VINES, and APPN/HPR) by using the network control protocol (NCP) packets. Each Layer 3 protocol has its own associated network control protocol. For example IP has IP Control Protocol (IPCP). NCP negotiation is independently managed for every network control protocol and the specific state of the NCP (up or down) indicates if that network protocol traffic will be carried over the link.

AUTHENTICATION PROTOCOLS

PPP authentication protocols provide a form of security between two nodes connected via a PPP link. There are different authentication protocols supported:

- **Password Authentication Protocol (PAP)**—PAP is described in RFC 1334. It provides a simple mechanism of authentication after link establishment. One peer sends an ID and a password to the other peer and waits to receive an acknowledgment. Passwords are sent in clear text and there is no encryption involved.
- **Challenge/Handshake Authentication Protocol (CHAP)**—CHAP is described in RFC 1994. It is used periodically to check the identity of the peer, not only at the establishment of the link. The authenticator sends a challenge message to the peer, which responds with a value calculated with a hash function. The authenticator verifies the value of the hash function with the expected value to accept or terminate the connection.
- **Microsoft PPP CHAP (MS-CHAP)**—MS-CHAP is used to authenticate Windows workstations and peer routers.

■ **Shiva Password Authentication Protocol (SPAP)**—The SPAP is a Shiva proprietary protocol. The authentication mechanism starts at the LCP exchange, because if one of the end systems refuses to use an authentication protocol requested by the other, the link setup fails. Some authentication protocols, for instance CHAP, may require the end systems to exchange the authentication messages during connection setup.

THE NETWORK CONTROL PROTOCOL (NCP)

PPP has many NCPs for establishing and configuring different network layer protocols. They are used individually to set up and terminate specific network layer protocol connections and include:

- AppleTalk Control Protocol (ATCP)
- Banyan VINES Control Protocol (BVCP)
- Bridging protocols (BCP, NBCP, and NBFCP)
- Callback Control Protocol
- DECnet Control Protocol (DNCP)
- IP Control Protocol (IPCP)
- IPv6 Control Protocol (IPv6CP)
- IPX Control Protocol (IPXCP)
- OSI Control Protocol (OSICP)
- APPN High Performance Routing Control Protocol (APPN HPRCP)
- APPN Intermediate Session Routing Control Protocol (APPN ISRCP)

IPCP is described in RFC 1332 and specifies some features such as the Van Jacobson header compression mechanism or the IP address assignment mechanism. An endstation can either send its IP address to the peer or accept an IP address. Moreover it can supply an IP address to the peer if the peer requests that address. The first situation to handle is an unnumbered interface in which both ends of the point-to-point connection will have the same IP address; they will be seen as a single interface. This does not create problems in the IP routing algorithms. Otherwise the other end system of the link will be provided with its own address.

The router will automatically add a static route directed to the PPP interface for the address that is successfully negotiated, allowing data to be properly routed. When the IPCP connection is ended this static route is subsequently removed. This is a common configuration for dial-in users.

MULTILINK PPP (MP)

MP is an important enhancement to the PPP extensions to allow multiple parallel PPP physical links to be bundled together as if they were a single physical path. The implementation of multilink PPP can accomplish dynamic bandwidth allocation and also on-demand features to increase the available bandwidth for a single logical connection. Multilink PPP can have importance in the area of multimedia application support.

Multilink PPP is based on the process of fragmentation of large frames and rebuilding them, sequentially. When the PPP links are configured for multilink PPP support they are said to be *bundled*. The multilink PPP sender is allowed to fragment large packets and the fragmented frames are delivered with an added multilink PPP header that basically consists of a sequence number identifying each fragmented packet. The multilink PPP receiver reassembles the input packets in the correct order following the sequence numbers in the multilink PPP header.

The virtual connection made up by multilink PPP has more bandwidth than the original PPP link. The resulting MP bundled bandwidth is almost equal to the sum of the bandwidths of the individual links. The advantage is that large data packets can be transmitted within a shorter time.

The multilink PPP implementation in the Nways 221x family can accomplish both the Bandwidth Allocation Protocol (BAP) and the Bandwidth Allocation Control Protocol (BACP) to dynamically add and drop PPP dial circuits to a virtual link. Multilink PPP also uses Bandwidth On Demand (BOD) to add dial-up links to an existing multilink PPP bundle.

The multilink PPP links can be defined in two different ways:

- **Dedicated link**—A multilink PPP-enabled interface that has been configured as a link to a particular multilink PPP interface. If this link attempts to join another multilink PPP bundle, it is terminated.
- **Enabled link**—One that is not dedicated and can become a link in any multilink PPP bundle.

The BAP and the BACP are used to increase and decrease the multilink PPP interface bandwidth. These protocols make it possible, when the actual bandwidth utilization thresholds are reached, to add an enabled multilink PPP dial circuit to the MP bundle, if any is available and the negotiation process with the partner does not fail. The dedicated links have the priority for being added to the bundle before the enabled ones.

The Bandwidth On Demand protocol (BOD) adds dial links to the MP bundle using the configured dial circuit's telephone numbers. These are added in sequence and last for the time that the bundle is in use.

Using multilink PPP requires careful planning of the configured bundles. Limitations exist for mixing leased lines and dial-up circuits in the same bundle. Multilink PPP capabilities are being investigated for support of multi-class functions in order to provide a reliable data-link layer protocol for multimedia traffic over low-speed links . The multilink PPP implementation in the Nways 221x router family also supports the multilink multi-chassis. This functionality is provided when a remote connection can establish a. Layer 2 tunnel with a phone hunt group that spans multiple access servers.

Asynchronous Transfer Mode (ATM)

ATM is a switching technology that offers high-speed delivery of information including data, voice and video. It runs at 25, 100, 155, and 622 Mbps or even up to 2.4 Gbps, and is suitable for deployment in a LAN or WAN environment. Due to its ubiquitous nature, it can be categorized as a LAN or a WAN technology.

Unlike LAN technologies such as Ethernet or token ring that transport information in packets called frames, ATM transports information in *cells*. In legacy LANs, frames can vary in size, while in ATM, the cells are of fixed size—53 bytes. ATM is a connection-oriented protocol, which means it does not use broadcast techniques at the data-link layer for delivery of information, and the data path is predetermined before any information is sent. It offers features not found in Ethernet or token ring, one of which is called Quality of Service (QoS). Another benefit of ATM is the concept of Virtual LAN (VLAN). Membership in a group is no longer determined by physical location. Logically similar workstations can now be grouped together even though they are separate.

Because ATM works differently from the traditional LAN technologies, new communication protocols and new applications have to be developed. Before this happens, something needs to be done to make the traditional LAN technologies and IP applications work across an ATM network. Today, there are two standards developed for this purpose: classical IP and LAN emulation.

Classical IP (CIP)

CIP (RFC 1577) is a way of running the IP protocol over an ATM infrastructure. As its name implies, it supports only the IP protocol. Since ATM does not provide broadcast service, something needs to be done to address the mechanism for ARP, which is important in IP for mapping IP addresses to hardware addresses. A device called the ARP server is introduced in this standard to address this problem, and all IP workstations must register with the ARP server before communication can begin.

In RFC 1577, all IP workstations are grouped into a common domain called a *logical IP subnet (LIS)*. Within each LIS there is an ARP server, whose purpose is to maintain a table containing the IP addresses of all workstations within the LIS and their corresponding ATM addresses. All other workstations in an LIS are called ARP clients and they place calls, ATMARP, to the ARP server, for the resolution of the IP address to the ATM address. After receiving the information from the ARP server, ARP clients proceed to make calls to other clients to establish the data path so that information can flow. Therefore, ARP clients need to be configured with the ATM address of the ARP server before they can operate in a CIP environment. In a large CIP network, this poses an administrative problem if there will be a change in an ARP server's ATM address. It is therefore advisable to configure the ARP server's End System Identifier (ESI) with a locally administered address (LSA) so that no reconfiguration is required on ARP clients. There is an update to the RFC, RFC 1577+, that provides the mechanism for multiple ARP servers within a single LIS. This is mainly to provide redundancy to the ARP server.

CLASSICAL IP OVER PERMANENT VIRTUAL CIRCUIT (CIP OVER PVC)

Another implementation of CIP, is called CIP over PVC. It is usually deployed over an ATM WAN connection, where the circuit is always connected. This is typically found in service providers that operate an ATM core switch (usually with switching capacity ranging from 50 Gbps to 100 Gbps), with limited or no support for SVC services. In CIP over PVC, there is no need to resolve the IP address of the destination to the ATM address, as it has been mapped statically to an ATM connection through the definition of virtual path identifier (VPI) and virtual channel identifier (VCI) values. Because the mapping has to be done statically, CIP over PVC is used in networks where the interconnections are limited; otherwise, it would be an administrative burden for the network manager.

Though it may have its limitations, CIP over PVC can be a good solution for certain specific requirements. If it is used to connect a remote network to a central backbone, the network manager can set up the PVC connection in the ATM switch to be operative only at certain times of the day. The operation of the PVC (for example, setup and teardown) can be managed automatically by a network management station. In this way, a network manager can limit the flow of the remote network's traffic to certain times of the day for security reasons or for a specific business requirement.

ADVANTAGES OF CIP

There are several advantages of using CIP, especially in the areas of performance and simplicity:

- **ATM provides higher speeds than Ethernet or token ring**—The specifications for ATM states connecting speeds of 25, 155, or even 622 Mbps. Some vendors have announced support of link speeds of up to 2.4 Gbps. These links offer higher bandwidth than what Ethernet or token ring can offer.
- **CIP has no broadcast traffic**—Since there is no broadcast traffic in the network, the bandwidth is better utilized for carrying information.
- **Benefits of switching**—All workstations can have independent conversation channels with their peers through the switching mechanism of ATM. This means all conversations can take place at the same time, and the effective throughput of the network is higher than in a traditional LAN.
- **Simplicity**—Compared to LAN Emulation (LANE), CIP is simpler to implement and uses fewer ATM resources, called VCs. Adding and deleting ARP clients requires less effort than in LANE, and this makes CIP simpler to troubleshoot in the event of a problem.
- **Control**—As mentioned in the example of CIP over PVC, traffic control can be enforced through the setup and teardown of the PVCs. This is like giving the network the ability to be "switched on" or "switched off."

LAN Emulation (LANE)

Unlike CIP, which provides for running only IP over ATM, LANE is a standard that allows multiprotocol traffic to flow over ATM. As its name implies, LANE emulates the operation of Ethernet or token ring so that existing applications that run on these two technologies can operate on ATM without any changes. It is useful in providing a migration path for the existing LAN to ATM because it protects the investment cost in the existing applications.

The components that make up LANE are much more complicated than those in CIP and include:

- **LAN Emulation Configuration Server (LECS)**—The LECS centralizes and disseminates information from the ELANs and LECs. It is optional to deploy LECS, although it is strongly recommended.
- **LAN Emulation Server (LES)**—The LES has a job role rather similar to that of the ARP server in CIP. It resolves LAN addresses to ATM addresses.
- **Broadcast and Unknown Server (BUS)**—The BUS is responsible for the delivery of broadcast, multicast, and unknown unicast frames.
- **Lan Emulation Client (LEC)**—A LEC is a workstation participating in a LANE network.

Although more complicated in terms of its implementation as opposed to CIP, LANE enjoys advantages in several areas:

- ■ LANE supports multiprotocol traffic. It supports all protocols and this makes migration of existing networks easier.
- ■ LANE supports broadcast. However much of a nuisance it may be, many protocols rely on broadcast to work. Many servers use broadcast to advertise their services or existence. Clients use protocols such as DHCP to get their IP addresses. These services would not be possible in a CIP environment.
- ■ LANE provides advanced features not found in CIP. One good example is Next Hop Resolution Protocol (NHRP), with which it is possible to improve the performance of a network through a reduction in router hops.

Table 3.5 shows the differences between ATM and LAN technologies.

TABLE 3.5
Comparing ATM with other LAN technologies.

	LAN	CIP	LANE
Speed	4/16/100/1000	25/155/622	25/155/622
Broadcast support	Yes	No	Yes, through the BUS
QoS	No	Yes	Yes
Multiprotocol	Yes	No, only IP	Yes
Share/dedicated bandwidth	Share/switch	Switch	Switch
Transport data/voice/ video natively	No	Yes	Yes
Need new protocol	No	Yes	Yes
Need new adapter	No (most PCs now have built-in LAN ports)	Yes	Yes
Administrative effort in installation of client	Minimal	Need to specify ARP server's ATM address	Can join an ELAN through any combination of the following: • LECS address • LES/BUS address • ELAN names
Overheads (header vs total packet size)	Low (<2%)	High (>10%)	High (>10%)

ATM is a technology that provides a ubiquitous transport mechanism for both LAN and WAN. In the past, LAN and WAN used different protocols to operate, such as Ethernet for LAN and ISDN for WAN. This complicated design and made maintaining the network costly because more protocols were involved, and managers needed to be trained on different protocols. With ATM, it is possible to use it for both LAN and WAN connections and to make the network homogeneous.

The Connecting Devices

A network can be as simple as two users sharing information through a diskette or as complex as the Internet that we have today. This Internet is made of thousands of networks interconnected through devices called hubs, bridges, routers, and switches. These devices are the building blocks of a network and each of them performs a specific task to deliver the information flowing in the network. Points to be considered in choosing which device is the most appropriate to implement are:

- **Complexity of the requirement**—If the requirement is just to extend the network length to accommodate more users, then a bridge will do the job.
- **Performance requirement**—With the advent of multimedia applications, more bandwidth must be made available to users. A switch, in this case, is a better choice than a hub for building a network.
- **Specific business requirement**—Sometimes, a specific business requirement dictates a more granular control of who can access what information. In this type of situation, a router may be required to perform sophisticated control of information flow.
- **Availability of expertise**—Some devices require very little expertise to operate. A bridge is a simpler device to operate than a router.
- **Cost**—Ultimately, cost is an important decision criterion. When all devices can do the job, the one with the least cost will usually be selected.

The connecting devices function at different layers of the OSI model, and it is important to know this so that a choice can be made in using them.

Hub

A *hub* is a connecting device that all end workstations are physically connected to, so that they are grouped within a common domain called a *network segment*. The hub functions at the physical layer of the OSI model (Figure 3.13); it merely regenerates the electrical signal produced by a sending workstation, and is also known as a *repeater*. It is a shared device, which means if all users are connected to a 10-Mbps Ethernet hub, then all the users share the same bandwidth of 10 Mbps. As more users are plugged into the same hub, the effective average bandwidth that each user has decreases. The number of hubs that can be used is also determined by the chosen technology.

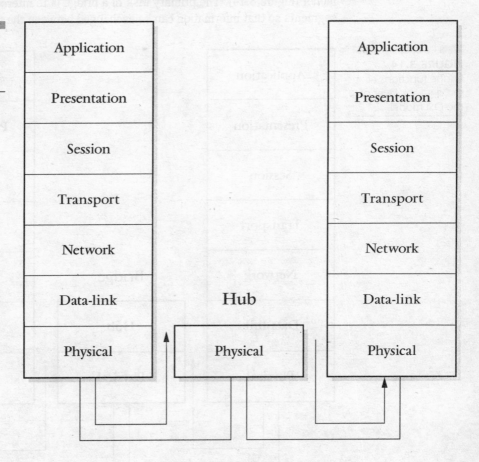

FIGURE 3.13
Hub functions at the physical layer of the OSI model.

Ethernet, for instance, has specific limitations in the use of hubs in terms of placement, distance and numbers. It is important to know these limitations so that the network can work within specifications and not cause problems.

Most, if not all, of the hubs available today are plug and play. This means very little configuration is required and probably everything works all right after it is unpacked from the box. With the increasing numbers of small offices and e-commerce, Ethernet hubs have become consumer products. With these hubs selling at a very low price and all performing a common function, the one important buying decision is the price per port.

Bridge

A *bridge* is a connecting device that functions at the data-link layer of the OSI model (Figure 3.14). The primary task of a bridge is to interconnect two network segments so that information can be exchanged between the two segments.

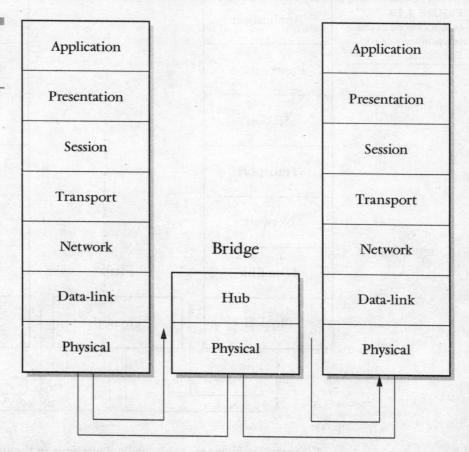

FIGURE 3.14
Bridge functions at the data-link layer of the OSI model.

A bridge basically stores a packet that comes into one port, and when required to, forwards it out through another port. When a bridge forwards information, it only inspects the data-link layer information within a packet. As such, a bridge is generally more efficient than a router, which is a Layer 3 device. The reasons for using a bridge can be any of the following:

■ **To accommodate more users on a network**—Networks such as token ring allow only 254 hosts to be in a single network segment, and any additional hosts need to be in another network segment.

- **To improve the performance of a network**—A bridge can be used to separate a network into two segments so that interference, such as collisions, can be contained within a certain group of users, allowing the rest to continue to communicate with each other undisturbed.
- **To extend the length of a network**—Technologies such as Ethernet specify certain maximum distances for a LAN. A bridge is a convenient tool to extend the distance so that more workstations can be connected.
- **To improve security**—A bridge can implement what is called *MAC filtering*; selectively allowing frames from certain workstations to pass through it. This allows network managers to control access to certain information or hosts.
- **To connect dissimilar networks**—A bridge can also be used to connect two dissimilar networks such as one Ethernet and one token ring segment.

Because there are a variety of reasons for using a bridge, bridges are classified into various categories for the functions they perform:

- **Transparent bridge**—A transparent bridge is one that forwards traffic between two adjacent LANs. It is unknown to the endstations, hence the name transparent. A transparent bridge builds a table of MAC addresses of the workstations that it learns and decides whether to forward a packet from the information. When the bridge receives a packet, it checks its table to see the packet's destination. If the destination is on the same LAN segment as where the packet comes from, the packet is not forwarded. If the destination is different from where the packet comes from, the packet is forwarded. If the destination is not in the table, the packet is forwarded to all interfaces except the one that the packet comes from. Transparent bridges are used mainly in Ethernet LANs.
- **Source route bridge**—A source route bridge is used in token ring networks. The sending workstation decides on the path to get to the destination, but before sending information to a destination, a workstation has to decide what the path should be. It does this by sending out an "explorer frame," and builds its forwarding path based on information received from the destination.
- **Source route transparent (SRT) bridge**—A source route transparent (SRT) bridge is one that performs source routing when source routing frames with routing information are received and performs transparent bridging when frames are received without routing information. The SRT bridge forwards transparent bridging frames without any conversions to the outgoing interface, while source routing frames are restricted to the source routing bridging domain. Thus, transparent frames are able to

reach the SRT and transparent bridged LAN, while the source-routed frames are limited only to the SRT and source route bridged LAN.

- **Source routing–Transparent bridge (SR-TB)**—In the SRT model, source routing is only available in the adjacent token ring LANs and not in the transparent bridge domain. An SR–TB, overcomes this limitation and allows a token ring workstation to establish a connection across multiple source route bridges to a workstation in the transparent bridging domain.

Another way of classifying bridges is to divide them into local and remote categories. A *local bridge* connects two network segments within the same building; *remote bridges* work in pairs and connect distant network segments.

A bridge is a good tool to use because it is simple and requires very little configuration effort. Its simplicity makes it very suitable for an environment where no networking specialist is available on site. Because it only inspects the data-link layer information, a bridge is truly a multiprotocol connecting device.

Router

As we mentioned earlier, a router functions at Layer 3 of the OSI model, the network layer (Figure 3.15). It inspects the information in a packet pertaining to the network layer and forwards the packet based on certain rules. Since it needs to inspect more information than just the data-link layer formation in a packet, a router generally needs more processing power than a bridge to forward traffic. However different in the way they inspect the information in a packet, both router and bridge attain the same goal: that of forwarding information to a designated destination.

A router is an important piece of equipment in an IP network since it is the connecting device for different groups of networks, called *IP subnets*. All hosts in an IP network have a unique identifier called the *IP address*. This address is made up of two parts, the *network number* and the *host number*. Hosts assigned different network numbers are said to be in different subnets and must be connected through an intermediate device, the router, before they can communicate. The router, in this case, is called the default gateway for the hosts. All information exchanged between two hosts in different subnets has to go through the router.

The reasons for using a router are the same as those for using a bridge. Since a router inspects more information within a packet than a bridge does, it has more powerful features in terms of making decisions based on protocol and network information such as the IP address. With the introduction of a more powerful CPU and more memory, a router can even inspect information within a packet at a higher layer than the network layer. New-generation routers can perform tasks such as blocking certain users from accessing such functions as FTP or TELNET. A router which performs that function is said to be *filtering*.

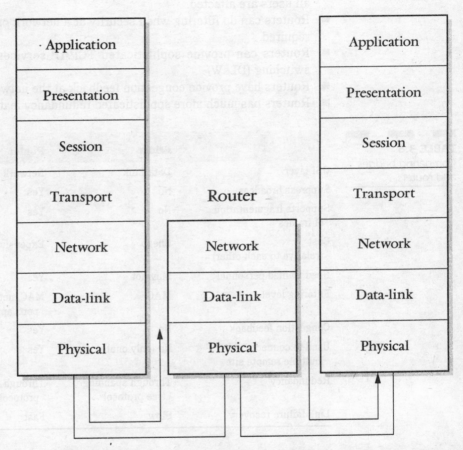

FIGURE 3.15
Router functions at the router layer of the OSI model.

A router is also often used to connect remote offices to a central office. In this scenario, the router located in the remote office usually comes with a port that connects to the local office LAN, and a port that connects to the wide area service, such as an ISDN connection. At the central office, there is a higher-capacity router that supports more connection ports for remote office connections.

Because a router is such a powerful device, it is difficult to configure and usually requires trained personnel to do the job. It is usually located within the data center and costs more than a bridge. Although the reasons for using a router can be the same as those mentioned for a bridge (Table 3.6), some of the reasons for choosing a router over a bridge are:

■ Routers can contain broadcast traffic within a certain domain so that not all users are affected.
■ Routers can do filtering when security at a network or application level is required.
■ Routers can provide sophisticated TCP/IP services such as data-link switching (DLsW).
■ Routers have provide congestion feedback at the network layer.
■ Routers has much more sophisticated redundancy features.

TABLE 3.6
Comparing bridges and routers.

	Bridge	Router
OSI layer	Data Link	Network
Suppress broadcast	No	Yes
Supports fragmentation of frames	No	Yes
Cost (relative to each other)	Cheap	Expensive
Need trained personnel	May not	Yes
Filtering level	MAC	MAC, network protocol, TCP port, application level
Congestion feedback	No	Yes
Used to connect multiple remote site	No (only one)	Yes
Redundancy	Through spanning-tree protocol	Through more sophisticated protocol such as OSPF
Link failure recovery	Slow	Fast

Switch

A switch functions at the same OSI layer as the bridge, the data-link layer. In fact, a switch can be considered a multiport bridge. While a bridge forwards traffic between two network segments, the switch has many ports, and forwards traffic between those ports.

One great difference between a bridge and a switch is that a bridge does its job through software functions, while a switch does its job through hardware implementation. A switch is more efficient than a bridge, and usually costs more. While the older-generation switches can work only in store-and-forward mode, some new switches offer a feature called *cut-through mode* whereby a packet is forwarded even before the switch has received the entire packet. This greatly enhances the performance of the switch. Another new method called *adaptive cut-through mode* has been introduced. In it the switch operates in cut-through mode and falls back to store-and-forward mode if it discovers that packets are forwarded with CRC errors. A switch with a switching capacity of the total bandwidth required by all the ports is considered to be *non-blocking*, an important factor in choosing a switch.

Switches are introduced to partition a network segment into smaller segments, so that broadcast traffic can be reduced and more hosts can communicate at the same time. This is called *microsegmentation* (Figure 3.16), and it increases the overall network bandwidth without a major upgrade to the infrastructure.

Virtual LAN (VLAN)

With hardware prices falling and users demanding more bandwidth, more segmentation is required and the network segments at the switch ports get smaller until one user is left on a single network segment. More functions are also added, one of which is VLAN, a logical grouping of endstations that share a common characteristic. At first, endstations were grouped by ports on the switch; that is, endstations connected to a certain port belonged to the same group. This is called *port-based VLAN*. Port-based VLAN is static because the network manager has to decide the grouping so that the switch can be configured before putting it to use. Later, enhancements were made so that switches can group endstations not by which ports they connect to, but by which network protocol they run, such as IP or IPX. This is called a *protocol VLAN* or *PVLAN*. Recently, more powerful features were introduced to group users on the basis of the IP network address. The membership of an endstation is not decided until it has obtained its IP address dynamically from a DHCP server.

It is worthwhile to note that when there are multiple VLANs created within a switch, inter-VLAN communication can be achieved only through a bridge, which is usually made available within the switch itself, or an external router. After all, switches at this stage are still Layer 2 devices.

As hardware gets more powerful in terms of speed and memory, more functions have been added to switches. A new generation of switches begins to appear. Some offer functions originally found only in routers. This makes inter-VLAN communication possible without an external router for protocols such as TCP/IP. This is called *Layer 3 switching*, as opposed to the original, *Layer 2 switching*.

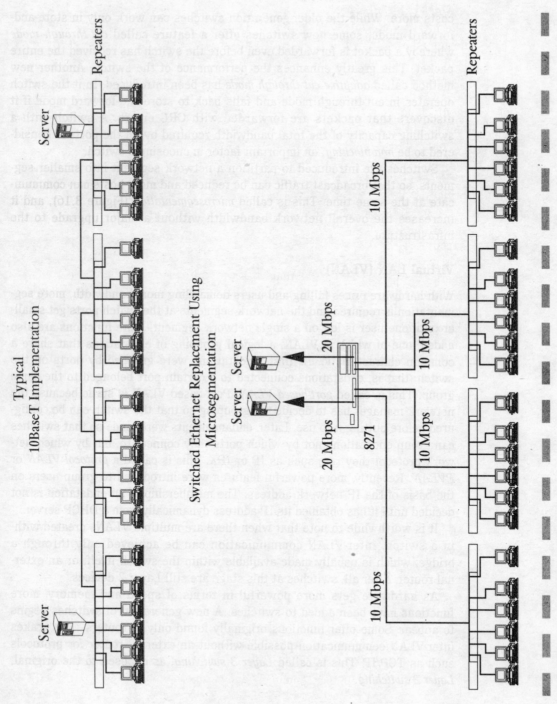

FIGURE 3.16 *Microsegmentation.*

Repeaters

Server

Typical
10BaseT Implementation

Switched Ethernet Replacement Using
Microsegmentation

Server   Server

8271

20 Mbps

20 Mbps

10 Mbps

10 Mbps

10 Mbps

10 Mbps

10 Mbps

Repeaters

ADVANTAGES OF VLAN

The introduction of the concept of VLANs created an impact on network design, especially with regard to physical connectivity. Previously, users connected to the same hub belonged to the same network. With the introduction of switches and VLANs, users are now grouped logically instead of by their physical connectivity. Companies are now operating in a dynamic environment: departmental structures change, employee movements, relocations, and mobility can only be supported by a network that can provide flexibility in connectivity. VLAN gives the network the flexibility required to support the logical grouping independent of physical wiring.

Because the forwarding of packets based on Layer 2 information (what a bridge does) and Layer 3 information (what a router does) is done at hardware speed, a switch is more powerful than a bridge or a router in terms of forwarding capacity. Because switches offer such a rich functionality at wire speed, more and more of them are being installed in corporate networks, and this is one of the fastest growing technologies in connectivity. Network managers have begun to realize that with the increase in the bandwidth made available to users, switching might be the way to solve the network bottleneck problem, as well as to provide a new infrastructure to support a new generation of applications. Vendors have begun to introduce new ways of building a network based on these powerful switches. One of them, Switched Virtual Networking (SVNz) is IBM's way of exploiting the enormous potential of a switching network in support of business needs.

LAN Switches

LAN switches, as the name implies, are found in a LAN environment and get users connected to the network. They come in different sizes, mainly based on the number of ports that they support. Stackable LAN switches are used for workgroup and low density connections and are usually doing only Layer 2 switching. Because of their low port density, they can be connected to each other (hence stackable) through their switch port to form a larger switching pool. Many other features are also added so that they can support ever-increasing need from the users. Among the features most wanted are:

■ **Link aggregation**—Link aggregation is the ability to interconnect two switches through multiple links to achieve higher bandwidth and fault tolerance in the connection. For example, two 10 Mbps Ethernet switches may be connected to each other using two ports on each switch in order to achieve a dual-link configuration that provides redundancy, in case one link fails, as well as a combined bandwidth of 20 Mbps.

- **VLAN tagging/IEEE 802.1Q**—VLAN tagging is the ability to share membership information of multiple VLANs across a common link between two switches. This enables endstations connected to two different switches but belonging to the same VLAN to communicate with each other as if they were connected to the same switch. IEEE 802.1Q is a standard for VLAN tagging and many switches offer this feature.
- **Multicast support/IGMP snooping**—Multicast support, better known as IGMP snooping, allows the switch to forward traffic only to the ports that require the multicast traffic. This greatly reduces the bandwidth requirement and improves the performance of the switch itself.

Campus Switches

As LAN switches get more powerful in terms of features, their port density increases as well. This gives rise to bigger LAN switches, called campus switches, that are usually deployed in the data center. Campus switches are usually Layer 3 switches, with more powerful hardware than the LAN switches. They do routing at the network layer as well. Because of their high port density, they usually have higher switching capacity and provide connections for LAN switches. Campus switches are used to form the backbone for large networks and usually provide feeds to even higher-capacity backbones, such as ATM networks.

ATM Switches

Because ATM technology can be deployed in a LAN or WAN environment, many different types of ATM switches are available:

- **ATM LAN switch**—The ATM LAN switch is usually a desktop switch, with UTP ports for the connection of 25-Mbps ATM clients. It most often comes with a higher-bandwidth connection port, called an *uplink*, for connection to higher-end ATM switches that usually run at 155 Mbps.
- **ATM campus switch**—The ATM campus switch is usually deployed in the data center and is for concentrating ATM uplinks from the smaller ATM switches or LAN switches with ATM uplink options. The ATM campus switch has a high concentration of ports that run in 155 Mbps and maybe a few with 622 Mbps.
- **ATM WAN switch**—The ATM WAN switch, also called *broadband switch*, is usually deployed in large corporations or telcos for carrying data on wide area links. Support ranges from very low to high-speed connections. It can connect to services such as frame relay and ISDN, or multiplex data across a few links by using the technology called *Inverse Multiplexing over ATM*.

As switches develop over time, it seems apparent that switching is the way to build a network because it offers the following advantages:

- **It is fast**—With its hardware implementation of forwarding traffic, a switch is faster than a bridge or a router.
- **It is flexible**—Due to the introduction of VLANs, the grouping of workstations is now no longer limited by physical location. Instead, workstations are grouped logically, whether or not they are located together.
- **It offers more bandwidth**—As opposed to a hub that provides shared bandwidth to endstations, a switch provides dedicated bandwidth to the endstations. More bandwidth is introduced to the network without a redesign. With dedicated bandwidth, a greater variety of applications, such as multimedia, can be introduced.
- **It is affordable**—The prices for LAN switches have been dropping with advances in hardware design and manufacturing. In the past, it was normal to pay about $500 per port for a LAN switch. Now, vendors are offering switches below $100 per port.

With vendors offering a wide array of LAN switches at different prices, it is difficult for a network manager to select an appropriate switch. However, there are a few issues to consider when buying a LAN switch:

- **Standards**—It is important to select a switch that supports open standards. An open standards-based product means there is a smaller chance of encountering problems in connecting to another vendor's product, if you need to.
- **Support for Quality of Service (QoS)**—The switching capacity, the traffic control mechanism, the size of the buffer pool, and the support for multicast traffic are all important criteria to ensure that the switch can support the demand for the QoS network.
- **Features**—Certain standard features must be included because they are important in building a switched network. These include support for the 801.D spanning tree protocol, SNMP protocol, and remote loading of the configuration.
- **Redundancy**—This is especially important for backbone switches. Because backbone switches concentrate the entire company's information flow, a downed backbone switch means the company is paralyzed until the switch is back up again. Hardware redundancy, which includes duplicate hardware as well as hot swappability, helps to reduce the risk and should be a deciding factor in choosing a backbone switch.
- **Management capability**—It is important to have a management software that makes configuration and changes easy. Web-based management is a

good way of managing the devices because it only requires a browser. But Web-based management usually accomplishes a basic management task, such as monitoring, and does not provide sophisticated features. A specialized management software to manage switches may be necessary.

TIP

Beware of Those Figures

It is important to find out the truth about what vendors claim on the specification of their products. It is common to see vendors claiming their switches have an astronomical 560 Gbps switching throughput. Vendors seem to have their own mathematics when making statements like this and this is usually what happens:

There is a chassis-based backbone switch that can support one master module with 3-Gbps switching capacity, and 10 media modules each with 3-Gbps switching capacity. Vendors will claim that their backbone switch is (3+10x3) which is 33, multiply by 2 because it supports duplex operation, and voila, you have a 66 Gbps switch. What the vendor did not say is that all traffic on all media modules has to pass through the master module, which acts as a supervisor. In fact, the switch at most can provide 6 Gbps switching capacity, if you agree that duplex mode does provide more bandwidth.

ATM vs. Switched High-Speed LAN

One of the most debated topics in networking recently is the role of ATM in an enterprise network. ATM was initially promoted as the technology of choice, from desktop connections to backbone and the WAN. It was supposed to be the technology that would replace others and unify all connecting protocols. The fact is, this is not happening, and will not happen for quite some time. ATM is a good technology but not everybody needs it. Its deployment has to be very selective and so far, it has proven to be an appropriate choice for some of the following situations:

- When there is a need for image processing, for example, in a hospital network where X-ray records are stored digitally and need to be shared electronically.
- In a graphics-intensive environment, such as a CAD/CAM network, for use in design and manufacturing companies.
- When there is a need to transport high-quality video across the network, such as when advertising companies are involved in video production.
- When there is a need to consolidate data, voice, and video on a single network to save cost on WAN connections.

ATM technology also has its weak points. Because it transports cells in a fixed size of 53 bytes, and with its 5-byte header, it has a considerable overhead. With more and more PCs having pre-installed LAN ports, adopting ATM technology to the desktops means having to open them up and install an ATM NIC. An additional driver is also required for using the ATM NIC. For network managers not familiar with the technology, the LES, BUS, LECS, VCs, VCCs, and other acronyms are just overwhelming.

While some vendors are pushing very hard for ATM's deployment, many network managers are finding that their good old LANs, though crawling under a heavy load, are still relevant. The reasons for feeling so are none other than the legacy LANs' low cost of ownership, familiarity with the technology, and ease of implementation.

While some people may still argue over which is better, others have found a perfect solution: combining both technologies. Many have found that ATM as a backbone, combined with switched LANs at the edge, provides a solution with the benefits of both technologies.

As a technology for backbones, ATM provides features such as PNNI, fast reroute, VLAN capabilities and high throughput, and is both fast and resilient to failure. The switched LAN protects the initial investment on the technologies, continues to keep connections to the desktop affordable, and through sheer volume, makes deployment easy.

It is important to know that both ATM and switched LANs solve the same problem: the shortage of bandwidth on the network. Some managers have implemented networks based entirely on ATM and have benefited from it. Others have stayed away from it because it is too difficult. It is important to know how to differentiate the technologies, and appreciate their implications to the overall design.

Factors that Affect a Network Design

Designing a network is more than merely planning to use the latest gadget in the market. A good network design takes into consideration various factors:

Size

At the end of the day, size does matter. Designing a LAN for a small office with a few users is different from building one for a large company with 2,000 users. In building a small LAN, a flat design is usually used, where all connecting devices may be connected to each other. For a large company, a hierarchical approach should be used.

Geography

The geographical locations of the sites that need to be connected are important in a network design. The decision-making process for selecting the right technology and equipment for remote connections, especially those of cross-country nature, is different from that for a LAN. Tariffs, local expertise, and quality of service from service providers are some of the important criteria.

Politics

Politics in the office ultimately decides how a network should be partitioned. Department A may not want to share data with department B, while department C allows only department D to access its data. At the network level, requirements such as these are usually done through filtering at the router so as to direct traffic flow in the correct manner. Business and security needs determine how information flows in a network and the right tool must be chosen to carry this out.

Types of Application

The types of application deployed determine the bandwidth required. While a text-based transaction may require a few kbps of bandwidth, a multimedia help file with video explanations may require 1.5 Mbps of bandwidth. The performance requirement mainly depends on application need and the challenge of a good network is to be able to satisfy different application needs.

Need for Fault Tolerance

In a mission-critical network, performance may not be a key criterion but fault tolerance is. The network is expected to be up every minute and the redundancy required is both at the hardware level and at the services level. To this end, many features must be deployed, such as hardware redundancy, re-route capabilities, etc.

To Switch or Not to Switch

One of the factors that influences network design is whether to deploy switching technology. Although switching seems to be enjoying popularity, it may not be suitable in terms of cost for a small office of four users. In a large network design, switching to the desktop may not be suitable because it would drive up the entire project cost. On the other hand, a small company that designs multimedia applications for its clients may need a switching network to share all the video and voice files. The decision a network manager has to make is when to switch and where to switch.

Strategy

One important factor is a networking strategy. Without a networking blueprint, one may end up with a multivendor, multiprotocol network that is difficult to manage and expand. It has been estimated that 70% of the cost of owning a network is in maintaining it. Having a network strategy ensures that technology is deployed at the correct place and products are chosen carefully. A network built upon a strategy ensures manageability and scalability.

Cost Constraints

The one major decision that makes or breaks a design is cost. Many times, network managers have to forego a technically elegant solution for a less sophisticated design.

Standards

Choosing equipment that conforms to standards is important. Standards mean having the ability to deploy an industry-recognized technology supported by the majority of vendors. This provides flexibility in choice of equipment, and allows network managers to choose the most cost-effective solution.

As more business and transactions are conducted through the network, the network infrastructure has become more important than ever. Network managers need to choose the right technologies, from the backbone to the desktops, and tie everything together to support the needs of their businesses. By now, it is obvious that designing a network is not just about raw speed. Adopting a balanced approach, weighing features against cost, and choosing the right technology based on open standards to meet the business requirement is the right way to begin.

Cisco Router Configuration Basics

Router Basics I

This section describes the configurable components, bootup sequence, and basic command modes of a Cisco router. We will also examine a router's external and internal configuration components, and the router initialization process, and discuss the different command modes available in Cisco routers.

Configuration Components

Router configuration information can come from many sources. Broadly speaking, they may be divided into external and internal components. All Cisco router models include an asynchronous serial port. This console port provides local access to the router using a console terminal (an ASCII terminal or a PC running terminal emulation software). Routers also have an auxiliary port, so they can be configured remotely using a modem.

A router can be configured over any of its network interfaces (Figure 4.1). Configuration information can be supplied to a router using:

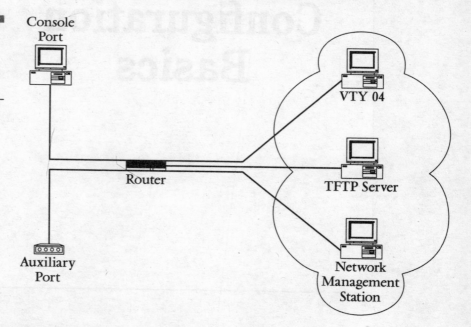

FIGURE 4.1
Router configuration information can come from many sources.

- **Console Port**—Upon initial installation, configure the router from a console terminal, which is connected to the router via the console.
- **Auxiliary Port**—Configure a router using the auxiliary port.

- **Virtual Terminals**—Configure a router from virtual terminals 0 through 4 after the router is installed on the network. Note that a VTY can typically be accessed via TELNET.
- **TFTP Server**—Configuration information can also be downloaded from a TFTP server on the network. The TFTP server can be UNIX or PC workstation that acts as a central depository for files. Configuration files can be kept on the TFTP server and then downloaded to the router.
- **Network Management Stations**—Router configuration can be managed from a remote system running network management software such as CiscoWorks or HP OpenView.

The internal configuration components (Figure 4.2) of a router include:

- **RAM/DRAM**—RAM/DRAM is the main storage component for the router. RAM is also called *working storage* and contains the dynamic configuration information.
- **NVRAM**—NVRAM contains a backup copy of the configuration. If the power is lost or the router is turned off for a period of time, the backup copy of the configuration enables the router to return to operation without needing to be reconfigured.
- **Flash Memory**—Flash memory is a special kind of erasable, programmable read-only memory. It contains a copy of Cisco IOS software. Flash memory has a structure that enables it to store multiple copies of the Cisco IOS software, so a new level of the operating software can be loaded in every router in your network and then, at some convenient time, the whole network can be upgraded to that new level. Flash memory content is retained upon power down or restart.
- **ROM**—ROM contains an initializing bootstrap program and a small monitoring system that can be used for recovery from a catastrophe. The Cisco 2500, 4000, and 4500 router series have a subset of the Cisco IOS software in ROM. The Cisco 7000 and 7500 router series have full Cisco IOS software in ROM. The ROM software can be upgraded by replacing pluggable chips on the CPU.
- **Interfaces**—Interfaces are the network connections through which packets enter and exit the router. Depending on the specific router, the interfaces supported are Ethernet, token ring, serial, BRI, ATM, FDDI, and Channel Interface Protocol (CIP) for SNA support. Some Cisco routers also support BRI, ATM, FDDI, Channel Interface Processor for SNA, HSSI, FEIP, and MIP interfaces.
- **Auxiliary Ports**—Cisco IOS software also allows the auxiliary port to be used for asynchronous routing as a network interface.

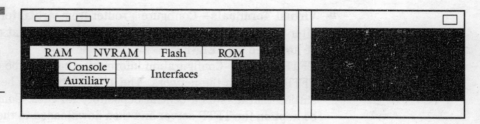

RAM	NVRAM	Flash	ROM
Console		Interfaces	
Auxiliary			

Router Initialization and Command Modes

Each time the router is switched on, it goes through power-on self-test diagnostics to verify basic operation of the CPU, memory and network interfaces. The system bootstrap software in ROM (boot image) executes and searches for valid router operating system software (Cisco IOS image).

There are three places to find the Cisco IOS image to load from flash: memory, a TFTP server on the network, or ROM. The source of the Cisco IOS image is determined from the boot field setting of the router's configuration register. The default setting for the configuration register indicates that the router should attempt to load a Cisco IOS image from flash memory. The default setting for the configuration register indicates that the router should attempt to load a Cisco IOS image from flash memory.

If the router finds a valid IOS image, it searches for a valid configuration file. If it does not find a valid system image, or if its configuration file is corrupted at startup, and the configuration register (bit 13) is set to enter ROM monitor mode, the system enters ROM monitor mode. The configuration file, saved in NVRAM, is loaded into main memory and executed one line at a time. These configuration commands start routing processes, supply addresses for interfaces, and set media characteristics. If no configuration file exists in NVRAM, the operating system executes a question-driven initial configuration routine called the system configuration dialog. This special mode is also called the *Setup mode* (Figure 4.3).

The Cisco IOS use interface is divided into many different modes. The commands available at any given time depend on which mode you are currently in.

NOTE

Entering a question mark (?) at the system prompt allows you to obtain a list of commands available for each command mode.

When you start a session on the router, you begin in user mode, often called *EXEC mode*. Only a limited subset of the commands are available in EXEC mode. In order to have access to all commands, enter privileged EXEC mode. Normally, you must enter a password to enter *privileged EXEC mode*.

From privileged mode, enter any EXEC command or enter global configuration mode. Most of the EXEC commands are one-time commands, such as `show` commands, which show the current status of something, and the `clear` command, which clear counters or interfaces. The EXEC commands are not saved across reboots of the router.

FIGURE 4.3
The entire startup
sequence of a router.

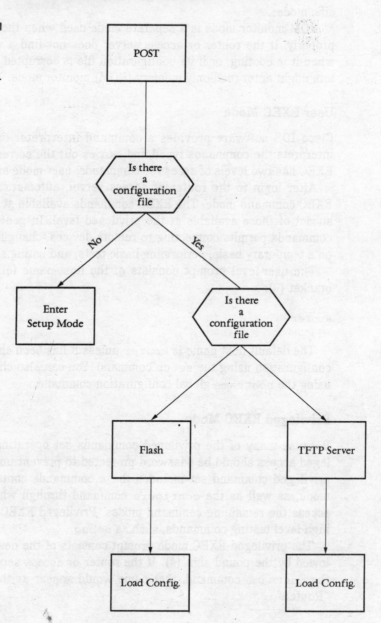

The configuration modes permit making changes to the running configuration. If the configuration is later saved, these commands are stored across router reboots. In order to get to the various configuration modes, start at global configuration mode. From global configuration, enter interface configuration mode, subinterface configuration mode, and a variety of protocol-specific modes.

ROM monitor mode is a separate mode used when the router cannot boot properly. If the router or access server does not find a valid system image when it is booting, or if its configuration file is corrupted at startup, the system might enter read-only memory (ROM) monitor mode.

User EXEC Mode

Cisco IOS software provides a command interpreter called EXEC, which interprets the commands typed and carries out the corresponding operation. EXEC has two levels of access to commands: user mode and privileged mode.

After login to the router or access server, automatically results in user EXEC command mode. The EXEC commands available at the user level are a subset of those available at the privileged level. In general, the user EXEC commands permits connecting to remote devices, changing terminal settings on a temporary basis, performing basic tests, and listing system information.

The user-level prompt consists of the host name followed by the angle bracket (>):

```
Router>
```

The default host name is Router unless it has been changed during initial configuration using the setup command. You can also change the host name using the hostname global configuration command.

Privileged EXEC Mode

Because many of the privileged commands set operating parameters, privileged access should be password protected to prevent unauthorized use. The privileged command set includes those commands contained in user EXEC mode, as well as the configure command through which it is possible to access the remaining command modes. Privileged EXEC mode also includes high-level testing commands, such as debug.

The privileged EXEC mode prompt consists of the devices' host name followed by the pound sign (#). If the router or access server was named with the hostname command, that name would appear as the prompt instead of "Router."

```
Router#
```

The following example shows how to access privileged EXEC mode:

```
Router> enable
Password:
Router#
```

Global Configuration Mode

Global configuration commands apply to features that affect the system as a whole, rather than just one protocol or interface. Use the configure terminal privileged EXEC command to enter global configuration mode. Commands to enable a particular routing or bridging function are also global configuration commands. For information on protocol-specific global configuration commands, see the appropriate configuration guide in the Cisco IOS software documentation.

The following example shows how to access global configuration mode:

```
Router# configure terminal
Enter configuration commands, one per line. End with CNTL/Z.
Router(config)#
```

Interface Configuration Mode

Many features are enabled on a per-interface basis. Interface configuration commands modify the operation of an interface such as an Ethernet FDDI or serial port. Interface configuration commands always follow an interface global command, which defines the interface type.

In the following example, serial interface is about to be configured. The new prompt Router(config-if)# indicates interface configuration mode.

```
Router(config)# interface serial 0 <CR>
Router(config-if)#
```

To exit interface configuration mode and return to global configuration mode, enter the exit command. To exit configuration mode and return to privileged EXEC mode, use the end command or press **Ctrl-Z**.

Subinterface Configuration Mode

Multiple virtual interfaces (called *subinterfaces*) can be configured on a single physical interface. Subinterfaces appear to be distinct physical interfaces to the various protocols. For example, frame relay networks provide multiple point-to-point links called *permanent virtual circuits (PVCs)*. These can be grouped under separate subinterfaces that in turn are configured on a single physical interface. From a bridge, a spanning-tree can be sent out on another subinterface.

Subinterfaces also allow multiple encapsulations for a protocol on a single interface. For example, a router or access server can receive an ARPA-framed IPX packet and forward the packet back out on he same physical interface as a SNAP-framed IPX packet.

In the following example, a subinterface is configured for serial line 2, which is configured for frame relay encapsulation. The subinterface is called 2.1 to indicate that it is subinterface 1 of serial interface 2. The new prompt Router(config-subif)# indicates the subinterface configuration mode. The subinterface can be configured to support one or more frame relay PVCs.

```
Router(config)# interface serial 2
Router(config-if)# encapsulation frame-relay
Router(config-if)# interface serial 2.1
Router(config-subif)#
```

To exit subinterface configuration mode and return to global configuration mode, enter the exit command. To exit configuration mode and return to privileged EXEC mode, press **Ctrl-Z**.

ROM Monitor Mode

If the router or access server does not find a valid system image, or if the boot sequence is interrupted, the system might enter ROM monitor mode. From this mode, the device can be booted or diagnostic tests can be performed.

It is also possible to enter ROM monitor mode by entering the reload EXEC command and then pressing the **Break** key during the first 60 seconds of startup. If the configuration has been changed, use the copy running-config startup-config command then issue the reload command to save configuration changes.

The ROM monitor is the angle bracket (>):

>

To return to user EXEC mode, type continue. To initialize the router or access server, enter the i command. This command causes the bootstrap program to reinitialize the hardware, clear the contents of memory, and boot the system. It is best to issue the i command before running any tests or booting software. To boot the system image file, use the b command.

OTHER CONFIGURATION MODES

There are more than 17 different specific configuration modes. Most of these can entered from global configuration mode. Other modes must be entered from another configuration mode. To learn more about them, refer to **www.cisco.com**.

Router Basics II

This section describes how to log into a Cisco router and examine its configurable components using Cisco IOS commands. We will examine how to log into and out of a Cisco router, how to use enhanced editing and context-sensitive help features, how Cisco IOS commands can be used to examine router status, log in to a Cisco router, access privileged mode, log out of a Cisco router, and use Cisco IOS commands to examine the configurable components of a Cisco router.

Logging in to a Cisco Router

The login process is not complicated, but there are certain features to be aware of. The login screen displays the name of the router: KENT. It announces that the console zero port, the only console port of the router, is available.

```
Kent con0 is now available

Press RETURN to get started.
```

The login screen requires you to hit the **Return** or **Enter** key, to continue to the next stage of the login process.

If no password is required, pressing **Return** may be the only step required to log in and you will be granted access to the IOS. There are many cases in which a console password is not required and you may intentionally choose not to set one. However, without a properly configured password anyone can gain instant access to the IOS. A password is a recommended first step in maintaining network security.

If a password has been set, pressing the **Return** key will return a prompt for a password. The User Access Verification on the console port is a request for the one and only console password. If you know the password, you are allowed access to the IOS. If not, you cannot proceed. The passwords are case sensitive, so insure that the **Caps-Lock** button is not engaged on your console terminal.

```
Press RETURN to get started.
User Access Verification
Password:
```

The router allows a finite period of 30 seconds to login and enter the password. If you fail to enter any portion of the password within 30 seconds of the initial prompt, it prompts again.

```
Press RETURN to get started.
User Access Verification
Password:
%Password: timeout expired!
Password:
```

The router keeps track of the number of login attempts and allows only three. An attempt is either a failure to enter any password, or an incorrect password. After three attempts you are returned to the "Press Return to get start" prompt. The router has no internal logs that track the number of failed console logins. When you are thrown back to "Press Return", you can then re-enter the console password.

```
User Access Verification
Password:
%Password: timeout expired!
Password:
Password:
%Bad passwords·
```

When you enter a password no characters will appear on the screen. Since you cannot track your progress as you enter the password, you only know if you entered it wrong when the IOS prompts you for another password. When you enter the console password correctly, you are allowed passage to the IOS. However, knowledge of the console password does not grant you access to critical commands or information within the router. There are various access levels available in the IOS as discussed previously.

To log out, use Exit, Logout, or Quit. The IOS has a default, auto-logout security feature that disconnects the console session after approximately ten minutes of inactivity. If you leave the console for an extended period of time, or forget to log out, this prevents access by someone without a valid login. The ten-minute inactivity limit can be changed with a configuration command. Value range is from one second to infinity.

On-line Help

User Mode Command List

When you first log in you see the user EXEC mode prompt. Type **?** at the prompt to display a list of available commands. (Examples in this book may vary based on the version of the Cisco IOS and may not be accurate in this particular section but are only to demonstrate commands and their usage.)

```
Router> ?
Exec commands:
<1-99>          Session number to resume
connect         Open a terminal connection
disconnect      Disconnect an existing telnet session
enable          Turn on privileged commands
exit            Exit from the EXEC
help            Description of the interactive help system
lat             Open a lat connection
lock            Lock the terminal
login           Log in as a particular user
logout          Exit from the EXEC

menu Start a menu-based user interface
mbranch  Trace multicast route for branch of tree
-- more --
```

The More prompt indicates that there are more commands to see. If you press **Return**, you will see the next line. You can see the contents of the next whole screen by pressing the **Space bar**.

Privileged Mode Command List

As in the user EXEC mode, display the available commands for the privileged EXEC mode by typing **?** at the privileged prompt.

```
Router# ?
Exec commands:
<1-99>            Session number to resume
access-enable     Create a temporary Access-List entry
access-template   Create a temporary Access-List entry
bfe               For manual emergency modes setting
clear             Reset functions
clock             Manage the system clock
configure         Enter configuration mode
connect           Open a terminal connection
copy              Copy configuration or image data
debug             Debugging functions (see also 'undebug')
disable           Turn off privileged commands
disconnect        Disconnect an existing telnet session
```

```
enable              Turn on privileged commands
erase               Erase flash or configuration memory
exit                Exit from the EXEC
help                Description of the interactive help system
lat                 Open a lat connection
lock                Lock the terminal
login               Log in as a particular user
logout              Exit from the EXEC
menu                Start a menu-based user interface
mbranch             Trace multicast route for branch of tree
-- more --
```

Once again the More prompt indicates further information is available. See the next line by pressing **Return**. Or the contents of the next whole screen by pressing the **Space bar**. Notice that many more commands are now available in privileged mode. Press any key to return to the system prompt.

Context-Sensitive Help

Use the context-sensitive help features of the Cisco IOS to determine the command required to perform a given task (Table 4.1).

TABLE 4.1
To get help specific to a command mode, a command, a keyword, or arguments, perform one of the following tasks.

Command	Task
help	Obtain a brief description of the help system in any command mode.
abbreviated-command-entry ?	Obtain a list of commands that begin with a particular character string.
abbreviated-command-entry <Tab>	Complete a partial command line.
?	List all commands available for a particular character string.
command ?	List a command's associated keywords.
command keyword ?	List a keyword's associated arguments.

Suppose you want to set the router clock. You can obtain a list of commands that begin with a particular character sequence by typing those characters followed immediately by a question mark. When using context-sensitive help, the space (or lack of a space) before the question mark is significant. This form of help, in which characters are followed immediately by a question mark, is called *word help* because it completes a word.

Example: Enter the letters cl at the system prompt followed by a question mark. Do not leave a space between the last letter and the question mark (?). The system provides the commands that begin with cl.

```
Router# cl?
clear  clock
```

When you discover the correct command to use, it still may not be complete on its own.

```
Router# clock
%Incomplete command
```

You can use help to check the syntax for setting the router clock. Type the command, add a space, and then type **?**. The help output shows that the set keyword is required. This form of help is called *command syntax help*, because it reminds you which keywords or arguments are required to continue a command.

```
Router# clock ?
set  Set the time and date
```

Next you can check the syntax for entering the time.

```
Router# clock set ?
Current Time (hh:mm:ss)
```

Then enter the current time using hours, minutes, and seconds, as shown here.

```
Router# clock set 15:00:00
%Incomplete command
```

In the above example, the system indicates that additional arguments must be provided to complete the command. Press **Ctrl+P** to repeat the previous command entry automatically. Then add a space and a question mark to reveal additional arguments. The output indicates that two more arguments are needed.

```
Router# clock set 15:00:00 ?
<1-31>   Day of the month
MONTH    Month of the year
```

NOTE

The Cisco user interface provides a history of commands entered. This feature is particularly useful for recalling long or complex commands or entries.

Use the command history feature to recall commands. Command history is set by default and the system records ten command lines in its history buffer. The command history feature can be disabled for the current session using the Terminal No History *command.*

Recall the most recent command by pressing **Ctrl+P** *(or the up* **arrow** *key). Repeat this step to display successively older commands. Alternatively, display the last several commands entered using the* Show History *command.*

Return to more recent commands, after recalling several using **Ctrl+P**, *by pressing* **Ctrl+N** *(or the* **down arrow** *key).*

If you can't remember a complete command name, use the **Tab** *key to complete a partial entry. Similarly, abbreviate commands and keywords to the number of characters that allow a unique abbreviation. For example, abbreviate the* show *command to* sh.

If an incorrect command is entered, the caret symbol (^) and help response indicate the error. Notice that the caret symbol character is displayed at the point in the command string where the IOS detected that an incorrect command, keyword, or argument. This error location facility together with the interactive help system makes it possible to find and correct syntax errors easily.

```
Router# clock set 15:00:00 15 5
                                ^
%Invalid input detected at '^' market.
```

In this case, press **Ctrl+P** to recall the last command you typed, and you add a space and type **?**. Here, another required parameter is displayed.

```
Router# clock set 15:00:00 15 May ?
  <1993-2005> Year
```

Now complete the command entry and press **Return** to execute the command.

```
Router# clock set 15:00:00 15 May 1999
```

Using Enhanced Editing Commands

The Cisco user interface includes an enhanced editing mode that provides a set of editing key functions. Enhanced editing mode is automatically enabled. It is possible to disable enhanced editing mode and revert to the editing mode of previous Cisco IOS releases. It might be desirable to disable enhanced editing mode if there are pre-built scripts that don't interact well if it is enabled.

NOTE

Perform the following tasks to move the cursor around on the command line:

- *Press* **Ctrl+B** *(or the left arrow key) repeatedly to scroll back to the start of the line one character at a time.*
- *Press* **Esc+B** *to move back a word at a time.*
- *Press* **Ctrl+A** *to return directly to the start of the line.*
- *Press* **Ctrl+F** *(or the right arrow key) repeatedly to move to end of the command line.*
- *Press* **Esc+F** *to move forward one word.*
- *Press* **Ctrl+E** *to jump to the end of the line.*

Do the following to delete command entries:

- *Press* **Delete** *or* **Backspace** *to erase the character to the left of the cursor.*
- *Press* **Ctrl+D** *to delete the character at the cursor.*
- *Press* **Ctrl+K** *to delete all characters from the cursor to the end of the command line.*
- *Press* **Ctrl+U** *or* **Ctrl+X** *to delete all characters from the cursor to the beginning of the command line.*
- *Press* **Ctrl+W** *to delete the word to the left of the cursor.*
- *Press* **Esc+D** *to delete from the cursor to the end of the word.*

The editing command set provides a horizontal scrolling feature for commands that extend beyond a single line on the screen. When the cursor reaches the right margin, the command line shifts ten spaces to the left. The dollar sign ($) indicates that the line has been scrolled (see the following example).

```
Router# config
Configuring from terminal, memory, or network [terminal]?
Enter configuration commands, one per line. End with CNTL/Z.
Router(config)# $16.2.5 255.255.255.0 172.16.2.6 255.255.255.0 eq
45
```

Scroll back to the start of the line by pressing **Ctrl+B** (or the **left arrow** key) repeatedly. Press **Esc+B** to move back a word at a time. Alternatively, press **Ctrl+A** to return directly to the start of the line.

```
Router# config
Configuring from terminal, memory, or network [terminal]?
Enter configuration commands, one per line. End with CNTL/Z.
Router(config)# access-list 101 permit tcp 172.16.2.5
255.255.255.0 172.16.1 (Ö)
```

Router Examination

Several Cisco IOS commands can be used to examine the status of a router (Figure 4.4). Each command permits examination of a different configurable component of the router.

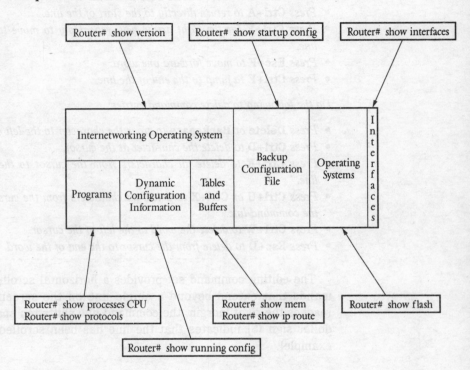

FIGURE 4.4
Many commands are available to monitor router configuration.

Router status commands are as follows:

- show version—To display the configuration of the system hardware, the software version, the names and sources of configuration files, and the boot images, use the show version EXEC command.
- show processes—Use the show processes EXEC command to display information about the active processes.
- show buffers—Use the show buffers EXEC command to display statistics for the buffer pools on the network server.
- show ip protocol—To display the parameters and current state of the active routing protocol process, use the show ip protocols EXEC command.
- show protocols—Use the show protocols EXEC command to display the configured protocols. This command shows the global and interface-

specific status of any configured Level 3 protocol; for example, IP, DEC-net, IPX, AppleTalk, and so forth.

- `show memory`—Use the `show memory` EXEC command to show statistics about memory, including memory-free pool statistics.

- `show ip route`—Use the `show ip route` EXEC command to display the current state of the routing table.

- `show flash`—List information about flash memory, including system image filenames and amounts of memory used and remaining.

- `show running-config`—To display the configuration information currently running on the terminal, use the `show running-config` EXEC command. This command replaces the `write terminal` command.

- `show startup-config`—To display the contents of NVRAM (if present and valid) or to show the configuration file pointed to by the CONFIG_FILE environment variable, use the `show startup-config` EXEC command. This command replaces the `show configuration` command.

- `show interfaces`—Use the `show interfaces` EXEC command to display statistics for all interfaces configured on the router or access server. The resulting output varies, depending on the network for which an interface has been configured.

show version Command

This command first appeared in Cisco IOS Release 10.0. Log in to the router and enter privileged mode. Type `show version` to display the configuration of the system hardware, the software version, the names and sources of configuration files, and the boot images.

```
Router> enable
Password:
Router# show version

IOS (tm) 3000 Software (IGS-J-L), Version 11.3, RELEASE SOFTWARE
(fc1)
Copyright (C) 1986-1997 by cisco Systems, Inc.
Compiled Tue 06-May-97 by mkamson
Image text-base: 0x030372E0, data-base: 0x00001000

ROM: System Bootstrap, Version 5.2(8a), RELEASE SOFTWARE
ROM: 3000 Bootstrap Software (IGS-RXBOOT), Version 10.2(8a),
RELEASE SOFTWARE

Router uptime is 1 week, 3 days, 32 minutes
System restarted by reload
System image file is "c2500-js-1", booted via tftp from
171.69.1.129
```

```
Cisco 2500 (68030) processor (revision D) with 8192K/2048K bytes
of memory
Processor board ID 03272326, with hardware revision 00000000
Bridging software.
SuperLAT software copyright 1990 by Meridian Technology Corp.
X.25 software, Version 2.0, NET2, BFE and GOSIP compliant.
TN3270 Emulation software (copyright 1994 by TGV Inc).
Basic Rate ISDN software, Version 1.0.
1 Ethernet/IEEE 802.3 interface.
2 Serial network interfaces.
1 ISDN Basic Rate interface.
```

Here you can see:

- The current version of the Cisco IOS being used: Version 11.3
- How long the router has been up: router uptime is 1 week, 3 days, 32 minutes
- How the system was restarted: System restarted by reload
- Where the operating system was loaded from:

```
System image file is "c2500-js-1", booted via tftp from
171.69.1.129
```

Press the **Space bar** to see the next screen and find information about the router's interfaces. Check the value of the configuration register.

```
ROM: System Bootstrap, Version 5.2(8a), RELEASE SOFTWARE
ROM: 3000 Bootstrap Software (IGS-RXBOOT), Version 10.2(8a),
RELEASE SOFTWARE

Router uptime is 1 week, 3 days, 32 minutes
System restarted by reload
System image file is "c2500-js-1", booted via tftp from
171.69.1.129

Cisco 2500 (68030) processor (revision D) with 8192K/2048K bytes
of memory
Processor board ID 03272326, with hardware revision 00000000
Bridging software.
SuperLAT software copyright 1990 by Meridian Technology Corp.
X.25 software, Version 2.0, NET2, BFE and GOSIP compliant.
TN3270 Emulation software (copyright 1994 by TGV Inc).
Basic Rate ISDN software, Version 1.0.
1 Ethernet/IEEE 802.3 interface.
2 Serial network interfaces.
1 ISDN Basic Rate interface.
32K bytes of non-volatile configuration memory.
8192K bytes of processor board System flash (Read ONLY)

Configuration register is 0x2102
```

If several routers are exhibiting the same behavioral problems, use the show version *command. Perhaps all problem routers obtained the same image file from the same TFTP server, which could indicate that the image file on the TFTP server is corrupted.*

show processes Command

To display information about the active processes type show processes. First check the overall CPU utilization in the previous five seconds, minute, and five minutes. PID represents the ID number of each process.

```
Router# show processes

CPU utilization for five seconds: 2%/2%; one minute: 5%; five minutes: 5%
 PID Q Ty      PC Runtime (ms)    Invoked   uSecs   Stacks  TTY Process
   1 M E  305109C         36         21     1714 1426/2000    2 Virtual Exec
   2 L E  3040184   74254712     708734   104775  908/1000    0 Check heaps
   3 M E  30676AE          0          2        0  964/1000    0 Timers
   4 L E  3096BFE        156        334      467  734/1000    0 ARP Input
   5 L E  30C06B2          0          1        0  924/1000    0 Probe Input
   6 M E  30C024A          0          1        0  962/1000    0 RARP Input
   7 H E  30B294C     287160     263357     1090 1572/2000    0 IP Input
   8 M E  30D9192       3592     487257        7  706/1000    0 TCP Timer
   9 L E  30DAE6E        100         62     1612  648/1000    0 TCP Protocols
  10 M E  30BD382       2176       6733      323  790/1000    0 BOOTP Server
  11 M E  3118FFC     158256     366449      431  822/1000    0 CDP Protocol
  12 M *        0       1264        145     8717 1140/2000    0 Exec
  13 L T  318A9A2        132      40586        3  878/1000    0 IP Cache Ager
  14 M E  322B58E         12          2     6000 1740/2000    0 SNMP Traps
  15 M E  3036610         68          8     8500  740/1000    0 Net Background
  16 L E  30618D0          8          7     1142  884/1000    0 Logger
  17 M P  3040EB2    1101876    2435192      452  758/1000    0 TTY Background
  18 H E  30368C2     108248     583920      185  374/500     0 Net Input
  19 M P  3036544    1137656      40587    28030  734/1000    0 Per-minute Job
  20 M E  30ECB98          0          2        0 1806/2000    0 IP SNMP
  21 M E  32D696C          0          2        0 1948/2000    0 IPX SNMP
  22 M E  31795C0      27868      40602      686  926/1000    0 IP-RT Background
  23 M E  31AD32A    2250872     343468     6533 1152/1500    0 RIP Router
```

Q indicates the process queue priority (High, Medium, or Low). Ty represents a test of the status of the process. PC is the current program counter. Runtime (in milliseconds) denotes the CPU time that the process has used. Invoked represents the number of times the process has been invoked. uSecs tells the microseconds of CPU time for each process invocation. Stacks shows the low watermark/total stack space available, in bytes. TTY tells which terminal controls the process. Process displays the name of the process.

show memory Command

To see how the management system allocates memory for different purposes in the router type show memory. The first section of the display includes summary statistics about the activities of the system memory allocator. The information here includes the amount of memory in use and the size of the largest available free block (highlighted).

```
Router# show memory

          Head     Total(b)   Used(b)   Free(b)   Lowest(b)   Largest(b)
Processor B0EE38   5181896    2210036   2971860   2692456     2845368
```

The second section of the display is a block-by-block listing of memory use. Scroll down to see more, and type q to quit back to the privileged mode prompt.

```
Processor memory
Address   Bytes   Prev.    Next     Ref  PrevF  NextF  Alloc PC   What
B0EE38    1056       0     B0F280   1                  18F132     List Elements
B0F280    2656    B0EE38   B0FD08   1                  18F132     List Headers
B0FD08    2520    B0F280   B10708   1                  141384     TTY data
B10708    2000    B0FD08   B10F00   1                  14353C     TTY Input Buf
B10F00     512    B10708   B11128   1                  14356C     TTY Output Buf
B11128    2000    B10F00   B11920   1                  1A110E     Interrupt Stack
B11920      44    B11128   B11974   1                  970DE8     *Init*
B11974    1056    B11920   B11DBC   1                  18F132     messages
B11DBC      84    B11974   B11E38   1                  19ABCE     Watched Boolean
B11E38      84    B11DBC   B11EB4   1                  19ABCE     Watched Boolean
B11EB4      84    B11E38   B11F30   1                  19ABCE     Watched Boolean
B11F30      84    B11EB4   B11FAC   1                  19ABCE     Watched Boolean
```

show buffers Command

Get a closer look at the buffers by typing show buffers. The example shown here indicates that there are different buffer sizes available.

```
Router# show buffers

Buffer elements:
     334 in free list (500 max allowed)
     2235660 hits, 0 misses, 0 created

Public buffer pools:
Small buffers, 104 bytes (total 50, permanent 50):
     50 in free list (20 min, 150 max allowed)
     731498 hits, 0 misses, 0 trims, 0 created
Middle buffers, 600 bytes (total 25, permanent 25):
     25 in free list (10 min, 150 max allowed)
```

```
                    263838 hits, 0 misses, 0 trims, 0 created
Big buffers, 1524 bytes (total 50, permanent 50):
       50 in free list (5 min, 150 max allowed)
       121827 hits, 0 misses, 0 trims, 0 created
VeryBig buffers, 4520 bytes (total 10, permanent 10):
       10 in free list (0 min, 100 max allowed)
       0 hits, 0 misses, 0 trims, 0 created
Large buffers, 5024 bytes (total 0, permanent 0):
       0 in free list (0 min, 10 max allowed)
       0 hits, 0 misses, 0 trims, 0 created
Huge buffers, 18024 bytes (total 0, permanent 0):
       0 in free list (0 min, 4 max allowed)
       0 hits, 0 misses, 0 trims, 0 created
Interface buffer pools:
Ethernet0 buffers, 1524 bytes (total 64, permanent 64):
       16 in free list (0 min, 64 max allowed)
       48 hits, 0 fallbacks
       16 max cache size, 16 in cache
Ethernet1 buffers, 1524 bytes (total 64, permanent 64):
       16 in free list (0 min, 64 max allowed)
       48 hits, 0 fallbacks
       16 max cache size, 16 in cache
Serial0 buffers, 1524 bytes (total 64, permanent 64):
       16 in free list (0 min, 64 max allowed)
       48 hits, 0 fallbacks
       16 max cache size, 16 in cache
Serial1 buffers, 1524 bytes (total 64, permanent 64):
       16 in free list (0 min, 64 max allowed)
       48 hits, 0 fallbacks
       16 max cache size, 16 in cache
TokenRing0 buffers, 4516 bytes (total 48, permanent 48):
       0 in free list (0 min, 48 max allowed)
       48 hits, 0 fallbacks
       16 max cache size, 16 in cache
TokenRing1 buffers, 4516 bytes (total 32, permanent 32):
       32 in free list (0 min, 48 max allowed)
       16 hits, 0 fallbacks

0 failures (0 no memory)
```

show flash Command

Examine flash memory more closely by typing `show flash`. This will also
show the size of the files and the amount of flash memory free.

```
Router# show flash
System flash directory:
File   Length    Name/status
  1    5596900   igs-j-1.103-10
[5596964 bytes used, 2791644 available, 8388608 total]
8192K bytes of processor board System flash (Read ONLY)
```

NOTE

Use show flash, *to check whether another copy of the operating system is being kept in flash. Two different versions of the IOS may be kept in flash memory. This is generally done in an upgrade from one version of the IOS to another when you want to return to the older one. It is also possible to keep two copies of the same IOS version in case one becomes corrupt.*

show interfaces Command

To see what hardware interfaces are on the router type show interfaces. In this example, press the **Space bar** to see the details of the Ethernet (E0) interface.

```
Router# show interfaces

Ethernet0 is up, line protocol is up
   Hardware is Lance, address is 0000.0c8d.c30d (bia 0000.0c8d.c30d)
   Internet address is 172.16.168.1 255.255.255.0
   MTU 1500 bytes, BW 10000 Kbit, DLY 1000 usec, rely 255/255, load 1/255
   Encapsulation ARPA, loopback not set, keepalive set (10 sec)
   ARP type: ARPA, ARP Timeout 4:00:00
   Last input 0:00:05, output 0:00:02, output hang never
   Last clearing of "show interfaces" counters never
   Output queue 0/40, 0 drops; input queue 0/75, 0 drops
   5 minute input rate 0 bits/sec, 0 packets/sec
   5 minute output rate 0 bits/sec, 0 packets/sec
      189272 packets input, 30218862 bytes, 0 no buffer
      Received 188063 broadcasts, 0 runts, 0 giants
      222 input errors, 222 CRC, 1 frame, 0 overrun, 0 ignored, 0 abort

      0 input packets with dribble condition detected
      373246 packets output, 36074209 bytes, 0 underruns
      1 output errors, 1850 collisions, 1 interface resets, 0 restarts
      0 output buffer failures, 0 output buffer trapped out
--more--
```

show protocols Command

Show what protocols are configured on the router by typing show protocols. In the example shown here, IP is running, but the other protocol options are not. IP is configured on the Ethernet interface and on the serial ports.

```
Route# show protocols

Global values:
   Internet Protocol routing is enabled
BRI0 is administratively down, line protocol is down
```

```
Ethernet0 is up, line protocol is up
  Internet address is 172.16.128.1 255.255.255.0
Serial0 is up, line protocol is up
  Internet address is 172.16.65.2 255.255.255.0
Serial1 is up, line protocol is up
  Internet address is 172.16.67.1 255.255.255.0
```

show ip protocol Command

Examine IP further by typing show ip protocol. In this example, IP is
using RIP as its routing protocol.

```
Router# show ip protocol

Routing Protocol is "rip"
  Sending updates every 30 seconds, next due in 1 seconds
  Invalid after 180 seconds, hold down 180, flushed after 240
  Outgoing update filter list for all interfaces is not set
  Incoming update filter list for all interfaces is not set
  Redistributing: rip
  Routing for Networks:
    194.125.0.0
    172.16.0.0
  Routing Information Sources:
    Gateway          Distance      Last Update
    172.16.128.3       120         0:00:25
    172.16.67.2        120         0:00:00
    172.16.65.1        120         0:00:21
Distance: (default is 120)
```

NOTE

*Recall that a routing protocol is a language used to communicate between routers. The
router uses RIP to get information about the location of objects on the network. It uses
this information to create structures called* routing tables. *To examine the routing
table that IP is using you type* show ip route.

show running-config Command and show start-up Command

Use the show running-config command in conjunction with the show
startup-config command to compare the information in running memory
to the information stored in NVRAM or in a location specified by the CON-
FIG_FILE environment variable. In the Cisco 7000 family, this variable specifies the configuration file used for initialization (startup). Use the boot config command in conjunction with the copy running-config
startup-config command to set the CONFIG_FILE environment variable.
  The following partial sample output displays the running configuration:

```
Router# show running-config

Building configuration...

Current configuration:
!
version 11.2
no service udp-small-servers
no service tcp-small-servers
!
hostname Router2
!
...
!
end
```

NVRAM stores the configuration information on the network server in text form as configuration commands. For all platforms except the Cisco 7000 family, the `show startup-config` command shows the version number of the software used when you last executed the copy `running-config startup-config` command.

For the Cisco 7000 family, the `show startup-config` command shows the configuration file specified by the CONFIG_FILE environment variable. The Cisco IOS software indicates whether the displayed configuration is complete or a distilled version. A *distilled configuration* is one that does not contain access lists. If the CONFIG_FILE environment variable does not exist or is not valid, the software displays the NVRAM configuration (if it is a valid, complete configuration).

The following sample output from the `show startup-config` command displays the contents of NVRAM:

```
Router# show startup-config

Using 5057 out of 32768 bytes
!
version 10.3
!
enable-password xxxx
service pad
!
boot system dross-system 172.16.13.111
boot system dross-system 172.16.1.111
!
exception dump 172.16.13.111
!
no ip ipname-lookup
!
decnet routing 13.1
```

```
                    decnet node-type area
                    decnet max-address 1023
                    !
                    interface Ethernet 0
                    ip address 172.16.1.1 255.255.255.0
                    ip helper-address 172.30.1.0
                    ip accounting
                    ip gdp
                    decnet cost 3
                    !
                    ip domain-name BOSTON.COM
                    ip name-server 255.255.255.255
                    !
                    end
```

show ip route Command

When you specify that you want information about a specific network displayed, more detailed statistics are shown. The following is sample output from the show ip route command entered with the address 131.119.0.0.

```
Router# show ip route 131.119.0.0

Routing entry for 131.119.0.0 (mask 255.255.0.0)
   Known via "igrp 109", distance 100, metric 10989
   Tag 0
   Redistributing via igrp 109
   Last update from 131.108.35.13 on TokenRing0, 0:00:58 ago
   Routing Descriptor Blocks:
 * 131.108.35.13, from 131.108.35.13, 0:00:58 ago, via TokenRing0
     Route metric is 10989, traffic share count is 1
     Total delay is 45130 microseconds, minimum bandwidth is 1544 Kbit
     Reliability 255/255, minimum MTU 1500 bytes
     Loading 2/255, Hops 4
```

When an IS-IS router advertises its link state information, it includes one of its own IP addresses to be used as the originator IP address. When other routers calculate IP routes, they can store the originator IP address with each route in the routing table.

The following example shows the output from the show ip route command looking at an IP route generated by IS-IS. Each path shown under the Routing Descriptor Blocks report displays two IP addresses. The first address (10.22.22.2) is the next-hop address, the second is the originator IP address from the advertising IS-IS router. This address helps you determine where a particular IP route has originated in the network. In the example the route to 10.0.0.1/32 was originated by a router with IP address 223.191.255.247.

```
Router# show ip route 10.0.0.1

   Routing entry for 10.0.0.1/32
   Known via "isis", distance 115, metric 20, type level-1
   Redistributing via isis
   Last update from 223.191.255.251 on Fddi1/0, 00:00:13 ago
   Routing Descriptor Blocks:
   * 10.22.22.2, from 223.191.255.247, via Serial2/3
       Route metric is 20, traffic share count is 1
       223.191.255.251, from 223.191.255.247, via Fddi1/0
       Route metric is 20, traffic share count is 1
```

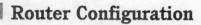

Router Configuration

This section introduces Cisco router configuration. We will examine the initial configuration of a Cisco router, how to generate and display router configuration information, how to approach router configuration, and how to configure a router with a new name.

Initial Configuration

The Cisco AutoInstall procedure permits configuring a router automatically and remotely over the network. AutoInstall is particularly useful for establishing new routers in remote locations where, for example, the branch office staff have very limited networking knowledge and experience. The new router must be connected to an existing router on either a WAN or a LAN link.

For the AutoInstall procedure (Figure 4.5) to work, the system must meet the following requirements:

- Routers must be physically attached to the network using one or more of the following interface types: Ethernet, token ring, Fiber Distributed Data Interface (FDDI), serial with High-Level Data Link Control (HDLC) encapsulation, or serial with frame relay encapsulation. HDLC is the default serial encapsulation. If the AutoInstall process fails over HDLC, the Cisco IOS software automatically configures frame relay encapsulation.
- The existing preconfigured router must be running Software Release 9.1 or later. For AutoInstall over frame relay, this router must be running Cisco IOS Release 10.3 or later.
- The new router must be running Software Release 9.1 or later. For AutoInstall over frame relay, the new router must be running Cisco IOS Release 10.3 or later.

NOTE

Of token ring interfaces, only those that set ring speed with physical jumpers support AutoInstall. AutoInstall does not work with token ring interfaces for which the ring speed must be set with software configuration commands. If the ring speed is not set, the interface is set to shutdown mode.

FIGURE 4.5
AutoInstall enables
you to configure
a new router
automatically and
remotely.

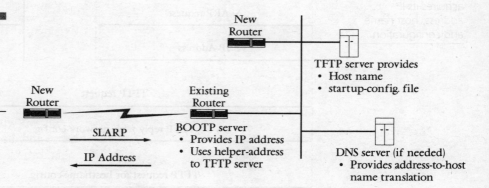

The existing router acts as a Bootstrap Protocol (BOOTP) or Reverse Address Resolution Protocol (RARP) server. It must be set up to help the new router acquire its IP address. This existing router also contains a helper address for the TFTP server. Configuring a helper address means that all incoming TFTP requests are forwarded to a particular address, in this case a particular TFTP server.

NOTE

Make sure that the new router configuration files reside on the TFTP server. Prepare new router configuration files for AutoInstall in the Cisco IOS software configuration mode. Move the new router configuration files using the copy running-config tftp *command to store the current configuration in RAM on a network TFTP server.*

The TFTP server provides a host name file for the new router. If this file is not available on the TFTP server, then the new router uses a Domain Name Server (DNS) server. Finally, the new configuration is downloaded from the TFTP server to the new router (Figure 4.6).

The AutoInstall procedure has several steps. First the new router sends a SLARP or BOOTP request for an IP address. The new router learns its IP address from the first valid BOOTP or RARP reply it receives. Once the new router has obtained an IP address, it requests a file from the TFTP server to resolve this IP address into a hostname. The response to this request comes in the form of a file named network-confg containing the hostname for the new router. Finally, the new router uses its newly acquired hostname to request the `hostname-confg` file that contains its specific configuration entries. The TFTP server downloads this file to the new router.

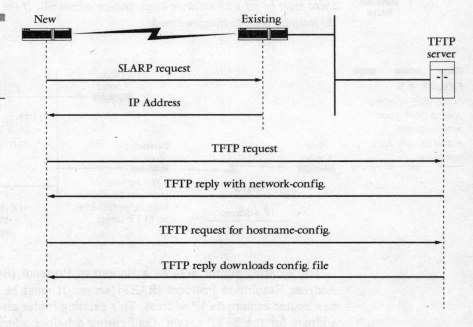

FIGURE 4.6
The new router acquires its IP address, host name, and configuration.

The AutoInstall process includes several fallback features to use if a common scenario fails to provide the proper response to the new router's requests. If the hostname request to the TFTP server fails to provide the new router with a host name, it will use another request procedure (Figure 4.7). The new router sends a request to the DNS server to obtain IP address-to-hostname translation.

If the new router requests a `hostname-config` file, but the TFTP server cannot send the requested file, it will send a more generic configuration named `router-confg`. Then TELNET the new router and make specific configuration changes necessary for the new router.

A new router can AutoInstall from an existing router and TFTP server using an Ethernet, token ring, or FDDI interface. In the example shown here, the commands are entries on the existing router.

```
interface ethernet 0
ip address 172.16.25.5 255.255.255.0
ip helper-address 172.16.10.10
```

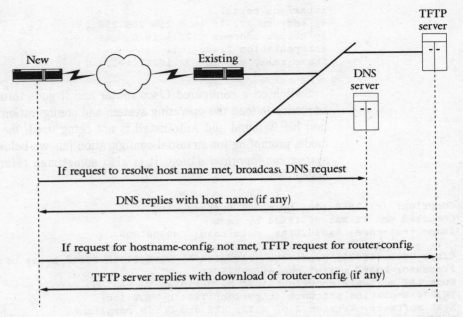

FIGURE 4.7
If host name
resolution from TFTP
network-config fails,
the new router sends
a request to the DNS
server.

The `Interface` command defines an Ethernet interface on the existing router. The `IP address` command defines the IP address and subnet mask for the Ethernet (E0) on the existing router. The `IP Helper-Address` command defines the address of the TFTP server that all incoming TFTP requests at the E0 interface are forwarded to that address.

A new router can receive an AutoInstall from an existing router and TFTP server across a WAN. In this example, the command entries are on the existing router, which uses HDLC. The commands define the serial interface being used, the IP address and subnet mask for the serial interface, and the helper address of the TFTP server.

```
interface serial 1
ip address 172.16.16.5 255.255.255.0
ip helper-address 172.16.16.0
```

In the example shown below, the existing router and new router connect over a frame relay link. The first three commands shown here define the serial interface, the IP address and subnet mask for the serial interface, and the address of the TFTP server. In addition, the `Encapsulation` command defines frame relay encapsulation. The `Frame-relay map ip` command statically maps the new router's IP address, 172.16.11.10, to its designated data-link connection identifier (DLCI), 39.

```
interface serial 1
ip address 172.16.16.5 255.255.255.0
ip helper-address 172.16.16.0
encapsulation frame-relay
frame-relay map ip 172.16.11.10.39
```

Switch on a configured Cisco router and it goes through an initialization sequence to load the operating system and configuration file. If no configuration file is found and AutoInstall is not being used, the router enters setup mode, prompting for an initial configuration (shown below). This is called the *system configuration dialog*. It is also sometimes referred to as the *setup dialog*.

```
Copyright (c) 1986-1996 by cisco Systems, Inc.
Compiled Mon 11-Mar-96 19:34 by tamb
Image text-base: 0x0302E6A8, data-base: 0x00001000

Cisco 2500 (68030) processor (revision L) with 6144K/2048K bytes of memory.
Processor board serial number 02975066
SuperLAT software copyright 1990 by Meridian Technology Corp.
TN3270 Emulation software (copyright 1994 by TGV Inc).
X.25 software, Version 2.0, NET2, BFE and GOSIP compliant.
Bridging software.
Basic Rate ISDN software, Version 1.0.
1 Ethernet/IEEE 802.3 interface.
2 Serial network interfaces.
1 ISDN Basic Rate interface.
32K bytes on non-volatile configuration memory
8192K bytes of processor board System flash (Read ONLY)
        --- System Configuration Dialog ---
At any point you may enter a question mark '?' for help.
Use ctrl-c to abort configuration dialog at any prompt.
Default settings are in square brackets '[]'.
Would you like to enter the initial configuration dialog? [yes]:
```

You begin the initial configuration process by typing yes, or pressing **Return**. (Remember: At this point you can choose not to continue with the system configuration dialog by entering no at the prompt. You can press **Ctrl+C** to terminate the process and start over at any time.) If you choose to see it, the router displays a summary of the configuration information, if any, for each interface.

```
First, would you like to see the current interface summary? [yes]:

Any interface listed with OK? value "NO" does not have a valid configuration

Interface     IP-Address    OK?   Method    Status      Protocol
BRI0          unassigned    NO    not set   up          up
Ethernet0     unassigned    NO    not set   up          down
```

```
Serial0      unassigned      NO    not set    down         down
Serial1      unassigned      NO    not set    down         down
```

NOTE

*For many of the prompts in the system configuration dialog, default answers appear in square brackets ([]) following the question. Press **Return** to accept the defaults. If the system was previously configured, the defaults that appear are the currently configured values. If you are configuring the system for the first time, the factory defaults are provided, and if there is no factory default, nothing is displayed after the question mark.*

Next, you are prompted for global parameters, such as a router name and passwords, at the console. Use the configuration values determined for the router, entering them at the appropriate prompts.

```
Configuring global parameters:

    Enter host name [Router]: sandox
    Enter enable password: shovel
    Enter virtual terminal password: pail
    Configure SNMP Network Management? [no]:
    Configure IP? [yes]:
    Configure IGRP routing? [yes]:
    Your IGRP autonomous system number [1]: 200
    Configure DECnet? [no]:
    Configure XNS? [no]:
    Configure Novell? [no]: yes
    Configure Apollo? [no]:
    Configure AppleTalk? [no]: yes
    Multixone networks? [no]: yes
    Configure Vines? [no]:
    Configure bridging? [no]:
```

NOTE

At any prompt during the setup dialog, you can request help by typing a question mark. If the prompt requires a Yes or No answer, no further help is available, but if there is a range of acceptable answers, the help facility will give some guidance. For example, if you are prompted to select the number of bits in a subnet mask, the help facility might inform you that you can choose a decimal number between 0 and 16 for a class B address.

You are prompted for parameters for each installed network interface. In the example shown here, there is a token ring interface and there are also two serial interfaces. Enter the configuration values determined for each interface at the appropriate prompt.

```
Configuring interface parameters:

Configuring interface Ethernet0:
```

```
    Is this interface in use? [yes]:
       Tokenring ring speed (4 or 16)? [16]:
    Configure IP on this interface? [no]: yes
       IP address for this interface: 172.16.92.67
       Number of bits in subnet field [0]:
       Class B network is 172.16.0.0, 0 subnet bits; mask is
255.255.0.0
    Configure Novell on this interface? [no]: yes
       Novell network number [1]:
Configuring interface Serial0:
    Is this interface in use? [yes]:
    Configure IP on this interface? [yes]:
    Configure IP unnumbered on this interface? [no]:
       IP address for this interface: 172.16.97.67
       Number of bits in subnet field [0]:
       Class B network is 172.16.0.0, 0 subnet bits; mask is
255.255.0.0
    Configure Novell on this interface? [yes]: no

Configuring interface Serial1:
    Is this interface in use? [yes]: no
```

When you complete the configuration process for all installed interfaces on the router, the setup command facility displays the configuration command script created. You are asked whether you want to use the new configuration.

```
interface Ethernet0:
ip address 172.16.92.67 255.255.0.0
novell network 1
no mop enabled
!
interface Serial0:
ip address 172.16.97.67 255.255.0.0
interface Serial1:
shutdown
!
router igrp 200
network 172.16.0.0
!
end
Use this configuration? [yes/no]: yes
[ok]
Use the enabled mode 'configure' command to modify this
configuration.
```

If you enter Yes, the configuration file is executed and saved to NVRAM. If you enter No, the configuration file is not saved and you can use the Setup command to begin the process again. There is no default for this prompt; you must answer Yes or No. Once you have answered Yes to this last question, the system is ready to use. If you want to alter the configuration in any way, you have to do it manually.

For AutoInstall examples, commands, and details, refer to the Cisco documentation or go to **www.cisco.com**.

Working with Configuration Files

The commands that determine a router's configuration are held in configuration files. There are two principal configurations associated with each router:

- **Startup configuration file**—The startup configuration file is stored in NVRAM and is accessed when the router is restarted. Enter `show startup-config` to see the startup configuration. Use the `show config` command with Cisco IOS versions 10.3 and earlier.
- **Running configuration**—The running configuration is held in RAM and changes as you modify interfaces and make other configuration changes. Enter `show running-config` to examine the running configuration. Use the `write term` command with Cisco IOS versions 10.3 and earlier.

The following sample output from the `show startup-config` command displays the contents of NVRAM.

```
Router# show startup-config

Using 5057 out of 32768 bytes
!
version 10.3
!
enable-password xxxx
service pad
!
boot system dross-system 172.16.13.111
boot system dross-system 172.16.1.111
!
exception dump 172.16.13.111
!
no ip ipname-lookup
!
decnet routing 13.1
decnet node-type area
decnet max-address 1023
!
interface Ethernet 0
ip address 172.16.1.1 255.255.255.0
ip helper-address 172.30.1.0
ip accounting
```

```
ip gdp
decnet cost 3
!
ip domain-name CISCO.COM
ip name-server 255.255.255.255
!
end
```

The following partial sample output displays the running configuration.

```
Router# show running-config

Building configuration...

Current configuration:
!
version 11.3
no service udp-small-servers
no service tcp-small-servers
!
hostname Router
!
...
!
end
```

When administrators want to make changes and test configurations, they first change the running configuration. When they are happy with the new configuration, they copy the running configuration to the startup configuration file.

```
copy running-config to startup-config
```

There are several ways to generate router configuration information. First, use the privileged mode configure command to enter global configuration mode.

```
Router> enable
Password:
```

In global configuration mode you have access to a set of commands that affect the system configuration as a whole. Cisco commands are not case sensitive.

```
Router# configure
Configuring from terminal, memory, or network [terminal]?
```

When you use the `configure` command you are prompted for the source of the configuration commands. Specify the terminal, NVRAM, or a file stored on a TFTP server on the network as the source. Alternatively specify terminal configuration by typing `configure terminal` at the command line. The `configure terminal` command is often shortened to `config term` or `Config` followed by two returns.

The default method is to enter commands from the terminal console. You can configure the router from a virtual (remote) terminal, or from a console terminal. This allows you to change the existing router configuration at any time. You can access many other specific configuration modes from global configuration mode. For example, many router features are enabled on a router interface basis. Use the `interface` command to access interface configuration mode. In this example, a serial interface is configured to provide clocking.

```
Router> enable
Password:
Router# configure
Configuring from terminal, memory, or network [terminal]?
Enter configuration commands, one per line. End with CNTL/Z.
Router(config)# interface serial 0
Router(config-if)# clock rate 64000
```

NOTE

The configuration modes accessible access from Global Configuration mode include (and may be beyond the scope of this book):

- **Interface Configuration**—*Many features are enabled on a per-interface basis. Interface configuration commands modify the operation of an interface such as an Ethernet, FDDI, or serial port. Interface configuration commands always follow an interface global configuration command, which defines the interface type.*

- **Subinterface Configuration**—*Configure multiple virtual interfaces (called subinterfaces) on a single physical interface. Subinterfaces appear to be distinct physical interfaces to the various protocols. For example, frame relay networks provide multiple point-to-point links called permanent virtual circuits (PVCs). PVCs can be grouped under separate subinterfaces that in turn are configured on a single physical interface. From a bridging spanning-tree viewpoint, each subinterface is a separate bridge port, and a frame arriving on one subinterface can be sent out on another subinterface.*

- **Controller Configuration**—*Configure channelized T1 in the controller configuration mode. Refer to the "Configuring Channelized E1 and Channelized T1" chapter in the* Dial Solutions Configuration Guide *for more information at* **www.cisco.com**.

- **Map-List Configuration**—*Cisco IOS ATM and frame relay software support static mapping schemes that identify the protocol addresses of remote hosts or routers.*

For a listing of which Cisco platforms support ATM and frame relay, see the "Platform Support" appendix in the Configuration Fundamentals Command Reference *at* **www.cisco.com**. *Map-list configuration commands configure a map list. They always follow a map-list global configuration command. See the "ATM Commands" chapter in the* Wide-Area Networking Command Reference *at* **www.cisco.com.**

■ *Router Configuration—Router configuration commands configure an IP routing protocol and always follow a router command. See the relevant chapter on IP routing protocol in the* Network Protocols Configuration Guide, Part 1 *at* **www.cisco.com**

■ *Line Configuration—Line configuration commands modify the operation of an auxiliary, console, physical, or virtual terminal line. They always follow a line command, which defines a line number. These commands are generally used to connect to remote routers or access servers, change terminal parameter settings either on a line-by-line basis or for a range of line, and set up the auxiliary port modem configuration to support dial-on-demand routing (DDR). See the "Configuring Modem Support and Asynchronous Devices" chapter in the* Dial Solutions Configuration Guide *at* **www.cisco.com.**

■ *IPX-Router Configuration—Internet Packet Exchange (IPX) is a Novell network-layer protocol. The IPX-router configuration mode is used to configure IPX routing. Refer to the "Novell IPX Commands" chapter in the* Network Protocols Command Reference, Part 2 *at* **www.cisco.com.**

■ *Route-Map Configuration—Use the route-map configure mode to configure routing table and source and destination information. See the "Configuring IP Routing Protocol-Independent Features" chapter in the* Network Protocols Configuration Guide, Part 1 *at* **www.cisco.com.**

■ *ROM monitor—If the router or access server does not produce a valid system image, or if you interrupt the boot sequence, the system might enter read-only memory (ROM) monitor mode. From ROM monitor mode, you can boot the device or perform diagnostic tests.*

In the example below, a routing protocol has been enabled by a global configuration command. The router configuration mode prompt is displayed. Then the `network` command is used to associate a specific network with the routing protocol.

```
Router> enable
Password:
Router# configure
Configuring from terminal, memory, or network [terminal]?
Enter configuration commands, one per line. End with CNTL/Z.
Router(config)# router rip
Router(config-router)# network 172.16.0.0
```

Enter multiple boot system commands in the router's startup configuration file to provide a backup method for loading a system image into the router. An operating system image can be loaded in three ways:

- From flash memory:

```
Router# configure terminal
Router(config)# boot system flash gsnew-image
[Ctrl-Z]
Router# copy running-config startup-config
```

- From a network TFTP server:

```
Router# configure terminal
Router(config)# boot system test.exe 172.16.13.111
[Ctrl-Z]
Router# copy running-config startup-config
```

- From ROM:

```
Router# configure terminal
Router(config)# boot system rom
[Ctrl-Z]
Router# copy running-config startup-config
```

Enter the different types of boot system commands in any order in NVRAM configuration. If you enter multiple boot commands, the router tries them in the order in which they were entered.

Flash memory makes it possible to copy new system images without changing electrically erasable programmable read-only memories (EEP-ROMs). The information stored in flash memory isn't vulnerable to network failures that can occur when loading system images from servers.

In case flash memory becomes corrupted, you can specify a system image to be loaded from a TFTP server. This provides a backup boot method for the router. In case of both network failure and corrupted flash memory, you can specify that the system image load from ROM to provide a final backup boot method.

System images stored in ROM might not always be as complete or as current as those stored in flash memory or on network servers.

It is possible to create a backup of the Cisco IOS image by copying it to a network server. Use this copy of the system image to verify that the copy in flash memory is the same as the original disk file.

The example shown below uses the `show flash` command to learn the name of the system image file. In this case the filename is `igs-j-1`. Use the `Copy Flash TFTP` command to copy the image to a TFTP server.

```
Router# show flash
4096K bytes of flash memory on embedded flash (in XX).

file  offset      length      name
0     0x40        1294637     igs-j-1
   [903848/2097152 bytes free]

Router# copy flash tftp
IP address of remote host [255.255.255.255]? 172.16.13.111
filename to write on tftp host? igs-j-1
write igs-j-1 !!!!!!!!!!!!!!!!!!!!!!!!!!!!!!!!!!!!!!!!!!!!!!!!!!!!!!!
successful tftp write.
```

Load Cisco IOS software into flash from a TFTP server using the `Copy TFTP Flash` command.

```
Router# copy tftp flash
```

The system prompts for the IP address (or name) of the TFTP server, then for the name of the image file. There is the option of erasing the existing flash memory before writing to it.

```
IP address or name of remote host [255.255.255.255]? 172.16.13.111
Name of configuration file? [igs-j-1]? <Return>
copy igs-j-1 from 172.16.13.111 into flash memory? [confirm] <Return>
xxxxxxx bytes available for writing without erasure.
erase flash before writing? [confirm]<Return>
Clearing and initializing flash memory (please wait)####...###

Loading from 172.16.13.111: !!!!!!!!!!!!!!!!!!!!!!!!!!!!!!!!!!!!!!!!!
[OK - 324572/524212 bytes]
Verifying checsum...
vvvvvvvvvvvvvvvvvvvvvvvvvvvvvvvvvvvvvvvvvvvvvvvvvvvvvvvvvvvvvv
Flash veritification successful. Length = 1204637, checksum = 0x95D9
```

NOTE

If you attempt to copy a file into flash memory that is already there, a prompt indicates that a file with the same name already exists. This old file is marked deleted when you copy the new file into flash. The first copy of the file still remains in flash but it is rendered unusable in favor of the newest version. It is listed with a [deleted] tag when you use the show flash *command. If you abort the copy process, the newer file is marked* [deleted] *because the entire file was not copied and is therefore not valid.*

In the example shown above, a system image named `igs-j-1` is copied into flash memory. Each exclamation mark means that ten User Datagram Protocol (UDP) segments have successfully transferred. The series of Vs indicates successful checksum verification.

Configuration Control

Router configuration can be approached with a general method (Figure 4.8).

FIGURE 4.8
A general method to
router configuration.

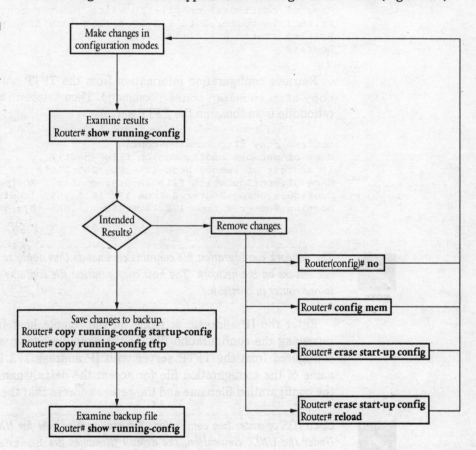

Initially, make certain changes to the router's configuration by entering commands in the appropriate configuration mode. Then examine the results of the changes made. Use the `show running-config` command to do this. If the results are satisfactory, save them to the backup file that the router will use when it starts up again. Otherwise remove the changes.

Load configuration information from a TFTP server on the network or NVRAM. Store the current router configuration (in RAM) on a network TFTP server using the `copy running-config tftp` command. Then configure the router by retrieving the configuration file. This makes it possible to maintain and store configuration information at a central location.

```
Router# copy running-config tftp
Remote host[]? 172.16.2.155
Name of configuration file to write [Router-config]? router.2
Write file router.2 to 172.16.2.155? [confirm] y
Writing router.2 !!!!!!!! [OK]
Router#
```

Retrieve configuration information from the TFTP server by entering the `copy tftp running-config` command. Then select an appropriate configuration file from those on the TFTP server.

```
Router# copy tftp running-config
Host of network configuration file [host]?
IP address of remote host [255.255.255.255]? 172.16.2.155
Name of configuration file [Router-config]? Router.2
Configure using Router.2 from 172.16.2.155? [confirm] y
Booting Router.2 from 172.16.2.155:!! [OK - 874/16000 bytes]
```

NOTE

The network configuration file contains commands that apply to all routers and terminal servers on the network. The host configuration file contains commands that apply to one router in particular.

Enter the IP address, or name, of the remote host from which you are retrieving the configuration file. In the example shown above, the router is configured from the TFTP server with IP address 172.16.2.155. Enter the name of the configuration file (or accept the default name). Finally, confirm the configuration filename and the server address that the system supplies.

NOTE

Cisco IOS operates two conventions for naming files, one for UNIX and one for DOS. Under the UNIX convention, the default filenames are `hostname-config` *for the host file, and* `network-config` *for the network configuration file. In a DOS environment, the server filenames are limited to eight characters plus a three-character extension (for example,* `router.cfg`*).*

Merge configuration information to the running configuration file from NVRAM using the `copy startup-config running-config` command.

This command adds startup commands to the running configuration. It is not a reset operation.

Alternatively use the `erase startup-config` command to erase the contents of NVRAM. When you reboot the router you can enter new configuration information in the setup dialog. To display the saved configuration use the `show startup-config` command. This displays the contents of NVRAM.

We will now look at examples of how to configure a Cisco router.

Secure the system by using passwords to restrict access. For example, use the `enable password` command to restrict access to the privileged exec mode. We will look here at how to establish passwords on individual terminal lines.

```
Router> enable
Password:
Router#
```

First enter global configuration mode using the `config term` command. (Type a question mark to see a list of available configuration commands.) To enable passwords on terminal lines use the `line` command.

```
Router# config term

Router(config)# line ?
  <0-6>    First Line number
  aux      Auxiliary line
  console  Primary terminal line
  vty      Virtual terminal
```

Enter `line console 0` to begin the password configuration process for the console terminal. Then enter `login` to enable password checking. Finally, enter `password` followed by the chosen password for this terminal line.

```
Router(config)# line console 0
Router(config-line)# login
Router(config-line)# password cisco
```

Enter `line vty 0 4` to establish password protection on incoming TELNET sessions from remote terminals 0 through 4. Again, using the `login` command enables password checking. Then use the `password` command with the chosen password.

```
Router(config)# line vty 0 4
Router(config-line)# login
Router(config-line)# password cisco
```

Now let's look at how to give a router a meaningful name.

Enter global configuration mode by typing `config term`. Because you want to change the hostname of the router, you can type `ho?` to check which command to use.

```
Router> enable
Password:
Router# config term
Router(config)# ho?
hostname
```

You need to use the `hostname` command. To find out more about the `hostname` command enter `hostname ?`.

```
Router(config)# hostname ?
  WORD    This system's network name
```

Now that you know the correct syntax to use, change the router's name. If you want to change the router's name to SanJose enter `hostname Boston`. Then you press **Ctrl+Z** to exit configuration mode.

```
Router(config)# hostname Boston^Z
```

A message is displayed letting you know that the router has been configured. Press **Return** to acknowledge the message. Notice that the router name has changed at the prompt.

```
Router#
%SYS-5-CONFIG_I: Configured from console by console
Boston#
```

Check the new configuration by entering `show running-config`. The router's name has changed. This can be contrasted with the startup configuration.

```
Boston# show running-config

Current configuration:
!
version 11.3
no service upd-small-servers
no service tcp-small servers
!
hostname Boston
!
enable secret 5 $1$xmb1$CW2.ZcrS8oDfh8IXCm5si1
```

```
enable password eve
!
!
interface Ethernet0
 ip address 172.16.128.1 255.255.255.0
 no mop enabled
!
interface Serial0
 ip address 172.16.65.2 255.255.255.0
!
interface Serial1
 ip address 172.16.67.1 255.255.255.0
 clockrate 64000
--more--
```

Enter show startup-config to see the startup configuration file. This still shows the old router name.

```
Current configuration:
!
version 11.3
no service upd-small-servers
no service tcp-small servers
!
hostname Router
!
enable secret 5 $1$xmb1$CW2.ZcrS8oDfh8IXCm5si1
enable password eve
!
!
interface Ethernet0
 ip address 172.16.128.1 255.255.255.0
 no mop enabled
!
interface Serial0
 ip address 172.16.65.2 255.255.255.0
!
interface Serial1
 ip address 172.16.67.1 255.255.255.0
 clockrate 64000
--more--
```

The changes made to the running configuration (in RAM) have not affected the configuration stored in the startup configuration file (in NVRAM). (To add the changes to the startup configuration, use the copy running-config startup-config command.) Restore the startup configuration by entering config mem. (This is the abbreviated version of the configure memory command.) Notice that the router name has now changed back to Router. Now, if you examine the running configuration file, you see that the original hostname has been restored.

```
Boston# config mem

Router#
%SYS-5-CONFIG_I: Configured from memory by console

Router#
Router# show running-config
Current configuration:
!
version 11.3·
no service upd-small-servers
no service tcp-small servers
!
hostname Router
!
enable secret 5 $1$xmb1$CW2.ZcrS8oDfh8IXCm5si1
enable password eve
!
!
interface Ethernet0
 ip address 172.16.128.1 255.255.255.0
 no mop enabled
!
interface Serial0
 ip address 172.16.65.2 255.255.255.0
!
interface Serial1
 ip address 172.16.67.1 255.255.255.0
 clockrate 64000
--more--
```

Accessing Configuration

This section explains how to access remote Cisco routers. We will examine how to use the Cisco Discovery Protocol (CDP) to get information about a router's neighbors, how to use the TELNET utility to log in to remote Cisco routers, some basic connectivity methods, and how to access remote router using the TELNET utility.

Cisco Discovery Protocol

CDP provides a single proprietary command that enables access to a summary of the multiple protocols and addresses configured on other directly connected routers.

CDP runs over a data-link layer connecting lower physical media and upper network-layer protocols as seen in Figure 4.9. Because CDP operates at this level, two or more CDP devices that support different network layer protocols can learn about each other.

FIGURE 4.9
CDP enables
discovery on
multiprotocol
networks.

Upper-Layer Entry Addresses	TCP/IP	Novell IPX	AppleTalk	Others
Cisco Proprietary Data-Link Protocol	CDP discovers and shows information about directly connected Cisco devices.			
Media Supporting SNAP	LANs	Frame Relay	ATM	Others

FIGURE 4.9
CDP enables discovery on multiprotocol networks.

Physical media supporting the Subnetwork Access Protocol (SNAP) connect CDP devices. These include all LANs, frame relay and SMDS WANs, and ATM networks. Advertisement and discovery using CDP involves frame exchanges at the data-link layer. Only directly connected routers, bridges, access servers, and workgroup switches (neighbors) can exchange CDP information. Cisco devices never forward CDP packets. When new CDP information is received, Cisco devices discard old information.

When a Cisco device running Cisco IOS boots up, CDP runs by default. CDP can then automatically discover neighboring Cisco devices that are running CDP, regardless of which protocol they are running. Once CDP has discovered a device, it can display any of the various upper-layer protocol address entries used on the discovered device's port, such as IPX or AppleTalk Datagram Delivery Protocol.

Each router running CDP exchanges information about any protocol entries it knows with its neighbors. Display the results of this CDP information exchange on a console directly connected to a router configured to run CDP on its interfaces.

A router caches any information it receives from its CDP neighbors. If a subsequent CDP frame indicates that any of the information about a neighbor has changed, the router discards the older information in favor of the newer.

In the following example, use the show cdp interface command to display:

- **The interface status**—For Ethernet0, Serial0, and Serial0, the line protocol is up.
- **The encapsulation used by CDP for its advertisement and discovery frame transmissions**—For Ethernet0, encapsulation is ARPA, while for Serial0 and Serial1 the encapsulation is HDLC.

```
Router> enable
Password:
```

```
Router# config
Configuring from terminal, memory, or network [terminal]?
Enter configuration commands, one per line. End with CNTL/Z.
Router(config)# interface serial 0
Router(config-if)# cdp enable
Router(config-if)# ^Z
Router#
%SYS-5-CONFIG_I: Configured from console by console
Router# show cdp interface
Ehternet0 is up, line protocol is up, encapsulation is ARPA
  Sending CDP packets every 60 seconds
  Holdtime is 180 seconds
Serial0 is up, line protocol is up, encapsulation is HDLC
  Sending CDP packets every 60 seconds
  Holdtime is 180 seconds
Serial1 is up, line protocol is up, encapsulation is HDLC
  Sending CDP packets every 60 seconds
  Holdtime is 180 seconds
```

The timers for the frequency between CDP updates and the holdtime for older CDP entries are set by default at 60 seconds and 180 seconds respectively. If the router receives a more recent update, or if the holdtime value expires, the router must discard that CDP entry.

Display the results of CDP information exchange between neighboring routers. Use the show cdp entry command to display a single cached CDP entry.

```
Router# show cdp entry Vermont

Device ID: Vermont
Entry address(es):
  IP address: 198.92.68.18
  CLNS address: 490001.1111.1111.00
  AppleTalk address: 10.1
Platform: AGS, Capabilities: Router Trans-Bridge
Interface: Ethernet0, Port ID(outgoing port): Ethernet0
Holdtime: 155 sec
```

NOTE

The output from this command includes all Layer 3 addresses present in the neighboring router. You can see the IP, Apple Talk, and CLNS network addresses of the targeted CDP neighbor with a single command.

Use the show cdp neighbors command to display the CDP updates received on the local router. For each port the display shows the neighbor router's ID, the local port type and number, and a decremental holdtime value (in seconds).

```
Router# show cdp neighbors

Capability Codes: R - Router, T - Trans Bridge, B - Source Route Bridge
                  S - Switch, H - Host, I - IGMP
Device ID         Local Interface    Holdtime   Capability   Platform   Port ID
Maine             Ser 0              130        R            2500       Ser 0
New Hampshire     Ser 1              156        R            2500       Ser 1
```

You can also see the neighbor router's device capability code, hardware platform, and remote port type and number.

You can display information combined from the show cdp entry and show cdp neighbors commands by using the show cdp neighbor detail command. You can see device information for each of the router's CDP neighbors, in this case Vermont and Maine.

```
Router# show cdp neighbors all

Device ID: Maine
Entry address(es):
    IP address: 172.16.65.1
Platform: cisco 2500, Capabilities: Router
Interface: Serial0, Port ID (outgoing port): Serial0
Holdtime: 169 sec

Version:
Cisco Internetwork Operating System Software
IOS (tm) 3000 Software (IGS-J-L), Version 11.1(4), RELEASE SOFT-
WARE (fc1)
Copyright (c) 1986-1996 by cisco Systems, Inc.

Compiled Mon 17-Jun-96 14:55 by mkamson
-------------------------
Device ID: New Hampshire
Entry address(es):
    IP address: 172.16.67.2
Platform: cisco 2500, Capabilities: Router
Interface: Serial1, Port ID (outgoing port): Serial1
Holdtime: 134 sec

Version:
--more--
```

Virtual Terminal Connections

The TCP/IP remote login utility, TELNET, can be used to initiate console sessions with remote routers. It is possible to log into other Cisco routers without being physically attached to them. To access a remote router, use the TELNET command along with the IP address of one of the target router's interfaces. In the example shown here, a connection is established to one of the Maine router's serial ports.

```
Vermont> enable
Password:
Vermont# telnet 172.16.67.2
Trying 172.16.67.2 ... Open

User Access Verification

Password:
Maine>
```

If the target router's host name is available on the source router or if it can be reached from a DNS server to which the source router has access, then you can use the host name with the TELNET command. Here a connection is established with the Maine router.

A router's configuration or a Domain Name Service (DNS) server maps IP addresses to more meaningful router host names. For example, the IP address 172.16.67.2 corresponds to the host name Maine on the router.

In fact, given access to a DNS server or the router configuration, you can establish a TELNET connection with a remote router using just the host name. In the example shown here, enter Maine to access that router.

```
User Access Verification
Password:
Maine>exit
[Connection to Maine closed by foreign host]
Vermont# Maine
Trying Maine (172.16.67.2) ... Open

User Access Verification

Password:
Maine>exit
```

Once you have established a TELNET session with another router, you can enter the escape sequence Ctrl+Shift+6+X to get back to the command prompt of the source router without ending the TELNET session. It is possible to initiate another session from the router, this time to the Connecticut router.

```
Maine> <Ctrl+Shift+6+X>
Vermont# Connecticut
Trying Connecticut (172.16.65.1) ... Open
```

```
User Access Verification

Password:
Connecticut>
```

Display details of the currently open TELNET sessions from the router using the show sessions command. Each session has an associated connection number.

```
Connecticut> <Ctrl+Shift+6+X>
Vermont# show sessions
Conn Host          Address        Byte  Idle    Conn Name
   1 Maine          172.16.67.2     0     1      Maine
 * 2 Connecticut    172.16.65.1     0     1      Connecticut

Vermont#
```

Resume the session by pressing **Return**. By entering the appropriate session number you can resume that TELNET connection. In the example shown here, enter 1 to resume the connection to the Maine router.

```
Vermont# <Return>

[Resuming connection 2 to Connecticut ... ]
Connecticut> 1

[Resuming connection 1 to Maine ... ]
Maine>
```

From the local router prompt you can end (or disconnect) a TELNET session using the disconnect command. In this example, disconnect the second session to the Connecticut router.

```
Vermont# disconn 2
Closing connection to Connecticut [confirm]
Vermont#
```

You can also end a TELNET session by entering quit or exit at the remote target router's prompt. In the example shown here, end the session with the Maine router and return to the Vermont router.

```
Vermont# 1
Maine# exit
[Connection to Maine closed by foreign host]
Vermont#
```

Entering exit *logs you out of the remote router whereas the escape sequence* (**Ctrl+Shift+6+X**) *moves you back to your own router without ending any sessions.*

Basic Connectivity Testing

It is a good idea to perform basic testing of internetwork connectivity following the layers of the OSI model. Begin testing by focusing on upper-layer applications. Use TELNET to determine if a remote router can be accessed. If you can remotely access another router using TELNET, then you know that one TCP/IP application can reach that router. A successful TELNET connection indicates that the upper-layer application, and the services provided by the lower layers function properly.

You may find that you can TELNET to one router, but not to another. In this case it is likely that the TELNET failure is caused by specific addressing, naming, or access permission problems. These problems can exist on the local router or on the router that failed as a TELNET target.

The *Ping utility* provides a simple mechanism to determine whether packets are reaching a particular destination. When you use the Ping command the router sends a special datagram to the destination host. It then waits for a reply datagram from that host. The results of this echo protocol can help evaluate the path-to-host reliability, delays over the path, and whether the host can be reached or is functioning.

In the example shown here, the ping target responded successfully to all five datagrams sent. The exclamation marks indicate each successful echo.

```
Vermont> enable
Password:
Vermont# ping 172.16.65.1
Type escape sequence to abort.
Sending 5, 100-byte ICMP Echoes to 172.16.65.1, timeout is 2
seconds:
!!!!!
Success rate is 100 percent (5/5), round-trip min/avg/max =
36/38/40 ms
Vermont#
```

Here, the router timed out waiting for a datagram echo from the ping target. The periods indicate that the requests have timed out.

```
Vermont# ping 172.16.65.3
Type escape sequence to abort.
Sending 5, 100-byte ICMP Echoes to 172.16.65.3, timeout is 2
seconds:
```

```
. . . . .
Success rate is 0 percent (0/5)
Vermont#
```

NOTE

> *The* `ping` *user Exec command can be used to diagnose basic network connectivity on AppleTalk, CLNS, IP, Novell IPX, Apollo, VINES, DECnet, or XNS networks.*

Use the `trace` command to discover the routes that packets take when traveling to their destinations. The `trace` command takes advantage of the error messages generated by routers when a datagram exceeds its time-to-live (TTL) value. It starts by sending probe datagrams with a TTL value of 1. The low TTL value causes the router to discard the probe datagram and send back an error message. Several probes are sent at each TTL level and the round-trip time for each is displayed.

The next basic test focuses on the network layer. Use the `show ip route` command to determine whether a routing table entry exists for the target network. In the example shown below, the network (a subnet) 172.16.129.0 is present, but the network 172.16.192.0 is not available.

```
Vermont# show ip route

Codes: C - connected, S - static, I - IGRP, R - RIP, M - mobile, B - BGP
       D - EGIRP, EX - EGIRP external, O - OSPF, IA - OSPF inter area
       E1 - OSPF external type 1, E2 - OSPF external type 2, E - EGP
       i - IS-IS, L1 - IS-IS level 1, L2 - IS-IS level 2, * - candidate default

Gateway of last report is not set

    172.16.0.0  255.255.255.0 is subnetted, 4 subnets
R      172.16.129.0 [120/1] via 172.16.64.4, 00:00:28, Ethernet0
C      172.16.128.0 is directly connected, Ethernet0
C      172.16.67.0 is directly connected, Serial1
C      172.16.65.0 is directly connected, Serial0
Vermont#
```

The next step is to examine the data-link and physical layers. Use the `show interface` command to display the line and data link protocol status. A partial example is shown below.

```
Vermont# show interface serial1
Serial1 is up, line protocol is up
  Hardware is HD64570
  Internet address is 172.16.67.1 255.255.255.0
  MTU 1500 bytes, BW 1544 Kbit, DLY 2000 usec, rely 255/255, load
1/255
  Encapsulation HDLC, loopback not set, keepalive set (10 sec)
```

```
Last input 0:00:07, output 0:00:06, output hang never
Last clearing of "show interface" counters never
Output queue 0/40, 0 drops; input queue 0/75, 0 drops
5 minute input rate 0 bits/sec, 0 packets/sec
5 minute output rate 0 bits/sec, 0 packets/sec
1177 packets input, 75807 bytes, 0 no buffer
Received 1031 broadcasts, 0 runts, 0 giants
0 input errors, 0 crc, 0 frame, 0 overrun, 0 ignored, 0 abort
1300 packets output, 75807 bytes, 0 underruns
0 ouptput errors, 0 collisions, 16 interface resets, 0 restarts
```

The line status is triggered by a *carrier detect signal*. This refers to the physical layer. The line protocol is triggered by *keepalive frames*, which refer to the data-link layer.

If the line and line protocol are up, then the link is operational. If the line is up, but the line protocol is down, there is a connection or clocking problem. If the line is down and the line protocol is down, then there is an interface problem. If the line is displayed as being administratively down and the line protocol is down, then that interface is disabled.

The `show interface` command shows real-time statistics related to an interface that can help indicate the source of a problem. For example, an increasing number of input errors may indicate faulty equipment or a noisy line.

Use `debug` commands to see what protocol messages are being sent and received by a router. The `debug` privileged Exec commands can provide a wealth of information about the traffic being seen (or not seen) on an interface. Examine error messages generated by nodes on the network, protocol-specific diagnostic packets, and other useful troubleshooting data. A partial example is shown below.

```
Vermont# debug ip-rip
RIP protocol debugging is on
Vermont#
RIP: received update from 172.16.65.1 on Serial0
     172.16.68.0 in 1 hops
     172.16.66.0 in 2 hops
     172.16.32.0 in 1 hops
     172.16.1.0 in 2 hops
RIP: received update from 172.16.128.3 on Ethernet0
     172.16.129.0 in 1 hops
RIP: received update from 172.16.67.2 on Serial1
     172.16.192.0 in 1 hops
     172.16.68.0 in 2 hops
     172.16.66.0 in 1 hops
     172.16.1.0 in 2 hops
```

You should be aware that the debug commands often generate data of little use for a specific problem. Also, the high overhead of debug commands can disrupt router operation. You should use debug commands only when you have narrowed your problems to a likely subset of causes, not to monitor normal network operation. By default, the router sends output from system error messages and the debug commands to the console terminal. Messages can also be redirected to a UNIX host or to an internal buffer.

TCP/IP
Addressing

An IP network has two very important resources, its IP addresses and the corresponding naming structure within the network. To provide effective communication between hosts or stations in a network, each station must maintain a unique identity. In an IP network this is achieved by the IP address. The distribution and management of these addresses is an important consideration in an IP network design.

IP addresses are inherently not easy to remember. People find it much easier to remember names and have these names related to individual machines connected to a network. Even applications rarely refer to hosts by their binary identifiers; in general they use ASCII strings such as polo@westport.com. These names must be translated to IP addresses because the network does not utilize identifiers based on ASCII strings. The management of these names and the translation mechanism used must also be considered by the IP network designer.

After the network has been designed and implemented, it must be managed. Traffic flow, bottlenecks, security risks, and network enhancements must be monitored. Systems for this type of management are available and should be incorporated in the IP network's initial design, so as to avoid headaches because of ad hoc processes coupled together at a later date.

Address Management

As mentioned previously, the distribution and management of network-layer addresses is crucial. Addresses for networks and subnets must be well planned, administered, and documented. Because network and subnet addresses cannot be dynamically assigned, an unplanned or undocumented network will be difficult to debug and will not be scalable.

As opposed to the network itself, devices attached to the network can generally be configured for dynamic address allocation. This allows for easier administration and a more robust solution. The following section deals with the issues faced by technologies used in address management.

IP Addresses and Address Classes

The IP address is defined in RFC 1166—Internet Numbers as a 32-bit number having two parts.

```
IP address = <network number><host number>
```

The first part of the address, the network number, is assigned by a regional authority (see "IP Address Registration" section in this chapter), and will vary in its length depending on the class of addresses to which it belongs. The network number part of the IP address is used by the IP protocol to route IP datagrams throughout TCP/IP networks. These networks may be within your enterprise and under your control, in which case, to some extent, you are free to allocate this part of the address yourself without prior reference to the Internet authority. If you do so, you are encouraged to use the private IP addresses that have been reserved by the Internet Assigned Number Authority (IANA) for that purpose (see the "Private IP Addresses" section in this chapter). However, your routing may take you into networks outside your control, using, for example, the worldwide services of the Internet. In this second case, it is imperative that you obtain a unique IP address from your regional Internet address authority (see the "IP Address Registration" section in this chapter).

The second part of the IP address, the host number, is used to identify the individual host within a network. This portion of the address is assigned locally within a network by the authority that controls that network. The length of this number is, as mentioned before, dependent on the class of the IP address being used and also on whether or not subnetting is in use (subnetting is discussed in the "Subnets" section).

The 32 bits that make up the IP address are usually written as four 8-bit decimal values concatenated with dots (periods). This representation is commonly referred to as a *dotted decimal notation*. An example of this is the IP address 172.16.3.14. In this example the 172.16 is the network number and the 3.14 is the host number. The split into network number and host number is determined by the class of the IP address.

There are five classes of IP addresses. These are shown in Figure 5.1.

This diagram shows the division of the IP address into a network number part and a host number part. The first few bits of the address determine the class of the address and its structure. Classes A, B, and C represent *unicast addresses* and make up the majority of network addresses issued by the InterNIC. A unicast address is an IP address that refers to a single recipient. To address multiple recipients you can use *broadcast* or *multicast* addresses (see the "Special Case Addresses" section in this chapter).

Class A addresses have the first bit set to 0. The next 7 bits are used for the network number. This gives a possibility of 128 networks (27). However, it should be noted that there are two cases, the all-bits 0 number and the all-bits 1 number, which have special significance in classes A, B, and C. These are discussed in the "Special Case Addresses" section. These special case addresses are reserved, which gives us the possibility of only 126 (128–2) networks in Class A. The remaining 24 bits of a Class A address are used for the host number. Once again, the two special cases apply to the host number part of an IP address. Each Class A network can therefore have a total of 16,777,214 hosts (224–2). Class A addresses are assigned only to networks with very large numbers of hosts (historically, large corporations). An example is the 9.0.0.0 network, which is assigned to IBM.

The Class B address is more suited to medium-sized networks. The first two bits of the address are predefined as 10. The next 14 bits are used for the network number and the remaining 16 bits identify the host number. This gives a possibility of 16,382 networks each containing up to 65,534 hosts. The Class C address offers a maximum of 254 hosts per network and is therefore suited to smaller networks. However, with the first three bits of the address predefined to 110, the next 21 bits provide for a maximum of 2,097,150 such networks.

The remaining classes of address, D and E, are reserved classes and have a special meaning. Class E addresses are reserved for future use while Class D addresses are used to address groups of hosts in a limited area. This function is known as *multicasting* and is beyond the scope of this book.

FIGURE 5.1
IP Address classes.

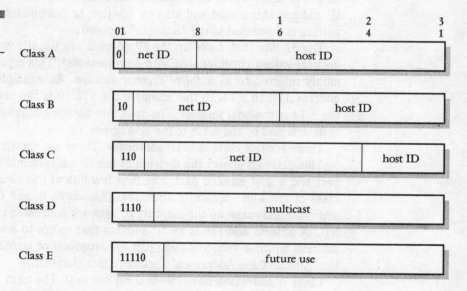

Special Case Addresses

We have already come across several addresses that have been reserved or have special meanings. We will now discuss these special cases in more detail.

Source Address Broadcasts

As we have seen, both the network number and host number parts of an address have the reserved values of all bits 0 and all bits 1. The first value of all bits 0 is seen only as a source IP address and can be used to identify this host on this network (both network and host number parts set to all bits 0—0.0.0.0) or a particular host on this network—<network part>, <host part>=whatever.

Both the cases described above would relate only to situations where the source IP address appears as part of an initialization procedure when a host is trying to determine its own IP address. The BootP protocol is an example of such a scenario (see the "Bootstrap Protocol (BootP)" section).

Destination Address Broadcasts

The all bits 1 value is used for broadcast messages and, again, may appear in several combinations. However, it is used only as a destination address.

When both the network number and host number parts of an IP address are set to the all bits 1 value, the IP protocol will issue a limited broadcast to all hosts on the network. This is restricted to networks that support broadcasting and will appear only on the local segment. The broadcast will never be forwarded by any routers.

If the network number is set to a valid network address while the host number remains set to all bits 1 then a directed broadcast will be sent to all hosts on the specified network. For example, 172.16.255.255 will refer to all hosts on the 172.16 network. This broadcast can be extended to use *subnetting*, but both the sender and any routers in the path must be aware of the subnet mask being used by the target host (subnetting is discussed in the "Subnets" section).

Loopback Address

Of all the broadcast addresses there is one with special significance: 127.0.0.0. This all-bits 1 Class A address is used as a loopback address and, if implemented, must be used correctly to point back at the originating host itself. In many implementations, this address is used to provide test functions. By definition, the IP datagrams never actually leave the host.

The use of broadcast addresses is very much dependent on the capabilities of the components of the network, including the application, the TCP/IP implementation and the hardware. All these must support broadcasting and must react in a given way depending on the type of broadcast address. Incorrect configurations can lead to unpredictable results, with broadcast storms flooding a network. Broadcasting is a feature that should be used with care. It should be avoided if possible, but in some cases, cannot be avoided.

Private IP Addresses

We have briefly discussed how the regional authorities assign official IP addresses when an organization is required to route traffic across the Internet (see "IP Address Registration" for further details). However, when building their networks, many organizations do not have the requirement (or at least they do not yet have the requirement) to route outside their own network. Under these circumstances the network can be assigned any IP address that the local network administrator chooses. This practice has now been formalized in RFC 1918 *Address Allocation for Private Internets*. This RFC details the following three ranges of addresses, which the IANA has reserved for private networks that do not require connectivity to the Internet:

10—The single Class A network
172.16 through 172.31—16 contiguous Class B networks
192.168.0 through 192.168.255—256 contiguous Class C networks

These addresses may be used by any organization without reference to any other organization, including the Internet authorities. However, they must not be referenced by any host in another organization, nor must they be defined to any external routers. All external routers should discard any routing information regarding these addresses, and internal routers should restrict the advertisement of routes to these private IP addresses.

Subnets

The idea of a subnet is to break down the host number part of an IP address to provide an extra level of addressability. We stated in "IP Addresses and Address Classes" that an IP address has two parts:

```
<network number><host number>
```

Routing between networks is based upon the network number part of the address only. In a Class A network this means that one byte of the IP address is used for routing (for example, the 9 in the IBM Class A address 9.0.0.0). This is fine for remote networks routing into the local 9 network. They simply direct everything for the IBM network at a specified router that accepts all the 9.0.0.0 traffic.

However, that router must then move the traffic to each of the 16,777,214 hosts that a Class A network might have. This will result in huge routing tables in the routers, as they need to know where every host is. To overcome this problem, the host number can be further subdivided into a subnet number and a host number to provide a second logical network within the first. This second network is known as the subnetwork or subnet. A subnetted address now has three parts:

```
<network number><subnet number><host number>
```

The subnet number is transparent to remote networks. Remote hosts still regard the local part of the address (the subnet number and the host number) as a host number. Only those hosts within the network that are configured to use subnets are aware that subnetting is in effect.

Only the local part of the address is divided into subnet number and host number is up to the local network administrator. Subnetting can be used with all three classes of IP addresses but there are precautions to be aware of in the different classes. Class C addresses have only a 1-byte host number to divide into subnet and host. Care must be taken not to use too many bits for the subnet, because this reduces the number of bits remaining for the host's allocation. For example, there are few networks that need to split a class C address into 128 subnets with one host each.

Subnet Mask

A subnet is created by the use of a subnet mask. This is a 32-bit number just like the IP address itself, and has bits relating to the network number, subnet number and host number. The bit positions in the subnet mask that identify the network number are set to 1s to maintain the original routing. In the remaining local part of the address, bits set to 1 indicate the subnet number and bits set to zero indicate the host number. You can use any number of bits from the host number to provide your subnet mask. However, these bits should be kept contiguous when creating the mask because this makes the address more readable and easier to administer. We also recommended that, whenever possible, you use eight or four bits for the mask. Again, this makes understanding the subnetting values a lot easier.

Let us look at a subnet mask of 255.255.255.0. This has a bit representation of:

```
11111111 11111111 11111111 00000000
```

In order for a host or router to apply the mask, it performs a `logical_AND` of the mask with the IP address it is trying to route (for example, 172.16.3.14).

```
10000000 00001010 00000011 00001110
11111111 11111111 11111111 00000000 logical_AND
10000000 00001010 00000011 00000000
```

The result provides the subnet value of 172.16.3. Notice that a subnet is normally identified as a concatenation of the network number and subnet number. The trailing zero is not normally shown. The original datagram can now be routed to its destination within the network, based on its subnet value.

The previous subnet mask uses a full eight bits for the subnet number. This is a practice we strongly recommend. However, you may decide to use a different number of bits. Another common split is to use four bits for the subnet number with the remaining bits for the host number. This may be your best option when subnetting Class C addresses. Remember that you have only one byte of host address to use. In the first scheme, it is clear what the available subnet numbers are. The eight bits provide an easily readable value which in our example is 3. When you use only four bits, things are not quite so clear at first sight.

Let us take the same Class B network address previously used (172.16) and this time apply a subnet mask of 255.255.240.0, which has only four significant bits in the third byte for the subnet number. The bit values for this mask are seen in Figure 5.2.

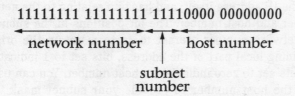

FIGURE 5.2
4-Bit subnet mask for a Class B address.

Applying this mask, the third byte of the address is divided into two 4-bit numbers: the first represents the subnet number, while the second is concatenated with the last byte of the address to provide a 12-bit host address.

Table 5.1 contains the subnet numbers that are possible when using this subnet mask.

For each of these subnet values, only 14 addresses (from 1 to 14) are valid because of the all-bits 0 and all-bits 1 number restrictions. This split will therefore give 14 subnets each with a maximum of 4,094 hosts. Notice that the value applied to the subnet number takes the value of the full byte with non-significant bits being set to zero. For example, the hexadecimal value 0001 in this subnet mask assumes an 8-bit value 00010000 and gives a subnet value of 16 and not 1 as it might seem.

TABLE 5.1
Subnet values for
subnet mask
255.255.240.0

Hexadecimal value	Subnet number
0000	0
0001	16
0010	32
0011	48
0100	64
0101	80
0111	112
1000	128
1001	144
1010	160
1011	176
1100	192
1101	208
1110	224
1111	240

Applying this mask to a sample Class B address 172.16.38.10 would break the address down as seen in Figure 5.3.

Notice that the host number shown above is a relative host number, that is, it is the 1,546th host on the 32nd subnet. This number bears no resemblance to the actual IP address this host has been assigned (172.16.38.10) and has no meaning in terms of IP routing.

Subnetting Example

As an example, a Class B network 172.16.0.0 is using a subnet mask of 255.255.255.0. This allocates the first two bytes of the address as the network number. The next eight bits represent the subnet number, and the last eight bits give us the host number. This allows us to have 254 subnets each having 254 hosts and the values of each are easily recognized.

FIGURE 5.3

An example of
subnet mask
implementation.

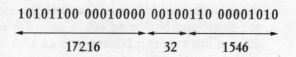

```
10101100 00010000 00100110 00001010
```

172.16   32   1546

or:

```
10101100 00010000 00100110 00001010
11111111 11111111 11110000 00000000  logical_AND
─────────────────────────────────────
10101100 00010000 00100000 00000000  = 172.16.32 (subnet)
```

and leaves a host address of:

```
-------- -------- ----0110 00001010
```

that represents host 1546

The Class B address 172.16.3.14 implies host 14 on subnet 3 of network 172.16. Figure 5.4 shows how this example can be implemented with three subnets. All IP traffic destined for the 172.16 network is sent to Router 1. Remember, all remote networks have no knowledge of the subnets used within the 172.16 network. Router 1 will apply the subnet mask (255.255.255.0) to the destination address in the incoming datagrams (a logical_AND of the subnet mask with the address). The result identifies the subnet 172.16.3. Router 1 will now route the datagrams to Router 2 according to its routing tables. Router 2 again applies the subnet mask to the address and again results in 172.16.3. Router 2 identifies this as a locally attached subnet and delivers the datagram to host 14 on that subnet.

Subnet Types

We stated earlier that a major reason for using subnets is to ease the problem of routing to large numbers of hosts within a network. There are a number of other reasons why you might consider the use of subnets; for example, the allocation of host addresses within a local network without subnets can be a problem.

Building networks of different technologies, LANs based on token ring or Ethernet, point-to-point links over SNA backbones, and so on, can impose severe restrictions on network addressing and may make it necessary to treat each as a separate network. If the limits of a network technology are reached, particularly in terms of the numbers of connected hosts, then adding new hosts requires a new physical network. There may also be a subset of the hosts within a network that monopolizes bandwidth and causes network congestion. Grouping these hosts on physical networks based on their high mutual communication requirements can ease the problem for the rest of the network. In each of the cases above it would be necessary to allocate multiple IP addresses to accommodate these networks. Using subnets overcomes these problems and permits full use of the IP addresses that have been allocated.

FIGURE 5.4
Subnet configuration
example.

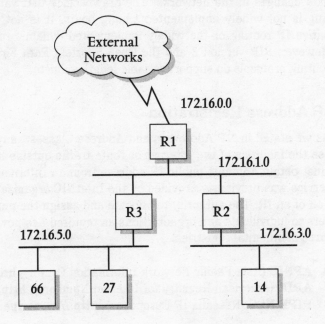

STATIC SUBNETTING

In the previous example, we used the same subnet mask in each of the hosts and routers in the 172.16 network. This can be referred to as static subnetting and implies the use of a single subnet mask for each network being configured. An internetwork may consist of networks of different classes, but each network will implement only one subnet within it. This is the easiest type of subnetting to understand and is simple to maintain. It is implemented in almost all hosts and routers and is supported in the Routing Information Protocol (RIP) and native IP routing. However, let us look at the allocation of hosts within a subnet. Our Class B network (172.16.0.0) uses a subnet mask of 255.255.255.0. This allows each subnet up to 254 hosts. If one of the subnets is a small network, perhaps a point-to-point link with only two host addresses, then we have wasted 252 of the host addresses that can have been allocated within that subnet. This is a major drawback of static subnetting.

VARIABLE-LENGTH SUBNETTING

This waste can be overcome by using variable-length subnetting. As the name implies, variable-length subnetting allows different subnets to use subnet masks of differing sizes. In this way, a subnet can use a mask appropriate to its size and avoid wasting addresses. By changing the length of the mask (by adding or subtracting bits), the subnet can easily be reorganized to accommodate changes in the networks. The drawback is that variable length subnetting is not widely implemented among hosts. It is not supported by either native IP routing or the widely implemented dynamic routing protocol, RIP. However, RIP Version 2 and the Open Shortest Path First (OSPF) Version 2 routing protocols do support variable-length subnets.

IP Address Registration

As we stated in "IP Addresses and Address Classes," any one who wishes to use the facilities of the Internet or route traffic outside his/her own network must obtain a unique public IP address from an Internet Registry (IR). This service was previously provided by the InterNIC organization and is the function of an IR. The authority to allocate and assign the numeric network numbers to individuals and organizations as required has now been distributed to three continental registries:

- **APNIC** (Asia-Pacific Network Information Center), **http://www.apnic.net**
- **ARIN** (American Registry for Internet Numbers), **http://www.arin.net**
- **RIPE NCC** (Réseaux IP Européens), **http://www.ripe.net**

These organizations have been delegated responsibility from IANA, which assigns all the various numeric identifiers required to operate the Internet. These identifiers can be seen in RFC 1700 *Assigned Numbers*. The three regional organizations do not cover all areas but they serve areas around their core service locations.

These three organizations rarely directly assign IP address for end-users. The growth in Internet activity has placed a heavy burden on the administrative facilities of the Internet authorities; many of the day-to-day registration services have been delegated to Internet service providers (ISPs).

The regional bodies that handle the geographic assignments of IP addresses assign blocks of Class C addresses to individual service providers who, in turn, re-assign these addresses to subscribers or customers.

The IANA has provided some guidelines for the allocation of IP addresses:

- RFC 2050—*Internet Registry IP Allocation Guidelines*

- RFC 1918—*Address Allocation for Private Internets*
- RFC 1518—*An Architecture for IP Address Allocation with CIDR*

When you apply for an IP address there are a number of points to consider before filling in the forms. Will you be registering your network as an *Autonomous System (AS)*? An Autonomous System is a group of IP networks operated by one or more network operators that has a single and clearly defined external routing policy. This implies that you plan to implement one or more gateways and use them to connect networks in the Internet. The term *gateway* is simply an historic name for a router in the IP community. The two terms can be used interchangeably. Each AS has a unique 16-bit number associated with it to identify the AS. An AS must therefore be registered with the IANA in a manner similar to that used for the IP network number. This AS identifier is also used for exchanging routing information between ASs using exterior routing protocols.

The creation of an AS is not a normal consideration for organizations seeking Internet connectivity. An AS is required only for exchanging routing information with other ASs. The simple case of a customer connecting a network to a single service provider will normally result in the customer's IP network being a member of the service provider's AS. All exterior routing is done by the service provider. The only time customers would want to create their own AS is when they have multi-homed networks connected to two or more service providers. In this case, there may be a difference in the exterior routing policies of the two service providers and, by creating an AS, the customer can adopt a different routing policy for each of the providers.

Another point of consideration is the establishment of a *domain name*, though this subject is beyond the scope of this chapter. Please refer to my book *Managing Dynamic IP Networks* for more information on the Domain Name System (DNS).

IP Address Exhaustion

The allocation of IP addresses by the IANA, and its related Internet Registries, proceeded almost unhindered for many years. However, the growth in Internet activity and the number of organizations requesting IP addresses in recent years has far surpassed all the expectations of the Internet authorities. This has created many problems, perhaps the most widely publicized being the exhaustion of IP addresses. The allocation of the Class A, B, and C addresses differs greatly, but with the number of networks on the Internet doubling annually, it became clear that very soon all classes of IP address would be exhausted.

Class A addresses, as we have already stated, are seldom allocated. Class B addresses, the preferred choice for most medium to large networks, became widely deployed and would soon have been exhausted, except that once the IR had realized the potential problem, it began allocating blocks of Class C addresses to individual organizations instead of a single Class B address.

The InterNIC has now had to change its policies on network number allocation in order to overcome the problems that it faces. These new rules are specified in RFC 1466 *Guidelines for Management of IP Address Space*, and are summarized as follows:

- Class A addresses from 64.0.0.0 through 127.0.0.0 will be reserved by the IANA indefinitely. Organizations may still petition for a Class A address, but they will be expected to provide detailed technical justification documenting their network size and structure.
- Allocations for Class B addresses have been severely restricted, and any organization requesting Class B addresses will have to detail a subnetting plan based on more than 32 subnets within its network and have more than 4,096 hosts in that network.
- Any petitions for a Class B address that do not fulfill these requirements and that do not demonstrate that it is unreasonable to build the planned network with a block of Class C addresses will be granted a consecutively numbered block of Class C addresses.
- The Class C address space will itself be subdivided. The range 208.0.0 through 223.255.255 will be reserved by the IANA. The range 192.0.0 through 207.255.255 will be split into eight blocks. This administrative division allocates the blocks to various regional authorities who will allocate addresses on behalf of the IR. The block allocation is as follows:
  192.0.0 – 193.255.255 Multi-regional
  194.0.0 – 195.255.255 Europe
  196.0.0 – 197.255.255 Others
  198.0.0 – 199.255.255 North America
  200.0.0 – 201.255.255 Central and South America
  202.0.0 – 203.255.255 Pacific Rim
  204.0.0 – 205.255.255 Others
  206.0.0 – 207.255.255 Others.
  The multi-regional block includes all those Class C addresses allocated before this new scheme was adopted. The blocks defined as Others are to provide for flexibility outside the regional boundaries.
- Assignment of Class C addresses from within the ranges specified will depend on the number of hosts in the network and will be based on the following.

- Less than 256 hosts—Assign 1 Class C network
- Less than 512 hosts—Assign 2 contiguous Class C networks
- Less than 1,024 hosts—Assign 4 contiguous Class C networks
- Less than 2,048 hosts—Assign 8 contiguous Class C networks
- Less than 4,096 hosts—Assign 16 contiguous Class C networks
- Less than 8,192 hosts—Assign 32 contiguous Class C networks
- Less than 16,384 hosts—Assign 64 contiguous Class C networks
- Less than 32,768 hosts—Assign 128 contiguous Class C networks

Using contiguous addresses in this way will provide organizations with network numbers having a common prefix: the IP prefix. For example, the block 192.32.136 through 192.32.143 has a 21-bit prefix common to all the addresses in the block: 192.32.136 or B "110000100010000010001".

Classless Inter-Domain Routing (CIDR)

Due to the impact of growth, the IP address space will near exhaustion soon if addresses are assigned as they are requested or as they used to be assigned. IPv6 will easily overcome that problem, but what can be done until IPv6 is fully deployed?

One idea has been to use a range of Class C addresses instead of a single Class B address. The problem is that each network must be routed separately because standard IP routing understands only class A, B, and C network addresses.

Within each of these types of network, subnetting can be used to provide better granularity of the address space but there is no way to specify that multiple Class C networks are actually related. The result of this is termed the routing table explosion problem: A Class B network of 3,000 hosts requires one routing table entry at each backbone router, whereas the same network, if addressed as a range of Class C networks, would require 16 entries.

The solution to this problem is a scheme called *Classless Inter-Domain Routing (CIDR)*. CIDR is described in RFCs 1518 to 1520. It does not route according to the class of the network number (hence the term classless) but solely according to the high-order bits of the IP address, which are termed the IP prefix. Each CIDR routing table entry contains a 32-bit IP address and a 32-bit network mask, which together give the length and value of the IP prefix. This can be represented as <IP_address network_mask>. For example, to address a block of eight Class C addresses with one single routing table entry, the following representation would suffice: <192.32.136.0 255.255.248.0>. This would, from a backbone point of view, refer to the Class C network range from 192.32.136.0 to 192.32.143.0 as one single network because of the identical IP prefix, as illustrated in Figure 5.5.

FIGURE 5.5
Classless Inter-
Domain Routing—IP
supernetting example
(TCP/IP technical
overview).

```
11000000 00100000 10001000 00000000 = 192.32.136.0 (class C address)
11111111 11111111 11111--- -------- = 255.255.248.0 (network mask)
==================================== = logical_AND
11000000 00100000 10001--- -------- = 192.32.136 (IP prefix)

11000000 00100000 10001111 00000000 = 192.32.143.0 (class C address)
11111111 11111111 11111--- -------- = 255.255.248.0 (network mask)
==================================== = logical_AND
11000000 00100000 10001--- -------- = 192.32.136 (same IP prefix)
```

This process of combining multiple networks into a single entry is referred to as *supernetting* because routing is based on network masks shorter than the natural network mask of an IP address, in contrast to subnetting where the subnet masks are longer than the natural network mask.

The current Internet address allocation policies and the assumptions on which those policies were based, are described in RFC 1518 *An Architecture for IP Address Allocation with CIDR*. They can be summarized as follows:

- IP address assignment reflects the physical topology of the network and not the organizational topology; wherever organizational and administrative boundaries do not match the network topology, they should not be used for the assignment of IP addresses.
- In general, network topology will closely follow continental and national boundaries and therefore IP addresses should be assigned on this basis.
- There will be a relatively small set of networks that carry a large amount of traffic between routing domains. They will be interconnected in a non-hierarchical way that will cross national boundaries. These are referred to as *transit routing domains (TRDs)*. Each TRD will have a unique IP prefix. TRDs will not be organized in a hierarchical way where there is no appropriate hierarchy. However, wherever a TRD is wholly within a continental boundary, its IP prefix should be an extension of the continental IP prefix.
- There will be many organizations that have attachments to other organizations that are for the private use of those two organizations and do not carry traffic intended for other domains (transit traffic). Such private connections do not have a significant effect on the routing topology and can be ignored.
- The great majority of routing domains will be single-homed. That is, they will be attached to a single TRD. They should be assigned addresses that begin with that TRD's IP prefix. All the addresses for all single-homed domains attached to a TRD can therefore be aggregated into a single routing table entry for all domains outside that TRD.

This implies that if an organization changes its Internet service provider, it should change all its IP addresses. This is not the current practice, but the widespread implementation of CIDR is likely to make it much more common.

- There are a number of address assignment schemes that can be used for multi-homed domains. These include:

  - The use of a single IP prefix for the domain. External routers must have an entry for the organization that lies partly or wholly outside the normal hierarchy. Where a domain is multihomed but all the attached TRDs themselves are topologically nearby, it would be appropriate for the domain's IP prefix to include those bits common to all the attached TRDs. For example, if all the TRDs were wholly within the United States, an IP prefix implying an exclusively North American domain would be appropriate.

  - The use of one IP prefix for each attached TRD, with hosts in the domain having IP addresses containing the IP prefix of the most appropriate TRD. The organization appears to be a set of routing domains.

  - Assigning an IP prefix from one of the attached TRDs. This TRD becomes a default TRD for the domain but other domains can explicitly route by one of the alternative TRDs.

  - The use of IP prefixes to refer to sets of multi-homed domains having the TRD attachments. For example, there may be an IP prefix to refer to single-homed domains attached to network A, one to refer to single-homed domains attached to network B and one to refer to dual-homed domains attached to networks A and B.

- Each of these has various advantages, disadvantages, and side effects. For example, the first approach tends to result in inbound traffic entering the target domain closer to the sending host than the second approach, and therefore a larger proportion of the network costs are incurred by the receiving organization.

Because multihomed domains can vary greatly in character and none of the above schemes is suitable for all such domains, there is no single policy that is best and RFC 1518 does not specify any rules for choosing between them.

CIDR Implementation

The implementation of CIDR in the Internet is primarily based on Border Gateway Protocol Version 4. The implementation strategy, described in RFC

1520 *Exchanging Routing Information Across Provider Boundaries in the CIDR Environment* involves a staged process through the routing hierarchy beginning with backbone routers. Network service providers are divided into four types:

- **Type 1**—Those that cannot employ any default inter-domain routing.
- **Type 2**—Those that use default inter-domain routing but require explicit routes for a substantial proportion of the assigned IP network numbers.
- **Type 3**—Those that use default inter-domain routing and supplement it with a small number of explicit routes.
- **Type 4**—Those that perform all inter-domain routing using only default routes.

The CIDR implementation involves an implementation beginning with the Type 1 network providers, then the Type 2, and finally the Type 3 ones. CIDR has already been widely deployed in the backbone and over 9,000 class-based routes have been replaced by approximately 2,000 CIDR-based routes.

The Next Generation of the Internet Address–IPv6, IPng

The next generation of IP addressing is the Internet Protocol version 6 (IPv6), the specifications of which can be found in RFC 1883. IPv6 addresses a number of issues that the Internet Engineering Task Force IPng working group published in RFC 1752. These problems included IP address exhaustion, the growth of routing tables in backbone routers, and QoS issues, such as traffic priority and type of service.

In the design of a network, the major concern with IPv6 is the future adoption of IPv6 addresses into the network. With few host systems ready for IPv6, those capable mostly consisting of a minority of UNIX platforms, and few if any routers able to cope with IPv6 addressing, a period of transition is required.

During this intermediate stage, IPv6 hosts and routers will need to be deployed alongside existing IPv4 systems. RFC 1933 *Transition Mechanisms for IPv6 Hosts and Routers* and RFC 2185 *Routing Aspects of IPv6 Transition* define a number of mechanisms to be employed to ensure these systems run in conjunction with each other, without compatibility issues.

These techniques are sometimes collectively termed Simple Internet Transition (SIT). The transition employs the following techniques:

- Dual-stack IP implementations for hosts and routers that must interoperate between IPv4 and IPv6

■ Embedding of IPv4 addresses in IPv6 addresses—IPv6 hosts will be assigned addresses that are interoperable with IPv4, and IPv4 host addresses will be mapped to IPv6
■ IPv6-over-IPv4 tunneling mechanisms for carrying IPv6 packets across IPv4 router networks
■ IPv4/IPv6 header translation

This technique is intended for use when implementation of IPv6 is well advanced and only a few IPv4-only systems remain. The techniques are also adaptable to other protocols, notably Novell IPX, which has similar internetwork layer semantics and an addressing scheme that can be mapped easily to a part of the IPv6 address space.

Address Management Design Considerations

There are various considerations that must be taken into account when designing the addressing scheme. These are split into two sections: those relating to the network and those relating to the devices attached, such as the hosts.

The Network and Clients

The network must be designed so that it is scalable, secure, reliable, and manageable. These attributes must go hand in hand with each other. A network that might be secure and scalable, but is unreliable and unmanageable is not much use. Would you like to manage an unmanageable system that fails twice a day?

To achieve a network design that meets the above requirements, the following issues, as well as their ramifications, must be considered:

1. The network design must precede network implementation. When a network is implemented following a well-structured design, as opposed to an ad hoc manner, many problems are avoided. These include:
   • Illegal addresses
   • Addresses that cannot be routed
   • Wasted addresses
   • Duplicate addresses for networks or hosts
   • Address exhaustion
2. The addressing scheme must be able to grow with the network. This includes being able to accept changes in the network, such as new subnets, new hosts, or even new networks being added. It may even take into account changes such as the introduction of IPv6.

3. Use of dynamic addressing schemes.
4. Blocks of addresses should be assigned in a hierarchical manner to facilitate scalability and manageability.
5. The choice of scheme, such as DHCP and BootP, depends on platform support for the protocol. Whatever platform limitations are imposed, the address assignment scheme that is implemented should be the one with the greatest number of features that simplify the management of the network.

Some Thoughts on Private Addresses

As presented in "Special Case Addresses," private IP addresses can be used to improve the security of the network. Networks that are of medium size, or larger, should use private addresses. If the network is to be connected to the Internet, address translation should be used for external routing.

Apart from the security features provided by using private addresses, there are other benefits. Fewer registered IP addresses are required, because in most networks not every host requires direct access to the Internet, only servers do. With the use of proxy servers, the number of registered IP addresses required is drastically reduced.

New networks are also much simpler to incorporate into the existing network. As the network grows, the network manager assigns new internal IP addresses rather than applying for new registered IP addresses from an ISP or a NIC.

As most companies will find it more feasible to obtain their IP addresses from ISPs, as opposed to the regional NICs (see "IP Address Registration"), one important consideration is what happens when, for business or other needs, the organization must change its ISP. If private IP addresses have not been used, this translates to going through and redefining all the addresses on the devices attached to the network. Even with DHCP, or some other address assignment protocol, all the routers, bridges, and servers will need to be reconfigured. Manually doing this can be expensive. If private IP addresses are used with address translation, all the configuration work is done on the address translation gateway.

However, there are some problems with address translation; there's always a price to pay. When two separate networks are developed with private IP addresses, if they are required to be merged at a later date, there are some serious implications. First, if the same address ranges in the private address blocks have been used, it is impossible to merge the two networks without reconfiguring one of the networks; the duplicate addresses see to this.

If the network manager decides to go to the expense of adding a couple of routers between the two networks, and continues to develop the networks separately, an unwise choice in any case, the routing between the two private networks will fail. For example, in Figure 5.6, we see a network configuration that will fail. Router A will advertise its connection to the 10.0.0.0 network, but as router B is also connected to the 10.0.0.0 network, it will ignore router A. The reverse is also true for the same reasons. Thus, the two networks in the 10.0.0.0 range cannot communicate with each other. This is solved by using a routing protocol that can support classless routing, such as RIP-2 or OSPF.

Another problem that might occur, and in fact will occur due to human nature, is that when private IP addresses are implemented, all semblance of developing a structured scheme for IP address allocation is forgotten. With the flood of IP addresses available, who needs to consider spending time designing a way to assign these addresses? There's a whole Class A addresses ready to be assigned.

FIGURE 5.6
Routing problems faced with discontinuous networks.

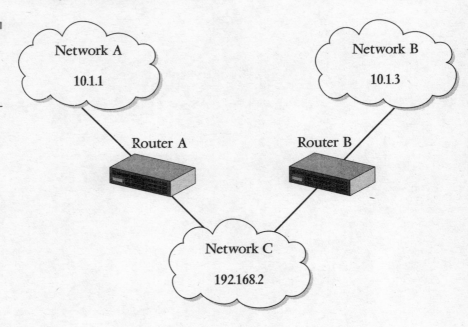

TCP/IP Routing Protocols

One of the basic functions of IP is its ability to form connections between different physical networks because of its flexibility since it can use almost any physical network below it, and because of the IP routing algorithm. A system that does this is termed a *router*, although the older term *IP gateway* is also used.

In other sections of the book, we show the position of each protocol in the layered model of the TCP/IP protocol stack. The routing function is part of the internetwork layer, but the primary function of a routing protocol is to exchange *routing information with other routers, and in this respect the protocols behave more like application protocols. Therefore, we do not attempt to represent the position of these protocols in the protocol stack with a diagram as we do with the other protocols.*

Basic IP Routing

The fundamental function for routers is present in *all* IP implementations: an *incoming* IP datagram that specifies a destination IP address other than one of the local host's IP address(es), is treated as a normal *outgoing* IP datagram. This outgoing IP datagram is subject to the IP routing algorithm of the local host, which selects the *next hop* for the datagram (the next host to send it to). This new destination can be located on any of the physical networks to which the intermediate host is attached. If it is a physical network other than the one on which the host originally received the datagram, then the net result is that the intermediate host has *forwarded* the IP datagram from one physical network to another (Figure 6.1).

The normal IP routing table contains information about locally attached networks and the IP addresses of other routers located on these networks, plus the networks they attach to. It can be extended with information on IP networks that are farther away, and can also contain a default route, but it still remains a table with limited information; that is, it represents only a part of the whole IP networks. That is why this kind of router is called a *router with partial routing information*.

Various considerations apply to these routers with partial information:

- They do not know about all IP networks.
- They allow local sites autonomy in establishing and modifying routes.
- A routing entry error in one of the routers can introduce inconsistencies, thereby making part of the network unreachable.

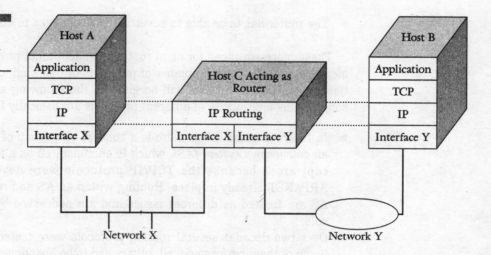

FIGURE 6.1
Router operation
of IP.

Some error reporting should be implemented by routers with partial information via the Internet Control Message Protocol (ICMP). These routers should be able to report the following errors back to the source host:

- Unknown IP destination network by an ICMP *Destination Unreachable* message.
- Redirection of traffic to more suitable routers by sending ICMP *Redirect* messages.
- Congestion problems (too many incoming datagrams for the available buffer space) by an ICMP *Source Quench* message.
- The time-to-live field of an IP datagram has reached zero. This is reported with an ICMP *Time Exceeded* message.
- Also, the following base ICMP operations and messages should be supported:
  - Parameter problem
  - Address mask
  - Time stamp
  - Information request/reply
  - Echo request/reply

A more intelligent router is required if:

- The router has to know routes to *all* possible IP networks, as was the case for the Internet backbone routers.
- The router has to have dynamic routing tables, which are kept up to date with minimal or no manual intervention.

Chapter Six

■ The router has to be able to advertise local changes to other routers.

These more advanced forms of routers use additional protocols to communicate with each other. A number of protocols of this kind exist, and descriptions of the important ones will be given in the following sections. The reasons for this multiplicity of different protocols are basically fourfold:

■ In Internet terminology, there is a concept of a group of networks, called an *autonomous system (AS)*, which is administered as a unit. The AS concept arose because the TCP/IP protocols were developed with the ARPANET already in place. Routing within an AS and routing outside an AS are treated as different issues and are addressed by different protocols.
■ Over two decades several routing protocols were tested in the Internet. Some of them performed well; others had to be abandoned.
■ The emergence of ASs of different sizes called for different routing solutions. For small- to medium-sized ASs a group of routing protocols based upon distance vector, such as RIP, became very popular. However, such protocols do not perform well for large interconnected networks. Link-state protocols, such as OSPF, are much better suited for such networks.
■ To exchange routing information between ASs, border gateway protocols were developed.

Routing Processes

In TCP/IP software operating systems, routing protocols are often implemented using one of two daemons:

■ **routeD**—Pronounced "route D." This is a basic routing daemon for interior routing supplied with the majority of TCP/IP implementations. It uses the RIP protocol.
■ **gateD**—Pronounced "gate D." This is a more sophisticated daemon on UNIX-based systems for interior and exterior routing. It can employ a number of additional protocols such as OSPF and BGP.

NOTE

Daemon, pronounced "demon," is a UNIX term for a background server process. Usually, daemons have names ending with a d. An analogous concept for MVS is a server running in a separate address space from TCP/IP; for VM it is a separate service virtual machine, for Windows NT it is a separate Windows NT process, and so on. Although TCP/IP servers are often implemented differently on different platforms, the routeD daemon is implemented like this on each of these platforms.

In TCP/IP hardware implementations, mainly in dedicated router operating systems such as the Common Code for IBM routers or Cisco's Internetworking Operating System (IOS), the routing protocols are implemented in the operating system.

Autonomous Systems

The dynamic routing protocols can be divided into two groups:

- **Interior Gateway Protocols (IGPs)**—Examples of these protocols are Open Short Path First (OSPF) and Routing Information Protocol (RIP).
- **Exterior Gateway Protocols (EGPs)**—An example of these routing protocols is Border Gateway Protocol Verson 4 (BGP-4).

In this book, the term gateway is frequently used to imply an IP router. Gateway protocols are referred to as interior or exterior depending on whether they are used within or between autonomous systems (ASs). Interior gateway protocols allow routers to exchange routing information within an AS. Exterior gateway protocols allow the exchange of summary reachability information between separately administered ASs.

An AS is defined as a logical portion of larger IP networks that are administered by a single authority. The AS would normally comprise the internetwork within an organization, and would be designated as such to allow communication over public IP networks with ASs belonging to other organizations. It is mandatory to register an organization's internetwork as an AS in order to use these public IP services. See Figure 6.2, which illustrates three interconnected ASs. It shows that IGPs are used within each AS, and an EGP is used between the three ASs.

Routing Algorithms

Dynamic routing algorithms allow routers to exchange route or link information, from which the best paths to reach destinations in an internetwork are calculated. Static routing can also be used to supplement dynamic routing.

Static Routing

Static routing requires that routes be configured manually for each router; this is one major reason why system administrators shy away from this technique if they have a choice. Static routing has the disadvantage that network reachability in this case is not dependent on the existence and state of the network itself. If a destination is down, the static routes remain in the routing table, and traffic is still sent toward that destination in vain without awareness of a possible alternate path to the destination.

FIGURE 6.2
Autonomous systems.

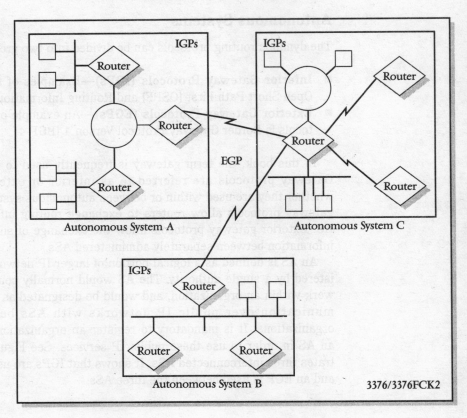

There are solutions to overcome this disadvantage including standard RFC 2338 VRRP and product implementation such as the next-hop awareness parameter.

NOTE

To simplify the task of network administrators, the manual configuration of routes is normally avoided especially in large network. However, there are circumstances when static routing can be attractive. For example, static routes can be used:

■ To define a default route, or a route that is not being advertised within a network.

- To supplement or replace exterior gateway protocols when:
  - Line tariffs between ASs make it desirable to avoid the cost of routing protocol traffic.
  - Complex routing policies are to be implemented.
  - It is desirable to avoid disruption caused by faulty exterior gateways in other ASs.

Distance Vector Routing

The principle behind *distance vector* routing is very simple. Each router in an internetwork maintains the distance from itself to every known destination in a *distance vector table*. Distance vector tables consist of a series of destinations (vectors) and costs (distances) to reach them and define the lowest costs to destinations at the time of transmission.

The distances in the tables are computed from information provided by neighbor routers. Each router transmits its own distance vector table across the shared network. The sequence of operations for doing this is as follows:

- Each router is configured with an identifier and a cost for each of its network links. The cost is normally fixed at 1, reflecting a single hop, but can reflect some other measurement taken for the link such as the traffic, speed, etc.
- Each router initializes with a distance vector table containing zero for itself, one for directly attached networks, and infinity for every other destination.
- Each router periodically (typically every 30 seconds) transmits its distance vector table to each of its neighbors. It can also transmit the table when a link first comes up or when the table changes.
- Each router saves the most recent table it receives from each neighbor and uses the information to calculate its own distance vector table.
- The total cost to each destination is calculated by adding the cost reported to it in a neighbor's distance vector table to the cost of the link to that neighbor.
- The distance vector table (the routing table) for the router is then created by taking the lowest cost calculated for each destination.

Figure 6.3 shows the distance vector tables for three routers within a simple internetwork.

The distance vector algorithm produces a stable routing table after a period directly related to the number of routers across the network. This period is referred to as the *convergence time* and represents the time it takes for distance vector information to traverse the network. In a large internetwork, this time may become too long to be useful.

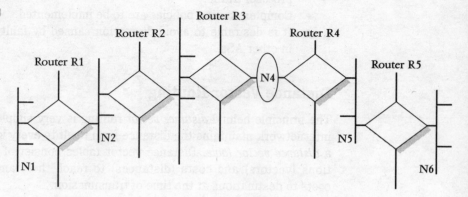

Router R2 Distance Vector Table				Router R3 Distance Vector Table				Router R4 Distance Vector Table		
Net	**Next Hop**	**Metric**		**Net**	**Next Hop**	**Metric**		**Net**	**Next Hop**	**Metric**
N1	R1	2		N1	R2	3		N1	R3	4
N2	=	1		N2	R2	2		N2	R3	3
N3	=	1		N3	=	1		N3	R3	2
N4	R3	2		N4	=	1		N4	=	1
N5	R3	3		N5	R4	2		N5	=	1
N6	R3	4		N6	R4	3		N6	R5	2

Routing tables are recalculated if a changed distance vector table is received from a neighbor, or if the state of a link to a neighbor changes. If a network link goes down, the distance vector tables that have been received over it are discarded and the routing table is recalculated.

The chief advantage of distance vector is that it is very easy to implement. There are also the following significant disadvantages:

■ The instability caused by old routes persisting in an internetwork
■ The long convergence time on large internetworks
■ The limit to the size of an internetwork imposed by maximum hop counts
■ The fact that distance vector tables are always transmitted even if their contents have not changed.

Enhancements to the basic algorithm have evolved to overcome the first two of these problems. They are described in the following subsections.

The Count-to-Infinity Problem

The basic distance vector algorithm will always allow a router to correctly calculate its distance vector table.

Using the example shown in Figure 6.4 you can see one of the problems of distance vector protocols known as *counting to infinity*. Counting to infinity occurs when a network becomes unreachable, but erroneous routes to that network persist because of the time for the distance vector tables to converge.

FIGURE 6.4
Counting to infinity—example network.

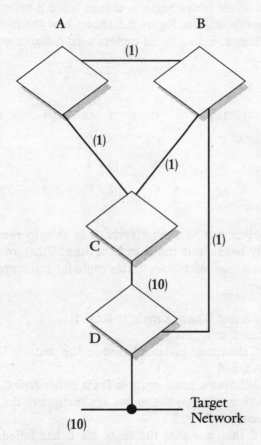

(n) = Network Cost

The example network shows four routers interconnected by five network links. The networks all have a cost of 1 except for that from C to D, which has a cost of 10. Each of the routers A, B, C, and D has routes to all networks. If we show only the routes to the target network, we will see they are as follows:

- For D : Directly connected network. Metric 1
- For B : Route via D. Metric 2
- For C : Route via B. Metric 3
- For A : Route via B. Metric 3

If the link from B to D fails, then all routes will be adjusted in time to use the link from C to D. However, the convergence time for this can be considerable.

Distance vector tables begin to change when B notices that the route to D has become unavailable. Figure 6.5 shows how the routes to the target network will change, assuming all routers send distance vector table updates at the same time.

FIGURE 6.5
Counting to infinity.

Time											
D: Direct	1	Direct	1	Direct	1	Direct	1	....	Direct	1	Direct	1
B: Unreachable		C	4	C	5	C	6		C	11	C	12
C: B	3	A	4	A	5	A	6		A	11	D	11
A: B	3	C	4	C	5	C	6	....	C	11	C	12

The problem can be seen clearly. B is able to remove the failed route immediately because it times out the link. Other routers, however, have tables that contain references to this route for many update periods after the link has failed.

1. Initially A and C have a route to D via B.
2. Link from D to B fails.
3. A and C then send updates based on the route to D via B even after the link has failed.
4. B then believes it has a route to D via either A or C. In reality it does not have such a route, as the routes are vestiges of the previous route via B, which has failed.
5. A and C then see that the route via B has failed, but believe a route exists via one another.

Slowly the distance vector tables converge, but not until the metrics have counted up, in theory, to infinity. To avoid this, practical implementations of distance vector have a low value for infinity; for example, RIP uses a maximum metric of 16.

The manner in which the metrics increment to infinity gives rise to the term *counting to infinity*. It occurs because A and C are engaged in an extended period of mutual deception, each claiming to be able to get to the target network, D, via one another.

Split Horizon

Counting to infinity can easily be prevented if a route to a destination is never reported back in the distance vector table that is sent to the neighbor from which the route was learned. *Split horizon* is the term used for this technique. The incorporation of split horizon would modify the sequence of distance vector table changes to that shown in Figure 6.6. The tables can be seen to converge considerably faster than before (see Figure 6.6).

FIGURE 6.6
Split horizon.

Time							
D:	Direct	1	Direct	1	Direct	1	Direct	1
B:	Unreachable		Unreachable		Unreachable		C	12
C:	B	3	A	4	D	11	D	11
A:	B	3	C	4	Unreachable		C	12

Split Horizon with Poison Reverse

Poison reverse is an enhancement to split horizon, whereby routes learned from a neighbor router are reported back to it, but with a metric of infinity (that is, network unreachable). The use of poison reverse is safer than split horizon alone because it breaks erroneous looping routes immediately.

If two routers receive routes pointing at each other, and they are advertised with a metric of infinity, the routes will be eliminated immediately as unreachable. If the routes are not advertised in this way, they must be eliminated by the timeout that results from a route's not being reported by a neighbor router for several periods (for example, six periods for RIP).

Poison reverse does have one disadvantage. It significantly increases the size of distance vector tables that must be exchanged between neighbor routers because all routes are included in the distance vector tables. While this is generally not a problem on LANs, it can cause real problems on point-to-point connections in large internetworks.

Triggered Updates

Split horizon with poison reverse will break routing loops involving two
routers. It is still possible, however, for there to be routing loops involving
three or more routers. For example, A may believe it has a route through B, B
through C, and C through A. This loop can only be eliminated by the timeout
that results from counting to infinity.

Triggered updates are designed to reduce the convergence time for routing
tables, and hence reduce the period during which such erroneous loops are
present in an internetwork. When a router changes the cost for a route in its
distance vector table, it must send the modified table immediately to neighbor routers. This simple mechanism ensures that topology changes in a network are propagated quickly, rather than at a rate dependent on normal periodic updates.

Link-State Routing

The growth in the size of internetworks in recent years has necessitated the
replacement of distance vector routing algorithms with alternatives that
address the shortcomings identified in the section above on distance vector
routing. These new protocols have been based on link-state or shortest-path-
first algorithms. The best example is the OSPF Interior Gateway Protocol.

The principle behind link-state routing is straightforward, although its
implementation can be complex:

- Routers are responsible for contacting neighbors and learning their identi-
ties.
- Routers construct link-state packets which contain lists of network links
and their associated costs.
- Link-state packets are transmitted to all routers in a network.
- All routers therefore have an identical list of links in a network, and can
construct identical topology maps.
- The maps are used to compute the best routes to all destinations.

Routers contact neighbors by sending *hello* packets on their network interfaces. Hello packets are sent directly to neighbors on point-to-point links and
non-broadcast networks. On LANs, hello packets are sent to a predefined
group or multicast IP address that can be received by all routers. Neighbors
who receive hellos from a router should reply with hello packets that include
the identity of that originating router. Once neighbors have been contacted in
this way, link-state information can be exchanged.

Link-state information is sent in the form of *link-state packets (LSPs)*, also known as link-state advertisements. LSPs provide the database from which network topology maps can be calculated at each router. LSPs are normally sent only under the following specific circumstances:

- When a router discovers a new neighbor
- When a link to a neighbor goes down
- When the cost of a link changes
- Basic refresh packets are sent every 30 minutes

Once a router has generated an LSP it is critical that it be received successfully by all other routers in a network. If this does not happen, routers on the network will calculate network topology based on incorrect link state information.

Distribution of LSPs would normally be on the basis of each router's routing tables. However, this leads to a "chicken and egg" situation. Routing tables would rely on LSPs for their creation and LSPs would rely on routing tables for their distribution. A simple scheme called *flooding* overcomes this, and ensures that LSPs are successfully distributed to all routers in a network.

Flooding requires that a router that receives an LSP transmit it to all neighbors except the one from which it was received. All LSPs must be explicitly acknowledged to ensure successful delivery, and they are sequenced and time stamped to ensure duplicates are not received and retransmitted.

When a router receives an LSP it looks in its database to check the sequence number of the last LSP from the originator. If the sequence number is the same as, or earlier than, the sequence number of the LSP in its database, then the LSP is discarded. Otherwise the LSP is added to the database.

The flooding process ensures that all routers in a network have the same link-state information. All routers are then able to compute the same shortest-path tree (see "Shortest-Path First [SPF]") topology map for the network, and hence select best routes to all destinations.

Shortest-Path First (SPF)

SPF is an algorithm that each router in the same AS has an identical link-state database, leading to an identical graphical representation by calculating a tree of shortest paths with the router itself as root. The tree is called the shortest-path tree giving an entire path to any destination network or host. Figure 6.7 shows the shortest-path tree example from router A. Each router, A, B, C, D, and E has an identical link-state database as shown. Router A generate its own shortest-path tree by calculating a tree of shortest paths with router A itself as root.

FIGURE 6.7
Shortest-Path First
(SPF) example.

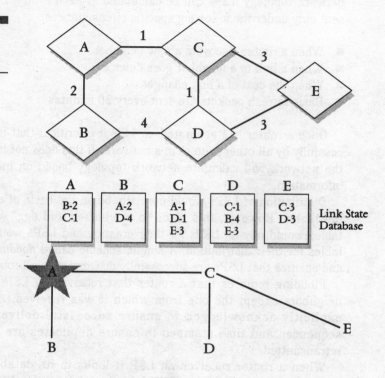

FIGURE 6.7
Shortest-Path First (SPF) example.

Interior Gateway Protocols (IGP)

There are many standard and proprietary interior gateway protocols. This section describes the following IGPs:

- Routing Information Protocol (RIP)
- Routing Information Protocol, Version 2 (RIP-2)
- Open Shortest Path First (OSPF)

Routing Information Protocol (RIP)

RIP is an IAB standard protocol; its status is elective. This means that it is one of several interior gateway protocols available, and it may or may not be implemented on a system. If a system does implement it, however, the implementation should be in line with the RFC 1058.

RIP is based on the Xerox PUP and XNS routing protocols. The RFC was issued after many RIP implementations had been completed. For this reason some protocols do not include all the enhancements to the basic distance vector routing protocol (such as poison reverse and triggered updates). RIP is a distance vector routing protocol suitable for small networks as compared to OSPF. This is because of the shortcomings of distance vector routing identified above.

There are two versions of RIP. Version 1 (RIP-1) is a widely deployed protocol with a number of known limitations. Version 2 (RIP-2) is an enhanced version designed to alleviate the limitations of RIP while being highly compatible with it. The term RIP is used to refer to Version 1, while RIP-2 refers to Version 2. Whenever the reader encounters the term RIP in TCP/IP literature, it is safe to assume that it is referring to Version 1 unless explicitly stated otherwise. We use this nomenclature in this section except when the two versions are being compared, when we use the term RIP-1 to avoid possible confusion. RIP is widely used because the code (known as *ROUTED*) was incorporated on the Berkeley Software Distribution (BSD) UNIX operating system, and in other UNIX systems based on it.

Protocol Description

RIP packets are transmitted onto a network in *User Datagram Protocol (UDP)* datagrams, which, in turn, are carried in IP datagrams. RIP sends and receives datagrams using UDP port 520. RIP datagrams have a maximum size of 512 octets and tables larger than this must be sent in multiple UDP datagrams.

RIP datagrams are normally broadcast onto LANs using the LAN MAC all-stations broadcast address and the IP network or subnetwork broadcast address. They are specifically addressed on point-to-point and multi-access non-broadcast networks, using the destination router IP address.

Routers normally run RIP in *active mode*; that is, advertising their own distance vector tables and updating them based on advertisements from neighbors. End nodes, if they run RIP, normally operate in *passive (or silent) mode*; that is, updating their distance vector tables on the basis of advertisements from neighbors, but not in turn advertising them.

RIP specifies two packet types: *request* and *response*. A request packet is sent by routers to ask neighbors to send part of their distance vector table (if the packet contains destinations), or all their table (if no destinations have been specified). A response packet is sent by routers to advertise their distance vector table in the following circumstances:

■ Every 30 seconds

- In response to a request packet
- When distance vector tables change (if triggered updates are supported)

Active and passive systems listen for all response packets and update their distance vector tables accordingly. A route to a destination, computed from a neighbor's distance vector table, is kept until an alternate is found with lower cost, or it is not re-advertised in six consecutive RIP responses. In this case the route is timed out and deleted.

When RIP is used with IP, the address family identifier is 2 and the address fields are four octets. To reduce problems of counting to infinity the maximum metric is 16 (unreachable) and directly connected networks are defined as having a metric of one.

The RIP packet format for IP is shown in Figure 6.8.

FIGURE 6.8
RIP message.

Number of Octets

Octets	Field	
1	Command	Request = 1, Response = 2
1	Version	Version = 1
2	Reserved	
2	2	Address Family Identifier for IP
2	Reserved	
4	IP Address	May be Repeated
8	Reserved	
4	Metric	

RIP makes no provision for passing subnet masks with its distance vector tables. A router receiving an RIP response must already have subnet mask information to allow it to interpret the network identifier and host identifier portions of the IP address correctly.

In the absence of subnet mask information a router will interpret routes as best as it can. If it knows an IP network has a specific subnet mask, it will interpret all other route information for that network on the basis of that single mask. If it receives a packet with bits set in the field that it regards as the host field, it will interpret it as a route to a host with a mask of

255.255.255.255. This makes it impossible for RIP to be used in an internetwork with variable-length subnet masks.

Routing Information Protocol Version 2 (RIP-2)

RIP-2 is a *draft standard protocol*. Its status is *elective*. It is described in RFC 1723. RIP-2 extends RIP-1. It is less powerful than other recent IGPs such as OSPF but has the advantages of easy implementation and lower overheads. The intention of RIP-2 is to provide a straightforward replacement for RIP that can be used on small- to medium-sized networks, can be employed in the presence of variable subnetting or supernetting, and can interoperate with RIP-1. In fact, the major reason for developing and deploying RIP-2 was the use of CIDR, which cannot be used in conjunction with RIP-1.

RIP-2 takes advantage of the fact that half the bytes in a RIP-1 message are reserved (must be zero) and that the original RIP-1 specification was well designed with enhancements in mind, particularly in the use of the version field. One notable area where this is not the case is in the interpretation of the metric field. RIP-1 specifies it as being a value between 0 and 16 stored in a four-*byte* field. For compatibility, RIP-2 preserves this definition, meaning that it agrees with RIP-1 that 16 is to be interpreted as infinity, and wastes most of this field.

Neither RIP-1 nor RIP-2 is properly suited for use as an IGP in an AS where a value of 16 is too low to be regarded as infinity, because high values of infinity exacerbate the counting-to-infinity problem. The more sophisticated link-state protocol used in OSPF provides a much better routing solution when the AS is large enough to have a legitimate hop count close to 16.

NOTE

Provided that an RIP-1 implementation obeys the specification in RFC 1058, RIP-2 can interoperate with RIP-1. The RIP message format is extended as shown in Figure 6.9.

The first entry in the message can be an authentication entry, as shown here, or it can be a route as in an RIP-1 message. If the first entry is an authentication entry, only 24 routes can be included in a message; otherwise the maximum is 25 as in RIP-1.

The fields in a RIP-2 message are the same as for a RIP-1 message except as follows:

- **Version**—Is 2. This tells RIP-1 routers to ignore the fields designated as "must be zero." (If the value is 1, RIP-1 routers are required to discard messages with non-zero values in these fields since the messages originate with a router claiming to be RIP-1-compliant but sending non-RIP-1 messages.)

FIGURE 6.9
RIP-2 message.

Number of Octets

Number of Octets		
1	Command	Request = 1
1	Version	Response = 2
2	Reserved	Version = 1
2	X}FFFF'	
2	Authentic Type	0 = No Authentication
16	Authentication Data	2 = Password Data
		Password if Type 2 Selected
2	2	
2	Reserved	
4	IP Address	
4	Subnet Mask	May be Repeated
4	Next Hop	
4	Metric	

- **Address Family**—May be X}FFFF} in the first entry only, indicating that this entry is an authentication entry.
- **Authentication Type**—Defines how the remaining 16 bytes are to be used. The only defined types are 0 indicating no authentication and 2 indicating that the field contains password data.
- **Authentication Data**—The password is 16 bytes, plain text ASCII, left adjusted and padded with ASCII NULLs (X}00}).
- **Route Tag**—Is a field intended for communicating information about the origin of the route information. It is intended for interoperation between RIP and other routing protocols. RIP-2 implementations must preserve this tag, but RIP-2 does not further specify how it is to be used.
- **Subnet Mask**—The subnet mask associated with the subnet referred to by this entry.
- **Next Hop**—A recommendation about the next hop that the router should use to send datagrams to the subnet or host given in this entry.

To ensure safe interoperation with RIP, RFC 1723 specifies the following restrictions for RIP-2 routers sending over a network interface where a RIP-1 router may hear and operate on the RIP messages:

1. Information internal to one network must never be advertised into another network.
2. Information about a more-specific subnet cannot be advertised where RIP-1 routers would consider it a host route.
3. Supernet routes (routes with a subnet mask shorter than the natural or unsubnetted network mask) must not be advertised where they could be misinterpreted by RIP-1 routers.

RIP-2 also supports the use of multicasting rather than simple broadcasting. This can reduce the load on hosts that are not listening for RIP-2 messages. This option is configurable for each interface, to ensure optimum use of RIP-2 facilities when a router connects mixed RIP-1/RIP-2 subnets to RIP-2-only subnets. Similarly, the use of authentication in mixed environments can be configured to suit local requirements.

RIP-2 is implemented in recent versions of the gateD daemon, often termed gateD Version 3.

RIPng for IPv6

RIPng is intended to allow routers to exchange information for computing routes through an IPv6-based network and documented in RFC2080.

Protocol Description

RIPng is a distance-vector protocol and similar to RIP-2 in IPv4. It is UDP based and sends and receives datagrams on UDP port number 521. RIPng should be implemented only in routers; IPv6 provides other mechanisms for router discovery. Any router that uses RIPng is assumed to have interfaces to one or more networks, otherwise it isn't really a router. RIPng has the following limitations, just as RIP-2 in IPv4, which are specific to a distance-vector protocol:

- Limited number of networks where longest path is 15.
- Dependence on counting to infinity. The resolution of the loop would require much more time.
- Fixed metric. It is not appropriate for situations where routers need to be chosen based on real-time applications.

The RIPng message format is extended as shown in Figure 6.10.

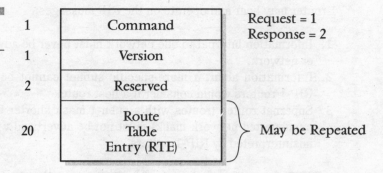

FIGURE 6.10
RIPng message.

The basic blocks of a RIPng message are the following:

1. **Command**—The same idea as in RIP-1 and RIP-2 in IPv4 (see Figures 6.8 and 6.9 also).
2. **Route Table Entry (RTE)**—A different idea from RIP-1 and RIP-2. RIPng provides the ability to specify the immediate next-hop IPv6 address to which packets to a destination specified by an RTE should be forwarded in much the same way as RIP-1 and RIP-2 (see RTE in Figure 6.11).

FIGURE 6.11
RIPng Route Table
Entry (RTE).

Number of Octets

16	IPv6 Prefix	
2	Route Tag	
1	Prefix Length	Between 0 and 128
1	Metric	Between 1 and 15 Infinity = 16

In RIP-2, each route table entry has a next-hop field. Including a next-hop field for each RTE in RIPng would nearly double the size of the RTE. Therefore, in RIPng, the next hop is specified by a special RTE and applies to all the address RTEs following the next-hop RTE until the end of the message or until another next-hop RTE is encountered.

3. **Next-Hop Route Table Entry (RTE)**—The next-hop RTE is identified by a value of 0xFF in the metric field of an RTE. The prefix field specifies the IPv6 address of the next hop (Figure 6.12).

Number of Octets

FIGURE 6.12
RIPng Next-Hop
Route Table Entry
(RTE).

Octets	Field	
16	IPv6 Next Hop Address	
2	Reserved	
1	Reserved	
1	Reserved	0xFF

Open Shortest Path First (OSPF)

The OSPF V2 Protocol is an interior gateway protocol defined in RFC 2328. A report on the use of OSPF V2 is contained in RFC 1246 *Experience with the OSPF Protocol*. It is an IAB standard protocol; its status is elective. However, RFC 1812 *Requirements for IPv4 Routers*, lists OSPF as the only required dynamic routing protocol.

OSPF is important because it has a number of features not found in other interior gateway protocols. Support for these additional features makes OSPF the preferred choice for new IP internetwork implementations especially in large networks. The following features are covered within OSPF:

■ Support for type of service (TOS) routing
■ Load balancing
■ Site partitioning into subsets by using areas
■ Information exchange between routers requires authentication
■ Support for host-specific routes as well as network-specific routes
■ Reduction of table maintenance overhead to a minimum by implementing a designated router
■ Definition of virtual links to provide support to a non-contiguous area
■ Allowing the use of variable length subnet masks
■ Will import RIP and EGP routes into its database

The use of TOS has been dropped in recent OSPF implementations.

NOTE

OSPF Terminology

OSPF uses specific terminology which must be understood before the protocol can be described.

AREAS

OSPF internetworks are organized into *areas*. An OSPF area consists of a number of networks and routers that are logically grouped together. Areas can be defined on a per location or a per region basis, or they can be based on administrative boundaries. All OSPF networks consist of at least one area, the backbone, plus as many additional areas as are demanded by network topology and other design criteria. Within an OSPF area all routers maintain the same topology database, exchanging link-state information to maintain their synchronization. This ensures that all routers calculate the same network map for the area.

Information about networks outside an area is summarized by an *area border* or *AS boundary routers* (see "Intra-Area, Area Border, and AS Boundary Routers" below) and flooded into the area. Routers within an area have no knowledge of the topology of networks outside the area, only of routes to destinations provided by area borders and AS boundary routers.

The importance of the area concept is that it limits the size of the topology database that must be held by routers. This has direct impact on the processing to be carried out by each router, and on the amount of link-state information that must be flooded into individual networks.

THE OSPF BACKBONE

All OSPF networks must contain at least one area, the *backbone*, which is assigned an area identifier of 0.0.0.0. (This is a different definition from IP address 0.0.0.0.) The backbone has all the properties of an area, but has the additional responsibility of distributing routing information between areas attached to it. Normally an OSPF backbone should be contiguous, that is, with all backbone routers attached one to another. This may not be possible because of network topology, in which case backbone continuity must be maintained by the use of *virtual links* (see below), which are backbone router-to-backbone router connections that traverse a non-backbone area. Routers within the backbone operate identically to other intra-area routers and maintain full topology databases for the backbone area.

INTRA-AREA, AREA BORDER, AND AS BOUNDARY ROUTERS

There are three possible types of routers in an OSPF network. Figure 6.13 shows the location of intra-area, area border, and AS boundary routers within an OSPF internetwork.

- **Intra-Area Routers**—Routers that are situated entirely within an OSPF area. All intra-area routers flood router link advertisements into the area to define the links they are attached to. If they are elected designated or backup-designated routers, they also flood network link advertisements to define the identity of all routers attached to the network. Intra-area routers maintain a topology database for the area in which they are situated.

- **Area Border Routers**—Routers that connect two or more areas. Area border routers maintain topology databases for each area to which they are attached, and exchange link-state information with other routers in those areas. Area border routers also flood summary link-state advertisements into each area to inform them of inter-area routes.

- **AS Boundary Routers**—Routers that are situated at the periphery of an OSPF internetwork and exchange reachability information with routers in other ASs using exterior gateway protocols. Routers that import static routes or routes from other IGPs, such as RIP, into an OSPF network are also AS boundary routers. AS boundary routers are responsible for flooding AS external link-state advertisements into all areas within the AS to inform them of external routes.

FIGURE 6.13
OSPF network.

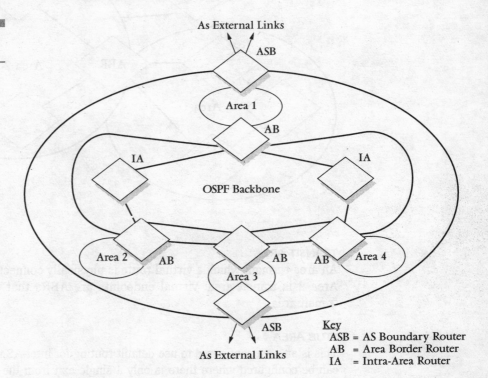

Key
ASB = AS Boundary Router
AB = Area Border Router
IA = Intra-Area Router

VIRTUAL LINK

A virtual link is part of the backbone. Its endpoints are two area border routers that share a common non-backbone area. The link is treated as a

point-to-point link with metrics cost equal to the intra-area metrics between
the endpoints of the links. The routing through the virtual link is done using
normal intra-area routing (see Figure 6.14). Virtual endpoints are area border
routers (ABRs) that share Area 2 as a transit area.

FIGURE 6.14
OSPF virtual link,
transit area.

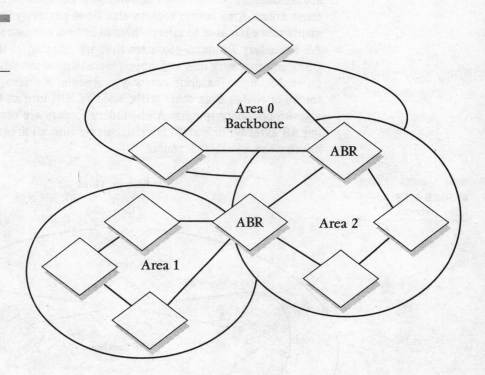

TRANSIT AREA

An area through which a virtual route is physically connected. In Figure 6.14,
Area 2 is transit area; virtual endpoints are ABRs that share Area 2 as a
transit area.

STUB AREA

This is an area configured to use default routing for inter-AS routing. A stub area
can be configured where there is only a single exit from the area, or where any
exit can be used without preference for routing to destinations outside the
autonomous system. By default inter-AS routes are copied to all areas, so the use
of stub areas can reduce the storage requirements of routers within those areas
for autonomous systems where a lot of inter-AS routes are defined.

NEIGHBOR ROUTERS

These are two routers that have interfaces to a common network. On multi-access networks, neighbors are dynamically discovered by the *Hello protocol*.

Each neighbor is described by a state machine, which describes the conversation between this router and its neighbor. A brief outline of the meaning of the states follows. See the section immediately following for a definition of the terms *adjacency* and *designated router*.

- **Down**—This initial state of a neighbor conversation indicates that there has been no recent information received from the neighbor.
- **Attempt**—A neighbor on a non-broadcast network appears down and an attempt should be made to contact it by sending regular Hello packets.
- **Init**—A Hello packet has recently been received from the neighbor. However, bidirectional communication has not yet been established with the neighbor. (That is, the router itself did not appear in the neighbor's Hello packet.)
- **2-way**—In this state, communication between the two routers is bidirectional. Adjacencies can be established, and neighbors in this state or higher are eligible to be elected as (backup) designated routers.
- **ExStart**—The two neighbors are about to create an adjacency.
- **Exchange**—The two neighbors are telling each other what they have in their topological databases.
- **Loading**—The two neighbors are synchronizing their topological databases.
- **Full**—The two neighbors are now fully adjacent; their databases are synchronized.

Various events cause a change of state. For example, if a router receives a Hello packet from a neighbor that is down, the neighbor's state changes to init, and an inactivity timer is started. If the timer fires (that is, no further OSPF packets are received before it expires), the neighbor will return to the down state. Refer to RFC 2173 for a complete description of the states and information on the events which cause state changes.

ADJACENT ROUTER

Neighbor routers can become *adjacent*. They are said to be adjacent when they have synchronized their topology databases through the exchange of link state information. Link-state information is exchanged only between adjacent routers, not between neighbor routers.

Not all neighbor routers become adjacent. Neighbors on point-to-point links do so, but on multi-access networks adjacencies are only formed between individual routers and the designated and backup designated routers. The exchange of link-state information between neighbors can create significant amounts of network traffic. Limiting the number of adjacencies on multi-access networks in this way achieves considerable reductions in network traffic.

DESIGNATED AND BACKUP DESIGNATED ROUTER

All multi-access networks have a *designated* and a *backup designated router*. These routers are elected automatically for each network once neighbor routers have been discovered by the Hello protocol.

The designated router performs two key roles for a network:

- It generates network links advertisements that list the routers attached to a multi-access network.
- It forms adjacencies with all routers on a multi-access network and therefore becomes the focal point for forwarding of all link-state advertisements.

The backup designated router forms the same adjacencies as the designated router. It therefore has the same topology database and is able to assume designated router functions should it detect that the designated router has failed.

PHYSICAL NETWORK TYPES

All OSPF areas consist of aggregates of networks linked by routers. OSPF categorizes networks into the following different types.

- **Point-to-point Network**—Point-to-point networks directly link two routers.
- **Multi-Access Network**—Multi-access networks are those that support the attachment of more than two routers. They are further subdivided into two types: broadcast and non-broadcast.
- **Point-to-Multipoint Network**—Point-to-multipoint networks describe a special case of multiaccess non-broadcast where not every router has a direct connection to any other router (also referred to as partial mesh).

Broadcast networks have the capability of directing OSPF packets to all attached routers, using an address that is recognized by all of them. An Ethernet LAN and token-ring LAN are examples of a broadcast multi-access network.

Non-broadcast networks do not have this capability and all packets must be specifically addressed to routers on the network. This requires that routers on a non-broadcast network be configured with the addresses of neighbors.

Examples of a non-broadcast multi-access network are the X.25 public data network or a frame relay network

INTERFACE

This is the connection between a router and one of its attached networks. Each interface has state information associated with it that is obtained from the underlying lower-level protocols and the OSPF protocol itself. A brief description of each state is given here. Please refer to RFC 2173 for more details, and for information on the events that will cause an interface to change its state.

- **Down**—The interface is unavailable. This is the initial state of an interface.
- **Loopback**—The interface is looped back to the router. It cannot be used for regular data traffic.
- **Waiting**—The router is trying to determine the identity of the designated router or its backup.
- **Point-to-point**—The interface is to a point-to-point network or is a virtual link. The router forms an adjacency with the router at the other end.

NOTE

The interfaces do not need IP addresses. Since the remainder of the internetwork has no practical need to see the routers' interfaces to the point-to-point link, just the interfaces to other networks, any IP addresses for the link would be needed only for communication between the two routers. To conserve the IP address space, the routers can dispense with IP addresses on the link. This has the effect of making the two routers appear to be one to IP but this has no ill effects. Such a link is called an unnumbered *link.*

- **DR other**—The interface is on a multiaccess network but this router is neither the designated router nor its backup. The router forms adjacencies with the designated router and its backup.
- **Backup**—The router is the backup designated router. It will be promoted to designated router if the present designated router fails. The router forms adjacencies with every other router on the network.
- **DR**—The router itself is the designated router. It forms adjacencies with every other router on the network, and must also originate a network links advertisement for the network node.

TYPE OF SERVICE (TOS) METRICS

In each type of link-state advertisement, different metrics can be advertised for each IP Type of Service. A metric for TOS 0 (used for OSPF routing protocol packets) must always be specified. Metrics for other TOS values can be specified; if they are not, these metrics are assumed equal to the metric specified for TOS 0.

The use of TOS has been dropped in recent OSPF implementations.

LINK STATE DATABASE

This is also called the *directed graph* or the *topological database*. It is created from the link-state advertisements generated by the routers in the area.

RFC 2328 uses the term link-state database in preference to topological database. The former term has the advantage that it describes the contents of the database, the latter is more descriptive of the purpose of the database, to describe the topology of the area. We have previously used the term topological database for this reason, but for the remainder of this section, where we discuss the operation of OSPF in more detail, we refer to it as the link-state database.

SHORTEST-PATH TREE

Each router runs the SPF algorithm on the link-state database to obtain its shortest-path tree. The tree gives the route to any destination network or host as far as the area boundary. It is used to build the routing table.

Because each router occupies a different place in the area's topology, application of the SPF algorithm gives a different tree for each router, even though the database is identical.

Area border routers run multiple copies of the algorithm but build a single routing table.

ROUTING TABLE

The routing table contains entries for each destination: network, subnet or host. For each destination, there is information for one or more types of service (TOS). For each combination of destination and type of service, there are entries for one or more optimum paths to be used.

AREA ID

This is a 32-bit number identifying a particular area. The backbone has an area ID of zero.

ROUTER ID

This is a 32-bit number identifying a particular router. Each router within the AS has a single router ID. One possible implementation is to use the lowest-numbered IP address belonging to a router as its router ID.

ROUTER PRIORITY

This is an 8-bit unsigned integer, configurable on a per-interface basis indicating this router's priority in the selection of the (backup) designated router. A router priority of zero indicates that this router is ineligible to be the designated router.

LINK-STATE ADVERTISEMENTS

Link-state information is exchanged by adjacent OSPF routers to allow area topology databases to be maintained and inter-area and inter-AS routes to be advertised.

Link-state information consists of four types of link-state advertisement (Figure 6.15). Together these provide all the information needed to describe an OSPF network and its external environment:

1. Router links
2. Network links
3. Summary links (type 3 and 4)
4. AS external links

- **Router link advertisements**—These are generated by all OSPF routers and describe the state of the router's interfaces (links) within the area. They are flooded throughout a single area only.
- **Network link advertisements**—These are generated by the designated router on a multi-access network and list the routers connected to the network. They are flooded throughout a single area only.
- **Summary link advertisements**—These are generated by area border routers. There are two types: one describes routes to destinations in other areas; the other describes routes to AS boundary routers. They are flooded throughout a single area only.
- **AS external link advertisements**—These are generated by AS boundary routers and describe routes to destinations external to the OSPF network. They are flooded throughout all areas in the OSPF network.

Protocol Description

The OSPF protocol is an implementation of a *link-state* routing protocol, as described in "Link State Routing."

FIGURE 6.15
OSPF link-state
advertisements.

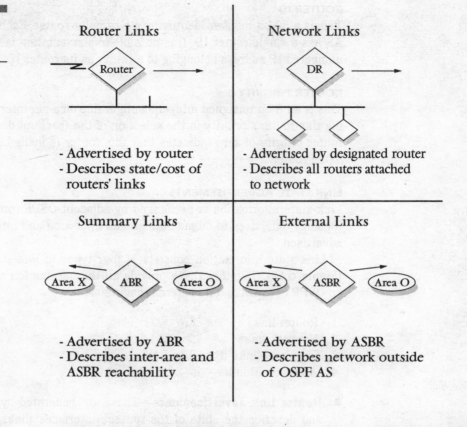

Router Links

Router

- Advertised by router
- Describes state/cost of
  routers' links

Network Links

DR

- Advertised by designated router
- Describes all routers attached
  to network

Summary Links

Area X — ABR — Area O

- Advertised by ABR
- Describes inter-area and
  ASBR reachability

External Links

Area X — ASBR — Area O

- Advertised by ASBR
- Describes network outside
  of OSPF AS

OSPF packets are transmitted directly in IP datagrams. IP datagrams containing OSPF packets can be distinguished by their use of *protocol identifier 89* in the IP header. OSPF packets are not, therefore, contained in TCP or UDP headers. OSPF packets are always sent with IP type of service set to 0, and the IP precedence field set to internetwork control. This is to aid them in getting preference over normal IP traffic.

OSPF packets are sent to a standard multicast IP address on point-to-point and broadcast networks. This address is 224.0.0.5, referred to as *AllSPFRouters* in the RFC. They are sent to specific IP addresses on non-broadcast networks using neighbor network address information that must be configured for each router. All OSPF packets share a common header, which is shown in Figure 6.16. This header provides general information such as area identifier and originating router identifier, and also includes a checksum and authentication information. A type field defines each OSPF packet as one of five possible types:

FIGURE 6.16
OSPF common
header.

Number of Octets

1	Version
1	Packet Type
2	Packet Length
4	Router ID
4	Area ID
4	Checksum
2	Authentication Type
8	Authentication Data

Version = 2
1 = Hello
2 = Database Description
3 = Link State Request
4 = Link State Update
5 = Link State Acknowledgement

0 = No Authentication
1 = Simple Password

Password if Type 1 Selected

1. Hello
2. Database description
3. Link state request
4. Link state update
5. Link state acknowledgment

The router identifier, area identifier, and authentication information are configurable for each OSPF router.

The OSPF protocol defines a number of stages which must be executed by individual routers. They are as follows:

- Discovering neighbors
- Electing the designated router
- Initializing neighbors
- Propagating link state information
- Calculating routing tables

The use of the five OSPF packet types to implement stages of the OSPF protocol are described in the following subsection.

During OSPF operation a router cycles each of its interfaces through a number of DR Other, BackupDR, or DR (DR stands for designated router) depending on the status of each attached network and the identity of the designated router elected for each of them. At the same time a router cycles each neighbor interface (interaction) through a number of states as it discovers them and then becomes adjacent. These states are: Down, Attempt, Init, 2-Way, ExStart, Exchange, Loading, and Full.

DISCOVERING NEIGHBORS—THE OSPF HELLO PROTOCOL

The Hello protocol is responsible for discovering neighbor routers on a network, and establishing and maintaining relationships with them. Hello packets are sent out periodically on all router interfaces. The format of these is shown in Figure 6.17.

Hello packets contain the identities of neighbor routers whose hello packets have already been received over a specific interface. They also contain the network mask, router priority, designated router identifier, and backup designated router identifier. The final three parameters are used to elect the designated router on multi-access networks. The network mask, router priority, hello interval, and router dead interval are configurable for each interface on an OSPF router.

A router interface changes state from Down to Point-to-Point (if the network is point-to-point), to DR Other (if the router is ineligible to become designated router), or otherwise to Waiting as soon as hello packets are sent over it. A router receives hello packets from neighbor routers via its network interfaces. When this happens the neighbor interface state changes from Down to Init. Bidirectional communication is established between neighbors when a router sees itself listed in a hello packet received from another router. Only at this point are the two routers defined as true neighbors, and the neighbor interface changes state from Init to 2-Way.

ELECTING THE DESIGNATED ROUTER

Each multi-access network has a designated router. There is also a backup designated router that takes over in the event that the designated router fails. The use of a backup, which maintains an identical set of adjacencies and an identical topology database to the designated router, ensures that there is no extended loss of routing capability if the designated router fails. The designated router performs two major functions on a network:

■ It originates network link advertisements on behalf of the network.

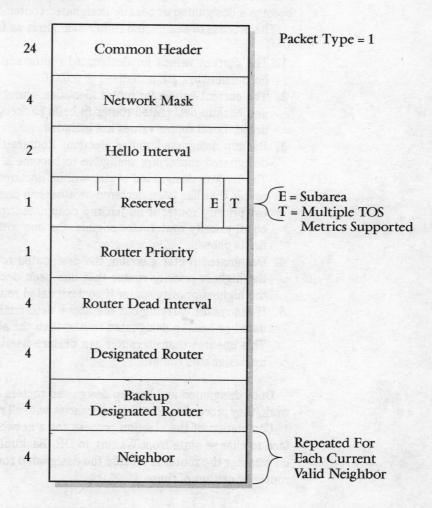

FIGURE 6.17
OSPF Hello packet.

Number of Octets

Packet Type = 1

Octets	Field
24	Common Header
4	Network Mask
2	Hello Interval
1	Reserved E T
1	Router Priority
4	Router Dead Interval
4	Designated Router
4	Backup Designated Router
4	Neighbor

E = Subarea
T = Multiple TOS Metrics Supported

Repeated For Each Current Valid Neighbor

- It establishes adjacencies with all other routers on the network. Only routers with adjacencies exchange link-state information and synchronize their databases.

The designated router and backup designated router are elected on the basis of the router identifier, router priority, designated router, and backup designated router fields in hello packets. Router priority is a single-octet field that defines the priority of a router on a network. The lower the value of the priority field the more likely the router is to become the designated router, hence the higher its priority. A zero value means the router is ineligible to become a designated or backup designated router.

The process of designated router election is as follows:

1. The current values for designated router and backup designated router on the network are initialized to 0.0.0.0.
2. The current values for router identifier, router priority, designated router, and backup designated router in hello packets from neighbor routers are noted. Local router values are included.
3. Backup designated router election: Routers that have been declared as designated router are ineligible to become a backup designated router. The backup designated router will be declared to be the highest priority router that has been declared as a backup designated router or the highest priority router if no backup designated router has been declared. If equal priority routers are eligible, the one with the highest router identifier is chosen.
4. Designated router election: the designated router will be declared to be the highest priority router that has been declared designated router or the highest priority router if no designated router has been declared.
5. If the router carrying out the above determination is declared the designated or backup designated router, then the above steps are re-executed. This ensures that no router can declare itself both designated and backup designated router.

Once designated and backup designated routers have been elected for a network, they proceed to establish adjacencies with all routers on the network.

Completion of the election process for a network causes the router interface to change state from Waiting to DR, BackupDR, or DR Other depending on whether the router is elected the designated router, the backup designated router or neither of these.

ESTABLISHING ADJACENCIES—DATABASE EXCHANGE

A router establishes adjacencies with a subset of neighbor routers on a network. Routers connected by point-to-point networks and virtual links always become *adjacent*. Routers on multi-access networks form adjacencies with the designated and backup designated routers only.

Link-state information flows only between adjacent routers. Before this can happen it is necessary for them to have the same topological database, and to be synchronized. This is achieved in OSPF by a process called *database exchange*.

Database exchange between two neighbor routers occurs as soon as they attempt to bring up an adjacency. It consists of the exchange of a number of database description packets that define the set of link-state information present in the database of each router. The link-state information in the database is defined by the list of link-state headers for all link-state advertisement in the database. (See Figure 6.22 for information on the link-state header.)

The format of database description packets is shown in Figure 6.18.

Number of Octets

FIGURE 6.18
OSPF database
description packet.

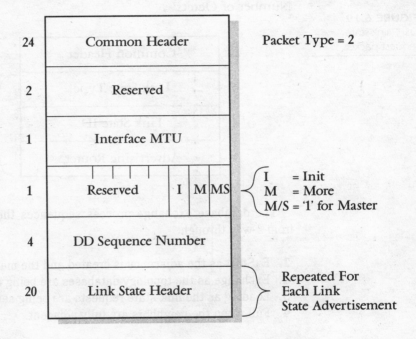

During the database exchange process the routers form a *master/slave* relationship, the master being the first to transmit. The master sends database description packets to the slave to describe its database of link-state information. Each packet is identified by a sequence number and contains a list of the link-state headers in the master's database. The slave acknowledges each packet by sequence number and includes its own database of headers in the acknowledgments.

Flags in database description packets indicate whether they are from a master or slave (the M/S bit), the first such packet (the I bit), and if there are more packets to come (the M bit). Database exchange is complete when a router receives a database description packet from its neighbor with the M bit off.

During database exchange each router makes a list of the link-state advertisements for which the adjacent neighbor has a more up-to-date instance (all advertisements are sequenced and time stamped). Once the process is complete, each router requests these more up-to-date instances of advertisements using link-state requests. The format of link-state request packets is shown in Figure 6.19.

FIGURE 6.19
OSPF link-state
request packet.

Number of Octets

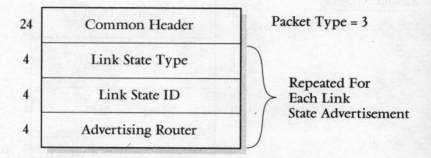

The database exchange process sequences the neighbor interface state from 2-way through:

1. ExStart as the adjacency is created and the master agreed upon.
2. Exchange as the topology databases are being described.
3. Loading as the link-state requests are being sent and responded to.
4. Full when the neighbors are fully adjacent.

In this way, the two routers synchronize their topology databases and are able to calculate identical network maps for their OSPF area.

LINK-STATE PROPAGATION

Information about the topology of an OSPF network is passed from router to router in link-state advertisements. These pass between adjacent routers in the form of link-state update packets, the format of which is shown in Figure 6.20.

Link-state advertisements are of five types: router links, network links, summary links (two types), and AS external links, as noted earlier in this section.

Link-state updates pass as a result of link-state requests during database exchange, and also in the normal course of events when routers wish to indicate a change of network topology. Individual link-state update packets can contain multiple link-state advertisements.

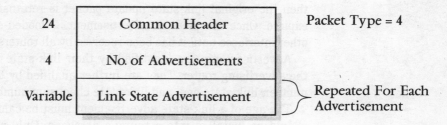

It is essential that each OSPF router in an area have the same network topology database; hence the integrity of link state information must be maintained. For that reason link-state update packets must be passed without loss or corruption throughout an area. The process by which this is done is called *flooding*.

A link-state update packet floods one or more link-state advertisements one hop further away from their originator. To make the flooding procedure reliable, each link-state advertisement must be acknowledged separately. Multiple acknowledgments can be grouped together into a single link-state acknowledgment packet. The format of such a packet is shown in Figure 6.21.

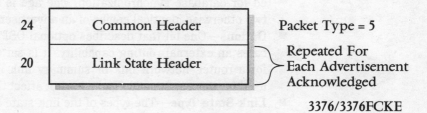

3376/3376FCKE

In order to maintain database integrity it is essential that all link-state advertisements be rigorously checked to ensure validity.

The following checks are applied and the advertisement discarded if:

- The link-state checksum is incorrect.
- The link-state type is invalid.

- The advertisement's age has reached its maximum.
- The advertisement is older than or the same as one already in the database.

If an advertisement passes the above checks, then an acknowledgment is sent back to the originator. If no acknowledgment is received by the originator, then the original link-state update packet is retransmitted after a timer has expired. Once accepted, an advertisement is flooded onward over the router's other interfaces until it has been received by all routers within an area.

Advertisements are identified by their link-state type, link-state ID, and the advertising router. They are further qualified by their link-state sequence number, link-state age, and link-state checksum number.

The age of a link-state advertisement must be calculated to determine if it should be installed into a router's database. Only a more recent advertisement should be accepted and installed. Valid link-state advertisements are installed into the topology database of the router. This causes the topology map or graph to be recalculated and the routing table to be updated.

Link-state advertisements all have a common 20-byte header. This is shown in Figure 6.22. The four link-state advertisement types are shown in Figures 6.23 through 6.26.

The fields in the link state advertisement header are:

- **Link Stage Age**—A 16-bit number indicating the time in seconds since the origin of the advertisement. It is increased as the link state advertisement resides in a router's database and with each hop it travels as part of the flooding procedure. When it reaches a maximum value, it ceases to be used for determining routing tables and is discarded unless it is still needed for database synchronization. The age is also to determine which of two otherwise identical copies of an advertisement a router should use.
- **Options**—One bit that describes optional OSPF capabilitiy. The E-bit indicates an external routing capability. It is set unless the advertisement is for a router, network link or summary link in a stub area. The E-bit is used for information only and does not affect the routing table.
- **Link-State Type**—The types of the link-state advertisement are:
  - *Router links*—These describe the states of a router's interfaces.
  - *Network links*—These describe the routers attached to a network.
  - *Summary links*—These describe inter-area, intra-AS routes. They are created by area border routers and allow routes to networks within the AS but outside the area to be described concisely.
  - *Summary links*—These describe routes to the boundary of the AS (that is, to AS boundary routers). They are created by area border routers and are very similar to type 3.

FIGURE 6.22
OSPF link-state
header.

Number of Octets

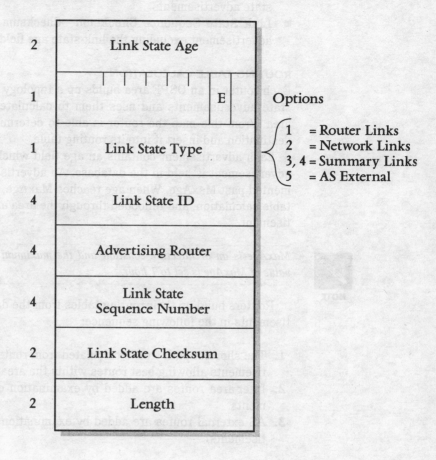

Octets	Field
2	Link State Age
1	E / Options
1	Link State Type
4	Link State ID
4	Advertising Router
4	Link State Sequence Number
2	Link State Checksum
2	Length

Options

1 = Router Links
2 = Network Links
3, 4 = Summary Links
5 = AS External

- • *AS external links*—These describe routes to networks outside the AS. They are created by AS boundary routers. A default route for the AS can be described this way.
- ■ **Link State ID**—A unique ID for the advertisement dependent on the link-state type. For types 1 and 4 it is the router ID, for types 3 and 5 it is an IP network number, and for type 2 it is the IP address of the designated router.
- ■ **Advertising Router**—The router ID of the router that originated the link-state advertisement. For type 1 advertisements, this field is identical to the link-state ID. For type 2, it is the router ID of the network's designated router. For types 3 and 4, it is the router ID of an area border router. For type 5, it is the router ID of an AS boundary router.

LS Sequence Number—Used to allow detection of old or duplicate link-state advertisements.
- **Link State Sequence Checksum**—Checksum of the complete link-state advertisement excluding the link-state age field.

ROUTING TABLE CALCULATION

Each router in an OSPF area builds up a topology database of validated link-state advertisements and uses them to calculate the network map for the area. From this map the router is able to determine the best route for each destination and insert it into its routing table.

Each advertisement contains an age field which is incremented while the advertisement is held in the database. An advertisement's age is never incremented past MaxAge. When age reaches MaxAge, it is excluded from routing table calculation, and reflooded through the area as a newly originated advertisement.

NOTE

MaxAge is an architecture constant and the maximum age an LSA can attain. The value of MaxAge is set to 1 hour.

Routers build up their routing tables from the database of link-state advertisements in the following sequence:

1. The shortest-path tree is calculated from router and network links advertisements allowing best routes within the area to be determined.
2. Inter-area routes are added by examination of summary link advertisements.
3. AS external routes are added by examination of AS external link advertisements.

The topology graph or map constructed from the above process is used to update the routing table. The routing table is recalculated each time a new advertisement is received.

The fields in the router link advertisement (Figure 6.23) header are:

- **V Bit**—When set, this router is the endpoint of a virtual link that is using this area as a transit area.
- **E Bit**—When set, the router is an AS boundary router.
- **B Bit**—When set, the router is an area border router.
- **Number of Links**—The number of links described by this advertisement.
- **Link ID**—Identifies the object that this link connects to. The value depends upon the field type.

FIGURE 6.23
OSPF router links
advertisement.

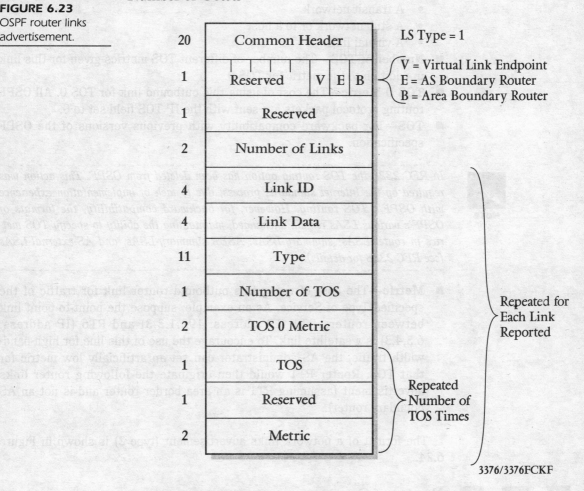

Number of Octets

20	Common Header
1	Reserved / V E B
1	Reserved
2	Number of Links
4	Link ID
4	Link Data
11	Type
1	Number of TOS
2	TOS 0 Metric
1	TOS
1	Reserved
2	Metric

LS Type = 1

V = Virtual Link Endpoint
E = AS Boundary Router
B = Area Boundary Router

Repeated for
Each Link
Reported

Repeated
Number of
TOS Times

3376/3376FCKF

- Neighboring router's router ID
- IP address of the designated router
- IP network/subnet number. This value depends on what the inter-area route is to: For a stub network it is the IP network/subnet number. For a host it is X}FFFFFFFF}. For the AS-external default route it is X}00000000}.
- Neighboring router's router ID

■ **Link Data**—This value also depends upon the type field (see RFC 2328 for details).

■ **Type**—This link connects to a:

- Point-to-point connection to another router
- A transit network
- A stub network or to a host
- A virtual link

■ **Number of TOS**—The number of different TOS metrics given for this link in addition to the metric for TOS 0.

■ **TOS 0 Metric**—The cost of using this outbound link for TOS 0. All OSPF routing protocol packets are sent with the IP TOS field set to 0.

■ **TOS**—For backward compatibility with previous versions of the OSPF specification.

In RFC 2328 the TOS routing option has been deleted from OSPF. This action was required by the Internet standards process, due to lack of implementation experience with OSPF's TOS routing. However, for backward compatibility, the formats of OSPF's various LSAs remain unchanged, maintaining the ability to specify TOS metrics in router-LSAs, summary-LSAs, ASBR-summary-LSAs, and AS-external-LSAs (see RFC 2328 for details).

■ **Metric**—The cost of using this outbound router link for traffic of the specified Type of Service. As an example, suppose the point-to-point link between routers RT1 (IP address: 192.1.2.3) and RT6 (IP address: 6.5.4.3) is a satellite link. To encourage the use of this line for high-bandwidth traffic, the AS administrator can set an artificially low metric for that TOS. Router RT1 would then originate the following router links advertisement (assuming RT1 is an area border router and is not an AS boundary router).

The format of a network links advertisement (type 2) is shown in Figure 6.24.

FIGURE 6.24
OSPF network links advertisement.

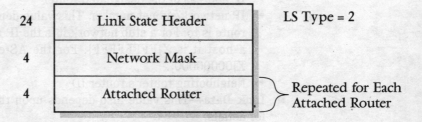

The fields in the network link advertisement header are:

- **Network Mask**—The IP address mask for the network. For example a CIDR prefix length /20 network would have the mask 255.255.240.0 (dotted-decimal) and the mask 1111 1111 1111 1111 1110 0000 0000 0000 (binary).
- **Attached Router**—The router IDs of each of the routers attached to the network that are adjacent to the designated router (including the sending router). The number of routers in the list is deduced from the field length in the header.

The fields in the summary link advertisement header (Figure 6.25) are:

- **Network Mask**—For a type 3 link-state advertisement, this is the IP address mask for the network. For a type 4 link-state advertisement, this is not meaningful and must be zero.
- **Reserved**—All zero.
- **Metric**—The cost of this route for this type of service in the same units used for TOS metrics in type 1 advertisements.
- **TOS**—Zero or more entries for additional types of service. The number of entries can be determined from the length field in the header.

Number of Octets

FIGURE 6.25
OSPF summary links advertisement.

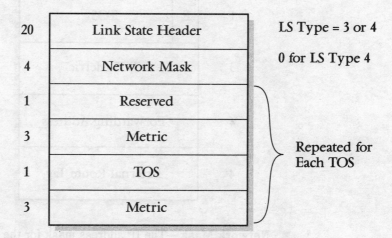

The fields in the external link advertisement (Figure 6.26) header are:

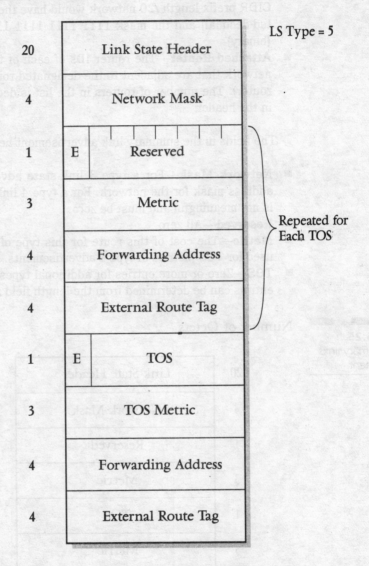

FIGURE 6.26
OSPF external links
advertisement.

- **Network Mask**—The IP address mask for the network.
- **Bit E**—The type of external metric. If set, the type is 2, otherwise it is 1. The metric is directly comparable to OSPF link-state metrics. The metric is considered larger than all OSPF link state metrics.

- **Reserved**—All zero.
- **Metric**—The cost of this route. Interpretation depends on the E-bit.
- **Forwarding Address**—The IP address to which data traffic for this type of service intended for the advertised destination is to be forwarded. The value 0.0.0.0 indicates that traffic should be forwarded to the AS boundary router that originated the advertisement.
- **External Route Tag**—A 32-bit value attached to the external route by an AS boundary router. This is not used by the OSPF itself. It can be used to communicate information between AS boundary routers.
- **TOS**—Zero or more entries for additional types of service. The number of entries can be determined from the length field in the header.

Exterior Routing Protocols

Exterior Routing Protocols or Exterior Gateway Protocols (EGPs) are used to exchange routing information between routers in different autonomous systems. Two EGPs are commonly used: Exterior Gateway Protocol (see Chapter 3, the section on "Exterior Gateway Protocol (EGP)") and Border Gateway Protocol.

NOTE

The term exterior routing protocol has no abbreviation commonly used, so we shall use the abbreviation EGP as is usual in TCP/IP literature.

Exterior Gateway Protocol (EGP)

EGP is a *historic protocol* described in RFC 904. Interestingly, its status is still listed as *recommended*. The Exterior Gateway Protocol is a protocol used for exchange of routing information between *exterior* gateways (not belonging to the same autonomous system). EGP assumes a single backbone, and therefore only one single path between any two ASs. Therefore, the practical use of EGP today is virtually restricted to someone who wants to build a private Internet. In the real world, EGP is being replaced progressively by BGP.

EGP is based on periodic polling using Hello/I Hear You message exchanges, to monitor neighbor reachability and poll requests to solicit update responses. EGP restricts exterior gateways by allowing them to advertise only those destination networks reachable entirely within that gateway's autonomous system. Thus, an exterior gateway using EGP passes along information to its EGP neighbors but does not advertise reachability information about its EGP neighbors (gateways are neighbors if they exchange routing information) outside the autonomous system. The routing information from inside an AS must be collected by this EGP gateway, usually via an Interior Gateway Protocol (IGP). This was shown in Figure 6.2.

Border Gateway Protocol (BGP-4)

The Border Gateway Protocol (BGP) is a draft standard protocol and its status is elective. It is described in RFC 1771. The Border Gateway Protocol is an exterior gateway protocol used to exchange network reachability information among ASs (see Figure 6.2). BGP-4 was introduced in the Internet in the loop-free exchange of routing information between autonomous systems. Based on Classless Inter-Domain Routing (CIDR), BGP has since evolved to support the aggregation and reduction of routing information.

In essence, CIDR is a strategy designed to address exhaustion of Class B address space and routing table growth. CIDR eliminates the concept of address classes and provides a method for summarizing n different routes into single routes. This significantly reduces the amount of routing information that BGP routers must store and exchange.

Before giving an overview of the BGP protocol, we should define some terms used in BGP:

- **BGP speaker**—This is a system running BGP (see Figure 6.27).
- **BGP neighbors**—This pair of BGP speakers exchanges inter-AS routing information. BGP neighbors may be of two types:
  - *Internal*—This is a pair of BGP speakers in the same autonomous system. Internal BGP neighbors must present a consistent image of the AS to their external BGP neighbors. This is explained in more detail below.
  - *External*—This is a pair of BGP neighbors in different autonomous systems. External BGP neighbors must be connected by a BGP connection as defined below. This restriction means that in most cases where an AS has multiple BGP inter-AS connections, it will also require multiple BGP speakers.
- *BGP session*—This is a TCP session between BGP neighbors exchanging routing information using BGP. The neighbors monitor the state of the session by sending a *keepalive* message regularly. (The recommended interval is 30 seconds.)

This keepalive message is implemented in the application layer, and is independent of the keepalive message available in many TCP implementations.

NOTE

FIGURE 6.27
BGP speaker and
AS relationship.

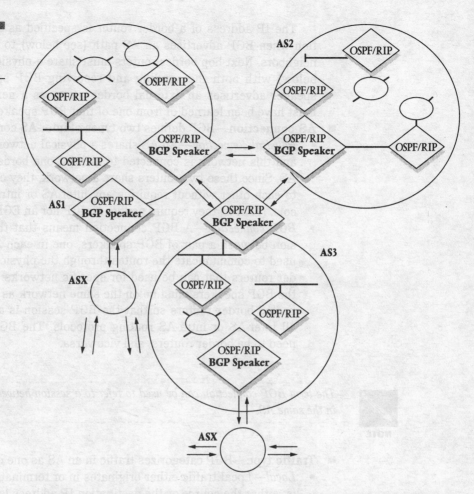

- **AS border router (ASBR)**—This router has a connection to multiple autonomous systems.

NOTE

The nomenclature for this type of router is somewhat varied. RFC 2328, which describes OSPF, uses the term AS boundary router. *RFC 1771 and 1772, which describe BGP, use the terms* border router *and* border gateway. *We use the first term consistently when describing both OSPF and BGP. BGP defines two types of AS border routers, each depending on its topological relationship to the BGP speaker that refers to it.*

- *Internal*—This next-hop router is in the same AS as the BGP speaker.
- *External*—This next-hop router is in an AS different from the BGP speaker.

The IP address of a border router is specified as a next-hop destination when BGP advertises an AS path (see below) to one of its external neighbors. Next-hop border routers must share a physical connection (see below) with both the sending and receiving BGP speakers. If a BGP speaker advertises an external border router as a next hop, that router must have been learned of from one of that BGP speaker's peers.

- **AS connection**—BGP defines two types of inter-AS connections:
  - *Physical connection*—An AS shares a physical network with another AS, and this network is connected to at least one border router from each AS. Since these two routers share a network, they can forward packets to each other without requiring any inter-AS or intra-AS routing protocols. (That is, they require neither an IGP nor an EGP to communicate.)
  - *BGP connection*—A BGP connection means that there is a BGP session between a pair of BGP speakers, one in each AS. This session is used to communicate the routes through the physically connected border routers that can be used for specific networks. BGP requires that the BGP speakers must be on the same network as the physically connected border routers so that the BGP session is also independent of all inter-AS or intra-AS routing protocols. The BGP speakers do not need to be border routers, and vice versa.

NOTE

The term BGP connection can be used to refer to a session between two BGP speakers in the same AS.

- **Traffic type**—BGP categorizes traffic in an AS as one of two types:
  - *Local*—Local traffic either originates in or terminates in that AS. That is, either the source or the destination IP address is in the AS.
  - *Transit*—Transit traffic is all non-local traffic. One of the goals of BGP is to minimize the amount of transit traffic.
- **AS type**—An AS is categorized as one of three types:
  - *Stub*—A stub AS has a single inter-AS connection to one other AS. A stub AS carries only local traffic.
  - *Multihomed*—A multihomed AS has connections to more than one other AS but refuses to carry transit traffic.
  - *Transit*—A transit AS has connections to more than one other AS and carries both and local transit traffic. The AS may impose policy restrictions on what transit traffic will be carried.
- **AS number**—This 16-bit number uniquely identifies an AS. This is the same AS number used by EGP.

- **AS path**—This is a list of all of the AS numbers traversed by a route when exchanging routing information. Rather than exchanging simple metric counts, BGP communicates entire paths to its neighbors.
- **Routing policy**—This set of rules constrains routing to conform to the wishes of the authority that administers the AS. Routing policies are not defined in the BGP protocol, but are selected by the AS authority and presented to BGP in the form of implementation-specific configuration data. Routing policies can be selected by the AS authority in whatever way that authority sees fit. For example:
  - A multihomed AS can refuse to act as a transit AS. It does this by not advertising routes to networks other than those directly connected to it.
  - A multihomed AS can limit itself to being a transit AS for a restricted set of adjacent ASs. It does this by advertising its routing information to this set only.
  - An AS can select which outbound AS should be used for carrying transit traffic.

  An AS can also apply performance-related criteria when selecting outbound paths:
  - An AS can optimize traffic to use short AS paths rather than long ones.
  - An AS can select transit routes according to the service quality of the intermediate hops. This service quality information could be obtained using mechanisms external to BGP.

The definitions above indicate that a stub AS or a multihomed AS has the same topological properties as an AS in the ARPANET architecture. That is, it never acts as an intermediate AS in an inter-AS route. In the ARPANET architecture, EGP was sufficient for such an AS to exchange reachability information with its neighbors, and this remains true with BGP. Therefore, a stub AS or a multihomed AS can continue to use EGP (or any other suitable protocol) to operate with a transit AS. However, RFC 1772 recommends that BGP be used instead of EGP for these types of AS because it provides an advantage in bandwidth and performance. Additionally, in a multihomed AS, BGP is more likely to provide an optimum inter-AS route than EGP, since EGP addresses only reachability and not distance.

Path Selection

Each BGP speaker must evaluate different paths to a destination from the border router(s) for an AS connection, select the best one that complies with the routing policies in force, and then advertise that route to all its BGP neighbors at that AS connection. BGP is a vector-distance protocol but, unlike traditional vector-distance protocols such as RIP where there is a single metric, BGP determines a preference order by applying a function mapping each path to a preference value and selects the path with the highest value. The function applied is generated by the BGP implementation according to configuration information. However, BGP does not keep a cost metric to any path. This is sometimes considered a shortcoming, but there is no mechanism in place for BGP to collect a uniform cost for paths across the multitude of today's service provider networks.

Where there are multiple viable paths to a destination, BGP maintains all of them but only advertises the one with the highest preference value. This approach allows a quick change to an alternate path should the primary path fail.

Routing Policies

RFC 1772 includes a recommended set of policies for all implementations:

■ A BGP implementation should be able to control which routes it announces. The granularity of this control should be at least at the network level for the announced routes and at the AS level for the recipients. For example, BGP should allow a policy of announcing a route to a specific network to a specific adjacent AS. Care must be taken when a BGP speaker selects a new route that cannot be announced to a particular external peer, while the previously selected route was announced to that peer. Specifically, the local system must explicitly indicate to the peer that the previous route is now infeasible.

■ BGP should allow a weighting policy for paths. Each AS can be assigned a weight and the preferred path to a destination is then the one with the lowest aggregate weight.

■ BGP should allow a policy of excluding an AS from all possible paths. This can be done with a variant of the previous policy; each AS to be excluded is given an *infinite* weight and the route selection process refuses to consider paths of infinite weight.

See Figure 6.28 regarding the BGP process and routing policies:

1. Routing updates are received from other BGP routers.
2. An input policy engine filters routes and performs attribute manipulation.
3. The decision process decides what routes the BGP router will use.

4. An output policy engine filters routes and performs attribute manipulation for routes to be advertised.
5. Routing updates are advertised to other BGP routers.

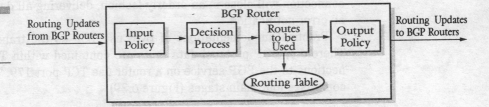

FIGURE 6.28
BGP process and
routing policies.

AS Consistency

BGP requires that a transit AS present the same view to every AS using its services. If the AS has multiple BGP speakers, they must agree on two aspects of topology: intra-AS and inter-AS. Since BGP does not deal with intra-AS routing at all, a consistent view of intra-AS topology must be provided by the interior routing protocol(s) employed in the AS. Naturally, a protocol such as OSPF that implements synchronization of router databases lends itself well to this role. Consistency of the external topology may be provided by all BGP speakers in the AS having BGP sessions with each other, but BGP does not require that this method be used, only that consistency be maintained.

Routing Information Exchange

BGP advertises only routes that it uses itself to its neighbors. That is, BGP conforms to the normal Internet hop-by-hop paradigm, even though it has additional information in the form of AS paths and theoretically could be capable of informing a neighbor of a route it would not use itself.

When two BGP speakers form a BGP session, they begin by exchanging their entire routing tables. Routing information is exchanged via UPDATE messages (see below for the format of these messages). Since the routing information contains the complete AS path to each listed destination in the form of a list of AS numbers in addition to the usual reachability and next-hop information used in traditional vector distance protocols, it can be used to suppress routing loops and to eliminate the counting-to-infinity problem found in RIP. After BGP neighbors have performed their initial exchange of their complete routing databases, they exchange only updates to that information.

Protocol Description

BGP runs over a reliable transport-layer connection between neighbor routers. BGP relies on the transport connection for fragmentation, retransmission, acknowledgment, and sequencing. It assumes that the transport connection will close in an orderly fashion, delivering all data, in the event of an error notification.

Practical implementations of BGP use TCP as the transport mechanism. Therefore, BGP protocol data units are contained within TCP packets. Connections to the BGP service on a router use TCP port 179. The BGP protocol comprises four main stages (Figure 6.29):

FIGURE 6.29
BGP messages flow between BGP speakers,

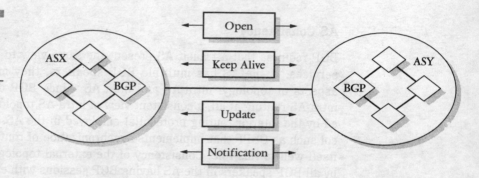

- Opening and confirming a BGP connection with a neighbor router
- Maintaining the BGP connection
- Sending reachability information
- Notification of error conditions

OPENING AND CONFIRMING A BGP CONNECTION

BGP communication between two routers commences with the TCP transport protocol connection being established. Once the connection has been established, each router sends an *OPEN* message to its neighbor.

The BGP OPEN message, like all BGP messages, consists of a standard header plus packet-type specific contents. The standard header consists of a 16-octet marker field, which is set to all ones when the authentication code is 0, the length of the total BGP packet, and a type field that specifies the packet to be one of four possible types:

1. OPEN
2. UPDATE
3. NOTIFICATION

4. KEEPALIVE

The format of the BGP header is shown in Figure 6.30.

Number of Octets

16	Marker	Set to '1s'
2	Length	
1	Type	1 = Open 2 = Update 3 = Notification 4 = Keep Alive

FIGURE 6.30
BGP message header.

NOTE

RFC 1771 uses uppercase to name BGP messages, so we do the same in this section.

The open message defines the originating router's AS number, its BGP router identifier, and the hold time for the connection. If no KEEPALIVE, UPDATE, or NOTIFICATION messages are received for a period of hold time, the originating router assumes an error, sends a notification message, and closes the connection. The OPEN message also provides an optional parameter length and optional parameters. These fields may be used to authenticate a BGP peer. The format of the OPEN message is shown in Figure 6.31.

An acceptable OPEN message is acknowledged by a *KEEPALIVE* message. Once neighbor routers have sent KEEPALIVE messages in response to opens, they can proceed to exchange further KEEPALIVES, NOTIFICATIONS, and UPDATES.

MAINTAINING THE BGP CONNECTION

BGP messages must be exchanged periodically between neighbors. If no messages have been received for the period of the hold timer calculated by using the smaller of its configured hold time and the hold time received in the OPEN message, then an error on the connection is assumed. BGP uses KEEPALIVE messages to maintain the connection between neighbors. KEEPALIVE messages consist of the BGP packet header only, with no data. The RFC recommends that the hold time timer be 90 seconds and keepalive timer be 30 seconds.

FIGURE 6.31
BGP OPEN message.

Number of Octets

19	Common Header	Type = 1
1	Version	
2	AS Number of Transmitter	
2	Hold Time	
4	BGP Identifier	
1	Optional Parameter Length	
12	Optional Parameters	

SENDING REACHABILITY INFORMATION

Reachability information is exchanged between BGP neighbors in UPDATE messages. An UPDATE message is used to advertise a single feasible route to a peer, or to withdraw infeasible routes from service. An UPDATE may simultaneously advertise a feasible route and withdraw multiple infeasible routes from service. The following are the basic blocks of an UPDATE message:

1. Network Layer Reachability Information (NLRI)
2. Path attributes
3. Withdrawn routes

The format of these is shown in Figure 6.32.

NETWORK LAYER REACHABILITY INFORMATION (NLRI)

NLRI is the mechanism by which BGP-4 supports classless routing. It is a variable-field indication, in the form of an IP prefix route, of the networks being advertised. The NLRI is also represented by the tuple <length,prefix>. A tuple of the form <14,220.24.106.0> indicates a route to be reachable of the form 220.24.106.0 255.252.0.0 or 220.24.106.0/14 in the CIDR format (see Figure 6.33).

FIGURE 6.32
BGP UPDATE
message.

Number of Octets

Octets	Field	
19	Common Header	Type = 2
2	Unfeasible Route Length	
Variable	Withdrawn Routes	
2	Total Path Attribute Length	
Variable	Path Attribute	
Variable	Network Layer Reachability Information	

FIGURE 6.32
BGP UPDATE
message.

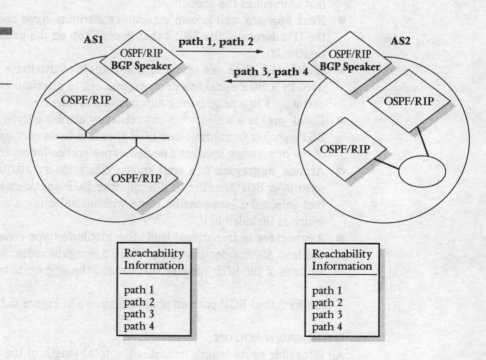

FIGURE 6.33
BGP exchanging
NLRI.

PATH ATTRIBUTES

Each path attribute consists of a triple set of values: attribute flag, attribute type, and attribute value. Three of the attribute flags provide information about the status of the attribute types, and may be optional or well known, transitive or non-transitive, and partial or complete.

Attribute flags must be read in conjunction with their associated attribute types. There are seven attribute types that together define an advertised route:

- **Origin** is a well-known mandatory attribute (type code 1), and defines the origin of the route as an IGP, an EGP, or INCOMPLETE (for example a static route).
- **AS path** is a well-known mandatory attribute (type code 2), and defines the ASs which must be crossed to reach the network being advertised. It is a sequence of AS numbers a route has traversed to reach a destination. The AS that originates the route adds its own AS number when sending the route to its external BGP peer. Each AS that receives the route and passes it on to other BGP peer will prepend its own AS number as the last element of the sequence.
- **Next hop** is a well-known mandatory attribute (type code 3), and defines the IP address of the ASBR that is next hop on the path to the listed destination(s).
- **Multi_exit_disc**, an optional non-transitive attribute (type code 4), is used by a BGP speaker's decision process to discriminate among multiple exit points to a neighboring autonomous system.
- **Local_pref** is a well-known discretionary attribute (type code 5) used by a BGP speaker to inform other BGP speakers in its own autonomous system of the originating speaker's degree of preference for an advertised route.
- **Atomic_aggregate** is a well-known discretionary attribute (type code 6) used by a BGP speaker to inform other BGP speakers that the local system selected a less-specific route without selecting a more-specific route which is included in it.
- **Aggregator** is an optional transitive attribute (type code 7), and indicates the last AS number that formed the aggregate route, followed by the IP address of the BGP speaker that formed the aggregate route.

The format of BGP path attributes is shown in Figure 6.34.

WITHDRAWN ROUTES

An infeasible route length indicates the total length of the withdrawn routes field in octets. A value equaling 0 indicates that no routes are being withdrawn from service, and that the Withdrawn Routes field is not present in this update message.

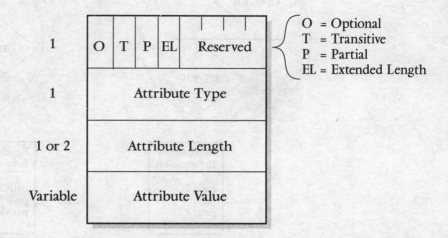

FIGURE 6.34
BGP path attributes.

Number of Octets

O = Optional
T = Transitive
P = Partial
EL = Extended Length

Withdrawn Routes is a variable-length field. Updates qualify if they are not feasible or are no longer in service and need to be withdrawn from BGP routing table. The withdrawn routes have the same formats as the NLRI. Withdrawn routes are also represented by the tuple `<length,prefix>`. A tuple of the form `<15,220:24.106.0>` indicates a route to be withdrawn of the form 220.24.106.0 255.254.0.0 or 220.24.106.0/15 in the CIDR format (see Figure 6.35).

NOTIFYING ERRORS

NOTIFICATION messages are sent to a neighbor router when error conditions are detected. The BGP transport connection is closed immediately after a notification message has been sent.

NOTIFICATION messages consist of an *error code* and an *error subcode*, which further qualifies the main error. The format of NOTIFICATION messages is shown in Figure 6.36.

Error codes provided by BGP are Message Header Error, Open Message Error, Update Message Error, Hold Timer Expired, Finite State Machine Error, and Cease.

A data field is included in the NOTIFICATION message to provide additional diagnostic information.

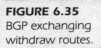

FIGURE 6.35
BGP exchanging
withdraw routes.

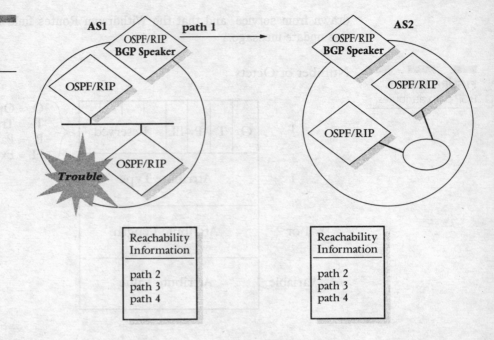

Number of Octets

FIGURE 6.36
BGP NOTIFICATION
message.

Number of Octets		
19	Common Header	Type = 3
1	Error Code	
1	Error Subcode	
Variable	Data	

References

For more information on IP routing protocols, please see the following RFCs:

RFC 904 – *Exterior Gateway Protocol Formal Specification*
RFC 1058 – *Routing Information Protocol*

RFC 1245 – *OSPF Protocol Analysis*
RFC 1246 – *Experience with the OSPF Protocol*
RFC 1721 – *RIP Version 2 Protocol Analysis*
RFC 1722 – *RIP Version 2 Protocol Applicability Statement*
RFC 1723 – *RIP Version 2 – Carrying Additional Information*
RFC 1724 – *RIP Version 2 MIB Extension*
RFC 1771 – *A Border Gateway Protocol 4 (BGP-4)*
RFC 1772 – *Application of the Border Gateway Protocol in the Internet*
RFC 1812 – *Requirements for IP Version 4 Routers*
RFC 1850 – *OSPF Version 2: Management Information Base*
RFC 2080 – *RIPng for IPv6*
RFC 2328 – *OSPF Version 2*

Implementing
IP-Enhanced
IGRP

Enhanced IGRP Concepts

To introduce the IP-enhanced IGRP routing protocol we present an outline of the various features of Enhanced IGRP, then list the network-layer protocols supported by Enhanced IGRP, and list the types of packets used by Enhanced IGRP routers to maintain routing information. We describe the specific use of each packet type and explain how Enhanced IGRP uses neighbor tables and topology tables to update routing tables. We describe how DUAL is used to determine successors and consider a scenario in which Enhanced IGRP routers update their routing tables using two separate methods.

Overview

Enhanced interior gateway routing protocol (IGRP) is an advanced distance-vector routing protocol that offers features available in distance-vector routing protocols such as IGRP. It combines these with advantages found in link state routing protocols such as OSPF. For more information on distance-vector and link-state routing see Chapter 5.

Enhanced IGRP is compatible with IGRP routers. In fact, an automatic redistribution mechanism allows the routes from either of these protocols to be imported into the other. The metrics of both protocols can easily be compared because they can be directly translated. This facilitates the gradual implementation of Enhanced IGRP in existing IGRP networks. Enhanced IGRP treats IGRP routes as external routes, and provides a way for the network administrator to customize them.

Enhanced IGRP includes the following features:

- Fast convergence
- Partial, bounded updates
- Variable-length subnet masks
- Multiple network-layer support.

Routers running Enhanced IGRP support fast convergence by using the *diffusing update algorithm (DUAL)*. A router's DUAL finite state machine is the process responsible for determining the routes along which packets are sent. It selects routes to be inserted into the routing table based on feasible successors. An Enhanced IGRP feasible successor is a neighboring router used for packet forwarding that has a least-cost path to a destination guaranteed not to be part of a routing loop.

Each Enhanced IGRP router stores every routing table belonging to its neighbors. (In the context of Enhanced IGRP, neighbors are routers that are directly connected to each other and also running Enhanced IGRP.)

These tables are received when a router first communicates with its neighbors. This means that an alternate route can be adapted quickly if a routing change becomes necessary. This helps to eliminate routing loops.

When a route becomes unusable, a router running Enhanced IGRP examines the routing table compiled from its neighbors and selects the most appropriate route. If no such route is immediately apparent, the router queries its neighbors in an attempt to discover an alternative route. These queries are propagated until a new route is found.

Enhanced IGRP routers update their routing tables only when there is a specific need to do so. These updates are made when the routing path changes or when the metric for that route changes. This distinguishes these routers from those that run pure distance-vector routing protocols, which perform periodic updates to routing tables.

When an update is made to a routing table, an Enhanced IGRP router sends that update to its neighbors. It is automatically bounded so that it sends only the information that needs to be updated and it sends that information only to those routers affected by the update.

By default, Enhanced IGRP uses a flat (non-hierarchical) topology. Subnet routes are automatically summarized at a network number boundary. This is sufficient for most IP networks.

NOTE

Route summarization allows a single router to act as the interface between the subnetwork and the rest of the network. This means that a single, summary route can be advertised for the entire subnetwork.

Route summarization can also be configured at any interface with any bit boundary. This allows ranges of networks to be summarized arbitrarily.

Enhanced IGRP permits using bit-wise subnetting in conjunction with variable-length subnetwork masks when assigning addresses. This saves address space. For more information on assigning addresses and defining subnet masks, see Chapter 3.

Enhanced IGRP supports some of the most commonly used protocols: TCP/IP, AppleTalk, and Novell IPX. The functionality of Enhanced IGRP can be divided into two areas: tasks that are shared between protocols and tasks that are separate for each supported protocol.

For each network-layer protocol supported by Enhanced IGRP, a separate set of tables must be maintained. To facilitate this, Enhanced IGRP offers a specific protocol-dependent module for each supported protocol.

Protocol-dependent modules are responsible for network layer protocol-specific tasks. For example, the IP Enhanced IGRP module is responsible for sending and receiving Enhanced IGRP packets that are encapsulated in IP.

Each protocol-dependent module is responsible for sending and receiving packets associated with that specific protocol. This includes the reception and redistribution of packets containing protocol-specific routing data. The protocol used by the source router determines which set of tables is used to store the incoming data. The AppleTalk implementation learns its routes from the routing table maintenance protocol. The Novell IPX implementation receives its information from the Novell routing information protocol (RIP) or service advertisement protocol (SAP). There are a variety of sources from which the IP implementation can gather its routing information. These include OSPF, RIP, intermediate system-to-intermediate system (IS-IS), EGP, and BGP.

The protocol-dependent modules parse the incoming packets and pass the relevant data to DUAL, which uses the data to make routing decisions. The results of these decisions are stored in routing tables—one for each supported protocol. There is also a neighbor table and a topology table for each protocol.

Enhanced IGRP's protocol engine allows for some tasks to be shared between protocols, such as route processing using DUAL, neighbor discovery, and reliable transport.

Although Enhanced IGRP maintains separate routing tables for each supported protocol, the process of making routing decisions is performed by one common algorithm. The DUAL algorithm applies a common metric structure to each protocol when performing this task.

An Enhanced IGRP router uses neighbor discovery to attempt to locate other Enhanced IGRP routers. It does this by sending protocol-dependent *hello packets*. This process, critical to proper Enhanced IGRP operation, is the same for all supported protocols.

Enhanced IGRP depends on sending partial route updates to notify other routers of route changes. Reliable transport is essential in order to ensure a loop-free network topology. To achieve this, routers receiving certain types of packets send a packet back to the source router acknowledging reception.

Enhanced IGRP guarantees ordered delivery of all packets by using the Reliable Transport Protocol (RTP). RTP supports intermixed transmission of multicast and unicast packets.

Hello packets that are multicast over an Ethernet network are examples of certain packets that do not need to be transmitted reliably by Enhanced IGRP routers. In such cases, an indicator is set in the packet to inform receiving routers that no acknowledgment to the packet is required. This increases efficiency by reducing unnecessary network traffic.

Enhanced IGRP Packet Types

Let's take a closer look at the types of packets used by Enhanced IGRP routers to maintain routing information. These packets are exchanged between neighbors only. Enhanced IGRP supports the following message types: hellos, acknowledgments, updates, queries, replies, and requests.

Enhanced IGRP routers use *hello* packets to discover neighbors. To achieve this purpose each router multicasts such packets at regular intervals. Routers determine that a neighbor is operating based on regular reception of the transmitting router's packets. Generally, these packets are transmitted unreliably, and no acknowledgment is required. When a packet is transmitted reliably a response is required from the router receiving the packet. In such a case, the receiving router sends an acknowledgment packet to the source router.

An *acknowledgment* packet is a hello packet that has no data. Instead, it contains a non-zero acknowledgment number. Unlike hello packets, acknowledgments are always sent using a unicast address.

Update packets are sent by routers to inform neighbors of network topology changes. Because they are reliably transmitted they require acknowledgments. Depending on the nature of the update they can be either multicast or unicast transmissions. When a router discovers a new neighbor it informs all its other neighbors by sending a unicast update packet to each established neighbor. The neighbors use this information to amend their topology tables. Some updates are sent as a result of a metric change. For example, when a router is informed of a link cost change it sends an update to all its neighbors. This type of update is multicast.

In the event that a router can no longer avail itself of a specific route to a destination, (i.e. the destination has no feasible successors), a new route must be determined. In order to establish the new route it sends *query* packets to all its neighbors, as a multicast address. In this way the router attempts to identify an alternate route by inquiring how neighbors reach the same destination.

An Enhanced IGRP feasible successor *is a neighboring router used for packet forwarding that has a least-cost path to a destination guaranteed not to be part of a routing loop. The router determines feasible successors by recomputing the route to a destination when no feasible successors exist in the router's routing table and neighboring routers are advertising the destination.*

Each Enhanced IGRP router that receives a query packet must unicast a *reply* packet. This indicates that the originator of a query packet does not need to recompute the route because there are feasible successors. A router receiving the query packet may not know how to reach the requested destination. In such a case, it sends a similar query to *its* neighbors. Reply packets ensure that query packets are broadcast reliably. They are also broadcast reliably, so must be acknowledged.

Request packets are used to get specific information from one or more neighbors. They are used in route server applications can be either multicast or unicast, and are transmitted unreliably.

Discovery Methods

A protocol-dependent module is provided for every network layer protocol supported by Enhanced IGRP. These modules are used to manage a set of tables corresponding to each protocol. Enhanced IGRP uses these tables to facilitate its specific discovery methods.

Every Enhanced IGRP router remains aware of its neighbors by maintaining a *neighbor table* for each supported protocol. These tables are built based on the reception of hello packets from neighbors.

NOTE

Neighbor tables record the address and interface of each directly connected router. They also record information required by RTP, which uses sequence numbers in order to match packets with data. The last sequence number transmitted by a neighbor is recorded so that out-of-sequence packets can be detected. Neighbor tables are also used to store round-trip timers. The timers are used in connection with the possible retransmission of packets on a per-neighbor basis.

When a router sends a hello packet it advertises a *hold* time. This is the amount of time that it can be assumed by the receiving neighbor to be reachable and operational. This relationship is maintained provided that the router transmits the next hello packet before the hold time expires. If a hello packet is not transmitted within its specified hold time, a topology change is indicated. The router expecting the hello packet informs DUAL that the packet has not been received and a change is made to the neighbor table.

Enhanced IGRP routers use *topology* tables to store their neighbors' routing table information. This information is used when a new route to a destination needs to be identified. Each entry in a topology table includes a destination address and a list of neighbors that have advertised the address. For every listed neighbor, the metric that the neighbor advertises for reaching the destination is also listed, as is. The information relating to the router containing the topology table.

NOTE

Enhanced IGRP uses the same vector of metrics as IGRP: bandwidth, delay, reliability, and load.

The bandwidth value *is based on the type of interface and can be modified by using the* bandwidth *router command.*

Delay *refers to propagation delay and the command can be used to modify this value, which can be useful when optimizing routing in networks with satellite links.*

Reliability *and* load *are both dynamically computed as a rolling weighted average over five seconds. By default, Enhanced IGRP computes the metric for a route by using the minimum bandwidth of each hop in the path and adding a media-specific delay for each hop.*

Every neighbor advertising a destination associates a route with that destination. Since Enhanced IGRP is a distance-vector protocol, it must follow the rules associated with that type of protocol. In other words, in this example, if the router is advertising a route to a destination, it must itself be using that route to forward packets.

NOTE

The metric that a router advertises to its neighbors (and uses itself) is the sum of the best-advertised metric from its neighbors plus the link cost to the best neighbor.

An Enhanced IGRP router's topology tables are used by the DUAL finite state machine in order to generate its *routing* tables. Updates to the routing table occur whenever the router is made aware of a routing change. This can be caused by a change in a neighbor's metric or there may be a problem on the network, such as when a router malfunctions.

When a routing change becomes necessary, DUAL seeks to identify successors (neighbors with routes to the destination) from its host routers topology tables. DUAL performs a feasibility calculation to determine which successor provides the most cost-effective route. Then the appropriate routing table is updated to include that successor and its destination. This eliminates the need to recompute the route.

There may be occasions when DUAL can find no successors in the topology table that are associated with a specific destination. When this occurs, DUAL must perform a computation to find a new successor. This process begins by changing the state of the topology table entry for that destination.

Destinations listed in a topology table can be in one of two states—active or passive. A destination is in the *passive* state providing that the current path is in operation, or a successor can be identified from the list of possible successors associated with the destination in the topology table.

If no successor can be found in a topology table, the listed destination is changed to be in an *active* state. The router then multicasts query packets to determine whether neighbors' routing tables contain a successor. When each neighbor has replied, the topology table's destination entry is returned to the passive state. A router cannot change a destination's routing table information while the topology table lists that destination as being in an active state. Then DUAL identifies a feasible successor from information that neighbors return in reply packets. Once a feasible successor is identified, DUAL updates the appropriate routing table on its host router.

NOTE

DUAL uses the following method to compute a feasible successor:

It determines which neighbors advertise a distance to the destination that is less than the best metric during an active-to-passive transition, then it calculates the minimum computed cost to the destination and determines which neighbor(s) offer a computed cost to the destination that is equal to the minimum cost as calculated by DUAL.

Network Routing Table Updates

Let's look at a hypothetical situation that demonstrates how routing tables might be updated by Enhanced IGRP. For this example, assume that there are five Enhanced IGRP routers connected as shown. At present, the network is stable. No packets containing routing information are being transmitted because no updates are required.

The routing information stored in router C specifies that router C reaches router A by way of router B. This has been set by a network administrator, and based on local network policy. For router E, DUAL has dynamically determined that its best path to router A is through routers C and B.

Let's say that a link failure is detected between routers C and B. Router B can still transmit packets to router A. Router C has lost the route specified by the network administrator and router E has lost its dynamically established route.

The routing updates performed by routers C and E occur at virtually the same moment. However, the way in which they re-establish a path to router A is different for each. This is because their routes were established by different methods.

Because router E established its path to router A dynamically, router E has topology table entries that include all neighbors with a path to router A. In this example, that includes router D as well as router C.

When DUAL searches through router E's topology table entries it identifies router D as a successor. This means that the path to router A remains in the passive state. There is no need for router E to send query packets and recompute a path. Instead, a local calculation is performed and a routing table entry is made specifying the new path to router A.

In this example, router E's convergence time is almost instantaneous. This is because the path to router A remained in the passive state.

Because router C's path to router A was determined by local network policy, router C's topology table contains no list of successors for that router. This means the table entry for that destination goes into the active state and the route needs to be recomputed. In order to recompute the path to router A, router C multicasts query packets to all its neighbors. In this example there is only one neighbor that can reply to router C's query. On a larger network there could be other routers directly connected to router C. The more routers that reply to a router's query, the longer the convergence time.

The reply that router E sends to router C contains routing table information about router E's path to router A. Because router E did not need to recompute the route it was able to update its routing table before router C. So the reply contains the new path to router A. Once router C receives router E's reply, the topology table entry for router A is returned to a passive state. Next, DUAL calculates the new successor to router A. Then router C must multicast an update to its neighbors. When this occurs, the network is once again stable.

It is worth noting that the routing update did not affect all the network's routers. It is possible, although not inevitable, that routers A and B would need to determine a new path to router C, router E, or both. However, in this example, there is no possibility of router D's routing table being updated.

Configuring IP-Enhanced IGRP

In our discussion of how to configure IP Enhanced IGRP on a network, we describe how IP Enhanced IGRP can integrate several existing networks that use different routing protocols, outline how to configure Enhanced IGRP routing on a network, and enable IP Enhanced IGRP routing on a network.

IP-Enhanced IGRP Configuration

Use Enhanced IGRP to integrate several existing networks that are using different routing protocols. Enhanced IGRP supports three network-level routing protocols: IPX RIP, AppleTalk RTMP, and IP RIP. Each of these has protocol-specific, value-added functionality.

Routers running IPX Novell Enhanced IGRP support incremental Service Advertisement Protocol (SAP) updates, remove the RIP limitation of 15 hop counts, and provide optimal path use. For more information on this see Chapter 12.

Routers running AppleTalk Enhanced IGRP support partial, bounded routing updates, provide load sharing, and provide optimal path use. For more information on this see Chapter 15.

The IP implementation of Enhanced IGRP supports *variable-length subnet masks (VLSMs)* (Figure 7.1) to allow network administrators to more efficiently allocate IP addresses. This implementation can redistribute routes learned by OSPF, IP RIP, IS-IS, EGP, or BGP. For example, two routers could use Enhanced IGRP to convert and exchange IP RIP routing information.

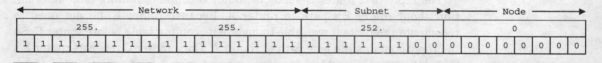

◄──────── Network ────────►	◄──── Subnet ────►	◄──── Node ────►
255.	255.	252.	0
1 1 1 1 1 1 1 1	1 1 1 1 1 1 1 1	1 1 1 1 1 1 0 0	0 0 0 0 0 0 0 0

FIGURE 7.1   *IP implementation of Enhanced IGRP supports variable-length subnet masks.*

A router may be sending updates for Enhanced IGRP for IP, Enhanced IGRP for IPX, and Enhanced IGRP for AppleTalk. This would appear to cast heavy demands on bandwidth. However, Enhanced IGRP saves on WAN link bandwidth by sending routing updates only when routing information changes. The updates sent contain information only about the link that has changed. In addition, they are bounded, meaning that they go only to affected routers.

Since Enhanced IGRP routers exchange information from their own routing tables, WAN link bandwidth is not consumed with routing updates from non-adjacent routers.

Unlike routing protocols that use a single metric such as a hop count, Enhanced IGRP uses a composite set of metrics to determine the best path to a destination. Enhanced IGRP can determine that a single 19.2 kbps hop between networks is significantly slower than a three-hop path through multiple T1 links.

Enhanced IGRP routers use a metric structure similar to that used by IGRP routers. As a result, they can easily exchange routing information.

When you are integrating Enhanced IGRP into existing networks plan a phased implementation. In a large network the configuration of all routers cannot be changed simultaneously. To achieve minimal disruption, begin by adding Enhanced IGRP to the routers at the periphery of the network.

Since peripheral routers generally talk to each other through the core, you cannot change the routing protocol in the core if the peripheral routers are not configured for the new protocols. When the peripheral routers are configured for Enhanced IGRP, then concentrate on changing the core.

If the network contains only one autonomous system (AS), route redistribution between the routers is automatic. During migration from IGRP to Enhanced IGRP configure the routers within the same AS with both IGRP and Enhanced IGRP. The routers then have both an IGRP and an Enhanced IGRP process active, sharing the same AS number. Once Enhanced IGRP has acquired all the routing information in the IGRP tables, you terminate the IGRP process.

If there are two ASs, the AS boundary router will run separate routing processes with different AS numbers. In this case, the network administrator must configure redistribution manually.

Once the boundary routers are configured for Enhanced IGRP, Enhanced IGRP can be integrated into the core network.

Enhanced IGRP for IP Integration

Your company wants you to implement Enhanced IGRP on your network. To do this you must enable IP Enhanced IGRP at each router and define the directly connected networks with which each router interfaces.

In order to configure the routers you must be in Privileged mode. Enter Configuration mode by typing `config` at the prompt and pressing **Return** to configure from terminal.

Starting with the Connecticut router you enter the command `router eigrp 109`. This enables Enhanced IGRP routing on the Connecticut router (Figure 7.2).

The number 109 is the number of the AS to which this router belongs.

NOTE

Next, define the networks with which the Connecticut router interfaces. Enter the command `network 172.16.0.0` (172.16.0.0 is the number of the network which will be advertised by the Connecticut router.) The Connecticut router is now configured for Enhanced IGRP. Exit Configuration mode by pressing **Ctrl+Z**. Save the configuration in NVRAM by entering `copy runn start`.

Next, configure the Maine router. Log on remotely to the Maine router using TELNET by entering `telnet maine` and then entering the Maine router's logon password, `linux`. As before, you need to be in Privileged mode on the Maine router before you can configure it. Enter Privileged mode by typing `enable` at Maine's command prompt and entering its password, `cisco`. Then enter Configuration mode by typing `config` and pressing **Return** to configure from terminal.

FIGURE 7.2
Implementing
Enhanced IGRP on
Connecticut router.

```
Connecticut# config
Configuring from terminal, memory, or network [terminal]?
Enter configuration commands, one per line. End with CNTL/Z.
Connecticut(config)# router eigrp 109
Connecticut(config-router)# network 172.16.0.0
Connecticut(config-router)# ^Z
Connecticut#
%SYS-5-CONFIG_I: Configured from console by console
Connecticut# copy runn start
Building configuration...
[OK]
Connecticut#
```

You enable Enhanced IGRP routing on the Maine router (Figure 7.3) by entering `router eigrp 109`. Define the networks with which the Maine router interfaces by entering `network 172.16.0.0`.

The Maine router is now configured for Enhanced IGRP routing. Exit the Configuration mode by pressing **Ctrl+Z**. Save the configuration in NVRAM by entering `copy runn start`. Then log out of the Maine router and exit back to the Connecticut router by typing `exit`.

The Vermont and New Hampshire routers are configured in the same way.

Routing and Monitoring

To show how routing is monitored in the IP Enhanced IGRP process we describe how to minimize routing updates and how route summarization procedures condense routing information. We also monitor IP Enhanced IGRP operation on a network.

Minimizing Routing Updates

There are several methods to use to minimize routing updates:

FIGURE 7.3
Implementing
Enhanced IGRP
remotely on Maine
router.

```
Connecticut# telnet Maine
Trying Maine (172.16.65.1)... Open


User Access Verification

Password:
Maine> enable
Password:
Maine# config
Configuring from terminal, memory, or network [terminal]?
Enter configuration commands, one per line. End with CNTL/Z.
Maine(config)# router eigrp 109
Maine(config-router)# network 172.16.0.0
Maine(config-router)# ^Z
Maine#
%SYS-5-CONFIG_I: Configured from console by console
Maine# copy runn start
Building configuration...
[OK]
Maine# exit

[Connection to Maine closed by foreign host]
Connecticut#
```

- Prevent updates being generated on the interface
- Eliminate routing protocols
- Filter routing updates
- Minimize route advertising with redistribution

Use the `Passive-Interface` command to prevent routing protocol updates from being generated on the interface (Figure 7.4). Because updates are not sent, the router cannot discover any neighbors on that interface. This means that the router does not learn about networks linked to a passive interface.

The syntax is:

```
passive-interface interface-name
```

Specify the interface type and number with the `Interface-Name` parameter.

You can eliminate the routing protocol `Network` command for an interface using an address from a separate network. Do not use this command to configure the routing protocol on the interfaces that connect to that network.

```
router rip
network 172.16.0.0
redistribute eigrp 90
default-metric 2
passive-interface serial0
```

FIGURE 7.4   Use the Passive-Interface command to prevent routing protocol updates from being generated on the interface.

You can set up route filters on any interface to prevent it inappropriately learning or propagating routing information. This is a useful security feature in Enhanced IGRP. Route filtering means that certain routes are not advertised to some parts of the network. To do this use *access lists* to filter routing updates on one or more interfaces. Use the Distribute-List command to filter networks received in updates. The syntax for the command is:

```
distribute-list access-list-number {out | in} [interface-name |
routing-process]
```

The Access-List-Number parameter is a standard IP number. The list explicitly specifies which networks are to be received and which are to be suppressed. The optional Interface-Name parameter is an interface on which the access list should be applied to incoming updates. If no interface is specified, the access list is applied to all incoming updates. The routing-process parameter can contain the optional name of the particular routing process, or it can contain the keywords static or connected. The Distribute-List command can be applied to transmitted (outbound) or received (inbound) routing updates.

In this route filtering example you apply access list 7 to outbound packets (Figure 7.5).

FIGURE 7.5
Apply access list 7 to
outbound packets.

```
router eigrp 1
network 172.16.0.0
network 192.168.7.0
distribute-list 7 out s0
!
access-list 7 deny 10.0.0.0 0.255.255.255
access-list 7 permit 172.16.0.0 0.0.255.255
```

The access list does not allow routing information from network 10.0.0.0 to be distributed out of the S0 interface. As a result, network 10.0.0.0 is hidden on the S0 interface. This command applies access list 7 as a route redistribution filter on routing updates sent on Serial 0.

The `Permit` keyword allows traffic matching the parameters to be forwarded.

The network number and wildcard mask are used to verify source addresses. The first two address octets must match and the rest don't care.

You can minimize route advertising using redistribution, which allows routing information discovered through one routing protocol to be distributed in the update messages of another routing protocol. Do this using the `Distribute-List` command with access lists.

Let's look at the redistribution filtering example in Figure 7.6. It filters the redistribution of routing updates between different routing processes such as IP RIP and Enhanced IGRP.

FIGURE 7.6
The redistribution of routing updates between different routing processes such as IP RIP and Enhanced IGRP.

```
router rip
network 192.168.7.0
redistribute eigrp 1
default metric 3
distribute-list 7 out eigrp 1
!
router eigrp 1
network 172.16.0.0
redistribute rip
default metric 56 2000 255 1 1500
!
access-list 7 deny 10.0.0.0 0.255.255.255
access-list 7 permit 0.0.0.0 255.255.255.255
```

This command enables routes learned from Enhanced IGRP on autonomous system 1 to be redistributed into IP RIP. It specifies that all routes learned from Enhanced IGRP will be advertised by RIP as reachable in three hops. Here the command applies to routes defined by distribute list 7. These routes leaving the Enhanced IGRP process will be filtered prior to being given to the RIP process. This distribute list redistributes all routing information except updates from network 10.0.0.0.

You can reduce routing updates over an interface by defining a *static route* on that interface. A static route is explicitly configured and entered into the routing table and takes precedence over a route chosen by a dynamic routing protocol.

You can configure static route redistribution on one router only. This eliminates the possibility of routing loops created by static route redistribution on routers with parallel routes between networks and allows updates to converge on the configured router.

Define a static route using the IP Route command. The router configuration command:

```
ip route network[mask] address[distance]
```

defines a path to an IP destination network or subnet. The default administrative distance is 1. This configuration requires redistribution.

This router configuration:

```
ip route network[mask] interface[distance]
```

has a default administrative distance of 0. Use the interface parameter instead of the address parameter when the router is directly connected to the network. This configuration is automatically redistributed.

Figure 7.7 shows an example of a configuration for static route distribution. The Redistribute Static command applies to routes learned from static entries in the routing table. It redistributes them into Enhanced IGRP.

FIGURE 7.7
A configuration for static route distribution.

```
ip route 172.16.0.0 255.255.0.0 192.68.8.18
ip route 192.168.7.0 255.255.255.0 192.68.8.10
!
router eigrp 1
network 192.13.7.0
default-metric 10000 100 255 1 1500
redistribute static
distribute-list 3 out static
!
access-list 3 permit 172.16.0.0 0.0.255.255
```

This command filters routes, specified in distribute list 3, learned from static entries. This occurs before the routes are passed to the Enhanced IGRP process.

Packets from source IP addresses that match the first two octets of 172.16 (and the other octets that exist don't care) will be forwarded.

Enhanced IGRP Route Summarization

Route summarization procedures condense routing information. Using summarization, routers can reduce some sets of routes to a single advertisement. This reduces the load on the router and the perceived complexity of the network.

Without summarization each router in a network must retain a route to every subnet in the network. Some routing protocols summarize automatically. Other routing protocols require manual configuration to support route summarization.

With Enhanced IGRP, subnet routes of directly connected networks are automatically summarized at network number boundaries. In addition, a network administrator can configure route summarization at any interface with any bit boundary. This allows ranges of networks to be summarized arbitrarily.

Network-level route summarization—class A, B, or C—is automatic and is enabled by default. It is possible to turn off automatic route summarization using the No Auto-Summary command.

Use the IP-Summary-Address Enhanced IGRP command to specify summary routes on a particular interface. It is helpful if you want to advertise summary routes on a subnet boundary, rather than class A, B, or C addresses.

The As-Number parameter specifies the autonomous system number of the network being summarized.

The Address parameter is the IP address being advertised as the summary address. The address does not need to be aligned on class A, B, or C boundaries.

The Mask parameter contains the IP subnet mask being used to create the summary address.

In Figure 7.8, automatic route summarization has been disabled to allow discontiguous subnets 172.17.1.0 and 172.17.2.0 to communicate.

FIGURE 7.8
Route summarization example.

```
router eigrp 1
network 172.17.1.0
network 172.17.2.0
no auto-summary
```

The command Router Enhanced IGRP 1 starts an Enhanced IGRP process for autonomous system 1. The No Auto-Summary command disables automatic summarization at the point between major network numbers, such as 172.168.5.0 and 172.16.0.0.

In Figure 7.9 eigrp 1 specifies that routes learned from Enhanced IGRP autonomous system 1 will be manually summarized at the interface Serial 0.

FIGURE 7.9
Routes learned from Enhanced IGRP autonomous system 1 will be manually summarized at the interface Serial 0.

```
router eigrp 1
network 172.16.0.0

int s0
ip address 172.168.4.2 255.255.255.0
ip summary-address eigrp 1 172.168.5.0 255.255.0.0
```

Implementing BGP and Route Redistribution

Understanding and Configuring BGP

To understand the function of the Border Gateway Protocol (BGP) and to show how to configure it on a router, we outline the function of the Border Gateway Protocol (BGP) and explain how the BGP routes data and routing information. We outline the tasks required to configure BGP on a router and those required to enable communication between BGP routers. We configure and monitor BGP on routers and explain how to use default networks and static routes as alternatives to BGP.

BGP Fundamentals

Exterior gateway protocols are designed to route between routing domains. In the terminology of the Internet, a routing domain is called an *autonomous system (AS)*, a set of routers that operate under the same administration and share a common routing strategy.

The first exterior gateway protocol to achieve widespread acceptance in the Internet was the Exterior Gateway Protocol (EGP). Although EGP was a useful technology, it had several weaknesses, including the fact that it is more of a reachability protocol than a routing protocol. The Border Gateway Protocol (BGP) overcomes many of EGP's weaknesses. As a result BGP has replaced EGP in the Internet.

The Border Gateway Protocol is an inter-autonomous system (or inter-AS) routing protocol created for use in the Internet. However, it can be used for routing packets both within and between ASs.

Unlike EGP, BGP guarantees the loop-free exchange of routing information within and between ASs. A *loop* is a route in which packets never reach their destination, but cycle repeatedly through a series of network nodes.

Routers that belong to different ASs and exchange BGP updates are said to be running *external BGP (EBGP)*. These routers are usually adjacent to each other and share the same media and subnet. Peer routers in different autonomous systems use BGP to maintain a consistent view of the internetwork topology.

Routers that belong to the same AS and exchange BGP updates are said to be running internal BGP (IBGP). IBGP coordinates and synchronizes the routing policy within the AS. IBGP routers do not have to be adjacent to each other for communication to occur. They can be located anywhere in the AS, even several hops away from each other. BGP is also used to determine which router will serve as the connection point for specific external autonomous systems.

The commands for configuring IBGP and EBGP are essentially the same, except for the `Neighbor EBGP-Multihop router configuration` command.

BGP routers within the same AS communicate with one another to ensure that they share a consistent view of the AS. They also determine which BGP router within that AS will serve as the connection point to or from certain external ASs. BGP neighbors communicating between ASs must reside on the same physical network.

Before it exchanges information with an external AS, BGP ensures that networks within the AS are reachable. It does this by a combination of internal peering among routers within the AS, and redistributing BGP routing information to Interior Gateway Protocols (IGPs), that run within the AS. Examples of IGPs are the RIP and OSPF.

Some BGP ASs are merely "pass-through" channels for network traffic. Such an AS will transport network traffic that did not originate within it, and is addressed to destinations in other ASs. However, BGP must be able to interact with whatever IGP is used within the pass-through AS.

BGP uses the Transport Control Protocol (TCP). When two routers running BGP form a TCP connection they exchange messages to open and confirm the connection parameters. There are four BGP message types specified in RFC 1771, *A Border Gateway Protocol 4 (BGP-4)*. Once the connection is established the routers can communicate with each other.

The initial data exchange between two BGP-speaking routers is the entire BGP routing table. This message is known as an *open message*. An open message is confirmed using a keepalive message sent by the peer device. An open message must be confirmed before updates, notifications, and keepalives can be exchanged. Unlike some other routing protocols, BGP does not require a periodic refresh of the entire routing table. Instead, routers running BGP receive incremental updates that contain the latest version of each peer's routing table. Incremental updates are sent out as the routing tables change. BGP update messages consist of a network number and domain path pairs. The domain path contains the string of domains through which the specified network may be reached.

BGP maintains a routing table with all feasible paths to a particular network. It advertises only the optimal (primary) path in its update messages. Update messages can withdraw one or more unfeasible routes from the routing table and can simultaneously advertise a route while withdrawing others. They do this by using the *BGP metric*.

NOTE

There are two other messages. The notification message *is sent when an error condition is detected. Notifications are used to close an active session after an error is detected and to inform any connected routers of why the session is being closed. The* keepalive message *notifies the BGP peers that a device is active. Keepalives are sent often enough to keep the session from expiring.*

The BGP metric is an arbitrary unit number specifying the degree of preference of a particular path. The metric may be based on any number of criteria, including AS hop count, type of link, bandwidth, path cost, and other factors. These metrics are typically assigned by the network administrator through configuration files.

Configuring and Monitoring BGP

BGP is mainly used to route packets between ASs. Let's look at configuring BGP on two routers, Maine and Vermont. These are located in different ASs. The commands used for configuring BGP on routers in different ASs and within the same AS are essentially the same.

Router Maine is in AS 100 and is connected to a network with an IP address of 192.168.5.0. Router Vermont is in AS 200 and is connected to a network with an IP address of 172.16.0.0. Both routers will exchange information by forming a TCP connection through their serial interfaces.

The two basic tasks required to configure BGP are enabling BGP routing and configuring BGP neighbors.

First we'll look at configuring BGP on the Maine router. The first step to enabling BGP routing is to issue the BGP command in Configuration mode: `router bgp autonomous-system`.

This command activates the BGP protocol and identifies the local autonomous system the router belongs to.

For router Maine type `router bgp 100` and press **Return**. This indicates that router Maine is running BGP and belongs to AS 100 (Figure 8.1). Once the Router BGP command has been issued you are in Router Configuration mode.

```
Maine(config)# router bgp 100
```

FIGURE 8.1   *The router Maine is running BGP and belongs to AS 100.*

The second step for enabling BGP on router A is to issue the Network command in Router Configuration mode: `network network-number`.

This command permits BGP to advertise a network if the network is listed in the IP routing table. Because the network (192.168.5.0) connected to router Maine is already in the routing table, it can be advertised. The router advertises networks configured as static routes and those it learns about dynamically.

When issuing the `Network` command for router Maine enter `network 192.168.5.0`. This enables router Maine to generate an entry in the BGP routing table for network 192.168.5.0 (Figure 8.2).

```
Maine(config)# router bgp 100
Maine(config-router)# network 192.168.5.0
```

FIGURE 8.2   Issuing the network command enables router Maine to generate an entry in the BGP routing table for network 192.168.5.0.

The `BGP Network` command operates differently from an `IGP Network` command. In most IGP configurations, the `Network` command creates a route in the routing table. With BGP, the `Network` command creates the route in the BGP table only if the routes are already present in the IP routing table. When BGP is configured, the `Redistribute` command can be used instead of the `Network` command, but precautions have to be taken to prevent routing loops.

The `BGP Network` command is used to inject IGP routes into the BGP table. For this reason BGP must work with an IGP such as RIP, OSPF, or Enhanced IGRP in order to advertise routes into an autonomous system.

Once BGP is enabled on a router, the next step is to define its BGP neighbors. Any two routers that have formed a TCP connection to exchange BGP routing information are called *neighbors* or *peers*. Even if they are physically connected, routers are not defined as neighbors unless they form a TCP connection.

The command used to configure BGP neighbors is: `neighbor ip-address remote-as autonomous-system`.

This command is used to identify a neighbor router with which the local router will establish a communication session.

BGP supports internal (IBGP) and external (EBGP) communication sessions. An EBGP session occurs between routers in two different ASs. An IBGP session occurs between routers in the same AS.

The `neighbor` part of the command indicates the routers to which we are trying to connect using BGP. For EBGP the IP address is the next-hop directly connected address (this is usually the IP address of the interface at the other end of the connection). For IBGP the IP address can be the IP address of any of the router's interfaces.

The `remote-as autonomous-system` identifies the AS number of the router to which we are trying to connect using BGP. The value placed in the *autonomous-system* part of the command determines whether the communication between the local router and the neighbor is an EBGP or an IBGP session. If the value of the autonomous system is the same as the local router's value, then BGP will initiate an internal session. If the field values are different, then BGP will have an external session.

Before issuing the `Neighbor Remote-As` command for router Maine you need to find out how many neighbors it has. Router Maine has one neighbor—router Vermont. Router Vermont is in AS 200 and uses its serial interface (IP address 172.16.66.1) to form a TCP connection with the serial interface of the Maine router.

To issue the `Neighbor Remote-AS` command for router Maine enter neighbor 172.16.66.1 remote-as 200 in Router Configuration mode (Figure 8.3)

```
Maine(config)# router bgp 100
Maine(config-router)# network 192.168.5.0
Maine(config-router)# neighbor 172.16.66.1 remote-as 200
Maine(config-router)# ^Z
Maine#
```

FIGURE 8.3 Both routers establish an EBGP session when communicating with each other because they both have different AS numbers in the AS parameter part of the command.

Both routers establish EBGP sessions when communicating with each other. This is because they both have different AS numbers in the AS parameter part of the command.

BGP configuration on router Maine is now complete. Now we will go on to look at configuring BGP on router Vermont.

To enable BGP on router Vermont type router bgp 200 in Config mode and press **Return**. Enter network 172.16.0.0 in Router Configuration mode (Figure 8.4).

FIGURE 8.4
Setting up BGP configuration on router Vermont.

```
Vermont(config)# router bgp 200
Vermont(config-router)# network 172.16.0.0
Vermont(config-router)# neighbor 172.16.66.2 remote-as 100
Vermont(config-router)# ^Z
```

Router Vermont has router Maine as its neighbor. When configuring BGP neighbors on router Vermont, type neighbor 172.16.66.2 remote-as 100 in Router Configuration mode and press **Return**. Because router Vermont and router Maine are in different ASs they establish an EBGP session with each other.

There are a number of commands that can be used to monitor and check a router's BGP configuration. You can display the entries in the BGP routing table by issuing the following command in Privileged mode: show ip bgp.

```
Maine# show ip bgp
BGP table version is 3, local router ID is 192.168.6.1
Status codes: s suppressed, d damped, h history, * valid, > best, i internal
Origin codes: i - IGP, e - EGP, ? - incomplete

   Network          Next Hop          Metric LocPrf Weight Path
*> 172.16.0.0       172.16.66.1            0             0 200 i
*> 192.168.5.0      0.0.0.0                0         32768 i
Maine#
```

FIGURE 8.5   A sample output from the show ip bgp command.

The output of this command for router Maine is shown in Figure 8.5. Look at the Network part of the output; router Maine learns network 172.16.0.0 from the serial interface 172.16.66.1 on router Vermont.

NOTE

The Show IP BGP *command provides useful BGP information. The BGP table version indicates the internal version number of the table. This number is incremented whenever the table changes. The local router ID is the IP address of the router.*

The status codes *indicate the status of the table entry. The status is displayed at the beginning of each line in the table. It can have one of the following values:*

- **s**—*suppressed: Entry is suppressed.*
- ***—valid: Entry is valid.*
- **>**—*best: Entry is the best to use for that network.*
- **i**—*internal: Entry learned via an internal BGP session.*

The origin codes *indicate the origin of the entry and are placed at the end of each line in the table. They can have one of the following values:*

- **i**—*IGP: Entry originated from IGP and was advertised with a Network command in Router Configuration mode.*
- **e**—*EGP: Entry originated from EGP.*
- **?**—*incomplete: Origin of the path is not clear. Usually, this is a route that is redistributed into BGP from an IGP.*

The Network field is the IP address of a network entity.

The Next-Hop field is the IP address of the next system that is used when forwarding a packet to the destination network. An entry of 0.0.0.0 indicates that the router has some non-BGP routes to this network.

The Metric field (if shown) is the value of the inter-autonomous system metric. This is frequently not used.

The LocPrf field is the local preference value as set with the Set Local-Preference Route-Map configuration command. The default value is 100.

The Weight field is the weight of the route as set by means of autonomous system filters.

The Path field is the AS's path to the destination network. There can be one entry in this field for each autonomous system in the path.

To see the current state of the IP routing table issue the following command in User mode (Figure 8.6):

```
show ip route
```

```
Maine# show ip route
Codes: C - connected, S - static, I - IGRP, R - RIP, M - mobile, B - BGP
       D - IEGRP, EX - EIGRP external, O - OSPF, IA - OSPF inter area
       E1 - OSPF external type 1, E2 - OSPF external type 2, E - EGP
       i - IS-IS, L1 - IS-IS level-1, L2 - IS-IS level-2, * - candidate default
       U - per-user static route

Gateway of last resort is not set

C    192.168.5.0/24 is directly connected, Ethernet0
     172.16.0.0/16 is variably subnetted, 2 subnets, 2 masks
B       172.16.0.0/16 [20/20] via 172.16.66.1, 00:46:15
C       172.16.66.0/24 is directly connected, Serial1
Maine#
```

FIGURE 8.6   A sample output of the show ip route command.

This command on router Maine shows two networks directly connected (C), and one route that has been learned from BGP (B).

NOTE

Understanding what each field represents enables you understand the BGP information displayed. The Code field indicates the protocol that derived the route. The Network Address field 172.16.0.0 *indicates the address of the remote network.*

In the [20/0] *field, the first number in the bracket is the administrative distance of the information source; the second number in the bracket is the metric for the route.*

The via network number field via `172.16.66.1` *specifies the address of the next router to the remote network.*

The Time field `0:01:03` *specifies the last time the route was updated.*

The Interface field `E2` *specifies the interface through which the specified network can be reached.*

To check that a neighbor connection is up, issue the following command in User mode (Figure 8.7):

```
show ip bgp neighbors
```

```
Maine# show ip bgp neighbors
  BGP neighbor is 172.16.66.1, remote AS 200, external link
  BGP version 4, remote router ID 172.16.192.1
  BGP state = Established, table version = 3, up for 00:52:08
  Last read 00:00:07, hold time is 180, keepalive interval is 60 seconds
  Minimum time between advertisement runs is 30 seconds
  Received 56 messages, 0 notifications, 0 in queue
  Sent 56 messages, 0 notifications, 0 in queue
  Connections established 1; dropped: 0
Connection state is ESTAB, I/O status: 1, unread input bytes: 0
Local host: 172.16.66.2, Local port: 179
Foreign host: 172.16.66.1, Foreign port: 11002

Enqueued packets for retransmit: 0, input: 0, saved: 0

Event Timers (current time is 0x44816C):
Timer          Starts      Wakeups              Next
Retrans            57            0              0x0
TimeWait            0            0              0x0
AckHold            56            1              0x0
SendWnd             0            0              0x0
KeepAlive           0            0              0x0
GiveUp              0            0              0x0
PmtuAger            0            0              0x0

iss: 4120253810   snduna: 4120254918   sndnxt: 4120254918    sndwnd:     15277
irs: 4118793731   rcvnxt: 4118794838   rcvwnd:      15278   delrcvwnd:    1106
```

FIGURE 8.7 *A sample output of the show ip bgp neighbors command.*

The `BGP state = Established` field indicates that a connection has been made between router Maine and router Vermont. Any other state other than Established indicates that the connection has not been made.

Once you have defined two routers as BGP neighbors, they will form a BGP connection and exchange routing information. If you subsequently change the configuration, such as the BGP version, you need to reset BGP connections in order for the configuration change to take effect. The command used to do this is:

```
clear ip bgp *|address
```

To reset a BGP connection with a particular neighbor, issue this command in User mode. To reset all BGP connections issue the Clear IP BGP * command in User mode.

Static Routes and Default Networks

BGP is used in the networks of many Internet service providers (ISPs). As a result many organizations have BGP configured on their AS to facilitate easier communication with an ISP.

When an AS is connected to an ISP, the routing policy that will be implemented in the AS may be identical to or a subset of the policy implemented in the ISP's AS. In these cases it may not be necessary or desirable to configure BGP in the local autonomous system. This is because connectivity can be achieved using a combination of static routes and default networks.

Static routes are user-defined routes that cause packets moving between a source and a destination to take a specified path. A default network is used when no next hop is explicitly listed in the routing table. To define a static route entry in the IP routing table use the IP Route command (Figure 8.8).

```
ip route network mask {interface | ip-address} [distance]
```

FIGURE 8.8   To define a static route entry in the IP routing table use the IP Route command.

The Network Mask parameter describes a remote network to be entered into the IP routing table. The Interface parameter identifies the local router's outbound interface that will be used to access the remote network. The IP-Address parameter defines the IP address of an adjacent interface on a peer router. The Distance parameter overrides the default values by assigning an administrative distance.

An *administrative distance* is a rating of the trustworthiness of a routing information source. In Cisco routers, administrative distance is expressed as a numerical value between 0 and 255. The higher the value of the administrative distance, the lower its trustworthiness rating.

The default administrative distance of a static route specified with an IP-Address parameter is set to 1. An Interface parameter's default value is set to 0.

Apart from establishing a static route you can also establish a *floating static route*, which is a variety of static route that can be overridden by dynamically learned routes. You can configure a floating static route by using an administrative distance larger than the default distance used by a dynamic routing protocol.

Floating static routes make it possible to switch to another path whenever routing information for a destination is lost. They provide backup routes in topologies where dial-on-demand routing is used. For example floating static routes can provide another connection to the Internet using an alternate service provider.

If you configure a floating static route, the router checks to see if an entry for the route already exists in the IP routing table. If a dynamic route already exists, the floating static route is placed in reserve as part of the floating static route table. When the router detects that the dynamic route is no longer available, it replaces the dynamic route in the IP routing table with the floating static route for that destination. If the route is later relearned dynamically, the dynamic route replaces the floating static route and the floating static route is again placed in reserve. To avoid the possibility of a routing loop's occurring, by default floating static routes are not redistributed into other dynamic protocols.

We will now look at a static route being redistributed in RIP as an alternative to running BGP. In this example the static route enables router A to connect to router B and the ISP's AS.

Figure 8.9 is an example of code that uses a static route in an OSPF default configuration. Look at the IP Route command. 0.0.0.0 has been defined as the static route. The serial interface parameter, S, and the interface's default administrative distance, 0, have also been specified.

FIGURE 8.9
An example of code that uses a static route in an OSPF default configuration.

```
ip route 0.0.0.0 s1 0
!
router rip
network 10.0.0.0
redistribute static
```

The 0.0.0.0 route is a default route in the IP routing table. The 0.0.0.0 route ensures that if there is no matching route for the destination IP address in the routing table, then it will match the address. If the default route is chosen, the packets are routed using router A's S1 interface to the ISP's AS.

The default route is only defined for router A. By using the `Redistribute Static` command the default route can be advertised by means of RIP to all routers in the autonomous system. Advertising the default route enables the other routers in the AS to send packets that don't match other routes in the IP routing table to router A. Router A will then forward the packets to the Internet service provider's autonomous system.

NOTE

Static routes that point to an interface will be advertised by means of RIP, IGRP, and other dynamic routing protocols, regardless of whether Redistribute Static commands were specified for those routing protocols. This is because static routes that point to an interface are considered in the routing table to be connected, and hence lose their static nature. However, if you define a static route to an interface that is not one of the networks defined in a `Network` *command, no dynamic routing protocols will advertise the route unless a* `Redistribute Static` *command is specified for these protocols.*

To generate a default route into an OSPF routing domain, use the following router configuration command:

```
default-information originate always
```

Figure 8.10 shows an example of code that results in the default configuration of OSPF using a static route. This has an effect similar to redistributing a static route using RIP.

FIGURE 8.10
Code that results in the default configuration of OSPF using a static route.

```
ip route 0.0.0.0 s0
!
router ospf 111
network 19.0.0.0 0.255.255.255 area 0
default-information originate always
```

Route Filtering

This section will show how BGP filters update information. It outlines how transit policies are used to determine the best routes through an AS and how BGP learns and advertises routes. It discusses how access lists and distribute lists are used to filter routing update information and how AS path access lists are used to filter routing update information, as well as how route maps are used to filter routing update information.

Transit Policies

A transit policy ensures that the best route is chosen when transferring information through an AS. A transit policy is drawn up after decisions have been made on issues such as performance, reliability, security, and cost. Transit policies are especially important when dealing with complex or convoluted routes through Internet service providers (ISPs).

In relation to BGP, a transit policy is generally applied to two basic types of inter-AS configurations, *single-homed* and *multi-homed*.

An AS is single-homed when it connects to one other AS (usually an Internet service provider). There may be multiple exit points connecting the two ASs. An AS has at least two connections to an ISP, but only one of these connections is used. The other connection is used as a backup.

An AS is said to be multi-homed when it connects to more than one AS. A multi-homed connection enables you to choose between two or more ISPs. There are advantages in having a multi-homed connection:

- If a route to one ISP becomes congested, you can improve throughput by accessing the Internet through another ISP.
- If an ISP's server is down, you can still use the services of the other ISP.
- You can avail of the different services that each ISP provides.

Sometimes routers can choose between multiple paths to reach a given destination. The preferred path is the path that traffic takes from one AS, AS 100 for example, to its destination, AS 400 for example, may not be the same path as that used by traffic moving from AS 400 to AS 100. Deciding which path network traffic will take depends on decisions made when drawing up the transit policy.

In a single-homed AS the transit policy would probably reflect decisions about backup paths, alternate providers, and performance considerations. It would be implemented using IGP techniques for preferring one path over another.

In a multi-homed ISP system, transit policy decisions may be implemented by a combination of IGP and BGP techniques, including routing update filtering and redistribution filtering.

In both single- and multi-homed ASs you can filter routes that BGP advertises by using access lists, distribute lists, and route maps.

Before looking at BGP route filtering we will see how BGP learns and advertises routes. BGP always passes on routing information that it learns from one neighbor to its other neighbors. It also redistributes routes that it has learned into the IP routing table, but only if there is no route with a better administrative distance already in the IP table. (The administrative distance is used to select an optimum route.)

BGP routes derived from internal neighbors (IBGP sessions) are placed into the IP table (Figure 8.11) with an administrative distance of 200. External routes derived from external neighbors (EBGP sessions) are placed into the IP table with an administrative distance of 20.

FIGURE 8.11
BGP routes derived from internal neighbors are placed into the IP table.

IP Routing Table	
Route	Distance
Internal	200
External	20

In an IP routing table, with two or more routes to the same destination, the route with the lowest administrative distance is preferred and is installed in the table. Because external routes have lower administrative distances, they are preferred.

Just as BGP routes can be installed in IP routing tables, static and dynamic P routes can be redistributed into BGP routing tables. This happens only if they are present in the IP routing table and have been specified in the BGP Network command or by the Redistribute command.

Using the Redistribute command is not usually required or recommended, except to inject BGP routes into IGP. This is because of the precautions that have to be taken when using it to avoid creating routing loops.

Access Lists and Distribute Lists

It is possible to restrict the information that the router learns or advertises by filtering BGP routing updates to and from a particular neighbor. This helps prevent routing loops. To filter routing updates, use an access list, which is a sequential collection of permit and deny conditions applied to IP addresses. The router tests addresses against the conditions in an access list one by one.

If an IP address matches a condition and the Permit parameter is specified, the router includes the address in its updates. But if the Deny parameter is specified, the router rejects it. The order of the conditions is critical because the router stops testing conditions after the first match. If an IP address does not match any conditions it is rejected.

To create an access list, for example access list 1, that prevents a router from transmitting routes for network 172.16.0.0 and have that router transmit all other routes from other networks, refer to Figure 8.12.

FIGURE 8.12
Note that distribute list filters are applied to network numbers and not autonomous system paths.

```
!Router C    172.16.54.2
router bgp 300
network 192.168.5.0
neighbor 172.16.54.2 remote-as 200
neighbor 10.2.5.6 remote-as 100
neighbor 10.2.5.6 distribute-list 1 out

access-list 1 deny 172.16.0.0 0.0.255.255
access-list 1 permit 0.0.0.0 255.255.255.255
```

Use the `Neighbor Distribute-List` command to distribute the filtered BGP update information specified in an access list to a router's neighbors. To remove an entry, use the `no` form of this command.

In the `Neighbor` part of the `Neighbor Distribute-List` command, specify either the IP address of the neighbor, or the name of a BGP peer group. If you specify a BGP peer group, all the members of the peer group will inherit the keywords and the parameter values configured with this command. Specifying the command with an IP address will override the keywords and values inherited from the peer group.

You can permit or deny routes from being advertised in routing updates according to the action specified in the access list. Every access list has an associated access list number, which is a decimal number in the range from 1 to 99.

Access lists can be applied to both incoming and outgoing routes. Redistributed routing information should always be filtered by the `Distribute-List Out` router configuration command. This ensures that only those routes intended by the administrator are passed along to the receiving routing protocol. To filter networks received in updates, use the `Distribute-List In` command.

Below is an example of how to use the `Neighbor Distribute-List` command to filter routing updates to a particular neighbor.

It is desirable to prevent Router C from transmitting updates for network 172.16.0.0 to AS 100. Router B is including network 172.16.0.0 in updates it sends to Router C. You can exclude network 172.16.0.0 from updates by applying an access list to filter those updates that Router C exchanges with Router A.

The configuration for Router C is shown in Figure 8.12. Note that distribute list filters are applied to network numbers and not autonomous system paths.

The combination of the `Neighbor Distribute-List` command and Access List 1 prevents Router C from transmitting routes for network 172.16.0.0 when it sends routing updates to neighbor 10.2.5.6, that is Router A.

AS Path Access Lists

Using distribute lists is one way to filter BGP advertisements. Another way is to use AS path filters, which use access lists to filter BGP advertisements to routing updates. AS path filters can be applied to both incoming and outgoing updates.

An access list is based on the value of an update's AS path attribute, the list of AS numbers that an update has crossed in order to reach a destination. The AS path attribute is represented by a *regular expression*, a pattern of characters that define strings, using wildcard characters such as:

- The period (.), which matches any single character in the string.
- The asterisk (*), which matches any sequence of characters.
- The caret (^), which refers to the rightmost characters in the string.
- The dollar sign ($), which refers to the leftmost characters in the string.

To verify that your regular expressions work as intended, use the following syntax or the EXEC command:

```
show ip bgp regular-expression
```

This displays all paths that match the specified regular expression.

Wildcards can be used in combination to represent any value of the AS path attribute. For example, ^200$ is a regular expression that represents all AS path attributes that start with the characters "200" (as specified by ^), and end with "200" (as specified by $). Or you could match patterns of characters such as "ABC" or "120" with the regular expression ".*", represents any number of occurrences (*) of any character (.).

A BGP filter applies a specific AS path access list. To configure BGP path filtering, you need to define an AS path access list and apply a BGP filter.

To define an AS system path access list use the IP As-Path Access-List command (Figure 8.13).

The Access-List-Number parameter is an integer in the range from 1 to 199, which indicates the number of the access list that contains the regular expression. The `Permit` or `Deny` parameters either permit or deny matching conditions. The `As-Regular-Expressions` parameter is a regular expression that represents the AS path attribute in the access list.

```
ip as-path access-list access-list-number
{permit | deny} as-regular-expression
```

FIGURE 8.13   To define an AS system path access list you use the IP As-Path Access-List command.

To apply a specific AS path access list to updates to and from particular neighbors, use the `Neighbor Filter-List` command.

This command can establish filters on both inbound and outbound BGP routes.

The `Weight` parameter is an integer in the range from 0 to 65,535. It assigns a relative importance to incoming routes that match specified AS paths. The route with the highest weight will be chosen as the preferred route.

```
neighbor {ip-address | peer-group-name} filter-list
access-list-number {in | out | weight}
```

FIGURE 8.14   To apply a specific AS path access list to updates to and from particular neighbors, use the Neighbor Filter-List command.

The weight ascribed to a route affects BGP's route-selection rules. The implemented weight is based on the first matched AS path and overrides the weights assigned by the `Neighbor` commands. In other words, the weights assigned with the `Match As-Path` and `Set Weight Route-Map` commands override the weights assigned using the `Neighbor Weight` and `Neighbor Filter-List` commands.

Any number of weight filters are allowed on a per-neighbor basis, but only one in- or out-filter is allowed.

Now we will look at an example of how to use the `AS Path Filtering` commands to filter routing updates to a particular neighbor.

Router C needs to transmit updates it receives from AS 400 to AS 100, but to filter out any updates that originate from AS 200. Remember that an AS path access list filters updates based on the value of an update's AS path attribute. Updates from AS 400 have an AS path attribute that starts with 200 and ends with 400. Updates from AS 200 have an AS path attribute that starts with 200 and ends with 200.

Now we will consider the AS path access list, Access List 1 (Figure 8.15). The first access list statement uses the regular expression ^200$. The effect of this statement is to deny any update whose AS path attribute starts with 200 (as specified by ^) and ends with 200 (as specified by $). Because Router B sends updates about network 172.16.0.0 whose AS path attributes start and end with 200, these updates will match the condition in the access list and will be denied.

FIGURE 8.15
The AS path access
list, Access List 1.

```
!Router C
neighbor 172.16.54.2 remote-as 200
neighbor 10.2.5.6 remote-as 100
neighbor 10.2.5.6 filter-list 1 out

ip as-path access-list 1 deny ^200$
ip as-path access-list 1 permit .*
```

The access list permits updates from AS 400 because the AS path attribute of an update from this AS ends with 400. If the access list specified ^200 as the regular expression for its deny condition, updates from AS 400 would be denied. This is because the regular expression, ^200, matches any update whose AS path attribute starts with 200.

In the second access list statement, the permit condition uses the regular expression (.*) which matches any value of the AS path attribute. This permits any update that has not been denied by the previous access list statement. So updates from AS 400 are permitted.

The Neighbor Filter List command given to Router C allows the transmission of updates from AS 400 to AS 100.

Route Maps

Route maps are used in BGP to control and modify routing information. They also define the conditions subject to which routes are redistributed between routing systems. Route maps can be applied to both incoming and outgoing updates.

Route maps use Match commands with AS path access lists to identify information in BGP updates. They use Set commands to change attributes within those updates. As a result, BGP route maps provide more sophisticated route filtering than other filtering options.

The syntax for the command used to define a route map is shown in Figure 8.16.

```
route-map map-tag [[permit | deny] | [sequence-number]]
```

FIGURE 8.16   *Syntax for the command used to define a route map.*

The `Map-Tag` parameter is a name that identifies the route map, for example `MAP`. It is possible to define multiple instances of the same route map. Use multiple instances of a route map to create a series of conditions for testing different attributes of updates (Figure 8.17). For example, one instance may try to match an update's route-type and route-source while another instance may try to match an update's metric.

```
route-map MAP permit 10
!first set of conditions goes here

route-map MAP permit 20
!second set of conditions goes here
```

FIGURE 8.17   *Use multiple instances of a route map to create a series of conditions for testing different attributes of updates.*

The `Sequence Number` parameter indicates an instance of a route map. The sequence number of each instance is set at varying intervals. For example, if you define two instances of route map `MAP`, the first instance will have a sequence number, 10 for example, and the second will have another sequence number, 20 for example. This helps identify the position a new route map is to have in the list of route maps already configured with the same name.

Each instance of a route map is applied to an update in ascending order.

The `Match` and `Set Route Map` configuration commands are used to define the condition portion of a route map. The `Match` command specifies a condition that the routing update must match, for example `Match Route-Type`. If the condition does not match, the next instance of the route map is applied to the routing update. The `Set` command specifies an action that is to be taken if a routing update meets the condition defined by the `Match` command.

```
route-map MAP permit 10 ip address 1.1.1.1
```

FIGURE 8.18   *The Match command specifies a condition that the routing update must match and the Set command specifies an action that is to be taken if a routing update meets the condition defined by the Match command.*

NOTE

The related commands for `Match` *are:*

```
Match AS-Path
Match Community
Match Clns
Match Interface
Match IP Address
Match IP Next-Hop
Match IP Route-Source
Match Route-Type
Match Tag
```

The related commands for `Set` *are:*

```
Set AS-Path
Set Clns
Set Automatic-Tag
Set Community
Set Interface
Set Default Interface
Set IP Default Next-Hop
Set Level
Set Local-Preference
Set Metric-Type
Set Next-Hop
Set Origin
Set Tag
Set Weight
```

When BGP applies route map `MAP` to routing updates, it applies the lowest instance first, in this case instance 10. If the first conditions in instance 10 are not met, we proceed to a higher instance of the route map, in this case instance 20. This is done until either a set of conditions has been met, or there are no more sets of conditions to apply.

If a condition has been fulfilled and the `Permit` parameter has been specified, the update is allowed. But if the `Deny` parameter has been specified, the update is discarded. This will also happen if an update does not match any condition, that is, it fails to match any of the available conditions.

To apply a route map to incoming and outgoing routes use the `Neighbor Route-Map` configuration command (Figure 8.19).

```
neighbor {ip-address | peer-group-name} route map route-map-name {in | out}
```

FIGURE 8.19   To apply a route map to incoming and outgoing routes use the Neighbor Route-Map configuration command.

Now we will look at a network that uses multiple instances of a route map to filter BGP updates.

Router C should deny updates from AS 400. You also want to change to 20 the weight attribute for updates from AS 200. For all other updates the weight attribute should be changed to 10.

The configuration for Router C shown in Figure 8.20.

FIGURE 8.20
The configuration
for Router C.

```
!Router C
router bgp 300
network 172.16.0.0
neighbor 172.16.54.2 remote as-200
neighbor 172.16.54.2 route-map STAMP in

route-map STAMP permit 10
match as-path 1
set weight 20
!
route-map STAMP permit 20
match as-path 2
!
route-map STAMP permit 30
set weight 10
!
ip as-pat access-list 1 permit ^200$
ip as-pat access-list 2 deny_400_
```

Updates from AS 200 match the first instance (instance 10) of the route map. This is because the Match As-Path condition has been met by Access List 1. Access List 1 permits these updates because the AS path attribute begins with 200 and ends with 200 (that is, it permits updates that originate in AS 200). The set condition in the route map then changes the weight attribute of the permitted update to 20.

Updates from AS 400 match the second instance of the route map, but Access List 2 denies updates whose AS path attribute contains 400. These updates are discarded. All other updates have a weight of 10 (by means of instance 30 of the STAMP route map) and will be permitted.

Route Redistribution

The following sections help us to understand what redistribution is and show how redistribution occurs between various protocols. We explain the commands that are used to redistribute routes and outline how route redistribution occurs between Enhanced IGRP and IGRP. We discuss the ability to integrate Enhanced IGRP into IGRP in the same AS and redistribute routes between both protocols and describe how OSPF is added to the backbone of a RIP network. We outline how route redistribution occurs between RIP and OSPF. Finally, we consider how to add OSPF to the center of a RIP network and redistribute routes between the two protocols.

Understanding Redistribution

Typically, an AS consists of one or more routers connecting multiple IP network numbers. Routes originating from one AS that need to be advertised into another AS must be *redistributed*.

Redistribution enables routing information discovered through one protocol to be advertised in the update messages of another routing protocol. Redistribution can also occur between two different protocols, such as Enhanced IGRP and IGRP, in the same AS. It can take place between routers running the same protocol, for example IGRP, in different ASs.

The command used to redistribute routing information is shown here in Figure 8.21. The Redistribution command is not used when both protocols are in the same AS because redistribution occurs automatically in that case.

```
redistribute protocol [options]
```

FIGURE 8.21   The command used to redistribute routing information.

The Protocol parameter in the Redistribute command names the source protocol from which routes are being redistributed. The Options parameter provides a number of options that can be used with the Redistribute command, for example an AS number or a process-ID.

Redistributed routes advertise a metric, the method by which a routing algorithm determines that one route is better than another. Metrics include bandwidth, communication cost, delay, hop count, load, MTU, path cost, and reliability. Because metrics for different protocols cannot be directly compared, the Default-Metric command is generally used with the Redistribute command. It sets the metric used during redistribution.

Most protocols, with the exception of IGRP and Enhanced IGRP, use the same format of the Default-Metric command.

Figure 8.22 shows the syntax for the Default-Metric command for IGRP and Enhanced IGRP.

```
default-metric bandwidth delay reliability loading mtu
```

FIGURE 8.22   *The syntax for the Default-Metric command for IGRP and Enhanced IGRP.*

The `Bandwidth` parameter in the `Default-Metric` command is the minimum bandwidth of the route in kilobits per second. The `Delay` parameter is the route delay, measured in microseconds. `Reliability` is the likelihood of successful packet transmission and is normally expressed as a number between 0 and 255. `Loading` is the effective bandwidth of the route, expressed as a number from 0 to 255, while `Mtu` is the maximum transmission unit (MTU) size of the route in bytes.

For OSPF, RIP, EGP, and BGP, the `Default-Metric` command is:

```
default-metric number
```

The `Number` parameter is the value of the metric. For example, in redistributing RIP, this parameter would be the hop count. If no value is specified using the `Default-Metric` command in both cases, the default-metric value is set to 0.

When you issue the `Redistribute` command for a routing protocol it will advertise in its updates all the routes in its routing table. But you may not want all routes to be advertised. To filter routes (or networks) sent or received in updates use the `Distribute-List` command (Figure 8.23). This ensures that only selected routes are redistributed. The syntax for the `Distribute-List` command is:

```
distribute-list access list-number
{out|in} [interface-name|routing-process]
```

```
distribute-list access list-number {out | in} interface-name | routing-process
```

FIGURE 8.23   To filter routes (or networks) sent or received in updates use the Distribute-List command.

The `Access-List` number is a standard IP access list number. An access list explicitly specifies which networks are to be received and which are to be suppressed. The `Interface-Name` option is the interface on which the access list should be applied to incoming updates. If no interface is specified, the access list is applied to all incoming updates. The `Routing-Process` option is the name of the particular routing process, or either of the keywords `static` or `connected`. Specifying a process causes the access list to be applied to only those routes derived from the specified routing process. If no process is specified then the access list will be applied to all routes.

Enhanced IGRP and IGRP Redistribution

Networks using the Interior Gateway Routing Protocol (IGRP) can benefit from the use of Enhanced IGRP. To avail themselves of the benefits that Enhanced IGRP provides, such as faster convergence, many organizations are integrating Enhanced IGRP into their existing IGRP network environment. Enhanced IGRP can be added to an IGRP network using the same IGRP AS number.

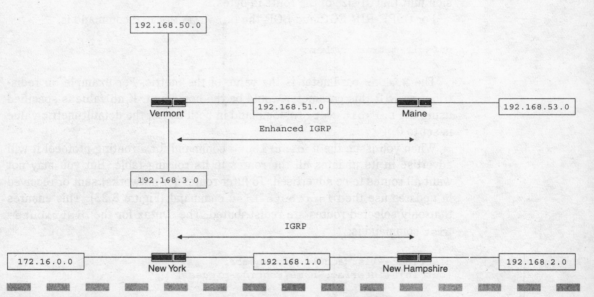

FIGURE 8.24   Integrating Enhanced IGRP into an existing IGRP network environment.

Let's look at how Enhanced IGRP can be added to IGRP in the same AS, and how redistribution of routing information takes place between them. An AS, AS 100 for example, is divided into two sections. One section is running IGRP and the other is running Enhanced IGRP. Initially there is no link between the two sections.

The section running IGRP contains two routers, router NewYork and router New Hampshire. Router NewYork advertises network 172.16.0.0 and 192.168.1.0, and router New Hampshire advertises network 192.168.2.0 and 192.168.1.0. The section running Enhanced IGRP contains two routers, Vermont and Maine. Router Vermont advertises networks 192.168.50.0,

192.168.51.0, and 192.168.3.0, and router Maine advertises networks 192.168.53.0 and 192.168.51.0.

To connect the two sections, designate a boundary router, router NewYork for example, that will run both IGRP and Enhanced IGRP. A boundary router exchanges routing information with routers belonging to other ASs. Since router NewYork is already running IGRP, you need to configure it with Enhanced IGRP.

In order to configure router NewYork with Enhanced IGRP you must be in Privileged mode. Enter Configuration mode by typing `config` at the prompt and pressing **Return** to configure from terminal. Then enter `router eigrp 100`. The number 100 is the process-ID for the Enhanced IGRP routing process. This enables Enhanced IGRP routing on router NewYork (Figure 8.25).

FIGURE 8.25
Router NewYork will become the designated boundary router that will run both IGRP and Enhanced IGRP.

```
NewYork> enable
Password:
NewYork# config
Configuration from terminal, memory, or network [terminal]?
Enter configuration commands, one per line. End with CNTL/Z.
NewYork(config)# router eigrp 100
NewYork(config-router)# network 192.168.3.0
NewYork(config-router)# ^Z
NewYork# copy runn start
Building configuration...
[OK]
NewYork#
```

Next enter `network 192.168.3.0.` to identify the network that will be advertised by the router. This provides the link between the NewYork and Vermont routers. This command assumes that the serial interfaces on both routers have been configured with the 192.168.3.0 address and the appropriate subnet addresses.

The NewYork router is now configured for Enhanced IGRP routing. Exit the Configuration mode by pressing **Ctrl+Z**. Save the configuration in NVRAM by entering `copy runn start`.

Since the AS number for both IGRP and Enhanced IGRP is the same, you need not use the `Redistribute` command, because redistribution occurs automatically within an AS.

Once you have Enhanced IGRP running on router NewYork, there are a number of commands that can be used to check that the redistribution configuration was successful.

Display the current state of the routing table by entering `show ip route` in Privileged mode (Figure 8.26).

```
NewYork# show ip route
Codes: C - connected, S - static, I - IGRP, R - RIP, M - mobile, B - BGP
       D - IEGRP, EX - EIGRP external, O - OSPF, IA - OSPF inter area
       E1 - OSPF external type 1, E2 - OSPF external type 2, E - EGP
       i - IS-IS, L1 - IS-IS level-1, L2 - IS-IS level-2, * - candidate default
       U - per-user static route

Gateway of last resort is not set

D     192.168.51.0/24 [90/2195456] via 192.168.3.2, 00:04:30, Serial1
D     192.168.53.0/24 [90/2707456] via 192.168.3.2, 00:04:30, Serial1
D     192.168.50.0/24 [90/2681856] via 192.168.3.2, 00:04:30, Serial1
C     192.168.1.0/24 is directly connected, Serial0
I     192.168.2.0/24 [100/8576] via 192.168.1.1, 00:00:19, Serial0
C     192.168.3.0/24 is directly connected, Serial1
C     172.16.0.0/16 is directly connected, Ethernet0
NewYork#
```

FIGURE 8.26   Display the current state of the routing table by entering show ip route in Privileged mode.

You can see from the output of Show IP Route that the routing table of the router NewYork contains networks that are directly connected (C); routes learned from IGRP (I); and routes learned from Enhanced IGRP (D).

To issue a Show IP Route command for router Vermont log on remotely to 192.168.3.2 on the Vermont router using Telnet. To do this enter telnet 192.168.3.2 and then enter the Vermont router's logon password, linux. Enter Privileged mode by typing enable at Vermont's command prompt and entering its password, cisco. Then type show ip route (Figure 8.27).

You can see from the output that the routing table of the Vermont router contains networks that are directly connected (C) and routes learned via Enhanced IGRP (D).

Looking at the routes learned via Enhanced IGRP (D) you can see that network 191.168.53.0 is as an internal route. All other IGRP routes are external (D EX) because they were learned via IGRP in router NewYork and redistributed into Enhanced IGRP.

Display the Enhanced IGRP topology table by entering show ip eigrp topology in Privileged mode (Figure 8.28). The output of this command on router Vermont shows:

- All the destination networks to which the router can send routing updates.
- The IP address of the interface on which the network was learned.
- The cost and metric used by the router for each route.

```
NewYork# telnet 192.168.3.2
Trying 192.168.3.2... Open


User Access Verification

Password:
Vermont> enable
Password:
Vermont# show ip route
Codes: C - connected, S - static, I - IGRP, R - RIP, M - mobile, B - BGP
       D - IEGRP, EX - EIGRP external, O - OSPF, IA - OSPF inter area
       E1 - OSPF external type 1, E2 - OSPF external type 2, E - EGP
       i - IS-IS, L1 - IS-IS level-1, L2 - IS-IS level-2, * - candidate default
       U - per-user static route

Gateway of last resort is not set

C    192.168.50.0/24 is directly connected, Ethernet0
C    192.168.51.0/24 is directly connected, Serial0
C    192.168.3.0/24 is directly connected, Serial1
D EX 172.16.0.0/16 [170/2169856] via 192.168.3.1, 00:19:33, Serial1
D EX 192.168.1.0/24 [170/2169856] via 192.168.3.1, 00:19:33, Serial1
D    191.168.53.0/24 [90/2195456] via 192.168.51.2, 00:19:33, Serial 0
D EX 192.168.2.0/24 [170/2707456] via 192.168.3.1, 00:19:33, Serial1
Vermont#
```

FIGURE 8.27   Issue a show ip route command for router Vermont remotely via Telnet.

FIGURE 8.28

Display the
Enhanced IGRP
topology table by
entering show ip
eigrp in Privileged
mode.

```
Vermont# show ip eigrp topology
IP-EIGRP Topology Table for process 100

Codes: P - Passive, A - Active, U - Update, Q - Query, R - Reply,
       r - Reply status

P 172.16.128.0/24, 1 successors, FD is 216985
        via 192.168.3.1 (2169856/1), Serial1
P 192.168.50.0/24, 1 successors, FD is 281600
        via Connected, Ethernet0
P 192.168.51.0/24, 1 successors, FD is 216985
        via Connected, Serial0
P 192.168.53.0/24, 1 successors, FD is 270745
        via Connected, Serial0
P 192.168.1.0/24, 1 successors, FD is 2169856
        via 192.168.3.1 (2169856/1), Serial1
P 192.168.2.0/24, 1 successors, FD is 2707456
        via 192.168.3.1 (2707456/2195456), Serial1
P 192.168.3.0/24, 1 successors, FD is 2169856
        via Connected, Serial1
Vermont#
```

If Enhanced IGRP uses a different AS number when it is added to an IGRP network, you need to configure redistribution manually with the `Redistribute` command.

In Figure 8.29 you want to integrate two different ASs, one running IGRP and the other Enhanced IGRP. Router NewYork is running IGRP in AS 200 and is advertising network 172.16.0.0. and is running Enhanced IGRP in AS 300 and is advertising network 192.168.50.0.

FIGURE 8.29   Integrating two different ASs, one running IGRP and the other Enhanced IGRP.

Assume that Enhanced IGRP and IGRP have been configured on the router with the Router and Network commands. To redistribute routes from both protocols into each other you need to issue the `Redistribute` command for each protocol.

Starting with Enhanced IGRP configuration, enter `redistribute igrp 200` in Router Configuration mode. The number 200, the process-ID for the IGRP routing process, is the number of the AS from which you want to distribute the routing information. This redistributes IGRP-derived routing information received from IGRP AS 200 into Enhanced IGRP AS 300 (Figure 8.30).

FIGURE 8.30
Redistribution of
IGRP-derived routing
information received
from IGRP AS 200
into Enhanced IGRP
AS 300.

```
NewYork# conf term
Enter configuration commands, one per line. End with CNTL/Z.
NewYork(config)# router eigrp 300
NewYork(config-router)# network 192.168.50.0
NewYork(config-router)# redistribute igrp 200
NewYork(config-router)# default-metric 56 2000 255 1 1500
NewYork(config-router)# router igrp 200
NewYork(config-router)# network 172.16.0.0
NewYork(config-router)# redistribute eigrp 300
NewYork(config-router)# default-metric 56 2000 255 1 1500
NewYork(config-router)# ^Z
NewYork#
```

The `Default-Metric` command need not be specified because both IGRP and Enhanced IGRP use similar metrics. The command has been added here but it is not necessary. The NewYork router is now able to redistribute Enhanced IGRP routes from AS 300.

Next, configure router NewYork to enable the redistribution of IGRP routes from AS 200. Enter `redistribute eigrp 300` in Router Configuration mode. This redistributes route information received from Enhanced IGRP AS 300 into IGRP AS 200. These commands can also be used to redistribute routes between routers running the same protocol, such as IGRP, in different ASs. Both ASs can now exchange routing information.

When you redistribute Enhanced IGRP information to and from dynamic routing protocols other than IGRP, you must use the `Redistribute` and `Default-Metric` commands.

In Figure 8.31, these protocols are implemented in different ASs. RIP is implemented in AS 400 and is advertising network 192.168.50.0, while Enhanced IGRP is implemented in AS 500, and is advertising network 172.16.0.0.

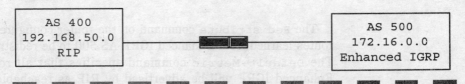

FIGURE 8.31   An example that deals with redistribution of routes between RIP and Enhanced IGRP.

The commands that enable the redistribution of routing protocols between these two protocols are now shown. The `Redistribute` command on router Vermont enables the redistribution of routes learned from Enhanced IGRP AS 500 into RIP. The default metric specifies that Enhanced IGRP learned routes are two hops away. The `Redistribute` command on router Vermont enables the redistribution of routes learned from the RIP into Enhanced IGRP AS 500. The `Default-Metric` command configured on router Vermont specifies that the bandwidth is 1,544 kilobits per second, delay is 100 microseconds, reliability is 100% (255/255), loading is less than 1% (1/255), and Mtu is 1,500 bytes. Mutual redistribution occurs when two or more routing protocols redistribute information between each other.

You can filter the redistribution of routing updates between different routing protocols, such as RIP and Enhanced IGRP by using the `Distribute-List` command.

The commands that enable an AS running RIP to receive filtered updates from a different AS running Enhanced IGRP are shown in Figure 8.32.

```
Vermont(config)# router rip
Vermont(config-router)# network 172.16.0.0
Vermont(config-router)# redistribute eigrp 500
Vermont(config-router)# default-metric 2
Vermont(config-router)# passive-interface serial0
Vermont(config-router)# router eigrp 500
Vermont(config-router)# network 192.168.50.0
Vermont(config-router)# redistribute rip
Vermont(config-router)# default-metric 1544 100 255 1 1500
Vermont(config-router)# distribute-list 1 in
Vermont(config-router)# passive-interface serial0
Vermont(config-router)# access-list 1 permit ip 172.16.0.0 255.255.0.0
Vermont(config-router)# access-list 1 deny ip
```

FIGURE 8.32   Commands that enable an AS running RIP to receive filtered updates from a different AS running Enhanced IGRP

The Redistribute command on the router configured with RIP enables routes learned from Enhanced IGRP AS 500 to be redistributed into AS 400. The Default-Metric command specifies that all routes learned from Enhanced IGRP will be advertised by RIP as reachable in two hops. The Distribute-List in router configuration command causes the router to use access list 1 to filter networks learned from RIP and allows only those networks that match the list to be redistributed into Enhanced IGRP. This prevents route feedback loops from occurring.

The passive-interface router configuration command disables the sending of routing updates on serial interface 0. In this case, the Passive-Interface command is used with RIP, which means the router does not send out any updates on a passive interface, but the router still processes updates that it receives on that interface. The result is that the router still learns of networks that are behind a passive interface. (The same is true when the passive-interface command is used with IGRP.)

The Distribute-List command sets up access list 1 as the input for the RIP process. Access list 1 permits networks 172.16.0.0 and denies all other networks.

RIP and OSPF Redistribution

The Routing Information Protocol (RIP) is a relatively old but still commonly used IGP created for use in small, homogeneous networks. The Open System Path First (OSPF) protocol is generally used in larger networks because it is a link-state routing algorithm, one in which each router broadcasts information regarding the cost of reaching each of its neighbors to all nodes in the internetwork. This creates a more consistent view of the network and prevents routing loops.

When an organization's network becomes too large for RIP to run effectively, many network managers decide to migrate to OSPF. A common first step in converting an RIP network to OSPF is to add OSPF to the backbone of a RIP network.

Now we will look at how OSPF can be added to the backbone of a RIP network and how the redistribution of routes between the two protocols is achieved. The backbone is currently running RIP but when RIP routes are advertised in the backbone, it will be running OSPF.

The RIP network in this example contains four domains, A, B, C, D, and the backbone. The network addresses are class B network addresses that are subnetted using a subnet mask of 255.255.255.0. The router sees subnets as different networks so a routing protocol has to be in place in order to route between the various subnets. These networks are connected to each other through four backbone routers—NewYork, Maine, New Hampshire, and Vermont. The backbone of the RIP network is made up of the serial line connections between these routers.

The tasks involved in adding OSPF to the backbone of a RIP network (Figure 8.33) and allowing redistribution between the two protocols are:

1. Suppressing RIP on the backbone router's interfaces.
2. Enabling OSPF on the backbone.
3. Redistributing RIP routes into the OSPF backbone.
4. Redistributing OSPF routes into the RIP network.

FIGURE 8.33
The RIP network in this example contains four domains, A, B, C, D, and the backbone.

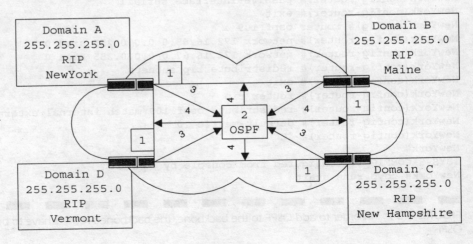

These tasks need to be performed on each backbone router.

In order to add OSPF to the backbone, the backbone's routers have to be configured with OSPF (Figure 8.34). Because OSPF must run on the backbone, RIP does not need to run between the backbone routers. The first task is to suppress RIP on a router's serial interfaces (S0, S1), router NewYork for example.

Starting with router NewYork, enter `router rip` in Configuration mode. Then enter `passive-interface serial 0` in Router Configuration mode and press **Return**. This disables the sending of RIP routing updates on router NewYork's S0 interface.

Next enter `passive-interface serial 1` to suppress the RIP updates on router NewYork's S1 interface. Enter `exit` to return to Configuration mode.

Once RIP has been suppressed on the serial interfaces, OSPF can be configured on router NewYork. To do this, enter `router ospf 109` in Configuration mode. This enables OSPF routing on the router NewYork. (The number 109 is the OSPF AS number.)

Next, configure OSPF on the router's serial interfaces. Enter the command `network 172.16.65.0 0.0.0.255 area 0`. This defines the serial interface whose address is 172.16.65.0 as an OSPF interface. It also defines the area ID for this interface.

```
NewYork> enable
Password:
NewYork# config
Configuring from terminal, memory, or network [terminal]?
Enter configuration commands, one per line. End with CNTL/Z.
NewYork(config)# router rip
NewYork(config-router)# passive-interface serial0
NewYork(config-router)# passive-interface serial1
NewYork(config-router)# exit
NewYork(config)# router ospf 109
NewYork(config-router)# network 172.16.65.0 0.0.0.255 area 0
NewYork(config-router)# network 172.16.67.0 0.0.0.255 area 0
NewYork(config-router)# redistribute rip subnets
NewYork(config-router)# exit
NewYork(config-router)# router rip
NewYork(config-router)# redistribute ospf 109 match internal external 1 external 2
NewYork(config-router)# default-metric 10
NewYork(config-router)# ^Z
NewYork#
%SYS-5-CONFIG_I: Configured from console by console
NewYork# coyp runn start
```

FIGURE 8.34   In order to add OSPF to the backbone, the backbone's routers have to be configured with OSPF.

The Serial 1 interface, 172.16.67.0, on router NewYork is configured in the same way.

Once OSPF has been configured on the backbone routers, these routers become OSPF AS boundary routers. Each AS boundary router controls the flow of routing information between OSPF and RIP. Router NewYork's Ethernet interface is still configured with RIP.

Once OSPF is enabled on the boundary routers you can redistribute the RIP routes into the OSPF backbone. To do this, enter `redistribute rip subnets` in Router Configuration mode. This command redistributes the RIP routes from Domain A (NewYork) into the OSPF backbone.

The `Subnets` parameter in the `Redistribute` command tells OSPF to redistribute all subnet routes. Without the `Subnets` parameter, only networks that are not subnetted will be redistributed by OSPF. The redistributed RIP routes appear as external type 2 routes in OSPF.

The redistribution of Domain A's RIP routes into the OSPF backbone is now complete. Enter `exit` to return to Configuration mode.

Now you want to redistribute the OSPF routes into the RIP networks of Domain, so that Domain A receives information about the networks in other RIP domains as well as in the OSPF backbone area. Domain A learns about the other domain's RIP routes as external OSPF routes.

Enter RIP configuration commands on router NewYork by entering `router rip` in Configuration mode.

Next enter `redistribute ospf 109 match internal external 1 external 2` in Router Configuration mode. This redistributes the OSPF routes (both internal and external) into Domain A.

The `OSPF` parameter in the `Redistribute` command specifies that OSPF routes are to be redistributed into RIP. The number 109 specifies the AS from which routes are to be redistributed. The `Match Internal External 1 External 2` parameters specify the types of routes that are to be redistributed into RIP. Note that the `Match` parameter allows any of the routes that have been specified to be redistributed. OSPF routes can be:

- **Internal**—These are routes that are internal to a specific AS.
- **External 1**—These are routes that are external to the AS, but are imported into OSPF as type 1 external routes.
- **External 2**—These are routes external to the AS, but imported into OSPF as type 2 external routes.

A type 1 external route uses a metric comparable to the link-state metric, which is calculated by adding the internal route metric to the external route metric.

A type 2 external route metric assumes that routing between two ASs is the major cost of routing a packet. This type of metric eliminates the need for conversion of external costs to internal link-state metrics. Type 1 and type 2 external routes are the external metric types used by OSPF.

The Internal, External 1, and External 2 parameters are used as the default setting. Because the Redistribute command in the example uses the default behavior, these parameters may not appear when you use the Write Terminal or Show Configuration commands.

When you are redistributing between two different protocols the Default-Metric command must be specified. To do this, enter default-metric 10 in Router Configuration mode. This designates the cost of the redistributed route used in RIP updates. All routes that are redistributed will use this default metric.

Router NewYork is now configured for the redistribution of routes between both protocols. You exit the Configuration mode by pressing **Ctrl+Z**. Save the configuration in NVRAM by entering copy runn start.

Since routers Maine, New Hampshire, and Vermont are also OSPF AS boundary routers, they can be configured in the same way.

There are a number of commands to use to monitor redistribution on the network. For example, you can display the current state of router NewYork's routing table by entering show ip route in Privileged mode. The output of the Show IP Route for router NewYork is shown in Figure 8.35.

You can see from the output that the routing table of the NewYork router contains networks that are directly connected (C); routes learned from RIP (R); and routes learned from OSPF (O).

The RIP routes in the other domains are redistributed into router NewYork as OSPF external type 2 routes (O E2). A Show IP Route command on the other routers will display a similar output.

You can discover the routes a router's packets follow when traveling to their destination by using the following command:

```
Trace [destination]
```

The Destination parameter is generally the IP address for a network.

To trace the routes from router Maine that can be used to reach network 172.16.128.1 on router NewYork, enter trace 172.16.128.1 in Privileged mode. The output of this command shows two routes that can be used to reach network 172.16.128.1 (Figure 8.36). One goes through the Vermont router to the 172.16.67.1 (S1) interface on the NewYork router. The other goes through the New Hampshire router to the 172.16.65.2 (S0) interface on the NewYork router.

```
NewYork> enable
Password:
NewYork# show ip route
Codes: C - connected, S - static, I - IGRP, R - RIP, M - mobile, B - BGP
       D - IEGRP, EX - EIGRP external, O - OSPF, IA - OSPF inter area
       E1 - OSPF external type 1, E2 - OSPF external type 2, E - EGP
       i - IS-IS, L1 - IS-IS level-1, L2 - IS-IS level-2, * - candidate default
       U - per-user static route

Gateway of last resort is not set

     172.16.0.0 255.255.255.0 is subnetted,
C        172.16.128.0 is directly connected,
R        172.16.129.0 [120/1] via 172.16.128.3, 00:00:15, Ethernet0
O E2     172.16.192.0 [110/20] via 172.16.67.2, 00:01:03, Serial1
O E2     172.16.32.0 [110/20] via 172.16.65.1, 00:01:03, Serial0
O E2     172.16.1.0 [110/20] via 172.16.67.2, 00:01:03, Serial1
                     [110/20] via 172.16.65.1, 00:01:03, Serial0
O        172.16.68.0 [110/128] via 172.16.65.1, 00:01:03, Serial0
C        172.16.65.0 is directly connected, Serial0
O        172.16.66.0 [110/128] via 172.16.67.2, 00:01:03, Serial1
C        172.16.67.0 is directly connected, Serial1
NewYork#
```

FIGURE 8.35   You can display the current state of router NewYork's routing table by entering show ip route.

FIGURE 8.36
The output of this command shows two routes that can be used to reach network 172.16.128.1.

```
Maine# trace 172.16.128.1

Type escape sequence to abort.
Tracing the route to NewYork (172.16.128.1)

   1 Vermont (172.16.66.2) 32 msec
     New Hampshire (172.16.68.1) 16 msec

   2 NewYork (172.16.65.2) 68 msec
     NewYork (172.16.67.1) 52 msec *
Maine#
```

A command that can be used to monitor OSPF is show IP OSPF events, which displays all the events that have occurred to OSPF on the backbone router (Figure 8.37). For example, the "Insert route list" event (number 21) shows that an OSPF route has been added to the NewYork router.

FIGURE 8.37
Show ip ospf events displays all the events that have occurred to OSPF on the backbone router.

```
NewYork# show ip ospf events
1    318352    DB free:   172.16.32.0   0xF86BC 5
2    318380    Insert MAXAGE lsa:   0xF86BC   172.16.32.0
3    320408    End Suspend:   0x0   0x0
4    320408    Suspend:   0x31AEAD8   0x0
5    320408    Generic:   ex_delete_old_routes   0x0
6    320408    Insert route list INFO:   0x101E9C   0x0 2
7    320408    Insert route list:   172.16.192.0   0x118DC8 5
8    320408    Insert route list:   172.16.192.0   0x118DC8 5
9    320412    Insert route list INFO:   0x100BF4   0x0 2
10   320412    Insert route list:   172.16.67.0   0x101E9C 5
11   320412    Insert route list:   172.16.67.0   0x101E9C 5
12   320412    Insert route list INFO:   0x1029A8   0x0 2
13   320412    Insert route list:   172.16.65.0   0x100BF4 5
14   320412    Insert route list INFO:   0x100808   0x0 2
15   320412    Insert route list:   172.16.32.0   0x1029A8 5
16   320412    Insert MAXAGE lsa:   0xF86BC   172.16.32.0
17   320416    Generic:   build_ex_lsa   0xAC102000
18   320416    Redist summary-address check:   172.16.32.0   0x20
19   320416    Generic:   ex_route_callback   0xF2934
20   320416    Insert route list INFO:   0x0   0x0 2
21   320416    Insert route list:   172.16.1.0   0x100808 5
22   320416    Delete route list:   172.16.1.0   0x100808 5
23   320416    Delete route list:   172.16.1.0   0x100808 5
```

Managing Traffic

Managing Complex Internetworks

To describe the major tasks that must be performed when managing a complex internetwork we explain the use of a hierarchical design model when planning complex internetworks and discuss the characteristics of a complex internetwork. We describe internetwork management issues associated with complex internetworks and methods of controlling network congestion in a complex internetwork.

Internetworking Growth and Hierarchical Design

The trend towards more complex environments is making internetwork design increasingly difficult. This means that careful planning by internetwork administrators is required to prevent inefficient use of resources.

An internetwork that comprises 50 routers can pose complex problems that lead to unpredictable results. If you attempt to optimize internetworks that feature hundreds or thousands of routers, you run into even bigger problems.

A hierarchical design helps to avoid certain common operational problems. In such a design, routers are distributed by function. This minimizes the complexity of the internetwork and makes routers easier to manage. For example, you can accomplish phased upgrades to software and hardware more easily when you use a hierarchical design approach.

A hierarchical design divides internetworks into three logical services: backbone, distribution, and local area access (Figure 9.1). Backbone (or core) services aim to optimize communication between routers at different sites or in different logical groups. Distribution services provide a way to implement internetwork traffic control. Local access services support communication between workstations and routers.

If host 3 and host 2 need to communicate, such a transmission could be routed through router X to router D to router C to router B to host 2. The path from router X to router D travels through a portion of the backbone network. Communication between router D and router C (and subsequently router B) is controlled by traffic-handling policy rules associated with distribution services. Router B and host 2 communicate using local access services. Controlling access to resources on this network is router B's primary goal.

LANs are at the heart of most corporate internetworks and form the backbone of most routed internetworks. The easiest way to witness growth in a routed internetwork is to study the technology employed in the backbone.

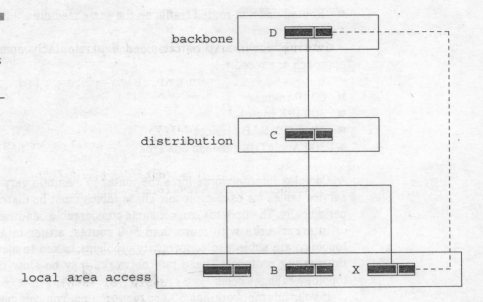

FIGURE 9.1
A hierarchical design divides internetworks into three logical services.

Some networks consist of a single Ethernet segment that connects hosts to a mainframe. As the number of hosts within the building increases, routers link multiple Ethernet segments together.

When the network evolves to a multiple building or campus topology, a fiber optic cable in a high-speed ring configuration connects the buildings, while Ethernet is kept in place in individual buildings. Many corporations use an FDDI/CDDI ring as the backbone in their current networks.

As corporations become more global in nature, multiple campus networks require connectivity. New technologies, such as ATM, use high-speed fiber optic cable as a backbone to provide global connectivity for both private and public networks.

Networks have differing design requirements. As your network grows, it must evolve to meet the needs of users. Once it has done this, you have to deal with the next set of management issues, such as controlling traffic flow and reducing overhead traffic.

Introducing Complex Internetworks

To identify a complex internetwork, look for the following characteristics:

- More than 500 routes
- Global topology with multiple remote connections
- Emphasis on security

- Routed and non-routed traffic on the same medium

Internetworks may be considered particularly complex when they approach or exceed:

- 00 IP routes
- 300 IPX routes
- 1000 IPX SAP services
- 300 AppleTalk zones in one area

Complex internetworks force the router to maintain very large routing and service tables for each protocol. These tables must be distributed or updated periodically. The updates can consume considerable bandwidth on all links.

Internetworks with more than 500 routes, either in a local or remote topology, are subject to connectivity problems linked to metric limitations of the routing protocol. These internetworks may be slow to converge when topology changes occur.

If your internetwork has 500 or more routes, you can manage router overhead by using route summarization and advanced routing protocols.

The problems caused by maintaining more than 500 entries in a routing table can be managed by reducing the overall number of entries using route summarization.

Route summarization occurs at major network boundaries for most routing protocols, consolidating address advertisement with a summary address. Some IP protocols, such as OSPF and Enhanced IGRP, allow manual summarization on arbitrary boundaries within the major network. Careful planning and address allocation are required for manual summarization to be most effective.

Advanced routing protocols, such as OSPF and Enhanced IGRP, reduce bandwidth consumption by sending only topology changes rather than the entire routing table contents. These topology updates are sent at regular intervals. Enhanced IGRP further reduces overhead processing in the router because it uses a single algorithm to calculate IP, IPX, and AppleTalk routes.

If you manage geographically remote networks (global topology), there is the challenge of tracing, logging, and accounting for resource usage. Keeping records of line usage, CPU time, and server time is a major challenge. Designing and managing internetworks with many remote links usually involves trading off cost against reliability.

As internetworks become more widely distributed geographically, maintaining connectivity becomes more of a problem. Often, connections are maintained by service providers rather than by the individual company itself, and network segments are not always located in the same building or even in the same city. It is vital to plan the management and repair of links. This requires strategic planning with fallback positions defined in advance.

You can manage a global topology (incorporating different carriers and service providers) by using dial-on-demand routing (DDR), data compression, and packet-switched networks. You can maintain infrequent connectivity requirements using Cisco's dial-on-demand routing (DDR) feature. Active links are created only after traffic is detected by the router. This service replaces nailed-up circuits that accumulate costs even when the link is idle.

Data compression of headers or entire frames is one way to reduce traffic. The router software accomplishes the compression before the frame is placed on the medium. Packet-switched networks, such as X.25 and Frame Relay, offer the advantage of global connectivity through a large number of service providers with established circuits to most major cities.

As an internetwork administrator you must be conscious of maintaining security in your internetwork. You need to block unauthorized access and verify authorized access. Even then access to certain connections may need to be restricted.

An internetwork that delivers both routed and non-routed traffic has some unique problems. Most non-routable protocols lack a mechanism to provide flow control, so they are very sensitive to delays in delivery. Delivery delays, or packets arriving out of sequence, can result in loss of an application session.

Some non-routable traffic, such as LAT and link protocols, for example IBM's SDLC, must be encapsulated inside a routable protocol. This allows delivery to remote hosts, but also requires additional resources within the router.

Non-routable (or bridged) traffic depends heavily on broadcasts for host delivery. In mixed-media environments, such as Ethernet connected to Token Ring, address and header differences create problems that can be overcome only by additional CPU processing power in the router.

Cisco's concurrent routing and bridging feature allows the same protocol to be both routed and bridged (albeit on different interfaces) within the router. This feature is very important during migration from bridged to routed environments.

Filters and Queues

Network congestion occurs when the amount of data to be transmitted by a particular medium exceeds the bandwidth of the medium. A network has many sources of data traffic and overhead traffic. Data traffic is usually generated by user applications. These may initiate file transfers using protocols such as FTP and TFTP. Client/server applications are another common source of data traffic.

Overhead traffic is generated when the traffic is not directly related to user applications. Examples of overhead traffic include routing updates and broadcast requests, such as for a Domain Name server.

Traffic generated by different protocols can cause problems for routers and other hardware devices. The routers have to maintain separate tables and caches for each protocol, wasting resources on what is effectively duplicated information.

The physical presence of additional traffic from another protocol on the medium creates competition for the fixed bandwidth of that medium.

Multiprotocol traffic presents problems for internetwork designers as well as for internetwork administrators. When you use only a single protocol, internetwork design can be tailored to suit the idiosyncrasies of that protocol suite. But when multiple-protocol traffic is present, the internetwork must be balanced between the needs of each protocol.

To resolve congestion, traffic must be either reduced or rescheduled. With Cisco routers you can control network congestion by filtering traffic, prioritizing traffic with queues, and limiting broadcast/multicast traffic.

Reducing traffic is the most obvious method of solving congestion problems. Traffic filters prevent user traffic from accessing portions of the network.

Use access lists to implement filters based on source and destination address characteristics, application type, and data size. Traffic filters can help to keep certain traffic from reaching critical links.

Service filters prevent access by hiding some services from designated groups of users. Of course, if you reduce the number of advertised services, you reduce bandwidth consumption on WAN links.

You can use route redistribution filters to prevent routing information from reaching routing tables on certain routers. This limits communication with remote devices connected to those routers.

You can reduce serial link congestion by establishing a corporate priority policy for user traffic. To do this on Cisco routers, you can use different types of traffic queuing systems: priority queuing, custom queuing, or weighted fair queuing.

Priority queuing means that high-priority traffic gets through at the risk of losing lower-priority traffic. If you use custom queuing, each traffic type gets a share of the available bandwidth. Weighted fair queuing sorts and assigns priorities to traffic streams automatically. This approach is acceptable on most networks, but can be overridden by manual configuration of either priority or custom queuing.

You can establish a queuing policy that gives priority to non-routable traffic. This can be useful, since applications that depend on non-routable protocols are very sensitive to traffic delays.

Some periodic broadcasts have configurable transmission timers to lengthen the interval between broadcasts. If you lengthen the timer, you reduce overall traffic load on that link.

You can use static entries in routing tables to eliminate the need to dynamically advertise routes across a link. This technique can be very effective for serial lines.

Implementing Traffic Filters

We introduce IP access lists and describe how to configure standard access lists on a Cisco router, explaining the use of IP access lists, describing how to configure standard access lists on a Cisco router and configuring a standard access list.

IP Access Lists

Packet filtering facilitates control packet movement through the network. Such control can help limit network traffic and restrict network use by certain users or devices. Use access lists to permit or deny packets' crossing of specified interfaces.

An access list is a sequential collection of permit and deny conditions that apply to IP addresses. The Cisco IOS tests addresses against the conditions in an access list one by one. The first match determines whether the Cisco IOS accepts or rejects the address. Because the Cisco IOS stops testing conditions after the first match, the order of the conditions is critical. If no conditions match, the Cisco IOS rejects the address.

Use access lists in several ways:

- To control the transmission of packets on an interface.
- To control virtual terminal line access.
- To restrict contents of routing updates.

After you create an access list, you can apply it to one or more interfaces. You can apply access lists on either inbound or outbound traffic on interfaces.

When you define an inbound access list, and the router receives a packet, the router checks the source address of the packet against the access list. If the access list permits the address, the router continues to process the packet.

If the access list denies the address, the router discards the packet. The router then returns an ICMP Host Unreachable message.

When you define outbound access lists, the incoming packet is routed to a controlled interface. The router then checks the source address of the packet against the access list. If the access list permits the address, the router transmits the packet.

If the access list rejects the address, the router discards the packet, and then returns an ICMP Host Unreachable message.

Standard Access List Configuration

Define a standard access list using the `Access-List` command in global configuration mode. The syntax of the command is:

```
access-list access-list-number {permit|deny}
{source[source-wildcard]|any}
```

`access-list-number` identifies the list to which the entry belongs. It can be any number from 1 to 99. In Figure 9.2, it is 3.

FIGURE 9.2
Define a standard access list using the Access-List command in global configuration mode.

```
Connecticut> enable
Password:
Connecticut# config term
Enter configuration commands, one per line. End with CNTL/Z.
Connecticut(config)# access-list 3 permit 172.16.128.3
Connecticut(config)# access-list 3 deny 172.16.128.0 0.0.0.2!
Connecticut(config)# interface ethernet0
Connecticut(config-if)# ip access-group 3 in
Connecticut(config-if)# ^Z
Connecticut#
%SYS-5-CONIFG_I: Configured from console by console
Connecticut# copy runn start
```

Specifying the permit or deny keywords indicates whether this entry allows or blocks traffic from the specified address. The *source* identifies the traffic source's IP address. Source could represent a range of IP addresses if a subnet address is specified. `source-wildcard` identifies which bits in the address field are matched. Specifying the keyword `any` means that the address 0.0.0.0 is used with the mask 255.255.255.255 and matches any address.

NOTE

If a 0 bit appears in the mask, then the corresponding bit location in the access list address and the packet address must match for the access list condition to apply.

If a 1 bit appears in the mask, then the corresponding bit in the packet address is ignored. This part of the source address plays no part in deciding whether to apply access list conditions. For this reason, 1 bits in the mask are sometimes called "don't care" bits.

Example address	Mask	Matches
0.0.0.0	*255.255.255.255*	*any address*
172.16.0.0	*0.0.255.255*	*network 172.16.0.0*
172.16.67.0	*0.0.0.255*	*only subnet 172.16.67.0*
172.16.67.2	*0.0.0.0*	*exactly host 172.16.67.2*
255.255.255.255	*0.0.0.0*	*local broadcast*

In Figure 9.3, traffic from 172.16.128.3 is permitted, so host B can reach the host A. But host C cannot reach host A. The 0.0.0.255 mask implies that traffic from all other hosts on the 172.16.128.0 subnet is denied.

FIGURE 9.3
Traffic from
172.16.128.3
is permitted.

```
Vermont(config)# access-list 2 permit 172.16.128.3
Vermont(config)# access-list 2 deny 172.16.128.0 0.0.0.255
Vermont(config)# access-list 2 permit 172.16.0.0 0.0.255.25
```

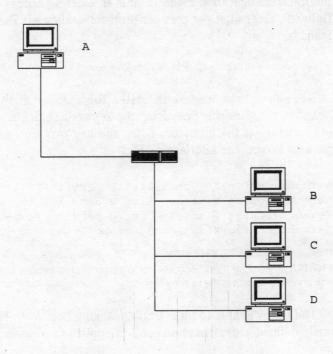

Traffic from other subnets on the 172.16.0.0 network is permitted. Host D can reach host A. It is a good idea to organize an access list so that more specific references in a network or subnet appear before more general ones. You should also place frequently occurring conditions before less frequent conditions.

If you omit the mask from an associated IP host address access list specification, 0.0.0.0 is assumed to be the mask. In this example, the 0.0.0.0 mask is implicit. This reduces the typing required for large numbers of individual addresses.

When you create an access list, by default the end of the list contains an implicit deny statement. Any addresses not accounted for in the list are denied. In the example shown here, all other access, such as from hosts on a different network (192.168.0.0), is denied.

Once you create an access list, you cannot selectively add or remove access list command lines from the list. Any subsequent additions you make are placed at the end of the list.

If you attempt to apply an access list that has not yet been defined, the software will act as though there is no access list. This situation is equivalent to a "permit any" statement and all packets will be accepted.

Once you have defined the conditions in the access list, you then need to associate it with a router interface. Use the IP Access-Group command in interface configuration mode to link an existing access list to an interface. Only one access list per port per protocol is allowed. The syntax of the command is:

```
ip access-group access-list-number {in|out}
```

access-list-number indicates the number of the access list to be linked to the interface. Specifying the keyword in defines processing of packets arriving on the interface. Using the keyword out defines processing of packets leaving the interface.

```
Vermont(config)# access-list 2 permit 172.16.128.3
Vermont(config)# access-list 2 deny 172.16.128.0 0.0.0.255
Vermont(config)# access-list 2 permit 172.16.0.0 0.0.255.255
Vermont(config)# ip access-group 2 in
```

FIGURE 9.4 Use the IP Access-Group command in interface configuration mode to link an existing access list to an interface.

The policy goal is to filter traffic reaching host A. In Figure 9.4, the previously defined access list number 2 is applied to incoming traffic on the Vermont router's E0 interface. Configuring the access list for inbound traffic saves processing time.

You can define access lists to restrict virtual terminal access. To restrict incoming and outgoing connections between a particular virtual terminal line (into a device) and the address in an access list, use the Access-Class command in line configuration mode. The syntax of the this command is:

```
access-class access-list-number {in|out}
```

access-list-number indicates the number of the access list to be linked to this terminal line. Using the keyword in applies the access list to inbound connections. Using the keyword out applies it to outbound connections.

In Figure 9.5, only hosts in subnet 172.16.192.0 are included in the access list. This access list is then applied to the Connecticut router's virtual terminal lines. Only those hosts can establish connections with the router's terminal ports. The implicit deny statement still applies in this case, restricting access to any addresses not explicitly mentioned in the access list.

FIGURE 9.5

Define access lists to restrict virtual terminal access.

```
Connecticut> enable
Password:
Connecticut# config term
Enter configuration commands, one per line. End with CNTL/Z.
Connecticut(config)# access-list 1 permit 172.16.192.0 0.0.0.255
Connecticut(config)# line vty 4
Connecticut(config-line)# access-class 1 in
Connecticut(config-line)# exit
Connecticut(config)# ^Z
Connecticut#
%SYS-5-CONFIG_I: Configured from console by console
Connecticut#
```

In Figure 9.6 an access list permitting access to network 10.0.0.0 is defined. It is then applied to the router's terminal lines, but this time to outbound connections. Outbound terminal line connections to networks other than 10.0.0.0 are denied.

Let's look at an example of configuring standard access lists on a Cisco router.

Network 172.16.0.0 is a class B network that has been subnetted; the third octet is now the subnet identifier (subnet mask 255.255.255.0). The purpose of the access list here is to restrict traffic from the 172.16.128.0 subnet.

The goal is to allow traffic from the server only (IP address 172.16.128.3), and restrict all other traffic from that subnet (Figure 9.7). Here, for example, any traffic from the workstation (IP address 172.16.128.4) will be denied by the router.

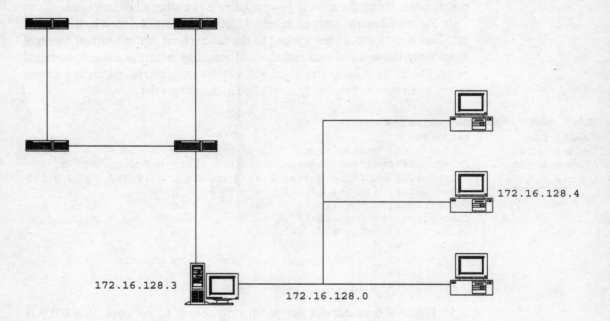

FIGURE 9.6
An access list
permitting access
to network
10.0.0.0.0 is defined.

```
Connecticut> enable
Password:
Connecticut# config term
Enter configuration commands, one per line. End with CNTL/Z.
Connecticut(config)# access-list 5 permit 10.0.0.0 0.255.255.255
Connecticut(config)# line vty 0 4
Connecticut(config-line)# access-class 5 out
Connecticut(config-line)# exit
Connecticut(config)# ^Z
Connecticut#
%SYS-5-CONFIG_I: Configured from console by console
Connecticut#
```

172.16.128.4

172.16.128.3

172.16.128.0

```
Connecticut# config term
Enter configuration commands, one per line. End with CNTL/Z.
Connecticut(config)# access-list 3 permit 172.16.128.3
Connecticut(config)# access-list 3 deny 172.16.128.0 0.0.0.255
Connecticut(config)# interface ethernet0
Connecticut(config-if)# ip access-group 3 in
Connecticut(config-if)# ^Z
Connecticut#
%SYS-5-CONFIG_I: Configured from console by console
Connecticut#
```

FIGURE 9.7   The goal is to allow traffic from the server only and restrict all other traffic from that subnet.

Assume now that you are logged in to the Connecticut router and that you have entered Privileged mode. Enter config term to access Global configuration mode.

Assume that this is access list number 3. To allow traffic from the server you enter access-list 3 permit 172.16.128.3. To prevent traffic from the rest of the subnet you enter access-list 3 deny 172.16.128.0 0.0.0.255.

Next specify an interface for access list number 3. In this case the access list will be applied to incoming traffic on the Connecticut router's E0 interface. Enter interface configuration mode by entering interface ethernet 0. Then enter ip access-group 3 in.

Press **Ctrl+Z** to leave configuration mode. You can save the new configuration in NVRAM by entering copy run start.

Let's look at the effect of the access list configuration. Of course, this assumes that no unforeseen events have affected connectivity with the host addresses.

The access list is applied to incoming traffic on the Connecticut router's E0 interface. To test the effects of access list operation (Figure 9.8), first log on to another router, in this case, the Vermont router. From the Vermont router you attempt to reach the server by entering ping 172.16.128.3. As you can see the attempt is successful.

```
Connecticut# telnet 172.16.67.2
Trying 172.16.67.2 ...  Open

User Access Verification

Password:
Vermont> ping 172.16.128.3

Type escape sequence to abort.
Sending 5, 100-byte ICMP Echoes to 172.16.128.3, timeout is 2 seconds:
!!!!!
Success rate is 100 percent (5/5), round-trip min/avg/max = 32/39/56 ms
Vermont> ping 172.16.128.4

Type escape sequence to abort.
Sending 5, 100-byte ICMP Echoes to 172.16.128.4, timeout is 2 seconds:
.....
Success rate is 0 percent (0/5)
```

FIGURE 9.8 Test the effects of access list operation.

Now you can attempt to reach a workstation on the server's LAN by entering ping 172.16.128.4. Here, the test fails. The access list prevents contact from being made.

Advanced Traffic Filters

Now we should explain how to configure extended IP access lists on Cisco routers and the use of extended IP access lists. We will describe how to configure extended IP access lists and an extended access list on a Cisco router.

Extended Access List Configuration

Standard access lists offer quick configuration and low overhead processing in limiting network traffic. Extended access lists provide a higher degree of control than standard access lists.

You can use extended access lists to enable filtering based on protocol, source, or destination address, or application port number.

These features make it possible to limit traffic based on the uses of the network.

Each packet processed by an extended access list entry must match all options configured in that entry. Then the packet is permitted or denied in accordance with the entry. Just as with standard access lists, the first matching entry in the access list determines how the packet will be treated. You can also specify inbound or outbound processing for extended access lists.

If no access list is present then, by default, the packet is permitted. If an extended access list is defined then the packet's source IP address is checked. If the source address matches, then the destination address is checked. If the destination address matches, then the protocol and any protocol options are checked. Only then is the packet explicitly permitted or denied.

Use the Access-List command to create an entry in an extended IP access list. The syntax of the command is:

```
access-list access-list-number {permit|deny}
    {protocol protocol-keyword}
    {source source-wildcard|any}
    {destination destination-wildcard|any}
    [precedence precedence] [tos tos]
```

This is the general syntax of the Access-List command for defining extended access lists. It can vary considerably depending on the aim of a given command.

The `access-list-number` can be any value from 100 to 199. The `protocol` parameter is the name or number of an IP protocol. The `protocol` parameter can be one of the following keywords: `eigrp`, `gre`, `icmp`, `igmp`, `igrp`, `ip`, `ipinip`, `nos`, `ospf`, `tcp`, or `udp`, or an integer in the range 0 through 255 representing an IP protocol number. To match any Internet protocol, including ICMP, TCP, and UDP, use the keyword `IP`.

The `Source` and `Destination` parameters are IP addresses, and are accompanied by corresponding wildcard masks. Use the keyword `Any` instead of configuring the address 0.0.0.0 and mask 255.255.255.255. Use the keyword `Host` before an IP address to replace the mask 0.0.0.0.

The `Precedence` parameter can have a value from 0 to 7. It indicates the precedence level at which packets are filtered. The `TOS` (Type of Service) parameter can have a value from 0 to 15. This value indicates the type of service level specified for packet filtering.

You can define an extended access list with protocol-specific options to filter traffic based on ICMP messages.

The syntax for the `Access-List ICMP` command is:

```
access-list access-list-number {permit|deny} icmp
    {source source-wildcard|any}
    {destination destination-wildcard|any}
    [icmp type [icmp-code]|icmp-message]
    [precedence precedence] [tos tos]
```

TABLE 9.1
An explanation of the parameters for the command Access-List ICMP.

Access-List ICMP command parameter	Description
`access-list number`	A number from 100 to 199.
`permit/deny`	Whether this entry is used to allow or block the specified address(es).
`source` and `destination`	IP addresses.
`source-wildcard` and `destination-wildcard`	Wildcard masks of address bits that must match.
`icmp-type`	Packets can be filtered by ICMP message type. The type is a number from 0 to 255.
`icmp-code`	Packets that have been filtered by ICMP message type can also be filtered by ICMP message code. The code is a number from 0 to 255.
`icmp-message`	Packets can be filtered by a symbolic name representing an ICMP message type or a combination of ICMP message type and ICMP message code.

The keyword ICMP indicates that a different syntax is being used for this command and that protocol-specific options are available.

Use the Access-List TCP command to define an extended access list that filters traffic based on TCP port number. See Table 9.3.

administratively-prohibited	information-reply	precedence-unreachable
alternate-address	information-request	protocol-unreachable
conversion-error	mask-reply	reassembly-timeout
dod-host-prohibited	mask-request	redirect
dod-net-prohibited	mobile-redirect	router-advertisement
echo	net-redirect	router-solicitation
echo-reply	net-tos-redirect	source-quench
general-parameter-problem	net-tos-unreachable	source-route-failed
host-isolated	net-unreachable	time-exceeded
host-precedence-unreachable	network-unknown	timestamp-reply
host-redirect	no-room-for-option	timestamp-request
host-tos-redirect	option-missing	traceroute
host-tos-unreachable	packet-too-big	ttl-exceeded
host-unknown	parameter-problem	unreachable
host-unreachable	port-unreachable	

Access-List TCP command parameter	Description
access-list number	A number from 100 to 199
permit/deny	Whether this entry is used to allow or block the specified address(es).
source and destination	IP addresses.
source-wildcard and destination-wildcard	Wildcard masks of address bits that must match.
source port and destination port	A decimal number between 0 and 65535 or a name that represents a TCP port number.
operator	A qualifying condition. It can be: lt (less than), gt (greater than), eq (equal to), neq (not equal to), and range (inclusive range).
established	A match occurs if the TCP datagram has the ACK or RST bits set. The first packet arriving is passed on down the list, until it is ultimately permitted or denied. If it is permitted, subsequent packets belonging to the now established connection are permitted by this first line and need no further processing.

continued on next page

	Access-List TCP command parameter	Description
TABLE 9.3 continued	precedence	Packets can be filtered by precedence level specified by a number from 0 to 7.
	tos	Packets can be filtered by type of service level specified by a number from 0 to 15.

The syntax for the `Access-List TCP` command is:

```
access-list access-list-number {permit|deny} tcp
    {source source-wildcard|any}
    [operator source-port|source-port]
    {destination destination-wildcard|any}
    [operator destination-port|destination-port]
    [established]
    [precedence precedence] [tos tos]
```

Packets can be filtered by precedence level specified by a number from 0 to 7 (Figure 9.9). The numbers correspond to the precedence names shown here.

FIGURE 9.9
Packets can be filtered by precedence level specified by a number from 0 to 7.

```
0    critical
1    flash
2    flash-override
3    immediate
4    internet
5    network
6    priority
7    routine
```

Packets can be filtered by type of service (TOS) level specified by a number from 0 to 15. Examples of TOS names are shown in Figure 9.10. The protocol keyword TCP indicates that an alternate syntax is being used for this command and that protocol-specific options are available.

FIGURE 9.10
Examples of TOS names.

```
max-reliability
max-throughput
min-delay
min-monetary-cost
normal
```

Use the `Access-List UDP` command to define an extended access list that filters traffic based on UDP port number (Figure 9.11). For a list of commands consult Table 9.4.

```
Connecticut(config)# access-list 102 permit udp any any eq domain
```

FIGURE 9.11   Use the Access-List UDP command to define an extended access list that filters traffic based on UDP port number

TABLE 9.4
An explanation of the parameters for the command Access-List UDP.

Access-list UDP	Description
`access-list number`	A number from 100 to 199.
`permit/deny`	Whether this entry is used to allow or block the specified address(es).
`source` and `destination`	IP addresses.
`source-wildcard` and `destination-wildcard`	Wildcard masks of address bits that must match.
`source port` and `destination port`	A decimal number between 0 and 65535 or a name that represents a TCP port number.
`operator`	A qualifying condition. It can be: lt (less than), gt (greater than), eq (equal to), neq (not equal to), and range (inclusive range).
`established`	A match occurs if the TCP datagram has the ACK or RST bits set.
`precedence`	Packets can be filtered by precedence level specified by a number from 0 to 7.
`tos`	Packets can be filtered by type of service level specified by a number from 0 to 15.

The syntax for the `Access-List UDP` command is:

```
access-list access-list-number {permit|deny} udp
{source source-wildcard|any}
[operator source-port|source-port]
{destination destination-wildcard|any}
[operator destination-port|destination-port]
[established]
[precedence precedence] [tos tos]
```

The `Precedence` and `TOS` (Type of Service) names are the same as for TCP. The protocol keyword UDP indicates that an alternate syntax is being used for this command and that protocol-specific options are available.

In Figure 9.12, the first line permits any incoming TCP connections with destination port numbers greater than 1,023. Source ports are defined as a number in the range from 0 to 255. Destination ports are defined as a number above 1,023. The next line permits incoming TCP connections to the SMTP port (25) of host 172.16.1.2. The last line permits incoming ICMP messages for error feedback.

```
Connecticut> enable
Password:
Connecticut# config term
Enter configuration commands, one per line. End with CNTL/Z.
Connecticut(config)# access-list 102 permit tcp any 172.16.0.0 0.0.255.255 gt 1023
Connecticut(config)# access-list 102 permit tcp any host 172.16.1.2 eq smtp
Connecticut(config)# access-list 102 permit icmp any host 172.16.1.2
```

FIGURE 9.12   This line permits any incoming TCP connections with destination port numbers greater than 1,023.

Let's consider another example of using an extended access list.

Suppose a network connected to the Internet. Any host on an Ethernet should be able to form TCP connections to any host on the Internet. Internet hosts should not be able to form TCP connections to hosts on the Ethernet, except to:

- The mail (SMTP: 25) port of a dedicated mail host.
- The appropriate ports of a DNS (42,53)/FTP (20,21) server.
- The WWW port (80) of a World Wide Web server.

The fact that the router will only accept particular types of connection on specified ports makes it possible to separately control incoming and outgoing services. The access list can be configured on either the inbound or the outbound interface. For example, SMTP uses TCP port 25 on one end of the connection and a random port number on the other end. The same two port numbers are used throughout the life of the connection. Mail packets coming in from the Internet will have a destination port of 25. Outbound packets will have the port numbers reversed.

In the access list shown in Figure 9.13, the first line allows existing TCP connections. The next line permits ICMP messages. The next line allows SMTP connections from any source to one host, 172.16.192.2, the mail server.

The access list allows WWW connections from any source to the World Wide Web server, 172.16.192.5, only. The remainder of the list allows DNS and FTP (command and data) connections from any source to the DNS/FTP server, 172.16.192.10.

```
Connecticut> enable
Password:
Connecticut# config term
Enter configuration commands, one per line. End with CNTL/Z.
Connecticut(config)# access-list 105 permit tcp any any established
Connecticut(config)# access-list 105 permit icmp any any
Connecticut(config)# access-list 105 permit tcp any host 172.16.192.5 eq smtp
Connecticut(config)# access-list 105 permit tcp any host 172.16.192.5 eq www
Connecticut(config)# access-list 105 permit tcp any host 172.16.192.10 eq domain
Connecticut(config)# access-list 105 permit tcp any host 172.16.192.10 eq 42
Connecticut(config)# access-list 105 permit tcp any host 172.16.192.10 eq ftp
Connecticut(config)# access-list 105 permit tcp any host 172.16.192.10 eq ftp-data
Connecticut(config)# access-list 105 permit tcp any host 172.16.192.10 eq smtp
Connecticut(config)# interface serial0
Connecticut(config-if)# ip access-group 102 in
```

FIGURE 9.13   An example of using an extended access list.

To apply the access list, first specify an interface. In this case it is the serial 0 interface. Use the IP Access-Group command to link the access list to the Serial 0 interface.

Let's look at an example of configuring an extended access list on a Cisco router. Network 172.16.0.0 is a class B network that has been subnetted; the third octet is now the subnet identifier (subnet mask 255.255.255.0). The purpose of the access list here is to restrict traffic from the 172.16.128.0 subnet so that only TELNET traffic from the server (172.16.128.3) is accepted. All other traffic from the subnet (for example FTP, SMTP) is denied. In this scenario, any traffic from the workstation (IP address 172.16.128.4) will be denied by the router.

Assume now that you are logged in to the Connecticut router and have entered Privileged mode. Enter config term to access global configuration mode. See Figure 9.14.

We will define this access list as number 102. First we permit TCP connections with any destination port on the 172.16.128.0 subnet greater than 1023. Remember, source ports are numbers in the range 0 to 255. Destination port numbers have values greater than 1,023 (though 1,024 is usually reserved).

To allow any incoming TCP connections with destination port numbers greater than 1023, enter access-list 102 permit tcp any 172.16.128.0.0.0.0.255 gt 1023. Next, we need to restrict access to incoming Telnet traffic. Enter access-list 102 permit tcp any host 172.16.128.3 eq telnet. Remember, the keyword Host can be used in front of an IP address in place of the mask 0.0.0.0. You can also use the TELNET source port number, 23, in the command instead of telnet.

```
Connecticut> enable
Password:
Connecticut# config term
Enter configuration commands, one per line. End with CNTL/Z.
Connecticut(config)# access-list 102 permit tcp any 172.16.128.0.0.0.0.255 gt 1023
Connecticut(config)# access-list 105 permit tcp any host 172.16.128.3 eq telnet
Connecticut(config)# access-list 105 permit icmp any host 172.16.128.3
Connecticut(config)# interface ethernet0
Connecticut(config)# ip access-group 102 out
Connecticut(config)# ^Z
Connecticut#
%SYS-5-CONFIG_I: Configured from console by console
Connecticut# copy run start
Building configuration...
[OK]
Connecticut#
```

FIGURE 9.14   An example of configuring an extended access list on a Cisco router.

Now we can make allowance for ICMP messages to facilitate error feedback. Enter `access-list 102 permit icmp any host 172.16.128.3`.

Next we specify an interface for access list number 102. In this case the access list will be applied to outbound traffic on the Connecticut router's E0 interface. Enter interface configuration mode by entering `interface ethernet 0`. Then enter `ip access-group 102 out`.

Press **Ctrl+Z** to leave Configuration mode. You can save the new configuration in NVRAM by entering `copy runn start`.

Let's look at the effect of the access list configuration. Here, the Connecticut router is connected to a LAN server (IP address 172.16.128.3). The access list is applied to outbound traffic on the Connecticut router's E0 interface. To test the effects of access list operation, first log on to another router, in this case the Vermont router. From the Vermont router attempt to reach the server by entering `ping 172.16.128.3`. As you can see the attempt is successful (Figure 9.15).

Now you can attempt to reach a workstation on the server's LAN by entering `ping 172.16.128.4`. Here, the test fails. The access list prevents contact using the `Ping` command from being made.

Queue Configuration

We will describe the operation of Cisco IOS queuing strategies: the need for queuing in a large network, priority queue operation, priority queue configuration, the operation of custom queuing, how to configure custom queues, the operation of weighted fair queuing, and how to configure weighted fair queuing.

```
Connecticut# telnet 172.16.67.2
Trying 172.16.67.2 ...  Open

User Access Verification

Password:
Vermont> ping 172.16.128.3

Type escape sequence to abort.
Sending 5, 100-byte ICMP Echoes to 172.16.128.3, timeout is 2 seconds:
!!!!!
Success rate is 100 percent (5/5), round-trip min/avg/max = 32/39/56 ms
Vermont> ping 172.16.128.4

Type escape sequence to abort.
Sending 5, 100-byte ICMP Echoes to 172.16.128.4, timeout is 2 seconds:
.....
Success rate is 0 percent (0/5)
```

FIGURE 9.15 The effect of the access list configuration.

Queuing Overview

Queuing is a mechanism that assigns a priority to one type of network traffic over other types. This is done by reordering the packets that constitute the traffic. Queuing is useful over congested serial lines, but it can be slow since it requires buffering in the router.

It is a good idea to establish a corporate queuing policy to decide which traffic on a congested line gets through first. Configure the Cisco IOS software to support the following types of queuing strategy: priority queuing, custom queuing, and weighted fair queuing.

You can configure priority, custom, and weighted fair queuing on a Cisco router, but you can assign only one queue type to an interface. The primary distinction between priority and custom queuing is that custom queuing guarantees some level of service to all traffic. Priority queuing guarantees that one type of traffic will get through at the expense of all others.

When there is a limited amount of bandwidth available, priority queuing consumes most, if not all, of the available bandwidth when it delivers the critical traffic. Priority queuing makes maximum use of low-bandwidth links for a few selected protocols.

When more bandwidth is available, custom queuing shares equitably between the different traffic types. It ensures that each traffic type gets to use some portion of the link. Custom queuing is more flexible than priority queuing, but priority queuing is more powerful when you need to assign a priority to a mission-critical protocol.

Weighted fair queuing provides traffic priority management that automatically sorts among individual traffic streams. You do not need to define access lists first. There are two categories of data streams in weighted fair queuing: high-bandwidth sessions and low-bandwidth sessions.

Low-bandwidth traffic has effective priority over high-bandwidth traffic. The high-bandwidth traffic shares the transmission service proportionally according to assigned weights.

Priority Queuing

Priority queuing is used to prioritize datagrams traveling on an interface. You can set priorities on the type of traffic passing through the network.

Packets are classified according to several criteria, including protocol and subprotocol type. They are then queued on one of four output queues: high, medium, normal, or low.

When the router is ready to transmit a packet, it scans the priority queues. This is done in order, from highest to lowest, until the highest priority packet is found. After the highest priority packet is transmitted, the router checks the priority queues again. If a priority queue fills up, packets are dropped, and the router does not process them. For IP, quench indications are sent to the original transmitter to notify it about the dropped packets.

With priority queuing, the high-priority queue is always emptied before the medium-priority queue, and so on. Priority queuing is appropriate for cases where the WAN links are congested from time to time. If the WAN links are never congested, priority queuing is probably unnecessary.

You can establish queuing priorities based on the protocol type. To do this, use the `Priority-List Protocol` command, which has the following syntax:

```
priority-list list-number
  protocol protocol-name
  {high|medium|normal|low}
  queue-keyword keyword-value
```

The *list-number* is a value between 1 and 10 that identifies the priority list. The *protocol-name* specifies protocols such as AppleTalk, CLNS, DECnet, IP, IPX, Banyan Vines, or X.25. Here we are primarily concerned with IP traffic. In Figure 9.16 you can see the priority list number and the type of protocol. The queue priority level is high.

FIGURE 9.16
Establish queuing
priorities based on
the protocol type
using the Priority-List
Protocol command.

```
Connecticut(config)# priority-list 1 protocol ip high tcp 23
Connecticut(config)# priority-list 1 protocol ip high list 1
Connecticut(config)# priority-list 1 protocol appletalk medium
Connecticut(config)# priority-list 1 protocol ipx medium
Connecticut(config)# priority-list 1 protocol ip normal
Connecticut(config)# priority-list 1 interface serial 1 high
Connecticut(config)# priority-list 1 default low
Connecticut(config)# priority-list 1 queue-limit 15 20 20 30
!
Connecticut(config)# access-list 1 permit 172.16.0.0 0.0.255.255
!
Connecticut(config)# interface serial 1
Connecticut(config-if)# priority-group 1
```

Other optional keywords that you can use with the Queue command include byte-count, TCP service and port number assignments. In this example you can see a protocol keyword, TCP, and an associated port number. This refers to *telnet traffic*.

Use the Priority-List Interface command to set the priority of traffic arriving on an interface. The command's syntax is:

```
priority-list list-number
   interface interface-type
   interface-number
   {high|medium|normal|low}
```

where *interface-type* and *interface-number* specify the name of the interface with incoming packets.

In Figure 9.6, packets arriving on Serial 1 are given high priority. Use the Priority-List Default command to assign previously unassigned traffic to a queue. The syntax for the Priority-List Default command is:

```
priority-list list-number
   default
   {high|medium|normal|low}
```

In Figure 9.16, the default priority level is low.

Use the Priority-List Queue-Limit command to define the maximum number of packets in each priority queue. The syntax for this command is:

```
priority-list list-number
   queue-limit high-limit medium-limit normal-limit low-limit
```

The queue limit defaults define the default number of datagrams in each queue. The default high limit is 20 datagrams. The default medium limit is 40 datagrams. The default normal limit is 60 datagrams. The default low limit is 80 datagrams. In general, it is not a good idea to change the default queue sizes.

In Figure 9.16, the high limit of datagrams is 15. The medium and normal limits are both 20. The low limit is 30.

Assign a priority list number to an interface using the Priority-Group command. You can assign only one list per interface. The syntax of the Priority-Group command is:

```
priority-group list-number
```

In Figure 9.16, Serial 1 has a priority queue.

IP TELNET traffic and traffic from source network 172.16.0.0, as specified by access list 1, enter the high queue. This allows the IP and TELNET traffic to be transmitted on the serial 1 interface ahead of other traffic, even if IP and TELNET traffic don't arrive at the router first.

Custom Queuing

Custom queuing assigns priorities traffic in a different way from priority queuing. Custom queuing assigns different amounts of queue space to each protocol and handles the queues in round-robin fashion. A particular protocol may have a higher priority because it has more queue space. The protocol will never monopolize the entire bandwidth and so there is no risk of losing lower priority packets.

Custom queuing is particularly important for time-sensitive protocols, such as those associated with SNA.

When custom queuing is enabled on an interface, the system maintains 17 output queues for that interface. You can specify queues 1 through 16. For queue numbers 1 through 16 the system cycles through the queues sequentially. Packets in the current queue are delivered before the system moves on to the next.

A configurable byte count is associated with each output queue. This specifies how many bytes of data from the current queue the system should deliver before it moves on to the next queue. When a particular queue is being processed, the router sends packets until the number of bytes sent exceeds the queue byte count. Or it will stop when the queue is empty.

Queue 0 is a system queue. The system uses it for high-priority packets, such as keepalives. It is emptied before any of the other queues. You cannot configure other traffic to use this queue.

You can establish queuing priorities based on the protocol type. To do this, use the `Queue-List Protocol` command, which has the following syntax:

```
queue-list list-number
     protocol protocol-name
     queue-number
     queue-keyword keyword-value
```

The `list-number` is a value between 1 and 16 that identifies the queue list. The `protocol-name` specifies protocols such as AppleTalk, CLNS, DEC-net, IP, IPX, Banyan Vines, or X.25. In the example shown here you can see the queue list number and the type of protocol. The `queue-number`, which may be between 1 and 16, in Figure 9.17 is 1.

FIGURE 9.17
Establish queuing priorities based on the protocol type using the Queue-List Protocol command.

```
Connecticut(config)# queue-list 1 protocol ip tcp 23
Connecticut(config)# queue-list 1 protocol ip 2
Connecticut(config)# queue-list 1 protocol ipx 3
Connecticut(config)# queue-list 1 protocol appletalk 4
Connecticut(config)# queue-list 1 protocol serial 1 1
Connecticut(config)# queue-list 1 default 5
Connecticut(config)# queue-list 1 limit 20
Connecticut(config)# queue-list 1 queue 1 byte-count 4554
Connecticut(config)# queue-list 1 queue 2 byte-count 1518
!
Connecticut(config)# interface serial 1
Connecticut(config)# custom-queue-list 1
```

Queue keywords provide additional options including byte-count, TCP service, and port number assignments. In this example you can see a protocol keyword, TCP, and associated port number.

Use the `Queue-List Interface` command to set the priority of all traffic arriving on an interface. The command's syntax is:

```
queue-list list-number
     interface interface-type
     interface-number
     queue-number
```

where `interface-type` and `interface-number` specify the name of the interface with incoming packets.

In Figure 9.17, packets arriving on Serial 1 get more bandwidth.

Use the `Queue-List Default` command to specify the queue to which traffic not previously specified will be assigned. The syntax for the `Queue-List Default` command is

```
queue-list list-number
    default queue-number
```

In Figure 9.17, the default queue is set to queue 5 on list 1.

Use the `Queue-List Queue` command to limit the length of a particular queue. The syntax for the command is:

```
queue-list list-number queue
    queue-number
    limit limit-number
```

where `list-number` and `queue-number` identify the numbers of the queue list and queue. The `Limit-Number` parameter defines the maximum number of packets that may be in the queue at any one time. The `Limit-Number` parameter can have a range from 0 to 32767. The default value is 20.

Use the `Queue-List Queue Byte-Count` command to define the maximum byte count transferred from the specified queue. The syntax for this command is:

```
queue-list list-number
    queue queue-number
    byte-count
    byte-count-number
```

where `list-number` and `queue-number` identify the numbers of the queue list and queue. `Byte-count-number` specifies the maximum number of bytes that the system allows to be delivered from the specified queue during a particular cycle. The default byte count is 1,500.

In Figure 9.17, the queue list number is 1. The queue number is also 1 and the byte count is 4,554.

You can assign a queue list to an interface using the `Custom-Queue-List` command. The syntax of the `Custom-Queue-List` command is:

```
custom-queue-list list-number
```

where `list-number` indicates the number of the queue list (between 1 and 16) made available to control the interface's bandwidth. You can assign only one list per interface.

In Figure 9.17, the `Custom-Queue-List` command is used to assign queue list 1 to the serial 1 interface. Different kinds of IP packets are assigned to queues 1 and 2. Queue 1 is assigned a maximum of 4,554 bytes. The default queue is queue number 5.

Weighted Fair Queuing

Cisco's implementation of weighted fair queuing divides traffic into *conversations* based on packet header addressing. A conversation is a series of messages that makes up a continuous data stream. A queuing weight is assigned to each conversation based on bandwidth requirements and other variables. A conversation index determines whether traffic represents low-volume or high-volume conversations. The switching logic within the Cisco IOS determines the selection of the data path through the router.

NOTE

Weighted fair queuing is dependent on encapsulation. *When the router initializes, the Cisco IOS checks the encapsulation type specified for each interface. Serial interfaces using HDLC, LAPB, PPP, Frame Relay, or SMDS encapsulation are candidates for fair queuing. Serial interfaces are further categorized by bandwidth (link speed). Fair queuing is enabled, by default, on serial interfaces with the proper encapsulation type operating at 2.048 Mbps (E1) or less. Fair queuing is not enabled on serial interfaces using X.25 or compressed PPP as the encapsulation type. LAN interfaces and serial lines operating at E3 or T3 speeds are also not available for fair queuing.*

Fair queuing is based on delivering messages across a serial link in a timely fashion. As the packets are switched through the router, they arrive in a precise order at the outgoing interface. The exact order of the packets is determined by the arrival of the first bit in each packet. As the packets arrive, the fair queue algorithm sorts them into messages that are part of a conversation.

The packets are placed in a holding queue before transmission. The transmission routine sorts the conversation queues "fairly" to determine the order in which messages will be handled. The order of removal of messages from each queue is determined by the value of the last bit in the last packet. So the order of removal is determined when a message ends, rather than when it begins.

File transfers cause high-volume conversations. Other application tasks are monitored by the user and are time sensitive. They do not require a lot of bandwidth. For example, interactive users create low-volume conversations.

The challenge for the queuing method is to provide the responsiveness required by the interactive user and still move lots of data to satisfy the file transfer.

You use the `Fair-Queue` command manually to enable fair queuing on an interface.

The syntax for the command is:

```
fair-queue congestive-discard-threshold-number
```

where the `congestive-discard-threshold-number` parameter has a value between 1 and 512 (default 64).

This defines a congestion threshold above which messages for high volume traffic will no longer be enqueued. Weighted fair queuing is enabled by default on serial links with the proper encapsulation type which operate at E1 speeds or less.

The congestive discard policy applies only to high-volume conversations that have more than one message in the queue. The discard policy tries to control conversations that would monopolize the link. The policy is invoked when the total number of messages on all queues is greater than the threshold, or the number of messages in a single queue is greater than one quarter of the threshold.

New messages for high-bandwidth conversations are discarded once the congestive-messages threshold (either as set, or its default value) is exceeded. However, low-bandwidth conversations, including control-message conversations, continue to enqueue data. The fair queue may occasionally contain more messages than are specified by the threshold number.

In Figure 9.18, Frame Relay encapsulation is set on interface serial 1. The congestive-discard threshold is set to 64 for fair weighted queuing. The interface is configured to operate at a 56 Kbps link speed.

FIGURE 9.18
Frame Relay
encapsulation is set
on interface serial 1.

```
!
interface Serial1
encapsulation frame-relay
fair-queue 64
bandwidth 56
!
ip address 172.16.121.1 255.255.255.0
```

You can monitor queue operation by using Cisco IOS commands to display information about input and output queues. Use the `Show Interface` command to display the status of the port and whether or not queuing is enabled. The syntax for the command is:

```
show interface interface-name
```

In the Figures 9.19 and 9.20, fair queuing is enabled by default on the Serial 0 interface. But priority queuing is enabled on Serial 1.

Use the `Show Queue` command to display detailed queuing information for a given interface. The syntax for the command is:

```
show queue interface-name
```

```
Connecticut# show interface Serial0

Serial0 is up, line protocol is up
  Hardware is HD64570
  Internet address is 172.16.66.2/24
  MTU 1500 bytes, BW 1544 Kbit, DLY 20000 usec, rely 255/255, load 1/255
  Encapsulation HDLC, loopback not set, keepalive set (10 sec)
  Last input 00:00:07, output 00:00:01, output hang never
  Last clearing of "show interface" counters never
  Output queue 0/40, 0 drops; input queue 0/75, 0 drops
  5 minute input rate 0 bits/sec, 0 packets/sec
  5 minute output rate 0 bits/sec, 0 packets/sec
    388267 packets input, 26154659 bytes, 0 no buffer
    Received 260253 broadcasts, 0 runts, 0 giants
    0 input errors, 0 CRC, 0 frame, 0 overrun, 0 ignored, 0 abort
    388313 packets output, 26068851 bytes, 0 underruns
    0 output errors, 0 collisions, 2 interface resets
    0 output buffer failures, 0 output buffers swapped out
    36 carrier transitions
    DCD=up DSR=up DTR=up RTS=up CTS=up
```

FIGURE 9.19 Use the Show Interface command to display the status of the port and whether or not queuing is enabled.

In Figure 9.21, queuing information is displayed for the Serial 1 interface.

Use the `Show Queuing` command to display detailed information about all interfaces where queuing is enabled. The command's syntax is:

```
show queuing
```

In Figure 9.22, you can see fair and priority queuing details displayed for the relevant interfaces. Custom queuing has not been configured here.

```
Connecticut# show interface Serial1

Serial1 is up, line protocol is up
  Hardware is HD64570
  Internet address is 172.16.66.2/24
  MTU 1500 bytes, BW 1544 Kbit, DLY 20000 usec, rely 255/255, load 1/255
  Encapsulation HDLC, loopback not set, keepalive set (10 sec)
  Last input 00:00:00, output 00:00:06, output hang never
  Last clearing of "show interface" counters never
  Input queue 0/75/0 (size/max/drops); Total output drops: 0
  Output queue 0/64/0 (size/thresholds/drops)
  5 minute input rate 0 bits/sec, 0 packets/sec
  5 minute output rate 0 bits/sec, 0 packets/sec
    403949 packets input, 26679996 bytes, 0 no buffer
    Received 249071 broadcasts, 0 runts, 0 giants
    135 input errors, 0 CRC, 0 frame, 0 overrun, 0 ignored, 0 abort
    399280 packets output, 27382600 bytes, 0 underruns
    0 output errors, 0 collisions, 28 interface resets
    0 output buffer failures, 0 output buffers swapped out
    199 carrier transitions
    DCD=up DSR=up DTR=up RTS=up CTS=up
```

FIGURE 9.20   Priority queuing is enabled on Serial 1.

FIGURE 9.21
Queuing information
is displayed for the
Serial 1 interface.

```
Connecticut# show queue serial 1
  Input queue: 0/75/0 (size/max/drops); Total output drops: 0
  Output queue: 0/64/0 (size/threshold/drops)
    Conversations 0/3 (active/max active)
    Reserved Consersations 0/0 (allocated/max allocated)

Connecticut#
```

Broadcast Management

This section will describe how to handle broadcast messages in an IP network, the types of broadcasting supported by Cisco IOS 11.1, the facility for selecting which broadcasts are forwarded by a router, and how helper addresses are used to assist the movement of broadcast traffic through a network.

Managing Broadcasts

A broadcast is a data packet destined for all hosts on a network. Broadcasts are identified by a broadcast address, a special address reserved for sending a message to all stations. The IP network administrator is responsible for controlling broadcast messages on the network.

FIGURE 9.22
Fair and priority queuing details displayed for the relevant interfaces.

```
Connecticut# show queuing
Current fair queue configuration:
interface BRI0

    Input queue: 0/75/0 (size/max/drops); Total output drops: 0
    Output queue: 0/64/0 (size/threshold/drops)
        Conversations 0/3 (active/max active)
        Reserved Consersations 0/0 (allocated/max allocated)

interface Serial1

    Input queue: 0/75/0 (size/max/drops); Total output drops: 0
    Output queue: 0/64/0 (size/threshold/drops)
        Conversations 0/3 (active/max active)
        Reserved Consersations 0/0 (allocated/max allocated)

Current priority queue configuration

List    Queue     Args
1       low       default
1       high      protocol ip          tcp port
1       high      protocol ip          list1
1       medium    protocol appletalk

List    Queue     Args
1       medium    protocol ipx
1       normal    protocol ip
1       high      interface Serial0
1       high      limit 15
1       medium    limit 20
1       normal    limit 20
1       low       limit 30
```

Cisco IOS 11.1 supports IP broadcasts on both LANs and WANs. It can be configured to generate any form of IP broadcast address. The default is an address consisting of four octets of ones (255.255.255.255). Cisco IOS 11.1 supports two types of broadcasting: *directed broadcasting* and *flooding*.

A directed broadcast is a packet sent to a specific network or series of networks. A flooded broadcast packet is sent to every network. A directed broadcast address includes the network or subnet fields. For example, if the network address is 172.16.0.0, the address 172.16.255.255 indicates all hosts on network 172.16.0.0. This would be a directed broadcast. If network 172.16.0.0 has a subnet mask of 255.255.255.0 (the third octet is the subnet field), the address 172.16.5.255 specifies all hosts on subnet 5 of network 172.16.0.0, another directed broadcast.

Broadcast packets can cause a serious network overload known as a *broadcast storm*, is an undesirable network event in which many broadcasts are sent simultaneously across all network segments. The old broadcast standard uses four octets of all zeros instead of all ones to indicate broadcast addresses. Many implementations using this standard do not recognize an all-ones broadcast address and fail to respond to the broadcast correctly. Others forward all-ones broadcasts, causing a serious network overload. Such broadcast storms use substantial network bandwidth and, typically, cause network time-outs.

Routers do not forward broadcast packets, by default. They provide some protection from broadcast storms by limiting their extent to the local cable. However, bridges will propagate broadcast storms, as they are OSI Layer 2 devices which forward broadcasts to all network segments.

The best solution to broadcast storms is to use a single broadcast address scheme on a network. Modern IP implementations allow the network administrator to set the address used as the broadcast address. Cisco IOS 11.1 accepts and interprets all possible forms of broadcast address.

The current broadcast standard provides specific addressing schemes for forwarding broadcasts. The IP Broadcast-Address command allows you to specify the IP broadcast address for your network. This takes the specified IP address as its only argument. When you wish to specify the IP broadcast address on a router without nonvolatile memory (NVRAM), you need to set jumpers in the processor configuration register (Bit 10 and Bit 14).

Consider an interface where directed broadcasts are translated to physical broadcasts. You can use the IP Directed-Broadcast command to enable "directed broadcast-to-physical broadcast" translation on the interface. Forwarding of directed broadcasts on this type of interface is enabled, by default, for those protocols configured using the IP Forward-Protocol Global Configuration command.

You have the option of defining an access list to control which broadcasts are forwarded. Only those IP packets permitted by the access list are eligible to be translated from directed broadcasts to physical broadcasts. You provide the access list number as the optional argument to the IP Directed-Broadcast command.

You can allow IP broadcasts to be flooded throughout your internetwork in a controlled fashion. This feature also helps prevent routing loops. Broadcast traffic received on an interface is sent out from all interfaces on that device, except the interface on which the information was originally received. In Figure 9.23, the broadcast packet arriving on interface E0 is flooded to interfaces E1, E2, and S0.

Broadcast flooding can be done in a controlled manner using the database created by the *Bridging Spanning-Tree* protocol. A spanning-tree is a loop-free subset of a network topology. The Spanning-Tree protocol is a bridge protocol that utilizes the spanning-tree algorithm, enabling a learning bridge to dynamically work around loops in a network topology by creating a spanning tree. Bridges exchange hello messages (Bridge Protocol Data Units—BPDUs) with other bridges to detect loops, and then remove the loops by shutting down selected bridge interfaces. Cisco IOS 11.1 provides the IP Forward-Protocol Spanning-Tree command to achieve flooding of UDP datagrams using the bridging spanning-tree database.

FIGURE 9.23
The broadcast packet arriving on interface E0 is flooded to interfaces E1, E2, and S0.

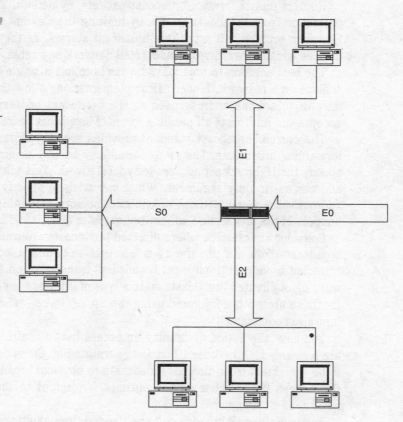

Bridging must be configured on each interface that is to participate in the flooding. In addition, the routing software must include transparent bridging. Transparent bridging refers to a scheme where bridges pass frames along one hop at a time, based on tables which associate end nodes with bridge ports. Its name derives from the presence of bridges transparent to network end nodes. If bridging is not configured on an interface, it can receive broadcasts but can never forward them.

Packets must meet all the following criteria before they can be considered candidates for flooding:

- The packet must be a MAC-level broadcast.
- The packet must be an IP-level broadcast (not all MAC-level broadcasts are IP broadcasts).
- The packet must be a TFTP, DNS, NetBIOS, ND, or BOOTP packet, or a UDP protocol specified by the `IP Forward-Protocol` command. These are the most common users of the broadcast feature and the ones you may want to flood.
- The packet's time-to-live (TTL) value must be two or greater.

A flooded UDP packet is given the destination address specified with the `IP Broadcast-Address` command on the output interface. The destination address may change as the packet propagates through the network, but the source address remains constant. The TTL value is also decreased as propagation continues.

The broadcast packet is handed to the normal IP output routines once the decision has been made to send it out on an interface. The broadcast packet is therefore subject to whatever filters and access lists are defined on the output interface.

Flooding of UDP packets based on the bridging spanning-tree database is implemented using the `IP Forward-Protocol Spanning-Tree` command. The spanning-tree algorithm can be used to significantly speed-up spanning-tree-based UDP flooding. This feature is called *turboflooding*. Enable it using the `IP Forward-Protocol Turbo-Flood` global configuration command.

Turboflooding is supported over Ethernet interfaces configured for ARPA encapsulated, Fiber Distributed Data Interface (FDDI), and HDLC-encapsulated serial interfaces. It is not supported on token ring interfaces. As long as the token rings and the non-HDLC serial interfaces are not part of the bridge group used for UDP flooding, turboflooding will behave normally.

IP Helper Address

Network hosts can use UDP broadcasts to determine address, configuration, and name information. If the network host is on a segment that has no server, UDP broadcasts are normally not forwarded. You can overcome this problem by configuring a *helper address* on the interface where broadcasts are expected.

The helper address is the address to which selected classes of broadcasts received on an interface will be sent. Helper address configuration provides proper connectivity by forwarding broadcast traffic that might not otherwise transit the network.

You can configure a number of helper addresses on each interface. Where a helper address has been defined for an interface, UDP and Network Disk (ND) forwarding are enabled by default. Cisco IOS gives you the option of specifying a UDP destination port to control which UDP services are forwarded. You are allowed to specify multiple UDP protocols.

If you configure the forwarding of UDP broadcasts without specifying a UDP port, you effectively configure the router to act as a BOOTP forwarding agent. BOOTP is a protocol used by diskless workstations to discover their IP address, the address of a server host, and the name of a file to be loaded into memory and executed at boot time. BOOTP packets can carry Dynamic Host Configuration Protocol (DHCP) information. This makes Cisco IOS compatible with DHCP clients.

Broadcast packets forwarded to a single network address using the IP helper address mechanism can be flooded. Only one copy of the packet is sent over each network segment.

Let's consider the IP helper address example presented in the graphic. The IP Forward-Protocol command specifies which class of broadcast packet will be forwarded. Here, the decision is to forward UDP broadcasts. No UDP port is specified, so the router will act as a BOOTP forwarding agent.

In Figure 9.24, broadcasts are expected on the Ethernet 0 interface. Therefore, this is the interface on which to configure helper addresses.

FIGURE 9.24
Broadcasts are expected on the Ethernet 0 interface, and this is the interface on which to configure helper addresses.

```
Connecticut> enable
Password:
Connecticut# config term
Enter configuration commands, one per line. End with CNTL/Z.
Connecticut(config)# ip forward-protocol udp
Connecticut(config)# interface ethernet0
Connecticut(config-if)# ip address 12 9.108.2.18 255.255.255
Connecticut(config-if)# ip helper-address 144.253.1.2
Connecticut(config-if)# ip helper-address 144.253.3.4
Connecticut(config-if)#
```

The IP Helper-Address command accomplishes the following: it enables forwarding and it specifies the destination address for UDP broadcast packets.

This effectively changes a destination address from a broadcast to a unicast address.

Here, two helper addresses are configured on the Ethernet 0 interface of the main router. Incoming UDP broadcast packets received on this interface are to be forwarded to host addresses 172.16.1.2 and 172.16.3.4. Subnetting is in operation in this example, with the third portion of the address acting as the subnet identifier. Thus, helper addressing provides a simple mechanism for controlling how broadcast traffic flows within and between networks.

IPX Overview and Addressing

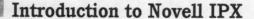

Introduction to Novell IPX

This chapter introduces Novell IPX, its protocols, addressing formats, and routing procedures and explains how the Novell/IPX protocol suite maps to the OSI model. We outline the features of Novell/IPX, describe the protocols in the Novell/IPX protocol stack, and outline the media access control protocols that support Novell IPX.

Novell/IPX Protocol Stack

NetWare is a network operating system (NOS) and related support services environment created by Novell. It was introduced to the market in the early 1980s. Its networking technology was derived from Xerox Networks Systems (XNS), a networking system developed in the late 1970s.

Today, NetWare is used worldwide. As internetwork connections increase, NetWare and its supporting protocols often operate on the same physical channel as other popular protocols such as TCP/IP, DECnet, and AppleTalk.

As a NOS environment, NetWare provides support for file sharing, printer sharing, electronic mail transfer, and database access.

NetWare is based on a client/server architecture. Clients or workstations request services such as file and printer access from servers. NetWare clients and servers can be represented by virtually any kind of computer system, from PCs to mainframes.

In the client/server system remote network access is transparent to the user. This is accomplished through remote procedure calls. A server receives a procedure call from a local computer program running on a client or workstation. The server then executes the remote procedure call and returns the requested information to the local computer client.

Novell's Internetwork Packet Exchange (IPX) is a proprietary protocol derived from the Xerox Network Systems (XNS) protocol (Figure 10.1).

Novell Internetwork Packet Exchange (IPX)—functioning at the heart of the NetWare protocol suite—is the original network-layer protocol used to route packets through an internetwork. IPX is a connectionless datagram-based network protocol and as such is similar to the Internet Protocol (IP) found in Transmission Control Protocols (TCP/IP) networks.

The Novell/IPX protocol stack corresponds loosely to the OSI model but does not map exactly onto it. NetWare protocol designers wanted to provide a high level of functionality rather than adhering strictly to existing standards.

As a NOS environment, NetWare specifies the upper five layers of the OSI reference model. The Novell/NetWare protocols can be grouped as shown.

FIGURE 10.1
Novell's Internetwork
Packet Exchange is a
proprietary protocol
derived from the
Xerox Network
Systems protocol.

Applications		NetWare Core Protocol (NCP)	RPC-basaed application	LU6.2 support
NetBIOS emulator	NetWare shell (client)		RPC	
	SPX		UDP	
		UDP		
RIP		SAP		NLSP
Ethernet /IEEE 802.3	Token Ring/ IEEE 802.5	FDDI	ARCnet	PPP

The NetWare Core Protocol (NCP) corresponds roughly to the OSI application, presentation, and session layers. The Network Basic Input/Output System (NetBIOS) emulator corresponds roughly to the session and transport layers, although it is usually known as a session layer interface specification. Servers and routers use the Service Advertisement Protocol (SAP) to advertise their services and network addresses. SAP corresponds to the OSI transport and network layers as well as the upper layers. Sequenced Packet Exchange (SPX) is a transport layer protocol. Internet Packet Exchange (IPX), Routing Information Protocol (RIP), and Novell Link Services Protocol (NLSP) are network layer protocols.

At the lower layer are the media access control (MAC) protocols on which Novell IPX can run. These are Ethernet/IEEE 802.3, Token Ring/IEEE 802.5, Fiber Distributed Data Interface (FDDI), ARCnet, and Point-to-Point protocol (PPP).

The higher level protocols such as NetBIOS, SAP, NCP, SPX, NLSP, and RIP rely on the MAC protocols and IPX to handle lower level communications, for example, node addressing.

Novell IPX Features

Novell IPX is a network-layer/transport-layer protocol. It defines internetwork and internode addresses, and routes packets in an IPX internetwork. To communicate with devices on different networks, IPX routes the information through intermediate networks. IPX uses the physical device address of the underlying hardware and its socket, that is, a service address, to address the packet to its final node destination.

Novell IPX is also a datagram connectionless protocol. A *datagram* is a logical grouping of information sent as a network layer unit over a transmission medium without prior establishment of a virtual circuit. When processes running on two separate nodes use IPX to communicate, no connection is established between the nodes before data is transmitted.

Because it is a connectionless protocol, IPX does not require an acknowledgment for each packet sent.

IPX uses the services of the dynamic distance vector routing protocol, Routing Information Protocol (RIP), or the link-state routing protocol, NetWare Link Services Protocol (NLSP). RIP is used by Novell IPX to route packets in an internetwork. RIP uses IPX and the Media Access Control (MAC) protocols for its transport. The IPX RIP metrics used for making decisions on the optimal path are *ticks* (a time measure), and *hop count*. The tick metric, in principle is the delay expected when using a particular path length. One tick is 1/18th of a second. In the case of two paths with an equal tick count, IPX RIP uses the hop count, the passage of a packet through a router, as the tie breaker.

Routing updates are sent at 60-second intervals. The high frequency of updates can cause excessive overhead traffic on some internetworks. For more on IPX RIP and NLSP see Chapter 11.

Novell IPX uses the proprietary Service Advertisement Protocol (SAP) to advertise network services. SAP allows nodes such as file servers or print servers to advertise both their addresses and the services they provide. Servers running SAP identify themselves and advertise their services by broadcasting a service identification packet.

Advertisements are sent via SAP every 60 seconds. Services are identified by a hexadecimal number which is called a SAP identifier, for example, 4=file server and 7=printer server. Routers gather this information and share it with other routers.

Workstations on the network can utilize SAP to determine which services are available on the network. This information is obtained by using a service query packet. Workstations can reference information in the IPX header to find a service address with which to initiate a session.

Novell has introduced a link-state protocol called *Novell Link Services Protocol (NLSP)* intended to replace RIP and SAP. NLSP was derived from ISO's Intermediate System-to-Intermediate System (IS-IS) protocol. NLSP routers exchange information to maintain a logical map of the internetwork. This information includes connectivity states path costs, maximum transmission unit size, and media types.

The Sequenced Packet Exchange (SPX) is a reliable connection-oriented protocol that supplements the datagram service provided by IPX, NetWare's network layer protocol. Under a connection-oriented protocol, data transfer must occur over a virtual circuit. SPX supplements the datagram service provided by network-layer protocols and provides the packet verification lacking in IPX routing.

The upper-layer NetWare Core Protocol (NCP) is used by IPX to provide client-to-server connections and applications. Services provided by NCP include file access, printer access, name management, accounting, security, and file synchronization.

As well as having its own protocol suite, Novell IPX supports a number of other upper-layer protocols and applications. For example Novell IPX supports the Network Basic Input/Output System (NetBIOS) session-layer interface specification from IBM and Microsoft. Novell's NetBIOS emulation software allows programs written to the industry-standard NetBIOS interface to run within the NetWare system.

NetWare Media Access

Novell IPX can run on any of the following lower-layer media access control (MAC) protocols:

- Ethernet/IEEE 802.3
- Token ring/IEEE 802.5
- Fiber Distributed Data Interface (FDDI)
- ARCnet
- Point-to-Point Protocol (PPP)

Ethernet and IEEE 802.3 specify similar technologies. They are both carrier-sense multiple access/collision detection (CSMA/CD) LANs. Today the term Ethernet is applied to all CSMA/CD LANs, including IEEE 802.3, that generally conform to Ethernet specifications. CSMA/CD stations are those that can detect transmission collisions occurring when two stations simultaneously transmit over a network; so that CSMA/CD stations know when data should be retransmitted.

Ethernet itself provides services which correspond to the physical and data-link layers of the OSI model.

The data-link layer in the OSI model corresponds to two sublayers, logical link control (LLC) and media access control (MAC), in IEEE architecture. IEEE 802.3 specifies the physical layer and the media-access portion of the OSI data-link layer. However it does not define a logical link control protocol. So there are very slight differences between Ethernet and IEEE 802.3 in relation to the OSI model as modified by IEEE.

The term token ring is generally used to refer to IBM's token ring network and IEEE 802.5 networks. The associated protocols use the token passing media access method. A small frame called a token is moved around the network. Token ring specifies the physical layer and the MAC, but not the LLC section of the data link layer.

FDDI is similar to token ring/IEEE 802.5 as it also uses the token passing media access method. It is based on the structure of two rings, one to move data and one to perform backup and other services. The FDDI ANSI standard consists of four parts. The Physical Media Dependent (PMD) and the Physical layer (PHY) correspond to the physical layer of the OSI model. The Media Access Control (MAC) corresponds to the lower half of the OSI data-link layer. The fourth part is Station Management, which fixes faults on the ring, gets data on and off the ring, and generates data.

Attached Resource Computer Network (ARCnet) is a simple network system that supports twisted-pair, coaxial, and fiber optic cable types. It combines the token-passing element of token ring with the bus and star topologies. ARCnet functions map evenly to the physical and data-link layers of the OSI model.

The Point-to-Point Protocol (PPP) also maps exactly to the data-link and physical layers of the OSI model. PPP provides router-to-router and host-to-host connections. At the data link layer it uses the Logical Link Control protocol to manage point-to-point connections. It also uses the High Level Data Link (HLDL) protocol as the basis of encapsulating datagrams over point-to-point links.

IPX Addressing

Here we present an overview of the elements and procedures involved in IPX addressing and routing.

We examine the format of IPX addresses and outline the encapsulation types used by Novell IPX and the elements of the IPX packet header. We discuss how to assign network numbers and encapsulation types when enabling IPX on interfaces.

IPX Address

A Novell IPX address is made up of a network number and a node element. In text format, these elements are separated by a period, so IPX addresses are represented in the form `network.node`. In IPX packets the address is represented in a sequence of 80 bits.

The network number identifies a physical network. It contains 32 of the 80 bits that make up the IPX address. A network must have a number that is unique throughout the entire IPX internetwork. A network administrator assigns the network number. A network number can be expressed as eight hexadecimals. For example, 0000004A is a valid network number.

When you use Cisco IOS software you need not enter all of the eight hexadecimal digits in a network number. You can omit leading zeros. So 0000004A becomes 4A.

The remaining 48 bits in the IPX address are used for the node number. The node number is represented by a dotted triplet of four-digit hexadecimal numbers. For example, an IPX network address might be 4A.0000.0C00.23FE. Here 0000.0C00.23FE is the node number. The node number contains the Media Access Control (MAC) address of the interface. A MAC address is a standardized, link-layer address required for every port or device connected to a LAN. MAC addresses are six bytes long.

IPX's use of a MAC address for the node number allows sending nodes to predict what MAC address to use on a data link. In contrast, because the host portion of an IP network address has no correlation to the MAC address, IP nodes must use the Address Resolution Protocol (ARP), an Internet protocol used to map an IP address to a MAC and defined in RFC 826, to determine the destination MAC address. Since with IPX, the interface MAC address is part of the logical address, an Address Resolution Protocol (ARP) is not needed. The MAC address is usually used to identify the interface.

IPX Encapsulation Types

Encapsulation is the process of packaging upper-layer protocol information and data into a frame. A frame is an information unit whose source and destination is a link-layer entity. Encapsulation uses the frame formats of the MAC protocols. Many MAC protocols are from the IEEE 802.x series and specify particular header types which are used in IPX encapsulation.

Depending on what interface type is used, there are many different encapsulation formats available when using IPX routing. In particular, Ethernet, token ring, FDDI, and PPP frame formats are used by IPX. The most common IPX Ethernet packet encapsulation formats are Ethernet version 2 and Ethernet 802.3. Ethernet version 2, also known as Ethernet II, is recommended for networks that handle both TCP/IP and IPX traffic. It includes the standard Version 2 header, Destination and Source Address fields, followed by an Ether Type # field.

NOTE

IEEE 802.2 and IEEE 802.3 are LAN protocols. IEEE 802.2 specifies an implementation of the Logical Link Control sublayer of the data link layer. It handles error, framing, flow control, and the network layer service interface. IEEE 802.3 specifies an implementation of the physical layer and the Media Access Control sublayer of the data link layer.

Ethernet 802.3 is Ethernet's *raw* format. This means that an IEEE 802.3 header is used alone, without the usual IEEE 802.2 frame information. 802.3 is the default frame type for NetWare 3.1, but you cannot send IPX packets containing checksums encapsulated in 802.3 frames. The default frame type for NetWare 4 and later releases is Ethernet 802.2.

For each Novell packet format, Cisco has a keyword. For example, the keyword for Ethernet 2.0 is `Arpa`. The keyword for Ethernet 802.3 is `Novell Ether`.

Novell developments now allow the encapsulation of IPX packets in standard 802.3 frames using Service Access Point (SAP), a field defined by the 802.2 specification which is part of an address. A SAP is also a logical interface between two adjacent OSI protocol layers. The Cisco keyword for this frame format is `SAP`.

The SubNetwork Access Protocol (SNAP) which extends the IEEE 802.2 headers has also been developed. In Cisco terms this frame format is known as *SNAP*.

Both SAP and SNAP encapsulations include the 802.2 Logical Link Control protocol (LLC). This protocol handles error control, flow control, framing, and MAC sublayer addressing.

Cisco routers support all these frame encapsulation formats. Comparable raw (802.3), SAP, and SNAP frame formats used by other media access control protocols are supported by IPX.

FDDI has a raw 802.3 frame format which has the Cisco keyword `Novell-FDDI`. The FDDI SAP format consists of a standard FDDI MAC header followed by an 802.2 LLC header. The FDDI SNAP format consists of an FDDI MAC header followed by an 802.2 SNAP LLC header. The SAP and SNAP Cisco keywords remain the same.

Token ring has no raw 802.3 format but has SAP and SNAP formats. The token ring SAP format is the standard 802.5 MAC header followed by an 802.2 LLC header. The SNAP format consists of the 802.5 header followed by a SNAP LLC header.

On serial interfaces, Novell IPX uses PPP's HDLC encapsulation. The PPP/HDLC frame format has the following fields:

■ Flag—marks start or end of frame

- Address—broadcast address
- Control—similar to LLC
- Protocol—encapsulated protocol name
- Datagram—datagram contained
- Frame check sequence—error control

IPX Packet Format

The IPX packet is similar to an XNS packet and consists of two parts:

- A 30-byte (minimum) IPX header containing various packet fields
- Data, including the header of a higher level protocol

The IPX Packet format has several fields. The checksum field is a 16-bit field that is set to 1s. The checksum is set to all 1s (FFFF) since it is not used. The packet length field is a 16-bit field. It specifies the length, in bytes, of the complete IPX datagram. The packet length is at least 30 bytes.

IPX packets can be any size up to the particular media maximum transmission unit (MTU). The MTU is the maximum packet size in bytes that a particular interface can handle. For example, Ethernet 2.0 packets are limited to a packet size of 1,500 bytes. The maximum packet size that IPX can transmit is 65,535 bytes.

The transport control field is 8 bits long. It indicates the number of routers that the packet has passed through. On a RIP-based IPX router, IPX packets whose transport control field reaches 16 are discarded under the assumption that a routing loop might be occurring. Sending nodes always set this field to zero when building an IPX packet. Routers receiving packets that require more routing increase the field by one and then route the packet.

The packet type field is also an 8-bit field. The information in this field specifies which upper-layer protocol, such as NCP, SAP, SPX, NetBIOS, or RIP, is to receive the packet's information. When the value is 5, the protocol will be SPX. When the value is 17, NCP is specified.

The destination network, destination node, and destination socket fields specify relevant destination information. The destination network is the number of the network to which the destination node is attached. When this field is zero, the sending and receiving nodes are assumed to be on the same network segment.

The destination node field represents the physical address of the destination node. The socket field is the socket address of the packet destination process. (A *socket* is a software structure operating as a communications end point within a network device.)

The corresponding source fields specify the following source information: source network, source node, and source socket.

The upper-layer data field contains information required for upper-layer processes such as headers of upper-level protocols like NCP or SPX. Data for these headers are contained in the data portion of the IPX packet.

Assigning IPX Network Addresses

When configuring IPX on Cisco routers you need to plan your network address assignment. During the course of IPX configuration you assign network numbers to individual interfaces. This enables IPX routing on those interfaces.

Your first step in configuring IPX is to enable IPX routing. This involves entering the IPX Routing command in Configuration mode, and then entering the node number of the router. If you do not specify the node number, the Cisco IOS software uses the hardware Media Access Control (MAC) address currently assigned to it. This might be, for example, the MAC address of the first Ethernet, token ring, or FDDI interface card.

Figure 10.2 shows the format of the command to enable IPX routing. The IPX host address is defaulted to the first IEEE conformance interface, Ethernet 0.

```
ipx routing
inteface ethernet0
```

FIGURE 10.2   The format of the command to enable IPX routing and the IPX host address is defaulted to the first IEEE conformance interface.

Once you have enabled IPX routing on an interface, you can specify an encapsulation or frame type for packets being transmitted. A single interface can support either a single network or multiple logical networks. If you use a single network, you can configure any encapsulation type as long as it matches that of the clients and servers using that network number.

Figure 10.3 shows the format of the command used to assign a network number to an interface that supports a single network. After you have entered ipx network you add in the network number you have specified, for example, 4A.

You then have the option of entering an encapsulation type using the appropriate Novell keyword. For example you may enter encapsulation arpa for an Ethernet interface.

In a manner different from that of single networks, if you are assigning network numbers to an interface that supports multiple networks you must specify different encapsulation types for each network. Multiple networks assigned to an interface all share the same physical medium. Assigning different encapsulation types allows Cisco IOS software to identify the packets that belong to each network.

```
ipx network network [encapsulation encapsulation type]
ipx network 4A encapsulation arpa
```

FIGURE 10.3 The format of the command used to assign a network number to an interface that supports a single network.

A network administrator is configuring IPX using a single Ethernet cable. There are four packet encapsulation types supported for Ethernet. Up to four IPX networks can be configured in accordance with the four Ethernet encapsulation types available. As with single networks, the encapsulation type for each of the multiple networks should match the servers and clients using the same network number.

To assign network numbers to interfaces that support multiple networks, you usually use *subinterfaces*, so that several logical interfaces or networks can be associated with a single hardware or physical interface.

To enable IPX on the multiple networks you first enable IPX routing and then follow two other configuration steps. In Figure 10.4 we see the command that allows you to complete the first step of specifying a subinterface. For more information on enabling IPX routing and practice sessions, see Chapters 11 and 12.

```
interface type number. subinterface number
interface ethernet 0.1
```

FIGURE 10.4 The command that makes it possible to complete the first step of specifying a subinterface.

Enter interface, then the interface type, for example Ethernet. The number segment refers to a port, connector, or interface card number. Following a period, type a subinterface number that is associated with the interface referred to earlier in the command. A subinterface number can be in the range 1 to 4,294,967,293.

Once you have specified the subinterface, the second step is identical to that used to enable IPX on a single network (Figure 10.5). Enter ipx network, add in the appropriate network number and assign an encapsulation type.

```
interface ethernet 0.1
 ipx network 1 encapsulation novell-ether
interface ethernet 0.2
 ipx network 2 encapsulation snap
interface ethernet 0.3
 ipx network 3 encapsulation arpa
interface ethernet 0.4
 ipx network 4 encapsulation sap
```

To configure more than one subinterface repeat these two steps, remembering to vary the encapsulation type each time. Another possible way of configuring multiple networks on an interface is first to assign a primary and then a secondary network. However, primary and secondary networks will not be supported by future Cisco IOS software releases.

When you specify an individual subinterface, any interface configuration parameters you use, for example a routing update timer, are applied only to that subinterface.

NetWare Transport and Upper Layers

This section describes IPX services and NetWare's transport and upper layer protocols. We describe how services are advertised and requested on IPX networks using Novell's Service Advertisement Protocol (SAP). We provide an overview of NetWare's transport layer protocols and describe NetWare upper layer protocols and services.

IPX SAP and GNS Overview

The complete Novell NetWare system provides the following services: file, print, message, application, and database. NetWare is based on a *server-centric architecture*. This means that remote devices appear local to the user.

All the servers on NetWare internetworks can advertise their services and addresses using Service Advertisement Protocol (SAP). All servers and routers keep a complete list of the services available throughout the network. Service advertisements synchronize the list of available services. Adding, finding, and removing services on an IPX network is dynamic because of SAP advertisements.

Each SAP service is identified by a hexadecimal number. Some typical examples would be:

- File server—hex 4
- Print server—hex 7
- Remote bridge server—hex 24

An IPX client needs to broadcast a Get Nearest Server (GNS) request when it requires a specific service. Responses to a GNS request can come from local servers, local routers, or remote servers.

A GNS request is a broadcast issued by a client using IPX SAP. A GNS packet requests a specific service from a server. The nearest NetWare server offering the service responds with another SAP. A GNS response allocates a server to the client, allowing the client to log in to the target server and proceed to use server resources.

The Cisco router can respond to a GNS request on a network segment, but does not perform the nearest-server function. A router acts like a server by building a SAP table. If real NetWare servers are located on the segment, they should be first, to respond to the client request.

The router's GNS response can be delayed to allow local servers to respond first. On Cisco routers you can use the IPX GNS-Response-Delay command to specify the length of time (in milliseconds) that a router should wait before sending a GNS response. The default is 0 milliseconds or no delay. Zero delay indicates the assumption that no server is present on this segment and a rapid response by the router is desirable.

By default, Cisco routers running IOS 11.1 respond to GNS requests with the most recently known and available server of the type requested. However, you can configure the router to use a *round-robin* strategy in an effort to spread work evenly among servers. With round robin, the router answers successive GNS requests for a particular server by providing the address of the next server available. One undesirable side effect of round robin is the tendency to allocate remote servers when closer ones are available. To configure a router for round-robin operation use the IPX GNS-Round-Robin command.

A Cisco router does not forward individual SAP broadcasts. SAP tables are created and maintained by routers to state advertised internetwork server information. Instead, the SAP table is advertised at regular intervals. The default interval is 60 seconds.

A router will always accept service information as long as the server's network is reachable. When a server for a GNS response is chosen, the *tick value* of the route to each eligible server is used as the metric. The tick value is a delay time measurement used as the primary metric in determining the best path to a destination. If the tick values are equal, then hop count is used as the tiebreaker.

NetWare Transport Layer

NetWare has a large variety of protocols and programming interfaces associated with it. These protocols are modular and layered, but they do not fit neatly into OSI's seven-layer model.

The transport layer handles conversations between end nodes. This type of flow control is called *end-to-end flow control*: just the sender and the receiver are involved in recovering lost or delayed packets on the internetwork.

Sequenced Packet Exchange (SPX) is the most commonly used NetWare transport protocol. Novell derived this protocol from the Sequenced Packet Protocol (SPP) of the XNS protocol suite. SPX uses *segment sequencing* to reorder segments that are received in a different order to that transmitted. Segment sequencing numbers are unique. When all the segments for a given message have arrived at their destination, the message is rebuilt by shuffling the segments into their correct order.

SPX is a reliable, connection-oriented protocol. SPX supplements the datagram service provided by Layer 3 protocols. It monitors network transmissions to ensure successful delivery.

Data segments can be lost, delayed, or corrupted as they travel through the network. SPX verifies and acknowledges successful packet delivery to any network destination. SPX requests verification from the destination that transmitted data was successfully received. Received verifications must include a value or checksum that matches a value calculated from the data before transmission. By comparing checksums, SPX can ensure error-free delivery of the transmitted data packet.

SPX can track data transmissions consisting of a series of separate packets. If an acknowledgment request is not received within a specified time, SPX will retransmit the entire series of packets in the transmission. When a specific number of retransmissions fail to return a positive acknowledgment, SPX assumes the connection has failed and warns the operator.

Cisco IOS 11.1 supports SPX *spoofing*, a scheme used by Cisco routers to cause a host to treat an interface as if it were up and supporting a session. The router "spoofs" replies to keepalive messages from the host in order to convince the host that the session still exists. This feature allows clients and servers to create their own *watchdog keepalive* packets at a user-defined rate. Watchdog spoofing allows a router to act for a NetWare client by sending watchdog packets to a NetWare server to keep the session between client and server active.

SPX spoofing receives, recognizes, and successfully acknowledges these packets at both the client and server ends of a wide-area link. Requests for the transmission of legitimate information triggers the dial-up connection, resulting in reduced WAN costs.

Novell also offers Internet Protocol (IP) support in the form of User Datagram Protocol/Internet Protocol (UDP/IP) encapsulation of other Novell packets. IPX/SPX datagrams are encapsulated inside UDP/IP headers for transport across an IP-based internetwork.

The User Datagram Protocol (UDP), like TCP, provides transport services. Unlike TCP, it is not connection-oriented, does not acknowledge data receipt, and simply accepts and transports datagrams. Datagram delivery is accomplished by assigning a port address, a pointer to a local process rather than a virtual circuit connection. UDP usually transfers data faster than TCP. This is because UDP is not concerned with processes such as establishing and maintaining connections, controlling data flow, or other overheads incurred by connection-oriented protocols.

NetWare Upper Layer Protocols and Services

NetWare supports a wide variety of upper-layer protocols.

The NetWare shell (or NetWare DOS Requester) runs on clients or workstations. It consists of a number of Virtual Loadable Modules (VLMs). A VLM is a modular executable program with a set of logically grouped features. For example, transport-related functions such as "send packets" and "receive packets" fit logically into a VLM.

The NetWare shell intercepts application I/O calls to determine whether they require network access for satisfaction. If network access is required, the NetWare shell packages the requests and sends them to lower-layer software for processing and network transmission. Where network access is not required, the requests are simply passed to local I/O resources. Client applications are unaware of any network access required for completion of application calls.

NetWare Remote Procedure Call (NetWare RPC) is another more general redirection mechanism supported by Novell. RPC is a session-layer protocol. It allows local applications to call functions on other networks. Local function calls are passed to software usually called a *redirector*, *shell*, or *virtual file system interface*.

This software determines whether the call can be satisfied locally or requires a network access. If the call can be satisfied locally, then it is sent to the local operating system and completed. Otherwise the call is packaged and sent over the network to a server.

RPC servers are usually specialized service providers that can handle many RPC calls and store many files. The server executes the function call and puts the results in a reply packet. The reply packet is then returned to the original operating system or client.

The *NetWare Core Protocol (NCP)* is a series of server routines designed to satisfy application requests coming from, for example, the NetWare shell. NCPs exist for every service a workstation might request from a server. Services provided by NCP include file access, printer access, name management, accounting, security, and file synchronization. Common requests handled by NCP include creating or destroying a service connection, manipulating directories and files, opening *semaphores* (a flag used to coordinate access to global data in a multiprocess environment), and printing.

NCP comprises numerous function calls that support network services. NetWare client software running on workstations uses NCP function calls to provide transparent file and printer access to service clients.

NetWare application-layer services include:

- NetWare Message Handling Service (NetWare MHS)
- Btrieve
- NetWare Loadable Modules (NLMs)
- Various IBM connectivity features

Messaging is a core network service. NetWare Message Handling Service (NetWare MHS) is a message delivery system that provides electronic mail transport. Basic MHS is the starter product in the NetWare MHS family. It provides message delivery among users on the same file server.

Global MHS is a scalable, full-featured MHS platform that provides network-wide message delivery. It supports message delivery among users at multiple file servers. NetWare Remote MHS provides laptop users with convenient asychronous access to the MHS network.

Basic MHS is fully compatible with Global MHS and offers the following features:

- It allows full-name user addressing.
- It supports third-party message applications such as electronic mail.
- Users can be imported from the NetWare bindery, to a database that contains definitions for entities such as users, groups, and workgroups, into the Basic MHS database on installation.

Typical operation of Basic MHS would be as follows. Users create messages with an MHS-compatible electronic mail application that complies with Novell's

Standard Message Format (SMF) interface. The application submits the message to Basic MHS, which delivers it to the recipient's mailbox.

Btrieve is Novell's implementation of the binary tree (btree) database access mechanism. The Btrieve key-indexed record management system is designed for high performance data handling and improved programming productivity. Btrieve allows your application to retrieve, insert, update, or delete either by key value or by sequential or random access methods.

NetWare Btrieve is server based rather than client based. It automatically creates and maintains file indexes as records are inserted, updated, and deleted. Btrieve allows file sizes of up to 4 Gigabytes. It offers consistent file structures and management routines. Btrieve permits specifying the amount of memory to reserve for the I/O cache buffers it uses to hold pages previously read. It also allows concurrent access to records in multiuser environments while ensuring file integrity.

A Btrieve application running on a server can access data on the local server or on a remote server. A Btrieve application running on a workstation can access local, remote, or local and remote data.

A NetWare Loadable Module (NLM) is a program you can load and unload from server memory while the server is running. NLMs are implemented as add-on modules that attach into the NetWare system. NLMs for alternative protocol stacks, communication services, database services, and many other services are currently available from Novell and third parties.

Novell also supports IBM Logical Unit (LU) 6.2 network addressable units (NAUs). LU 6.2 allows peer-to-peer connectivity across IBM communication environments. It allows NetWare nodes to exchange information across an IBM network. The NetWare packets are encapsulated within LU 6.2 packets for transport across the IBM network.

NetWare also supports the Network Basic Input/Output System (NetBIOS) session layer interface specification from IBM and Microsoft. NetWare's NetBIOS emulation software allows workstations within the NetWare system to run applications that support IBM's NetBIOS calls.

Implementing NLSP and IPXWAN

NLSP and IPXWAN Operation

This section looks at NLSP operation and IPXWAN features, and offers practice in the configuration of NLSP and IPXWAN on Cisco routers. We identify the advantages of using NLSP instead of RIP/SAP and identify the main features of NLSP. We describe IPXWAN explain how NLSP and IPXWAN are configured and monitored.

NLSP Benefits

The NetWare Link Services Protocol (NLSP) is a link-state routing protocol based on the Open Systems Interconnection (OSI) Intermediate System to Intermediate System (IS-IS) protocol.

In the past, IPX/SPX networks tended to be relatively small and simple. IPX RIP and SAP were generally adequate for routing over such networks. SAP is used by NetWare servers to advertise their services and addresses. For more information see Chapter 10. As networks increased in size and complexity, IPX RIP and SAP did not always offer the facilities needed for optimal routing. RIP and SAP are used in combination by IPX and in this context are referred to as RIP/SAP.

NLSP was designed to cope with the increasing complexity and size of IPX/SPX networks, and in particular to improve the scalability of IPX networks, route more effectively and efficiently, and reduce overhead and management demands.

In addition, NLSP routers are backward compatible with RIP-based routers.

NLSP's link-state operation makes it a more efficient protocol than RIP/SAP. One disadvantage of RIP/SAP is the broadcast of updates every 60 seconds; this consumes a large amount of bandwidth. In contrast, NLSP transmits information only when a change occurs in a route or service, or every two hours, whichever is first.

Multicast is a transmission method whereby only devices primed for a specified multicast packet address accept the routing information packet. When packets are broadcast, as opposed to multicast, all nodes receive the information. The multicast method uses less bandwidth than the broadcast method.

With NLSP, route or service information can be multicast instead of broadcast, if the network interface driver supports multicast transmission. With multicast addressing, routing information is sent only to other NLSP routers, not to all other devices, as with RIP. The transmission features of NLSP result in less traffic and use of bandwidth in an internetwork than RIP or SAP produce.

As a link-state protocol, NLSP allows updates resulting from topology changes to be received by routers simultaneously. In this way, NLSP supports fast convergence—where all routers share the same view of the network. Distance vector protocols like RIP are prone to slow convergence; the problem of routing loops often results.

NLSP's fast convergence has several advantages:

- It reduces the occurrence of routing loops.
- It makes it possible to discover network problems more quickly.
- It reduces the loss of in-transit packets while routers are rebuilding their databases.

NLSP's cost metric is based on a hop count of 127, in contrast to RIP's hop count of 15. This means that packets relayed by NLSP can travel through 127 routers. NLSP also permits hierarchical addressing of network nodes, allowing networks to contain thousands of LANs and servers. So NLSP supports larger IPX internetworks.

NLSP has other beneficial features such as load balancing, whereby forwarded traffic is automatically distributed across network interfaces. If two or more routes between network nodes are ascribed the same cost, NLSP will distribute the traffic evenly between them. Over WAN links, NLSP provides greater efficiency by supporting IPX header compression to reduce packet size.

NLSP improves link integrity. It periodically checks its links for connectivity and the data integrity of routing information. If a link fails, NLSP switches to an alternate link. When there are connectivity changes anywhere in the routing area NLSP updates the network topology databases stored in each node.

NLSP is fully compatible with IPX RIP and SAP. You can use NLSP and RIP routers together in the same network. NLSP can also encapsulate and propagate the routing and service information it receives from RIP/SAP devices and networks.

NLSP Features

NLSP is designed for a hierarchical routing environment where networked systems are grouped into *routing areas*. A routing area is an administrative domain where all users have network layer access to the same services. Link-state routing within a single routing area is known as *level 1 routing*.

The terminology of levels, domains, and areas is also used in OSI internetworking. However, the layer numbers for NLSP routing do not correspond with the numbering of layers in the OSI model.

Level 2 routing allows the combination of routing areas into routing domains. A level 2 router acts as a level 1 router within its own area. A domain is a group of end and intermediate systems which operates under a single set of administrative rules. It can be a company, university, or even a public carrier connecting two or more organizations.

Level 3 routing allows several domains to be grouped into a global internetwork. A level 3 router also acts as a level 2 router within its own domain.

Routing areas establish hierarchy within a network. Hierarchical routing simplifies the process of enlarging a network. It reduces the amount of information that each router must store and process to route packets in a domain.

The router at each level of the topology stores all the information for its level. For instance level 1 routers store link-state information about the level 1 area, including a record of all routers in the area, links connecting routers, and whether or not links and devices are active.

To exchange traffic with other areas, a level 1 router needs only to find the nearest level 2 router. Between areas, level 2 routers advertise the area address(es) only for their respective area, not their entire link-state databases. Between domains, level 3 routers perform similarly.

The use of routing areas results in better scaling of growing internetworks, allowing for more LANs, servers, and routers. Routing areas separate an internetwork into more manageable components.

You can manage traffic and user access to networks by using routing areas. For example, you may want to assign a route information filter which can restrict general users' access to accounting data. If you use hierarchical addressing in your internetwork then a single filter will be able to identify all the systems within a particular routing area.

NLSP routers maintain several databases to store internetwork routing information. These are the *adjacency database*, the *link-state database*, and the *forwarding database*.

An NLSP adjacency database is a router's record of the state of its connections with its immediate neighbors. It also contains information on the neighbors' attributes.

There is a particular adjacency procedure for establishing and maintaining adjacencies over a LAN. When a link becomes active, an NLSP router begins periodic transmission of hello packets to initiate a relationship with its neighbors. The router then waits for its neighbor to reply with a hello packet. Once both routers have identified each other they create an entry for each other in their adjacency databases.

An adjacency state is said to be "down" when the neighbor is in a different routing area. It is "initializing" when a one-way connection is established between a router and its neighbor. The link is "up" once hello packets have been exchanged and a two-way connection is established. If neighboring routers do not discover each other, make sure that you have defined an IPX internal network number on the routers.

Like all link-state protocols, NLSP sends information through link-state packets (LSPs). The link-state packet includes connectivity information from the adjacency database. It also contains route and services information for each of the links. LSPs are used to synchronize *link-state databases* because they are propagated throughout the routing area when routers observe topology state changes.

Two methods ensure that accurate change information is propagated: flooding and receipt confirmation. Link-state information is "flooded" (sent to all individual routers simultaneously) when a router detects a topology change. When a router receives an LSP it checks the sequence number in the packet to see if it is a newer LSP than that in its own database. If it is newer, it retransmits the LSP to all its neighbors, except those on the circuit from where the LSP was received.

LSP flooding occurs as a directed broadcast on WANs. By default, NLSP also uses broadcasts to transmit LSPs on LANs. However it is possible to multicast LSPs on LANs if all devices on the LAN support multicast.

The second method used to ensure that accurate change information is propagated is *receipt confirmation*. Under NLSP, a designated router is a router responsible for exchanges of link-state information on behalf of all other NLSP routers on the same LAN. NLSP assigns a particular router as a designated router by checking the priority field in its hello packets. You can set a priority parameter for each LAN interface on a router. The router with the highest priority is the designated router.

All routers in the same routing area should have identical link-state databases. To ensure that this is the case, the designated router on a LAN periodically floods a summary of its LSP database to all routers on that LAN. The summary is sent in a *complete sequence number packet (CSNP)*. The CSNP contains the following information about the LSPs in the sending router's database: ID, sequence number, and remaining lifetime.

If a router on a LAN has a more up-to-date LSP than the designated router's CSNP broadcast, it floods the information to all routers on the LAN. If a router has missing or out-of-date information, it multicasts a *partial sequence number packet (PSNP)*. The PSNP identifies, using its sequence number, which LSPs it needs. The designated router will then retransmit the required LSPs.

On WAN links, PSNPs are used by non-designated routers to acknowledge receipt of LSPs. This method is used instead of CNSP broadcast for synchronizing LSPs.

Routers aggregate local routing area LSP information into their link-state databases. NLSP uses fictitious *pseudonodes* to keep link-state databases to a manageable size. In a link-state database, a fictitious pseudonode represents an entire LAN. Each router represents itself as being directly connected to the pseudonode. Designated routers send out LSPs on behalf of the fictitious pseudonodes in a link-state database.

Each router uses the information in its link-state database when calculating the optimal route to a destination. *Cost* is the metric used by NLSP. It is an arbitrary value that can be based on hop count, media bandwidth, or other measures. It is assigned by a network administrator and is used by NLSP to choose the most favorable path to a destination.

Like other link-state protocols such as OSPF, NLSP uses Dijkstra's Shortest Past First (SPF) algorithm to calculate optimal routes. The paths selected by the SPF calculation are recorded in the router's forwarding database. The set of paths contained in each router's *forwarding database* is unique since it is based on that particular router's perspective. A router waits for changes to accumulate before it recomputes its forwarding database. Its calculations are made five seconds after it receives an LSP.

NLSP and IPXWAN

IPXWAN is a link-layer negotiation protocol that sets up connections for IPX over WAN links. IPXWAN was developed by Novell to standardize how IPX treats all supported wide area links. Cisco IOS software supports the IPXWAN protocol as defined in RFC 1634.

IPXWAN allows a router running IPX routing to connect through a serial link to another router also routing IPX and using IPXWAN. Network administrators can use IPXWAN when connecting over PPP, X.25, or frame relay links. IPXWAN can also be used over HDLC but the devices at both ends of the serial link must be Cisco routers.

Although IPX is a connectionless datagram protocol, WANs often use a connection-oriented call setup process. When a WAN link comes up, IPX packets are sent across to negotiate IPXWAN startup options. Once these options are agreed, normal IPX transmission can begin.

In the IPXWAN adjacency establishment procedure, the routers on each side of the WAN link use a hello process to identify each other. WAN hello packets allow routers to discover each other's identity, decide if they are in the same routing area, and determine whether other routers and their links are operational.

To establish a WAN adjacency, first both sides of the link send timer requests. The timer request includes information on the routing protocol type and the IPX network number.

The router with the higher internal address number is then designated the *requester* or *master*. The router with the lower number is known as the *responder* or *slave*. The responder sends a timer response agreeing to the link details proposed by the requester's timer request.

The two link nodes can agree to use either RIP/SAP or NLSP. Negotiations between the two link nodes vary according to which protocol is chosen.

When IPX RIP/SAP is chosen, the routers finalize negotiations by exchanging the following information:

- Delay (time for packet to reach link, measured in microseconds)
- Throughput (the interval between packets measured in seconds)
- Network number for the link
- Router names

If the link is maintained through the media access Point-to-Point protocol then the compression of header information may also need to be negotiated. Once the IPXWAN link is up, RIP/SAP can use the WAN link without any further IPXWAN processes being necessary.

When NLSP is chosen, extra negotiations are required before the final information exchange. The requester sends a pair of equally sized throughput request packets. The responder calculates the throughput value by measuring the time between the arrival of the first and second packets.

Next, the responder sends two throughput responses back to the requester node. The requester calculates the average response time of the two packets. If the requester receives no response it will repeat sending the throughput request a specified number of times. You can set both the number of retries and the length of time the node should wait for a response.

Once the throughput response has been received, a delay request and delay response are exchanged by the two nodes. These exchanges measure the time taken to get bits onto the link and propagate packets to the other side of the link.

After these interactions the NLSP protocol acts like RIP/SAP, in that the nodes exchange IPXWAN information request and response packets. NLSP routing on the link can then begin.

Once hello and information packets have been exchanged, the routers on each side of the serial link make entries for each other in their adjacency databases. For each adjacency in the database, a router will maintain a state variable indicating whether the link is up, down, or initializing. If the neighbor is not heard from during the time specified by the holding timer, the router generates a link "down" message and deletes the adjacency.

Since IPXWAN can dynamically assign parameters such as delay, throughput, and compression, it is especially appropriate when connecting Cisco routers over a WAN link. In particular, IPXWAN allows the accurate calculation of the tick value for a WAN link. If IPXWAN is not used, a default value of 6 ticks is assigned, regardless of the true speed of the link. IPXWAN must be used when connecting a Cisco router to a NetWare MultiProtocol Router (MPR).

NLSP Configuration

Assume that you want to set up NLSP routing between routers in Maine and Vermont (Figure 11.1). The connection will be made between Maine's Serial 1 interface and Vermont's Serial 0 interface. You need to assign a common network address over these two interfaces. You also assign a network address to the routers' own Ethernet interfaces to allow these networks to be accessed through NLSP.

FIGURE 11.1
Setting up NLSP routing between routers in Maine and Vermont.

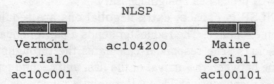

It is important to remember to assign internal network numbers to each of the routers so that neighboring routers can discover each other. In this case, you just want to use NLSP only as your protocol, so you must disable the default protocol, RIP.

You have logged on and put the Maine router in Configuration mode. The first step in configuring NLSP is to enable IPX routing on the router (Figure 11.2). As with IPX RIP routing, the command you enter to enable IPX routing on a router is ipx routing.

You then assign an internal network number to the router. (An internal network number must be assigned to each router on the network for NLSP to work.) You can assign the router the number ac100101. To do this, type

```
ipx internal-network ac100101
```

```
Maine# config terminal
Enter configuration commands, one per line. End with CNTL/Z.
Maine(config)# ipx routing
Maine(config)# ipx internal-network ac100101
Maine(config)# ipx router nlsp
Maine(config-ipx-router)# area-address 0 0
Maine(config-ipx-router)# interface ethernet0
Maine(config-if)# ipx network ac100100
Maine(config-if)# ipx nlsp enable
Maine(config-if)# interface serial1
Maine(config-if)# ipx network ac104200
Maine(config-if)# ipx nlsp enable
Maine(config-if)# exit
Maine(config)# no ipx router rip
Maine(config)# ^Z
Maine# copy running-config startup-config
Building configuration...
[OK]
Maine#
```

FIGURE 11.2   *Setting up NLSP routing in Configuration mode.*

You next enable NLSP on the router. You type `ipx router nlsp` in Configuration mode to enable NLSP routing on the Maine router.

Now you are in Router Configuration mode. Your next step is to configure an area address for the router. The syntax for the `Area-Address` command is:

```
area-address address mask
```

You can assign a set of network numbers to be included in the area or include all numbers in the area. You include all networks by setting the address and mask both to zero. Here, all networks will be included so you enter `area-address 0 0`.

Next you configure the interfaces that you want included in your NLSP internetwork. In this case you want to configure the Ethernet 0 interface for NLSP. Similarly to when you configure IPX RIP, you must put the router in Interface configuration mode.

If you type `interface ethernet 0` you are now in Interface Configuration mode and can configure additional details for the Ethernet 0 interface.

The network associated with Ethernet 0 is ac100100. To assign network ac100100 to the Ethernet 0 interface type `ipx network ac100100`.

Since IPX RIP is the default protocol for IPX routing, you don't have to specify RIP routing on interfaces when configuring ordinary IPX routing. However, NLSP routing must be specified and configured both on the router and on individual interfaces.

You enable NLSP on the Ethernet 0 interface by typing `ipx nlsp enable` in Interface mode. Maine's Serial 1 interface is connected to Vermont, so that interface also has to be configured, be assigned with a network number, and have NLSP enabled.

One other step needs to be taken to complete the configuration. Your first task in the configuration process was to enable IPX routing. When you did this, IPX RIP was enabled by default. Since you just want to run NLSP, you will have to turn off RIP routing. The correct entry to turn off IPX RIP routing on the Maine router is `no ipx router rip`.

Press **Ctrl+Z** to exit Configuration mode. Then enter `copy running-config startup-config` to save the changes.

To link the Vermont router with Maine through NLSP routing (Figure 11.3), you have logged on to the Vermont router. You have already enabled IPX routing on the Vermont router. Enter `ipx internal-network ac10c001` to assign an internal network number. The `Internal-Network` command will not be recognized if it is not hyphenated.

NLSP is enabled on the router with the `IPX Router NLSP` command. You are now in Router Configuration mode.

Once you have enabled NLSP on the router, assign an NLSP area address by entering `area-address 0 0`. Again, the hyphenation of the `Area-Address` command is essential. Enter Interface Configuration mode and configure Ethernet 0 by typing `interface ethernet 0`. Then assign the network address with `ipx network ac10c000`. Then enable NLSP on the interface with `ipx nslp enable`.

Vermont's Serial 0 interface has a connection to Maine so it is being configured for NLSP. The same network number assigned for Maine's Serial 1 port is being assigned to Vermont's Serial 0 port. This is because the two routers are linked by the same interface, although the port names are different on each side. NLSP is enabled on Vermont's Interface connection.

IPX RIP is still running by default, so you must turn it off. Enter `no ipx router rip`. The configuration is complete, so you can exit Configuration mode and save the changes.

You can check the router to see which routes are connected internally, directly, or through NLSP. For example, you can view Vermont's routing table (Figure 11.4). As with IPX RIP routing, the command to show the routing table is `Show IPX Route`.

FIGURE 11.3

Linking Vermont
router with Maine
through NLSP
routing.

```
Maine# telnet dublin
Trying Vermont (172.16.66.2)... Open

User Access Verification

Password:
Vermont> enable
Password:
Vermont# config terminal
Enter configuration commands, one per line. End with CNTL/Z.
Vermont(config)# ipx routing
Vermont(config)# ipx internal-network ac10c001
Vermont(config)# ipx router nlsp
Vermont(config-ipx-router)# area address 0 0
Vermont(config-ipx-router)# interface ethernet0
Vermont(config-if)# ipx network ac10c000
Vermont(config-if)# ipx nlsp enable
Vermont(config-if)# interface serial0
Vermont(config-if)# ipx network ac104200
Vermont(config-if)# ipx nlsp enable
Vermont(config-if)# exit
Vermont(config)# no ipx router rip
Vermont(config)# ^Z
Vermont# copy running-config startup-config
Building configuration...
[OK]
Vermont#
```

```
Vermont# show ipx route
Codes: C - Connected primary network, c - Connected secondary network
       S - Static, F - Floating static, L - Local (internal), W - IPXWAN
       R - RIP, E - EIGRP, N - NLSP, X - External, A - Aggregate
       s - seconds, u - uses

5 Total IPX routes. Up to 1 parallel paths and 16 hops allowed.

No default route known.

L    AC10C001 is the internal network
C    AC104200 (HDLC),          Se0
C    AC10C000 (NOVELL-ETHER),  Et0
N    AC100100 [27][01/01] via AC100101.0000.0000.0001,  143s, Se0
N    AC100101 [27][02/01] via AC100101.0000.0000.0001,  143s, Se0
Vermont#
```

FIGURE 11.4   Use Show IPX Route to view Vermont's IPX RIP routing.

You can see that Maine's networks are now accessible to Vermont through NLSP routing.

You can also check what LSPs the link-state database contains. To view the router's NLSP link-state database type show ipx nlsp database (Figure 11.5).

The database is a level 1 routing link-state database. You can see details of both Vermont's and Maine's LSPs; for example the LSP ID number, the LSP sequence number, and the LSP checksum.

```
Vermont# show ipx nlsp database
NLSP Level-1 Link State Database: Tag Identifier = notag
LSPID                 LSP Seq Num   LSP Checksum   LSP Holdtime   ATT/P/OL
Vermont.00-00       * 0x0000000F    0xF3E9         7336           0/0/0
Vermont.01-00       * 0x00000002    0x9B48         6263           0/0/0
Vermont.02-00       * 0x00000002    0x592A         0 (6269)       0/0/0
Vermont.03-00       * 0x00000003    0x5031         0 (7335)       0/0/0
Maine.00-00           0x00000011    0xB1D7         7243           0/0/0
Maine.01-00           0x00000002    0x147D         6404           0/0/0
Vermont#
```

FIGURE 11.5   Use show ipx nlsp database to view a router's NSLP link-state database.

If you type show ipx nlsp neighbors at Vermont's Privileged mode prompt, you can see which routers are connected to it through NLSP (Figure 11.6). We can see that Maine has been logged as Vermont's neighbor.

FIGURE 11.6

Use show ipx nlsp neighbors to view which routers are connected through NLSP.

```
Vermont# show ipx nlsp neighbors
NLSP Level-1 Neighbors: Tag Identifier = notag

System Id      Interface    State   Holdtime   Priority   Circuit Id
Maine          Se0          Up      43         0          03
Vermont#
```

You can view the details of the SPF algorithm calculation by entering show ipx nlsp spf-log (Figure 11.7). For instance, the SPF log shows the triggers for recalculation and the time at which the calculation was made.

Using the Show IPX Route command at the Maine terminal lets us see that NLSP routing is connecting Vermont's networks (Figure 11.8).

FIGURE 11.7
Use show ipx nlsp
spf-log to view the
details of the SPF
algorithm calculation.

```
Vermont# show ipx nlsp spf-log

    Level 1 SPF log
     When    Duration  Nodes  Count   Triggers
   00:22:38      4       4      4      NEWLSP
   00:21:11      4       4      2      TLVCONTENT
   00:21:06      4       3      1      TLVCONTENT
   00:21:01      4       3      3      NEWLSP TLVCONTENT
   00:19:27      4       3      1      TLVCONTENT
   00:18:47      4       3      1      TLVCONTENT
   00:09:47      8       6      1      TLVCONTENT
   00:04:50      8       5      2      TLVCONTENT
   00:03:19      4       4      1      TLVCONTENT
   Vermont#
```

```
Maine# show ipx route
Codes: C - Connected primary network, c - Connected secondary network
       S - Static, F - Floating static, L - Local (internal), W - IPXWAN
       R - RIP, E - EIGRP, N - NLSP, X - External, A - Aggregate
       s - seconds, u - uses

5 Total IPX routes. Up to 1 parallel paths and 16 hops allowed.

No default route known

L    AC100101 is the internal network
C    AC100100 (NOVELL-ETHER),  Et0
C    AC104200 (HDLC),          Se1
N    AC10C000 [27][01/01] via AC10C001.0000.0000.0001,  393s, Se1
N    AC10C001 [27][02/01] via AC10C001.0000.0000.0001,  393s, Se1
Maine#
```

FIGURE 11.8   The Show IPX Route command at the Maine terminal lets us see that NLSP routing is connecting Vermont's networks.

Typing show ipx nlsp neighbors at the Maine router shows us that Vermont is logged there (Figure 11.9). If you we show ipx nlsp neighbors detail the internal address of the Vermont router is also given (Figure 11.10).

```
Maine# show ipx nlsp neighbors
NLSP Level-1 Neighbors: Tag Identifier = notag

System Id          Interface    State  Holdtime  Priority  Circuit Id
Vermont            Se1          Up     44        0         02
Maine#
```

```
Maine# show ipx nlsp neighbors detail
NLSP Level-1 Neighbors: Tag Identifier = notag

System Id          Interface    State  Holdtime  Priority  Circuit Id
Vermont            Se1          Up     44        0         02
   IPX Address:  AC10C001.0000.0000.0001
   IPX Areas:   00000000/00000000
   Uptime: 00:25:11
Maine#
```

A way of rechecking connectivity is to ping the internal network address (Figure 11.11). Include the node number in the `Ping` command. Once you enter ping ipx ac10c001.0000.0000.0001, you see that the connection between the two routers is active.

```
Maine# show ipx nlsp neighbors detail
NLSP Level-1 Neighbors: Tag Identifier = notag

System Id          Interface    State  Holdtime  Priority  Circuit Id
Vermont            Se1          Up     44        0         02
   IPX Address:  AC10C001.0000.0000.0001
   IPX Areas:   00000000/00000000
   Uptime: 00:25:11
Maine#
```

IPXWAN Configuration

IPXWAN is used to make a connection between two IPX routers over a serial link. IPXWAN can run over PPP, X.25, or frame relay links. If Cisco routers are at both ends, it can run under HDLC. You need to change the encapsulation type on the interface to one of these formats.

It is important to ensure you have no IPX addresses on the serial interfaces when configuring IPXWAN. IPXWAN does not support numbered links.

The Maine and Vermont routers have to be connected by a serial link, so you want to configure IPXWAN as the startup protocol for the link. You have logged on to the Maine router and are in Configuration mode. The connection is on Maine's Serial 1 interface. You first have to put the router in Interface Configuration mode. Type `interface serial 1` to put the router in Configuration mode for the Serial 1 interface (Figure 11.12).

```
Maine# config terminal
Enter configuration commands, one per line. End with CNTL/Z.
Maine(config)# interface serial 1
Maine(config-if)# encapsulation ppp
%LINEPROTO-5-UPDOWN:  Line protocol on Interface Serial1, changed state to down
Maine(config-if)# no ipx network
Maine(config-if)# ipx ipxwan
Maine(config-if)# ipx nlsp enable
Maine(config-if)# ^Z
Maine# copy runn start
Building configuration...
[OK]
Maine#
```

FIGURE 11.12   *Setting up IPXWAN on the Maine router.*

You need to specify an encapsulation for one of the interface types over which IPXWAN can run. In this case you have chosen to configure the link as a PPP interface. So type `encapsulation ppp`.

You can see that the line has gone down between Maine and Vermont. This is because the Serial 0 connection on the Vermont side is using the serial link HDLC method of encapsulation. Later, you will configure PPP encapsulation on Serial 0 Vermont to restore the link.

IPXWAN does not support numbered links, so it is necessary to remove assigned network addresses from the interface over which IPXWAN is running. Enter `no ipx network` to remove assigned network numbers from Maine's Serial 1 interface.

You next enable IPXWAN on the interface by typing `ipx ipxwan`.

Now you can enable NLSP on the Maine router's Serial 1 interface. Typing `ipx nlsp enable` allows NLSP to be configured on Maine's Serial 1 IPXWAN interface. Exit Configuration mode as usual by pressing **Ctrl+Z**. Then save the changes by typing `copy runn start`.

You have logged on at the Vermont router and are now in Configuration mode. First, you put the router in Interface Configuration mode. The Vermont interface that connects to Maine is its Serial 0 interface. Type `interface serial 0` (Figure 11.13).

You can set the encapsulation type for the interface as PPP by typing `encapsulation ppp` at Vermont's Interface Configuration mode prompt.

FIGURE 11.13
Setting up IPXWAN
on the Vermont
router.

```
Vermont# config terminal
Enter configuration commands, one per line. End with CNTL/Z.
Vermont(config)# interface serial 0
Vermont(config-if)# encapsulation ppp
Vermont(config-if)# no ipx network
Vermont(config-if)# ipx ipxwan
%IPXWAN Resetting Interface Serial0
Vermont(config-if)# ipx nlsp enable
Vermont(config-if)# ^Z
Vermont# copy runn start
Building configuration...
[OK]
Vermont#
```

Type no ipx network first as IPXWAN does not support network addresses. An attempt to configure IPXWAN while network addresses are still assigned on a router's interface results in an error message. Enter ipx ipxwan after networks have been disabled. The line feedback shows that the interface Serial 0 is being reset for IPXWAN.

Now you can enable NLSP on the link. The correct format of the command is ipx nlsp enable. You then exit Configuration mode and save the changes.

To monitor IPXWAN you can check the routing table to see which networks are connected (Figure 11.14). Typing show ipx route displays Vermont's routing table.

```
Vermont# show ipx route
Codes: C - Connected primary network, c - Connected secondary network
       S - Static, F - Floating static, L - Local (internal), W - IPXWAN
       R - RIP, E - EIGRP, N - NLSP, X - External, A - Aggregate
       s - seconds, u - uses

6 Total IPX routes. Up to 1 parallel paths and 16 hops allowed.

No default route known.

L    AC10C001 is the internal network
C    AC104300 (HDLC),          Se1
C    AC10C000 (NOVELL-ETHER),  Et0
N    AC100100 [45][10/01] via AC100101.0000.0000.0001,  35s, Se0
N    AC100101 [45][11/01] via AC100101.0000.0000.0001,  35s, Se0
N    AC104400 [45][10/01] via AC100101.0000.0000.0001,  35s, Se0
Vermont#
```

FIGURE 11.14   To monitor IPXWAN you can check the routing table to see which networks are connected.

You can see the internal and interface network numbers that were assigned. Maine networks are now also accessible through NLSP routing.

Much as in IPX RIP routing, you can view the details of a particular interface connection. When you type show ipx interface serial 0 you can view configuration details for the Serial 0 interface (Figure 11.15).

```
Vermont# show ipx interface serial 0
Serial0 is up, line protocol is up
  IPX address is 0.ac10.c001.0000 [up] line-up, RIPPQ: 0, SAPPQ: 0
  Delay on this IPX network, in ticks is 16 throughput 64000 link delay
  Local IPXWAN Node ID:         AC10C001/Vermont
  Network when IPXWAN master:        0 IPXWAN delay (master owns): 16
  IPXWAN Retry Interval:            20 IPXWAN Retry limit:        3
  IPXWAN Routing negotiated: NLSP
  IPXWAN State:                 Master: Connect
  State change reason: Received Router Info Rsp as Master
  Last received remote node info: AC100101/Maine
  Client mode disabled, Static mode disabled, Error mode is reset
  IPX SAP update interval is 1 minute(s)
  IPX type 20 propagation packet forwarding is disabled
  Incoming access list is not set
  Outgoing access list is not set
  IPX helper access list is not set
  SAP GNS processing enabled, delay 0 ms, output filter list is not set
  SAP Input filter list is not set
  SAP Output filter list is not set
  SAP Router filter list is not set
  Input filter list is not set
  Output filter list is not set
  Router filter list is not set
  Netbios Input host access list is not set
  Netbios Input bytes access list is not set
  Netbios Output host access list is not set
  Netbios Output bytes access list is not set
  Updates each 60 seconds, aging multiples RIP: 3 SAP: 3
  SAP interpacket delay is 55 ms, maximum size is 480 bytes
  RIP interpacket delay is 55 ms, maximum size is 432 bytess
  Watchdog spoofing is disabled, SPX spoofing is disabled, idle time 60
  IPX accounting is disabled
  IPX fast switching is configured (enabled)
  RIP packets received 52, RIP packets sent 31
  SAP packets received 1, SAP packets sent 2
  IPX NLSP is running on primary network 0
    RIP compatibility mode is AUTO (OFF)
    SAP compatibility mode is AUTO (OFF)
    Level 1 Hello interval 20 sec
    Level 1 Designated Router Hello interval 10 sec
    Level 1 CSNP interval 30 sec, LSP retransmit interval 5 sec
    Level 1 adjacency count is 1
    Level 1 circuit ID is Maine.04
Maine#
```

FIGURE 11.15   Type show ipx interface serial 0 to view configuration details for the Serial 0 interface.

Additional IPXWAN details include:

- IPXWAN retry interval
- IPXWAN retry limit
- The type of IPXWAN routing (NLSP)
- The router's IPXWAN link relationship (master)

As well as RIP and SAP packet details, you can see information on Level 1 routing such as:

- The router's NLSP Hello interval.
- The designated router's Hello interval.
- The interval between broadcast of the designated router's CSNP.

If you log on to the Maine router and enter the Show IPX Route command, you can see that the router has access to Vermont's networks (Figure 11.16).

```
Maine# show ipx route
Codes: C - Connected primary network, c - Connected secondary network
       S - Static, F - Floating static, L - Local (internal), W - IPXWAN
       R - RIP, E - EIGRP, N - NLSP, X - External, A - Aggregate
       s - seconds, u - uses

6 Total IPX routes. Up to 1 parallel paths and 16 hops allowed.

No default route known.

L    AC100101 is the internal network
C    AC100100 (NOVELL-ETHER),   Et0
C    AC104400 (HDLC),           Se0
N    AC104300 [45][10/01] via AC10C001.0000.0000.0001,   150s, Se1
N    AC10C000 [45][10/01] via AC10C001.0000.0000.0001,   150s, Se1
N    AC10C001 [45][11/01] via AC10C001.0000.0000.0001,   150s, Se1
Vermont#
```

FIGURE 11.16   Log on to the Maine router and enter the Show IPX Route command; you can see that the router has access to Vermont's networks.

The connection between Vermont and Maine is through Maine's Serial 1 interface. Type show ipx interface serial 1 to see Maine's Serial 1 details. In

Figure 11.17 we can see details similar to those in Vermont except that in this case the Maine router has assumed the role of slave or responder.

```
Maine# show ipx interface serial 1
Serial1 is up, line protocol is up
  IPX address is 0.ac10.0101.0000 [up] line-up, RIPPQ: 0, SAPPQ: 0
  Delay on this IPX network, in ticks is 16 throughput 64000 link delay 14928
  Local IPXWAN Node ID:          AC100101/Maine
  Network when IPXWAN master:        0 IPXWAN delay (master owns): 16
  IPXWAN Retry Interval:            20 IPXWAN Retry limit:        3
  IPXWAN Routing negotiated: NLSP
  IPXWAN State:                 Slave: Connect
  State change reason: Received Router Info Req as Slave
  Last received remote node info: AC10C001/Dublin
  Client mode disabled, Static mode disabled, Error mode is reset
IPX SAP update interval is 1 minute(s)
IPX type 20 propagation packet forwarding is disabled
Incoming access list is not set
Outgoing access list is not set
IPX helper access list is not set
SAP GNS processing enabled, delay 0 ms, output filter list is not set
SAP Input filter list is not set
SAP Output filter list is not set
SAP Router filter list is not set
Input filter list is not set
Output filter list is not set
Router filter list is not set
Netbios Input host access list is not set
Netbios Input bytes access list is not set
Netbios Output host access list is not set
Netbios Output bytes access list is not set
```

FIGURE 11.17   *Type show ipx interface serial 1 to see Maine's Serial 1 details.*

NLSP Route Aggregation

This section describes NLSP route aggregation, when it can be used, and how to practice configuration between different NLSP 1.1 areas. We outline how route aggregation operates and explain the operation of route aggregation between NLSP 1.1 areas. We describe how route aggregation is configured between NLSP 1.1 areas and how it is monitored. We learn how to configure multiple NLSP 1.1 areas with route aggregation.

Route Aggregation Overview

As your internetwork grows, you will require ways of managing it more efficiently. You may want to divide your internetwork into smaller, more manageable units. You may also want to control the flow of traffic from one part of the network to another.

Cisco IOS Release 11.1 has a route aggregation feature which is compatible with Novell's NLSP specification, revision 1.1.

Route aggregation allows you to:

■ Divide large IPX internetworks into multiple interconnected areas without the use of IPX RIP.
■ Redistribute route and service information directly from one NLSP area into other areas.
■ Enable route summarization between multiple NLSP areas or between NLSP and Enhanced IGRP or IPX RIP areas.

Cisco's implementation of NLSP's revision 1.1 also allows multiple instances of NLSP to run on the same router.

Novell recommends that networks containing more than 400 addresses should be split into smaller NLSP areas. Each of the multiple NLSP areas must be assigned with a unique area address. An area address consists of a pair of 32-bit hexadecimal numbers: an area number and a corresponding mask.

An example of an area address might be 01234500 ffffff00. The number 01234500 is the network address for this routing area. Every network number within that area starts with the identification 012345.

The number ffffff00 is the mask. It indicates how much of the network address identifies the area itself and how much identifies the individual networks in the area. In the area address 01234500 ffffff00, the first 24 bits (012345) identify the routing area. The remaining 8 bits are used to identify individual network numbers within the routing area, for example: 012345ab, 012345c1, or 01234511.

Area addresses are used as unique identifiers of the routers in an area. NLSP 1.1 routers within an area must have at least one area address common to all, or they cannot identify and communicate with each other. For example, for routers with the hexadecimal addresses 2845, 2425, 2122, the common area address might be 2000 f000. An area address does not necessarily have to resemble the network addresses used in the area.

A routing area can have as many as three different area addresses. Having more than one area address allows the routing area to be reorganized without interrupting operations. Any combination of area addresses can be used within a domain.

A route summary defines a set of explicit routes used by a router to generate an aggregated route. An aggregated route is a single, compact data structure that describes many IPX networks simultaneously as a single route.

When area addresses are being summarized, the bits in the mask portion indicated by the hexadecimal digit f are the common element of all addresses to be summarized. This portion of the summary is known as the *prefix*. The bits in the mask indicated by a 0 refer to the portion of the area address that specifies the individual networks having that common prefix. So for example, an area address of 11100000 with a mask of fff00000 summarizes all addresses beginning with 111 into 11100000 fff00000.

A portion of an aggregated route's 32-bit network number is common to all the addresses summarized within it. In an LSP, an aggregated route is shown as a hexadecimal number relating to the size in bits of the common prefix for all the network addresses. In this case there are 24 bits in common, the hexadecimal conversion is 18. So the aggregated route for 12345600 ffffff00 is 18 12345600.

When routers use segregated areas they are generally unaffected by changes in adjacent areas. This reduces computational overheads on network links because the SPF algorithm only runs when an LSP noting changes is received. The frequency of recalculating the forwarding database is lowered. Because multiple addresses can be summarized as a single address, the size of the link-state database is reduced.

Since most changes in aggregated explicit routes do not have to be propagated to neighboring areas, there is less use of bandwidth. Route aggregation allows for filtering of route and service information at area boundaries. Information flow within and between networks can be managed more efficiently.

Route Aggregation NLSP 1.1 Areas

Before Cisco IOS Release 11.1, multiple NLSP areas were possible but could only be linked using IPX RIP. Each router had its own adjacencies database, link-state database, and forwarding database. Each router's link-state database was identical to that of other routers.

Pre-release 11.1 routers (NLSP 1.0 routers) and the current NLSP 1.1 routers use what is called a *single process*. Within any particular router in an area, the adjacencies, forwarding, and link-state databases work together as one process. This joint process allows the router to discover, select, and maintain route information about the area.

NLSP 1.1 routers (release 11.1) have the route aggregation capability, which allows them to interconnect multiple NLSP areas. An NLSP 1.1 router must be able to manage sets of adjacencies and link-state databases for every area to which it is attached.

When linking multiple areas, the NLSP router must keep an *area address database*. This contains area addresses that the router uses to identify its adjacent routers and routers in the same area. If route aggregation is enabled, the entries in this database act as route summaries for use in aggregated routes.

When a router interconnects multiple areas, the *single process* is its collective maintenance of the adjacencies, link-state, and area address databases for any one area. The forwarding database is the only one shared between different processes. A router can be configured with an NLSP process for each NLSP area of which it is a member. It can have up to 28 processes, minus the number of IPX Enhanced IGRP processes configured on it.

The ability to pass route information learned from one NLSP area to another is known as *leaking* in Novell terms, and as *route redistribution* in Cisco terms. Route redistribution from one NLSP process can occur to another NLSP process, an Enhanced IGRP process, or a RIP process.

You can redistribute explicit routes through multiple areas. You are limited to six areas when redistributing route summaries. An *area count* field tracks the number of areas through which an aggregated route has already been redistributed. Each router that connects multiple areas decreases the field by one when it redistributes to another router that interconnects multiple areas.

Let's see how route information is discovered and redistributed in adjoining NLSP 1.1 areas. Process 1 receives an LSP about network 1001 and adds the LSP to its link-state database. After computing the SPF algorithm it adds an entry for network 1001 into the forwarding database. Process 1 automatically redistributes network 1001 information to process 2, since both areas are NLSP 1.1 areas.

Process 2 gets the entry for network 1001 from the shared forwarding database. If route aggregation is configured, Process 2 checks Process 1's area address database to see if it already has a summary that includes network 1001. If so, Process 2 creates a new LSP including the aggregated route 1000 f000 instead of the explicit route 1001. If there is no summary that includes network 1001, Process 2 adds 1001 as an explicit route in its LSP and then forwards the LSP.

Routers running NLSP use either the cost or the tick metric to calculate the best route to a destination. The choice of metric depends on whether the destination is within the same NLSP area as the router, or in a different one. As a link-state protocol, NLSP's default metric is cost, so cost is used to calculate the best path to a destination within an NLSP area.

As aggregated routes traverse different area boundaries, the tick field in the packet increments by one. The tick metric is used to determine the best path to a destination in another NLSP area or in areas running different protocols. If an NLSP 1.1 router that connects multiple areas receives several route summaries with equal tick values for a destination, cost becomes the tie breaker.

An NLSP 1.1 router can receive both an explicit route to a destination and the aggregated route that includes the explicit route. In this case the explicit route is selected as the best path.

Where there is a choice of two aggregated routes, the router chooses the more explicit route. This is the route whose prefix identifies a more specific subset of networks. It is also referred to as the route with the longest match. For example, the aggregated route aaaa0000 ffff0000 would be chosen in preference to a0000000 f0000000.

In connection with route aggregation, you should remember:

- Areas must be segregated according to common addressing schemes, with a maximum of three addresses for an area.
- If area addresses do not represent network addresses within the area, you must manually configure route aggregation and access lists.
- An advertised aggregated route that is a subset of an NLSP 1.1 router's aggregated route is integrated under the entries in the router's existing LSP.

One problem with route aggregation is that neighboring routers may not discover each other. If this happens, you need to check that you defined an internal network number on the router and make sure that the neighbors have at least one common area address defined.

Remote routers may not discover a WAN link, even though they can identify networks on the other side of the link. The difficulty is that NLSP does not support numbered WAN links, so WAN link addresses are not propagated across the link. To solve this problem you should configure the WAN link as unnumbered.

When route aggregation is in effect, the rules that usually govern SAP and Get Nearest Server (GNS) requests are modified. For instance, routers normally must have an explicit route to a destination service before the service is accepted. (This rule is stated in the IPX Router Specification, version 1.0.) However, for forwarding packets to a service, NLSP specification, revision 1.1 states that you can now use explicit routes, aggregated routes, or default routes.

The rule for responding to GNS requests is to compare the route ticks of the service entry in the SAP table. SAP tables are created and maintained by routers and servers to state advertised internetwork server information. When the entries for two or more routes show an equal number of ticks, hops are used as tie breakers for selecting paths. The hop count for a summary route is always considered to be greater than that of a specific route.

Aggregation Configuration of NLSP 1.1 Areas

You may want to configure route aggregation on your internetwork to make routing more efficient by reducing processing and bandwidth demands. In this case you wish to design a network that consists of three NLSP 1.1 areas and you want to organize the routing between them.

Area 1 has the address range aaaa0000 to aaaaffff. The Maine router connects it to Area 2 which has the address range bbbb0000 bbbbffff. Area 2 is connected to Area 3 by the Vermont router (Figure 11.18). Area 3 has the address range cccc0000 to ccccffff.

FIGURE 11.18
The Maine router connects to Area 1 and Area 2, while Area 2 is connected to Area 3 by the Vermont router.

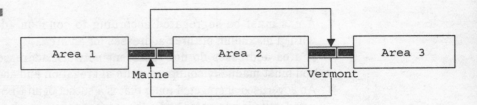

First we will see how to configure route aggregation between NLSP 1.1 Areas 2 and 3 on the Vermont router. Here you are logged on to the Vermont router and have entered the command to configure the terminal.

When you configure route aggregation between multiple NLSP areas, many of the configuration steps are the same as those used in standard NLSP configuration (Figure 11.19). For example, first you turn on IPX routing. You must assign an internal network number. In this case the number is 1000, so you enter `ipx internal-network 1000`.

Any router that interconnects multiple NLSP areas is responsible for managing the processes at work in each area with which it connects. When route aggregation is being configured between multiple areas, the router is managing multiple processes. To distinguish these processes from each other, each process must be assigned a process or *tag* identifier.

You assign each defined process to an *interface* that you want to configure. Your first step is to enter Interface Configuration mode. Enter `interface ethernet 0` and now you are in the Interface Configuration mode.

Next, assign a network number to the interface. The network number for the Ethernet 0 interface in Area 3 is cccc0001. Type `ipx network cccc0001` to assign this network number to the interface.

Now assign your first defined process to the interface and enable NLSP for that process. Use an area number as the tag identifier. In this case the tag identifier is "area3". Enable NLSP for this process by typing `ipx nlsp area3 enable`.

The Vermont router connects to Area 2 through the Serial 0 interface. Configure Serial 0 in the same way as you did the Ethernet interface. Enter `interface serial 0`.

FIGURE 11.9
Configuring route aggregation between multiple NLSP areas involves many of the configuration steps as those used in standard NLSP configuration.

```
Vermont# configure terminal
Enter configuration commands, one per line. End with CNTL/Z.
Vermont(config)# ipx routing
Vermont(config)# ipx internal-network 1000
Vermont(config)# interface ethernet 0
Vermont(config-if)# ipx network cccc0001
Vermont(config-if)# ipx nlsp area3 enable
Vermont(config-if)# interface serial 0
Vermont(config-if)# ipx network bbbb0001
Vermont(config-if)# ipx nlsp area2 enable
Vermont(config-if)# ipx router nlsp area3
Vermont(config-ipx-router)# area-address cccc0000 ffff0000
Vermont(config-ipx-router)# route-aggregation
Vermont(config-ipx-router)# ipx router nlsp area2
Vermont(config-ipx-router)# route-aggregation
Vermont(config-ipx-router)# ^Z
Vermont# copy runn start
Building configuration...
[OK]
Vermont#
```

Next assign a network number. The addresses in Area 2 are bbbb0000 to bbbbffff and the network for Serial 0 is bbbb0001. Assign network bbbb0001 by typing `ipx network bbbb0001`.

The correct format of the command to type to assign a process and enable NLSP on the interface is `ipx nlsp area2 enable`.

Next you need to enable NLSP on the router and define an NLSP process. Assign the tag identifier "area3" to process 3. The full command to enable NLSP on the router and define process 3 is `ipx router nlsp area3`.

Now you are in Router Configuration mode. Next you assign up to three area addresses for each defined process. Here, just one area address, cccc0000 ffff0000 is assigned. Type `area-address cccc0000 ffff0000` to assign that area address to the router for process 3.

Processes in different NLSP 1.1 areas redistribute information between them automatically. The process receiving the information gets the forwarding direction for the networks of which it is informed from the shared forwarding database.

If route aggregation is configured between NLSP 1.1 areas, the default route summarization technique is that area addresses are used as the basis of generating aggregated routes. A process will check the area address database of its informant to see if there is a route summary for the network on which it has received information.

If you want to enable route summarization, enter the Route-Aggregation command after the area address has been configured. Type route-aggregation in Router Configuration mode to enable route aggregation and default route summarization. If you enable route aggregation, all areas must be NLSP 1.1 areas. NLSP 1.0 areas do not recognize aggregated routes.

You configure the router with the second process tag identifier in the same way as you did the first. To configure the second process with the tag identifier "area2" on the router, type ipx router nlsp area2.

To configure the range of area addresses for Area 2, type area-address bbbb0000 ffff0000.

Finally you enable route aggregation and default route summarization by entering route-aggregation. Save and copy the changes.

At this point you can check that you have configured the two processes correctly on the Vermont router. Type show ipx route to see if all processes are configured correctly and if any routes have yet been sent as summaries (Figure 11.20). Here we can see that 1000 is the internal network configured on the router, and that the router connects Area 3 over the Ethernet 0 interface and Area 2 over the Serial 0 interface.

```
Vermont# show ipx route
Codes: C - Connected primary network, c - Connected secondary network
       S - Static, F - Floating static, L - Local (internal), W - IPXWAN
       R - RIP, E - EIGRP, N - NLSP, X - External, A - Aggregate
       s - seconds, u - uses

3 Total IPX routes. Up to 1 parallel paths and 16 hops allowed.

No default route known.

L       1000 is the internal network
C   CCCC0001 (NOVELL-ETHER),   Et0
C   BBBB0001 (HDLC),           Se0
Vermont#
```

FIGURE 11.20 Type show ipx route to see if all processes are configured correctly and if any routes have yet been sent as summaries.

Routes advertised as aggregated routes will be identified with an "A". No such routes have yet been advertised.

Mixed-Area Route Aggregation

In this section we discuss how to configure route aggregation between mixed NLSP areas and between NLSP 1.1 and Enhanced IGRP/RIP areas. We outline the commands used to aggregate routes between NLSP 1.1 and NLSP 1.0 areas and describe how to configure route aggregation between NLSP 1.1 and Enhanced IGRP/RIP areas. We also configure and monitor route aggregation between NLSP 1.1 and Enhanced IGRP/RIP areas.

Route Aggregation and Mixed NLSP Areas

A router may be configured with different IPX protocols such as NLSP 1.0, Enhanced IGRP, or RIP. Although these protocols operate as unique processes, they use the same forwarding database in the router. The forwarding database contains the routes to particular destinations.

Entries in the forwarding database need to be translated into a format that the particular protocol can understand before that information is redistributed to a protocol's process. Manually configuring route redistribution and aggregation may be necessary on an NLSP router when it coexists with a dissimilar protocol.

Let's look at an instance in which a router is managing mixed version NLSP areas simultaneously, that is NLSP 1.1 and NLSP 1.0. NLSP 1.0 routers do *not* support the route aggregation function. This is because they cannot interpret the route summary field in an LSP. They cannot learn about destinations included in address summaries. You can enable the summarization of routes from NLSP 1.0 areas to NLSP 1.1 areas but not from NLSP 1.1 to NLSP 1.0 areas. If an NLSP 1.1 router detects that the next-hop router on the path to an aggregated destination is an NLSP 1.0 router, it drops the packet. This prevents routing loops.

Since routes cannot be summarized from NLSP 1.1 areas to NLSP 1.0 areas you must customize your route summarization, to ensure aggregated routes are redistributed from NLSP 1.0 to NLSP 1.1 areas only.

Figure 11.21 shows that the syntax for configuring aggregation between mixed NLSP areas is very similar to that used for configuring it between NLSP 1.1 areas. Here, Area 1 is an NLSP 1.0 area and Area 2 is an NLSP 1.1 area.

FIGURE 11.21
The syntax for
configuring
aggregation
between mixed NLSP
areas is very similar
to that used for
configuring it
between NLSP 1.1
areas.

```
ipx routing
ipx internal-network 2000
interface ethernet 1
ipx network 1001
ipx nlsp area1 enable
interface ethernet 2
ipx network 2001
ipx nlsp area2 enable
access-list 1200 deny aaaa0000
access-list 1200 permit -1
ipx router nlsp area1
area-address 1000 fffff000
ipx router nlsp area2
area-address 2000 fffff000
route aggregation
redistribute nlsp area1 access-list 1200
```

For the NLSP 1.0 area you assign a process tag identifier and a network to the first interface as usual. However, for the NLSP 1.1 area, an access list is specified in Global Configuration mode. The access list specifies which routes to summarize and which routes to redistribute explicitly.

In this case, access list 1200 specifies that all routes except those in the range aaaa0000 can be redistributed to Area 2 from Area 1 as explicit routes. The deny keyword excludes explicit routes. The Permit -1 subcommand allows all explicit routes apart from the specified excluded ones.

Then, for the NLSP 1.0 area, NLSP is assigned to the router, along with the process tag identifier. You define an area address for the area as usual.

The same procedure is carried out for the NLSP 1.1 area. However, you also want to allow the routes specified in the previously defined access list to be redistributed to Area 2 in the form of an aggregated route.

First you configure route aggregation with the Route-Aggregation command. Next you specify that you want the range of routes defined in the access list to be redistributed from Area 1 (NLSP 1.0) to Area 2 (1.1) as an aggregated route.

You do not have to specify an access list for NLSP routes redistributed to the NLSP 1.0 area since it does not support route summarization. Routes redistributed into NLSP 1.0 areas should always be explicit ones.

NLSP 1.1 and Enhanced IGRP/RIP Areas

You may encounter a situation where your NLSP router needs to manage the flow of route information between an NLSP 1.1 area and Enhanced IGRP or

IPX RIP areas. In this case, we will look at setting up an internetwork consisting of:

- NLSP Area 1 with the address range aaaa0000 to aaaaffff.
- Enhanced IGRP autonomous system (AS) 100 with the network number bbbb0001.
- NLSP Area 2 with the address range cccc0000 to ccccffff.

Area 1 and the Enhanced IGRP AS are connected by the Maine router. The Enhanced IGRP AS and Area 2 are connected by the Vermont router (Figure 11.22).

FIGURE 11.22
Area 1 and the EIGRP AS are connected by the Maine router and EIGRP AS and Area 2 are connected by the Vermont router.

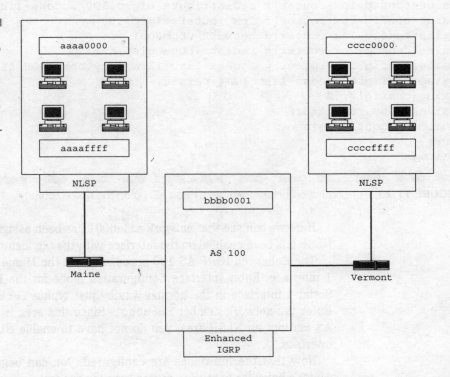

We begin by configuring Area 1 and AS100 on the Maine router (Figure 11.23). The initial steps of the configuration will be the same as those used when configuring mixed and same NLSP version areas.

Once you have put the router in Configuration mode, you enable IPX routing. Then you assign an internal network number.

The Maine router connects to Area 1 over an Ethernet 0 interface. Configure that interface in the usual way.

```
Maine# configure terminal
Enter configuration commands, one per line. End with CNTL/Z.
Maine(config)# ipx routing
Maine(config)# internal-network 3000
Maine(config)# interface ethernet 0
Maine(config-if)# ipx network aaaa0001
Maine(config-if)# ipx nlsp area1 enable
Maine(config-if)# interface serial 1
Maine(config-if)# ipx network bbbb0001
Maine(config-if)# ipx router nlsp area1
Maine(config-ipx-router)# area-address aaaa0000 ffff0000
Maine(config-ipx-router)# route-aggregation
Maine(config-ipx-router)# redistribute eigrp 100 access-list 1234
Maine(config-ipx-router)# ipx router eigrp 100
Maine(config-ipx-router)# network bbbb0001
Maine(config-ipx-router)# redistribute nlsp area1
Maine(config-ipx-router)# access-list 1234 deny bbbb0000 ffff0000
Maine(config)# access-list 1234 permit -1
Maine(config)# ^Z
Maine# copy runn start
Building configuraiton...
[OK]
Maine#
```

FIGURE 11.23   Configuration begins with Area 1 and AS100 on the Maine router.

Here we can see that network aaaa0001 has been assigned to the interface. NLSP has been enabled on the interface with the tag identifier "area1".

The Enhanced IGRP AS 100 is connected to the Maine router at the Serial 1 interface. Enter Interface Configuration mode for the Enhanced IGRP AS Serial 1 interface in the normal way by just typing `interface serial 1`. Enter the network number `bbbb0001`. Since this area is an Enhanced IGRP AS and not an NLSP area, you do not have to enable NLSP on the Serial 1 interface.

Now that the interfaces are configured, you can begin to configure the router's behavior in routing routes between the two areas. First configure the details for the Area 1 process on the router. Put the router in Configuration mode. Enable NLSP and specify a process tag identifier on the router, by typing `ipx router nlsp area1`.

Next assign the area address for the NLSP area as usual. The area address for the NLSP Area 1 is aaaa0000 ffff0000 so enter `area-address aaaa0000 ffff0000`.

Enable route aggregation for the NLSP area on the router. This allows the router to list aggregated routes in the NLSP routing table. Enter `route-aggregation`.

The procedure for the aggregation of Enhanced IGRP or IPX RIP routes to NLSP 1.1 is the same as that used for aggregation of NLSP 1.0 routes to NLSP 1.1. You must manually configure the `Redistribute` command with an access list number while in Router Configuration mode for the NLSP area. The access list you specify will list the range of routes from the Enhanced IGRP area that are to be advertised as aggregated routes. You can specify an access list at any point. However it is more convenient to wait until router configuration is complete because the `Access` command defaults out of Router Configuration mode.

You have decided that your access list will be number 1234. You want routes coming from Enhanced IGRP AS 100 to be aggregated. The correct syntax of the `Redistribute` command is:

```
redistribute eigrp
autonomous-system-number
[access-list access list number]
```

The correct format to redistribute aggregated routes from Enhanced IGRP to NLSP Area 1 is `redistribute eigrp 100 access-list 1234`. If you were configuring a RIP area with an access list 3456, the correct format would be `redistribute rip access-list 3456`.

You have now completed the configuration of details for the NLSP Area 1 on the Maine router. Next you need to configure details for the Enhanced IGRP AS 100 on the router. Enter `ipx router eigrp 100`. This command enables Enhanced IGRP on the router and identifies the local autonomous system to which this router is connected.

When configuring Enhanced IGRP, you don't assign area addresses, but you must enter a `Network` command instead. The `Network` command enables the router to generate an entry in the Enhanced IGRP routing table for the network you specify. Entering `network bbbb0001` enables the Maine router to generate an entry in the Enhanced IGRP routing table for `network bbbb0001`.

As with NLSP 1.0, Enhanced IGRP and IPX RIP do not recognize summarized route entries and only accept explicit routes from an NLSP 1.1 area. You need not enable route aggregation for either an Enhanced IGRP or RIP area.

Redistribution of an explicit route from an NLSP 1.1 area to an IPX RIP area is automatic. However you need to configure the `Redistribute` command to redistribute explicit route entries from NLSP 1.1 to Enhanced IGRP. The correct format of the command to redistribute routes from NLSP Area 1 to Enhanced IGRP AS 100 is `redistribute nlsp area1`.

You need not specify an access list because only explicit and not aggregated routes will be redistributed from NLSP 1.1 to the Enhanced IGRP AS. The configuration is not complete until you have specified the details of access list 1234.

You want to specify that all routes sent from the Enhanced IGRP area be redistributed as aggregated and not explicit routes. You deny all explicit routes in the range bbbb0000 ffff0000. The access list is defined by typing access-list 1234 deny bbbb0000 ffff0000.

You want to ensure that all other routes outside the Enhanced IGRP area are redistributed to NLSP 1.1 Area 1 as explicit routes. Use the Permit subcommand to allow all other routes. In Configuration mode, you type access-list 1234 permit -1.

You have configured the interfaces connecting the Maine router to NLSP Area 1 and Enhanced IGRP AS 100. You have also configured the aggregation details from the Enhanced IGRP area to the NLSP 1.1 area. You have redistributed explicit routes from NLSP 1.1 to Enhanced IGRP. If you are configuring for a RIP area, follow all the same steps except that explicit route entries are redistributed automatically from NLSP 1.1 to RIP. You can now exit Configuration mode and save the changes.

So far you have connected and configured route aggregation between NLSP Area 1 and the Enhanced IGRP area. You can check to see that all connections are working correctly. You can check Maine's routing table, by typing show ipx route (Figure 11.24). The Enhanced IGRP network bbbb0001 and the NLSP network aaaa0001 are connected.

```
Maine# show ipx route
Codes: C - Connected primary network, c - Connected secondary network
       S - Static, F - Floating static, L - Local (internal), W - IPXWAN
       R - RIP, E - EIGRP, N - NLSP, X - External, A - Aggregate
       s - seconds, u - uses

3 Total IPX routes. Up to 1 parallel paths and 16 hops allowed.

No default route known.

L      3000 is the internal network
C   AAAA0001 (NOVELL-ETHER),   Et0
C   BBBB0001 (HDLC),           Sel
Maine#
```

FIGURE 11.24   Type show ipx route to check Maine's routing table.

You can also check which interfaces are configured as Enhanced IGRP interfaces. Type show ipx eigrp interface. You can see that the Serial 1 interface is configured as the Enhanced IGRP interface (Figure 11.25).

```
Maine# show ipx eigrp interface

IPX EIGRP Interfaces for process 100

                  Xmit Queue   Mean  Pacing Time  Multicast    Pending
Interface  Peers  Un/Reliable  SRTT  Un/Reliable  Flow Timer   Routes
Se1        0      0/0          0     12/378       0            0
Maine#
```

FIGURE 11.25   Type show ipx eigrp interface to check which interfaces are configured as EIGRP interfaces.

Managing
IPX Traffic

Managing Complex Networks

In considering the management of complex networks and the issue of traffic congestion on IPX networks we describe the characteristics of complex networks and the management issues associated with complex networks, and we outline the causes of traffic congestion and the methods used to manage it in complex networks.

An Overview of Complex Networks

The trend toward more complex networks is making network management even more challenging. As a network grows, it must continue to meet the needs of its users. Once this is achieved, you need to deal with the next set of management issues, such as controlling traffic flow and reducing traffic overhead.

The following characteristics can identify a complex network:

- More than 300 IPX routes
- Global topology with multiple remote connections
- Emphasis on security
- Routed and non-routed traffic on the same medium.

Networks may be considered particularly complex when they approach or exceed: 500 IP routes, 300 IPX routes, 1,000 IPX SAP services, or 300 AppleTalk zones in one area.

Complex networks force the router to maintain very large routing and service tables for each protocol. These tables have to be updated or distributed periodically, which consumes considerable bandwidth on all links.

Networks with more than 300 IPX routes, either in a local or remote topology, are subject to connectivity problems linked to the metric limitations of the routing protocol. These networks may be slow to converge when topology changes occur. If your network has 300 IPX or more routes, you can manage router overhead by using route summarization and advanced routing protocols.

Route summarization manages problems caused when maintaining more than 300 entries in a routing table by reducing the overall number of entries. It occurs at major network boundaries for most routing protocols, consolidating address advertisement with a summary address.

Some routing protocols, such as NLSP and IPX Enhanced IGRP, allow manual summarization on arbitrary boundaries within a major network. Manual summarization is most effective when careful planning and address allocation is enforced.

Advanced routing protocols, such as NLSP and IPX Enhanced IGRP, reduce bandwidth consumption by sending only topology changes rather than the entire routing table contents. These topology updates are sent at regular intervals. Enhanced IGRP further reduces processing overhead in the router because it uses a single algorithm to calculate IP, IPX, and AppleTalk routes.

If you manage geographically remote networks (a global topology), there is the challenge of tracing, logging, and accounting for resource usage. Keeping records of line usage, CPU time, and server time is a major challenge. Managing networks with many remote links usually involves trading off cost against reliability. As a network becomes more geographically distributed, maintaining connectivity becomes more of a problem.

Often, connections are maintained by service providers rather than by the individual company itself, and network segments are not always located in the same building or even in the same city. You therefore need to plan the management and repair of links. This requires strategic planning with fallback positions defined in advance.

You can manage a global topology (incorporating different carriers and service providers) by using dial-on-demand routing (DDR), data compression, and packet-switched networks.

Infrequent connectivity requirements can be maintained using Cisco's dial-on-demand routing feature. Active links are created only after traffic is detected by the router. This service replaces nailed-up circuits that accumulate costs even when the link is idle.

Data compression of headers or entire frames is one way to reduce traffic. The router software accomplishes the compression before the frame is placed on the medium.

Packet-switched networks, such as X.25 and frame relay, offer the advantage of global connectivity through a large number of service providers with established circuits to most major cities.

As a network administrator, you need to be conscious of maintaining security in your network. You need to block unauthorized access. You also need to verify authorized access, and even then, access to certain connections may need to be restricted.

A network delivering both routed and non-routed traffic has certain unique problems. Most non-routable protocols lack a mechanism to provide flow control, and therefore are very sensitive to delays in delivery. Delivery delays, or packets arriving out of sequence, can result in an application session's being lost.

Some non-routable traffic, such as LAT, and link protocols, for example, IBM's SDLC, must be encapsulated inside a routable protocol. This allows delivery to remote hosts, but it also requires additional resources within the router.

Non-routable (or bridged) traffic depends heavily on broadcasts for host delivery. In mixed-media environments, such as Ethernet connected to token ring, address and header variances create differences that can be overcome only by additional CPU processing power in the router.

Cisco's concurrent routing and bridging feature allows the same protocol to be both routed and bridged (albeit on different interfaces) within the router. This feature is very important during migration from bridged to routed environments.

Traffic Congestion on IPX Networks

The problem of traffic congestion exists in all large networks. Congestion occurs when the quantity of data to be transmitted by a particular medium exceeds the bandwidth of that medium. Congestion anywhere in the path results in delays for user applications.

An IPX network has many sources of data traffic and overhead traffic. Data traffic is usually generated by user applications. These applications may initiate file transfers using protocols such as Novell's IPX/SPX. Client/server applications are another common source of data traffic.

Overhead traffic is generated when the traffic is not directly related to user applications. Examples of overhead traffic include routing updates and broadcast requests.

Traffic generated by different protocols can cause problems for routers and other hardware devices. The routers have to maintain separate tables and caches for each protocol, wasting resources on what is effectively duplicated information.

The physical presence of additional traffic from another protocol on the medium creates competition for the fixed bandwidth of that medium.

Multiprotocol traffic presents problems for network administrators. When you use only a single protocol, network design can be tailored to suit that protocol suite. When multiple protocol traffic is present, the network must be balanced to suit the needs of each protocol.

Much of the traffic in an IPX network is inherent to NetWare's enhanced support of client services. Service Advertisement Protocol (SAP) traffic is an overhead, but is required for announcements about service availability. While these service advertisements may work well on a LAN, a large IPX network will have lots of SAP traffic. This can require too much bandwidth to be acceptable on large networks, or networks linked on WAN serial connections. WAN links are capable of connecting geographically diverse sites. Therefore, they often make up the backbone network and are critical to corporate operations.

Novell IPX uses Routing Information Protocol (RIP) as the default routing protocol. IPX RIP is used to facilitate the exchange of routing information. As with SAP, IPX RIP updates can cause excessive overhead traffic on some networks. Routing updates are sent every 60 seconds.

SAP and RIP are enabled by default on all interfaces configured for IPX. These interfaces always respond to SAP and RIP requests. Novell IPX RIP is optimized for local use and does not scale well over large networks. It has limited route selection metrics and a maximum hop count of 15.

An IPX client broadcasts a Get Nearest Server (GNS) request when it requires a specific service. Responses to a GNS request can come from local servers, local routers, or remote servers.

Remote server GNS responses are undesirable because they needlessly increase traffic congestion on the network.

To resolve congestion, traffic must be either reduced or rescheduled. With Cisco routers, you can control network congestion by filtering traffic, prioritizing traffic with queues, or limiting broadcast/multicast traffic.

Reducing traffic is the most obvious method of solving congestion problems. *Traffic filters* prevent user traffic from accessing certain portions of the network. Traffic filters based on area or service type are used as primary distribution service tools in an IPX network. Using filters on a router interface allows or restricts different protocols and applications on individual networks. Such filters provide policy-based access control into backbone services.

Both area and service filtering are implemented using access lists. You can use traffic filters to keep certain traffic from reaching critical links. Service filters prevent access by hiding some services from designated groups of users. Of course, if you reduce the number of advertised services, you reduce bandwidth consumption on WAN links. Area, or network, access filters are used to enforce the selective transmission of traffic based on the network address.

You can use route redistribution filters to prevent routing information from reaching routing tables on certain routers. This limits communication with remote devices connected to those routers.

You can reduce serial link congestion by establishing corporate *priority policy* for user traffic. To do this on Cisco routers, you can use the following types of traffic *queuing* system: priority queuing, custom queuing, or weighted fair queuing.

Priority queuing means that high-priority traffic gets through at the risk of losing lower-priority traffic. If you use custom queuing, each traffic type gets a share of the available bandwidth. Weighted fair queuing sorts and prioritizes traffic streams automatically. The weighted fair queue approach is acceptable on most networks, but can be overridden by manual configuration of either priority or custom queuing.

You can establish a queuing policy that gives priority to non-routable traffic. This can be useful since applications that depend on non-routable protocols are very sensitive to traffic delays.

Some periodic broadcasts have configurable transmission timers to lengthen the interval between broadcasts. If you lengthen the timer, you reduce overall traffic load on that link.

You can use static entries in routing tables to eliminate the need to dynamically advertise routes across a link. This technique can be very effective for serial links.

Access Lists and Filters

We will discuss how IPX access lists, generic filters, and broadcast message filters manage traffic in an IPX network, by describing the four types of IPX access lists and gaining an understanding of the access list command syntax. We will describe the five groups of IPX filters and how to configure generic and broadcast message filters using standard and extended access lists. We will configure a generic filter using a standard access list and a broadcast message filter using an extended access list.

IPX Access Lists

An IPX access list is a sequence of statements, each of which permits or denies certain conditions or addresses from crossing specified interfaces. Access lists can be used to permit or deny messages from particular network nodes and messages sent using particular protocols and services. Cisco IOS tests addresses against the conditions in an access list one by one. An access list can be applied to either inbound or outbound traffic on interfaces.

When you define an inbound access list and the router receives a packet, it checks the source address of the packet against the access list. If the access list permits the address, the router continues to process the packet. If the access list denies the address, the router discards the packet and returns an ICMP Host Unreachable message.

When an outbound access list is applied, the incoming packet is routed to a controlled interface. The router checks the source address of the packet against the access list. If the access list permits the address, the router transmits the packet. If the address is rejected, the router discards the packet and returns an ICMP Host Unreachable message.

Using access lists to manage traffic routing is a powerful tool in overall network control. However, it requires a certain amount of planning and the appropriate application of several related commands. There are a number of factors you should keep in mind when configuring IPX access lists.

Access list entries are scanned in the order which you enter them. Given that the first matching entry is used, it is recommended to place the most commonly used entries near the beginning of the access list.

An implicit "deny everything" entry is defined at the end of an access list unless you include an explicit "permit everything" at the end of the list.

All new entries to an existing list are placed at the end of the list. This means that if you have previously included an explicit "permit everything" entry, new entries will never be scanned. The solution is to delete the access list and re-enter it with new entries.

You should take care that the conditions in your access list do not cause packets to be lost. For example, this could happen when a device or interface is configured to advertise services on a network that has access lists which deny these packets.

To control access to IPX networks, you create access lists and then apply them with filters to individual interfaces. The same access list can be assigned to different interfaces.

You cannot filter within an NLSP area. You can filter at the boundary of NLSP and RIP, or SAP, though restrictions do apply.

There are four types of IPX access lists to use to filter various kinds of traffic: standard, extended, SAP, and NetBIOS. The "No" version of all access list commands will remove the access list you have created.

A *standard access list* restricts traffic according to its source network number. You can further restrict traffic by specifying a destination address and a source and destination address mask (all of which are optional). Standard IPX access lists have numbers from 800 to 899.

You create a standard access list using the standard version of the `Access-List` command:

```
access-list access-list-number
{deny  permit}
source-network[options]
```

NOTE

The full syntax of the standard `Access-List` *command is:*

```
[no] access-list access-list-number {deny | permit}
source-network[.source-node[source-node-mask]]
[destination-network[.destination-node
[destination-node-mask]]]
```

The `.source-node` *is a node on the* `source-network` *from which the packet is being sent: a 48-bit value represented as a dotted triplet of four-digit hexadecimal numbers (xxxx.xxxx.xxxx).*

The `source-node-mask` *is a mask to be applied to the* `source-node`: *a 48-bit value represented as a triplet of four-digit hexadecimal numbers where ones are placed in the bit positions you want to mask.*

The `destination-network` *is an eight-digit hexadecimal address of the network to which the packet is being sent; it ranges 1 to FFFFFFFD; 0 is the local network, and -1 is all networks.*

The `.destination-node` *is a node on the destination-network to which the packet is being sent: a 48-bit value represented as a dotted triplet of four-digit hexadecimal numbers (xxxx.xxxx.xxxx).*

The `destination-node-mask` *is a mask to be applied to the destination-node: a 48-bit value represented as a triplet of four-digit hexadecimal numbers where ones are placed in the bit positions you want to mask.*

The `access-list-number` is a decimal number representing the access list (800-899). The keywords `Deny` or `Permit` determine whether access is blocked or allowed. The `source-network` is an eight-digit hexadecimal address of the network from which the packet is being sent; ranges 1 to FFFFFFFD, 0 is the local network, and −1 is all networks. Leading zeros do not need to be specified in the network address. For example, for the network address 000000AA, you can enter `AA`.

Figure 12.1 shows a network featuring two routers on two network segments.

Suppose you want to prevent clients and servers on Network AA from using the services on Network BB. However, you want to allow the clients and servers on Network BB to use the services on Network AA. A standard access list on Ethernet 1 on Router 2 will block all packets from Network AA to Network BB. You do not need any access list on Ethernet 0 on Router 1. You configure Ethernet 1 on Router 2 with the following commands:

```
access-list 800 deny aa bb01
access-list 800 permit -1 -1
```

An *extended access list* restricts traffic based on the IPX protocol type. You can further restrict traffic by specifying source and destination addresses and address masks, and source and destination sockets. Extended IPX access lists have numbers from 900 to 999.

You create an extended access list using the extended version of the `Access-List` command:

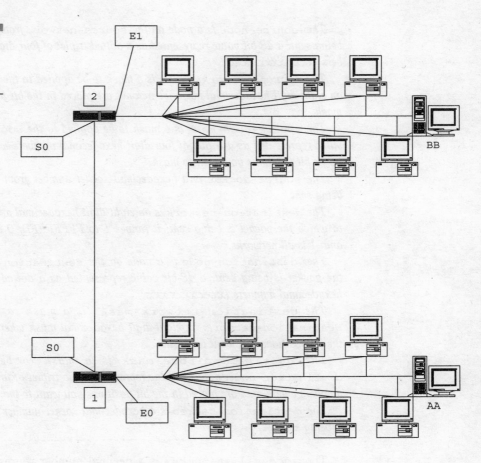

FIGURE 12.1
A network featuring
two routers on two
network segments.

```
access-list access-list number
{deny  permit} protocol [options]
```

NOTE

The full syntax of the extended Access-List *command is:*

```
[no] access-list access-list-number {deny | permit}
protocol [source-network][[[.source-node]
source-node-mask]|[.source-node source-network-mask.
source-node-mask]][source-socket]
[destination-network][[[.destination-node]
destination-node-mask]|[.destination-node
destination-network-mask.
destination-node-mask]][destination-socket]
```

The source-network *is an eight-digit hexadecimal address of the network from which the packet is being sent; it ranges 1 to FFFFFFFD; 0 is the local network, and −1 is all networks.*

The *.source-node* is a node on the *source-network* from which the packet is being sent: a 48-bit value represented as a dotted triplet of four-digit hexadecimal numbers (*xxxx.xxxx.xxxx*).

The *source-network-mask.* is a mask to be applied to the *source-network:* an eight-digit hexadecimal mask where ones are placed in the bit positions you want to mask.

The *source-node-mask* is a mask to be applied to the *source-node:* a 48-bit value represented as a triplet of four-digit hexadecimal numbers where ones are placed in the bit positions you want to mask.

The *source-socket* is a hexadecimal socket number from which the packet is being sent.

The *destination-network* is an eight-digit hexadecimal address of the network to which the packet is being sent; it ranges 1 to FFFFFFFD; 0 is the local network, and -1 is all networks.

The *.destination-node* is a node on the *destination-network* to which the packet is being sent: a 48-bit value represented as a dotted triplet of four-digit hexadecimal numbers (*xxxx.xxxx.xxxx*).

The *destination-network-mask.* is a mask to be applied to the *destination-network:* an eight-digit hexadecimal mask where ones are placed in the bit positions you want to mask.

The *destination-node-mask* is a mask to be applied to the *destination-node:* a 48-bit value represented as a triplet of four-digit hexadecimal numbers where ones are placed in the bit positions you want to mask.

The *destination-socket* is a hexadecimal socket number to which the packet is being sent.

The *access-list-number* is a decimal number representing the access list (900–999). The keywords Deny or Permit determine whether access is blocked or allowed. The protocol is a decimal number representing an IPX protocol type (0–255), sometimes referred to as the packet type; −1 is any IPX protocol type. For example, if you wanted to create an extended access list to deny traffic from the Printing protocol, you would type access-list 950 deny 47.

An SAP access list restricts traffic based on the IPX Service Advertisement Protocol (SAP) type. SAP access lists are numbered from 1,000 to 1,099. These lists are used for SAP filters and Get Nearest Server (GNS) response filters.

To create an SAP access list, use the SAP filtering form of the Access-List command:

```
access-list access-list-number
{deny  permit} network[options]
```

NOTE

The full syntax of the SAP `Access-List` *command is:*

```
[no] access-list access-list-number {deny | permit}
network[.node][network.node-mask][service-type]
[server-name]
```

The `.node` *is a node on the* `network`*: a 48-bit value represented as a dotted triplet of four-digit hexadecimal numbers (xxxx.xxxx.xxxx).*

The `network.node-mask` *is a mask to be applied to the* `network` *and* `node` *where ones are placed in the bit positions you want to mask.*

The `service-type` *is the type of service to be filtered: an eight-digit hexadecimal number where 0 is all services.*

The `server-name` *is the name of the server providing the specified service type; it can be any contiguous string of printable ASCII characters (for example, PRINT-ER_1).*

The `access-list-number` is a decimal number representing the access list (1000–1099). The keywords `Deny` or `Permit` determine whether access is blocked or allowed.

The `network` is an eight-digit hexadecimal address of the network from which the packet is being sent; it ranges 1 to FFFFFFFD; 0 is the local network, and -1 is all networks.

IPX NetBIOS allows messages to be exchanged between nodes using alphanumeric names as well as node addresses. An `IPX NetBIOS access list` restricts IPX NetBIOS traffic based on NetBIOS names, not numbers. When creating a NetBIOS access list, you can filter the IPX NetBIOS packets either by node name or by arbitrary byte pattern.

To create a NetBIOS access list for filtering IPX NetBIOS packets by node name, use the following command:

```
netbios access-list host name
{deny | permit} string
```

To create a NetBIOS access list for filtering IPX NetBIOS packets by arbitrary byte pattern, use the following command:

```
netbios access-list bytes name
{deny | permit} offset bytepattern
```

IPX Filters

IPX filters help control packet movement through a network. This control limits network traffic and restricts network use by certain users or devices.

There are 13 different IPX filters that you can define for IPX interfaces, each filter falling into one of five groups.

The full set of IPX filter groups includes: routing table, SAP, IPX NetBIOS, generic, and broadcast message filters.

Standard and extended access lists are applied when creating routing table filters, generic filters, and broadcast message filters.

Routing table filters control which Routing Information Protocol (RIP) updates are accepted and advertised by the Cisco IOS software. They also determine which devices the local router will accept RIP updates from. When RIP routing updates are received, you can control which networks are added to the Cisco IOS software's routing table using the IPX `Input-Network-Filter` command:

```
ipx input-network-filter
access-list-number
```

The `access-list-number` for standard access lists is a decimal number in the range 800–899; for extended access lists it is in the range 900–999.

To control which networks are advertised in RIP routing updates sent out by the Cisco IOS software, use the IPX `Output-Network-Filter` command:

```
ipx output-network-filter
access-list-number
```

In the same way as when dealing with repeat filters, the `access-list-number` for standard access list for output filters is a decimal number in the range 800–899, or an NLSP access list number in the range 1200–1299.

To control which networks are advertised in the Enhanced IGRP routing updates sent out by the Cisco IOS software, use the `Distribute-List Out` router configuration command:

```
distribute-list access-list-number out
```

NOTE

The full syntax of the `Distribute-List Out` *command is:*

```
distribute-list access-list-number out [interface-name | routing-process]
```

The `interface-name` *is the interface on which the access list should be applied to outgoing updates; if not specified, the access list is applied to all outgoing updates.*

The `routing-process` *is the name of a particular routing process, for example,* `eigrp @Bautonomous-system-number@b`, *rip, or* `nlsp [@Btag@b]`.

Again, the `access-list-number` for standard access lists is a decimal number in the range 800–899; for extended access lists it is in the range 900–999. The keyword `Out` applies the access list to outgoing routing updates.

To control the routers from which routing updates are accepted, use the `IPX Router-Filter` command:

```
ipx router-filter access-list-number
```

The `access-list-number` for standard access lists is a decimal number in the range 800–899; for extended access lists, it is in the range 900–999.

SAP filters control which SAP services the Cisco IOS software accepts and advertises, and which Get Nearest Server (GNS) response messages it sends out.

IPX NetBIOS filters control incoming and outgoing NetBIOS FindName packets by node name or by arbitrary byte pattern in the packet. These filters apply to IPX NetBIOS FindName packets only. They have no effect on other NetBIOS packets.

Keep in mind the following when configuring IPX NetBIOS access control:

- Host (node) names are case sensitive.
- Host and byte access lists can have the same names because these lists are independent of each other.
- When you are filtering by node name, the names in the access lists are compared with the destination name field for IPX NetBIOS FindName requests.

Also consider the following factors when configuring IPX NetBIOS:

- Access filters that filter by byte offset examine each packet, causing a slower packet transmission rate.
- If a node name is not found in an access list, the default action is to deny access.

To create an IPX NetBIOS filter for incoming NetBIOS FindName messages, use the `IPX NetBIOS Input-Access-Filter` command:

```
ipx netbios input-access-filter
{host | bytes} name
```

The keyword `host` identifies the `name` as a NetBIOS access filter previously defined with one or more NetBIOS `Access-List Host` commands. The keyword `bytes` identifies the *name* as a NetBIOS access filter previously defined with one or more NetBIOS `Access-List Bytes` commands. The *name* is the name of a NetBIOS access list.

To filter outgoing NetBIOS FindName messages, use the `IPX NetBIOS Output-Access-Filter` command:

```
ipx netbios output-access-filter
{host  bytes} name
```

The keyword `host` identifies the *name* as a NetBIOS access filter previously defined with one or more NetBIOS `Access-List Host` commands. The keyword `bytes` identifies the *name* as a NetBIOS access filter previously defined with one or more NetBIOS `Access-List Bytes` commands. The *name* is the name of a NetBIOS access list.

Generic filters determine which data packets are routed in or out of an interface based on the packet's source address, the packet's destination address, and IPX protocol type. Only one input filter and one output filter can be applied to each interface or sub-interface.

An output filter cannot be configured on an interface where autonomous switching is already configured. Similarly, autonomous switching cannot be configured on an interface where an output filter is already present. Autonomous switching is a feature on Cisco routers that provides faster packet processing by allowing packets to be switched independently without interrupting the system processor.

You cannot configure an input filter on an interface if autonomous switching is already configured on any interface. Likewise, you cannot configure input filters if autonomous switching is already enabled on any interface.

Use the `IPX Access-Group` interface configuration command to create a generic filter:

```
ipx access-group access-list-number {in | out}
```

The *access-list-number* for standard access lists is a decimal number in the range 800–899; for extended access lists it is in the range 900–999. The keywords `In` or `Out` determine whether inbound or outbound packets are filtered. The generic filter defaults to `Out` when neither keyword is specified in the command.

Figure 12.1 shows a network featuring two routers on two network segments.

Suppose you want to prevent clients and servers on Network AA from using the services on Network BB. However, you want to allow the clients and servers on Network BB to use the services on Network AA (refer to Figure 12.1).

A standard or extended access list on Ethernet 1 on Router 2 will block all packets from Network AA to Network BB. You do not need any access list on Ethernet 0 on Router 1.

You configure Ethernet 1 on Router 2 with the following sequence of commands:

- `ipx routing`
- `access-list 800 deny aa bb01`
- `access-list 800 permit -1 -1`
- `interface ethernet 1`
- `ipx network bb`
- `ipx access-group 800`

The IPX Access-Group command will filter all outgoing packets from Network BB through Ethernet 1.

You can accomplish the same result as the previous example more efficiently. For example, you can place the same generic output filter on Router 1, Serial 0. Alternatively, you could also place a generic input filter on interface Ethernet 0 of Router 1, as follows:

- `ipx routing`
- `access-list 800 deny aa bb01`
- `access-list 800 permit -1 -1`
- `interface ethernet 0`
- `ipx network aa`
- `ipx access-group 800 in`

Routers normally block all broadcast requests and do not forward them to other network segments. This prevents the degradation of performance inherent in broadcast traffic over the entire network. *Broadcast message filters* control which broadcast packets get forwarded to other networks.

To create a broadcast message filter, you first need to specify a helper address, one configured on an interface for forwarding broadcast messages. Create your broadcast message filter using the IPX Helper-Address interface configuration command:

`ipx helper-address network.node`

The *network* is the network from which the target IPX server resides: an eight-digit hexadecimal address that uniquely identifies a network cable segment and ranges 1 to FFFFFFFD; −1 is all-nets flooding. The *.node* is the node number of the target Novell server: a 48-bit value represented as a dotted triplet of four-digit hexadecimal numbers (xxxx.xxxx.xxxx).

A broadcast message filter has no effect unless you have issued an IPX Helper-Address or an IPX Type-20-Propagation command. These commands are issued on the interface to enable and control the forwarding of broadcast messages. Next, apply a broadcast message filter to an interface using the IPX Helper-List interface configuration command:

```
ipx helper-list access-list-number
```

The access-list-number defines outgoing packets with either standard (800–899) or extended (900–999) access list numbers. Use this command to assign an access list to an interface to control broadcast traffic (this includes type-20-propagation packets).

IPX services from SAP updates can be controlled. We will create static SAP entries on both the Vermont and Maine routers for a file server and a print server (Figure 12.2). These entries will simulate "live" entries on the network.

Assume you are logged onto the Vermont router and have entered Global Configuration mode by typing config term. You create a new IPX network, number AC200200, and create a loopback interface with this network number.

You need to create an IPX address for static SAP entry. The MAC address of the Ethernet 0 port was found to be 0000.0c92.9048. The IPX address formed is 0200.0c92.9048. We create the file server name 200FileServ and the print server name 200PrntServ.

Now we create the static SAP entries (Figure 12.3):

- 4—identifies the SAP service as a file server
- 7—identifies the SAP service as a print server
- 451—the NCP port for SAP
- 1—indicates that the service is one hop away

Finally, use the Show IPX Servers command to view the static entries you have created (Figure 12.4).

Now we will configure the Maine router in the same way. Create a new IPX network, number AC400400, and create a loopback interface with this network number.

Create an IPX address for static SAP entry (Figure 12.5). The MAC address of the Ethernet 0 port was found to be 0000.0c92.904e. The IPX address formed is 0200.0c92.904e. We create the file server name 400FileServ and the print server name 400PrntServ.

FIGURE 12.2
Creating static SAP
entries on the
Vermont routers for a
file server and a print
server.

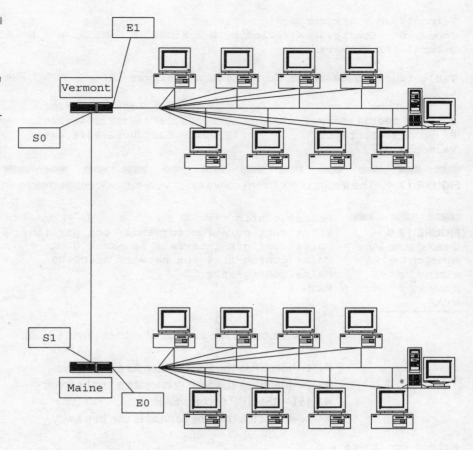

```
Vermont# config term
Enter configuration commands, one per line. End with CNTL/Z.
Vermont(config)# interface loopback 0
Vermont(config-if)# ipx network ac200200
Vermont(config-if)# ^Z
Vermont#
```

```
Vermont# config term
Enter configuration commands, one per line. End with CNTL/Z.
Vermont(config)# ipx sap 4 200FileServ ac200200.0200.0c92.9048 451 1
Vermont(config)# ipx sap 7 200PrntServ ac200200.0200.0c92.9048 451 1
Vermont(config)# ^Z
Vermont#
```

FIGURE 12.3   Creating static SAP entries on the Vermont router.

```
Vermont# snow ipx servers
Codes: S - Static, P - Periodic, E - EIGRP, N - NLSP, H - Holddown, + = detail
2 Total IPX Servers

Table ordering is based on routing and server info

     Type Name                      Net       Address      Port     Route Hops Itf
S      4 200FileServ                AC200200.0200.0c92.9048:0451     conn    1  Lo0
S      7 200PrntServ                AC200200.0200.0c92.9048:0451     conn    1  Lo0
Vermont#
```

FIGURE 12.4   Use the Show IPX Servers command to view the static entries created on the Vermont router.

FIGURE 12.5
Creating static SAP
entries on the Maine
routers for a file
server and a print
server.

```
Maine# config term
Enter configuration commands, one per line. End with CNTL/Z.
Maine(config)# interface loopback 0
Maine(config-if)# ipx network ac400400
Maine(config-if)# ^Z
Maine#
```

Now we create the static SAP entries (Figure 12.6):

- 4—identifies the SAP service as a file server.
- 7—identifies the SAP service as a print server.
- 451—the NCP port for SAP.
- 1—indicates that the service is one hop away.

```
Maine# config term
Enter configuration commands, one per line. End with CNTL/Z.
Maine(config)# ipx sap 4 200FileServ ac400400.0400.0c92.904e 451 1
Maine(config)# ipx sap 7 200PrntServ ac400400.0400.0c92.904e 451 1
Maine(config)# ^Z
Maine#
```

FIGURE 12.6   Creating the static SAP entries on the Maine router.

Finally, use the Show IPX Servers command to view the static entries you have created (Figure 12.7). There are now four "simulated" servers on the network, two print servers and two file servers.

Now, let's look at the steps involved in creating a generic filter on a Cisco router. To create a generic filter, you need to perform the following tasks: create a standard or extended access list and apply the filter to an interface.

```
Maine# show ipx servers
Codes: S - Static, P - Periodic, E - EIGRP, N - NLSP, H - Holddown, + = detail
4 Total IPX Servers

Table ordering is based on routing and server info

   Type Name                      Net        Address        Port    Route Hops Itf
S     4 400FileServ      AC400400.0400.0c92.904e:0451       conn    1   Lo0
P     4 200FileServ      AC200200.0200.0c92.9048:0451       7/02    2   Se1
S     7 400PrntServ      AC400400.0400.0c92.904e:0451       conn    1   Lo0
P     7 200PrntServ      AC200200.0200.0c92.9048:0451       7/02    2   Se1
Maine#
```

FIGURE 12.7   Use the Show IPX Servers command to view the static entries created on the Maine router.

Suppose you want to block all traffic sent from Network AC400400 in Maine to Network AC200200 in Vermont (Figure 12.8). However, you still want clients and servers on Network AC200200 to be able to send packets to Network AC400400.

FIGURE 12.8
Block all traffic sent
from Network
AC400400 in Maine
to Network
AC200200 in
Vermont.

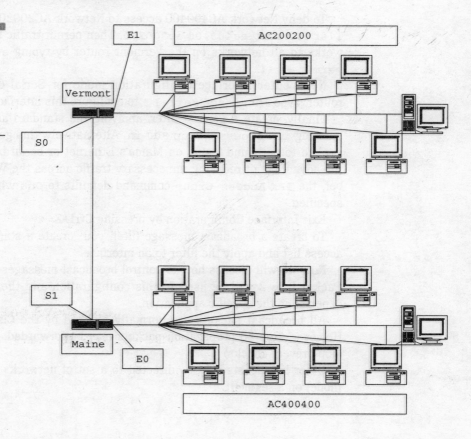

First, you need to create a standard access list on Serial 0 on Vermont to block all packets coming from Network AC400400 (Figure 12.9). Assume that you are logged in to the Vermont router and you have entered Privileged mode. To create a standard access list, you must enter Global Configuration mode. You do this by typing `config term` or `configure terminal` and pressing **Return**. If you type `config` or `configure`, and press **Return** twice, you also enter Global Configuration mode.

FIGURE 12.9
Create a standard access list on Serial 0 on Vermont to block all packets coming from Network AC400400.

```
Vermont# config term
Enter configuration commands, one per line. End with CNTL/Z.
Vermont(config)# access-list 800 deny ac400400 ac200200
Vermont(config)# access-list 800 permit -1 -1
Vermont(config)# interface serial 0
Vermont(config-if)# ipx access-group 800 in
Vermont(config-if)# ^Z
Vermont#
```

To deny Network AC400400 access to Network AC200200, enter `access-list 800 deny ac400400 ac200200`. Then permit traffic from all other networks to all networks on the Vermont router by typing `access-list 800 permit -1 -1`.

Next, enter Interface Configuration mode for Serial 0 on the Vermont router. Type `interface serial 0` to configure this interface.

Finally, create a generic filter, applying the standard access list to it by entering `ipx access-group 800 in`. Alternatively, this generic filter can be applied to outbound traffic on Maine's Ethernet or serial interface. This has the advantage of reducing unnecessary traffic across the WAN link. Remember, the `IPX Access-Group` command defaults to `Out` when no keyword is specified.

Exit Interface Configuration by pressing **Ctrl+Z**.

To create a broadcast message filter, you create a standard or extended access list and apply the filter to an interface.

Now we will discuss how to control broadcast messages on IPX networks. Packet type 2 will be used in this configuration and the actual type used depends on the specific application.

All broadcast packets are normally blocked by the Cisco IOS software. However, type 20 propagation packets may be forwarded, subject to certain loop-prevent checks.

Other broadcasts may be directed to a set of networks or a specific host (node) on a segment.

Figure 12.10 shows the Maine router connected to several Ethernet interfaces. All IPX clients are attached to segment AC100100, while all servers are attached to segments AC104200 and AC104300.

FIGURE 12.10
The Maine router
connected to several
Ethernet interfaces.

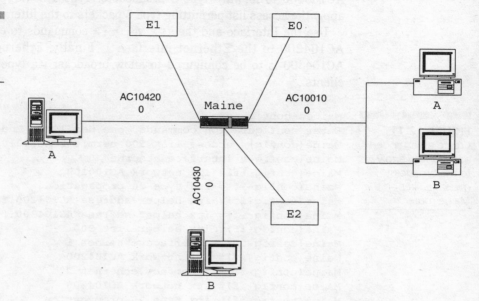

In controlling broadcasts on this router, the following conditions are to be applied:

- Only type 2 and type 20 broadcasts are to be forwarded.
- IPX clients on network AC100100 are allowed to broadcast via type 2 to any server on networks AC104200 and AC104300.
- IPX clients are allowed to broadcast via type 20 to any server on network AC104300.

To configure the Maine router, enter Global Configuration mode.

Let's create an extended access list to apply to the broadcast message filter (Figure 12.11). This list will permit type 2 broadcast traffic from Network AC100100. To do this, enter `access-list 900 permit 2 AC100100`.

The `IPX Interface` command enables you to configure the Ethernet 0 interface. To configure Network AC100100 on Ethernet 0, enter `ipx network ac100100`. The `IPX Type-20-Propagation` command allows Network AC100100 to broadcast via type 20 packets.

You now want to permit broadcast forwarding from Network AC100100 to Network AC104200 and from Network AC100100 to Network AC104300. To allow Network AC100100 to forward broadcasts, use the IPX Helper-Address command.

Now you need to set up the broadcast message filter to allow Network AC100100 to forward type 2 broadcasts. Type ipx helper-list 900 to apply the access list permitting type 2 packets to the filter.

Use the Interface and the IPX Network commands to configure Network AC104200 to the Ethernet interface 1. Finally, Ethernet 2 on Network AC104300 is to be configured to allow broadcast via type 20 from the IPX clients.

FIGURE 12.11
Create an extended access list to apply to the broadcast message filter on the Maine router.

```
Maine# config term
Enter configuration commands, one per line. End with CNTL/Z.
Maine(config)# access-list 900 permit 2 AC100100
Maine(config)# interface ethernet 0
Maine(config-if)# ipx network AC100100
Maine(config-if)# ipx type-20-propagation
Maine(config-if)# ipx helper-address AC104200.ffff.ffff.ffff
Maine(config-if)# ipx helper-address AC104300.ffff.ffff.ffff
Maine(config-if)# ipx helper-list 900
Maine(config-if)# interface ethernet 1
Maine(config-if)# ipx network AC104200
Maine(config-if)# interface ethernet 2
Maine(config-if)# ipx network AC104300
Maine(config-if)# ipx type-20-propagation
Maine(config-if)# ^Z
Maine#
```

The Type-20-Propagation command will enable IPX clients to broadcast via type 20 to any server on Network AC104300. Finally, press **Ctrl+Z** to return to Privileged mode.

This configuration means that any network downstream from Network AC100100 (for example, some arbitrary Network AC100111) cannot broadcast type 2 to Network AC104200 through the Maine router.

Broadcasts can only be achieved if the routers partitioning Networks AC100100 and AC100111 are configured to forward these broadcasts with a series of other configuration entries.

SAP/GNS and IP Tunneling

We will now consider how IP tunneling, SAP, and GNS filters manage IPX network traffic. We describe SAP and GNS filters and how to configure them using SAP access lists. We describe IP tunneling and how to configure an IP tunnel within an IPX network. We configure a SAP filter, and a GNS filter, and an IP tunnel within an IPX network.

SAP and GNS Filters

All servers on NetWare internetworks can advertise their services and addresses using SAP. All servers and routers keep a complete list of the services available throughout the network. Service advertisements synchronize the list of available services. Adding, finding, and removing services on an IPX network is dynamic because of SAP advertisements.

Each SAP service is identified by a hexadecimal number. Common examples are:

- 4—File server
- 7—Printer server
- 24—Remote bridge-server (router)

A Cisco router does not forward individual SAP broadcasts. Instead it will advertise the complete SAP table at regular intervals. The default interval is every 60 seconds.

SAP does not scale well over WANs. One solution to this problem is SAP filtering.

When a SAP advertisement arrives at the router interface, the contents are placed in the SAP table portion of main memory. The contents of the table are propagated during the next SAP update.

There is the option of configuring the interface to filter incoming and/or outgoing SAPs. The `IPX Input-SAP-Filter` and `IPX Output-SAP-Filter` commands place a SAP filter on an interface. You can apply only one of each type of SAP filter to an interface.

When an input SAP filter is in place, the services entered into the SAP table are reduced. The propagated SAP updates represent the entire table, but contain only a subset of all services.

To filter incoming service advertisements, use the `IPX Input-SAP-Filter` command:

```
ipx input-sap-filter access-list-number
```

The `access-list-number` is a decimal number from 1,000 to 1,099 indicating a SAP filter list.

Let's look at an example of an input SAP filter (Figure 12.12).

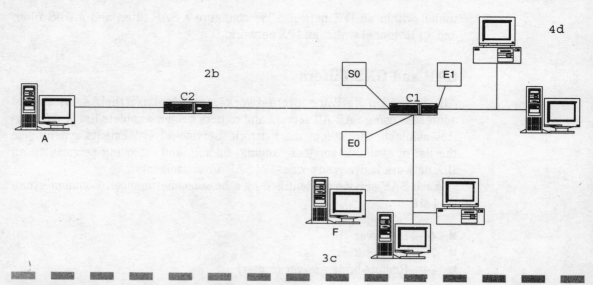

FIGURE 12.12   An example of an input SAP filter.

You want to configure Router C1 not to accept, and consequently not advertise, any information about Novell Server F. However, Router C1 will accept information about all other servers on Network 3c.

The following commands will set up the SAP access list to apply to the input SAP filter:

- `access-list 1000 deny 3c01.0000.0000.0001`
- `access-list 1000 permit -1`

Now that Server F has been denied, an input SAP filter needs to be placed on Router C1's Ethernet 0 interface to filter all incoming information for Network 3c. The following commands will filter the information through Router C1's Ethernet 0 interface:

- `interface ethernet 0`
- `ipx network 3c`
- `ipx input-sap-filter 1000`

Finally, you configure Router C1's other two interfaces so that information can be transmitted and received via the router:

- `interface ethernet 1`
- `ipx network 4d`

- interface serial 0
- px network 2b

When an output SAP filter is in place, the services propagated from the table are reduced. The propagated SAP updates represent a portion of the table contents and are a subset of all the known services.

To filter outgoing service advertisements, use the `IPX Output-SAP-Filter` command:

```
ipx output-sap-filter access-list-number
```

The `access-list-number` is a decimal number from 1,000 to 1,099 indicating a SAP filter list.

Now, let's look at an example of an output SAP filter. You want to configure Router C1 to prevent it advertising information about Novell Server A through interface Ethernet 1. However, Router C1 can advertise Server A on Network 3c.

The following commands set up the SAP access list to apply to the output SAP filter:

- access-list 1000 deny aa01.0000.0000.0001
- access-list 1000 permit -1

Now that Server A has been denied, an output SAP filter needs to be placed on Router C1's Ethernet 1 interface to filter all outgoing information from Network 4d. The following commands will filter information through Router C1's Ethernet 1 interface:

- interface ethernet 1
- ipx network 4d
- ipx output-sap-filter 1000

Finally, you configure Router C1's other two interfaces so that information can be transmitted and received via the router:

- interface ethernet 0
- ipx network 3c
- interface serial 0
- ipx network 2b

When you want to filter SAPs from a particular router, use the `IPX Router-SAP-Filter` command:

```
ipx router-sap-filter
access-list-number
```

The `access-list-number` is a decimal number from 1000 to 1099 indicating a SAP filter list.

A Get Nearest Server (GNS) request is a broadcast issued by a client using IPX SAP. A GNS packet requests a specific service from a server. The nearest NetWare server offering the service responds with another SAP. A GNS response allocates a server to the client, allowing the client to log in to the target server and proceed to use server resources.

A Cisco router can respond to a GNS request with the most recent server in the SAP table. A router acts like a server by building an SAP table. If real local NetWare servers are present, they should be the first to respond to GNS requests.

Use a SAP access list when creating a GNS filter. To create a GNS filter, use the IPX Output-GNS-Filter command:

```
ipx output-gns-filter access-list-number
```

The `access-list-number` is a decimal number from 1,000 to 1,099 indicating a SAP access list.

The router's GNS response can be delayed to allow local servers to respond first using the IPX GNS-Response-Delay command:

```
ipx gns-response-delay
milliseconds
```

The default is 0 milliseconds and 0 means no delay. The assumption is that no actual server is present on this segment and a rapid response by the router is desirable.

If a server is present, the router response can be delayed to allow the real server to respond first.

The router's GNS response can be configured in an effort to spread work evenly among servers using the IPX GNS Round-Robin command:

```
ipx gns-round-robin
```

This command enables the router to answer successive GNS requests for a particular type of server by providing the address of the next server available. Older versions of Cisco IOS had GNS round robin on by default; however, this has the undesirable side effect of allocating remote servers when closer ones are available. In current versions of Cisco IOS, this feature is off by default.

Cisco IOS responds to GNS requests with the most recently known available server of the type requested.

In the choice of a server for GNS response, the *tick value* of the route to each eligible server is used as the metric. The tick value is a delay time measurement used as the primary metric in determining the best path to a destination. If the tick values are equal, then hop count is used as the tie-breaker.

Let's configure a SAP filter to deny SAP traffic from the Vermont router to the Maine router. However, we do not want to stop all SAP traffic, just that for print servers.

You are currently logged onto the Maine router in Privileged mode. By typing show ipx servers, you can see that there are four servers on the network, two print servers and two file servers (Figure 12.13).

```
Maine# show ipx servers
Codes: S - Static, P - Periodic, E - EIGRP, N - NLSP, H - Holddown, + = detail
4 Total IPX Servers

Table ordering is based on routing and server info

   Type Name                    Net       Address        Port    Route Hops Itf
S    4 400FileServ     AC400400.0400.0c92.904e:0451       conn   1   Lo0
P    4 200FileServ     AC200200.0200.0c92.9048:0451       7/02   2   Se1
S    7 400PrntServ     AC400400.0400.0c92.904e:0451       conn   1   Lo0
P    7 200PrntServ     AC200200.0200.0c92.9048:0451       7/02   2   Se1
Maine#
```

FIGURE 12.13   By typing show ipx servers, you can see that there are four servers on the network, two print servers, and two file servers.

You want to create a SAP access list to block traffic from 200PrntServ on the Vermont router (Figure 12.14). This access list is best placed on the Vermont router to prevent SAP updates on the WAN link.

FIGURE 12.14
Create an SAP access list to block traffic from 200PrntServ on the Vermont router.

```
Vermont# config term
Enter configuration commands, one per line. End with CNTL/Z.
Vermont(config)# access-list 1000 deny AC200200.0200.0c92.9048 7
Vermont(config)# access-list 1000 permit -1
Vermont(config)# interface serial 0
Vermont(config-if)# ipx output-sap-filter 1000
Vermont(config-if)# ^Z
Vermont#
```

You are now logged onto the Vermont router and have entered Global Configuration mode.

To deny the print server on the Vermont router, you type:

```
access-list 1000 deny
ac200200.0200.0c92.9048 7
```

The next step is to permit SAP transmission between all other networks. This is done by entering:

```
access-list 1000 permit -1
```

Now that your SAP access list has been created, apply an output SAP filter on Vermont's Serial 0 interface. By typing interface serial 0, you enter Interface Configuration mode.

Finally, place the output SAP filter on Serial 0, ensuring that all outgoing traffic is monitored and any print server SAPs for the Maine router are denied. Type ipx output-sap-filter 1000 to create the SAP filter and press **Ctrl+Z** to return to Privileged mode.

To check that the print server has been removed from the Maine router, log onto it and type show ipx servers (Figure 12.15). You can see that the Vermont print server 200PrntServ has been removed.

```
Maine# show ipx servers
Codes: S - Static, P - Periodic, E - EIGRP, N - NLSP, H - Holddown, + = detail
3 Total IPX Servers

Table ordering is based on routing and server info

    Type Name                    Net       Address      Port     Route Hops Itf
S    4  400FileServ          AC400400.0400.0c92.904e:0451    conn   1  Lo0
P    4  200FileServ          AC200200.0200.0c92.9048:0451    7/02   2  Se1
S    7  400PrntServ          AC400400.0400.0c92.904e:0451    conn   1  Lo0
Maine#
```

FIGURE 12.15 Check that the print server has been removed from the Maine router, log onto it and type show ipx servers.

Now let's configure the Vermont router with a GNS response filter to deny it responding to any GNS requests from the Maine router. This filter will only deny the Vermont router from responding to requests sent by Maine to use its print server.

You are currently logged onto the Vermont router in Privileged mode. By typing show ipx servers, you can see that there are four servers on the network, two print servers and two file servers (Figure 12.16).

```
Vermont# show ipx servers
Codes: S - Static, P - Periodic, E - EIGRP, N - NLSP, H - Holddown, + = detail
4 Total IPX Servers

Table ordering is based on routing and server info

     Type Name                     Net       Address        Port    Route Hops Itf
S       4 400FileServ    AC400400.0400.0c92.904e:0451       conn   1  Lo0
P       4 200FileServ    AC200200.0200.0c92.9048:0451       7/02   2  Se1
S       7 400PrntServ    AC400400.0400.0c92.904e:0451       conn   1  Lo0
P       7 200PrntServ    AC200200.0200.0c92.9048:0451       7/02   2  Se1
Vermont#
```

FIGURE 12.16 Type show ipx servers, and you can see that there are four servers on the network, two print servers and two file servers.

You want to create a SAP access list to block GNS responses from Vermont to requests sent from Maine for the server 200PrntServ (Figure 12.17). Enter Global Configuration mode by typing config term.

FIGURE 12.17
Creating an SAP access list to block GNS responses from Vermont to requests sent from Maine for the server 200PrntServ.

```
Vermont# config term
Enter configuration commands, one per line. End with CNTL/Z.
Vermont(config)# access-list 1002 deny AC200200.0200.0c92.9048 7
Vermont(config)# access-list 1002 permit -1 -1
Vermont(config)# interface serial 0
Vermont(config-if)# ipx output-gns-filter 1002
Vermont(config-if)# ^Z
Vermont#
```

To deny the responses to requests for the print server on the Vermont router, type:

```
access-list 1002 deny
ac200200.0200.0c92.9048 7
```

The next step is to permit GNS responses to all other networks for all services. This is done by entering:

```
access-list 1000 permit -1 -1
```

Now that your SAP access list has been created, apply a GNS response filter on Vermont's Serial 0 interface. By typing interface serial 0, you enter Interface Configuration mode.

Finally, place the GNS response filter on Serial 0, ensuring that all outgoing traffic is monitored and any GNS responses to Maine for 200PrntServ are blocked. Type `ipx output-gns-filter 1002` to create the GNS filter and press **Ctrl+Z** to return to Privileged mode.

IP Tunneling

Communication within a LAN environment is relatively straightforward. The requirement for more global communication creates the following problems: how to connect isolated IPX LANs and how to connect the protocols operating in these LANs.

In a Novell IPX environment, the answer is to use a software-only IP tunnel interface when connecting IPX networks over IP networks (such as the Internet). A tunnel interface creates a virtual point-to-point link between isolated hosts. The tunnel is created by specifying a source and destination IP address. The use of a tunnel interface allows traffic from isolated hosts or discontiguous networks to be carried through an intermediate internetwork.

Reliability is achieved by using an IP network as the *transport mechanism*. This provides dynamic route selection for traffic passing through the tunnel. IP routing protocols allow more flexible route selection. They also scale better over large internetworks.

Different encapsulation methods carry protocol traffic. Encapsulation takes packets or frames from one network system and places them inside a frame from another network system. The *passenger* protocol traffic is encapsulated within a *carrier* protocol. The use of different encapsulations allows interoperability with vendor equipment.

Cisco's Generic Routing Encapsulation protocol over IP (GRE IP) is the default encapsulation method. The GRE carrier protocol encapsulates IPX packets inside IP tunnels.

Routing updates, SAP updates, and other administrative traffic may be sent over each tunnel interface. It is easy to saturate a physical link with routing information if several tunnels are configured over it.

Tunneling performance depends on:

- Routing and SAP update frequency
- Broadcasts
- Bandwidth of the physical interfaces
- The speed at which tunneled traffic can be switched by a router (CPU dependent)

In IPX environments, route filters and SAP filters cut down on the size of the updates that travel over tunnels.

To create an IP tunnel:

- Create a tunnel interface
- Assign an IPX network number to the tunnel
- Specify the source and destination of the tunnel
- Set the encapsulation method to use within the tunnel

The `Interface Tunnel` command creates a tunnel interface to carry protocol traffic:

```
interface tunnel interface-number
```

The `interface-number` is the number of the tunnel interface being created, ranging from 0 to 256.

You can assign the tunnel interface an IPX address so that it can be tested using extended `Ping` commands. To assign an IPX address, use the `IPX Network` command:

```
ipx network network
```

The `network` is an eight-digit hexadecimal number of the network to which the packet is being sent; it ranges from 1 to FFFFFFFD, where 0 is the local network, and –1 is all networks.

Now you need to establish the source and destination addresses for the tunnel. Use the `Tunnel Source` command to establish the source of the tunnel:

```
tunnel source {ip address | interface-type interface-number}
```

The `ip-address` is the IP address used as the source address for packets in the tunnel. The `interface-type` is the type of media, such as Ethernet or serial. The `interface-number` specifies the port, connector, or interface card number.

To establish the destination address for the tunnel, use the `Tunnel Destination` command. A single-hop direct connection to the tunnel destination is not required.

You need to include the hostname or IP address as an argument in the `Tunnel Destination` command:

```
tunnel destination {hostname | ip-address}
```

The *hostname* is the name of the host destination. The *ip-address* is the IP address of the host destination expressed in decimal in four-part, dotted notation.

The next step is to define the encapsulation method to be used within the tunnel. This is achieved using the Tunnel Mode command:

```
tunnel mode {aurp | cayman | eon | gre | ip | nos}
```

NOTE

----

aurp—*AppleTalk Update-based Routing Protocol*
cayman—*Cayman TunnelTalk AppleTalk encapsulation*
eon—*EON-compatible Connectionless Network Service (CLNS) tunnel*
gre ip—*Generic Route Encapsulation (GRE) protocol over IP, the default*
nos—*KA9Q/NOS compatible IP over IP*

Although the tunnel uses existing IP links to deliver encapsulated traffic, the tunnel itself does not require an IP address to function properly. Therefore, you can type the command no ip address to specify that the tunnel itself does not have an IP address.

Let's see how to configure an IP tunnel over an IP network. Figure 12.18 shows an IP network connecting two routers with Novell IPX networks on their LANs.

FIGURE 12.18 An IP network connecting two routers with Novell IPX networks on their LANs.

Before you create the tunnel interface, you can look at the current configuration using the Show IPX Route and the Show IP Route commands (Figure 12.19).

Here, there is an IP connection to the Maine router via 172.16.66.2, the IP address on Vermont's Serial 0 interface. The remote address is 172.16.66.1, the IP address on Maine's Serial 1 interface.

Using the Ping command, you can see that there is a successful connection between the Vermont router and the Maine router (Figure 12.20).

When creating a tunnel interface, you first need to enter Global Configuration mode (Figure 12.21).

```
Vermont# show ipx route
Codes: C - Connected primary network, c - Connected secondary network
       S - Static, F - Floating static, L - Local (internal), W - IPXWAN
       R - RIP, E - EIGRP, N - NLSP, X - External, A - Aggregate
       s - seconds, u - uses

1 Total IPX routes. Up to 1 parallel paths and 16 hops allowed.

No default route known.

C    AC10C000 (NOVELL-ETHER),  Et0
Vermont# show ip route
Codes: C - connected, S - static, I - IGRP, R - RIP, M - mobile, B - BGP
       D - EIGRP, EX - EIGRP external, O - OSPF, IA - OSPF inter area
       E1 - OSPF external type 1, E2 - OSPF external type 2, E - EGP
       i - IS-IS, L1 - IS-IS level-1, L2 - IS-IS level-2, * - candidate default
       U - per-user static route

Gateway of last resort is not set

     172.16.0.0/16 is subnetted, 1 subnets
C       172.16.66.0 is directly connected, Serial0
Vermont#
```

FIGURE 12.19   Current configuration viewed using the Show IPX Route and the Show IP Route commands.

```
Vermont# ping 172.166.66.1

Type escape sequence to abort.
Sending 5, 100-byte ICMP Echoes to 172.16.66.1, timeout is 2 seconds:
!!!!!
Success rate is 100 percent (5/5), round-trip min/avg/max = 56/60/80 ms
Vermont#
```

FIGURE 12.20   Using the Ping command, you can see that there is a successful connection between the Vermont router and the Maine router.

FIGURE 12.21
Configuring an IP
tunnel over an IP
network.

```
Vermont# config term
Enter configuration commands, one per line. End with CNTL/Z.
Vermont(config)# interface tunnel 0
Vermont(config-if)# ipx network aaabbbcc
Vermont(config-if)# tunnel source s0
Vermont(config-if)# tunnel destination 172.16.66.1
Vermont(config-if)# tunnel mode gre ip
Vermont(config-if)# no ip address
Vermont(config-if)# ^Z
Vermont#
```

Next, use the `Interface Tunnel` command to create the tunnel interface. Enter `interface tunnel 0` which enables Interface Configuration mode.

You can now assign the tunnel interface an IPX address so that it can be tested using extended `Ping` commands. To assign an IPX address, use the IPX `Network` command.

You need to establish the source and destination addresses for the tunnel.

Use the `Tunnel Source` command to establish the source of the tunnel. In this case, we are using Vermont's Serial 0 interface. Alternatively, you can use the IP address of Vermont's Serial 0 interface to establish the source of the tunnel.

The `Tunnel Destination` command establishes the destination address for the tunnel. The destination is Maine's Serial 1 router. A single-hop direct connection to the tunnel destination is not required.

Finally, define the encapsulation method to be used within the tunnel. To do this, type `tunnel mode gre ip`. This is default encapsulation mode.

Although the tunnel uses existing IP links to deliver encapsulated traffic, the tunnel itself does not require an IP address to function properly. Therefore, you can type the command `no ip address` to define that the tunnel itself does not have an IP address and exit Configuration mode.

Finally, the `Show IPX Route` command will show that the tunnel has been created. To show that the tunnel is operational and to see the IPX parameters associated with it (Figure 12.22), type `show ipx interface tunnel 0` (Figure 12.23).

The far side of the tunnel has not been configured, therefore you cannot see the remote IPX network. You can also type `show interface tunnel 0`, but this command will not show the tunnel's IPX parameters.

```
Vermont# show ipx route
Codes: C - Connected primary network, c - Connected secondary network
       S - Static, F - Floating static, L - Local (internal), W - IPXWAN
       R - RIP, E - EIGRP, N - NLSP, X - External, A - Aggregate
       s - seconds, u - uses

2 Total IPX routes. Up to 1 parallel paths and 16 hops allowed.

No default route known.

C    AAABBBCC (TUNNEL),        Tu0
C    AC10C000 (NOVELL-ETHER),  Et0
Vermont#
```

FIGURE 12.22   The Show IPX Route command.

```
Vermont# show ipx interface tunnel 0
Tunnel0 is up, line protocol is up
  IPX address is AAABBBCC.0000.0c92.9048 [up] line-up, RIPPQ: 0, SAPPQ: 0
  Delay of this IPX network, in ticks is 150 throughput 0 link delay
  Delay of this IPX network, in ticks is 150 throughput 0 link delay 0
  IPXWAN processing not enabled on this interface
  IPX SAP update interval is 1 minute(s)
  IPX type 20 propagation packet forwarding is disabled
  Incoming access list is not set
  Outgoing access list is not set
  IPX helper access list is not set
  SAP GNS processing enabled, delay 0 ms, output filter list is not set
  SAP Input filter list is not set
  SAP Output filter list is not set
  SAP Router filter list is not set
  Input filter list is not set
  Output filter list is not set
  Router filter list is not set
  Netbios Input host access list is not set
  Netbios Input bytes access list is not set
  Netbios Output host access list is not set
  Netbios Output bytes access list is not set
  Updates each 60 seconds, aging multiples RIP: 3 SAP: 3
  SAP interpacket delay is 55 ms, maximum size is 480 bytes
  RIP interpacket delay is 55 ms, maximum size is 432 bytes
  Watchdog spoofing is disabled, SPX spoofing is disabled, idle time 60
  IPX accounting is disabled
  IPX fast switching is configured (enabled)
  RIP packets received 0, RIP packets sent 6
  SAP packets received 0, SAP packets sent 6
Vermont#
```

FIGURE 12.23 Use show ipx interface tunnel 0 to show that the tunnel is operational and to see the IPX parameters associated with it.

CHAPTER 13

AppleTalk Overview and Addressing

AppleTalk Overview

In this section, we will explore the protocols that make up AppleTalk's protocol suite, explaining what AppleTalk is and outlining the function of the physical and data-link layers, their protocols and the function of each. We will do the same for the network and transport layers and the session, presentation, and application layers.

Understanding AppleTalk

AppleTalk is a proprietary distributed client/server networking system developed by Apple Computer. Such a system enables users to share network resources, such as files and printers, with other users. Computers supplying these network resources are called servers; computers using a server's network resources are called clients.

AppleTalk was designed with a transparent network interface. That is, the interaction between client computers and network servers requires little interaction from the user. The computer itself determines the location of the requested material and accesses it without further information from the user. In addition, the operations of the AppleTalk protocols are invisible to end-users, who see only the result of these operations.

In addition to ease of use, distributed systems afford an economic advantage over peer-to-peer systems because important materials can be located in a few, rather than many, locations.

AppleTalk provides the following features:

- Supporting for peer-to-peer networking
- Allowing a router to propagate client lookups for services, ensuring that all available services will be located by the user
- Enabling devices dynamically to acquire addresses
- Using the Routing Table Maintenance Protocol (RTMP) as its routing protocol.

There are two versions of AppleTalk: Phase 1 and Phase 2.

AppleTalk Phase 1 was developed in the early 1980s. It was designed specifically for use in local workgroups. AppleTalk Phase 2 is an enhanced version of Phase 1 that improves the routing capabilities of AppleTalk and was designed for use in larger internetworks.

AppleTalk specifies a series of communication protocols that make up Apple's network architecture (Figure 13.1). These protocols fall into distinct layers according to the Open System Interconnection (OSI) model. For more information on the OSI model, see Chapter 2.

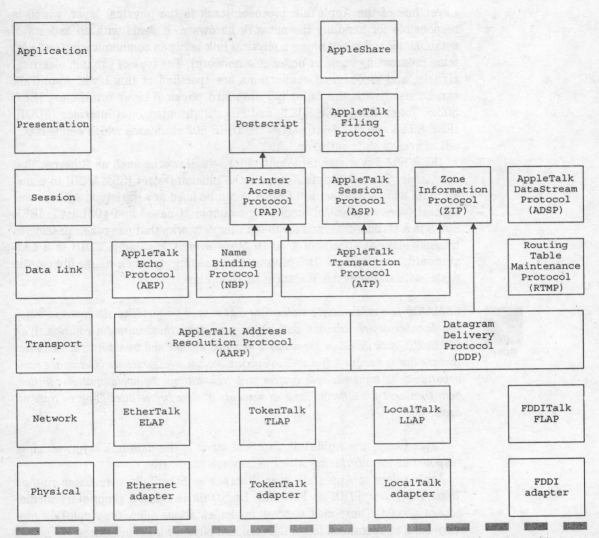

FIGURE 13.1 AppleTalk specifies a series of communication protocols that make up Apple's network architecture.

NOTE

Every form of network has its own way of transmitting data and divides the entire process into a series of specific functions. Each function requires a complete set of operating rules (or protocols).

AppleTalk's Physical and Data-link Layers

Layer one of the AppleTalk protocol stack is the physical layer, which is responsible for handling the network hardware. It deals with all aspects of establishing and maintaining a physical link between communicating end systems (nonrouting hosts or nodes in a network). The type of cabling, electrical signals, and mechanical connections are specified at this layer. AppleTalk can be used with the following standard physical-layer interfaces: IEEE 802.3, Token Ring/IEEE 802.5, and Fiber Distributed Data Interface (FDDI). IEEE 802.3 and 802.5 are part of the IEEE 802 standards which define methods of access and control on LANs.

IEEE 802.3 is a standard defined for bus networks such as Ethernet that use Carrier Sense Multiple Access with Collision Detect (CSMA/CD) to transmit data across a network. CSMA/CD can be used at a variety of speeds over several types of physical media, for example 10Base2 and 100BaseT. IEEE 802.5 is a standard defined for token ring networks that use token passing to transmit data at speeds of 4 or 16 Mbps over STP cabling. FDDI is a LAN standard, specifying a 100-Mbps token-passing network using fiber optic cable, with transmission distances of up to 2km.

NOTE

CSMA/CD is a media-access mechanism that is used for handling situations in which two or more devices transmit data at the same time, thus causing a collision. With CSMA/CD, each device on the network monitors the line and transmits when it senses that the line is not busy. If a collision occurs because another device is using the same opportunity to transmit, both devices stop transmitting. To avoid another collision, both then wait for differing random amounts of time before attempting to transmit again.

Layer two of the AppleTalk Protocol stack is the data-link layer, which is responsible for interfacing with the network hardware.

Apple refers to AppleTalk over Ethernet as EtherTalk, over token ring as TokenTalk, over FDDI as FDDITal; LocalTalk is Apple's proprietary media-access system. These media-access implementations allow the AppleTalk protocol suite to operate on top of the standard physical-layer interfaces.

EtherTalk, TokenTalk, and FDDITalk networks are organized exactly the same as the networks of the associated physical-layer interfaces that they represent. For example, FDDITalk supports the same speeds and the same number of active network nodes as an FDDI network.

LocalTalk is Apple's own network interface and is a proprietary data-link layer implementation developed by Apple for its AppleTalk protocol suite. It is designed as a cost-effective network solution for connecting local workgroups. LocalTalk hardware is typically built into Apple products, and is easily connected using inexpensive twisted-pair cabling. LocalTalk is based on contention access (CSMA/CD), a bus topology, and baseband signaling, and transmits data over shielded twisted-pair media at 230.4 Kbps. LocalTalk network segments can span up to 300 meters and support a maximum of 32 nodes. Many Apple products contain a LocalTalk interface, but Cisco products do not support this type of interface.

Link Access Protocol handles the interaction between the AppleTalk protocols and the associated media's data-link interface. A LAP is needed because upper-layer AppleTalk protocols do not recognize the standard interface's hardware addresses. In order for data to be transmitted across the physical layer, the network addresses have to be mapped to the hardware addresses. LAP uses the AppleTalk Address Resolution Protocol (AARP) to carry out this mapping process. AARP is an AppleTalk network-layer protocol.

Let's look at how LAP enables the interaction between upper-layer protocols and the physical layer.

Data from the upper-layer protocols are divided, at the network layer, into packets. LAP receives a Datagram Delivery Protocol (DDP) packet from the network layer that requires transmission. DDP is an AppleTalk network-layer protocol.

LAP finds the network address specified in the DDP packet's header and then requests AARP to find the corresponding hardware address. When AARP returns the hardware address, LAP creates a new header which contains the hardware address in its destination field. It then appends this header to the DDP packet. This enables the resulting frame (a logical grouping of information sent as a data-link layer unit over a transmission medium) to be transmitted across the physical medium. Headers that can be applied at this level are the IEEE 802.3, IEEE 802.5, FDDI, Subnetwork Access Protocol (SNAP), and the IEEE 802.2 Logical Link Control (LLC) header.

Each type of media-access implementation has it own link-layer protocol:

- EtherTalk uses the EtherTalk Link-Access Protocol (ELAP)
- TokenTalk uses the TokenTalk Link-Access Protocol (TLAP)
- FDDITalk uses the FDDITalk Link-Access Protocol (FLAP)
- LocalTalk uses the LocalTalk Link-Access Protocol (LLAP)

AppleTalk's Network and Transport Layers

Layer three of the AppleTalk protocol stack is the network layer, at which routing occurs. This layer is responsible for ensuring that data reach their destination when sent across a network. Layer 3 achieves this by using the Datagram Delivery Protocol (DDP). DDP is the primary network-layer routing protocol in the AppleTalk protocol suite. Its main function is to transmit packets to and receive packets from the data-link layer.

When DDP receives data from devices, it creates a DDP header using the appropriate destination network address and passes the packet to the data-link layer protocol. When DDP receives frames from the data-link layer, it examines the DDP header to find the destination network address, and routes the packet to the destination device.

Another protocol at the network layer is AppleTalk Address Resolution Protocol (AARP), whose function is to associate AppleTalk network addresses with hardware addresses. AARP services are used by other AppleTalk protocols.

AARP uses an Address Mapping Table (AMT) to simplify mapping between network and hardware addresses. By keeping the most recently used addresses in the AMT, AARP can efficiently map addresses as needed. Network configurations are constantly changing, so over time, the potential increases for an AMT entry to become invalid. To overcome this, each AMT entry typically has a timer associated with it. Every time the AARP receives a packet that verifies or changes the entry, the timer is reset. If the timer expires, the entry is deleted from the AMT.

When an AppleTalk protocol has data to send, it passes the network address of the destination node to AARP. AARP supplies the hardware address associated with that network address by checking the AMT to see whether the network address is already mapped to a hardware address. If the address is already mapped, the hardware address is passed to the inquiring AppleTalk protocol, which uses it to communicate with the destination.

If the address is not mapped, AARP transmits a broadcast using the network address in question, requesting that the destination node supply its hardware address. Once AARP receives the node's hardware address it creates an entry in the AMT for future reference. The hardware address is then passed to the inquiring AppleTalk protocol, which uses it to communicate with the destination node. If there is no node with the specified network address, no response is sent. After a specified number of retries, AARP assumes that the protocol address is not in use and returns an error to the inquiring AppleTalk protocol.

Layer four of the AppleTalk protocol stack is the transport layer. It is responsible for ensuring reliable network communication between network devices. The transport layer contains five protocols:

- AppleTalk Echo Protocol (AEP)

- AppleTalk Transaction Protocol (ATP)
- Name Binding Protocol (NBP)
- AppleTalk Update-Based Routing Protocol (AURP)
- Routing Table Maintenance Protocol (RTMP)

A router uses routing tables to select the optimal route to send data across a network. RTMP establishes and maintains AppleTalk routing tables. It can also be used by a device to learn a router's address.

RTMP defines what information is to be contained within each routing table and the rules for how this information is to be exchanged between routers so that they can maintain their routing tables. The periodic exchange of routing tables allows the routers in an internetwork to ensure that they supply current and consistent information.

The AppleTalk Transaction Protocol (ATP) ensures that DDP packets are delivered to a destination without any losses. It does this by means of transaction requests and transaction responses. Transaction requests are sent every time a packet is sent to a device. Upon receiving the request, the client performs the requested action and returns the appropriate information in a transaction response. By pairing transaction requests to transaction responses, ATP ensures that packets are transferred and acknowledged.

A device is generally represented by a numeric network address. To make network access easier for users, AppleTalk devices generally use names instead of a numeric address. For example, the sales printer could be represented as "sales_p".

The Name Binding Protocol (NBP) enables routing and communication to occur between devices by translating AppleTalk device names into numeric network addresses.

Before a node sends traffic across a network it checks to see if the destination address is reachable. It uses the AppleTalk Echo Protocol (AEP) to do this. One node sends a packet to another node and if it receives a duplicate, or echo, of that packet it knows that the node is reachable.

AppleTalk is most often used in LAN environments. However, the AppleTalk Update-Based Routing Protocol (AURP) makes it possible to connect two or more discontiguous AppleTalk internetworks through a foreign network (such as TCP/IP) to form an AppleTalk WAN. (This type of connection is called an *AURP tunnel*.) It achieves this by encapsulating AppleTalk traffic in the header of the foreign protocol.

In addition to its encapsulation function, AURP maintains routing tables for the entire AppleTalk WAN by exchanging routing information between exterior routers. (An exterior router is a router connected to an AURP tunnel.)

AppleTalk's Upper Layers

Situated on top of the transport layer is layer five, the session layer, whose main function is to establish and control data conversations ("Sessions") between devices.

The session layer contains four protocols:

- AppleTalk Session Protocol (ASP)
- AppleTalk's Printer Access Protocol (PAP)
- AppleTalk Data Stream Protocol (ADSP)
- Zone Information Protocol (ZIP). A zone is a logical collection of devices on an AppleTalk network, for example the sales zone.

ASP establishes and maintains sessions between AppleTalk clients and servers. It allows a client to establish a session with a server and to send commands to that server. ASP enables multiple client sessions to a single server to be maintained simultaneously. This allows a print server, for example, to process jobs from several different workstations at the same time.

To establish a session, for example between a client and a server, the workstation sends a request to the ASP asking it to establish a session with a particular server. When the PAP receives the request it uses the NBP to learn the network address of the requested server. PAP then uses the network address to open a connection between the client and server.

Once a connection is established the client and server can exchange information. When the communication is complete, PAP terminates the connection.

Like ASP, PAP establishes and maintains connections between clients and servers. The difference between them is that the PAP is mainly used to connect a client to a printer.

When a connection is made between two devices, the ADSP is responsible for the reliable transmission of data between them. ADSP provides full-duplex byte-stream delivery, which means that a conversation between two computers can take place in both directions at the same time. ATP, the transport-layer protocol, does not provide this type of delivery. The benefit of duplex byte-stream delivery is that it greatly speeds up data transfer.

ADSP ensures the reliable transfer of data by guaranteeing that data are correctly sequenced and that packets are not duplicated. It also controls the rate at which data are sent from one device to another by using a process called *flow control*, which enables the destination device to receive from the source device only the amount of data that its buffer allows.

The Zone Information Protocol (ZIP) coordinates NBP functions and maintains network number-to-zone name mappings. ZIP is used primarily by

AppleTalk routers. However, other network devices such as end nodes, use ZIP services at startup to assign their zone(s) and acquire internetwork zone information. NBP also relies on ZIP to help determine which networks belong to which zones.

ZIP maintains a zone information table (ZIT) in each router. These are lists maintained by ZIP that map specific network numbers to one or more zone names. Each ZIT contains a network number-to-zone name mapping for every network in the internetwork.

ZIP uses RTMP routing tables to keep up with network topology changes. When ZIP finds a routing table entry that is not in the ZIT, it creates a new ZIT entry.

The sixth layer of the AppleTalk protocol stack is the presentation layer, which is responsible for handling issues related to data files and formats.

The AppleTalk Filing Protocol (AFP) is used to provide remote access to files on a network. PostScript is a well-known page description language used in Apple's laser printers.

The last layer in the AppleTalk protocol stack is the application layer which defines the protocols used to provide services to application processes such as file transfer. AppleTalk has no specific protocols for the application layer, since printing and file services are all carried out at lower levels.

Network Entities

This section discusses the components of an AppleTalk network. It outlines what AppleTalk nodes and sockets are and what an AppleTalk network is. It describes the different categories of AppleTalk networks and outlines what AppleTalk zones are.

AppleTalk Nodes and Sockets

There are four basic components to an AppleTalk network: nodes, sockets, networks, and zones.

An AppleTalk *node* is any addressable device connected to an AppleTalk network. This device might be a Macintosh computer, a printer, an IBM PC, a router, or some other similar device. Each node in an AppleTalk network belongs to a single *network* and a specific *zone*. An AppleTalk zone is a logical group of nodes or networks.

Within each node are unique, addressable locations called *sockets*. A socket can be thought of as a software structure operating as a communications end-point within a network device. Sockets are the logical points at which upper-layer AppleTalk software processes and the network-layer Datagram Delivery Protocol (DDP) interact. The upper-layer software processes are known as socket clients. These are also referred to as *Network-Visible Entities (NVEs)*.

Socket clients can own one or more sockets, which they use to send and receive datagrams. For example, if a software process such as a communications program obtains a socket for receiving messages, that socket can only be used to receive messages for that program. Messages that arrive for some other program arrive through their own sockets.

Sockets can be assigned statically or dynamically. Statically assigned sockets are reserved for use by certain protocols or other processes. Dynamically assigned sockets are assigned by DDP to socket clients when needed.

An AppleTalk node can contain up to 254 different socket numbers.

AppleTalk Networks

An AppleTalk network consists of a single logical cable and multiple attached nodes. This logical cable is composed of either a single physical cable or multiple physical cables interconnected using bridges or routers.

AppleTalk networks fall into two categories: *nonextended* and *extended*. A nonextended AppleTalk network is a physical network segment assigned only a single network number. For example, Network 100 and Network 562 are both valid network numbers in a nonextended network. Because all nodes on a network have the same network number, each node is assigned a unique node number to distinguish it from other nodes on the network.

AppleTalk Phase 1 supports only nonextended networks. Nonextended network configurations are, as a rule, no longer used in new networks. They have been superseded by extended network configurations.

An extended AppleTalk network is a physical network segment that can be assigned multiple network numbers, or *cable-ranges*. AppleTalk cable-ranges can indicate a single (unary) network number or multiple consecutive network numbers. For example, the cable-ranges Network 3–3 (unary) and Network 3–6 are both valid in an extended network.

Nodes on an extended network can have the same node number. For example, a network with a cable-range of 3–4 can have two nodes with the same node number—3–20 and 4–20. In order to identify a particular node, each combination of network number and node number must be unique.

AppleTalk Phase 2 supports both extended and nonextended networks.

AppleTalk Zones

An AppleTalk zone is a logical group of nodes or networks. The assignment of zones is usually done according to:

- A logical scheme such as organizational departments, for example the marketing department.
- Physical location such as the floor of a building, for example the first floor.

The nodes or networks need not be physically contiguous in order to belong to the same AppleTalk zone. For example, a computer in one building can belong to the same zone as a file server in a different building.

Zones are defined when you configure the network. When configuring zones you assign each one a logical name in order to identify it. One of the main reasons for breaking a network into zones is to reduce the amount of searching a user must do to find a resource on a network. Zones also help reduce broadcast traffic because service requests are only sent to nodes in a particular zone, and not all nodes on a network. To use a particular printer on the network, the user can search through zones instead of searching the entire network. Let's look at how this is done using the *Chooser facility*.

The Chooser is a desk accessory included with the Macintosh software system and is used to select network services. It is the most common way of interfacing with an AppleTalk network.

First double-click the LaserWriter icon to select print services. Once this is done, the Chooser sends an NBP request to the nearest router for a list of all zones that contain LaserWriters. Since entities are represented by names, applications (and nodes) have to use NBP to discover the addresses of services (and nodes) such as printers.

When the router returns a list of all zones on the internetwork you can select the zone you want to print from. Once you select a zone, the Chooser sends another NBP request to the nearest router in that zone to find all the available printers in that zone. NBP requests use the following character string for controlling a search:

```
=:service type%004@zone name
```

double-clicking an icon in the Chooser defines the service type and selecting a zone defines the zone name. Depending on the size of the network this router may forward the NBP requests to other routers in the zone.

If a zone is made up of a number of cable-ranges, the router forwards these requests to each cable grouped in the selected zone. This type of request is in the form of a one-to-many *multicast* which goes to all the printers on the cable. A multicast is a transmission method in which single packets are copied by the network and sent to a specific subset of network addresses.

Any available printers in that zone reply to the request using NBP reply packets. An NBP reply, depending on the content of the request, generally contains the name, type, and network address (AppleTalk address) of the service provided by a node. Applications use the address to communicate with the device while users only have to relate to the service through its name. Routers in the path forward the NBP reply packets to the originating router (that sent the request) which then sends them to your computer.

The Chooser displays the NBP reply packets as a list of available printers. You can now select the printer you want to print from.

When a service has been chosen, a logical link for that service is retained by your computer for future reference. A list of services and zones is maintained within the router for local reference.

The number of zones you can assign to a network will depend on whether the network is extended or nonextended. Only one zone name is assigned to a nonextended network, so all nodes on that network belong to the same zone.

Extended networks can have multiple AppleTalk zones configured on a single network segment. Nodes on extended networks can belong to any single zone associated with the extended network. Let's look at how multiple zones on a network are dealt with.

When a network is associated with multiple zones, you configure the network with a zones list. This list contains the names of each zone associated with that network. A node on an extended network can belong to only one zone in that list.

Each zones list has a default zone. When a node first starts up, it resides in the default zone.

Each type of router can use its own method of defining which zone is the default zone. Generally the first zone in the zones list is used as the default zone.

Nodes belong to the default zone until another zone is chosen. (Zone names can be chosen from the Network Control Panel in the Chooser.) The zone in which a node is registered is the zone in which its services (if any) are advertised. Using the default zone does not restrict a user's ability to view and access network services in other AppleTalk zones by using the Chooser.

In order to ensure that each router has accurate information about the network, all routers must agree on which zone name is the default zone and the names in the zones list associated with that network.

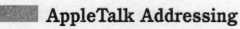

AppleTalk Addressing

This section describes how AppleTalk addresses are acquired and configured on an interface. We outline the components of an AppleTalk network address and discuss the AppleTalk network numbering systems. We describe how network addresses are assigned to nodes and how to manually configure a router's interface. We also investigate manual configuration of AppleTalk interfaces for nonextended and extended addressing. We describe how to dynamically configure a router's interface using Discovery mode.

Network Addresses

In order for a router to send data to the right destination, every node must have a unique address. AppleTalk network addresses consist of three elements: a network number, a node number, and a socket number.

The network number is a 16-bit value that identifies a specific AppleTalk network. The node number is an 8-bit value that identifies a particular AppleTalk node attached to the specified network. The socket number is an 8-bit number that identifies a specific socket running on a network node.

AppleTalk addresses are usually written as decimal values separated by a period. For example, 10.1.50 means network 10, node 1, socket 50. The address 10.1.50 might also be represented as 10.1, socket 50.

Two AppleTalk network numbering systems are currently in use: extended and nonextended. With nonextended addressing (used on LocalTalk, ARC-NET, and EtherTalk 1.0. networks) all nodes on a physical network have the same network address but a unique node number. Because each node is identified by an 8-bit node number, this limits the total number of addresses per network to 254. The highest number that can be represented in eight bits is 256, but only 254 addresses can be used because the node numbers 0 and 255 are reserved by AppleTalk. These 254 addresses can consist of up to 127 hosts and 127 servers.

With extended addressing, it is possible to assign a range of cable numbers to a network. Each network number can support up to 253 nodes (the node numbers 0, 254, and 255 are reserved to AppleTalk). These 253 nodes can consist of any combination of any number of hosts or servers.

Each node on an extended network uses the full 24-bit combination of network and node number as its unique identifier. This scheme increases the theoretical limit of the number of nodes per network to greater than 16 million.

AppleTalk Address Acquistion

AppleTalk nodes are assigned addresses dynamically when they first attach to a network. When an AppleTalk node is first attached to the network, it receives a provisional network-layer address.

The network portion of the provisional address (the first 16 bits) is selected from a startup range. The startup range is a reserved range of network addresses between the values of 65280 and 65534. The node portion (the next eight bits) of the provisional address is chosen dynamically.

The provisional address allows a node to communicate with a router attached to the same network, and to acquire a valid network number for the network. The node uses ZIP to locate a router that is attached to the same network.

When a router is located it replies with the valid cable-range for the network to which the node is attached. The node selects a valid network number from the cable-range supplied by the router, and then randomly chooses a node number.

The node uses AARP to verify the uniqueness of the address that it has chosen. Apart from mapping network and hardware addresses, AARP is also used to verify a node's dynamically assigned address. AARP broadcasts AARP probe packets on the network to determine whether the selected address is in use by another node.

If the address is not being used (that is, no other node responds to the AARP probe within a specific period), the node has successfully been assigned an address. If another node is using the address, that node responds to the AARP probe with a message indicating that the address is in use. In this case, AARP chooses another address and repeats this procedure until a usable address is found.

When a node acquires a network address it stores it in its memory. This enables a node to use the same address when it reconnects to the network after being turned off, unless another node has already obtained that address.

Manually Configuring AppleTalk Interfaces

A router is also a node on a network, so it has a node address just like any other node, such as a Mac or a LaserWriter. The router's node address can be acquired dynamically in the same manner as other nodes' AppleTalk addresses.

A router's interface needs to be assigned an address and one or more zone names before it can operate. It is possible to configure a router's interface for nonextended and extended AppleTalk routing either manually or dynamically.

To configure an interface manually for nonextended AppleTalk routing, the interface must be assigned an AppleTalk address and a zone name.

Let's look at an example. We want to configure the Ethernet interface 0 (E0) of the Vermont router with a network address of 206, the node number 79, and the zone name "sales" (Figure 13.2).

FIGURE 13.2
Configuring the Ethernet interface 0 of the Vermont router with a network address, node number, and zone name.

```
Vermont#
Vermont# configure terminal
Enter configuration commands, one per line. End with CNTL/Z.
Vermont(config)#
Vermont(config)# appletalk routing
Vermont(config)# interface ethernet 0
Vermont(config-if)# appletalk address 206.79
Vermont(config-if)# appletalk zone sales
Vermont(config-if)# ^Z
Vermont# copy run start
Building configuration...
[OK]
Vermont#
```

Let's assume an opened terminal session with the Vermont router. Before you can configure the interface you must put the router into Configuration mode and enable AppleTalk routing. To put the router into Configuration mode type configure terminal in Privileged mode and press **Enter**. Then, to enable AppleTalk routing on the router, type appletalk routing. Generally, the AppleTalk Protocol command is used after AppleTalk routing is enabled. It allows you to select the protocol that generates routing updates on this interface. If this command is not specified, RTMP is selected by default.

Once AppleTalk routing is enabled you specify the interface you want to configure. To configure router Vermont's Ethernet 0 interface, type interface ethernet 0. The router is now in Interface Configuration mode.

Once the router is in Interface Configuration mode you can assign the interface an AppleTalk address. To assign the AppleTalk address 206.79 to the interface type appletalk address 206.79. The network number is represented by the number 206 while the node number is represented by the number 79.

To assign the zone name "sales" to the interface type appletalk zone sales. You can use the AppleTalk Zone command only after an AppleTalk Address command. Only one zone name can be assigned to an interface configured with a nonextended address. If you assign more than one zone name, the second zone name will replace the first one.

Router Vermont's E0 interface is now configured with a nonextended address and a zone name. Exit the Configuration mode by pressing **Ctrl+Z**. Save the configuration in NVRAM by entering `copy run start`.

After you assign the address and zone names, the interface will attempt to verify them with another operational router on the connected network. If there are any discrepancies, for example, the interface has been assigned the wrong zone name, the interface will not become operational until the discrepancy is rectified. If there are no discrepancies the interface will become operational.

If there are no neighboring operational routers, the device will assume the interface's configuration is correct, and the interface will become operational. When an interface is restarted, it follows this procedure to check its configuration information, but the router acquires its configuration information from memory.

The commands used to configure an interface manually for nonextended and extended routing are very similar. The only difference is that for extended routing the `AppleTalk Cable-range` command is used instead of the `AppleTalk Address` command.

To assign an AppleTalk cable-range to an interface you issue the following command in Interface Configuration mode:

```
appletalk cable-range cable-range [network.node]
```

The `Cable-range` parameter specifies the start and end of the cable-range, separated by a hyphen. These values are decimal numbers from 0 to 65279. The starting network number must be less than or equal to the ending network number.

The optional `Network.node` parameter makes it possible to specify a unique address. Specifying the `Network.node` parameter is useful on mapped interfaces. When you assign this address the network number must fall within the specified range of network numbers. Let's look at an example.

You want to configure the Serial 1 interface (S1) on the Maine router with:

- The cable-range 2–2 (a range of one). The advantage of assigning it a cable-range of 1 is that it allows compatibility with nonextended networks. For example, if Maine's S0 interface was connected to the Vermont router that was configured earlier.
- A network address of 2.27
- The zone name "link1". Maine's E0 interface has already been configured.

Let's assume you have enabled AppleTalk routing and specified S1 as the interface you want to configure (Figure 13.3). To assign the cable-range 2–2 and the network address 2.27 to Maine's S1 interface, type `appletalk cable-range 2-2 2.27`. To assign the zone "link1" to this interface, type `appletalk zone link1`.

Repeated execution of the `AppleTalk Zone` command will not replace the interface's zone name with the newly specified zone name, but will add it to the zones list. This is because you can assign more than one zone name to a cable-range. The first zone name you assign is considered to be the default zone. The router always uses the default zone when registering NBP names for interfaces.

FIGURE 13.3
Enabling AppleTalk
routing and S1 as the
interface that you
want to configure.

```
Vermont#
Vermont# configure terminal
Enter configuration commands, one per line. End with CNTL/Z.
Vermont(config)#
Vermont(config)# appletalk routing
Vermont(config)# interface serial 1
Vermont(config-if)# appletalk cable-range 2-2 2.27
Vermont(config-if)# appletalk zone link1
Vermont(config-if)#
```

The zone list is cleared automatically when you issue an `AppleTalk Address` or `AppleTalk Cable-range` command. The list is also cleared if you issue the `AppleTalk Zone` command on an existing network; this can occur when zones are added to a set of routers until all routers are in agreement.

There are a number of commands to use to check that an interface's configuration is correct. You can display the status of an AppleTalk interface and the parameters configured on it by issuing the following command in Privileged mode:

```
show appletalk interface [type number]
```

The output of this command for Vermont's Ethernet 0 interface shown in Figure 13.4.

FIGURE 13.4
The status of an
AppleTalk interface
and the parameters
configured on it are
displayed by issuing
the Show Appletalk
Interface command.

```
Vermont# show appletalk interface ethernet 0
Ethernet0 is up, line protocol is up
   AppleTalk address is 206.79, Valid
   AppleTalk zone is "sales"
   AppleTalk address is gleaning is disabled
   AppleTalk route cache is enabled
Vermont#
```

The Show AppleTalk Interface command on router Vermont establishes:

- The type of interface. It states that it is currently active and inserted into the network.
- That the interface is usable.
- The address of the interface, and that the address is valid.
- The name of the zone this interface is in.

To verify that the interface is connected to the network you need to see if it can communicate with a node on that network. To check a node's reachability and network connectivity, issue the following command in Privileged mode (Ping stands for packet internet groper.)

```
ping [network.node]
```

The Ping command checks a node's reachability and network connectivity by sending AppleTalk Echo Protocol (AEP) datagrams to other AppleTalk nodes to verify connectivity and measure round-trip times.

The output of the Ping command for router Vermont is shown in Figure 13.5. If the system cannot map an address for a host name, it will return an "%Unrecognized host or address" error message. Here the router is sending five AEP datagrams to check the node's reachability and network connectivity. The five exclamation points indicate that the interface has received a reply (echo) from the target address for every AEP datagram, it sent. This 100% success rate indicates that the interface has been successfully connected to the network.

```
Vermont# ping appletalk 100.125

Type escape sequence to abort.
Sending 5, 100-byte AppleTalk Echoes to 100.125, timeout is 2 seconds:
!!!!!
Sucess rate is 100 percent (5/5), round-trip min/avg/max = 4/6/8 ms
Vermont#
```

FIGURE 13.5 *The Ping command checks a node's reachability and network connectivity by sending AppleTalk Echo Protocol datagrams to other AppleTalk nodes to verify connectivity and measure round-trip times.*

Different test characters displayed in a ping *response include:*
  .—The period indicates that the network server timed out while waiting for a reply from the target address.

NOTE

B—*This indicates that the echo received from the target address was bad or malformed.*

C—*This indicates that an echo with a bad DDP checksum was received.*

E—*This indicates that the transmission of an echo packet to the target address failed.*

R—*This indicates that the transmission of the echo packet to the target address failed due to lack of a route to the target address.*

A Cisco router can route packets between extended and nonextended AppleTalk networks that coexist on a single cable. This is important because Phase 2 AppleTalk supports both extended and nonextended addressing. This type of routing is often referred to as *transition routing*. Routers using it are said to be in Transition mode.

To use Transition mode, you must have two router interfaces connected to the same physical cable. One interface is configured as a nonextended AppleTalk network. The other is configured as an extended AppleTalk network. Routing is possible because packets are sent to one interface, translated, and sent out the other interface.

Each interface must have a unique network number, because you are routing between two separate AppleTalk networks: the *extended* and *nonextended*.

In order for the interfaces to communicate with each other you must ensure that each one has:

- The same interface type; for example, both are Ethernet.
- A different interface number; for example, 0 and 1.

The extended network must have a cable-range of one and a single zone in its zones list. This is required to maintain compatibility with the nonextended network, Network 3. This would also be the case if you connected an extended network to another interface on the router, E2 for example.

Dynamic Configuration with Discovery Mode

If a nonextended or an extended interface is connected to a network that has at least one other operational AppleTalk router, you can dynamically configure an interface. In order to do this, you need to place the interface often referred to as a *seed router*, in Discovery mode.

Once in Discovery mode, an interface can acquire information about the attached network from an operational router, and then use this information to configure itself. Seed routers seed, or initialize, the AppleTalk internet with configuration information. The type of information that can be acquired from an operational router is the network number or range, and zone name or list of the attached network.

Once an interface is configured it can seed the configuration of other routers on the connected network. Using Discovery mode does not affect an interface's ability to respond to configuration queries from other routers on the connected network once the interface becomes operational.

Discovery mode is useful when you are changing a network configuration, for example zone names, or when you are adding a router to an existing network. The benefit of using Discovery mode is that you need make the changes on only one operational (pre-configured) router. This router will then pass the information to other routers on the network.

Discovery mode can only be used if the interface is connected to a network that has at least one other operational AppleTalk router. If there is no operational router on the attached network, you must manually configure an interface. Also, if a Discovery mode interface is restarted, another operational router must be present before the interface will become operational. Discovery mode does not operate over serial lines.

It is important not to enable Discovery mode on all routers on a network. If you do so and all the devices restart simultaneously (for instance, after a power failure), the network will be inaccessible. That is, all routers on the network will be trying to get network information at the same time. This problem will only be overcome when you manually configure at least one router.

You can activate Discovery mode on an interface in one of two ways, depending on whether you know the network number of the attached network. If you know the address of the network, you first assign the address or cable-range to the interface. Then you explicitly enable Discovery mode by issuing the command `appletalk discovery` in Interface Configuration mode. The AppleTalk Discovery command should not be used if manually coded or hard-coded addresses are used. If AppleTalk Discovery is enabled by default you should disable it using the No AppleTalk Discovery command.

When activating Discovery mode, you need not assign a zone name, as the interface will acquire the zone name from another interface.

If you do not know the network number of the attached network you can place an interface into Discovery mode by:

- Assigning it the AppleTalk address of 0.0 if it is connected to a nonextended network.
- Assigning it the AppleTalk cable-range of 0–0 if it is connected to an extended network.

Figure 13.6 presents an example where both methods of activating Discovery mode are used by a router on an extended network. You want to enable Discovery mode on a router's E0 and E1 interfaces. You know the cable-range of the router's E1 interface but not the cable-range of its E0 interface.

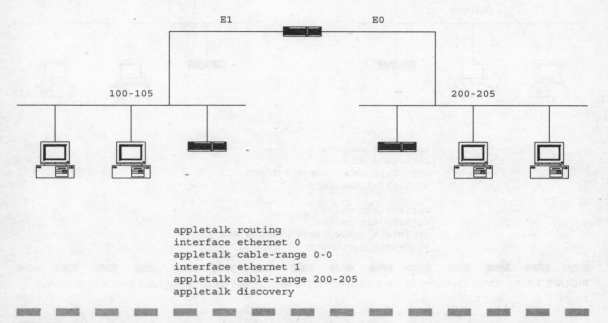

```
appletalk routing
interface ethernet 0
appletalk cable-range 0-0
interface ethernet 1
appletalk cable-range 200-205
appletalk discovery
```

FIGURE 13.6   *An example where both methods of activating Discovery mode are used by a router on an extended network.*

In order to enable Discovery mode for the E0 interface you assign it the cable-range 0–0. To enable Discovery mode on the E1 interface you assign it the cable-range 200–205 and enable Discovery mode using the Discovery command.

Once Discovery mode is enabled both interfaces will dynamically learn their addresses and zones (Figure 13.7). The E0 interface will use Router A to supply it with the cable-range 100–105, a valid network address, for example 102.6, and the zone name "production". The E1 interface will use Router C to supply it with a valid network address, for example 205.11, and the zone name "production".

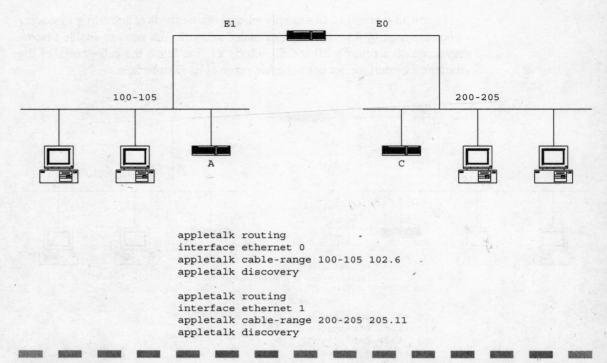

```
appletalk routing
interface ethernet 0
appletalk cable-range 100-105 102.6
appletalk discovery

appletalk routing
interface ethernet 1
appletalk cable-range 200-205 205.11
appletalk discovery
```

FIGURE 13.7 Once Discovery mode is enabled both interfaces will dynamically learn their addresses and zones.

Implementing Routing for AppleTalk

AppleTalk Routing

This section discusses protocols that AppleTalk uses to transmit packets and routing information across a network. It describes the function and operation of the Datagram Delivery Protocol (DDP) and of the Routing Table Maintenance Protocol (RTMP). It outlines the function and operation of the AppleTalk Update-Based Routing Protocol and identifies the components of a basic AppleTalk Update-Based Routing Protocol implementation, describing their operation.

Datagram Delivery Protocol

DDP is the primary network-layer routing protocol in the AppleTalk protocol suite. It provides a best-effort connectionless datagram service between AppleTalk sockets. A datagram is a logical grouping of information sent as a network layer unit over a transmission medium. An AppleTalk socket is a software structure operating as a communications end-point within a network device.

DDP performs two key functions: the transmission and reception of packets.

DDP receives data from socket clients, creates a DDP header using the appropriate destination address, and passes the packet to the data-link layer protocol. DDP receives frames from the data-link layer, examines the DDP header to find the destination address, and routes the packet to the destination socket.

There are two types of DDP headers: short and long. A short header addresses source and destination sockets by their 8-bit socket numbers and 8-bit node numbers. It is used in nonextended addressing. A long header consists of an extended address of the 8-bit socket number, 8-bit node number, and 16-bit network number. It is used in extended addressing.

DDP maintains the following information in every AppleTalk node:

- Cable-range of the local network.
- Network address of a router attached to the local network. In addition to this information, AppleTalk routers must maintain a routing table using the Routing Table Maintenance Protocol (RTMP).

DDP operates much as any routing protocol (Figure 14.1). Packets are addressed at the source, passed to the data link layer, and transmitted to the destination. Let's look at how DDP transmits packets.

First DDP receives data from an upper-layer protocol. It then determines whether the source and destination nodes are on the same network by examining the network number of the destination address.

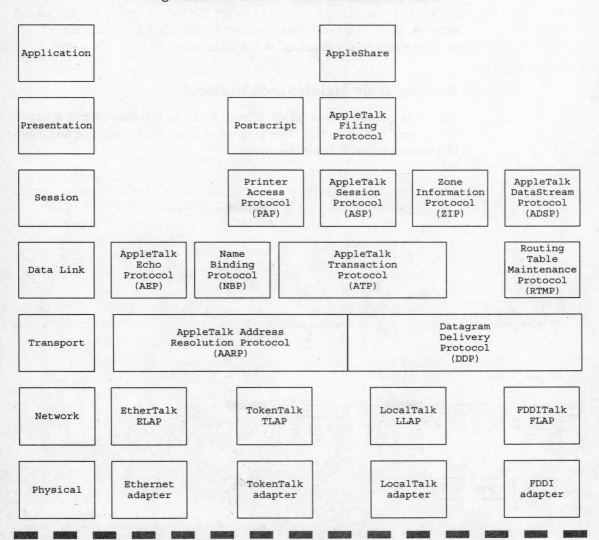

FIGURE 14.1   DDP operates much as any routing protocol.

If the destination network number is within the cable-range of the local network, the packet is encapsulated in a DDP header and is passed to the data-link layer for transmission to the destination node. If the destination network number is not within the cable-range of the local network, the packet is encapsulated in a DDP header and is passed to the data-link layer for transmission to a router.

When the packet is being transmitted across the network, intermediate routers use their routing tables to forward the packet toward the destination network. When the packet reaches a router attached to the destination network, the packet is transmitted to the destination node.

Routing Table Maintenance Protocol

AppleTalk generally uses RTMP (Figure 14.2) to transmit routing information to neighboring routers. This protocol is also used to establish and maintain routing tables in AppleTalk routers.

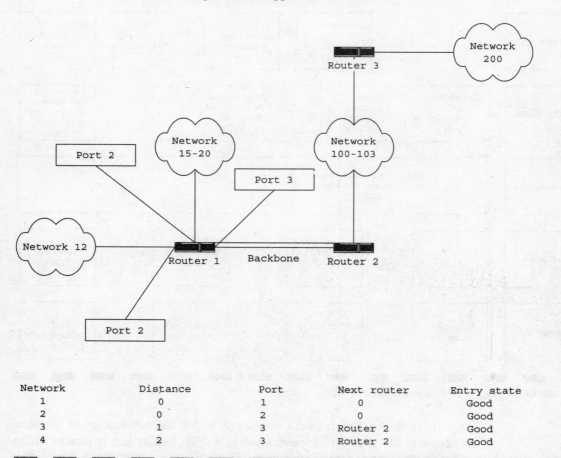

Network	Distance	Port	Next router	Entry state
1	0	1	0	Good
2	0	2	0	Good
3	1	3	Router 2	Good
4	2	3	Router 2	Good

FIGURE 14.2   An RTMP routing table contains information about each destination network known to the router.

RTMP is a transport-layer protocol in the AppleTalk protocol suite. It is based on the Routing Information Protocol (RIP). Like RIP, RTMP uses hop count as its metric for routing decisions. Hop count is calculated as the number of routers or other intermediate nodes through which a packet must pass to travel from the source network to the destination network.

The RTMP routing tables contain an entry for each network a packet can reach. If nodes on an AppleTalk internetwork are separated by more than 15 routers, they cannot communicate. This is because RTMP has a maximum hop count of 14.

An RTMP routing table contains the following information about each of the destination networks known to the router:

- Network cable-range of the destination network
- Distance in hops to the destination network
- Router port that leads to the destination network
- Address of the next-hop router
- Current state of the routing table entry (good, suspect, or bad)

A router uses the information in a routing table to forward packets to their destinations by the best possible route.

RTMP broadcasts its routing information every 10 seconds to all directly connected networks. This ensures that each router contains the most-current information in its routing table, and that the information is consistent across the internetwork.

A routing table is updated at set intervals. Let's look at how this is done. First, the status of all entries is changed from "good" to "suspect." Then the router sends an RTMP packet to all routers within the table.

If a response is not received within a set period of time, the entry for the nonresponding router is set to "bad" and removed from the routing table. If a response is received within a set period of time, the entry for the responding router is set to "good" and any changes in its routing information are added to the routing table.

RTMP saves network bandwidth by providing distance vector, split-horizoned routing. In distance vector routing, each router sends its entire routing table in each update, but only to its neighbors. In split-horizoned routing, a router does not advertise routes it learns from an interface through the same interface, because neighboring routers that can be reached through that interface know the information already.

AppleTalk Update-Based Routing Protocol

The AppleTalk Update-Based Routing Protocol (AURP) is an enhancement of RTMP. As well as transmitting routing information to routers, this transport-layer protocol provides the added feature of AppleTalk tunneling in Transmission Control Protocol/Internet Protocol (TCP/IP). *Tunneling* is described as the architecture designed to provide the services necessary to implement any standard point-to-point encapsulation scheme. This feature allows two or more AppleTalk internetworks to be interconnected through a TCP/IP network to form an AppleTalk WAN.

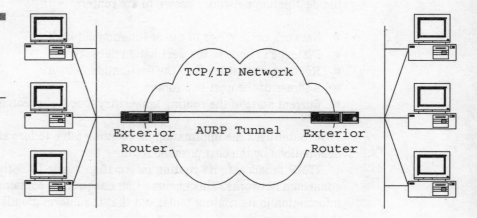

FIGURE 14.3
An AURP tunnel
acts as a virtual link
between remote
networks.

AURP allows two AppleTalk networks to be connected through a TCP/IP network because it encapsulates (wraps data in a particular header) AppleTalk packets in User Datagram Protocol (UDP) headers. UDP is a connectionless transport-layer protocol (layer 4) belonging to the Internet protocol family. UDP headers are used by the data-link layer protocol of the TCP/IP network to transmit data across its physical medium.

Once the AppleTalk packets are encapsulated they can be transported transparently through a TCP/IP network. Transportation is possible because the TCP/IP network sees the encapsulated packets as TCP/IP packets. Encapsulated packets benefit from any features normally enjoyed by IP packets, including default routes and load balancing.

Like RTMP, AURP also provides distance vector, split-horizoned routing and has a maximum hop count of 14. A tunnel counts as one hop.

AURP is useful in the following scenarios:

- To connect isolated AppleTalk networks by way of an existing TCP/IP internetwork.

■ To use only IP through the backbone network, when there are isolated AppleTalk networks to be connected.

An AURP implementation has two components: exterior routers and an AURP tunnel. Exterior routers connect a local AppleTalk internetwork to an AURP tunnel. They convert AppleTalk data and routing information to AURP, and perform encapsulation and de-encapsulation of AppleTalk traffic. Let's look at how this is done. When exchanging routing information or data through an AURP tunnel, AppleTalk packets must be converted from RTMP to AURP.

First, an exterior router receives AppleTalk routing information or data packets that need to be sent to a remote AppleTalk internetwork. It converts the packets to AURP packets and encapsulates them in UDP headers. The encapsulated packets are sent into the tunnel (that is, the TCP/IP network). The TCP/IP network treats the packets as normal UDP traffic.

The remote exterior router receives the UDP packets and removes the UDP header information. The AURP packets are converted back into their original format (routing information or data packets). If the AppleTalk packets contain routing information, the receiving exterior router updates its routing tables accordingly. If the packets contain data destined for an AppleTalk node on the local network, the traffic is sent out through the appropriate interface.

An exterior router has different applications depending on whether it is attached to the local network or to the TCP/IP network. It functions as an AppleTalk router in the local network and as an end node in the TCP/IP network.

When exterior routers first attach to an AURP tunnel, they exchange routing information with other exterior routers. After the initial exchange of routing information, exterior routers send routing information only when changes occur in the network's topology. This happens, for example, when a network is added to (or removed from) the routing table or when the distance to a network is changed. This type of exchange of routing information is often referred to as update-based routing. Routing information is also sent when a change in the path to a network causes the exterior router to access that network through its local internetwork rather than through the tunnel (or vice versa).

The relatively high bandwidth consumed by the frequent broadcasting of RTMP routing packets can severely hamper a backbone's network performance. Most of the time the information contained in the RTMP data packets is redundant. The benefit of using update-based routing is that it reduces the amount of bandwidth needed to exchange routing information because updates are sent infrequently, only when topology changes occur. This allows more bandwidth to be available for transmitting user data.

An AURP tunnel functions as a single, logical data link between remote AppleTalk internetworks. There can be any number of physical nodes in the path between exterior routers, but these nodes are transparent to the AppleTalk networks. There are two kinds of AURP tunnel: point-to-point and multipoint.

A *point-to-point AURP* tunnel connects only two exterior routers. This graphic shows two AppleTalk LANs connected via a point-to-point AURP tunnel. A *multipoint AURP* tunnel connects three or more exterior routers. There are two kinds of multipoint tunnel: fully-connected and partially-connected.

A fully-connected multipoint tunnel is one where all connected exterior routers are aware of each other and can send packets to one another. On a fully connected tunnel, the same number of routes should be reachable from each exterior router. A partially-connected multipoint tunnel is one where not all connected exterior routers are aware of and can communicate with one another.

A benefit of using a partially connected tunnel is that it can provide a level of network security. In a partially connected tunnel configuration, the routing tables on the different exterior routers can have a different number of entries. This means that not all networks connected to these exterior routers are equally reachable.

A partially connected tunnel makes it possible to isolate particular networks; for example you may want to isolate the accounts department's network because of the confidential information it contains. A problem with partially connected tunnels is that they can be created accidentally if the router is not configured properly. For example, you might create a partially connected tunnel by making an error when entering the list of peers with which the router should communicate.

Configuring AppleTalk for Routing

This section shows how AppleTalk routing is configured on a Cisco router. It outlines the tasks involved in configuring AURP and configures AppleTalk routing on a router.

AppleTalk Routing Configuration

The tasks involved in configuring AppleTalk on a router are:

- Enabling AppleTalk routing.
- Specifying a routing protocol.
- Assigning an AppleTalk address or cable-range to each interface.
- Assigning one or more zone names to each interface. An AppleTalk address (or cable-range) and zone name can be assigned either manually or dynamically.

Now we will look at manually configuring AppleTalk routing on a router, for example, the Vermont router. The Vermont router is connected to the Maine router through its Serial 0 interface. AppleTalk routing has already been configured on the Maine router. In this example you want to configure:

- The Vermont router with the routing protocol RTMP
- Vermont's Ethernet 0 interface with the AppleTalk address 206.79 and the zone name "sales"
- Vermont's Serial 0 interface with the AppleTalk address 2.26 and the zone name "link 1". The Vermont router's interfaces are to be configured for nonextended addressing.

Let's assume you have opened a terminal session on the Vermont router. In order to perform the AppleTalk routing tasks the router needs to be placed in Configuration mode (Figure 14.4). The router is placed in Configuration mode by typing `configure terminal` in Privilege mode and pressing **Return**.

FIGURE 14.4
Manually configuring AppleTalk routing on a router.

```
Vermont# configure terminal
Enter configuration commands, one per line. End with CNTL/Z.
Vermont(config)# appletalk routing
Vermont(config)# appletalk protocol rtmp
Vermont(config)# interface ethernet 0
Vermont(config-if)# appletalk address 206.79
Vermont(config-if)# appletalk zone sales
Vermont(config-if)# exit
Vermont(config)# interface serial 0
Vermont(config-if)# appletalk address 2.26
Vermont(config-if)# appletalk zone link1
Vermont(config-if)# ^Z
Vermont# copy runn start
Building configuration...
[OK]
Vermont#
```

To turn on AppleTalk routing on the router, type `appletalk routing`. Next, you select the routing protocol. To select RTMP as the router's AppleTalk routing protocol type `appletalk protocol rtmp`. AURP and Enhanced Interior Gateway Routing Protocol (E-IGRP) are other routing protocols that can be configured on an AppleTalk interface. There is no need to enter the `AppleTalk Protocol` command if you are specifying RTMP as the routing protocol because RTMP is selected by default.

Once the `AppleTalk Routing` and `Protocol` commands have been entered, specify the interface you want to configure. To configure Vermont's Ethernet 0 interface type `interface ethernet 0`.

Assign the AppleTalk address 206.79 to the E0 interface by typing `appletalk address 206.79`. The network number is represented by the number 206 while the node number is represented by the number 79. Assign the zone name "sales" to the interface by typing `appletalk zone sales`. Only one zone name can be assigned to an interface configured with a nonextended address. If you assign more than one zone name, the newly specified zone name will replace the existing interface's zone name. Router Vermont's E0 interface is now configured for AppleTalk routing.

To configure Vermont's S0 interface first type `exit` to return to Configuration mode. Then specify the Serial 0 interface that you want to configure by typing `interface serial 0`.

Once the router is in Interface Configuration mode you can assign the AppleTalk address 2.26 to the S0 interface by typing `appletalk address 2.26`. The network number is represented by the number 2 while the node number is represented by the number 26. You assign the zone name "link1" to the S0 interface by typing `appletalk zone link1`.

Router Vermont's S0 interface is now configured for AppleTalk routing and can now send AppleTalk packets and RTMP updates to, and receive AppleTalk packets and RTMP updates from, the Maine router.

To ensure that the router has AppleTalk routing enabled the next time it starts up, save the AppleTalk configuration in the router's memory. The router must be in Privileged mode to do this. Place the router into Privileged mode by pressing **Ctrl+Z**. Then enter `copy runn start` to save the configuration in NVRAM. NVRAM (nonvolatile RAM) is used to store configuration information because it retains its contents when a unit is powered off.

To test that RTMP routing is enabled (Figure 14.5) enter `ping 100.125` to see if the Vermont router can reach the E0 interface on router Maine. You can see from the output of this command that RTMP routing is enabled because the E0 interface on router Maine is reachable.

```
Vermont# ping 100.125

Type escape sequence to abort.
Sending 5, 100-byte AppleTalk Echoes to 100.125, timeout is 2 seconds
!!!!!
Success rate is 100 percent (5/5), round-trip min/avg/max = 32/32/32 ms
Vermont#
```

FIGURE 14.5   *Testing the RTMP routing using the ping command.*

> You can see the current state of the AppleTalk routing table by typing the following command in Privileged mode:
>
> ```
> show appletalk route
> ```
>
> You can see in Figure 14.6 that a Show AppleTalk Route command on router Vermont indicates:
>
> - Two routes directly connected (network 2–2 and 206). Network 206 is connected to the Vermont router through the router's E0 interface. Network 2–2 is connected to the Vermont router through the router's S0 interface.
> - One route that has been learned from RTMP (network 100–110). Network 100–110 is connected to the Maine's E0 interface. The Vermont router learns about network 100–110 through Maine's S1 interface.

```
Vermont# show appletalk route
Codes: R - RTMP derived, E - EIGRP derived, C - connected, A - AURP
       S - static, P - proxy
3 routes in internet

The first zone listed for each entry is its default (primary) zone.
C Net 2-2 directly connected, Serial0, zone link1
R Net 100-100 [1/G] via 2.27, 8 sec, Serial0, zone mrkting
C Net 206 directly connected, Ethernet0 zone sales
Vermont#
```

FIGURE 14.6   *The output of a Show AppleTalk Route command on router Vermont.*

Configuring AppleTalk for Tunneling

Next we will show how AURP tunneling is configured on a Cisco router; we outline the steps involved in configuring AURP and configure AURP on a router.

AURP Configuration

When two AppleTalk networks are connected with a non-AppleTalk backbone such as IP, the relatively high bandwidth consumed by broadcasting of RTMP data packets can severely hamper the backbone's performance. This problem can be solved by using AURP when tunneling AppleTalk through a foreign protocol, such as IP. AURP reduces the bandwidth consumed by packets because AURP updates occur less frequently and contain only information about changes in routes. RTMP updates contain full route information and occur more frequently (at 10-second intervals).

The tasks involved in configuring AURP on a router are:

- Enabling route-redistribution between protocols AURP is configured on an exterior router.
- Specifying a tunnel interface.
- Enabling AURP routing on the tunnel interface.
- Specifying the source and destination address of the tunnel.
- Enabling AURP encapsulation on the tunnel.
- Assigning an AppleTalk address and zone name to the tunnel. These tasks are carried out on every exterior router in an AURP implementation.

To allow the exchange of routing updates between RTMP and AURP, the routing information needs to be redistributed. The routing information in one protocol can be advertised in the update messages of another protocol. To enable the redistribution of routing updates between both protocols, issue the following command in Configuration mode:

```
appletalk route-redistribution
```

The default setting for the sending of AURP routing updates is every 30 seconds. If you want to change the interval between AURP routing updates, issue the following command in Configuration mode:

```
appletalk aurp update interval seconds
```

The number specified in the seconds parameter must be a multiple of 10. Update intervals can be applied only to tunnel interfaces (logical interfaces on exterior router). If the interval time is modified, the time must be the same on both ends of the tunnel.

A tunnel interface needs to be configured on an exterior router. Each physical interface on a router can support several logical interfaces. Do this by issuing the following command in Interface Configuration mode:

```
interface tunnel number
```

To select AURP as a routing protocol on this interface, issue the command:

```
appletalk protocol aurp
```

A sending and receiving interface needs to be specified for the tunnel. To specify the interface out of which the encapsulated packets will be sent, issue the command:

```
tunnel source {ip-address | type number}
```

The IP-Address parameter is the IP address of the serial interface on the router you are configuring which connects to the exterior router at the far end of the tunnel. This address will be used as the source address for packets in the tunnel. The Type parameter is the interface type, for example Ethernet or Serial. The Number parameter specifies the port, connector, or interface card number. These numbers are assigned at the factory at the time of installation or when added to a system. You can display an interface's number using the Show Interface command.

To specify the interface at the far end of the tunnel that is to receive the encapsulated packets, issue the command:

```
tunnel destination {hostname | ip-address}
```

The Hostname parameter is the name of the host destination. The IP-Address parameter is the IP address of the serial interface on the destination router that is used to connect it to the exterior router at the start of the tunnel.

AppleTalk packets need to be encapsulated by AURP into IP packets before they can be sent through the tunnel. To specify AURP-style encapsulation on the tunnel interface, issue the command:

```
tunnel mode aurp
```

GRE IP or Cayman tunneling mode can also be used with AppleTalk.

In order for the tunnel to receive packets from the AppleTalk network it needs to be assigned an AppleTalk address and zone name. This is done using the AppleTalk Address/Cable-range and Zone commands. The AppleTalk Address command is the network numbering system used on nonextended networks while the AppleTalk Cable-range command is

used on extended networks. If you are using the `Cable-range` command you
need to specify a cable-range of one to ensure that the tunnel supports both
extended and nonextended AppleTalk networks.

Let's look at configuring AURP on the serial links between the two routers
in the RTMP network you created earlier. IP routing is also enabled between
both routers. Vermont's S0 interface has been assigned the IP address
172.16.66.2 while Maine's S1 interface has been assigned the IP address
172.16.66.1.

Assume you have opened a terminal session with the Vermont router.
Before configuring AURP you should test that both RTMP and IP are operational. To test that IP routing is enabled you need to see if the Vermont router
can reach the S1 interface on router Maine. To do this you issue the following
command in Configuration mode:

```
ping 172.16.66.1
```

You can see from output of this command that IP routing is enabled
because the S1 interface on router Maine is reachable (Figure 14.7).

```
Vermont# ping 172.16.66.1

Type escape sequence to abort.
Sending 5, 100-byte ICMP Echoes to 172.16.66.1, timeout is 2 seconds:
!!!!!
Success rate is 100 percent (5/5), round-trip min/avg/max = 28/31/32 ms
Vermont#
```

FIGURE 14.7   To test that IP routing is enabled you need to see if the Vermont router can reach the S1 interface on router Maine.

To test that AppleTalk routing is enabled you need to see if the Vermont
router can reach the E0 interface on router Maine (Figure 14.8). To do this
you issue the following command in Configuration mode:

```
ping appletalk 100.125
```

You can see from output of this command that AppleTalk routing is
enabled because Maine's E0 is reachable.

In order to configure AURP between both routers (Figure 14.9) you need to
turn off AppleTalk on Vermont's S0 and Maine's S1 interface. It is not necessary that RTMP have been configured between the two networks, before an

AURP tunnel is configured. The command used to turn off AppleTalk must be entered in Interface Configuration mode. To put the Vermont router into Interface Configuration mode from Privileged mode, type:

- configure terminal in Privileged mode and press **Return**
- interface serial 0

```
Vermont# ping appletalk 100.125

Type escape sequence to abort.
Sending 5, 100-byte AppleTalk Echoes to 100.125, timeout is 2 seconds:
!!!!!
Success rate is 100 percent (5/5), round-trip min/avg/max = 32/32/36 ms
Vermont#
```

FIGURE 14.8   To test that AppleTalk routing is enabled you need to see if the Vermont router can reach the E0 interface on router Maine.

```
Vermont# configure terminal
Enter configuration commands, one per line. End with CNTL/Z.
Vermont(config)# interface serial 0
Vermont(config-if)# no appletalk address
Vermont(config-if)# ^Z
Vermont#
```

FIGURE 14.9   In order to configure AURP between both routers you need to turn off AppleTalk on Vermont's S0 and Maine's S1 interface.

To disable AppleTalk on this interface, type no appletalk address. Once this has been done, exit Interface Configuration mode by pressing **Ctrl+Z**.

Disable AppleTalk on Maine's S1 interface using the No AppleTalk Cable-range command (Figure 14.10).

To test that AppleTalk routing is disabled you need to see whether or not the Vermont router can now reach Maine's E0 interface. Do this by typing ping appletalk 100.125. You can see from the output of this command that AppleTalk routing is disabled because Maine's E0 interface is unreachable (Figure 14.11).

```
Maine# configure terminal
Enter configuration commands, one per line. End with CNTL/Z.
Maine(config)# interface serial 1
Maine(config-if)# no appletalk cable-range
Maine(config-if)# ^Z
Maine#
```

FIGURE 14.10   *Disable AppleTalk on Maine's S1 interface using the No AppleTalk Cable-range command.*

```
Maine# ping appletalk 100.125

Type escape sequence to abort.
Sending 5, 100-byte AppleTalk Echoes to 100.125, timeout is 2 seconds:
RRRRR
Success rate is 0 percent (0/5)
Vermont#
```

FIGURE 14.11   *The output of ping appletalk 100.125 shows that AppleTalk routing is disabled because Maine's E0 interface is unreachable.*

Once AppleTalk routing is disabled between the two routers you can start the AURP configuring process (Figure 14.12). The first step in configuring AURP is to enable route redistribution between the RTMP and AURP protocols. Do this by typing `appletalk route-redistribution` in Configuration mode.

You wish to change the AURP up-date interval to 60 seconds. Do this by typing `appletalk aurp update-interval 60`.

The next step in enabling AURP tunneling is to specify the tunnel interface. Specify the tunnel interface 0 by typing `interface tunnel 0`. Then create an AURP routing process on this interface by typing `appletalk protocol aurp`. Next, assign a source and destination address to the tunnel.

The source of the tunnel is the IP address of the Vermont router's S0 interface while the destination address is the IP address of the Maine router's S1 interface. To specify the source address of the tunnel, type `tunnel source 172.16.66.2`. To specify the destination address of the tunnel, type `tunnel destination 172.16.66.1`. Once both addresses have been assigned, enable AURP encapsulation on the tunnel by typing `tunnel mode aurp`.

The last step in configuring AURP on the Vermont router is to assign the tunnel interface an AppleTalk address and zone name. To assign the interface the AppleTalk address 2140.3, type `appletalk cable-range 2140-2140 2140.3`. To assign the interface the zone name "tunnel zone," type `appletalk zone tunnel zone`.

```
Vermont# configure terminal
Enter configuration commands, one per line. End with CNTL/Z.
Vermont(config)# appletalk route-distribution
Vermont(config)# appletalk aurp update-interval 60
Vermont(config)# interface tunnel 0
Vermont(config-if)# appletalk protocol aurp
Vermont(config-if)# tunnel source 172.16.66.2
Vermont(config-if)# tunnel destination 172.16.66.1
Vermont(config-if)# tunnel mode aurp
Vermont(config-if)# appletalk cable-range 2140-2140 2140.3
Vermont(config-if)# appletalk zone tunnel zone
Vermont(config-if)# ^Z
Vermont#
Vermont# copy runn start
Building configuration...
 [OK]
Vermont#
```

FIGURE 14.12   Once AppleTalk routing is disabled between the two routers, start the AURP configuring process.

The Vermont router's S0 interface is now configured for AURP routing. Exit the Configuration mode by pressing **Ctrl+Z**. You save the configuration by typing copy runn start.

To complete the AURP implementation, configure AURP on Maine's S1 interface using the same commands.

To test that the tunnel is working you can use the Ping AppleTalk command (Figure 14.13). For example, to test that the Vermont router can send AppleTalk packets to Maine's E0 interface type ping appletalk 100.125 in Privileged mode on the Vermont router. You can see from the output of this command that the tunnel is working because the E0 interface on router Maine can receive AppleTalk packets.

```
Vermont# ping appletalk 100.125

Type escape sequence to abort.
Sending 5, 100-byte AppleTalk Echoes to 100.125, timeout is 2 seconds:
!!!!!
Success rate is 100 percent (5/5), round-trip min/avg/max = 32/32/36 ms
Vermont#
```

FIGURE 14.13   To test that the tunnel is working you can use the Ping AppleTalk command.

There are a number of commands that you can use to check the Vermont router's tunnel configuration. You can display the status of the tunnel interface and the parameters configured on it by typing the following command in Privileged mode (Figure 14.14):

```
show appletalk interface tunnel 0
```

FIGURE 14.14
Display the status of the tunnel interface and the parameters configured on it by using the show appletalk interface tunnel 0 command.

```
Vermont# show appletalk interface tunnel 0
Tunnel0 is up, line protocol is up
  AppleTalk port is an AURP Tunnel
    AURP Data Sender state is Connected
    AURP Data Receiver state is Connected
    AURP Tickle Time interval is 90 seconds
  AppleTalk discarded 34 packets due to input errors
  AppleTalk address gleaning is not support by hardware
  AppleTalk route cache is disabled, port down
Vermont#
```

The output of a Show AppleTalk Interface command on router Vermont displays:

- The type of interface; it states that it is currently active and inserted into the network.
- That the interface is usable.
- That the AURP sending and receiving sides are connected.

You can see the current state of the AppleTalk routing table by typing show appletalk route in Privileged mode (Figure 14.15).

```
Vermont# show appletalk route
Codes: R - RTMP derived, E - EIGRP derived, C - connected, A - AURP
       S - static, P - proxy
2 routes in internet

The first zone listed for each entry is its default (primary) zone.

A Net 100-110 [1/G] via 0.0, 344 sec, Tunnel0, zone marketing
C Net 206 directly connected, Ethernet0, zone sales
Vermont#
```

FIGURE 14.15   Display the current state of the AppleTalk routing table by using the Show Appletalk Route command.

You can see from the output of a `Show AppleTalk Route` command on router Vermont that one route is directly connected (network 206) and one route has been learned from AURP (network 100–110).

You can display all the entries in the Zone Information Table (ZIT) by typing `show appletalk zone` in Privileged mode. (Figure 14.16)

FIGURE 14.16
Display all the entries in the Zone Information Table (ZIT) by using the Show Appletalk Zone command.

```
Vermont# show appletalk zone
Name                                            Netork(s)
sales                                           206
marketing                                       100-110
tunnelz
Total of 3 zones
Vermont#
```

You can see from the output of this command on router Vermont that it contains three zones.

You can display information about the AppleTalk internetwork and other parameters by typing `show appletalk globals` in Privileged mode (Figure 14.17).

```
Vermont# show appletalk globals
AppleTalk global information:
  Internet is incompatible with older, AT Phasel, routers.
  There are 2 routes in the internet.
  There are 3 zones defined.
  Logging of significant AppleTalk events is disabled.
  ZIP resends queries every 10 seconds.
  RTMP updates are sent every 10 seconds.
  RTMP entries are considered BAD after 20 seconds.
  RTMP entries are discarded after 60 seconds.
  AARP probe retransmit count: 10, interval: 200 msec.
  AARP request retransmit count: 5, interval: 1000 msec.
  DDP datagrams will be checksummed.
  RTMP datagrams will be strictly checked.
  RTMP routes may not be propagated without zones.
  Routes will be distributed between routing protocols.
  Routing between local devices on an interface will not be performed.
  IPTalk uses the udp base port of 768 (Default).
  AppleTalk EIGRP is not enabled.
  AURP updates will be sent every 60 seconds.
  Alternate node address format will not be displayed.
  Access control of any networks of a zone hides the zone.
Vermont#
```

FIGURE 14.17   *Display information about the AppleTalk internetwork and other parameters by using the Show Appletalk Globals command.*

You can see that:

- The AppleTalk internetwork cannot interoperate with Phase 1 routers.
- There are two routes and two zones in the current AppleTalk internet configuration.
- Zone name queries are retried every 10 seconds.
- RTMP routing updates are sent every 10 seconds.
- RTMP entries are considered "bad" after 20 seconds and are deleted after 60 seconds.

The output also shows:

- The number of AARP probes and requests that will be sent to verify an address, followed by the time, in milliseconds, between retransmission of ARP probe and request packets set these values with the `AppleTalk ARP Retransmit-Count` and `AppleTalk ARP Interval` commands, respectively.
- That route redistribution is enabled.
- That AURP updates are sent every 60 seconds.

You can get periodic verification that the tunnel is up by entering `debug apple aurp-packet` (Figure 14.18). This command displays, at regular intervals, the outcome of sending probe packets through the tunnel. If the router receives an acknowledgment from the router at the far end of the tunnel it knows that the tunnel is up.

FIGURE 14.18
Get periodic verification that the tunnel is up by entering debug apple aurp-packet.

```
Vermont# debug apple aurp-packet
AURP packets debugging is on
Vermont#
AT: Tunnel0: Tickle sent
AT: Tunnel0: Tickle-Ack received
AT: Tunnel0: Tickle-received
AT: Tunnel0: Tickle-Ack sent
Vermont#
```

You can display AURP update activity on the router by entering `debug apple aurp-update` (Figure 14.19). This command shows when AURP update packets are being received. The `Debug Tunnel` command is useful for gaining additional information about the tunnel process.

FIGURE 14.19
Display AURP update
activity on the router
by entering debug
apple aurp-update.

```
Vermont# debug apple aurp-update
AURP routing updaes debugging is on
AT: Processing queued update events
AT: Tunnel0: Building updates
AT: Tunnel0: Null update suppressed
AT: Garbage collecting update events queue
Vermont#
```

15

Implementing AppleTalk Enhanced IGRP

 **Introduction to Enhanced IGRP**

This section describes the features of the Enhanced IGRP routing protocol and describes the types of packets used by Enhanced IGRP routers.

Overview

Enhanced IGRP (Interior Gateway Routing Protocol) is a routing protocol developed by Cisco Systems Incorporated. It is an advanced distance vector routing protocol which includes some of the features of link-state protocols.

Enhanced IGRP uses a nonhierarchical (or flat) topology by default. In a flat topology, addresses are organized into a single group where each device is identified by a single, unique address. In a hierarchical topology addresses are organized into numerous subgroups, each successively narrowing an address until it points to a single device.

Subnet routes of directly connected networks can be automatically summarized at a network number boundary. You can also configure route summarization at any interface using whatever bit boundary you choose to specify. This allows ranges of networks to be summarized arbitrarily. When Enhanced IGRP summarizes a group of routes, it uses the metric of the best route in the summary as the metric for that summary.

Enhanced IGRP offers the following features: fast convergence, partial, bounded updates, neighbor discovery, multiple network-layer support, and scaling to larger networks. Enhanced IGRP uses the Diffusing Update Algorithm (DUAL) to achieve rapid convergence. *Convergence* relates to the speed and ability of a group of internetworking devices running a specific routing protocol to agree on the topology of an internetwork after a change in that topology. This algorithm provides loop-free operation at every instant throughout a route computation. DUAL allows routers involved in a topology change to synchronize at the same time, while not involving routers unaffected by the change.

A Cisco router running Enhanced IGRP stores all its neighbors' routing tables so that it can quickly adapt to alternate routes. Such a router will query its neighbors for an alternate route only when none can be found in its own tables. In the context of Enhanced IGRP, neighbors are seen as directly connected routers running Enhanced IGRP.

Enhanced IGRP does not send periodic updates to other routers. Instead, it sends partial updates about a route when the path changes or the metric for that route changes. Routing updates are automatically bounded, in that only those routers affected by changes are updated.

Enhanced IGRP has four basic components: neighbor discovery/recovery, reliable transport protocol, DUAL finite state machine, and protocol-dependent modules. Neighbor recovery/discovery is the process used dynamically to locate other directly attached routers running Enhanced IGRP. This process also describes the way Enhanced IGRP routers discover whether any of their neighbors have become unreachable or inoperative. Neighbor discovery/recovery functions by periodically sending small protocol-dependent hello packets. As long as hello packets are received, a router can determine that a neighbor is alive and functioning.

The reliable transport protocol provides guaranteed, ordered delivery of Enhanced IGRP packets to all neighbors. Not all Enhanced IGRP packets need to be transmitted reliably. For example, it is not necessary to send individual hello packets to each neighbor when the network provides multicast functionality. Multicasting is where single packets are copied by the network and sent to a specific subset of network addresses. These addresses are specified in the destination address field of the packet. Instead, Enhanced IGRP sends a single multicast hello with an indicator set which informs receivers that no acknowledgment is required. This would be typical of a multiaccess network like Ethernet.

Reliable delivery is required for routing updates. This ensures that all routers have an accurate, loop-free picture of the network topology. Therefore, routing update packets include an indicator to show that acknowledgment is required.

The DUAL finite state machine is the decision process for all route computations. DUAL tracks all routes advertised by all neighboring routers. It uses the distance information (or metric) to select efficient, loop-free paths. DUAL selects routes to be inserted into a routing table based on feasible successors. The term "successor" means a route to a destination. It can also be thought of as a neighboring router with a route to the destination.

When a topology change occurs, DUAL will test for a feasible successor, which represent the least-cost path to a destination that is guaranteed not to be part of a routing loop. DUAL picks the best feasible successor and inserts it, along with its destination, into the routing table. If no feasible successor exists, a *route recomputation*—also known as a *diffusing computation*—is required. A policy of using any feasible successor that exists avoids the need for recomputation. This leads to more efficient use of processor resources and faster convergence times.

The protocol-dependent modules are responsible for network-layer protocol-specific tasks. One such responsibility is to parse Enhanced IGRP packets and inform DUAL of the new information received. Protocol-dependent modules are also responsible for redistributing routes learned by other routing protocols.

Enhanced IGRP provides multiple network-layer support. Protocols supported are TCP/IP, Novell IPX, and AppleTalk. AppleTalk Enhanced IGRP provides the following features: automatic redistribution, increased network width, and the configuration of routing protocols on individual interfaces.

AppleTalk RTMP routes are automatically redistributed into Enhanced IGRP. Similarly, AppleTalk Enhanced IGRP routes are automatically redistributed into RTMP. AppleTalk Enhanced IGRP offers the option of disabling automatic redistribution. You can also completely turn off AppleTalk Enhanced IGRP and RTMP, either on the device or on individual interfaces.

RTMP allows a maximum network width of 15 hops. When Enhanced IGRP is enabled, the maximum hop count increases to 224. This restriction on network size is dictated by the transport-layer hop counter. Cisco IOS 11.1 increments the Transport Control field only when an RTMP packet has traversed 15 routers and the next hop to the destination was learned via Enhanced IGRP. When an RTMP route is being used as the next hop to the destination, the Transport Control field is incremented as normal.

You can configure interfaces that have been configured for AppleTalk to use either RTMP, Enhanced IGRP, or both routing protocols. If two neighboring routers are configured to use both RTMP and Enhanced IGRP, the Enhanced IGRP routing information will supersede the RTMP information. However, both devices will continue to send RTMP routing updates.

The fact that Enhanced IGRP routing information takes precedence over RTMP information allows you to control the excessive bandwidth usage of RTMP on WAN links. Because a WAN link is a point-to-point link, there are no other devices on the link, so there is no need to run RTMP to perform end-node router discovery. Using Enhanced IGRP on WAN links makes it possible to save bandwidth and, in the case of Packet Switched Digital Networks (PSDNs), traffic charges.

Enhanced IGRP for AppleTalk provides optimal path selection. While RTMP uses hop count to determine the best route, AppleTalk Enhanced IGRP uses a more sophisticated metric that includes bandwidth, delay, reliability, and load.

Enhanced IGRP Packet Types

Routers communicate with one another and maintain their routing tables using packets. Enhanced IGRP supports a number of different packet types: hellos/acknowledgments, updates, queries, replies, and requests. These packets are exchanged only between neighbors.

Enhanced IGRP routers use hello packets to discover neighbors. To achieve this purpose each router multicasts hello packets at regular intervals. Generally, these packets are transmitted unreliably, and no acknowledgment is required. Routers determine that a neighbor is operating based on regular reception of the transmitting router's packets.

When a packet is transmitted reliably, a response is required from the router receiving the packet. In this case, the receiving router sends an acknowledgment packet to the source router. An acknowledgment packet is a hello packet that has no data. Instead, it contains a non-zero acknowledgment number. Unlike hello packets, acknowledgments are always sent using a unicast address. A *unicast* is a message sent to a single network destination, so a unicast address is an address specifying a single-network device.

Update packets are sent by routers to inform neighbors of network topology changes. Because they are reliably transmitted they require acknowledgments. Depending on the nature of the update, they can be either multicast or unicast transmissions.

When a router discovers a new neighbor it informs all its other neighbors by sending a unicast update packet to each established neighbor. The neighbors use this information to amend their topology tables.

Some updates are sent as a result of a metric change. For example, when a router is informed of a link cost change it sends an update to all its neighbors. This type of update is multicast.

Query and reply packets are sent when a destination has no feasible successors. An Enhanced IGRP *feasible successor* is a neighboring router used for packet forwarding that has a least-cost-effective path to a destination guaranteed not to be part of the routing loop. The router determines feasible successors by recomputing the route to a destination when no feasible successors exist in the router's routing table and neighboring routers are advertising the destination. In order to establish the new route it sends query packets to all its neighbors as a multicast address. In this way the router attempts to identify an alternative route by inquiring how neighbors reach the same destination.

Each Enhanced IGRP router that receives a query packet must unicast a reply packet. This indicates that the originator of the query packet does not need to recompute the route because there are feasible successors. It can happen, however, that a router receiving the query packet does not know how to reach the requested destination. In such a case it sends a similar query to its neighbors. Reply packets ensure that query packets are broadcast reliably. Reply packets are also broadcast reliably, and so must be acknowledged.

Request packets are used to get specific information from one or more neighbors. They are used in route server applications, and can be either multicast or unicast, and are transmitted unreliably.

Using Routing Tables in Enhanced IGRP

This section explains how Enhanced IGRP uses neighbor tables and topology tables to update routing tables. It describes a scenario in which Enhanced IGRP routers update their routing tables using two distinct methods.

Discovery Methods

A protocol-dependent module is provided for every network-layer protocol supported by Enhanced IGRP. These modules are used to manage a set of tables corresponding to each protocol. Enhanced IGRP uses these tables to facilitate its discovery methods.

Every Enhanced IGRP router remains aware of its neighbors by maintaining a neighbor table for each supported protocol. Neighbor tables record the address and interface of each directly connected router. They also record information required by Routing Table Protocol (RTP). RTP uses sequence numbers to match packets with data. The last sequence number transmitted by a neighbor is recorded in a neighbor table so that out-of-sequence packets can be detected. If this happens, a transmission list is used to queue packets for possible retransmission on a per-neighbor basis. Round-trip timers are kept in the neighbor table entry to estimate an optimal retransmission interval. These tables are built based on the information contained in hello packets sent by neighboring routers.

When a router sends a hello packet it advertises a *hold time*. This is the length of time that the receiving neighbor can assume the sender to be reachable and operational. This relationship is maintained provided that the sending router transmits the next hello packet before the hold time expires. If a hello packet is not transmitted within its specified hold time, a topology change is indicated. The router expecting the hello packet informs DUAL that the packet has not been received. Change is made to the neighbor table.

Enhanced IGRP routers use *topology tables* to store routing information about their neighbors. This information is used when a new route to a destination needs to be identified.

Each entry in a topology table includes a destination address and a list of neighbors that have advertised the address. For every listed neighbor, the metric that the neighbor advertises for reaching the destination is also listed. Enhanced IGRP uses the following metrics: bandwidth, delay, reliability, and load. The bandwidth value is deduced from the interface type. This value can be modified by using the Bandwidth command. Delay refers to propagation delay. You can use the Delay command to modify this value; this can be useful for optimizing routing in networks with satellite links. Reliability and load are both dynamically computed as a rolling weighted average over 5 seconds.

By default, Enhanced IGRP computes the metric for a route by using the minimum bandwidth of each hop in the path and adding a media-specific delay for each hop. The metric that a router advertises to its neighbors (and uses itself) is the sum of the best-advertised metric from its neighbors plus the link cost to the neighbor that advertised that metric. Information relating to the router that contains the topology table is also included in this list.

Every router that advertises a destination associates a route with that destination. Since Enhanced IGRP is a distance vector protocol, it must follow the rules associated with that type of protocol. In this example, the router is advertising a route to a destination, so it must itself be using that route to forward packets.

An Enhanced IGRP router's topology tables are used by the DUAL finite state machine to generate its *routing* tables. Updates to the routing table occur whenever the router is made aware of a routing change, from a change in a neighbor's metric, or from a problem on the network, such as a router malfunction.

When a routing change becomes necessary, DUAL seeks to identify successors from its host router's topology tables. A successor is another neighbor with a route to the same destination. DUAL performs a feasibility calculation to determine which successor provides the most cost-effective route.

When DUAL has calculated the feasibility figure, it updates the appropriate routing table to include that successor and its destination. This eliminates the need to recompute the route.

It may happen that DUAL can find no successors in the topology tables associated with a specific destination. When this occurs, DUAL must perform a computation to find a successor. This process begins by changing the state of the topology table entry for the destination.

Destinations listed in a topology table can be either passive or active. A destination is in the passive state when the router is not performing a recomputation. In this case the current path can be in operation. Or a successor can be identified from a list of possible successors associated with the destination in the topology table.

If no successor can be found in the topology table, the listed destination is changed to be in an *active* state. The router then multicasts query packets to determine whether neighbors' routing tables contain a successor.

When each neighbor has replied, the topology table's destination entry is returned to the passive state. While a destination is in the active state, a router cannot change the destination's routing table information. Then DUAL identifies a feasible successor from information that neighbors sent in reply packets. DUAL uses the following method to compute a feasible successor: it determines which neighbors advertise a distance to the destination less than the best metric, DUAL calculates the minimum computed cost to the destination and determines which neighbor(s) offer a computed cost to the destination equal to the minimum cost as calculated by DUAL. Once a feasible successor has been identified, DUAL updates the appropriate routing table on its host router.

Routing Table Updates

Let's look at a situation that demonstrates how routing tables might be updated by Enhanced IGRP. For this example, assume that there are five Enhanced IGRP routers connected as shown in Figure 15.1.

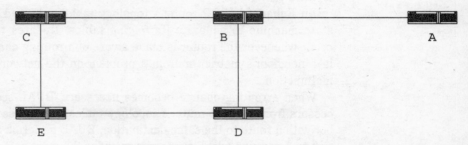

At present, the network is stable. No packets containing routing information are being transmitted because no updates are required. The routing information stored in Router C specifies that Router C reaches Router A by way of Router B (Figure 15.2). This has been set by a network administrator, and is based on local network policy.

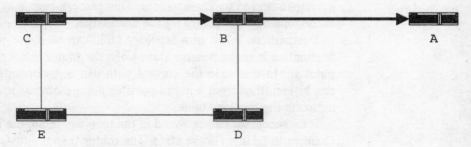

For Router E, DUAL has dynamically determined that its best path to Router A is through Routers C and B (Figure 15.3).

Let's say that a link failure is detected between Routers C and B (Figure 15.4). Router B can still transmit packets to Router A. But Router C has lost the route specified by the network administrator and Router E has lost its dynamically established route.

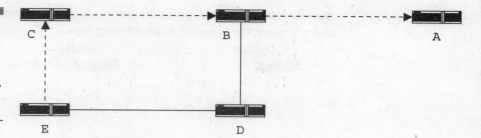

FIGURE 15.3
For Router E, DUAL
has dynamically
determined that its
best path to Router A
is through Routers C
and B.

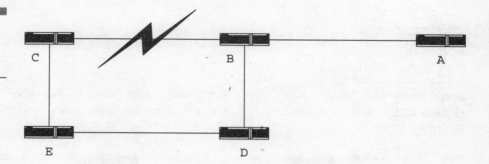

FIGURE 15.4
A link failure is
detected between
Routers C and B.

The routing updates performed by Routers C and E occur at virtually the same moment. However, the way in which they re-establish a path to Router A differs. This is because their routes were established by different methods.

Because Router E established its path to Router A dynamically, it has topology table entries that include all neighbors with a path to Router A (see Figure 15.3). In this example, that includes Router D as well as Router C.

When DUAL searches through Router E's topology table entries, it identifies Router D as a successor (Figure 15.5). This means that the path to Router A remains in the passive state. There is no need for Router E to send query packets and recompute a path. Instead, a local calculation is performed and a routing table entry is made specifying the new path to Router A.

In this example, Router E's convergence time is almost instantaneous. This is because the path to Router A remained in the passive state.

Because Router C's path to Router A was determined by local network policy, Router C's topology table contains no list of successors for that router. This means the table entry for that destination goes into the active state and the route needs to be recomputed.

In order to recompute the path to Router A, Router C multicasts query packets to all its neighbors (Figure 15.6). In this example only one neighbor can reply to Router C's query. On a larger network there could be other

routers directly connected to Router C. The more routers that reply to a
router's query, the longer the convergence time.

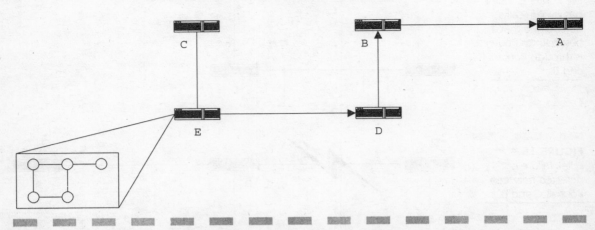

FIGURE 15.5   When DUAL searches through Router E's topology table entries, it identifies Router D as a
successor.

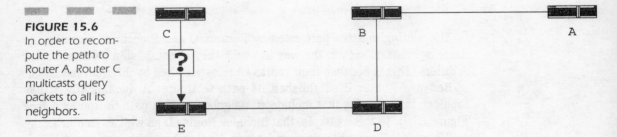

FIGURE 15.6
In order to recom-
pute the path to
Router A, Router C
multicasts query
packets to all its
neighbors.

The reply that Router E sends to Router C contains routing table information about Router E's path to Router A (Figure 15.7). Because Router E did
not need to recompute the route, it was able to update its routing table before
Router C. The reply contains the new path to Router A.

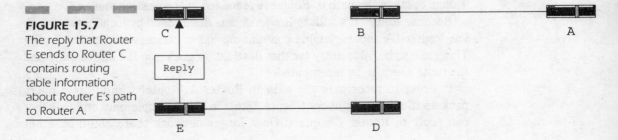

FIGURE 15.7
The reply that Router
E sends to Router C
contains routing
table information
about Router E's path
to Router A.

Once Router C receives Router E's reply, the topology table entry for Router A is returned to a passive state. Next, DUAL calculates the new successor to Router A. Then Router C must multicast an update to its neighbors. Once this occurs, the network is once again stable.

It is worth noting that the routing update did not affect all the network's routers. It is possible, but not inevitable, that Routers A and B would need to determine a new path to Router C, Router E, or both. However, in this example there is no possibility of Router D's routing table being updated.

Configuring AppleTalk Enhanced IGRP

This section shows how AppleTalk Enhanced IGRP is configured on a Cisco router.

Enabling AppleTalk Enhanced IGRP

The tasks involved in configuring Enhanced IGRP on a Cisco router are enabling an AppleTalk Enhanced IGRP routing process, assigning an AppleTalk address or cable range to each interface, assigning one or more zone names to each interface, and enabling Enhanced IGRP on each interface.

To enable an AppleTalk Enhanced IGRP routing process, issue the following command in Configuration mode appletalk `routing eigrp router-number`.

The `Router-Number` argument specifies the router ID and is a decimal integer in the range from 0 to 65535. IP and IPX Enhanced IGRP use an autonomous system number to enable Enhanced IGRP. The `Router-Number` argument is a unique number and must not be duplicated anywhere in the AppleTalk internetwork. If you configure a device with a router ID the same as that of a neighboring router, the Cisco IOS software will refuse to start AppleTalk Enhanced IGRP on interfaces that connect with that neighboring router. You can configure multiple AppleTalk Enhanced IGRP processes on a router. To do so, assign each a different router ID number.

Route redistribution occurs automatically between RTMP and Enhanced IGRP and vice versa. It may have been previously disabled on the router. To make sure that route redistribution occurs between both protocols, issue the `AppleTalk Route-Redistribution` command in Configuration mode.

To assign an AppleTalk address or cable range to an interface, issue the `AppleTalk Address` or `Cable-Range` command in Interface Configuration mode. To assign one or more zone names to an interface, issue the `AppleTalk Zone` command in Interface Configuration mode.

To enable Enhanced IGRP on an interface, issue the following command in Interface Configuration mode:

```
appletalk protocol eigrp
```

This command selects Enhanced IGRP as the protocol that generates routing updates on this interface. An interface can have more than one routing protocol configured on it.

You can completely turn off AppleTalk Enhanced IGRP routes and AppleTalk RTMP on the router or on individual interfaces. When Enhanced IGRP routing is disabled with the No AppleTalk Routing EIGRP command, all interfaces enabled for Enhanced IGRP alone (that is, not also for RTMP) lose their AppleTalk configuration.

To disable Enhanced IGRP and use RTMP on specific interfaces instead, you must enable RTMP on each interface using the AppleTalk Protocol RTMP command. Then, disable Enhanced IGRP routing using the No AppleTalk Routing EIGRP command. This process ensures that you do not lose AppleTalk configurations on interfaces for which you want to use RTMP. The same process is used to turn off RTMP on an interface and use Enhanced IGRP instead.

A number of miscellaneous AppleTalk Enhanced IGRP parameters can be configured on a router. Depending on the parameter you choose, you can perform any of the following tasks: disabling the redistribution of routing information, adjusting the interval between hello packets and the hold time, disabling split horizon, adjusting the active-state time for Enhanced IGRP routes, logging Enhanced IGRP neighbor adjacency changes, and configuring the percentage of link bandwidth used by Enhanced IGRP.

By default, AppleTalk RTMP routes are redistributed into AppleTalk Enhanced IGRP, and vice versa. Internal Enhanced IGRP routes are always preferred over external Enhanced IGRP routes. Redistributed RTMP routes are always advertised in Enhanced IGRP as external.

To disable the redistribution of RTMP routes into Enhanced IGRP and Enhanced IGRP routes into RTMP, issue the following command in Configuration mode:

```
no appletalk route-redistribution
```

Routers periodically send hello packets to each other to learn dynamically of other routers on their directly attached networks. The routers use this information to discover who their neighbors are and to learn when their neighbors become unreachable or inoperative. By default, hello packets are sent every five seconds.

You can configure the hold time, in seconds, on a specified interface for the AppleTalk Enhanced IGRP routing process designated by the router ID. The hold time is advertised in hello packets and indicates to neighbors the length of time they should consider the sender valid. The default hold time is three times the hello interval, or 15 seconds.

On very congested and large networks, 15 seconds may not be sufficient time for all routers to receive hello packets from their neighbors. In this case, you may want to increase the hold time. To change the interval between hello packets and the hold time, the command you issue in Interface Configuration mode is:

```
appletalk eigrp-timers hello-interval hold-time
```

Split horizon controls the sending of AppleTalk Enhanced IGRP update and query packets. When split horizon is enabled on an interface, these packets are not sent to destinations for which this interface is the next hop. This reduces the possibility of routing loops. By default, split horizon is enabled on all interfaces.

Split horizon prevents route information from being advertised by a router out of the interface from which the information originated. This behavior usually optimizes communication among multiple routers, particularly when links are broken. However, with nonbroadcast networks, such as frame relay and Switched Multimegabit Data Service (SMDS), situations can arise in which this behavior is less than ideal. Frame relay is a high-performance WAN protocol that provides a data communication interface between user devices and network devices. SMDS is a high-speed, packet-switched, datagram-based WAN networking technology offered by the telephone companies. For these situations, you may wish to disable split horizon. To disable split horizon, issue the following command in Interface Configuration mode:

```
no appletalk eigrp-split horizon
```

By default, Enhanced IGRP routes remain active for 1 minute. When a route reaches this active-state time limit, the Cisco router logs an error and removes the route from the routing table. You can adjust this active-state time limit by issuing the following command in Configuration mode in the following form:

```
appletalk eigrp active-time {minutes | disabled}
```

The Minutes parameter can be any number between 1 and 4,294,967,295 minutes; the default is 1 minute. The alternative Disabled parameter prevents routes remaining active indefinitely by disabling the Enhanced IGRP active state time limit.

You can enable the logging of neighbor adjacency changes by issuing the following command in Configuration mode:

```
appletalk eigrp log neighbor changes
```

This enables you to monitor the stability of the routing system and to detect problems. By default, adjacency changes are not logged.

To set a bandwidth value for an interface, use the `Bandwidth` command in Interface Configuration mode. The syntax is `bandwidth kilobits`. The intended bandwidth is expressed in *kilobits* per second.

By default, Enhanced IGRP packets consume a maximum of 50 percent of the link bandwidth. You can use the `AppleTalk EIGRP Bandwidth Percent` command to specify a different value. The syntax for this command is `appletalk eigrp bandwidth percent percent`. This command is entered in Interface Configuration mode.

The `AppleTalk EIGRP Bandwidth Percent` command is useful if a different level of link utilization is required. Or if the configured bandwidth does not match the actual link bandwidth, for example, it may have been configured to influence route metric calculations.

In this example, Enhanced IGRP is configured to use a maximum of 25 percent, or 32 kbps, of a 128 kbps circuit.

```
interface serial 0
bandwidth 128
appletalk eigrp-bandwidth-percent 25
```

Here we will look at configuring AppleTalk Enhanced IGRP on the Vermont router (Figure 15.8). In this example, we want RTMP and Enhanced IGRP routing on the Vermont router's Ethernet 0 (E0) interface and Enhanced IGRP routing only on its Serial 0 (S0) interface. The Vermont router is already configured for RTMP routing and route redistribution has previously been disabled on the router. The Vermont router is connected to the Maine router through its Serial 0 interface. The Maine router's E0 interface is configured for RTMP and Enhanced IGRP routing, and its S1 interface is configured for Enhanced IGRP routing only.

Assume that you have logged in to the Vermont router and are in Configuration mode. Use the `AppleTalk Routing` command to start an AppleTalk routing process. You use the keyword `EIGRP` and the router number, for example, 101, to enable Enhanced EIGRP for AppleTalk.

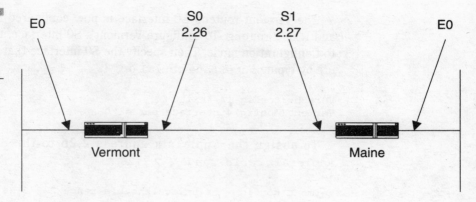

FIGURE 15.8
Configuring
AppleTalk Enhanced
IGRP on a router.

```
Vermont>enable
Password:
Vermont# config term
Enter configuration comands, one per line. End with CNTL/Z.
Vermont(config)#appletalk routing eigrp 101
```

To make sure that route redistribution occurs between both protocols, enter `appletalk route-redistribution` in Configuration mode.

```
Vermont(config)#apple route-redistribution
```

To configure Vermont's E0 interface, enter `interface ethernet 0`. Once the E0 interface is in Interface Configuration mode you can assign it a network address and zone name.

```
Vermont(config)#interface ethernet 0
```

To assign the E0 interface the AppleTalk address 206.69, type `appletalk cable-range 206-206 206.69`. To assign the interface the zone name "vermontlan", type `appletalk zone vermontlan`.

```
Vermont(config-if)#appletalk cable-range 206-206 206.69
Vermont(config-if)#appletalk zone vermontlan
```

Once the E0 interface has been assigned an AppleTalk address and zone name, you can enable RTMP and Enhanced IGRP routing on the interface. You don't need to configure RTMP on the interface because it has already been configured on it. To enable Enhanced IGRP routing on the interface, enter `appletalk protocol eigrp`.

```
Vermont(config-if)#appletalk protocol eigrp
```

The Vermont router's E0 interface is now configured for Enhanced IGRP and RTMP routing. To configure Vermont's S0 interface, type `exit` to return to Configuration mode. Then specify the S0 interface that you want to configure by typing `interface serial 0`.

```
Vermont(config-if)#exit
Vermont(config)#interface serial 0
```

To assign the AppleTalk address 2.26 to the S0 interface, type `appletalk cable-range 2-2 2.26`.

```
Vermont(config-if)#appletalk cable-range 2-2 2.26
```

To assign the zone name "vermontwanlon" to the S0 interface, type `appletalk zone vermontwanlon`.

```
Vermont
(config-if)#appletalk zone vermontwanlon
```

The Vermont router's S0 interface is to be configured for Enhanced IGRP only, so RTMP must be turned off on Vermont's S0 interface. Remember that you cannot disable RTMP without first enabling Enhanced IGRP.

To enable Enhanced IGRP on the S0 interface, type `appletalk protocol eigrp`. Then to turn off RTMP on this interface, type `no appletalk protocol rtmp`.

```
Vermont(config-if)#appletalk protocol eigrp
Vermont(config-if)#no appletalk protocol rtmp
```

You wish to configure the percentage of bandwidth that may be used by Enhanced IGRP on an interface to 75. Remember that Enhanced IGRP packets consume a maximum of 50 percent of the bandwidth assigned to an interface. Before you can do this job you must set the bandwidth value. To set the bandwidth value to 64 kilobits per second, type `bandwidth 64`.

```
Vermont(config-if)#bandwidth 64
```

To configure the percentage of bandwidth used by Enhanced IGRP on an interface to 75, type `appletalk eigrp-bandwidth-percent 75`.

```
Vermont(config-if)#appletalk eigrp-bandwidth-percent 75
Router Vermont's S0 interface is now configured for Enhanced IGRP
routing.
```

To ensure that the router has Enhanced IGRP routing enabled the next time it starts up, save the AppleTalk configuration in the router's memory. First exit Interface Configuration mode and return to Privileged mode by pressing **Ctrl+Z**. Then enter `copy runn start` to save the configuration in NVRAM.

```
Vermont(config-if)#^Z
Vermont#copy runn start
Building configuration...
[OK]
Vermont#
```

You can use a number of commands to check a router's configuration and monitor its activity on the network. For example, you can display the status of Vermont's E0 interface and the parameters configured on it by entering `show appletalk interface ethernet 0` in Privileged mode.

```
Vermont#show appletalk interface ethenet 0
Ethernet 0 is up, line protocol is up
  AppleTalk cable range is 206-206
  AppleTalk address is 206.69, Valid
  AppleTalk zone is "dublan"
  Routing protocols enabled: RTMP & EIGRP
  AppleTalk discarded 2 packets due to input errors
  AppleTalk address is disabled
  AppleTalk route cache is enabled
Vermont#
```

The output of a `Show AppleTalk Interface` command on Vermont's E0 interface displays the type of interface, states that it is currently active and inserted into the network, that the interface is usable, the address of the interface and name of the zone in which this interface is situated, and the routing protocols enabled on the interface.

To test that Enhanced IGRP routing is enabled on Vermont's serial interfaces you need to use the `Ping AppleTalk` command to see if the Vermont router can send Enhanced IGRP packets to Maine's E0 interface. The `Ping` command sends Echo Protocol datagrams to other AppleTalk nodes to verify connectivity and measure round-trip times. Do this by typing `ping 100.125` in Privileged mode. You can see from the output of this command that Enhanced IGRP is enabled because Maine's E0 interface can receive Enhanced IGRP packets.

```
Vermont#ping 100.125
Type escape sequence to abort.
Sending 5, 100-byte Apple to Echoes to 100.125, timeout is 2
```

```
seconds:
!!!!!
Success rate is 100 percent (5/5), round-trip min/avg/max =
32/33/36
Vermont#
```

You can see the current state of the AppleTalk routing table by typing the tshow appletalk route command in Privileged mode.

```
Vermont#
show appletalk route
Codes: R - RTMP derived, E - EIGRP derived, C - connected, A -
AURP
       S - static, P - proxy
3 routes in internet
The first zone listed for each entry is its default (primary)
zone.
C Net 2-2 directly connected, Serial0, zone dubwanlon
E Net 100-100 [1/G] via 2.27, 664 sec, Serial0, zone lonlan
C Net 206-206 directly connected, Ethernet0, zone dublan
Vermont#
```

You can see from the output of a Show AppleTalk Route command on router Vermont that it shows two routes directly connected (network 2–2 and 206–206) and one route that has been learned from EIGRP (network 100–100). Network 206 is connected to the Vermont router through the router's E0 interface. Network 2 is connected to the Vermont router through the router's S0 interface. Network 100–100 is connected to the Maine's E0 interface. The Vermont router learns about network 100–100 through Maine's S1 interface.

You can display information about the AppleTalk internetwork and specific parameters for the router by typing the show appletalk globals command in Privileged mode.

```
Vermont#show appletalk globals
AppleTalk global information
   Internet is compatible with older, AT Phase1, routers.
   There are 3 routes in the internet.
   There are 3 zones defined.
   Logging of significant AppleTalk events is disabled.
   ZIP resends queries every 10 seconds.
   RTMP updates are sent every 10 seconds.
   RTMP entries are considered BAD after 20 seconds.
   RTMP entries are discarded after 60 seconds.
   AARP probe retransmit count: 10, interval: 200 msec.
   AARP request retransmit count: 5, interval: 1000 msec.
   DDP datagrams will be checksummed.
   RTMP datagrams will be strictly checked.
```

```
RTMP routes may not be propagated without zones.
Routes will be distributed between routing protocols.
Routing between local devices on an interface will not be
performed.
IPTalk uses the udp base port of 768 (Default).
EIGRP router id is: 101
EIGRP maximum active time is 3 minutes.
Alternate node address format will not be displayed.
Access control of any networks of a zone hides the zone.
Vermont#
```

You can see from the output of a Show AppleTalk Globals command on router Vermont that there are three routes and three zones in the current AppleTalk internet configuration, route redistribution between both protocols is enabled, the router ID is 101, and the Enhanced IGRP's active state time is 3 minutes. The three routes specified are the two directly connected networks and the route learned through Enhanced EIGRP. The three zones specified are the two zones configured on Vermont's and Maine's E0 interface and the zone name of the serial link between both routers. The output of this command also shows the activity of other AppleTalk protocols on the network.

The Debug Apple Routing command enables debugging output from the RTMP routines. For example, a Debug Apple Routing command on router Vermont can be used to monitor the acquisition of routes, display the aging of routing table entries, and display the advertisement of known routes. The Debug Routing command also reports conflicting network numbers on the same network if the network is misconfigured.

```
Vermont#debug apple routing
AppleTalk RTMP routing debugging is on
AppleTalk EIGRP routing debugging is on
atigrp2_router: received HELLO from 2.27
atigrp2_router: received HELLO from 2.27
AT: src=Ethernet0:206.69, dst=206-206, size=22, 2 rtes, RTMP pkt
sent
AT: Route ager starting on Main AT RoutingTable (3 active nodes)
AT: Route ager finished on Main AT RoutingTable (3 active nodes)
atigrp2_router: received HELLO from 2.27
atigrp2_router: received HELLO from 2.27
AT: src=Ethernet0:206.69, dst=206-206, size=22, 2 rtes, RTMP pkt
sent
AT: Route ager starting on Main AT RoutingTable (3 active nodes)
Vermont#
```

Managing AppleTalk Traffic

 **Managing Complex Networks**

This section describes how complex networks are managed. We will describe the causes of traffic congestion and the methods used to manage it in complex networks.

Overview

As a network grows, it must continue to meet the needs of its users. The popularity of more complex networks is making network management even more challenging. A complex network has more than 500 routes, global topology with multiple remote connections, an emphasis on security, and routed and non-routed traffic on the same medium. Networks may be considered particularly complex when they approach or exceed 300 AppleTalk zones in one area.

Complex networks force the router to maintain large routing and service tables for each protocol. These tables have to be updated or distributed periodically and this consumes a lot of bandwidth on all links.

Networks with more than 500 routes, whether in a local or distributed topology, can have connectivity problems because of the metric limitations of the routing protocol. Convergence can be slow on these networks after changes in their topology.

If your network has 500 or more routes, you can use *route summarization* to manage router overheads. Route summarization (also known as *route aggregation*) reduces the overall number of entries in the routing table. Summarization of routes occurs at major network boundaries for most routing protocols.

Corporate networks often connect sites in different continents. However, managing geographically remote networks (global topology) usually involves trading off cost against reliability.

Maintaining connectivity is a common problem with geographically remote networks. Often, network administrators must rely on several carriers and service providers to maintain corporate connectivity requirements. The choice of connection type depends on tariff considerations balanced by service needs. Connection types, and as a result response times, can change during the day to take advantage of different fee structures.

You can manage global topology by using Cisco's dial-on-demand routing (DDR) feature. Under DDR, active links are created only after "interesting" traffic is detected by the router. "Interesting traffic" means packets that pass the restrictions of the access lists. This service replaces *nailed-up circuits* charges for even when the link is idle. DDR reduces the costs of managing a global network.

Data compression of headers or entire frames is a simple way to reduce the volume of traffic on a serial link. The router compresses a frame before it is placed on the medium.

Packet-switched networks, such as X.25 and frame relay, can also be used in global networks. These networks provide connectivity through a large number of service providers with established circuits to most major cities throughout the world.

Let's look now at routed and non-routed traffic. A network delivering both routed and non-routed traffic has some unique problems. Traffic that cannot be routed (for example, IBM's SDLC) relies on routed protocols for transport over integrated networks. Many applications that use non-routable protocols were never intended to operate outside a local LAN environment. These applications are usually sensitive to delays, and any delay can lead to an application session being lost.

In general, non-routed networks rely heavily on broadcast traffic to maintain communication with peer devices. However, routers are designed to block broadcast traffic, so special configurations are needed for routers that act as bridges.

Non-routable (or bridged) traffic can be encapsulated in a routable protocol to establish remote connections. However, you should establish a queuing policy that gives non-routable traffic priority in the network because application programs depend on timely responses.

Cisco's concurrent routing and bridging feature in IOS Release 11.0 and later allows the same protocol to be both routed and bridged (though on different interfaces) in the router. This feature is important during migration from bridged to routed networks.

Traffic Congestion on Networks

All large networks may be subject to traffic congestion. Congestion occurs when the volume of data transmitted by a particular medium exceeds the bandwidth of that medium. Congestion anywhere in the path leads to delays for user applications. Network users perceive the network as slow, but may not understand the cause of the slowness.

Data traffic is usually generated by user applications, electronic mail for example, because the applications initiate file transfers. Overhead traffic in an AppleTalk network is generated when the traffic isn't directly related to user applications. Examples of overhead traffic are routing updates and broadcast requests.

An AppleTalk network has the following sources of data and overhead traffic: user applications, routing protocol updates, Zone Information Proto col (ZIP) requests, and Name Binding Protocol (NBP) inquiries. The underlying architecture of AppleTalk networks generates a lot of traffic. The use of names for services rather than direct addresses means that NBP is needed to translate names to addresses before the actual address is used on the media link. User requests for services such as printers generate broadcast traffic and use ZIP to support that function.

A multiprotocol network has several different protocol suites active at the same time. The user data traffic for the different protocols is all active at the same time and many concurrent data transfers are taking place. In addition, the overhead traffic for each protocol requires a portion of the bandwidth of the medium.

Some underlying traffic on the medium is associated with the lower layers of the OSI model. All the following need some portion of the medium's data carrying capacity: AppleTalk Address Resolution Protocol (AARP) to resolve logical-to-physical addressing issues, keepalives to maintain connectivity, tokens for accessibility, and time-to-live updates.

Network congestion results from too much traffic trying to use the network medium at one time. To resolve congestion, traffic must be reduced or rescheduled. Reducing traffic is the most obvious solution for network congestion. Traffic filters can keep the volume of some traffic from reaching critical links. They can limit the size of routing updates and the number of networks that receive the updates.

Some periodic broadcasts have configurable transmission timers to extend the interval between broadcasts. Extending the interval reduces the overall traffic load on a link.

Using static entries in a routing table can eliminate the need to advertise network routes dynamically across a link. Traffic that uses a slow link such as a serial line can be given a priority to ensure that critical applications don't time out. You can reorder the application from its first-come-first-served order to give preference to some types of traffic.

The Cisco router can help control network congestion. Standard access lists generally use source addressing characteristics to filter traffic. Extended access lists should be used to filter source and destination address, application type, and data size. To customize the link, you can change the timers for low-level periodic announcements, such as keepalives.

You can statically configure most tables to reduce broadcasting as the means to learn dynamically about topology or reachability. You can also reorder application traffic flowing across a serial link in a priority queue (so that all traffic of a particular type gets through first) and a custom queue where traffic gets a certain percentage of the bandwidth.

AURP reduces congestion on a WAN link by sending routing updates only when a change in the network topology occurs.

■ ■ Queue Configuration

This section describes the operation of Cisco IOS queuing strategies. We will examine the need for queuing in a large network and describe priority queue operation, priority queue configuration, the operation of custom queuing, how to configure custom queues, the operation of weighted fair queuing, and how to configure weighted fair queuing.

Overview

Queuing is a mechanism that gives one type of network traffic priority over other types. This is done by reordering the packets that constitute the traffic. Queuing is useful over congested serial lines, but can be slow because it requires buffering in the router.

It is a good idea to establish a corporate queuing policy to decide which traffic on a congested line gets through first.

The Cisco IOS software can be configured to support the following types of queuing strategy: priority queuing, custom queuing, and weighted fair queuing. You can configure priority, custom, and weighted fair queuing on a Cisco router, but you can assign only one queue type to an interface.

The primary distinction between priority and custom queuing is that custom queuing guarantees some level of service to all traffic. Priority queuing guarantees that one type of traffic will get through at the expense of all others.

When there is a limited amount of bandwidth available, priority queuing consumes most, if not all of the available bandwidth when it delivers the critical traffic. Priority queuing makes maximum use of low-bandwidth links for a few selected protocols.

When more bandwidth is available, custom queuing shares it determinably between the different traffic types. It ensures that each traffic type gets to use some portion of the link. Custom queuing is more flexible than priority queuing, but priority queuing is more powerful when you need to prioritize a mission-critical protocol.

Weighted fair queuing provides traffic priority management that automatically sorts among individual traffic streams. You do not need to define access lists first. There are two categories of data streams in weighted fair queuing: high-bandwidth and low-bandwidth sessions.

Low-bandwidth traffic has effective priority over high-bandwidth traffic. The high-bandwidth traffic shares the transmission service proportionally according to assigned weights.

Priority Queuing

Use priority queuing to assign priorities to datagrams traveling on an interface. You can set priorities on the type of traffic passing through the network. Packets are classified according to several criteria, including protocol and subprotocol type. They are then queued on one of four output queues: high, medium, normal, and low.

·When the router is ready to transmit a packet, it scans the priority queues. This is done in order, from highest to lowest, until the highest priority packet is found. After the highest priority packet is transmitted, the router checks the priority queues again. If a priority queue fills up, packets are dropped, and the router does not process them.

With priority queuing, the high-priority queue is always emptied before the medium-priority queue, and so on. Priority queuing is appropriate for cases where the WAN links are congested from time to time. If the WAN links are never congested, priority queuing is probably unnecessary.

You can establish queuing priorities based on the protocol type. To do this, use the `Priority-List Protocol` command, which has the syntax `priority-list list-number protocol protocol-name {high medium normal low} queue-keyword keyword-value`.

```
Connecticut(config)#priority-list 1 protocol appletalk high
Connecticut(config)#priority-list 1 protocol ipx medium
Connecticut(config)#priority-list 1 protocol ip normal
Connecticut(config)#priority-list 1 interface serial 0 high
Connecticut(config)#priority-list 1 default low
Connecticut(config)#priority-list 1 queue-limit 15 20 20 30
!
Connecticut(config)#interface serial 0
Connecticut(config-if)#priority-group 1
Connecticut(config-if)#
```

The *list-number* is a value between 1 and 10 that identifies the priority list. The *protocol-name* specifies the protocol, AppleTalk for example. Examples of other protocols that can be specified are CLNS, DECnet, IP, IPX, Banyan Vines, and X.25. In the example shown here, you can see the priority list number and the type of protocol. The queue priority level is high. Queue keywords provide additional options including byte count and list.

Use the `Priority-List Interface` command to set the priority of traffic arriving on an interface. The command's syntax is `priority-list list-number interface interface-type interface-number {high medium normal low}`. The *interface-type* and *interface-number* specify the name of the interface with incoming packets.

In the example shown here, packets arriving on Serial 0 are given high priority.

```
Connecticut(config)#priority-list 1 interface serial 0 high
```

Use the `Priority-List Default` command to assign previously unassigned traffic to a queue. The syntax for the `Priority-List Default` command is priority-list *list-number* default {high medium normal low}. In this example, the default priority level is low.

```
Connecticut(config)#priority-list 1 default low
```

Use the `Priority-List Queue-Limit` command to define the maximum number of packets in each priority queue. The syntax for this command is priority-list *list-number* queue-limit *high-limit medium-limit normal-limit low-limit*. The queue limit defaults define the default number of datagrams in each queue. The default high limit is 20 datagrams. The default medium limit is 40 datagrams. The default normal limit is 60 datagrams. The default low limit is 80 datagrams. In general, it is not a good idea to change the default queue sizes. In the example below, the high limit of datagrams is 15. The medium and normal limits are both 20. And the low limit is 30.

```
Connecticut(config)#priority-list 1 queue-limit 15 20 20 30
```

You can assign a priority list number to an interface using the `Priority-Group` command in Interface Configuration mode. You can assign only one list per interface. The syntax of the `Priority-Group` command is priority-group *list-number*. In this example, Serial 0 has a priority queue.

```
Connecticut(config)#interface serial 0
Connecticut(config-if)#priority-group 1
```

Since AppleTalk traffic enters the high queue, it can be transmitted on the serial 0 interface ahead of the IP and IPX traffic.

Custom Queuing

Custom queuing uses a different method to assign priority to traffic. It assigns different amounts of queue space to each protocol and handles the queues in round-robin fashion. A particular protocol may be given higher priority by assigning it more queue space. The protocol will never monopolize the entire bandwidth and there is no risk of losing lower priority packets. Custom queuing is particularly important for time-sensitive protocols.

When custom queuing is enabled on an interface, the system maintains 17 output queues for that interface. You can specify queues 1 through 16. For queue numbers 1 through 16, the system cycles through the queues sequentially. Packets in the current queue are delivered before the system moves on to the next.

A configurable byte count is associated with each output queue. This specifies how many bytes of data from the current queue the system should deliver before it moves on to the next queue. When a particular queue is being processed, the router sends packets until the number of bytes sent exceeds the queue byte count. It will stop when the queue is empty.

Queue 0 is a system queue. It is emptied before any of the other queues. The system uses queue 0 for high-priority packets such as keepalives. You cannot configure other traffic to use this queue.

You can establish queuing priorities based on the protocol type. To do this, use the Queue-List Protocol command, which has the following syntax: queue-list *list-number* protocol *protocol-name queue-number queue-keyword keyword-value.*

```
Connecticut(config)#queue-list 1 protocol appletalk 1
Connecticut(config)#queue-list 1 protocol ip 2
Connecticut(config)#queue-list 1 protocol ipx 3
Connecticut(config)#queue-list 1 interface serial 0 1
Connecticut(config)#queue-list 1 default 5
Connecticut(config)#queue-list 1 queue 1 limit 20
Connecticut(config)#queue-list 1 queue 1 byte-count 4554
Connecticut(config)#queue-list 1 queue 1 byte-count 1518
!
Connecticut(config)#interface serial 0
Connecticut(config-if)#custom-queue-list 1
```

The *list-number* is a value between 1 and 16 that identifies the queue list. The *protocol-name* specifies a protocol, AppleTalk for example. Other examples of protocols that can be specified are CLNS, DECnet, IP, IPX, Banyan Vines, or X.25. In the example shown here, you can see the queue list number and the type of protocol. The *queue-number*, which may be between 1 and 16, is 1 in this example. Queue keywords provide additional options including byte-counts and lists.

Use the Queue-List Interface command to set the priority of all traffic arriving on an interface. The command's syntax is queue-list *list-number* interface *interface-type interface-number queue-number* where *interface-type* and *interface-number* specify the name of the interface with incoming packets. In the example below, packets arriving on Serial 0 get more bandwidth.

```
Connecticut(config)#queue-list 1 interface serial 0 1
```

Use the Queue-List Default command to specify the queue to which traffic not previously specified will be assigned. The syntax for this command is queue-list *list-number* default *queue-number*. In the example below, the default queue is set to queue number 5 on list 1.

```
Connecticut(config)#queue-list 1 default 5
```

Use the Queue-List Queue command to limit the length of a particular queue. The syntax for the command is queue-list *list-number* queue *queue-number* limit *limit-number*. Here *list-number* and *queue-number* identify the numbers of the queue list and queue. The limit-number parameter defines the maximum number of packets that may be in the queue at any one time. It can have a range from 0 to 32,767. The default value is 20.

```
Connecticut(config)#queue-list 1 queue 1 limit 20
```

Use the Queue-List Queue Byte-Count command to define the minimum byte count transferred from the specified queue. The syntax for this command is queue-list *list-number* queue *queue-number* byte-count *byte-count-number*.

List-number and *queue-number* identify the numbers of the queue list and queue. *Byte-count-number* specifies the minimum number of bytes that the system allows to be delivered from the specified queue during a particular cycle. The default byte count is 1,500.

In the example shown below, the queue list number is 1. The queue number is also 1. The byte count is 4,554.

```
Connecticut(config)#queue-list 1 queue 1 byte-count 4554
```

You can assign a queue list to an interface using the Custom-Queue-List command, but you can assign only one list per interface. The syntax of the Custom-Queue-List command is custom-queue-list *list-number* where the *list-number* indicates the number of the queue list (between 1 and 16) made available to control the interface's bandwidth.

In the example below, the Custom-Queue-List command is used to assign queue list 1 to the serial 0 interface. Different kinds of packets are assigned to queues 1 and 2. Queue 1 is assigned a maximum of 4,554 bytes. And the default queue is queue 5.

```
Connecticut(config)#interface serial 0
```

Weighted Fair Queuing

Cisco's implementation of weighted fair queuing divides traffic into conversations based on packet header addressing. Weighted fair queuing is dependent on encapsulation. When the router initializes, the Cisco IOS checks the encapsulation type specified for each interface. Serial interfaces using HDLC, LAPB, PPP, frame relay, or SMDS encapsulation are candidates for fair queuing. Serial interfaces are further categorized by bandwidth (link speed). Fair queuing is enabled by default on serial interfaces with the proper encapsulation type operating at 2.048 Mbps (E1) or less. Fair queuing is not enabled on serial interfaces using X.25 or compressed PPP as the encapsulation type. LAN interfaces and serial lines operating at E3 or T3 speeds are also not available for fair queuing. A *conversation* is a series of messages that makes up a continuous data stream. A queuing weight is assigned to each conversation based on bandwidth requirements and other variables.

A conversation index determines whether traffic represents low-volume or high-volume conversations. The switching logic within the Cisco IOS determines the selection of the data path through the router.

Fair queuing is based on delivering messages across a serial link in a timely fashion. As the packets are switched through the router, they arrive in a precise order at the outgoing interface. The exact order of the packets is determined by the arrival of the first bit in each packet. As the packets arrive, the fair queue algorithm sorts them into messages that are part of a conversation.

The packets are placed in a holding queue before transmission. The transmission routine sorts the conversation queues "fairly" to determine the order in which messages will be handled. The order of removal of messages from each queue is determined by the value of the last bit in the last packet. It is determined when a message ends, rather than when it begins.

File transfers cause high-volume conversations. Other application tasks are monitored by the user and are time-sensitive, but they do not require a lot of bandwidth. For example, interactive users create low-volume conversations.

The challenge for the queuing method is to provide the responsiveness required by the interactive user and still move lots of data to satisfy the file transfer.

The `Fair-Queue` command is used manually to enable fair queuing on an interface.

```
fair-queue congestive-discard-threshold-number
```

The `congestive-discard-threshold-number` parameter defines a congestion threshold above which messages for high-volume traffic will no longer be encapsulated. The number of messages can range from 1 to 512. The default for this field is 64 messages. The congestive-discard policy applies only to high-volume conversations that have more than one message in the queue.

The discard policy tries to control conversations that would monopolize the link. It is invoked when the total number of messages on all queues is greater than the threshold and the number of messages in a single queue is greater than one quarter of the threshold.

The `Show Queuing` command is used to display detailed queuing information about all interfaces where queuing is enabled.

```
show queuing [fair  custom  priority]
```

Access Lists and Filters

This section demonstrates how to configure AppleTalk access lists and filters. We will examine what access lists are, outline the different commands that make up access lists, describe what filters are, and outline the commands that enable filters to be applied to a router's interface. We will demonstrate how to configure an access list and filter, configure an access list on a router to filter traffic based on networks and cable-ranges, and configure an access list on a router to filter traffic based on zones.

AppleTalk Access Lists

Cisco provides access lists to permit or deny packets' crossing specified router interfaces. An AppleTalk access list is a list of AppleTalk network numbers, zones, or NBP named entities maintained by the Cisco IOS software. The lists are used to control access to or from specific zones, networks, or NBP named entities. Access lists can be used in three ways: to control the transmission of packets on an interface, to select the interesting traffic that initiates a dial-on-demand (DDR) connection, and to restrict the contents of routing updates.

To define an access list, issue the following command in Configuration mode: `access-list` *access-list-number* {permit deny} [options].

The `Access-List-Number` parameter is the number of the access list. Each access list is identified by a decimal number in the range from 600 to 699. The `Permit` and `Deny` parameters indicate whether the entry allows or blocks traffic of the type specified in the option. Different types of access lists can be defined depending on what option is specified, for example, the `Access-List Network` command is defined by specifying the `Network` option.

Cisco IOS software supports two general types of AppleTalk access lists: AppleTalk-style access lists and IP-style access lists. AppleTalk-style access lists regulate the internetwork using zone names and NBP named entities.

A zone access list is effectively a dynamic list of network numbers. When the user specifies a zone name, it is as if the user had specified all the network numbers belonging to that zone. Zone names can be expressed either explicitly, for example "sales" zone, or by using generalized argument keywords, for example zone "Sales". Thus, using AppleTalk zone name access lists simplifies network management. It also allows for greater flexibility when adding segments, because reconfiguration requirements are minimal.

An NBP named entity access list provides a means of controlling access at the network entity level. By using NBP named entities, you can permit or deny NBP packets from a class of objects, a particular NBP named entity, or all NBP named entities within a particular area.

The main advantage of AppleTalk-style access lists is that because they are based on zones and NBP named entities they make it possible to define access regardless of the existing network topology or any changes in future topologies.

IP-style access lists control network access based on network numbers. This feature can be useful in defining access lists that control the disposition of networks that overlap, are contained by, or exactly match a specific network number range. Using IP-style access lists overcomes the potential problem of assigning conflicting network numbers to different networks. For example, using an access list helps restrict the network numbers and zones that a department can advertise, thereby limiting advertisement to an authorized set of networks.

In general, however, using IP-style access lists is not recommended because the controls are not optimal; they ignore the logical mapping provided by AppleTalk zones. One problem with IP-style access lists is that when you add networks to a zone, you must reconfigure each secure router. Another problem is that because network segments can be easily added, the potential for confusion and misconfiguration is significant.

You can define IP-style access lists for networks and cable-ranges. To define an access list for a single network number (that is, for a nonextended network), issue the `Access-List Network` command in Configuration mode: `access-list` *access-list-number* `{permit deny}` `network` *network*. In the example below, you can see that the `Access-List Network` command forwards all packets from network 1 and denies all packets from network 2.

```
access-list 650 permit network 1
access-list 650 deny network 2
```

To define an AppleTalk access list for a cable-range (for extended networks only), issue the `Access-List Cable-Range` command in Configuration mode: `access-list` *access-list-number* `{permit deny}` `cable-range` *cable-range*. In the example below, you can see that the access list forwards all packets destined for cable-range 10 to 20.

```
access-list 600 permit cable-range 10-20
```

You can define an AppleTalk access list for an extended or a nonextended network that is included entirely within a specified cable-range. To do this, issue the `Access-List Within` command in Configuration mode: `access-list` *access-list-number* `{permit deny}` `within` *cable-range*. In the example shown, you can see that the access list permits access to any network or cable-range completely included in the range 10 to 20. This means, for example, that cable-range 13 to 16 will be permitted, but cable-range 17 to 25 will not be.

```
access-list 600 permit within 10-20
```

You can define an AppleTalk access list that overlaps any part of a range of network numbers or cable-ranges (for both extended and nonextended networks). To do this, issue the `Access-List Includes` command in Configuration mode: `access-list` *access-list-number* `{permit deny}` `includes` *cable-range*. In the example below, you can see that the access list permits access to any network or cable-range that overlaps any part of the range 10 to 20. This means, for example, the cable-range 17 to 25 will also be permitted.

```
access-list 600 permit includes 10-20
```

You can create AppleTalk-style access lists for zones and NBP named entities. To create access lists which define access conditions for zones, issue the

`Access-List Zone` command in Configuration mode: `access-list access-list-number {permit deny} zone zonename`. The `Zone Name` parameter can include special characters from the Apple Macintosh character set. To include a special character, type a colon followed by two hexadecimal characters. For zone names with a leading space character, enter the first character as the special sequence :20. In the example shown, you can see that the access list permits packets from the sales zone.

```
access-list 600 permit zone sales
```

To define an access list for NBP named entities, issue the `Access-List NBP` command in Configuration mode: `access-list access-list-number {deny permit} nbp seq {type object zone} string`.

This command allows you define an AppleTalk access-list entry for a particular NBP named entity (object), for example a particular application; a class of NBP named entities (type), for example a printer; and NBP named entities belonging to a specific area (zone). These three classifications make up an NBP name, which is also referred to as an NBP tuple.

For each access-list entry that you enter, you must specify a sequence number. The principal purpose of the sequence number is to allow you to associate two or three portions of an NBP name. To do this, enter two or three commands that have the same sequence number. Each command specifies a different keyword and NBP name portion—type, object, or zone. The same sequence number binds them together. This enables you to restrict the forwarding of NBP packets at any level, down to a single named entity. The sequence number also allows you to keep track of the number of access-list NBP entries you have made. You must enter a sequence number even if you do not use it to associate portions of an NBP name.

The `string` parameter is a portion of an NBP name identifying the type, object, or zone of a named entity. The name string can be up to 32 characters long, and can include special characters from the Apple Macintosh character set. To include a special character, type a colon followed by two hexadecimal characters. For an NBP name with a leading space, enter the first character as the special sequence :20.

In the example below, access list 607 allows the forwarding of NBP packets from all printers of type LaserWriter, AppleTalk file servers of type AFPServer, and applications called HotShotPaint. The `Access-List Object` command allows the forwarding of NBP packets from all applications that share the same name, regardless of the zone they are in, but it denies the forwarding of NBP packets from all other sources.

```
access-list 607 permit nbp 1 type LaserWriter
access-list 607 permit nbp 2 type AFPServer
access-list 607 permit nbp 3 object HotShotPaint
access-list 607 deny other-nbps
```

In the example below, you can see that access-list number 608 denies the forwarding of NBP packets from two specific servers (whose fully-qualified NBP names are specified) and permits the forwarding of NBP packets from all other sources.

```
access-list 608 deny nbp 1 object ServerA
access-list 608 deny nbp 1 type AFPServer
access-list 608 deny nbp 1 zone Bld3
access-list 608 deny nbp 2 object ServerB
access-list 608 deny nbp 2 type AFPServer
access-list 608 deny nbp 2 zone Bld3
access-list 608 permit other-nbps
access-list 608 permit other-access
```

It is a good idea to specify explicitly how to handle packets or routing updates that do not satisfy any of the access control statements in the access list. If you do not, the packets or routing updates will be automatically denied access and, in the case of data packets, they will be discarded.

To define the default action to take for access checks that apply to networks or cable-ranges, issue the Access-List Other-Access command in Configuration mode: access-list access-list-number {permit deny} other-access. In the example below, you can see that the access list forwards all packets except those destined for networks 1 and 2.

```
access-list 650 deny network 1
access-list 650 deny network 2
access-list 650 permit other-access
```

You can define the action to take for access checks not explicitly defined with the Access-List Zone command. To do this, issue the Access-List Additional-Zones command in Configuration mode: access-list access-list-number {permit deny} additional-zones. In the example shown, you can see that the access list allows packets from all zones except the accounts zone.

```
access-list 610 deny zone accounts
access-list 610 permit additional-zones
```

You can define the default action to take for access checks that apply to NBP packets from named entities not otherwise explicitly denied or permit-

ted. To do this, issue the `Access-List Other-Nbps` in Configuration mode:
`access-list access-list-number {permit deny} other-nbps`.

All access-list commands that specify the same access-list number create a single access list, which can contain any number and any combination of access-list commands. You can specify only one each of the commands that specify default actions to take if none of the access conditions are matched.

```
access-list 650 deny zone accounts
access-list 650 deny network 1
access-list 650 deny network 2
access-list 650 permit other-access
```

It is important to add the appropriate `Access-List Permit Other-Access` or `Access-List Permit Additional-Zones` statement to the end of the access list when using only one type of filtering. This is because the Cisco IOS software by default automatically includes an `Access-List Deny Other-Access` entry to the end of each access list.

If you do not want any network filtering to occur, you must create an access list that explicitly permits access to all networks. If you want to create an access list that denies access to a zone, for example zone Z, include the following entries in the access list: an `Access-List Deny Zone Z` entry to deny zone Z, an `Access-List Permit Additional-Zones` entry to permit all other zones, and an `Access-List Permit Other-Access` to explicitly permit all networks.

```
access-list 650 deny zone z
access-list 650 permit additional-zones
access-list 650 permit other-access
```

Unlike the access lists of other protocols, the ordering of conditions is unimportant. As a result, no network entry can overlap any other entry in a single list. In order to ensure that overlapping does not occur, care must be taken when designing access lists. An overlap occurs when, for example, a `permit network 10` command is entered followed by a `deny network 10` command.

```
access-list 607 permit network 10
access-list 607 deny network 10
```

If an entry is overlapped, the last one entered overwrites and removes the previous one from the access list. In the example above, this means that the "permit network" statement would be removed from the access list when the "deny network" statement was entered.

To remove an entire access list from the router's configuration, issue the No Access-List command with the access list number. For example, to remove access list 650 from the router's configuration, issue the no access-list 650 command.

```
access-list 650 deny network 1
access-list 650 deny network 2
access-list 650 permit other-access
no access-list 650
```

To remove a particular clause from an access list, specify the optional arguments. For example, to allow packets previously denied from network 2, issue the no access-list 650 deny network 2 command in Interface Configuration mode. A "No" version is not applicable to the Access-List Additional-Zones and Other-Access command.

```
access-list 650 deny network 1
access-list 650 deny network 2
access-list 650 permit other-access
no access-list 650 deny network 2
```

AppleTalk Filters

A filter examines specific packets that pass through a router's interface. It then permits or denies the packets based on the conditions defined in the access lists that have been applied to that interface. Any number of filters can be applied to each interface. Each filter applied to an interface can use the same access list or different access lists.

Packet filtering helps control movement through the network. Such control can help to limit network traffic and restrict network use by certain users or devices.

The following types of AppleTalk packets can be filtered: NBP packets, data packets, routing table updates, ZIP reply packets, and GetZoneList (GZL) request and reply packets.

To create a filter, first define an access list for that packet type. Then apply it to a router's interface. Before the access list can be applied to the interface, the interface must be configured with AppleTalk routing, an AppleTalk address, and a zone name.

A data packet filter checks data packets being sent out of a particular interface. If the packets' source network has access denied, these packets are discarded. Data packet filters use access lists which define conditions for networks, cable-ranges, and zones, but they ignore any zone information that may be in the access list.

When you apply a data packet filter to an interface, ensure that all networks or cable-ranges within a zone are governed by the same filters. This ensures that routers in the same zone contain the same information in their routing tables. For example, if a router receives a packet from a network in a zone that contains an explicitly denied network, it discards the packet.

To make a data packet filter, create an access list using any of the Access-List commands that define conditions for networks, cable-ranges, and zones. Data packet filters can be created using a single network number or cable-range. Then apply the data packet filter to an interface using the AppleTalk Access-Group command.

Routing table update filters determine which updates the local routing table accepts, and which routes the local router advertises in its routing updates. The filtering of routing updates is controlled by using distribution lists.

When incoming routing updates are filtered, each network number and cable-range in the update is checked against the access list. If no access list has been applied to an interface, all network numbers and cable-ranges in the routing update are added to the routing table. If an access list has been applied to an interface, only network numbers and cable-ranges that are not explicitly or implicitly denied are added to the routing table.

The following conditions are also applied when filtering routing updates generated by the local router: the network number or cable-range is not a member of a zone explicitly or implicitly denied; if partial zones are permitted, at least one network number or cable-range that is a member of the zone is explicitly or implicitly permitted; and if partial zones are not permitted (the default), all network numbers or cable-ranges that are members of the zone are explicitly or implicitly permitted.

To make a filter for incoming routing updates, you create an access list that defines conditions for networks or cable-ranges. Cisco IOS software ignores zone entries. Therefore, you should ensure that access lists used to filter incoming routing updates do not contain any zone entries. Filters for outgoing routing updates also define conditions for zones.

To apply the filter to incoming routing updates on an interface, issue the AppleTalk Distribute-List In command in Interface Configuration mode: appletalk distribute-list access-list-number in. This command controls which networks and cable-ranges in routing updates will be entered into the local routing table.

To apply the filter to outgoing routing updates on an interface, issue the AppleTalk Distribute-List Out command: appletalk distribute-list access-list-number out. This command controls which network numbers and cable-ranges are included in routing updates.

To create an AppleTalk NBP access-list entry, issue the `Access-List NBP` command in Configuration mode. To apply an NBP filter (data packet filter) to an interface, issue the `appletalk access-group access-list-number` command in Interface Configuration mode. An NBP filter is applied against the inbound traffic when the filter is used with the `AppleTalk Access-Group` command. When used with dialer lists, the NBP filter is applied against outbound traffic.

The Macintosh Chooser uses ZIP GZL requests to compile a list of zones from which the user can select services. Any router on the same network as the Macintosh can respond to these requests with a GZL reply.

To make a GZL filter, create an access list using the `Access-List Zone` and `Additional-Zones` commands. Then apply the access list to an interface by issuing the `appletalk getzonelist-filter access-list-number` command in Interface Configuration mode. You can create a GZL filter to control which zones the Cisco IOS software mentions in its GZL replies. This has the effect of controlling the list of zones that are displayed by the Chooser.

When defining GZL filters, you should ensure that all routers on the same network filter GZL reply identically. Otherwise, the Chooser will list different zones depending on which device responded to the request. Also, inconsistent filters can result in zones, appearing and disappearing every few seconds when the user remains in the Chooser. Because of these inconsistencies, you should normally apply GZL filters only when all routers in the internetwork are Cisco routers. Other vendors' routers can be used if they have a similar feature.

When a ZIP GZL reply is generated, only zones that satisfy the following conditions are included: if partial zones are permitted, at least one network number or cable-range that is a member of the zone is explicitly or implicitly permitted; if partial zones are not permitted (the default), all network numbers or cable-ranges that are members of the zone are explicitly or implicitly permitted; and the zone is explicitly or implicitly permitted.

Replies to GZL requests also are filtered by any outgoing routing update filter that has been applied to the same interface. You need to apply a GZL filter only if you want additional filtering to be applied to GZL replies. This filter is rarely needed except to eliminate zones that do not contain user services.

To prevent users from seeing a zone, all routers must implement the GZL filter. If there are any devices on the network from other vendors, the GZL filter will not have a consistent effect.

ZIP reply filters limit the visibility of zones from routers in unprivileged regions throughout the internetwork. They filter the zone list for each network provided by a router to neighboring devices to remove restricted zones.

To make a ZIP reply filter, create an access list using the `Access-List` commands that define conditions for zones. To apply a ZIP reply filter to an interface, issue the `appletalk zip-reply-filter` *access-list-number* command in Interface Configuration mode.

ZIP reply filters apply to downstream routers, not to end stations on networks attached to the local router. With ZIP reply filters, when downstream routers request the names of zones in a network, the local router replies with the names of visible zones only. It does not reply with the names of zones hidden with a ZIP reply filter. To filter zones from end stations, use GZL filters.

ZIP reply filters determine which networks and cable-ranges the Cisco IOS software sends out in routing updates. Before sending out routing updates, the software excludes the networks and cable-ranges whose zones have been completely denied access by ZIP reply filters. Excluding this information ensures that routers receiving these routing updates do not send unnecessary ZIP requests.

AppleTalk Access List and Filter Configuration

Let's look at configuring IP-style access lists on the serial link between two routers, Vermont and Maine. In this example, two access lists are used, access list 601 and 602 (Figure 16.1).

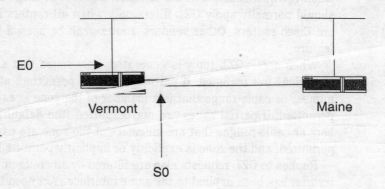

FIGURE 16.1
An IP-style access list on the serial link between two routers, Vermont and Maine, with two access lists, 601 and 602

Access list 601 (Figure 16.2) allows routing packets from network 2, 50, and from any network or cable-range in the cable-range 900–950. Packets are denied access if any packet's source network lies in the cable-range 970–990. While packets are accepted from any network or cable-range that is included entirely within the cable-range 991–995.

Access list 602 allows packets from network 206 and from any network or cable-range in the cable-range 210–215 (Figure 16.3). It also allows packets whose source network lies in the cable-range 220–223 and packets from any network or cable-range included entirely within the cable-range 201–202. You can assume that no AppleTalk configuration has been performed on the routers yet.

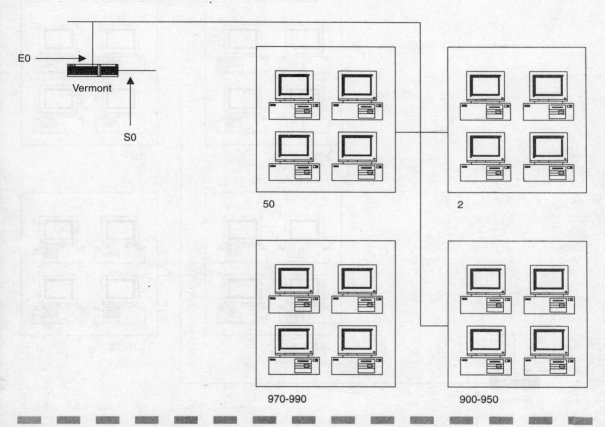

E0

Vermont

S0

50

2

970-990

900-950

FIGURE 16.2   *An illustration of Access list 601.*

Before you create both access lists, enable AppleTalk routing on the Vermont router by typing `appletalk routing` in Configuration mode.

```
Vermont>enable
Password:
Vermont#config term
Vermont(config)#appletalk routing
```

Once AppleTalk routing is enabled, create access list 601 by typing, in Configuration mode, `access-list 601 permit network 2` and `access-list 601 permit network 500` to allow packets from network 2 and 500 and `access-list 601 permit cable-range 900-950` to allow packets from the cable-range 900–950.

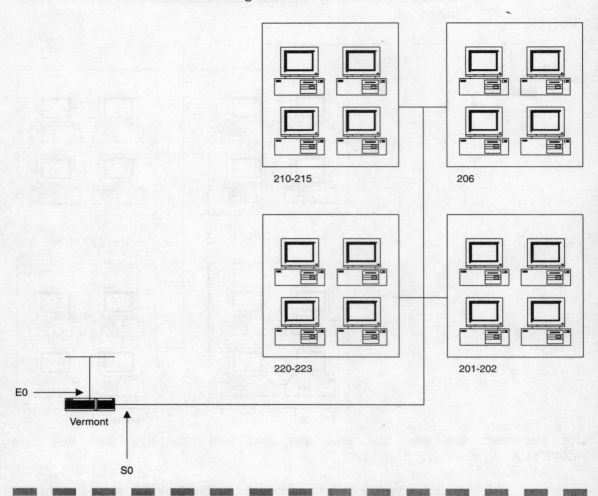

FIGURE 16.3 *Access list 602 allows packets from network 206 and from any network or cable-range in the cable-range 210–215.*

```
Vermont(config)#access-list 601 permit network 2
Vermont(config)#access-list 601 permit network 500
Vermont(config)#access-list 601 permit cable-range 900-950
```

To complete access list 601, type `access-list 601 deny includes 970-990` in Configuration mode to deny any packets from any network numbers or cable-ranges that include cable-range 970–990 and `access-list 601 permit within 991-995` to allow packets from any network number or cable-range within the cable-range 991–995.

```
Vermont(config)#access-list 601 deny includes 970-990
Vermont(config)#access-list 601 permit within 991-995
```

To define the default action to take, type `access-list 601 deny other-access`. This command denies packets from all other networks and cable-ranges.

```
Vermont(config)#access-list 601 deny other-access
```

To create access list 602, type `access-list 602 permit network 206` in Configuration mode to allow packets from network 206 and `access-list 602 permit cable-range 210-215` to allow packets from cable-range 210–215.

```
Vermont(config)#access-list 602 permit network 206
Vermont(config)#access-list 602 permit cable-range 210-215
```

To complete access list 602, type `access-list 602 permit includes 220-223` in Configuration mode to allow any packets from network numbers or cable-ranges that include cable-range 220–223 and `access-list 602 permit within 201-202` to allow packets from any network number or cable-range within the cable-range 201–202.

```
Vermont(config)#access-list 602 permit includes 220-223
Vermont(config)#access-list 602 permit within 201-202
```

When both access lists are created, apply them to an interface. Access list 601 is to be applied to Vermont's Ethernet 0 interface while access list 602 is to applied to its Serial 0 interface.

To configure Vermont's E0 interface with access list 602, type `interface ethernet 0` to place the router into Interface Configuration mode. Then assign it an AppleTalk address and zone name.

```
Vermont(config)#interface ethernet 0
Vermont(config-if)#appletalk cable-range 206-206
Vermont(config-if)#appletalk zone sales
```

You want to filter routing updates received on the E0 interface according to the conditions specified in access list 602. To do this, type `appletalk` `distribute-list 602 in` in Interface Configuration mode. This ensures that only network numbers and cable-ranges that are permitted by the access list are inserted into the Cisco IOS software AppleTalk routing table.

```
Vermont(config-if)#appletalk distribute-list 602 in
```

Vermont's E0 interface is now configured with access list 602. To configure Vermont's S0 interface with access list 601, type `exit` to return to Configuration mode. Then place the router into Interface Configuration mode by typing `interface serial 0`.

```
Vermont(config-if)#exit
Vermont(config)#interface serial 0
```

Once the router is in Interface Configuration mode, assign it an AppleTalk address and a zone name. Note that this interface is configured for non-extended addressing. Then apply access list 601 to the interface by typing `appletalk access-group 601` in Interface Configuration mode.

```
Vermont(config-if)#appletalk address 2.26
Vermont(config-if)#appletalk zone link1
Vermont(config-if)#appletalk access-group 601
```

Both interfaces on the Vermont router are now configured with access lists. To complete the filtering configuration, exit Interface Configuration mode and save the configuration in Configuration mode.

```
Vermont(config-if)#^Z
Vermont# copy runn start
Building configuration...
[OK]
Vermont#
```

With the flexibility allowed by access-list implementation, determining the optimal method to segment an AppleTalk environment using access control lists can be unclear. Now we will look at two ways of creating an AppleTalk-style access list, access list 603, that controls access to AppleTalk zones.

Access list 603 allows access to the Technical Support and Resource Library zones but denies access to the Accounts zone. This access list controls access to these zones by allowing the Technical Support and Resource Library zones to be advertised in routing updates but prevents the Accounts zone being advertised. Access list 603 is to be applied to router Vermont's Ethernet 0 (E0) interface.

Assume that you have logged on to the Vermont router.

```
Vermont>enable
Password:
Vermont#config term
```

To create access list 603, type `access-list 603 permit zone techni-cal support` to permit access to the Technical Support zone. Then type `access-list 603 permit zone resource library` to permit access to Resource Library zone. Next, type `access-list 603 deny additional-zones` to deny access to all other zones. Finally, type `access-list 603 permit other-access` to enable access to all networks in both zones.

```
Vermont(config)# access-list 603 permit zone technical support
Vermont(config)# access-list 603 permit zone resource library
Vermont(config)# access-list 603 deny additional-zones
Vermont(config)# access-list 603 permit other-access
```

Access List 603 makes the Technical Support and Resource Library zones public and all other zones secure.

When access list 603 has been configured, type `interface ethernet 0` to specify this interface as the interface to which you want access list 603 to be applied.

```
Vermont(config)# interface ethernet 0
```

To permit the two zones to be advertised in routing updates sent out Vermont's E0 interface, type `appletalk distribute-list 603 out` in Interface Configuration mode. To apply the access list to the interface, type `appletalk access-group 603` in Interface Configuration mode.

```
Vermont(config-if)# appletalk distribute-list 603 out
Vermont(config-if)# appletalk access-group 603
```

Router Vermont's E0 interface is now configured to allow customers access only to the organization's Technical Support and Resource Library zones. To complete the filtering configuration, exit Interface Configuration mode and save the configuration in Configuration mode.

```
Vermont(config-if)# ^Z
Vermont# copy runn start
Building configuration...
[OK]
Vermont#
```

Another solution to this scenario is to deny access to the Accounts zone and permit access to all other zones and networks. In the configuration below, the Accounts zone is secured, but all other zones are publicly accessible.

```
Vermont(config)# access-list 603 deny zone accounts
Vermont(config)# access-list 603 permit additional-zones
Vermont(config)# access-list 603 permit other-access
```

Both configurations satisfy the basic goal of isolating the accounts zone. Because the first example permits access to only two zones, it will continue to be secure when more zones are added in the future.

Setting Network and Cable-Range Filters

Your organization is experiencing traffic congestion on the serial link between two routers, Vermont and Maine (Figure 16.4). The IT manager wants to reduce the amount of traffic being transmitted on this link. Your job, as network administrator, is to configure two IP-style access lists, 601 and 602, on the Maine router. These access lists will reduce network traffic by filtering packets from certain networks and cable-ranges. The Maine router will have to be configured for AppleTalk.

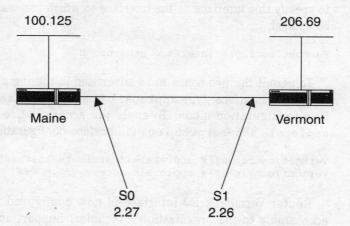

FIGURE 16.4
An illustration of a network experiencing traffic congestion on the serial between two routers.

Access list 601 (Figure 16.5) allows packets from network 2, 50, and from any network or cable-range in the cable-range 900–950. A packet is denied access if the packet's source network lies in the cable-range 970–990. However packets are accepted from any network or cable-range included entirely within the cable-range 991–995.

Access list 602 (Figure 16.6) allows packets from network 206 and from any network or cable-range in the cable-range 210–215. It also allows packets whose source network lies in the cable-range 220–223 and packets from any network or cable-range included entirely within the cable-range 201–202.

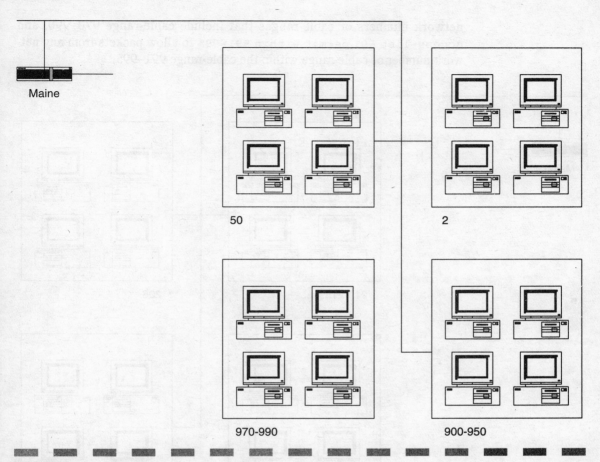

Maine

50

2

970-990

900-950

FIGURE 16.5   *An illustration of access list 601.*

Before you create both access lists, enable AppleTalk routing on the router by typing `appletalk routing` in Configuration mode.

```
Maine>enable
Password:
Maine#config term
Maine(config)#appletalk routing
```

Once AppleTalk routing is enabled, create access list 601 by entering `access-list 601 permit network` and `access-list 601 permit network 500` to allow packets from network 2 and 50, `access-list 601 permit cable-range 900-950` to allow packets from cable-range 900–950, `access-list 601 deny includes 970-990` to deny any packets from any

network numbers or cable-ranges that include cable-range 970–990, and
`access-list 601 permit within 991-995` to allow packets from any network number or cable-range within the cable-range 991–995.

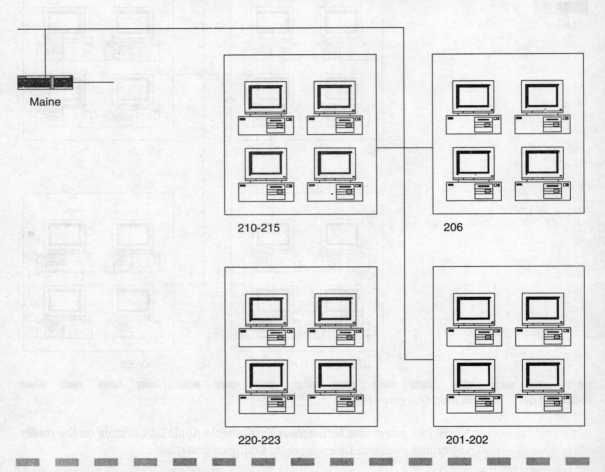

210-215

206

220-223

201-202

FIGURE 16.6 *An illustration of access list 602.*

```
Maine(config)#access-list 601 permit network 2
Maine(config)#access-list 601 permit network 500
Maine(config)#access-list 601 permit cable-range 900-950
Maine(config)#access-list 601 deny includes 970-990
Maine(config)#access-list 601 permit within 991-995
```

To create access list 602, enter in Configuration mode `access-list 602`
`permit network 206` to allow packets from network 206 and `access-list`
`602 permit cable 210-215` to allow packets from cable-range 210–215.

```
Maine(config)#access-list 602 permit 206
Maine(config)#access-list 602 permit cable 210-215
```

Also enter `access-list 602 permit includes 220-223` to allow any packets from network numbers or cable-ranges that include cable-range 220–223 and access-list `602 permit within 201-202` to allow packets from any network number or cable-range within the cable-range 201–202.

```
Maine(config)#access-list 602 permit includes 220-223
Maine(config)#access-list 602 permit within 201-202
```

When both access lists are created, apply them to an interface. Access list 601 is to be applied to Maine's Ethernet 0 interface, while access list 602 is to applied to its Serial 0 interface. To configure Maine's E0 interface with access list 602, type `interface ethernet 0` to place the router into Interface Configuration mode. Then assign it an AppleTalk address and zone name.

```
Maine(config)#interface ethernet 0
Maine(config-if)#appletalk cable-range 206-206
Maine(config-if)#appletalk zone sales
```

You want to filter routing updates received on the E0 interface according to the conditions specified in access list 602. To do this, type `appletalk distribute-list 602 in` in Interface Configuration mode. This ensures that only network numbers and cable-ranges that are permitted by the access list are inserted into the Cisco IOS software AppleTalk routing table.

```
Maine(config-if)#appletalk distribute-list 602 in
```

Maine's E0 interface is now configured with access list 602. To configure Maine's S0 interface with access list 601, type `exit` to return to Configuration mode. Then place the router into Interface Configuration mode by typing `interface serial 0`.

```
Maine(config-if)#exit
Maine(config)#interface serial 0
```

Once the interface is in Interface Configuration mode, assign it an AppleTalk address and a zone name. Non-extended addressing is in use here. Then apply access list 601 to the interface by typing `appletalk access-group 601` in Interface Configuration mode.

```
Maine(config-if)#appletalk address 2.27
```

```
Maine(config-if)#appletalk zone link1
Maine(config-if)#appletalk access-group 601
```

Both interfaces on the Maine router are now configured with access lists. Exit Interface Configuration mode by pressing **Ctrl+Z**. Then enter `copy runn start` to save Maine's access list configuration in NVRAM.

```
Maine(config-if)#^Z
Maine#copy runn start
Building configuration...
[OK]
Maine#
```

CHAPTER **17**

WAN
Connections

Introduction to WAN Services

This section describes the fundamentals of WAN service. We will examine the types of services available from a WAN provider, describe the terminology used in interfacing to a WAN provider, describe the DTE/DCE interface, and describe the forms of WAN services that can be accessed using Cisco routers.

Overview of WAN Service Providers

A WAN operates beyond the geographic scope of local LANs. Implementing a WAN requires access to network resources that you do not own. To gain access to these resources, you need to subscribe to a WAN service provider.

Plain old telephone service (POTS) is the most widely used WAN service. Customer voice and data traffic interfaces with the WAN service provider at a point called the central office (CO).

A WAN provider can be thought of as offering three main types of service: call setup service or signaling, time division multiplexing (TDM), X.25 or frame relay service. Call setup service sets up and clears calls between telephone users. All signaling is done using a separate telephone channel not available to other traffic. Signaling System 7 (SS7) is the most common call setup service. TDM allows information from multiple sources (or demand channels) to share a single medium's available bandwidth. Bandwidth is allocated based on preassigned time slots. Circuit switching uses the call setup service to determine the call route. POTS and Integrated Services Digital Network (ISDN) both use TDM circuits.

With X.25 and frame relay, information contained in packets or frames shares non-dedicated bandwidth. X.25 packet switching uses Layer 3 routing, with sender and receiver addressing contained in the packets. X.25's use of virtual circuits avoids any delay that might be encountered with call setup.

Virtual circuits can be permanent or switched (temporary) to cater for the type of traffic being transmitted. *Permanent virtual circuits (PVCs)* are preferred for the most frequently used data transfers, while *switched virtual circuits (SVCs)* are used for more sporadic data transfers.

Frame relay uses Layer 2 identifiers and permanent virtual circuits. It provides a means of statistically multiplexing virtual circuits. This feature can be used on its own or in tandem with standard TDM techniques.

Frame relay has been designed to take account of improved hardware reliability and reduced error rates and to be more streamlined and efficient than X.25. By streamlining functions, frame relay can adjust its bandwidth to match traffic conditions. Frame relay includes a cyclic redundancy check

(CRC), but unlike X.25, has no mechanism for correcting bad data. Frame relay replaces the flow control procedures of X.25 with a simpler congestion notification mechanism.

Interfacing WAN Service Providers

An outside WAN provider assigns each subscriber the parameters needed for connecting WAN calls. Subscribers make connections to destinations as point-to-point calls.

WAN service providers use the following common terms to describe the main parts of a WAN: customer premises equipment (CPE), demarcation, local loop, central office (CO), and toll network. CPE refers to devices physically located on the subscriber's premises. The demarcation (or demarc) point forms the boundary between the CPE and the local-loop part of the service. It separates the local loop from the CPE.

The local loop (or "last-mile") refers to the cabling that extends from the demarc into the central office of the WAN service provider. The central office is a switching facility for all local loops in a given area. The toll network refers to the collection of switches and facilities (termed "trunks") made available by the WAN service provider. Switches operate in provider offices with toll charges based on tariffs or authorized rates.

A key interface exists between the data terminal equipment (DTE) and the data circuit-terminating equipment (DCE) in the customer's premises. The DTE device is located at the subscriber end of the subscriber-provider interface and serves as a data source, destination, or both. DTEs include devices such as computers, terminals, protocol translators, and multiplexers.

The DCE device makes up the provider end of the subscriber-provider interface. It is used to convert data from the DTE into a form acceptable to the WAN service's facility. DCE also provides a clocking signal used to synchronize data transmission between DCE and DTE devices.

The attached DCE device could be any one of the following: modem, channel service unit/data service unit (CSU/DSU), and terminal adapter/network termination 1 (TA/NT1). A CSU is a digital interface device connecting DTE to the local digital telephone loop. DSU is used in digital transmission to adapt the physical interface on a DTE device to a transmission facility such as T1 or E1. E1 and T1 are wide-area digital transmission schemes capable of data rates of 2.048 Mbps and 1.544 Mbps, respectively. A terminal adapter is a device used to connect ISDN BRI connections to interfaces such as EIA/TIA-232. NT1 and NT2 are network termination devices that connect the four-wire subscriber wiring to the conventional two-wire local loop.

The DTE/DCE interface acts as a boundary where responsibility for traffic passes from WAN subscriber to WAN provider. The WAN path between DTEs may be referred to as a link, circuit, channel, and line. The protocol used by the DTE/DCE interface establishes how call setup operates and the way user traffic crosses the WAN.

WAN Services with Routers

Cisco routers allow access to three forms of WAN services: switched or relayed services, services providing connection to IBM's Enterprise Data Center range of computers, and services available using protocols that connect peer devices.

The first form uses switched or relayed services. This requires the use of a special device to interface with the WAN service provider. Examples of this type of WAN would be X.25, Frame Relay, and ISDN.

The X.25 specification defines a point-to-point interaction between DTE and DCE. X.25 provides for the transmission of multiple network-layer protocols across virtual circuits. X.25 Layer 3 achieves this by encapsulating source Layer 3 packets inside its own Layer 3 packets for transport across the network. X.25 specifies Link Access Procedure, Balanced (LAPB) as the data-link layer protocol. LAPB checks that frames are received error free and in the correct sequence. LAPB allows either the DTE or DCE to initiate communication.

Frame relay is a switched data-link layer protocol that operates over permanent virtual circuits (PVCs). It uses High-Level Data Link Control (HDLC) encapsulation between connected devices. HDLC specifies a data encapsulation method on synchronous links using frame characters and checksums.

Multiple PVCs can interconnect DTEs across the frame relay network to a destination. Each PVC is identified by a data-link connection identifier (DLCI) that provides the major addressing mechanism of the router's Frame Relay support to the Frame Relay WAN service.

Integrated Services Digital Network (ISDN) offers a set of digital services to end-users. It is the product of an effort to standardize subscriber services, user/network interfaces, and network and internetwork capabilities. Components of ISDN include terminals, terminal adapters (TAs), network-termination devices, line-termination equipment, and exchange-termination equipment. ISDN caters to high-speed image applications, additional telephone lines to the home, high-speed file transfer, and video conferencing.

The second form of WAN service that Cisco routers can access provides an interface front end to IBM's Enterprise Data Center range of computers. Synchronous Data Link Control (SDLC) is used in the point-to-point or point-to-multipoint connection of remote devices to IBM central mainframes. It is a System Network Architecture (SNA) data-link layer serial protocol.

Finally, you can access the services of WAN providers using protocols that connect peer devices. The peer devices use HDLC or Point-to-Point (PPP) encapsulation. PPP is a replacement for Serial Line IP. This type of access can use dial-on-demand routing (DDR) to trigger the Cisco router to make a WAN call.

Introduction to the Point-to-Point Protocol (PPP)

This section describes the main connection issue in implementing a wide area network. We will examine the general features of Point-to-Point Protocol (PPP).

Overview of PPP

PPP provides a method for transmitting packets over serial point-to-point links. It allows the simultaneous use of multiple network layer protocols. PPP implements multiple protocol encapsulation using its Network Control Protocols (NCPs) component. The HDLC protocol is used as the basis for encapsulating packets over point-to-point links.

PPP uses its extensible Link Control Protocol (LCP) to negotiate and set up control options on the WAN data link. Once LCP frames have established the link, the originating PPP sends NCP frames to select and configure one or more network-layer protocols. Packets from each of the configured network layer protocols can then be sent over the link. The link remains configured until closed by explicit LCP or NCP frames, or until some external event occurs.

PPP's LCP frames provide a way of establishing, configuring, maintaining, and terminating the point-to-point connection. There are four distinct phases associated with LCP. In the first phase, LCP opens the connection and negotiates configuration parameters. This phase completes when a configuration acknowledgment frame has been sent and received.

The second phase is optional and is used to test the quality of the established link. LCP can delay transmission of network layer protocol information until this phase is completed.

In the third phase, network layer protocols are separately configured by the appropriate NCP. These protocols can be brought up and taken down at any time.

The final phase is link termination. LCP can terminate the link at any time. Although termination is usually done at the request of a user, it can also be triggered by the loss of the carrier or the expiration of an idle-period timer. When LCP closes the link, it informs the network-layer protocols.

PPP uses a layered architecture and can operate across any DTE/DCE interface. PPP's lower-level functions support the use of synchronous and asynchronous media. PPP places no restriction on transmission rate.

Options within LCP provide a rich set of services for setting up a data link. These mainly consist of negotiating and checking frames used to implement the point-to-point controls for the call. LCP configuration options include authentication options, data compression options, and error detection mechanisms.

PPP's higher-level functions are responsible for carrying several network-layer protocols in NCPs. The NCPs are functional fields containing standardized codes. These codes indicate which network layer protocol PPP encapsulates.

PPP configuration commands most commonly used for ISDN on Cisco routers include Encapsulation PPP, PPP Authentication PAP, PPP Authentication CHAP, and Username *name* Password *secret-pwd*.

The Encapsulation PPP command defines the encapsulation type. The PPP Authentication PAP (Password Authentication Protocol) command sets password checking for incoming calls. The PPP Authentication CHAP (Challenge-handshake Authentication Protocol) command forces incoming calls to answer password challenges. The network administrator may use either PAP or CHAP, but not both, on a PPP link. PAP uses the exchange of clear-text passwords between the calling and called sides of the links. CHAP is more secure in that it authenticates the caller without disclosing the password on the link. The Username command sets host name and password for call verification.

For further information on PPP please see Chapter 21.

 # Introduction to Dial-on-Demand Routing (DDR)

This section introduces dial-on-demand routing. We will examine its general features and configure dial-on-demand routines on an ISDN BASIC rate interface.

Overview of DDR

Traditionally, WAN connections over POTS or PSTN have used dedicated leased lines. This can prove expensive when traffic is low in volume and is periodic. DDR was designed to reduce the need for dedicated lines. Cisco IOS

11.1 supports DDR for IP, Novell IPX, and AppleTalk.

DDR refers to a technique whereby a Cisco router can automatically initiate and close a circuit-switched session as transmitting stations demand. The router spoofs keepalives so that end-stations treat the session as active. DDR permits routing over ISDN or telephone lines using an external ISDN terminal adaptor or modem.

DDR initiates a WAN call to a remote site only when there is traffic to transmit. A router activates the DDR feature when it receives a bridged or routed packet destined for a location on the other side of the dial-up line. Only traffic specified as "interesting" will initiate DDR dial-up.

Once a connection has been established, packets from any supported protocol can be transmitted. The line is automatically disconnected when transmission is complete. DDR reduces cost by automatically terminating unneeded connections.

Be aware that WAN service providers increase their charges in line with WAN traffic. Therefore, you should specify static routes on links used by DDR to remote sites. This prevents routing updates across the DCE and over the PSTN network.

Only packets marked as "interesting" can trigger DDR connections. The most general option is to mark all packets in a protocol suite as either interesting or uninteresting for DDR. You can achieve this using Cisco's `Dialer-List Protocol` global command. However, this approach is less than satisfactory for most networks as it fails to eliminate unneeded traffic.

You can avoid unwanted DDR connections by configuring packets to be uninteresting or by setting up access list statements denying the packets. Packet types you may want to configure as uninteresting include regular routing updates, service advertisements, and serialization.

DDR configuration commands include the `Dialer-List Protocol`, the `Dialer Group`, the `Dialer Map`, the `Dialer Wait-For-Carrier-Time`, and the `Dialer Idle-Timeout`.

The `Dialer-List Protocol` command identifies all packets in the protocol suite as interesting or uninteresting for DDR. There is also a `Dialer-List Protocol List` command which allows more precision in specifying details about how to trigger the DDR call.

The `Dialer Group` command places the interface in a group associated with a list of interesting packets. The `Dialer Map` command defines how to reach a DDR destination. It must be used with the `Dialer Group` command and its associated access list to initiate dialing.

The `Dialer Wait-For-Carrier-Time` command specifies the time to wait for the carrier to come up when a call initiates. The `Dialer Idle-Timeout` command specifies the idle time before circuit disconnect.

WAN Scalability

Scalability Features for WANs

This section describes the main connection issues in implementing a wide area network. We will examine the various characteristics used in evaluating different WAN connection types, and describe the main connection types in a WAN environment, Cisco's implementation of these connection types, and the concept of packet switching. We will outline the main packet-switched services available through WAN service providers.

Network Connection Considerations

LANs provide connectivity within a limited geographical area. They afford multiple connected desktop devices (usually PCs) access to common information on high-bandwidth media. Users outside the local geographical area often rely on asynchronous connections to gain access to the services offered by the network. With the advent of LAN desktop devices which run more powerful applications, a single LAN's geographic scope is reduced.

As organizations grow and become more geographically diverse, they require LAN-like operation across their private internetworks. Organizations can either install their own dedicated WAN connections or look at other wide-area connectivity options. Therefore, as networks expand and their nodes become more remote, the connection methods that they use must be closely evaluated.

Connection decisions are a key element in any internetwork design process. Connectivity between users or groups of users, whether within LAN or WAN environments, needs careful consideration. Subscribing to a WAN provider may be the only way of realizing desired connectivity for an organization with widely distributed locations.

All connection types have characteristics inherent to their design, usage, and implementation. The main characteristics include availability, bandwidth, cost, ease of management, application traffic, and routing protocol specifics.

Not all connection types are available in all geographic locations. For example, Asynchronous Transfer Mode (ATM) is a technology widely used for high-speed transfer of voice, video, and data in public networks. However, ATM's availability in private networks cannot be relied upon.

Users increasingly require greater amounts of bandwidth, as evidenced by the growth in multimedia driven applications. WANs operating over serial links can have a limited bandwidth, such as 56 Kbps. Bandwidth limitation can lead to a bottleneck in the connection between source and destination. This might arise where broadcast traffic, such as Novell SAP advertisements, must share the link with application traffic.

The degree of difficulty in managing connections is another concern of the network designer. Connection management deals with configuration at initial startup and ongoing configuration tasks of normal operation. This management is the connection's ability to adjust to varying rates of traffic. This ability should not be affected by the nature of the traffic.

Another important consideration is the type of application traffic that will be carried. Application traffic may consist of many small packets, like those transmitted during a terminal session. At the other extreme, application traffic may consist of very large packets, as during a file transfer.

You also need to be concerned with the type of routing protocols in use. Different routing protocols inject overhead traffic in the form of broadcasts and routing updates. Such overhead traffic can easily cause degradation of performance across low bandwidth serial lines.

Connection Services

When designing for a WAN environment, you need to recognize the different types of connection services that can be used. The following connection services are available: dial-in using modems, dedicated (leased) lines, dial-up connections using a router, and packet-switched services.

Users with asynchronous modems can make temporary serial connections using PSTN. A modem is a device that converts digital and analog signals, allowing data to be transmitted over voice-grade telephone lines. Cisco implements this asynchronous dial-in capability in its Access Servers.

Dedicated links (or leased lines) provide full-time synchronous connections. Cisco implements this service as point-to-point connections over serial lines. Dedicated links are available only to Cisco products which have a DSU/CSU attached to the synchronous serial port.

Dial-up connections provide cost-effective, infrequent connectivity between routers. Examples of dial-up implementations include dial-on-demand routing (DDR) and dial backup. DDR is a technique whereby a Cisco router can dynamically initiate and close a circuit-switched session as transmitting end stations demand. Circuit switching is a WAN switching method which establishes and maintains a dedicated physical circuit through a carrier network for the duration of each communication session. Dial backup is a service that activates a backup serial line under certain conditions, such as primary link failure or excessive primary link loading.

These circuit-switched calls are placed using PSTN or ISDN networks. DDR implementation is available on Cisco products that have asynchronous auxiliary ports, synchronous serial ports, or ISDN ports.

Packet-switched Services

Packet-switched networks (PSNs) use virtual circuits that provide end-to-end connectivity. The physical connections are accomplished by statically programmed switched devices.

X.25, frame relay, and SMDS are supported on all Cisco products with synchronous serial interfaces. ATM is currently supported on Cisco 4000 and 7000 Series products only. Some switched services require specialized equipment to connect the router to the switching device.

An access server serves as a concentration point for dial-in and dial-out connections. Multiple dial-in clients can be connected to an access server. These can retrieve e-mail or data files from LAN-based servers via a PSTN network.

The choice of medium and technology will primarily depend on the bandwidth requirements of the servers in the LAN environment. The amount of bandwidth required by each dial-in client in retrieving a file should not be a concern.

Security is a very important issue in dial-in access environments. For example, PPP provides call authentication using password checking. Call authentication can also be achieved by applications such as TACACS+. Terminal Access Controller Access Control System (TACACS) is an authentication protocol providing remote access authentication and related services, such as event logging. TACACS+ is a Cisco enhancement of TACACS providing additional support for authentication, authorization, and accounting.

Dedicated, full-time connectivity is provided by point-to-point serial links. Connections are made using the router's synchronous serial ports.

Cisco's point-to-point implementation allows two types of transmission: datagram transmission which is composed of individually addressed frames, and data stream transmission which is composed of a stream of data for which address checking occurs only once.

The use of generic channel service unit/data service unit (CSU/DSU) equipment can yield a possible bandwidth utilization of up to 2Mb (E1). Reliability for user traffic is provided by the different encapsulation methods at the data-link layer.

Dedicated links are ideal for environments with a steady-rate traffic pattern. Tariffs are charged on dedicated lines even in the idle state. Therefore, efficient bandwidth utilization is an important concern.

Cisco's dial-on-demand routing (DDR) feature allows you to use existing telephone lines to form a WAN. While using existing telephone lines, you can analyze traffic patterns to determine whether the installation of leased lines is appropriate.

DDR routing is the best option when full-time circuit availability is not required. Connections are made only when traffic dictates a need. This makes DDR very cost efficient. DDR calls are made only when traffic marked "interesting" is detected by the router.

When the router receives interesting traffic destined for a remote network, a circuit is established and the traffic is transmitted normally. If the router receives uninteresting traffic, and a circuit is already established, this traffic is also transmitted normally.

The router maintains an idle timer which is reset only when interesting traffic is detected. Expiry of the idle timer triggers termination of the circuit.

If uninteresting traffic is received, and no traffic exists, the circuit is dropped. Periodic routing updates and other broadcast traffic should be treated as uninteresting for the purpose of a DDR implementation.

In general, routing protocols need to have a clear picture of network topology and reachability. With DDR, connections are brought up and taken down as transmitting stations demand. When the connection is down (inactive), some mechanism is required to convince the routing protocol that the destination is reachable.

For example, a Novell IPX session can be kept alive by having the router "spoof" keepalives to the remote destination. This makes the routing protocol believe that the interface is connected to a live network when, in fact, the link is down. With the DDR WAN link in the down state, tariffs are avoided.

Packet-switched networks (PSNs) consist of DCEs connected through packet switching exchanges (PSEs), or simply *switches*. Switches can be viewed as multiport internetworking devices that operate at the data link layer of the OSI reference model.

PSNs can be accessed by multiple end-stations via DCE equipment. The path between two end-stations is indirect, utilizing a series of intervening nodes. Network nodes share bandwidth with each other by carrying data within frames, packets, or cells.

Packets are passed from node to node as they transit the network. Packets contain a source and destination address, together with other control information. The network nodes treat the packets like envelopes to be delivered to a remote address.

The switching technology is transparent to the user. Its only responsibility is the internal delivery of the data.

In LAN environments, routers are connected to a common "wire" and each device receives all transmissions—hence the term broadcast media. In a WAN switched service, routers do not share a common medium. This, by definition, represents a nonbroadcast environment. Therefore, a PSN can be accurately described as a nonbroadcast multi-access environment (NBMA).

A broadcast environment can be created by transmitting the data on each individual circuit. This simulated broadcast requires significant buffering and CPU resource in the transmitting router. It can also result in lost user data due to contention for the virtual circuits.

Packet-switched networks can be privately or publicly maintained. Packet-switched services include X.25, frame relay, and SMDS/ATM.

X.25 is a packet-switched service more widely available in Europe than in the US. X.25 operates at the lower three levels of the OSI reference model. It uses packet-based analog technology. Its implementation standards are very well understood. X.25 is a connection-oriented service offering very good traffic control. It uses both PVCs and SVCs. X.25 contains extensive packet error checking.

Individual transmissions between switches require acknowledgment. Any packets not correctly received or acknowledged are retransmitted. This feature makes X.25 a good choice in environments where line quality is low.

Frame relay is a packet-switched service widely available in both Europe and the US. It uses a frame-based digital technology. Like X.25, frame relay is a connection-oriented service whose implementation standards are very well understood. Frame relay currently uses PVCs. New SVC standards are now under test.

Frame relay can operate over a broad range of data rates. Speeds between 56/64 Kbps and 1.544 Mbps (T1) are typical. Implementations capable of operating over 45 Mbps (DS-3) links are possible. DS-3 (digital signal level 3) is a framing specification used for transmitting digital signals at 44.736 Mbps on a T3 facility.

Frame relay exploits recent advances in WAN transmission technology, such as the use of fiber media and digital links. Higher-quality, more-reliable links allow frame relay to dispense with time-consuming error correction algorithms, leaving these to be performed at higher protocol layers.

Frame relay offers error detection for frames at the data-link layer, but any bad frames detected are dropped without notifying the user. Frame relay's error-detection feature takes the form of a cyclic redundancy check (CRC) for detecting corrupted bits.

Frame relay has a number of extended features which provide additional capabilities for complex internetworking environments. These are collectively known as the local management interface (LMI). Some LMI extensions are referred to as "common" and are expected to be implemented by everyone who adopts the specification. Other LMI extensions are "optional." LMI extensions include virtual circuit status messages (common), multicasting (optional), global addressing (optional), and simple flow control (optional).

Both switched multi-megabit services (SMDS) and asynchronous transfer mode (ATM) are cell-relay services that use fiber cable as the transmission medium. Cell relay is based on the idea of organizing information into fixed-size cells. These can then be processed and switched in hardware at very high speeds, producing very tight delay characteristics. SMDS and ATM are designed for high-speed transfer of voice, video, and data over WAN networks.

SMDS and ATM are both widely available in the US and are growing rapidly in Europe. SMDS has proprietary implementation standards, while those for ATM are still evolving.

SMDS and ATM both rely on the low error rates of the medium to achieve high throughput rates. SMDS and ATM have no error checking or retransmissions. Although SMDS is described as a fiber-based service, Digital Signal 1 (DS-1) access can be provided over either fiber- or copper-based media with significantly good error characteristics.

SMDS is a LAN-like datagram service. It relies on SMDS servers to forward traffic within the network and can operate at speeds of 100 Mbps.

Access to the SMDS network is accomplished by means of SMDS Interface Protocol (SIP). SMDS allows a packet size large enough to encapsulate entire IEEE 802.3, IEEE 802.4, IEEE 802.5, and FDDI frames.

SMDS supports group addresses, a feature analogous to multicasting on LANs. This allows a single data unit (datagram) to be sent and then delivered by the network to multiple recipients. SMDS also offers source and destination address screening. This feature allows a subscriber to establish a private virtual network that excludes unwanted traffic.

ATM is a connection-oriented service. It primarily uses PVCs to establish connections. ATM supports two connection types: unidirectional or bidirectional point-to-point connections and unidirectional point-to-multipoint connections.

Specialized ATM switches are used to forward the traffic within the network. ATM's switching fabric provides additive bandwidth. As long as the switch can handle the average cell transfer rate, additional connections to the switch can be made. The total bandwidth of the system increases accordingly.

ATM currently operates at speeds up to 155 Mbps, but new technologies now make transmission rates in excess of 600 Mbps possible.

ATM differs from synchronous transfer mode methods, where TDM techniques are used to preassign users to fixed time slots. In contrast to TDM, ATM time slots are made available on demand, allowing more-efficient use of the available bandwidth. An ATM station can send cells whenever necessary.

An important ATM characteristic is its star topology. The ATM switch acts as a hub in the ATM network, with all devices directly attached. This provides all the traditional benefits of star-topology networks, including easier troubleshooting and flexibility for network change.

Any ATM end station connecting to the ATM network essentially makes a *contract* with the network based on quality of service (QoS) parameters. An ATM contract specifies an envelope describing intended traffic flow.

An ATM device uses *traffic shaping* to ensure that traffic will fit within the promised envelope. Traffic shaping uses queues to constrain data bursts, limit peak data rate, and smooth jitter.

ATM switches have the option of using *traffic policing* to enforce the contract. This allows switches to drop offending cells during periods of congestion.

Serial Encapsulation Protocols

This section describes encapsulation protocols. We will examine the issues involved in selecting encapsulation protocols on Cisco routers and outline the configuration of HDLC, PPP, and LAPB.

HDLC, PPP, and LAPB

WAN connectivity is an important requirement of any modern business. One key element is the choice of encapsulation protocol for the WAN serial links. The following are examples of encapsulation protocols: HDLC, PPP, and LAPB.

The selection of an appropriate encapsulation protocol should take account of both reliability and interoperability within the internetwork. For example, consider the case where Link Access Procedure, Balanced (LAPB) is chosen as the encapsulation protocol on a noisy, fixed-delay land line. LAPB is the data-link layer protocol specified by X.25.

LAPB's retransmission characteristic will provide the desired reliability. However, if LAPB is used over a satellite link, needless retransmissions caused by unpredictable delays may seriously degrade performance. This makes LAPB a bad choice for links where unpredictable delays are common.

Cisco's `Encapsulation` command is used to set the IP encapsulation method used by a serial interface. The syntax for this Interface configuration command is:

```
encapsulation encapsulation-type
```

The choice of encapsulation type will depend on the interface. Each type of medium has a default *encapsulation type*.

Synchronous serial connections allow a wide range of encapsulation methods, including frame relay, X.25, LAPB, PPP, SMDS, and HDLC, which is the default.

Asynchronous serial connections are restricted to PPP or SLIP, which is the default. Other types of connection allow the following encapsulation methods: Ethernet—SAP, SNAP, or ARPA, the default; Token Ring—SNAP, the default; FDDI—SNAP, the default; ATM—SNAP, the default; ISDN BRI—PPP or HDLC, the default.

HDLC is the default encapsulation method for synchronous serial lines. It identifies three types of network node: primary, secondary, and combined, that is, the node can act as a primary or secondary. A primary node controls one or more secondary nodes. It polls secondaries in a predetermined order. The primary also sets up and tears down links and manages the link while it is operational.

HDLC supports three transfer modes: normal response mode (NRM), asynchronous response mode (ARM), and asynchronous balanced mode (ABM). ARM and ABM provide HDLC with greater flexibility in defining which nodes can initiate communication.

In NRM, secondaries can only communicate with the primary when the primary has given permission to do so. ARM allows secondaries to initiate communication with a primary without receiving permission.

With ABM, all communication is between multiple combined nodes. Any combined station can initiate data transmission without permission from any other station.

HDLC primaries and secondaries can be connected in two basic configurations: point-to-point which involves only two nodes, one primary and one secondary, and multipoint which involves one primary and multiple secondaries.

HDLC supports multiple protocols but does not provide authentication. HDLC is explicitly configured on an interface by typing `encapsulation hdlc` in Interface configuration mode. However, this command is only used where a different encapsulation type was previously configured on the interface.

The `Encapsulation HDLC` command will not show up in the configuration files as it is the default encapsulation type.

```
interface serial0
encapsulation hdlc
ip address 172.16.18.1 255.255.252.0
ipx network 10
```

PPP encapsulation must be configured at both ends of a link. This can be achieved by entering the command `encapsulation ppp` during the configuration of the serial interfaces at either end of the link.

PPP performs address negotiation and authentication. It supports multiple protocols and is interoperable with other vendors' hardware.

```
interface serial0
encapsulation ppp
ip address 172.16.18.1 255.255.252.0
ipx network 10
```

LAPB is best known for its presence in the X.25 protocol stack. LAPB has the same frame formats and types as HDLC. However, LAPB is restricted to the ABM transfer mode. It is therefore appropriate only for combined stations.

LAPB circuits can be established by either DTE or DCE. The station initiating the call is designated the primary, while the responding station is the secondary.

When you want to select LAPB encapsulation, use the Encapsulation LAPB command. This Interface configuration command has the following syntax:

```
encapsulation lapb [dte | dce] [multi | protocol]
```

DTE and DCE are optional keywords used to indicate whether the router is to function as a DCE or DTE device over the X.25 link. Multi is an optional keyword used to specify that multi-protocol traffic is to be carried over the link. Alternatively, you can specify a single protocol to be carried on the LAPB line.

Protocols that can be carried within LAPB are: IP, the default; XNS, DECnet, AppleTalk, VINES, CLNS, IPX, and Apollo. Cisco also provides the LAPB Protocol command as a way of selecting protocols to be carried within LAPB encapsulation. The syntax is as follows:

```
lapb protocol protocol-name
```

Only one protocol can be selected with each usage of this command.

Cisco also provides separate LAPB commands to alter the retransmission characteristics of LAPB. LAPB commands can change the maximum number of bits per frame (multiple of 8); the retransmission timer period; the transmission count, which specifies how many times a frame can be transmitted; and the frame count, which sets an upper limit on the number of outstanding frames awaiting acknowledgment.

Serial Compression and Channelized T1/E1

This section describes serial compression techniques. We will examine the data compression options available on Cisco routers, describe the channelized T1/E1 interface, and outline the issues involved in configuring channelized T1/E1.

Serial Compression Techniques

The default method of transmitting data (header and payload) across a serial link is in uncompressed format. This allows the header information to be used in the normal switching operation. However, sending data in an uncompressed format makes heavy demands on available bandwidth.

Data compression leads to more efficient use of the available bandwidth. Although compression involves an element of overhead, this is outweighed by the increased rate of transmission of compressed data over serial lines. You have the option of compressing either the header or payload, or both. For example, the *Van Jacobsen algorithm* is used to compress the fixed-length headers of small packets. A different algorithm is used for each protocol being transported.

TCP header compression can be accomplished using the IP TCP Header-Compression command. The syntax is:

```
ip tcp header-compression [passive].
```

Passive is an optional keyword used to restrict compression of outgoing TCP packets. When the Passive keyword is omitted, the router compresses all traffic. When Passive is included, outgoing TCP packets are compressed only if incoming TCP packets on the same interface are compressed.

Header compression can be used for a number of applications, including Telnet, DEC LAT, rlogin, and acknowledgments. It is supported for HDLC and X.25 encapsulations.

Payload compression leaves the header intact. This allows the packet to be routed through a switched network in the normal way. Payload compression is suitable for virtual network services like X.25, SMDS, frame relay, and ATM.

Link compression involves compressing both the header and the payload. Proper delivery of the compressed data is ensured using PPP or LAPB encapsulation. Link compression is protocol independent, unlike header compression.

Compression involves running the data to be transmitted through a "lossless" predictor algorithm. The predictor algorithm has the ability to learn data patterns, allowing it to predict the next character in the data stream. It is termed lossless because no data are lost during the compression and decompression process.

Cisco's `Compress Predictor` command can be used to configure point-to-point software compression for LAPB, PPP, and HDLC.

Channelized T1/E1 Overview

Traditionally, the implementation of multiple WAN connections has taken the form of a dedicated CSU/DSU for each line. Each of these low-speed lines (64 kbps) was located on a multiple-port synchronous serial interface card, like the 4-port FSIP unit seen in the graphic. Fast Serial Interface Processor (FSIP) is the default serial interface processor for Cisco 7000 series routers. The FSIP provides four or eight high-speed serial ports.

The number of WAN connections that a router could support was limited by port density of the interface card and backplane capacity. The backplane refers to the physical connection between an interface processor or card and the data buses and power distribution buses inside a Cisco chassis.

Cisco's 7000 series routers support the MultiChannel Interface Processor (MIP) which provides two full channelized T1 or E1 serial ports. T1 and E1 are wide-area digital transmission schemes. T1 can transmit data at 1.544 Mbps, while E1 can transmit at 2.048 Mbps. Cisco 4000 models support a single port interface for channelized T1/E1.

The MIP card allows you to configure up to 24 T1 or 30 E1 subchannels on one physical port. Each line (subchannel) can be separately configured as though it were a dedicated interface. Subchannels will all have the same configuration options and characteristics as ordinary serial ports.

Line-encoding and framing must be set to match the carrier equipment.

The output of a port on the MIP card can be carried by a private network. Alternatively, the MIP card can be directly connected to the service provider's facility. The channel output is then carried by a public data network (PDN). Multiple MIP cards can be configured into a single Cisco 7000 chassis. Complex configurations, like those needed in a back-to-back maintenance environment, will have MIP cards connected to other MIP cards.

Let's look at an example of how channelized T1/E1 might be configured on a Cisco 7000 series router. Controller configuration begins by indicating the channel type (T1 or E1) and the MIP card being configured.

In this example the `Controller` command initiates configuration of a T1 channel using the MIP card in slot 4 / port 1 of the Cisco 7000 router.

Next, the line code and framing types for the line are defined. These are T1 and E1 specific.

The `Framing` command for a T1 line allows only the following frame types: SF—super frame and ESF—extended super frame. SF (also called D4 framing) consists of 12 frames of 192 bits each, with the 193rd bit providing error checking and other functions. ESF is an enhanced version of SF, consisting of 24 frames of 192 bits each.

This example specifies ESF as the frame type. If you were implementing an E1 channel, the choice of frame types would be limited to CRC4 (cyclic redundancy check 4) with the default frame type and No-CRC4 which indicates that CRC checking is disabled.

A T1 channel can have the following line-code types: AMI—alternate mark inversion and B8ZS—binary 8-zero substitution.

An E1 channel can have AMI or HDB3. In the example shown, the T1 channel is assigned linecode type B8ZS via the `Linecode` command.

When configuring channelized T1/E1, you need to define the channel group (subchannel) associated with each timeslot. This can be accomplished using the `Channel-Group` command. The syntax is:

```
channel-group number timeslots range [speed {48 | 56 | 64}]
```

Number refers to the channel-group number, 0–23 for T1 and 0–29 for E1. *Range* refers to the range of timeslots belonging to the channel group, 1–24 for T1 and 1–31 for E1. `Speed` is an optional parameter, with a default value of 56 kbps.

In the first line of the following example, channel group 0 (circuit 0) is specified to have a single timeslot, running at the default speed of 56 kbps. In the second line, Channel group 8 has been assigned seven time slots (5, 7, 12–15, and 20), all operating at 64 kbps.

```
channel-group 0 timeslots 1
channel-group 8 timeslots 5,7,12-15,20 speed 64
```

Finally, you need to assign each subchannel an IP address and an encapsulation type. You can see here that both subchannels have been assigned to different subnets. PPP encapsulation has been chosen for subchannel 0, while the default encapsulation type (HDLC) applies to subchannel 8.

In a simple configuration like this, the MIP card receives its clock signals from the T1/E1 line. In more complex environments, where MIP cards are directly connected to one another, you need to specify which clock source to use—T1/E1 line or internal. This is accomplished via the `Clock Source` command.

19

X.25
Configuration

Introduction to X.25

This section introduces the features of the X.25 protocol. We will examine its characteristics and describe how X.25 encapsulates data.

X.25 Overview

The X.25 protocol is an International Telecommunication Union Telecommunication Standardization Sector (ITU-T, formerly known as CCITT) standard for WAN communications. It defines how connections between user devices and network devices are established and maintained across public data networks (PDNs).

X.25 is designed to operate effectively regardless of the type of systems connected to the network. It is typically used in the packet-switched networks (PSNs) of common carriers. Packet switching is a WAN switching method in which network devices share a single point-to-point link to transport packets from a source to a destination across a carrier network. Subscribers are charged based on their use of the network.

The X.25 specification defines a point-to-point interaction between data terminal equipment (DTE) and data circuit-terminating equipment (DCE) (Figure 19.1). DTE devices are end systems that communicate across the X.25 network. They are usually terminals, personal computers, or network hosts, and are located on the premises of individual subscribers. DCE devices are communications hardware such as modems and packet switches. They provide the interface between DTE devices and a packet-switching exchange (PSE), and are generally located in the carrier's facilities.

PSEs are switches that make up the bulk of the carrier's network. They transfer data from one DTE device to another through the X.25 packet switched network (PSN).

An X.25 session is initiated by one DTE device contacting another to request a communication session. The DTE device that receives the request can either accept or refuse the connection. If the request is accepted, the two systems begin full-duplex information transfer, is the simultaneous transmission of data between a sending station and a receiving station. Either DTE can terminate the connection.

A simple DTE device, such as a character-mode terminal, may not support full X.25 functionality. In this case, a DTE can be connected to a DCE through a translation device called a *packet assembler/disassembler (PAD)*. A PAD performs three primary functions: buffering, packet assembly, and packet disassembly (Figure 19.2). It buffers data sent to or from the DTE device.

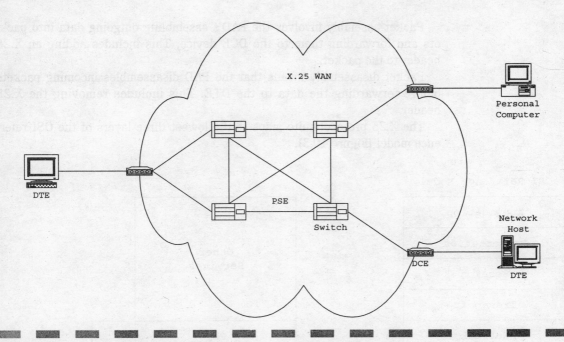

FIGURE 19.1 DTEs, DCEs, and PSEs make up an X.25 network.

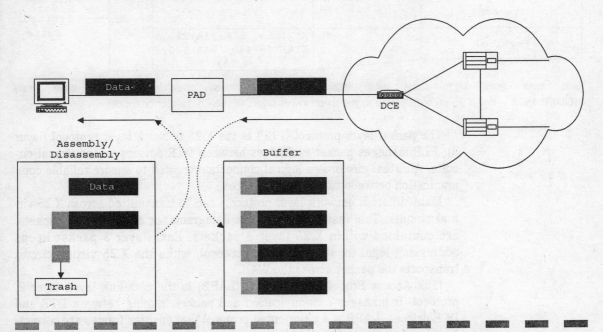

FIGURE 19.2 The PAD buffers, assembles, and disassembles data packets.

Packet assembly involves the PAD's assembling outgoing data into packets and forwarding them to the DCE device. This includes adding an X.25 header to the packet.

Packet disassembly means that the PAD disassembles incoming packets before forwarding the data to the DTE. This includes removing the X.25 header.

The X.25 protocol suite maps to the lowest three layers of the OSI reference model (Figure 19.3).

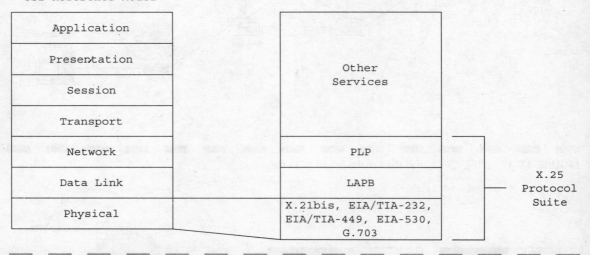

OSI Reference Model

FIGURE 19.3   Key X.25 protocols map to the three lower layers of the OSI reference model.

The packet-layer protocol (PLP) is the X.25 network layer protocol (layer 3). PLP manages packet exchanges between DTE devices across virtual circuits. A virtual circuit is a logical connection created to ensure reliable communication between two network devices.

Many different network-layer protocols can be transmitted across X.25 virtual circuits. This results in *tunneling*: datagrams, or other layer 3 packets, are contained within X.25 layer 3 packets. Each layer 3 packet keeps addressing legal for its respective protocol, while the X.25 virtual circuit transports the packet across the WAN.

Link Access Procedure, Balanced (LAPB) is the data-link layer, layer 2, protocol. It manages communication and packet framing between DTE and DCE devices. LAPB is a bit-oriented protocol that ensures frames are correctly ordered and error-free.

PLP, at layer 3, and LAPB, at layer 2, provide reliability and sliding windows. Sliding window flow control is a method of flow control in which a receiver gives transmitter permission to transmit data until a window is full. When the window is full, the transmitter must stop transmitting until the receiver advertises a larger window. Layers 3 and 2 were designed with strong flow control and error checking.

X.21bis is a physical-layer, layer 1, protocol used in X.25. It defines the electrical and mechanical procedures for using the physical medium. Other physical-layer serial interfaces, such as EIA/TIA-232, EIA/TIA-449, EIA-530, G.703, and so on, are also used in X.25 implementations.

X.21bis handles the activation and deactivation of the physical medium connecting DTE and DCE devices. It supports point-to-point connections and speeds up to 19.2 Kbps. It also supports synchronous, full-duplex transmission over four-wire media.

Communication between DTEs is accomplished across a virtual circuit (VC). VC is used interchangeably with the terms virtual circuit number (VCN), logical channel number (LCN), and virtual circuit identifier (VCI). A virtual circuit is a logical connection created to ensure reliable communication between two network devices. X.25 can maintain up to 4095 virtual circuits, numbered 1 through 4095, on an interface. A virtual circuit (Figure 19.4) indicates the existence of a logical, bidirectional path from one DTE to another across an X.25 network. The connection can pass through any number of intermediate nodes, such as DCE devices and PSEs.

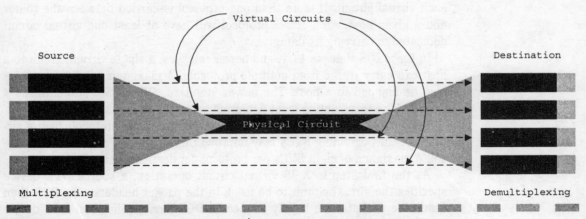

FIGURE 19.4 Virtual circuits can be multiplexed onto a single physical circuit.

Multiple virtual circuits, or logical connections, can be multiplexed onto a single physical circuit. Multiplexing is a process in which multiple data channels are combined into a single data or physical channel at the source. Virtual circuits are demultiplexed at the remote end, and data are sent to the appropriate destinations.

There are two types of X.25 virtual circuits: switched virtual circuit (SVC) and permanent virtual circuit (PVC). SVCs are temporary connections used for sporadic data transfers. They require that two DTE devices establish, maintain, and terminate a session each time the devices need to communicate.

SVCs can be combined to improve throughput for encapsulating a specific protocol. Multiple SVCs provide a larger effective window size, especially for protocols that offer their own higher-layer resequencing. Combining SVCs does not benefit traditional X.25 applications, such as those available from a timesharing host.

PVCs are permanently established connections. They are used for frequent and consistent data transfer between DTEs. PVCs do not require that sessions be established and terminated. A DTE device can therefore begin transferring data whenever necessary, because the session is always active.

A PVC is similar to a leased line. Both the network provider and the attached X.25 subscriber must provision the virtual circuit. Any provisioned PVCs are always present, even when no data traffic is being transferred.

The X.25 protocol offers simultaneous service to many hosts, for example multiplex connection service. An X.25 network can support any legal configuration of SVCs and PVCs over the same physical circuit attached to the X.25 interface.

A Cisco router's traditional encapsulation method assigns a protocol to each virtual circuit. If more than one protocol is carried between the router and a given host, each active protocol will have at least one virtual circuit dedicated to carrying its datagrams.

In Cisco IOS Release 11.1, and newer releases, a single virtual circuit to a host can carry traffic from multiple protocols. A maximum of nine protocols may be mapped to a host. The newer standard, RFC 1356, standardizes a method for encapsulating most datagram protocols over X.25.

Higher traffic loads are generated by routing multiple protocols over a virtual circuit. Combining SVCs may improve throughput for a particular protocol. A maximum of eight SVCs per protocol per destination is allowed.

As the first step in X.25 virtual circuit operation, a source DTE device specifies the virtual circuit to be used, in the packet headers. The DTE then sends the packets to a locally connected DCE device. The local DCE device examines the packet headers to determine which virtual circuit to use. Then it sends the packets to the closest PSE in the path of that virtual circuit.

PSEs, or switches, pass the traffic to the next intermediate node in the path, for example, another switch or the remote DCE device. When the traffic arrives at the remote DCE device, the packet headers are examined, and the destination address is determined. The packets are then sent to the destination DTE device. If communication occurred over an SVC, and neither device has additional data to transfer, the virtual circuit is terminated.

The format of X.25 addresses is defined by the ITU-T X.121 standard. X.121 addresses are used by the PLP to establish SVCs. In an X.121 address the first four digits specify the data network terminal identifier code (DNIC) (Figure 19.5). This field consists of the country code and provider number assigned by the ITU to the packet switched network (PSN) in which the destination DTE device is located. The field is sometimes omitted in calls within the same PSN.

FIGURE 19.5
The X.121 address
includes an IDN field.

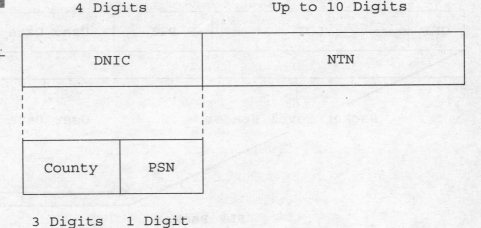

The remaining eight to ten digits specify the network terminal number (NTN) assigned by the PSN provider. Private X.25 networks may assign addresses that best fit their network architecture. Only decimal digits are legal for X.121 addresses. The router accepts an X.121 address with as few as 1 or as many as 15 digits.

Some networks allow subscribers to use subaddresses. The subaddress matches the X.121 address, but has one or more additional digits after the base address.

Different network protocols can be connected across X.25 using X.121 addressing. Statements are entered on the router to map the next-hop network layer address to an X.121 address. For example, an IP network layer address is mapped to an X.121 address to identify the next-hop host on the other side of the X.25 network.

X.25 Encapsulation

Movement of network-layer data through the internetwork usually involves encapsulation of datagrams inside media-specific frames. Encapsulation is the wrapping of data in a particular protocol header.

In an X.25 environment, Link Access Procedure, Balanced (LAPB) is the data-link layer protocol that manages communication and packet framing between DTE and DCE devices (Figure 19.6).

Field Length, in Bits

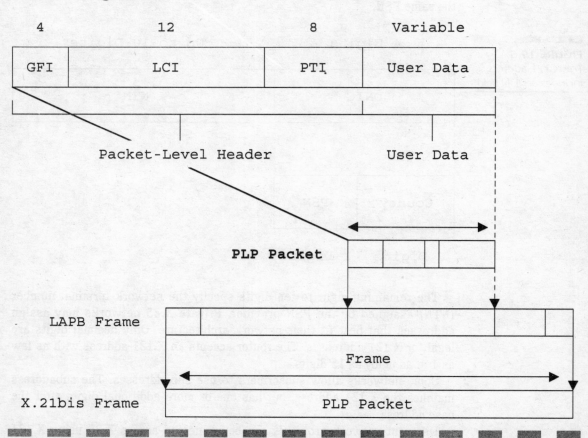

FIGURE 19.6 *The PLP packet is encapsulated within the LAPB frame and the X.21bis frame.*

An LAPB frame arrives at a router, which extracts the datagram from the packet or packets. The router discards the encapsulating frame. Then it analyzes the datagram to identify its format and next hop. Based on the route determination, the router re-encapsulates the datagram in framing suitable for the outgoing media as it forwards the traffic.

An X.25 frame is made up of a series of layer 3 and layer 2 fields. Layer 3, or PLP, fields make up an X.25 packet and include a header and user data.

The PLP header is made up of the following fields: General Format Identifier (GFI), Logical Channel Identifier (LCI), Packet Type Identifier (PTI), and User Data. A GFI is a 4-bit field that identifies packet parameters, such as whether the packet carries user data or control information. It also identifies what kind of windowing is being used and whether delivery confirmation is required. The LCI is a 12-bit field that identifies the virtual circuit across the local DTE/DCE interface. The PTI field identifies the packet as one of 17 different PLP packet types. The User Data field contains encapsulated upper-layer information. This field is only present in data packets. Otherwise, additional fields containing control information are added.

The PLP operates in five distinct modes when managing packet exchanges between DTE devices: call setup, data transfer, idle, call clearing, and restarting.

SVCs use all five modes. PVCs are always in data transfer mode because these circuits have been permanently established.

Call setup mode is used to establish SVCs between DTE devices. PLP uses the X.121 addressing scheme to set up an SVC.

Once a call is established, the PSN uses the LCI field of the data packet header to specify the particular SVC to the remote DTE.

Call setup mode is executed on a per-virtual-circuit basis. That is, one virtual circuit can be in call setup mode while another is in, for example, data transfer mode.

Data transfer mode is used for transferring data between two DTE devices across a virtual circuit. In this mode, PLP breaks up and reassembles user messages if they are too long for the maximum packet size of the circuit. Each data packet is given a sequence number, so error and flow control can occur across the DTE/DCE interface. Data transfer mode is executed on a per-virtual-circuit basis.

Idle mode is used when an SVC is established, but data transfer is not occurring. It is executed on a per-virtual-circuit basis.

Call clearing mode is used to end communication sessions between DTE devices and to terminate SVCs. It is executed on a per-virtual-circuit basis.

Restarting mode is used to synchronize transmission between a DTE device and a locally connected DCE device. This mode is not executed on a per-virtual-circuit basis. It affects all the DTE device's established virtual circuits.

Layer 2 X.25 is implemented by LAPB, which manages communication and packet framing between DTE and DCE devices. During information transfer, LAPB checks that the frames arrive at the receiver in the correct sequence and error-free. LAPB frames include a header, encapsulated data, and a trailer (Figure 19.7).

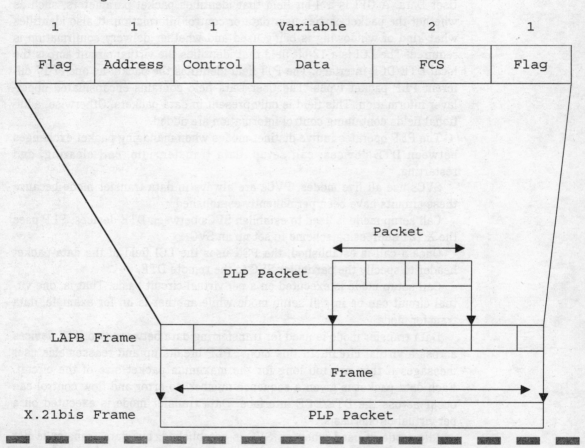

Field Length, in Bits

1	1	1	Variable	2	1
Flag	Address	Control	Data	FCS	Flag

Packet

PLP Packet

LAPB Frame

Frame

X.21bis Frame   PLP Packet

FIGURE 19.7   An LAPB frame includes a header, a trailer, and encapsulated data.

The Flag field delimits the beginning and end of the LAPB frame. Bit stuffing is used to ensure that the flag pattern does not occur within the body of the frame.

The Address field indicates whether the frame carries a command or a response.

The Control field qualifies command and response frames. It also indicates the frame format: whether the frame is an I-frame, an S-frame, or a U-frame. It indicates the frame function, for example, receiver ready or disconnect, and the sequence number of the frame.

The Data field contains upper-layer data in the form of an encapsulated PLP packet. The maximum length of this field is set by agreement between a PSN administrator and the subscriber at subscription time.

The Frame Check Sequence (FCS) field ensures the integrity of the transmitted data.

There are three types of LAPB frames: Information frame (I-frame), Supervisory frame (S-frame), and Unnumbered frame (U-frame). Information frames carry upper-layer information and some control information. Their functions include sequencing, flow control, and error detection and recovery. I-frames carry *send* and *receive* sequence numbers. The send sequence number refers to the number of the current frame. The receive sequence number records the number of the frame to be received next.

Supervisory frames carry control information. Their functions include requesting and suspending transmissions, reporting on status, and acknowledging the receipt of I-frames. S-frames carry only receive sequence numbers.

Unnumbered frames (U-frames) are not sequenced. They are used for control purposes. Their functions include link setup and disconnection, and error reporting.

Configuring X.25

This section shows how to configure and monitor X.25. We will examine X.25 configuration tasks, describe how to set a router as a switch, how to configure and monitor X.25, and will configure and monitor X.25 operation.

X.25 Configuration Tasks

When you select X.25 as a WAN protocol, you must set appropriate interface parameters. Certain parameters are essential for correct X.25 behavior, such as selecting the X.25 encapsulation style, and assigning the X.121 address. You should also define map statements to associate X.121 addresses with higher-level protocol addresses.

Use the X25 Encapsulation command to specify the encapsulation style to be used on the serial interface. The syntax is:

```
encapsulation x25 [dte  dce]
```

A router using X.25 layer 3 encapsulation can act as a DTE or DCE device, according to the needs of your X.25 service supplier. DTE is the default. A router typically is configured as an X.25 DTE when the X.25 PDN is used to transport more than one protocol. The router can be configured as an X.25 DCE, which is typically used when the router acts as an X.25 switch.

The `X25 Address` command defines the local router's X.121 address. Each interface has its own address. The syntax is:

```
x25 address x.121-address
```

The value specified must match the address designated by the X.25 public data network (PDN) service provider. If your router does not originate or terminate calls but only participates in X.25 switching, this task is optional.

Encapsulation is a cooperative process between a router and another X.25 host. Because X.25 hosts are reached with an X.121 address, the router must have a means to map a host's protocols and addresses to its X.121 address.

A defined protocol cannot dynamically determine LAN protocol-to-remote host mappings. You must explicitly enter all the information for each host with which the router may exchange X.25 encapsulation.

The `X25 Map` command provides a static conversion of higher-level addresses to X.25 addresses. This command correlates the network layer addresses of the peer host to the peer host's X.121 address. The syntax is:

```
x25 map protocol-keyword protocol-address x.121-address [options]
```

The `Protocol-Keyword` parameter specifies the protocol type. Supported protocols are entered by keyword. Supported protocols are IP, XNS, DECnet, IPX, AppleTalk, VINES, Bridge, CLNS, Apollo, PAD, QLLC, and Compressed TCP.

These are the protocols, and their keywords, supported by X.25.

NOTE

Keyword	Protocol
apollo	*Apollo Domain*
appletalk	*AppleTalk*
bridge	*Bridging*
clns	*ISO Connectionless Network Service*
cmns	*ISO Connection-Mode Network Service*
compressedtcp	*TCP/IP header compression*
decnet	*DECnet*
ip	*IP*
ipx	*IPX*

```
qllc          System Network Architecture (SNA) encapsulation in X.25
vines         Banyan VINES
xns           XNS
```

The `Protocol-Address` parameter specifies the protocol address. This is not specified for bridged or CLNS connections. Connectionless Network Service (CLNS) is an OSI network layer service that does not require a circuit to be established before data are transmitted.

The `X.121-Address` parameter specifies the X.121 address of the remote host. Both the protocol address and the X.121 addresses are required to specify the complete network protocol-to-X.121 mapping.

The `Options` parameter is used to customize the connection. You can use it to specify additional functionality for originated calls.

You can specify how multiple protocols reach a specified destination using a single virtual circuit. The syntax is:

```
x25 map protocol address [protocol2 address2[...[protocol9
address9]]] x121-address [options]
```

Use this command only when trying to communicate with a host that understands multiple protocols over a single virtual circuit. This communication requires the multiprotocol encapsulations defined by RFC 1356. Bridging is not supported.

With Cisco routers you can map an X.121 address to a maximum of nine protocol addresses. Each protocol can be mapped only once in the command line.

Let's look at an example of X.25 configuration on the Connecticut and New Hampshire routers (Figure 19.8).

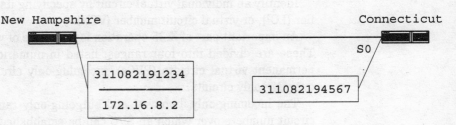

FIGURE 19.8
A layout of the Connecticut and New Hampshire routers.

Set the encapsulation style on Connecticut's Serial0 interface to X.25. Then establish Serial0's X.121 address.

```
interface serial0
encapsulation x25
x25 addresss 311082194567
```

Use the X25 Map command to specify the IP protocol, the IP address that is mapped, and New Hampshire's X.121 address.

```
ip address 172.16.8.1 255.255.248.0
x25 map ip 172.16.8.2 311082191234

New Hampshire's configuration:
interface serial0
encapsulation x 25
x25 address 311082191234
ip address 172.16.8.2 255.255.248.0
x25 map ip 172.16.8.1 311082194567
```

In this example, IP routing on the Connecticut router forwards datagrams destined for address 172.16.8.2 to interface Serial0. The interface map identifies the destination to the X.25 "cloud". Here, when Connecticut sends packets to 172.16.8.2, it tries to establish an SVC to New Hampshire using its own X.121 source address and New Hampshire's X.121 destination address of 311082191234.

When it receives the setup request, New Hampshire identifies the remote device's IP address from the source X.121 address contained in the setup request. New Hampshire then accepts the connection. Once the SVC is connected, each router uses it as a point-to-point data link for its destination.

The two X.25 attachments need complementary map configurations to establish the virtual circuit that will encapsulate IP datagrams.

You might need to perform some additional configuration tasks so that a router will work correctly with the service provider network. Important X.25 parameters specify the virtual circuit range, default packet sizes, default window sizes, and window modulus.

Identify an individual virtual circuit by specifying its logical channel identifier (LCI), or virtual circuit number (VCN).

An important part of X.25 operation is the range of virtual circuit numbers. These are divided into four ranges, listed in numerically increasing order: permanent virtual circuits (PVCs), incoming-only circuits, two-way circuits, outgoing-only circuits.

The incoming-only, two-way, and outgoing-only ranges define the virtual circuit numbers over which an SVC can be established. Cisco refers to a call received from the interface as an incoming call, and a call sent out the interface as an outgoing call. A PVC cannot be established by the placement of an X.25 call. However, an SVC can be established in this way.

There are rules about how DCE and DTE devices may initiate calls. Only a DCE device may initiate a call using a circuit number in the incoming-only range. Only the DTE device may initiate a call using a circuit number in the outgoing-only range. Both the DCE and DTE device may initiate a call using a circuit number in the two-way range.

A virtual circuit's operation is not affected by the range to which it belongs, except as regards the restrictions on which device can initiate a call. These ranges can be used to prevent one side of a connection from monopolizing the virtual circuits. This can be useful for X.25 interfaces that have a small number of SVCs available to them.

Figure 19.9 summarizes additional configuration tasks for virtual circuit number assignment. The complete range of virtual circuits can be allocated to PVCs or SVCs depending on your requirements. SVCs are most commonly used. If both limits of a range are zero, the range is not used.

	Range	Default	Command
PVCs	1-4095		x25 pvc circuit
	1-4095		
SVC Incoming only	1-4095	0	x25 lic circuit
DCE initiated	1-4095	0	x25 hic circuit
SVC Two-way	1-4095	0	x25 ltc circuit
	1-4095	1024	x25 htc circuit
SVC Outgoing only	1-4095	0	x25 loc circuit
DTE initiated	1-4095	0	x25 hoc circuit

FIGURE 19.9   A summary of additional configuration tasks for virtual circuit number assignment.

The circuit numbers must be assigned so that an incoming range comes before a two-way range. Both incoming and two-way ranges must come before an outgoing range. If you set up any PVCs, they must take a circuit number that comes before any SVC range.

Six X.25 parameters define the upper and lower limits of each of the three SVC ranges. A PVC must be assigned a number less than the numbers assigned to the SVC ranges. An SVC range is not allowed to overlap another range.

This numbering scheme in the figure lists the correct order for the virtual circuit number assignment commands. In this scheme, "lic" stands for low incoming circuit number and "hic" stands for high incoming circuit number. "Ltc" stands for low two-way circuit number and "htc" stands for high two-way circuit number. "Loc" stands for low outgoing circuit number and "hoc" for high outgoing circuit number.

```
1 ≤ PVCs ≤ (lic ≤ hic) ≤ (ltc ≤ htc) ≤ (loc ≤ hoc) ≤ 4095
```

The network administrator specifies the virtual circuit ranges for an X.25 attachment. An SVC range is not used if its lower and upper limits are set to 0. Apart from marking unused ranges, virtual circuit 0 is not available.

```
1 ≤ PVCs ≤ (lic ≤ hic) ≤ (ltc ≤ htc) ≤ (loc ≤ hoc) ≤ 0
```

For correct operation, the X.25 DTE and DCE must have identically configured ranges. Values configured must be the same on both ends of an X.25 link.

X.25 networks have a default maximum input and output packet size defined by the network administrator. You must set the Cisco IOS software default input and output maximum packet sizes to match those of the network. These defaults are the values that an SVC assumes if it is set up without explicitly negotiating its maximum packet sizes. PVCs will also use these default values, unless different values are configured for them.

The X25 IPS and X25 OPS commands set the default maximum input and output packet size. The input and output values should match unless the network supports asymmetric transmissions.

The X25 IPS command specifies the default incoming packet size. The syntax is:

```
x25 ips bytes
```

The X25 OPS command specifies the default outgoing packet size. The syntax is:

```
x25 ops bytes
```

The Bytes parameter is the maximum packet size assumed for virtual circuits that do not negotiate a size. Supported values are 16, 32, 64, 128, 256, 512, 1,024, 2,048, and 4,096.

The default packet size usually used on PDNs throughout the world is 128 bytes. In the US and Europe default packet sizes of 1,024 bytes are also common. Some other countries can also provide higher packet sizes. The layer 3 default maximum packet size is subject to the limit that lower layers are able to support.

The window size specifies the number of packets that can be received or sent without sending or receiving an acknowledgment. Both ends of an X.25 link must use the same default window size.

Use the x25 Win command to set the default input window size. The syntax is:

```
x25 win packets
```

The x25 Wout command sets the default output window size. The syntax is:

```
x25 wout packets
```

The Packets parameter states the packets in the window. The range of acceptable values is from 1 to M–1, where M is the modulus. The default is two packets.

X.25 supports flow control with a sliding window sequence count. The window counter restarts at zero upon reaching the upper limit, which is called the window modulus.

The x25 Modulo command sets the interface's data packet numbering count. Virtual circuit window sizes are limited to a maximum value equal to this modulo value minus 1. The syntax is:

```
x25 modulo modulus
```

The Modulus parameter is either 8 or 128. Modulo 8 is widely used and allows virtual circuit window sizes of up to seven packets.

Modulo 128 is rare. It allows virtual circuit window sizes of up to 127 packets. Modulo 128 operation is also referred to as *extended packet sequence numbering*, which allows larger packet windows. Both ends of an X.25 link must use the same modulo.

Here's an example of configuring X.25 tasks.

```
interface serial0
encapsulation x25

x25 address 311082198756
x25 ips 1024
x25 ops 1024
x25 win 7
x25 wout 7
```

An X.121 address is assigned to the Serial0 interface.

```
interface serial0
encapsulation x25

x25 address 311082198756
```

The input and output packet sizes are defined. Both the input and output window sizes are set to 1,024 bytes. This matches the values defined for the network attachment.

```
x25 ips 1024
x25 ops 1024
```

Here, the input and output window sizes are set to 7. This matches the values defined for the network attachment.

```
x25 win 7
x25 wout 7
```

Setting the Router as a Switch

The X.25 software implementation allows virtual circuits to be routed from one X.25 interface to another and from one router to another. A router's behavior can be controlled with switching and X.25-over-TCP (XOT) configuration commands. Transmission Control Protocol (TCP) is a connection-oriented transport layer protocol that provides reliable full-duplex data transmission.

Switching or forwarding of X.25 virtual circuits can be done in two ways: local X.25 switching and XOT switching. During local switching, incoming calls received from a local serial interface running X.25 can be forwarded to another local serial interface running X.25. Local X.25 switching indicates that the router handles the complete path. In other words, the router doesn't rely on any other device to complete routing data to its destination. It does not matter whether the devices are configured as DTE or DCE devices, because the router's software takes the appropriate actions.

During XOT switching, an incoming call can be forwarded to another Cisco router over a LAN using the TCP/IP protocols. XOT switching is sometimes called *remote switching*. Upon receipt of an incoming call, a TCP connection is established to the router acting as the switch for the destination. All X.25 packets are sent and received over this reliable data stream. Flow control is maintained end to end.

Running X.25 over TCP/IP provides a number of benefits. The datagram containing the X.25 packet can be switched by other routers using their high-speed switching abilities. X.25 connections can be sent over networks running only the TCP/IP protocols. The TCP/IP protocol suite runs over many different networking technologies, including Ethernet, Token Ring, T1 serial, and FDDI. X.25 data can therefore be forwarded over these media to another router, to be output to an X.25 interface.

When the connection is made locally, the switching configuration is used. When the connection is across a LAN, the XOT configuration is used. The basic function is the same for both types of connections, but different configuration commands are required for each type of connection.

You must enable X.25 routing to use either local or XOT switching. Use the x25 Routing Global Configuration command to do this.

```
x25 routing
x25 route 1012 interface serial0
x25 route 100 cud ^pud$ interface serial2
x25 route .*ip 172.16.16.2
```

Use the x25 Route command to establish a static route for local switching. The syntax is:

```
x25 route [# position] x.121-address [cud pattern] interface
interface-number
```

A static route is one explicitly configured and entered into a routing table. Static routes take precedence over routes chosen by dynamic routing protocols.

In the # Position parameter, the number that follows the # character specifies the line number in the routing table where this entry will be placed. If no value is specified, the entry is added to the bottom of the table. This parameter is optional.

The X.121-Address parameter represents the destination's X.121 address. This parameter can contain either an actual X.121 destination address or a regular expression such as 1111*, representing a group of X.121 addresses. A regular expression is a pattern of characters matched against an input string. You can use wildcard characters such as the dot (.) which matches any single character in the string; the asterisk (*) which matches any sequence of characters: the caret (^) which refers to the rightmost characters in the string; and the dollar sign ($) which refers to the leftmost characters in the string.

The CUD (call user data) pattern parameter is specified as a regular expression of ASCII text. This parameter is optional. The first few bytes, commonly four bytes, identify a protocol. The specified pattern is applied to any user data after the protocol identification.

The `Interface-Number` parameter is the destination interface, such as Serial0, used in local switching.

The X.25 routing table is consulted when an incoming call is received which is to be forwarded to a remote destination. Two fields in the table are used to determine the route to the call's destination. These are the destination X.121 Address and, optionally, the X.25 packet's CUD fields. When the destination address and the CUD of the incoming packet fit the X.121 and CUD patterns in the routing table, the call is forwarded.

Let's look at an example of X.25 switching.

Use the `x25 Routing Global Configuration` command to turn on the local and XOT switching function.

```
x25 routing
```

The following line forwards calls for any X.121 address containing the digits 1012 anywhere in it to interface Serial0. It is followed by the next line, which forwards calls for X.121 addresses containing 100. A CUD string of "pad" only will be forwarded onto interface Serial2.

```
x25 route 1012 interface serial0
x25 route 100 cud ^pad$ interface serial2
```

Calls not matching these criteria will fall through to the next line in the configuration and will be routed to an IP network device.

```
x25 route .*ip 172.16.16.2
```

This line specifies the X.121 address of interface Serial0 as 3110821876543.

```
x25 address 31108218766543
```

Calls that match address and CUD patterns will have those calls locally switched to the appropriate serial interfaces.

When calls do not match the specified parameters, the router will use the Ethernet0 interface to forward them to an IP network device at address 172.16.16.2. The circuit will be made using a TCP connection through the IP network.

```
interface ethernet0
ip address 172.16.16.1 255.255.255.0
```

Configuring and Monitoring X.25

Let's look at how to configure the Maine router for X.25. In this example, it will communicate with another router over an X.25 switched virtual circuit.

Assume that you are logged on to the Maine router and are currently in Privileged Exec mode. The first step is to enter Global Configuration mode. To do this, type `configure terminal` at the command prompt.

```
Maine>enable
Password:
Maine#configure terminal
Enter configuration commands, one per line. End with CNTL/Z.
```

Then enter Interface Configuration mode for the Ethernet0 interface. Assign the IP address for the Ethernet0 interface. Use the `IP Address` command to do this. The syntax is:

```
ip address ip-address mask
Maine(config)#interface ethernet0
Maine(config-if)#ip address 172.16.1.1 255.255.255.0
```

Now we will begin configuring the Serial1 interface. Set the encapsulation style to X.25 DTE. Remember, DTE is the default encapsulation style.

```
Maine(config-if)#interface serial1
Maine(config-if)#encapsulation x25
```

Use the `Bandwidth` command to specify the link bandwidth. `Bandwidth` commands are used by IGRP to determine which lines are the best choices for traffic. IGRP was developed by Cisco to address the problems associated with routing in large, heterogeneous networks. The default is 1,544 Kbaud, but X.25 service is not generally available at this rate. Baud is the unit of signaling speed equal to the number of discrete signal elements transmitted per second and is synonymous with bits per second (bps), if each signal element represents exactly 1 bit. You will need to specify the bandwidth setting for most X.25 interfaces used with IGRP. You specify a 9.6 Kbaud line by entering `bandwidth 10`.

```
Maine(config-if)#bandwidth 10
```

You can set default X.25 flow control values. Here the default incoming and outgoing packet sizes are set to 1,024 bytes. They should match the PDN defaults. The values used by an SVC are negotiable on a per-call basis.

```
Maine(config-if)#x25 ips 1024
Maine(config-if)#x25 ops 1024
```

Then set the default input and output X.25 window sizes. These are set to 7 packets; this means that 7 packets can be received or sent before an acknowledgment is required.

```
Maine(config-if)#x25 win 7
Maine(config-if)#x25 wout 7
```

Define the X.121 address for the Serial1 interface using the X25 Address command. Then set the IP address for the Serial1 interface.

```
Maine(config-if)#x25 address 311082194567
Maine(config-if)#ip address 172.16.66.1 255.255.255.0
```

You generally need to change some layer 3 parameters, most often those highlighted on screen. Specify a highest two-way virtual circuit (htc) number of 30. Next define the period of inactivity after which the router can clear an SVC of calls.

```
Maine(config-if)#x25 htc 30
```

Set the idle period to 5 minutes with the X25 Idle command. Calls originated and terminated by the router are cleared, SVCs are not cleared. To clear one or all virtual circuits at once, use the Privileged Exec command Clear X25-Virtual Circuit.

```
Maine(config-if)#x25 idle 5
```

Specify the maximum number of SVCs that X.25 can have open simultaneously to a single host. Then set the default to 2 SVCs.

```
Maine(config-if)#x25 nvc 2
```

You can override default values that have been specified for the Idle and NVC parameters, using the X25 Facility command.

Finally, map the IP address 172.16.66.2 to the X.121 address 311082191234. Exit Configuration mode by pressing **Ctrl+Z**.

```
Maine(config-if)#x25 map ip 172.16.66.2 3110821912345
Maine(config-if)#^Z
Maine#copy running-config startup-config
Buildiing configuration...
[OK]
Maine#
```

When you have configured the Maine router for X.25, you can then monitor its operation.

Use the `Show Interface Serial` command to display status and counter information about a serial interface. The syntax is:

```
show interface serial number
Maine#show interface serial1
Serial1 is up, the protocol is up
  Hardware is HD64570
  Internet address is 172.16.66.1/24
  MTU 1500 bytes, BW 10 Kbit, DLY 20000 usec, rely 255/255,
  load 1/255
  Encapsulation X25, loopback not set
  LAPB DTE, state CONNECT, modulo 8, k 7, N1 12056, N2 20
    T1 3000, interface outage (partial T3) 0, T4 0
    VS 0, VR 0, Remote VR 0, Retransmission 2
    Queues: U/S frames 0, I frames 0, unack. 0, reTx 0
    IFRAMEs 1523246/1542127 RNRs 0/0 REJs 0/0 SABMs 3/2 FRMRs 0/0
    DISCs 0/0
```

Here you can see general information about the Serial1 interface. The first line shows that the Serial1 interface hardware is currently active and the line is usable. The encapsulation method in use on it is X.25.

The output for the `Show Interface` command displays LAPB information. LAPB is a data-link layer protocol in the X.25 protocol stack.

On the Serial1 interface the state of the LAPB protocol is CONNECT. This means that a normal connect state exists between the Vermont router and its peer.

You can see the current parameter settings of the protocol. The modulo value, window size (k), and transmit counter (N2) are set at their default values. N2 is the number of unsuccessful transmit attempts that may be made before the link is declared down. The maximum number of bits per frame (N1) is 12056.

The `retransmission timer` (T1) parameter is set to 3000 seconds, which is the default. T1 determines how long a transmitted frame can remain unacknowledged before the Cisco IOS software polls for an acknowledgment. The hardware outage period is disabled. The idle link period (T4) is used to detect unsignaled link failures. Here it is disabled.

The `VS` parameter indicates the modulo frame number of the next outgoing information frame (I-Frame). The `VR` parameter indicates the modulo 8 frame number of the next information frame expected to be received.

The `Remote VR number` shows the number of the next information frame the remote device expects to receive. The `Retransmissions` parameter is a count of current retransmissions due to the expiration of T1.

There are no frames queued for transmission.

The IFRAMEs parameter displays a count of information frames sent and received. In this, 1523246 I-Frames have been sent and 1542127 received. You can also see the count of Receiver Not Ready (RNR), Reject (REJ), and Frame Reject (FRMR) frames sent and received.

The SABMs parameter is a count of Set Asynchronous Balanced Mode commands sent and received. The DISC's parameter is a count of Disconnect commands that have been sent and received.

This part of the output for the Serial1 interface displays information about X.25 operation on the Maine router.

```
X25 DTE, address 311082194567, state R1, modulo 8, timer 0
     Defaults: cisco encapsulation, idle 5, nvc 2
        input/output window sizes 7/7, packet sizes 1024/1024
     Timers: T20 180, T21 200, T22 180, T23 180, TH0
     Channels: Incoming-only none, Two-way 1-30, Outgoing-only
none
     RESTARTs 2/2 CALLs 132+130/176+174/0+0 DIAGs 0/0
  Last input 00:10:00, output 00:00:00, output hang never
  Last clearing of "show interface" counters never
  Output queue 0/40, 0 drops; input queue 0/75, 0 drops
  5 minute input rate 0 bits/sec, 3 packets/sec
  5 minute output rate 0 bits/sec, 3 packets/sec
     165233 packets input, 19261118 bytes, 0 no buffer
     Received 12120 broadcasts, 0 runts, 0 giants
     8 input errors, 8 CRC, 0 frame, 0 overrun, 0 ignored, 0 abort
     167894 packets output, 11378654 bytes, 0 underruns
     0 output errors, 0 collisions, 15 interface resets
     0 output buffer failures, 0 output buffers swapped out
     140 carrier transitions
     DCD=up  DSR=up  DTR=up  RTS=up  CTS=up
Maine#
```

The X.121 address used to originate and accept calls on the Serial1 interface is 311082194567. Next, the state of the interface is displayed. This can be R1, R2, or R3. R1 is the normal ready state. R2 is the DTE restarting state and R3 is the DCE restarting state. If the state is R2 or R3, the interface is awaiting acknowledgment of a Restart packet.

The modulo value is 8, its default value. The interface timer field value is 0. This value is zero unless the interface state is R2 or R3.

In the Defaults section you can see the layer 3 parameters set during the configuration of the Maine router. Also displayed are the flow control values that have been specified.

The Timers section displays the values of the X.25 timers and the packet acknowledgment threshold (TH). The X.25 layer 3 retransmission timers determine the number of seconds the Cisco IOS software waits for acknowledgment of control packets.

X.25 timer values from T20 to T23 are used for DTE devices. X.25 timer values from T10 to T13 are used for DCE devices.

The TH field value determines how many packets are received before an explicit acknowledgment is sent. The default value (0) sends an explicit acknowledgment only when the incoming window is full.

The `Channels` section displays the virtual circuit ranges for the interface. Remember, a highest two-way virtual circuit (htc) number of 30 was specified during configuration.

The `RESTARTs` field displays the Restart packet statistics for the interface. Two packets have been sent and two received.

The `CALLs` field displays the number of calls that have been sent, received, and forwarded. It shows details of failed calls.

The format for the `Calls` field is successful calls sent + failed calls, calls received + calls failed, and calls forwarded + calls failed. Calls forwarded are counted as calls sent. The `DIAGs` field displays the number of diagnostic messages sent and received.

The next section of the output for the `Show Interface` command displays information about packets sent and received by the interface. Here you can see that there are no packets in the output and input queues. The maximum size of the output queue is 40 packets, and the input queue is 75. No packets have been dropped due to either queue's being full.

165,233 error-free packets have been received by the interface, consisting of 19,261,118 bytes. No received packets were discarded because there was no buffer space in the system.

There were eight input errors; these were CRC (cyclic redundancy checksum) errors. CRCs on a serial link usually indicate transmission problems on the data link.

167,893 packets were transmitted by the interface, consisting of 11,378,654 bytes.

The interface has been completely reset 15 times. On a serial line, resets can be caused by a malfunctioning modem that is not supplying the transmit clock signal, or by a cable problem.

The output displays 140 in the carrier transitions field. This indicates that the carrier detect signal of the interface has changed state 140 times. For example, if data carrier detect (DCD) goes down and comes up, the carrier transition counter will increase twice. If the carrier detect line changes state often, this indicates modem or line problems.

X.25 Configuration

Here we will configure and monitor X.25 on the Vermont router from a terminal. Assume that you are logged in to the Vermont router, which has not yet
been configured.

```
Vermont>enable
Password:
Vermont#configure terminal
Enter configuration commands, one per line. End with CNTL/Z.
Vermont(config)#
```

Enter `interface ethernet0` to enter Interface Configuration mode for
the Ethernet0 interface. Then assign an IP address to the Ethernet0 interface.

```
Vermont(config)#interface ethernet0
```

Enter `ip address 172.16.192.1 255.255.255.0` to assign this
address and subnet mask to the Ethernet0 interface.

```
Vermont(config-if)#ip address 172.16.192.1 255.255.255.0
```

Now enter `interface serial0` to begin configuring that interface for
X.25 operation.

```
Vermont(config-if)#interface serial0
```

Enter `encapsulation x25` to set the encapsulation style to DTE.

```
Vermont(config-if)#encapsulation x25
```

You should specify the bandwidth that X.25 uses. Enter `bandwidth 10` to
specify a 9.6 Kbaud link bandwidth. Next set the default X.25 flow control
values.

```
Vermont(config-if)#bandwidth 10
```

Enter `x25 ips 1024` to set the default incoming packet size to 1,024
bytes. Enter `x25 ops 1024` to set the default outgoing packet sizes to 1,024
bytes.

```
Vermont(config-if)#x25 ips 1024
Vermont(config-if)#x25 ops 1024
```

Enter x25 win 7 to set the default input window size to 7 packets. Enter x25 wout 7 to set the default output window size to 7 packets.

```
Vermont(config-if)#x25 win 7
Vermont(config-if)#x25 wout 7
```

Enter x25 address 311082191234 to set 311082191234 as the X.121 address for the interface.

```
Vermont(config-if)#x25 address 311082191234
```

Set an IP address for the Serial0 interface.

```
Vermont(config-if)#ip address 172.16.66.2 255.255.255.0
```

Enter x25 htc 30 to set the highest two-way virtual circuit (htc) number to 30.

```
Vermont(config-if)#x25 htc 30
```

Enter x25 idle 5 to set the idle period to 5 minutes.

```
Vermont(config-if)#x25 idle 5
```

Enter x25 nvc 2 to specify that the maximum number of SVCs that X.25 can have open simultaneously to one host is two.

```
Vermont(config-if)#x25 nvc 2
```

Map the IP address 172.16.66.1 to the X.121 address 311082194567 by entering x25 map ip 172.16.66.1 311082194567.

```
Vermont(config-if)#x25 map ip 172.16.66.1 311082194567
```

Exit Configuration mode by pressing **Ctrl+Z**.

```
Vermont(config-if)#^Z
Vermont#copy running-config startup-config
Building configuration...
[OK]
Vermont#
```

When you have configured the Vermont router for X.25, you then monitor its operation.

Display status and counter information about the s0 (serial0) interface by entering `show interface serial0`.

```
Vermont#show interface serial0
Serial0 is up, line protocol is up
  Hardware is HD64570
  Internet address is 172.16.66.2/24
  MTU 1500 bytes, BW 10 Kbit, DLY 20000 usec, rely 255/255
  load 1/255
  Encapsulation X25, loopback not set
  LAPB DTE, state CONNECT, modulo 8, k 7, NI 12056, N2 20
      T1 3000, interface outage (partial T3) 0, T4 0
      VS 0, VR 0, Remote VR 0, Retransmission 2
      Queues: U/S frames 0, I frames 0, unack. 0, reTx 0
      IFRAMEs 1623445/1582125 RNRs 0/0 REJs 0/0 SABM/Es 4/2 FRMRs
      0/0 DISCs 0/0
  X25 DTE, address 311082191234, state R1, modulo 8, timer 0
      Defaults: cisco encapsulation, idle 5, nvc 2
        input/output window sizes 7/7, packet sizes 1024/1024
      Timers: T20 180, T21 200, T22 180, T23 180, TH 0
      Channels: Incoming-only none, Two-way 1-30, Outgoing-only none
      RESTARTs 2/2 CALLs 121+118/145+143/0+0 DIAGs 0/0
  Last input 00:12:09, output 00:00:00, output hang never
  Last clearing of "show interface" counters never
  Output queue 0/40, 0 drops; input queue 0/75, 0 drops
  5 minute input rate 0 bits/sec, 3 packets/sec
  5 minute output rate 0 bits/sec, 3 packets/sec
      17333 packets input, 1126909 bytes, 0 no buffer
      Received 10920 broadcasts, 0 runts, 0 giants
      10 input errors, 10 CRC, 0 frame, 0 overrun, 0 ignored, 0 abort
      17371 packets output, 1130299 bytes, 0 underruns
      0 output errors, 0 collisions, 119 interface resets
      0 output buffer failures, 0 output buffers swapped out
      260 carrier transitions
      DCD=up  DSR=up  DTR=up  RTS=up  CTS=up
Vermont#
```

In the output for the Show Interface Serial command the interface hardware is currently active and the line protocol is up, or usable. The window size (k) is 7 packets. The retransmission timer (T1) is set to 3,000 seconds. The interface is in the normal ready state, as indicated by the R1 parameter.

The values for the flow control parameters Window Size and Packet Size are displayed. There are no packets in the output queue. The Interface Resets and Carrier Transitions fields can indicate the existence of a modem problem.

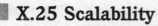 # X.25 Scalability

This section describes issues affecting X.25 scalability. We will examine how throughput can be increased on an X.25 network, describe how to configure X.25 facilities, explain how regular expressions can be used to specify routes, and how an X.25 network can carry broadcast traffic.

X.25 Throughput v. Bandwidth

As organizations grow and become more geographically diverse, they require LAN-like operations across their private internetworks. Organizations can either install their own dedicated WAN connections or look at other wide-area connectivity options. Therefore, as networks expand and their nodes become more widely dispersed, the connection methods that they use must be closely evaluated. Subscribing to a WAN provider may be the only way of realizing desired connectivity for an organization with widely distributed locations.

All connection types have characteristics inherent to their design, usage, and implementation. The main characteristics include availability, bandwidth, cost, ease of management, application traffic, and routing protocol specifics. Bandwidth is the data-carrying capacity of a link. Users increasingly require greater amounts of bandwidth, as evidenced by the growth in multimedia-driven applications.

WANs operating over serial links can have a limited bandwidth, such as 56 Kbps. Bandwidth limitation can lead to a bottleneck in the connection between source and destination. This might arise where broadcast traffic, such as Novell SAP advertisements, must share the link with application traffic. If heavy traffic consumes the bandwidth of an access link, user throughput is affected. Throughput is the amount of traffic that is delivered to a destination. Reducing the congestion on a link will restore user throughput. Congestion can occur when the amount of data transmitted by a particular medium exceeds its bandwidth. Temporary congestion can be expected in every network. Periodic congestion often occurs due to the bursty nature of today's network applications.

X.25 networks are composed of switching devices that forward data packets based on the X.121 address contained in an LAPB encapsulated frame.

If bandwidth is available on a link and throughput problems exist, you can adjust several parameters to improve throughput on an X.25 network. You can increase the window and packet sizes, and the number of virtual circuits to a destination. Use these commands to set the default flow control values: x25

WIN/WOUT, X25 IPS/OPS, and X25 Modulo. These values must match the X.25 network settings specified by the service provider for proper operation.

Use the X25 NVC command to establish the default maximum number of SVCs that can be open to any host or router. The syntax is:

```
x25 nvc count
```

The Count parameter is a circuit count from 1 to 8. To increase throughput across networks, you can establish up to eight SVCs to a host and protocol. The default is one.

A new SVC will be opened to a host or router when the windows and their output queues are all full. If the bandwidth of a link is already fully used, opening another SVC will have no effect on throughput.

Call User Facilities

The X.25 software provides commands to support X.25 user facilities. These allow you to implement features such as accounting, user identification, and flow control negotiation.

You can choose to configure facilities on a per-interface or a per-map basis. Use the X25 Facility command to force facilities on a per-call basis for calls initiated by this router interface. Use the X25 Map command to configure facilities on a particular host or router.

The X25 Facility commands specify the values sent for all encapsulation calls originated by the interface. These facilities can be overridden by optional fields specified in the X25 Map command. The facilities values must match the settings in the X.25 switch. The syntax for the X25 Facility command is:

```
x25 facility [option]
```

Use the CUG Number parameter to select a closed user group (CUG). The syntax is:

```
x25 facility cug number
```

CUGs 1 to 99 are allowed. CUGs can be used by a PDN to create a virtual private network within the larger network and to restrict access.

The Packetsize In-size Out-size parameter sets the maximum input packet size (In-size) and output packet size (Out-size) for flow control parameter negotiation. The syntax is:

```
x25 facility packetsize in-size out-size
```

Both values must belong to this set of values: 16, 32, 64, 128, 256, 512, 1,024, 2,048, or 4,096.

The `Windowsize In-size Out-size` parameter sets the packet count for input windows (`In-size`) and output windows (`Out-size`) for flow control parameter negotiation. The syntax is:

```
x25 facility windowsize in-size out-size
```

Both values must be in the range 1 to 127 and must not be greater than or equal to the value set for the `X25 Modulo` command.

The `Windowsize` and `Packetsize` parameters are supported for PVCs, although they have a slightly different meaning because PVCs do not use the call setup procedure. If the PVC does not use the interface defaults for the flow control parameters, these options must be used to specify the values. Not all networks will allow a PVC to be defined with arbitrary flow control values.

The `Reverse` keyword sets reverse charging to be in effect on all calls originated by the interface. The syntax is:

```
x25 facility reverse
```

The `Accept-Reverse` keyword allows reverse charging acceptance. The syntax is:

```
x25 facility accept-reverse
```

The `Throughput In Out` parameter sets the throughput class negotiation values for input (`In`) and output (`Out`) throughput across the network. The syntax is:

```
x25 facility throughput in out
```

Values for *in* and *out* are expressed in bits per second (bps) and range from 75 to 64000 bps.

The `Transit-Delay` parameter sets a network transit delay for the duration of outgoing calls for networks that support transit delay. The syntax is:

```
x25 facility transit-delay value
```

The transit delay value can be between 0 and 65,534 milliseconds.

The Recognized Private Operation Agency (RPOA) parameter sets the name of packet network carriers to use in outgoing call request packets. The syntax is:

```
x25 facility rpoa name
```

This name is a list of RPOAs defined by the X25 RPOA command. This example sets an RPOA name and then sends the list through the X.25 user facilities.

```
x25 rpoa green_list 23 35 36
interface serial0
x25 facility rpoa green_list
x25 map ip 172.16.170.25 10 rpoa green_list
```

You can use the X25 Map command to define optional parameters for call setup to a particular host/router device. The syntax is:

```
x25 map protocol address x121-address [option]
```

The NUID parameter sets the Cisco standard network user identification. The syntax is:

```
x25 map protocol address x121-address nuid username password
```

This parameter should only be used when connecting to another Cisco router. The combined length of the username and password should not exceed 127 characters.

The Nudata parameter sets a user-defined network user identification. The format is set by the network administrator. The syntax is:

```
x25 map protocol address x121-address nudata string
```

This parameter is provided for connecting to non-Cisco equipment that requires a network user identification facility.

The string should not exceed 130 characters and must be enclosed in quotation marks (" ") if the string contains any spaces.

```
interface serial0
x25 map ip 172.20.174.32 2 nudata
"Network User ID 35"
```

The Passive keyword sets options to be used if the arriving packet has that option active. The syntax is:

```
x25 map protocol address x121-address passive
```

This option is available only for compressed TCP maps. For example, you can specify that the X.25 interface should send compressed outgoing TCP datagrams only if they were already compressed when they were received.

Regular Expressions

A regular expression is a pattern of characters matched against an input string. You can use wildcard characters discussed above.

Specify the pattern that a string must match when you compose a regular expression. Matching a string to the specified pattern is called *pattern matching*. Pattern matching either succeeds or fails.

You can use regular expressions to help specify routes in an X.25 routing table. For example, you can specify in an X.25 routing table that incoming packets with destination addresses beginning with 3107 are routed to interface Serial0. 3107 is the pattern to be matched.

The string is the initial portion of the destination address of any incoming X.25 packet. When the destination address string matches 3107, then pattern matching succeeds. The Cisco IOS software routes the packet to interface Serial0. When the initial portion of the destination address does not match 3107, then pattern matching fails and the software does not route the packet to interface Serial0.

When a router or access server receives an incoming call that should be forwarded to its destination, the Cisco IOS software consults the X.25 routing table to determine the route. To determine the route, the software compares the X.121 network interface address field and the CUD field of the incoming packet with the routing table.

When the destination address and the CUD of the incoming packet match the X.121 and CUD regular expressions you specified in the routing table, the access server or router forwards the call.

In this switching example, the x25 Route command causes all X.25 calls to addresses whose first four DNIC digits are 1111 to be routed to the interface Serial3.

```
x25 route ^1111(.*) substitute-dest 2222\1
    interface serial3
```

You can use parentheses around a pattern to remember a pattern for use elsewhere in a regular expression. The .* characters instruct the IOS software to match any number of occurrences of any character. The x25 Route command also changes the DNIC field to 2222 in the addresses presented to the equipment connected to that interface.

The backslash (\), followed by an integer (1), instructs memory to reuse the remembered pattern. This pattern consists of the DNIC digits 1111, followed by any number of occurrences of any character (.*), but substitutes 1111 with 2222.

OSPF Using X.25

In LAN environments, routers are connected to a common "wire" and each device receives all transmissions. Hence the term broadcast media. In a WAN switched service, routers do not share a common medium. This, by definition, represents a nonbroadcast environment.

Most datagram routing protocols, such as OSPF, rely on broadcasts or multicasts to send routing information to their neighbors. Broadcast means that data packets will be sent to all nodes on a network. Multicast means that single packets are copied by the network and sent to a specific subset of network addresses.

Can configure a nonbroadcast multiaccess network, such as X.25, to carry broadcast or multicast traffic to a destination. A multiaccess network allows multiple devices to connect and communicate simultaneously. You use the X25 Map command, with the Broadcast option, to run OSPF over X.25. The syntax is:

```
x25 map protocol address x.121-address broadcast
```

OSPF operation over X.25 requires the selection of a designated router. An OSPF designated router generates link-state advertisements (LSAs) for a multiaccess network and has other special responsibilities in running OSPF.

Each multiaccess OSPF network that has at least two attached routers has a designated router elected by the OSPF Hello protocol. The designated router enables a reduction in the number of adjacencies required on a multiaccess network. An *adjacency* is a relationship formed between selected neighboring routers and end nodes for the purpose of exchanging routing information. Adjacency is based upon the use of a common media segment. This in turn reduces the amount of routing protocol traffic and the size of the topological database.

This example maps IP address 172.16.2.5 to X.121 address 000000010300. The Broadcast parameter directs any broadcasts sent through interface Serial0 to the specified X.121 address.

```
interface serial0
x25 map ip 172.16.2.5 000000010300 broadcast
```

Permanent virtual circuits (PVCs) are required in the X.25 network for proper OSPF operation.

Use the `IP OSPF Network` command, with the broadcast option, to define that OSPF treat the X.25 network attached to this interface as a broadcast medium. The syntax is:

```
ip ospf network {broadcast  non-broadcast
point-to-multipoint}
```

If `IP OSPF Network` command is issued on an interface that does not allow it, it will be ignored.

This example sets OSPF network as a broadcast network.

```
interface serial0
ip address 172.16.77.17 255.255.255.0
ip ospf network broadcast
encapsulation x25
```

Using the `IP OSPF Network Broadcast` command eliminates the need to manually configure OSPF neighbors.

Using the broadcast option can dramatically increase the traffic between the two hosts, especially if more than one protocol is mapped. Particular attention should be paid to the throughput requirements of such maps.

Subinterfaces can be defined on an X.25 interface to forward routing information between neighbors when the network topology is not fully connected. Subinterfaces are virtual interfaces that can be used to connect several networks to each other through a single physical interface.

Subinterfaces are made available on Cisco routers because routing protocols may need help to determine which hosts need a routing table. This is necessary especially for routing protocols using the *split horizon* principle, which allows routing updates to be distributed to all routed interfaces except the interface on which the routing update was received. In a connection-oriented protocol, such as X.25, other routers reached through the interface that received the update might not have received it. Connection-oriented is a term used to describe data transfer that requires the establishment of a virtual circuit. Rather than forcing you to connect routers by separate physical interfaces, Cisco provides subinterfaces that are treated as separate physical interfaces.

You can separate hosts into subinterfaces on a physical interface. This leaves the X.25 protocol unaffected. The routing processes recognize each subinterface as a separate source of routing updates, and all subinterfaces are eligible to receive routing updates.

CHAPTER **20**

Frame Relay
Configuration

Introduction to Frame Relay

This section introduces the basic concepts of frame relay, its characteristics and features. We will describe the features of data link connection identifiers (DLCIs), and describe LMI extensions and the LMI frame format.

Overview of Frame Relay

Frame relay is a WAN packet-switching protocol that operates at the physical and data-link layers of the OSI model. Packet-switching is a WAN switching method in which network devices share a single point-to-point link to transport packets from a source to a destination across a carrier network.

Frame relay is more efficient than X.25, the protocol for which it is generally regarded a replacement. X.25 is an ITU-T standard that defines how connections between data terminal equipment (DTE) and data circuit-terminating equipment (DCE) are maintained for remote terminal access and computer communications in public data networks (PDNs).

Frame relay provides a packet-switching data communications interface between user devices and network devices. A packet switch routes packets along the most efficient path and allows a communications channel to be shared by multiple connections. This interface forms the basis for communication between user devices across a WAN.

Packet switches can also be referred to as DCE. DCE devices consist of carrier-owned internetworking devices, which, in most cases, are packet switches, although routers or other devices can be configured as DCE devices as well (Figure 20.1).

User devices such as terminals, personal computers, routers, and bridges are generally referred to as DTE. DTE and DCE devices are logical entities. DTE devices initiate a communications exchange, and DCE devices respond.

The core components of frame relay function at the lower two layers of the OSI model. Using physical-layer facilities such as fiber media and digital transmission links, frame relay offers high-speed WAN transmission for end stations, typically on LANs. Working at the data-link layer, frame relay encapsulates information from the upper layers of the OSI model.

Frame relay operations share some features with older WAN packet-switching protocols like X.25. For example, a frame relay interface between the user and the network equipment will transmit and receive frames using first in, first out (FIFO) queuing on a statistically multiplexed circuit. Multiplexing allows several logical connections, described as *virtual circuits*, to share the same physical link.

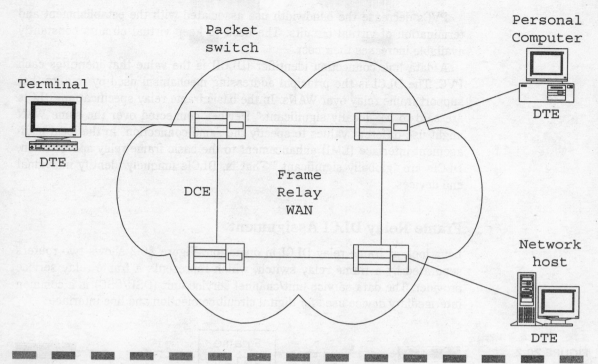

FIGURE 20.1 DCEs generally reside within carrier-operated WANs.

Frame relay offers a high-speed, streamlined service. Transmission speeds for frame relay span a wide range of data rates. Typical communication speeds for frame relay are between 56 Kbps and 2 Mbps. Digital Signal 3 (DS-3) speed (45 Mbps) is available from some service providers.

Frame relay streamlined service functions as a "best-effort" unreliable link. This assumes that improved digital or fiber facilities allow the connection to operate without needing time-consuming error-correction algorithms, acknowledgment schemes, and flow corrections. Frame relay has a high-speed throughput and minimal overhead, and so is suitable for connecting LANs across a WAN.

Frame relay operates over permanent virtual circuits (PVCs), which are permanently established connections. They are used when there is frequent and consistent data transfer between DTE devices across the frame relay network.

PVCs are in either a data transfer or an idle operational state. In the data transfer state, data are being transmitted between DTE devices over the virtual circuit. In the idle state, the connection between DTE devices is active, but no data are being transferred.

PVCs decrease the bandwidth use associated with the establishment and termination of virtual circuits. The need to keep virtual circuits constantly available increases their cost.

A data link connection identifier (DLCI) is the value that identifies each PVC. The DLCI is the principal addressing mechanism used by routers that support frame relay over WANs. In the basic frame relay specification, DLCIs are said to be "locally significant." Devices connected over the same WAN might use different values to specify the same connection. In the local management interface (LMI) enhancement to the basic frame relay specification, DLCIs are "globally significant." That is, DLCIs uniquely identify individual end devices.

Frame Relay DLCI Assignment

Let's look at frame relay DLCI in operation. Figure 20.2 shows two routers separated by a frame relay switch, which represents a frame relay service provider. The data service unit/channel service unit (DSU/CSU) is a common intermediary device used for digital circuit connection and line interface.

FIGURE 20.2
Two routers are separated by a frame relay switch.

Frame Relay

Public service frame relay is typically used by telephone companies which provide data communications market facilities. Frame relay can also be provided over a network of privately owned switches. In both cases, the frame relay provider creates a set of DLCI numbers to be used by routers for establishing PVCs. Certain DLCIs are reserved for special functions; for example, DLCIs 1019 to 1022 are used to designate multicast groups. DLCI 1023 is reserved for LMI use. Local network administrators can select available DLCIs to map to individual network addresses.

In Figure 20.3 you can see the structure of a frame relay frame.

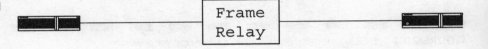

Flags	Address	Control	Data	FCS	Flags

FIGURE 20.3   Six fields comprise the frame relay frame.

The Flags fields delimit the beginning and end of the frame. After the first Flag field are the Address and Control fields which contain the address information. The Data field is a variable-length field that contains encapsulated upper layer data. The Frame Check Sequence (FCS) field is used for error-control purposes to ensure the integrity of transmitted data.

The DLCI value is at the heart of the frame relay header. It makes up the first six bits of the Address field and the first four bits of the Control field. It identifies the logical connection that is multiplexed into the physical channel.

In the basic mode of addressing, DLCIs have local significance. That is, the end devices at either end of a connection may use a different DLCI.

Let's look at an example of using locally significant DLCIs in frame relay addressing (Figure 20.4).

FIGURE 20.4
An example of using locally significant DLCIs in frame relay addressing.

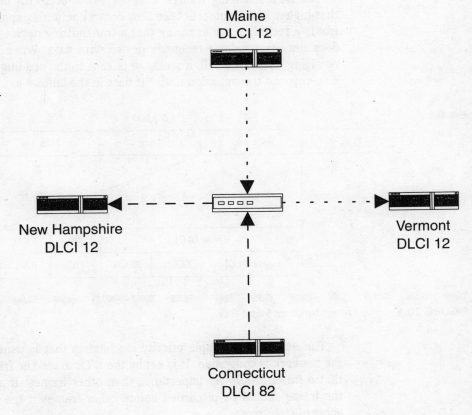

Maine
DLCI 12

New Hampshire
DLCI 12

Vermont
DLCI 12

Connecticut
DLCI 82

Assume there are two PVCs, one between New Hampshire and Connecticut, and one between Vermont and Maine. Connecticut uses DLCI 12 to refer to its PVC with New Hampshire, while New Hampshire refers to the same PVC as DLCI 82.

Similarly, the Vermont router uses DLCI 12 to refer to its PVC with Maine. The network uses internal proprietary mechanisms to keep the two locally significant PVC identifiers distinct.

Three bits in the 2-byte DLCI provide congestion control: the forward explicit congestion notification (FECN) bit, the backward explicit congestion notification (BECN) bit, and the discard eligibility (DE) bit.

The FECN bit is set by the frame relay network. It tells the DTE which receives that frame that congestion was experienced in the path from source to destination. The BECN bit is set by the frame relay network in frames that travel in the opposite direction from frames that encounter a congested path.

The DTE receiving frames with the FECN or BECN bits set can request that higher level protocols take flow control action as appropriate. Flow control is a technique for ensuring that a transmitting device, such as a modem, does not overwhelm a receiving device with data. When the buffers on the receiving device are full, a message is sent to the sending device instructing it to suspend transmission until the data in the buffers has been processed.

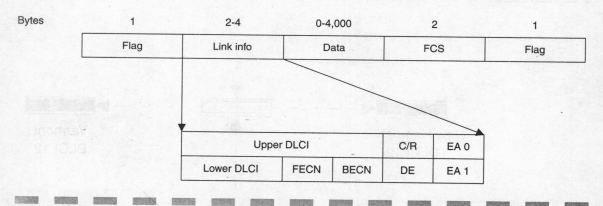

FIGURE 20.5 The frame format for frame relay.

The DE bit is a simple priority mechanism that is usually set only when the network is congested. It is set by the DTE to tell the frame relay network that a frame has lower importance than other frames. It also indicates that the frame should be discarded before other frames if the network becomes short of resources.

The eighth bit of each byte of the Address field is used to indicate the extended address (EA) bit. EA bit indicates the length of the Address field. The EA bits allow for the extension of address lengths beyond the usual 2 bytes.

The C/R bit follows the most significant DLCI byte in the Address field. This bit is not currently defined.

Cisco LMI Support

In 1990 Cisco Systems, StrataCom, Northern Telecom, and Digital Equipment Corporation formed a consortium to focus frame relay technology development and to accelerate the introduction of interoperable frame relay products. The consortium developed a specification conforming to the basic frame relay protocol being proposed by ANSI and ITU-T, but extended it with features that provide additional capabilities for complex internetworking environments. ANSI is the American National Standards Institute and ITU-T stands for the International Telecommunication Union Telecommunication Standardization Sector (formerly the CCITT). These frame relay extensions are referred to collectively as the local management interface (LMI).

LMI extensions promoted by the consortium include virtual circuit status messages, multicasting, global addressing, and simple flow control. Some LMI extensions, such as virtual circuit status messages, are referred to as *common* and are expected to be implemented by everyone who adopts the specification. Other LMI functions are referred to as *optional*.

Virtual circuit status messages provide communication and synchronization between the network and the user device. They periodically report the existence of new PVCs, the deletion of existing PVCs, and generally provide information about PVC integrity. Virtual circuit status messages prevent the sending of data into "black holes," that is, over PVCs that no longer exist.

Multicasting is an optional LMI extension. Multicast groups are designated by a series of four reserved values, 1019 to 1022. Frames sent by a device using one of these reserved DLCIs are replicated by the network and sent to all nodes that are members of the group in the designated set. The multicasting extension also defines LMI messages sent to user devices. These messages notify the user devices of the addition, deletion, and presence of multicast groups.

In networks that take advantage of dynamic routing, routing information must be exchanged among many routers. Dynamic routing is routing that adjusts automatically to network topology or traffic changes. Routing messages can be sent efficiently by using frames with a multicast DLCI. This allows messages to be sent to specific groups of routers.

Global addressing is an optional LMI extension. It gives connection identifiers global rather than local significance. This allows them to be used to identify a specific interface to the frame relay network. Global addressing provides significant benefits in a large, complex internetwork. The frame relay network now resembles a LAN in terms of addressing. Address resolution protocols therefore perform over frame relay exactly as they do over a LAN. Address resolution is a method for resolving differences between computer addressing schemes. It usually specifies a method for mapping network layer (Layer 3) addresses to data link layer (Layer 2) addresses.

Simple flow control is an optional LMI extension. It provides an XON/XOFF flow control mechanism that applies to the entire frame relay interface. It is intended for devices whose higher layers cannot use the congestion notification bits and which need some level of flow control.

The frame format for an LMI frame uses the basic frame relay protocol format, but with additional LMI features (Figure 20.6).

FIGURE 20.6
Nine fields comprise the frame relay that conforms to the LMI format.

Flag	LMI DLCI	Unnumbered information indicator	Protocol discriminator

Call reference	Message type	Information elements	FCS	Flag

The LMI DLCI field identifies the frame as an LMI frame instead of a basic frame relay frame. The LMI-specific DLCI value defined in the LMI consortium specification is 1020.

The Unnumbered Information Indication field has the poll/final bit set to zero. The poll/final bit is a bit in bit-synchronous data link layer protocols that indicates the function of a frame.

The Protocol Discriminator field is always set to a value indicating that the frame is an LMI frame.

The Call Reference field is always filled with zeros.

The Message Type field labels the frame as a status-enquiry or status message. A status-enquiry message allows a user device to enquire about the status of the network. A status message is used to respond to status-enquiry messages. Status messages include keepalives and PVC status messages. Status and status-enquiry messages help verify the integrity of logical and physical links. This information is important in a routing environment as routing algorithms make decisions based on link integrity.

The Information Elements field consists of a variable number of individual information elements (IEs). Each IE consists of a single-byte IE identifier, an IE length field, and one or more bytes containing the data being transmitted.

The Frame Check Sequence (FCS) field is used for error control purposes to ensure the integrity of transmitted data.

Frame Relay Configuration

This section examines how to configure a frame relay network and describes how to configure and monitor frame relay and frame relay operation.

Overview

To set frame relay encapsulation at the interface level, first specify an interface. Specify a serial interface using the `Interface Serial` command to enter Interface Configuration mode. The syntax is `interface serial` *number*.

```
interface serial1
```

To enable frame relay encapsulation, use the `Encapsulation Frame-Relay` command. The syntax is `encapsulation frame-relay [cisco | ietf]`.

```
encapsulation frame-rely cisco
```

The "`cisco`" keyword, which is optional, uses Cisco's own encapsulation, which was developed by the "gang of four": Cisco, Digital, Northern Telecom, and Stratacom. This encapsulation is a 4-byte header, with two bytes to identify the DLCI, and two bytes to identify the packet type. This is the default. And it does not operate with all vendors equipment.

The `IETF` keyword, which is optional, sets the encapsulation method to comply with the Internet Engineering Task Force (IETF) standard. This standard is specified in RFCs 1294 and 1490. Use the IETF keyword when connecting to another vendor's equipment across a frame relay network. IETF encapsulation is supported at either the interface level or on a map entry (per-DLCI) basis.

Use the `Encapsulation Frame-Relay` command with no keywords to restore the default Cisco encapsulation. The frame relay encapsulation can be specified globally or on a circuit-by-circuit basis.

Cisco frame relay software supports the industry-accepted standards for addressing the Local Management Interface (LMI). If the router or access server is attached to a public data network (PDN), the LMI type must match the type used on the public network. Otherwise, you can select an LMI type to suit the needs of your private frame relay network.

Use the `Frame-Relay LMI-Type` command to select the LMI type. The syntax is:

```
frame-relay lmi-type {ansi | cisco | q933a}
```

The default LMI type is `cisco`. To return to the default LMI type, use the No form of the command.

```
frame-relay lmi-type ansi
```

The router must be configured with the appropriate signaling to match the frame relay carrier implementation. All standard LMI signaling formats are supported: ANSI–Annex D defined by ANSI standard T1.617, ITU-T (or q933a)–Annex A defined by Q.933, and CISCO–LMI defined by the gang of four (default).

A keepalive interval must be set to enable the LMI. This is the period of time between each keepalive message sent by a network device. A keepalive message is sent by one network device to inform another network device that the virtual circuit between the two is still active. By default, this interval is 10 seconds and, as required by the LMI protocol, must be less than the corresponding interval on the switch.

Use the `Frame-Relay Keepalive` command to set the keepalive interval. The syntax is:

```
frame-relay keepalive number
```

This command has the same effect as the `Keepalive Interface Configuration` command. The `Number` parameter is an integer that defines the keepalive interval.

You can set a number of optional counters, intervals, and thresholds to fine-tune the operation of your LMI DTE and DCE devices.

A static map can be used to link a specified next-hop protocol address to a specified DLCI. Static mapping removes the need for Inverse ARP (Address Resolution Protocol) requests. Inverse ARP is a method of building dynamic address mappings in frame relay networks. It allows a router or an access server to discover the network protocol address of a device associated with a virtual circuit. When you supply a static map, Inverse ARP is automatically disabled for the specified protocol on the specified DLCI.

You must use static mapping if the router at the other end doesn't support Inverse ARP at all. You must also use static mapping if it doesn't support Inverse ARP for a specific protocol that you want to use over frame relay.

The Frame-Relay Map command defines static mappings between a specific protocol address and a designated DLCI. The syntax is:

```
frame-relay map protocol protocol-address DLCI
[broadcast] [ietf] [cisco]
```

The Protocol parameter specifies the supported protocols, such as AppleTalk, CLNS, DECnet, IP, XNS, IPX, VINES. The Protocol-Address parameter defines the address for the protocol.

The DLCI parameter specifies the DLCI number of the virtual circuit.

The Broadcast keyword specifies that broadcasts should be forwarded when multicast is not enabled. The IETF keyword enables the IETF form of encapsulation. The Cisco keyword enables Cisco encapsulation, which is the default.

This example maps the destination IP address 172.16.120.1 to DLCI 100.

```
interface serial1
frame-relay map ip 172.16.120.1 100
```

Configuring and Monitoring Frame Relay

Let's look at how to implement frame relay in a nonbroadcast multiaccess (NBMA) network and how to configure the Maine router for frame relay operation.

Assume that you are logged on to the Maine router and are currently in Privileged Exec mode. The first step is to enter Global Configuration mode. To do this, type configure terminal at the command prompt.

```
Maine>enable
Password:
Maine#configure terminal
Enter configuration commands, one per line. End with CNTL/Z.
```

Assign the IP address for the Ethernet0 interface. Use the IP Address command to do this. The syntax is ip address ip-address mask.

```
Maine(config)#interface ethernet0
Maine(config-if)#ip address 172.16.1.1 255.255.255.0
```

Here we will begin configuring interface Serial1. Set the frame relay encapsulation style to Cisco, which is the default. This means that the Maine router can send frames to other Cisco routers.

```
Maine(config-if)#interface serial1
Maine(config-if)#encapsulation frame-relay
```

Set the LMI type to Cisco using the `Frame-Relay LMI-Type` command. This is the default LMI type.

```
Maine(config-if)#frame-relay lmi-type cisco
```

Now set the IP address for the Serial1 interface.

```
Maine(config-if)#ip address 172.16.66.1 255.255.255.0
```

Here you use the `Frame-Relay Map` command to link the next hop address IP 172.16.66.3 to DLCI 82. Use the optional `Broadcast` keyword to specify that broadcast traffic will be carried to the destination.

```
Maine(config-if)#frame-relay map ip 172.16.66.3 82 broadcast
```

In this static mapping, IP address 172.16.66.2 is mapped to DLCI 76. Broadcast traffic can also be carried to this destination.

```
Maine(config-if)#frame-relay map ip 172.16.66.2 76 broadcast
```

Use the `Exit` command to exit Interface Configuration mode and return to Configuration mode. Exit Configuration mode by pressing **Ctrl+Z**.

```
Maine(config-if)#exit
Maine(config)#^Z
Maine#copy running-config startup-config
Building configuration...
[OK]
Maine#
```

When you have configured the Maine router for frame relay, you can then monitor its operation.

Use the `Show Interface Serial` command to display status and counter information about a serial interface. You can assume that the Vermont router has been configured at the far end. The syntax is `show interface serial` *number*.

```
Maine#show interface serial1
Serial1 is up, line protocol is up
  Hardware is HD64570
  Internet address is 172.16.66.1/24
  MTU 1500 bytes, BW 64Kbit, DLY 20000 usec, rely 255/255, load 1/255
  Encapsulation FRAME-RELAY, loopback not set, keepalives set (10 sec)
  LMI enq sent  4, LMI state recvd 0, LMI upd recvd 0, DTE LMI up
  LMI enq recvd 4, LMI state sent  0, LMI upd sent  0,
  LMI DLCI 1023 LMI type is CISCO frame relay DTE
  Broadcast queue 0/64, broadccasts sent/dropped 0/0,
  interface broadcasts 0
  Last input 0:00:50, output 0:00:04, output hang never
  Last clearing of "show interface" counters never
  Input queue: 0/75/0 (size/max/drops); Total output drops: 0
  Output queue: 0/64/0 (size/threshold/drops)
    Conversations 0/0 (active/max active)
    Reserved Conversations 0/0 (allocated/max allocated)
  5 minute input rate 0 bits/sec, 0 packets/sec
  5 minute output rate 0 bits/sec, 0 packets/sec
    3456 packets input, 234565 bytes, 0 no buffer
    Received 988 broadcasts, 0 runts, 0 giants
    1 input errors, 1 CRC, 0 frame, 0 overrun, 0 ingored, 0 abort
    7655 packets output, 3188765 bytes, 0 underruns
    0 output errors, 0 collisions, 11 interface resets
    0 output buffer failures, 0 output buffers swapped out
    1 carrier transitions
    DCD=up  DSR=up  DTR=up  RTS=up  CTS=up
Maine#
```

Here you can see general information about the Serial1 interface. The Serial1 interface hardware is currently active, and the line is usable.

The encapsulation method assigned to the Serial1 interface is frame relay. The keepalive interval has been set at ten seconds, which is the default.

You can see statistics for the Local Management Interface (LMI). The output displays the number of status-enquiry messages sent and received (LMI enq sent, LMI enq recvd), the number of status messages received and sent (LMI stat recvd, LMI stat sent), and the number of status updates received and sent (LMI upd recvd, LMI upd sent).

Remember, DLCI 1023 is reserved for LMI use. In the configuration, the LMI type was specified as Cisco.

The broadcast queue for this interface is set at its default level of 64 packets.

This section of the output for the Show Interface command displays details about packets that have been sent and received by the Serial1 interface.

The Last input field shows that fifty seconds have elapsed since the last packet was successfully received by the interface. Four seconds have elapsed since the last packet was successfully transmitted by the interface.

In the `Input queue` and `Output queue` fields you can see the number of packets in each field (0), the maximum size of the queue, and the number of packets dropped due to a full queue (0).

The `Conversations` field displays the number of currently active conversations, and the maximum number of conversations allowed on the interface.

3,456 error-free packets have been received by the interface, consisting of 234,565 bytes. Zero received packets were discarded because there was insufficient buffer space in the system.

The one error on the interface was a Cyclic Redundancy Checksum (CRC). On a serial link, CRCs usually indicate transmission problems on the data link.

7,655 packets were transmitted by the interface, consisting of 3,188,765 bytes. The interface has been completely reset 11 times. This can happen if packets queued for transmission were not sent within several seconds' time. On a serial line, this can be caused by a malfunctioning modem that is not supplying the transmit clock signal, or by a cable problem.

The output displays 1 in the carrier transitions field. This indicates that the carrier detect signal of the interface has changed state only once. If the carrier detect line changes state often this can indicate modem or line problems.

You use the `Show Frame-Relay Map` command to display the current map entries and information about the connections.

```
Maine#show frame-relay map
Serial1 (up):  ip 172.16.66.3 dlci 82(0x52, 0x1420), static,
               broadcast,
               CISCO, status defined, inactive
Serial1 (up):  ip 172.16.66.2 dlci 76(0x4C, 0x10C0), static,
               broadcast,
               CISCO, status defined, inactive
Maine#
```

The Serial1 interface is active, or up.

The destination IP address is displayed and the DLCI that identifies the logical connection being used to reach this interface. As well as displaying the DLCI's decimal value (82), the command also displays its hexadecimal value (0x52), and its value as it appears on the wire (0x1420).

You can see that this is a static entry and the encapsulation type is Cisco. Information about DLCI 76 is also displayed.

Configure and Monitor Frame Relay

As a network administrator you need to be able to configure a frame relay network. Figure 20.7 shows the configuration we will use, including the addresses and DLCIs assigned to each router.

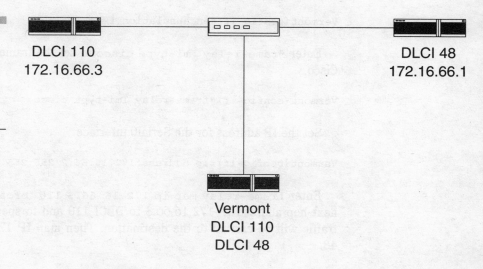

FIGURE 20.7
An illustration of frame relay network to be configured with addresses and DLCIs assigned to each router.

DLCI 110
172.16.66.3

DLCI 48
172.16.66.1

Vermont
DLCI 110
DLCI 48

Here you will configure and monitor frame relay on the Vermont router. Assume that you are logged in to the Vermont router, which has not yet been configured for frame relay.

```
Vermont>enable
Password:
Vermont#configure terminal
Enter configuration commands, one per line. End with CNTL/Z.
Vermont(config)#
```

Enter `interface ethernet0` to configure the interface and enter Interface Configuration mode. Then assign an IP address to the Ethernet0 interface.

```
Vermont(config)#interface ethernet0
```

Enter `ip address 172.16.192.1 255.255.255.0` to assign this address to the Ethernet0 interface.

```
Vermont(config-if)#ip address 172.16.192.1 255.255.255.0
```

Now enter `interface serial0` to begin configuring the Serial0 interface for frame relay operation.

```
Vermont(config-if)#interface serial0
```

To enable frame relay encapsulation, enter `encapsulation frame-relay`.

```
Vermont(config-if)#encapsulation frame-relay
```

Enter `frame-relay lmi-type cisco` to set the frame relay LMI type to Cisco.

```
Vermont(config-if)#frame-relay lmi-type cisco
```

Set the IP address for the Serial0 interface.

```
Vermont(config-if)#ip address 172.16.66.2 255.255.255.0
```

Enter `frame-relay map ip 172.16.66.3 110 broadcast` to map the next hop address IP 172.16.66.3 to DLCI 110 and to specify that broadcast traffic will be carried to the destination. Then map IP 172.16.66.1 to DLCI 48.

```
Vermont(config-if)#frame-relay map ip 172.16.66.3 110 broadcast
```

Enter `exit` to exit Interface Configuration mode and return to Configuration mode. Then exit Configuration mode by pressing **Ctrl+Z**.

```
Vermont(config-if)#exit
Vermont(config)#^Z
Vermont#copy running-config startup-config
Building configuration...
[OK]
Vermont#
```

When you have configured the Vermont router for frame relay, you then monitor its operation.

Display status and counter information about the Serial0 interface by entering `show interface s0`.

```
Vermont#show interface s0
Serial0 is up, line protocol is up
  Hardware is HD64570
  Internet address is 172.16.66.2/24
  MTU 1500 bytes, BW 64 Kbit, DLY 20000 usec, rely 255/255
  load 1/255
  Encapsulation FRAME-RELAY, loopback not set, keepalive set (10 sec)
  LMI enq sent 5, LMI stat recvd 0, LMI upd recvd 0, DTE LMI up
  LMI enq recvd 5, LMI stat sent 0, LMI upd sent 0
  LMI DLCI 1023  LMI stat is CISCO  frame relay DTE
  Broadcast queue 0/64, broadcasts sent/dropped 0/0,
  interface broadcasts 0
  Last input 0:01:23, output 0:00:08, output hang never
```

```
Last clearing of "show interface" counters never
Input queue: 0/75/0 (size/max/drops); Total output drops: 0
Output queue: 0/64/0 (size/threshold/drops); Total output drops: 0
   Conversations 0/0 (active/max active)
   Reserved Conversations 0/0 (allocated/max allocated)
5 minute input rate 0 bits/sec, 0 packets/sec
5 minute output rate 0 bits/sec, 0 packets/sec
   4565 packets input, 264217 bytes, 0 no buffer
   Received 1245 broadcasts, 0 runts, 0 giants
   1 input errors, 1 CRC, 0 frame, 0 overrun, 0 ignored, 0 abort
   9878 packets output, 3877654 bytes, 0 underruns
   0 output errors, 0 collisions, 12 interface resets
   0 output buffer failures, 0 output buffers swapped out
   2 carrier transitions
DCD=up  DSR=up  DTR=up  RTS=up  CTS=up
```

The Serial0 interface hardware is currently active, and the line is usable. Five status enquiry messages have been received, as displayed in the LMI enq recvd field.

The Last input field shows that one minute and 23 seconds have elapsed since the last packet was successfully received by the interface.

Enter show frame-relay map to display the current map entries and information about these connections.

```
Vermont#show frame-relay map
Serial0 (up): ip 172.16.66.3 dlci 110(0x6E, 0x18E0), static,
              broadcast,
              CISCO, status defined, inactive
Serial0 (up): ip 172.16.66.1 dlci 48(0x30, 0xC00), static,
              broadcast,
              CISCO, status defined, inactive
```

As well as displaying a DLCI's decimal value (110), the command also displays its hexadecimal value, 0x6E.

Frame Relay Options

This section describes frame relay options. We will examine how the non-broadcast multiaccess (NBMA) model works with frame relay, describe frame relay subinterfaces, configure frame relay subinterfaces, describe how to prioritize DLCI traffic, and how to configure a router as a frame relay switch.

Non-broadcast Multiaccess

In LAN environments, routers are often connected to a common "wire" and each device receives all transmissions, hence the term "broadcast media". frame relay is a WAN switched service and the routers do not share a common medium. By definition, without a common connection, frame relay is a non-broadcast environment.

A broadcast environment can be created by transmitting data on each individual circuit. This simulated broadcast requires significant buffering and CPU resources in the transmitting router. It can result in lost user data due to contention for the circuits.

One model for implementing frame relay in an internetwork is called non-broadcast multiaccess (NBMA). This model makes all routers connected by virtual circuits peers on the same IP network or subnetwork. Because frame relay does not support broadcasting, the routers must copy all broadcasts and transmit on each virtual circuit.

Full connectivity can be achieved in a partial mesh configuration for routing protocols that allow split horizon to be turned off. Protocols like AppleTalk RTMP do not allow split horizon to be turned off. Connectivity is restricted between routers that are directly connected by virtual circuits.

In an NBMA environment, routers trying to forward updates can encounter problems with the operation of split horizon on serial interfaces attached to WAN services. In split horizon, if a router learns a route from an interface, it does not propagate information about that route back out that same interface. For frame relay, this condition applies to all routing protocols except those in the IP suite, such as RIP, IGRP, and Enhanced IGRP. Split horizon applies to all service advertisements, such as IPX SAP or GNS traffic, and AppleTalk ZIP updates.

If you map DLCIs from a serial interface, for example S0 on Router A, only updates from Router A or to Router A can cross the S0 interface. If Router B attempts to send updates for Routers C or D through Router A, then Router A's split horizon process takes effect (Figure 20.8). Because the update comes in on S0, Router A with split horizon will not allow it to go back out on S0.

Since the split-horizon mechanism will not allow routers to receive updates from and then send them out to the same interface, you can provide for connectivity by operating frame relay with a full mesh. This sets up a frame relay data link from every route to every other destination. Then, at each router, you configure a DLCI to each destination of that router.

Connecting routers over a frame relay WAN using full point-to-point mesh requires many PVCs and configuration statements. The network administrator must order many frame relay PVCs from the service provider. The service provider will need to install each PVC. The enterprise will receive a bill for these services, and will also face ongoing, incremental bills for each PVC.

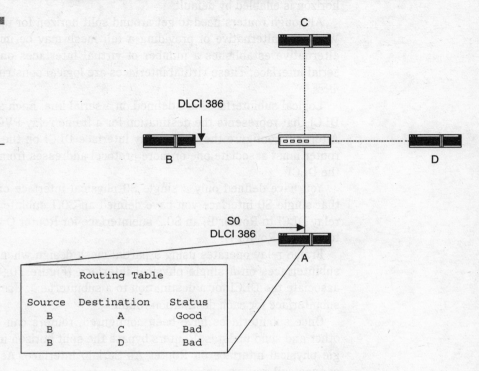

FIGURE 20.8
If Router B attempts to send updates for Routers C or D through A, then Router A's split horizon process takes effect.

The configuration of each router must include mapping statements for each DLCI it uses. To represent all its frame relay destinations, the configuration of all routers using this full-mesh approach will require many map statements. This configuration might be difficult to set up and support.

Frame Relay with Subinterfaces

Frame relay networks achieve full connectivity by design, through the use of virtual interfaces. In a full-mesh topology, there are virtual circuit connections to each possible destination. This method, although costly, provides the simplest, most straightforward design. It is the easiest to configure, at least until the number of connections becomes unmanageable. Using this approach, all routers are members of the same subnet and are considered peers in the network.

In a partial-mesh topology, only some destinations have direct virtual circuit connections to each other. Routers that forward traffic to another destination require multiple virtual interfaces to avoid split horizon issues. Split horizon is enabled by default.

Although routers need to get around split horizon for updates that use the WAN, the alternative of providing a full mesh may be impractical. Another alternative establishes a number of virtual interfaces on a single physical serial interface. These virtual interfaces are logical constructs called *subinterfaces*.

Logical subinterfaces are defined on a serial line. Each subinterface uses a DLCI that represents the destination for a frame relay PVC on your network. After you configure the frame relay interface DLCI on the subinterface, your router must associate one or more protocol addresses from the destination to the DLCI.

You have defined only a single S0 physical interface on Router A but on that single S0 interface you have defined an S0.1 subinterface for the frame relay DLCI to Router B, an S0.2 subinterface for Router C, and an S0.3 subinterface for Router D.

Frame relay operates using a partial-mesh design when you define logical subinterfaces on a single physical interface (Figure 20.9). To do this, you associate the DLCI for a destination to a subinterface. Use one DLCI and one subinterface for each destination router.

Once subinterfaces have been configured, routers can connect with each other and send updates. Routers bypass the split horizon in effect for the single physical interface on Router A's Serial0 interface. As a result, you can connect all routers without needing a separate frame relay PVC between each router.

The overall configuration to accomplish these connections is much simpler than using a map statement for each protocol address on each router's destination.

Before you can configure and use frame relay subinterfaces, you must first have a physical interface set up with encapsulation for frame relay.

Use the `Interface` command to define the logical subinterface for frame relay. The syntax is:

```
interface type number.subinterface [multipoint | point-to-point]
```

The `Type` parameter defines the type of interface that is to be configured. It is usually a serial interface.

The `Number` parameter refers to the number of the physical interface. This is a port, connector, or interface card number.

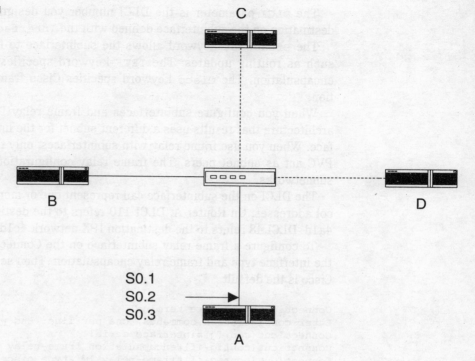

FIGURE 20.9
Frame relay operates
using a partial-mesh
design allowing
logical subinterrfaces
on a single physical
interface.

Following the dot (.), the `Subinterface` parameter is a unique integer on that interface.

The `multipoint | point-to-point` keywords specify either a multipoint or point-to-point subinterface. For multipoint subinterfaces, the destinations can be dynamically resolved through the use of frame relay Inverse ARP. Or they can be statically mapped using the `Frame-Relay Map` command. For point-to-point subinterfaces, specify the destination using the `Frame-Relay Interface DLCI` command.

The ability to change a subinterface from point-to-point to multipoint, or vice versa, is limited by the software architecture. The router must be rebooted for a change of this type to take effect.

As an alternative to rebooting, you can create another subinterface in the software. Then you can migrate the configuration parameters to the new subinterface using the proper point-to-point or multipoint setting, as required.

The `Frame-Relay Interface-DLCI` command assigns a frame relay DLCI to the subinterface on the router. The syntax is:

```
frame-relay interface-dlci dlci [broadcast | ietf | cisco]
```

The DLCI parameter is the DLCI number you designate to indicate the destination on the subinterface defined with the Interface command.

The Broadcast keyword allows the subinterface to forward broadcasts, such as routing updates. The IETF keyword specifies IETF frame relay encapsulation. The Cisco keyword specifies Cisco frame relay encapsulation.

When you configure subinterfaces and frame relay DLCIs, the network architecture that results uses a different subnet for the link on each subinterface. When you use frame relay with subinterfaces, only the two routers on a PVC act as subnet peers. The frame relay configuration contains multiple subnetworks.

The DLCI on the subinterface can represent one or more destination protocol addresses. On Router A, DLCI 110 refers to the destination IPX network 4a1d. DLCI 48 refers to the destination IPX network 4c1d.

To configure a frame relay subinterface on the Connecticut router, specify the interface type and frame relay encapsulation. Then select the LMI type—Cisco is the default.

```
Connecticut#configure terminal
Enter configuration commands, one per line. End with CNTL/Z.
Connecticut(config)#interface serial1
Connecticut(config-if)#encapsulation frame-relay
Connecticut(config-if)#frame-relay lmi-type cisco
```

Specify the subinterface, Serial1.1, and establish it as a point-to-point subinterface.

```
Connecticut(config-if)#interface serial1.1 point-to-point
```

In Subinterface Configuration mode, assign the IP address and subnet mask for the Serial1.1 subinterface.

```
Connecticut(config-subif)#ip address 172.16.66.3 255.255.255.0
```

Assign the DLCI, 152, to the Serial1.1 subinterface and specify that broadcasts can be forwarded out through this subinterface. Then enter exit to exit Subinterface Configuration mode, and enter it again to exit Configuration mode.

```
Connecticut(config-subif)#frame-relay interface-dlci 152 broad-
cast
Connecticut(config-subif)#exit
Connecticut(config)#exit
```

Subinterface Configuration

Now we will configure subinterfaces on the Vermont router from a terminal.

```
Vermont>enable
Password:
Vermont#configure terminal
Enter configuration commands, one per line. End with CNTL/Z.
Vermont(config)#
```

Enter `interface serial0` to enter Interface Configuration mode for the Serial0 interface.

```
Vermont(config)#interface serial0
```

Enter `encapsulation frame-relay` to set the encapsulation style to frame relay.

```
Vermont(config-if)#encapsulation frame-relay
```

To set the LMI type to cisco, enter `frame-relay lmi-type cisco`.

```
Vermont(config-if)#frame-relay lmi-type cisco
```

Enter `interface serial0.1 point-to-point` to enter Subinterface Configuration mode for the Serial0.1 subinterface and establish it as a point-to-point subinterface.

```
Vermont(config-interface serial0.1 point-to-point
```

Enter `ip address 172.16.76.1 255.255.255.0` to assign the IP address 172.16.76.1 to the Serial0.1 subinterface.

```
Vermont(config-subif)#ip address 172.16.76.1 255.255.255.0
```

Enter `frame-relay interface-dlci 48 broadcast` to assign DLCI 48 to the Serial0.1 subinterface and specify that broadcasts can be forwarded out through Serial0.1.

```
Vermont(config-subif)#frame-relay interface-dlci 48 broadcast
```

Enter `exit` to return to Configuration mode, from where you can begin configuring another subinterface.

```
Vermont(config-subif)#exit
```

Enter `interface serial0.2 point-to-point` to assign a second subinterface on the Serial0 interface and enter Subinterface Configuration mode for the Serial0.2 subinterface.

```
Vermont(config)#interface serial0.2 point-to-point
```

Assign an IP address and a DLCI to the subinterface. Then exit Subinterface Configuration mode and Configuration mode.

```
Vermont(config-subif)#ip address 172.16.66.2 255.255.255.0
Vermont(config-subif)#frame-relay interface-dlci 110 broadcast
Vermont(config-subif)#exit
Vermont(config)#exit
Vermont#copy runn start
Vermont configuration...
[OK]
Vermont#
```

Assigning Priorities to DLCI Traffic

Once connectivity is established to a frame relay network, administrators want to control the path the traffic takes to a destination. The path through a frame relay network cannot be controlled directly, but a virtual circuit, or DLCI, can be specified to carry different types of traffic.

Traffic is classified by the matching of parameters within a priority queue list. Each queue is linked to a specific DLCI.

If one DLCI has the best committed information rate (CIR), it can be selected to carry preferred, high-volume application traffic. The CIR is the rate at which a frame relay network transfers information under normal conditions. It is measured in bits per second.

A minimum of two DLCIs to the destination must be in place for DLCI prioritization to be effective. A maximum of four DLCIs to a single destination is allowed for each interface or subinterface. Redundancy and load sharing are other common reasons for multiple virtual circuits to a single destination.

Use the `Priority-List-Protocol` command to create a priority list for different protocols and traffic types. The syntax is:

```
priority-list group-number protocol protocol-name priority-level
equality byte-count
```

You use the `No` form of the `Priority-List-Protocol` command with the appropriate list number to remove an entry from the list. The syntax is:

```
no priority-list list-number protocol
```

The `Group-Number` parameter is the number of the priority list. This is a decimal number between 1 and 10. The `Protocol-Name` parameter specifies the protocol type.

The `Priority-Level` parameter is the priority queue level. This level can be high, medium, normal, or low.

The `Equality` parameter is a conditional value, such as fragments, `gt`, `lt`, `list`, `tcp`, and `udp`. The `Byte-Count` parameter is the number of bytes in the packet being classified.

The `Fragments` keyword assigns the priority level defined to fragmented IP packets (for use with IP packets only). IP packets whose Fragment Offset field is nonzero are matched by this command. The initial fragment of a fragmented IP packet has a fragment offset of zero, so such packets are not matched by this command.

The `GT` keyword specifies a greater-than byte-count. The priority level assigned goes into effect when a packet exceeds the value entered for the argument *byte-count*. The size of the packet must also include additional bytes due to MAC encapsulation on the outgoing interface.

The `LT` keyword specifies a less-than byte count. The priority level assigned goes into effect when a packet size is less than the value entered for *byte-count*. The size of the packet must also include additional bytes due to MAC encapsulation on the outgoing interface.

The `List` keyword assigns traffic priorities according to a specified list number when used with AppleTalk, bridging, IP, IPX, VINES, or XNS. The `List-Number` argument is the access list number as specified by the access-list `Global Configuration` command for the specified protocol name. For example, if the protocol is AppleTalk, *list-number* should be a valid AppleTalk access-list number.

The `TCP` keyword assigns the priority level defined to TCP segments originating from or destined to a specified port. It is used with the IP protocol only.

The `UDP` keyword assigns the priority level defined to UDP packets originating from or destined to the specified port. It is used with the IP protocol only.

When classifying a packet, the system searches the list of rules specified by `Priority List` commands for a matching protocol type. When a match is found, the packet is assigned to the appropriate queue. The list is searched in the order specified, and the first matching rule terminates the search.

Use the `Frame-Relay Priority-DLCI-Group` command to establish the DLCIs to be used by the four individual priority queues. It links the specified priority list to an interface. The syntax is:

```
frame-relay priority-dlci-group group-number high-dlci medium-
dlci normal-dlci low-dlci
```

The `Group-Number` parameter is the number of the priority list being linked to an interface. Next are the DLCI numbers assigned to the high, medium, normal, and low queues. If a DLCI value is not configured for a queue, the last assigned DLCI value used in the command syntax is propagated, by default, to complete the syntax.

The `Frame-Relay Priority-DLCI-Group` command applies at the subinterface level. The command defines different DLCIs for different categories of traffic. It does not itself define priority queuing but can be used in association with it.

You must define a global priority list before the `Frame-Relay Priority-DLCI-Group` command is used. Also, the DLCIs specified in the command must be defined before the command is used.

If you do not explicitly specify a DLCI for each of the levels, the last DLCI specified in the command line is used as the value of the remaining arguments. For example, the two commands below are equivalent.

```
frame-relay priority-dlci-group 1 40 50
frame-relay priority-dlci-group 1 40 50 50 50
```

When you configure `Frame-Relay Map` commands or use Inverse ARP, the high-level DLCI is the only one mapped. If you enter this command, you configure DLCI 40, but not DLCI 50, in a `Frame-Relay Map` command.

Figure 20.10 shows an example of DLCI prioritization on traffic transmitted from the multipoint S0.1 subinterface to Router C.

```
interface s0
no ip address
encapsulation frame-relay

interface s0.1 multipoint
ip address 172.16.11.1 255.255.255.0
frame-relay priority-dlci-group 2 41 42 42 42
frame-relay interface-dlci 41 broadcast
frame-relay interface-dlci 42 broadcast

priority-list 2 protocol ip high gt 576
priority-list 2 protocol ip low lt 128
priority-list 2 default normal
```

Here priority-list 2 is assigned to subinterface S0.1. The DLCI number for traffic transmitted by the high-priority queue is 4.

42 is the assigned DLCI number for traffic transmitted by the medium, normal, and low queues.

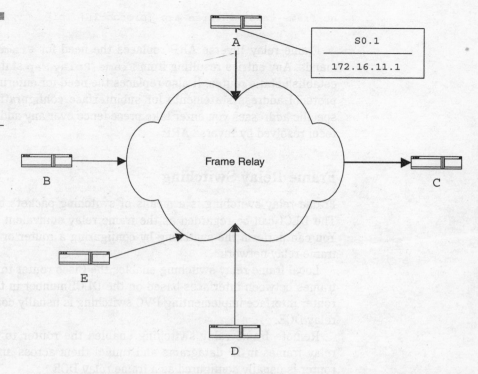

FIGURE 20.10
An example of DLCI
prioritization on
traffic transmitted
from the multipoint
S0.1 subinterface to
Router C.

Priority list 2 specifies that only IP packets larger than 576 bytes will be allowed to enter the high-priority queue. It specifies that only IP packets less than 128 bytes can enter the low-priority queue. Next, the normal queue is specified as the default queue for traffic that does not match the criteria of previous lines in priority-list 2.

Configurations using either subinterface DLCIs or NBMA groups can be simplified using Inverse Address Resolution Protocol (ARP). With Inverse ARP, the router needs to know only its own network protocol address on the NBMA network or subnet.

The router learns about the virtual circuits through LMI signaling from the frame relay switch. The router then learns the network address of each peer router by sending and receiving Inverse ARP messages on each DLCI. As soon as you specify DLCIs for frame relay, Inverse ARP automatically starts.

With Inverse ARP, the process resolves to a network address when given a DLCI. The router announces a network address and DLCI. Then frame relay Inverse ARP allows the frame relay network to propagate the information.

Because Inverse ARP for frame relay is on by default, if you need to disable Inverse ARP on a local DLCI, use the `No Frame-Relay Inverse-ARP` command. The syntax is:

```
no frame-relay inverse-arp [protocol][dlci]
```

Frame relay Inverse ARP replaces the need for `Frame-Relay Map` commands. Any entries resulting from `Frame-Relay Map` statements continue to establish static routes. It also replaces the need for entering specific network protocol address statements for subinterface configurations. However, any specific addresses you enter take precedence over any addresses for that protocol resolved by Inverse ARP.

Frame Relay Switching

Frame relay switching is a means of switching packets based on the DLCI. The DLCI can be regarded as the frame relay equivalent of a MAC address. You can perform the switching by configuring a router or access server as a frame relay network.

Local frame relay switching enables the Cisco router to switch frame relay frames between interfaces based on the DLCI number in the frame header. A router interface implementing PVC switching is usually configured as a frame relay DCE.

Remote frame relay switching enables the router to encapsulate frame relay frames in IP datagrams and tunnel them across an IP backbone. The router is usually configured as a frame relay DCE.

The Cisco Generic Route Encapsulation (GRE) tunnel protocol is used for remote frame relay switching. GRE was developed to encapsulate a wide variety of protocol types inside IP tunnels. It creates a virtual point-to-point link to Cisco routers at remote points over an IP network.

Use the `Frame Relay Switching` command to enable PVC switching on a frame relay DCE, DTE, or a network-to-network interface (NNI). This command has command has no arguments or keywords.

Use the `Frame-Relay Route` command to specify the static route within the router for PVC switching. The syntax is:

```
frame-relay route in-dlci out-interface out-dlci
```

The `In-DLCI` parameter is used to specify the DLCI on which the packet is received on the interface. The `Out-Interface` parameter is used to specify the interface the router uses to transmit the packet. The `Out-DLCI` parameter is used to specify the DLCI the router uses to transmit the packet over the specified out-interface.

Use the `Frame-Relay INFT-Type` command to configure a frame relay switch type. The syntax is:

```
frame-relay intf-type [dce | dte | nni]
```

The type of frame relay switch is determined by the router's function within the frame relay network.

The DTE option represents a router connected to a frame relay network. This option is the default. The DCE option represents a router connected to another router to another router and acts as a switch. The NNI option represents a router that functions as a switch and is connected to another switch performing network to network interface (NNI) support.

Figure 20.11 is an example of frame relay switching. Here Router B is configured as a remote frame relay switch.

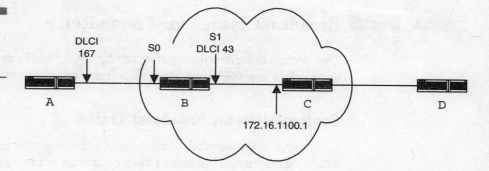

FIGURE 20.11

An illustration of frame relay switching.

Traffic arriving on Serial0 using DLCI 167 will be switched to output interface Serial1 and DLCI43 will be used in the source identifier. The traffic will be carried through the IP network using a GRE encapsulated tunnel having a next-hop destination of 172.16.100.1. The encapsulation mode for a tunnel interface defaults to GRE.

Here is the configuration for Router B.

```
frame-relay switching

interface serial0
no ip address
encapsulation frame-relay
frame-relay route 167 tunnel0 43
frame-relay intf-type dce

interface serial1
ip address 172.16.100.2 255.255.255.0

interface tunnel0
tunnel source serial1
tunnel destination 172.16.100.1
```

Enable frame relay switching. Specify the Serial0 interface. Then disable IP processing, and specify frame relay encapsulation.

Specify the static route for frame relay switching. 167 is the DLCI of the arriving or source, traffic to be switched. Tunnel0 is the outgoing interface to be used. 43 is the outgoing DLCI to be used when forwarding the traffic.

The Serial0 interface is established as a DCE.

Assign the IP address for the Serial1 interface.

Specify the Tunnel0 interface. Next specify that the software-only Tunnel0 interface will use physical interface Serial1 as the entry into the tunnel. Then specify that the tunnel will deliver traffic to 172.16.100.1.

Broadcast Issues for Frame Relay

This section describes issues affecting broadcast traffic over frame relay. We will explain how OSPF operates over a frame relay network.

Configuration for Broadcast Traffic

In a frame relay network, broadcast traffic must be replicated for each active connection. This means that each time a router sends a multicast frame, such as a routing or service advertisement protocol (SAP) update, the router must replicate the frame to each DLCI for the interface. Frame replication results in substantial overhead for the router and for the physical interface.

You should evaluate the amount of broadcast traffic and the number of virtual circuits terminating at each router during the design phase of a frame relay network. Overhead traffic can affect the delivery of critical user data, especially when the delivery path contains low bandwidth (56 Kbps) links.

Consider a Novell IPX environment with multiple DLCIs configured for a single physical serial interface. Every time an SAP update is detected, the router must replicate it and send it down the virtual interface associated with each DLCI.

SAP updates and RIP routing updates are seen as overhead traffic in the network and should be controlled locally to reduce the impact on user applications. Use the following methods to control SAP traffic: SAP filters, programmable SAP timers, and broadcast queues.

SAP filters are a special form of access list. They control which SAP services the Cisco IOS software accepts and advertises, and which Get Nearest Server (GNS) response messages it sends out.

Programmable SAP timers alter the interval between service advertisements. Changing the interval at which SAP updates are sent is most useful on limited-bandwidth, point-to-point links, or on X.25 and frame relay multipoint interfaces.

You can create a special broadcast queue for an interface, in order to better manage broadcast traffic. Broadcast queues limit the amount of available bandwidth that can be allocated to broadcast traffic. A queue will hold broadcast traffic that has been replicated for transmission on multiple DLCIs.

Use the `Frame-Relay Broadcast-Queue` command to set the capacity of a broadcast queue and to set the maximum transmission rate for broadcast traffic. The syntax is:

```
frame-relay broadcast-queue size byte-rate packet-rate
```

The `Size` parameter specifies the number of packets to hold in the broadcast queue. The default is 64 packets.

The `Byte-Rate` parameter specifies the maximum number of bytes to be transmitted per second. The default is 256,000 bytes per second.

The `Packet-Rate` parameter specifies the maximum number of packets to be transmitted per second. The default is 36 packets per second.

A `frame relay broadcast queue` is managed independently of the normal interface queue. It has its own buffers and a configurable service rate.

In this example, interface Serial0 has a broadcast queue establishing a connection to the frame relay network. The queue can hold 80 packets. A maximum of 240,000 bytes per second and 160 packets per second of broadcast traffic can be transmitted on each subinterface.

```
interface s0
encapsulation frame-relay
frame-relay broadcast-queue 80 240000 160
interface s0.1
ip address 172.16.100.1 255.255.255.0
ipx network 9ab
interface s0.2
ip address 172.16.101.1 255.255.255.0
ipx network 8cd
```

OSPF over Frame Relay

Open Shortest Path First (OSPF), an IP routing protocol, requires special configuration when operating over a non-broadcast network, such as frame relay. It typically operates in a broadcast LAN environment. Broadcast means that data packets will be sent to all nodes on a network. OSPF routers periodically send out link-state advertisements (LSAs) to all other routers, from which they require an acknowledgment.

When OSPF is used in a non-broadcast network, such as frame relay, OSPF must be configured to treat the network as a broadcast environment. This configuration is accomplished through the use of multiple Neighbor commands or by declaring the entire OSPF network to be a broadcast environment.

Use the IP OSPF Network command to specify that OSPF treats a non-broadcast multiaccess (NBMA) network, such as frame relay, as a broadcast network. The syntax is:

```
ip ospf network {broadcast | non-broadcast | point-to-
multipoint}
```

If this command is issued on an interface that does not allow it, it will be ignored.

The Broadcast keyword sets the network type to broadcast. The Non-Broadcast keyword sets the network type to non-broadcast.

The Point-to-Multipoint keyword sets the network type as a point-to-multipoint. In this case, routing between two routers that are not directly connected will go through the router that has virtual circuits to both routers.

Using the IP OSPF Network command eliminates the need to manually configure OSPF neighbors.

Use the Neighbor (OSPF) command to configure routers that interconnect to non-broadcast networks, such as frame relay. The syntax is:

```
neighbor ip-address [priority number] [poll-interval
seconds]
```

The IP-Address parameter, which is optional, specifies the IP address of the neighbor. The Priority parameter is an 8-bit number indicating the router priority value of the non-broadcast neighbor associated with the IP address. The default is 0.

The Poll-Interval parameter, which is optional, is an unsigned integer value reflecting the poll interval. Polling is a method in which a primary network device inquires, in an orderly fashion, whether secondaries have data to transmit. RFC 1247 recommends that this value be much larger than the Hello interval. The default is 120 seconds.

At the OSPF level you can configure a router as a broadcast network. One neighbor entry must be included in the Cisco IOS software configuration for each known nonbroadcast network neighbor. The neighbor address must be on the primary address of the interface.

If a neighboring router has become inactive, that is its hello packets have not been seen for the Router Dead Interval period, it may still be necessary to send hello packets to the dead neighbor. These packets will be sent at a reduced rate called Poll Interval.

When the router first starts up, it sends only hello packets to those routers with non-zero priority. Non-zero priority routers are eligible to become designated routers (DR) and backup designated routers (BDR). A designated router is an OSPF router that generates link-state advertisements (LSAs) for a multiaccess network and has other special responsibilities in running OSPF. After DR and BDR are selected, they will then start sending hello packets to all neighbors in order to form adjacencies.

In this example, OSPF is configured on Router A. Use the `Router OSPF` command to configure an OSPF routing process. The syntax is:

```
router ospf process-id
```

The `Process-ID` parameter is an internally used identification parameter for an OSPF process. It is locally assigned and can be any positive integer. A unique value is assigned for each OSPF routing process.

Use the `Network Area` command to define the interfaces on which OSPF runs. The syntax is:

```
network address wildcard-mask area area-id
```

The `Address` and `Wildcard-Mask` parameters specify the IP address and mask of the network to which the OSPF router is connected. The `Area-ID` parameter specifies the area to which the router belongs. It can be specified as either a decimal value or as an IP address.

One `Neighbor` command is required for each OSPF network neighbor. All the routers are part of subnet 172.16.100.0, and all are possible designated router candidates. They will poll one another after 180 seconds of inactivity.

PPP
Configuration

Introduction to PPP

This section describes the Point-to-Point Protocol (PPP) and its basic communication components. We will examine PPP and outline its connection negotiation process, define the use of Link Control Protocol (LCP) and Network Control Protocol (NCP) frames within PPP, and describe LCP and its use in PPP connection negotiation.

Overview

In the late 1980s, the Internet began to experience explosive growth in the number of hosts supporting the Internet Protocol (IP). The vast majority of these hosts were connected to LANS of various types, Ethernet being the most common. Most of the other hosts were connected through WANs. Relatively few hosts were connected with simple point-to-point (serial) links. Yet point-to-point links are among the oldest methods of data communications and almost every host supports point-to-point connections.

One reason for the small number of point-to-point IP links was the lack of a standard Internet encapsulation protocol. This problem was blocking the growth of serial-line access. The Point-to-Point Protocol (PPP) was created to solve remote Internet connectivity problems.

PPP is generally viewed as the successor to the Serial Link IP (SLIP) protocol. It provides router-to-router and host-to-network connections over both synchronous and asynchronous circuits. PPP is defined using several International Standards Organization (ISO) specifications. It uses the principles, terminology, and frame structure of the ISO High-Level Data Link Control (HDLC) procedures (ISO 3309-1979). ISO 3309-1979 specifies the HDLC frame structure for synchronous (bit-oriented) environments. ISO 3309:1984/PDAD1 specifies proposed modifications to ISO 3309-1979 to permit asynchronous (start/stop) use. ISO 4335-1979 and ISO 4335-1979/Addendum 1-1979 specify control procedures.

PPP is capable of operating across any DTE/DCE interface. The only absolute requirement imposed by PPP is the provision of a duplex circuit, either dedicated or switched. This circuit must operate in either asynchronous or synchronous bit-serial mode, transparent to PPP link-layer frames.

PPP does not impose any restrictions regarding transmission rate, other than those imposed by the particular DTE/DCE interface in use. Examples of supported physical interfaces include EIA/TIA-232-E, EIA/TIA-422, EIA/TIA-423, and V.35.

PPP deals with many issues: the most important include the assignment and management of IP addresses, asynchronous and synchronous encapsulation, network protocol multiplexing, and link configuration. PPP also provides link quality testing, error detection, and option negotiation for network-layer address negotiation and data compression negotiation.

PPP provides an extensible *Link Control Protocol (LCP)* and a family of *Network Control Protocols (NCPs)* to negotiate optional configuration parameters and facilities.

PPP provides a method for transmitting datagrams over serial point-to-point links. PPP datagram transmission employs three key components to provide effective data transmission. PPP supports the High-Level Data Link Control (HDLC) protocol to provide encapsulation.

Link Control Protocol (LCP) is extensible and is used to establish, configure, and test the data-link connection. Network Control Protocols (NCPs) are a family of NCPs used to establish and configure different network layer protocols.

PPP connections are established in stages. An originating PPP node first sends LCP frames to configure and optionally test the data link. Next, the link is established, and optional facilities are negotiated. The originating PPP node then sends NCP frames to choose and configure network-layer protocols. The chosen network-layer protocols are configured, and packets from each network layer protocol are sent.

The link will remain configured for communications until explicit LCP or NCP frames close the link. The link can also be closed by the occurrence of some external event (for example, an inactivity timer expires or a user intervenes).

PPP LCP Configuration

The PPP LCP provides a method of establishing, configuring, maintaining, and terminating the point-to-point connection. LCP goes through four distinct phases: link establishment and configuration negotiation, link quality determination, network layer protocol configuration negotiation, and link termination.

Before any network layer datagrams (for example, IP) can be exchanged, LCP must first open the connection and negotiate the configuration parameters. This phase is complete when a configuration acknowledgment frame has been both sent and received.

LCP allows an optional link-quality determination phase following the link establishment and configuration negotiation phase. In the link-quality determination phase, the link is tested to determine whether the link quality is sufficient to bring up network layer protocols. LCP can delay transmission of network layer protocol information until this phase is completed.

When LCP finishes the link-quality determination phase, network-layer protocols can be separately configured by the appropriate NCP, and can be brought up and taken down at any time. If LCP closes the link, it informs the network-layer protocols so that they can take appropriate action.

LCP can terminate the link at any time. This will usually be done at the request of a user, but can happen because of a physical event, such as the loss of carrier or the expiration of an idle-period timer.

Three PPP LCP frame types are used to accomplish the work of each of the LCP phases: link establishment frames—which establish and configure a link; link termination frames—which terminate a link; and link maintenance frames—which manage and debug a link.

There are six information fields in the PPP LCP Frame (Figure 21.1). The Flag field indicates the beginning or end of a frame and consists of the binary sequence 01111110. The Address field is the standard broadcast address, binary sequence 11111111. PPP does not assign individual station addresses.

Flag	Address	Control	Protocol	Data	FCS

FIGURE 21.1   Six fields make up the PPP frame.

The Control field is a single byte that consists of the binary sequence 00000011, which calls for transmission of user data in an unsequenced frame. A connectionless link service similar to that of Logical Link Control (LLC) Type 1 is provided.

The Protocol field is two bytes that identify the protocol encapsulated in the Data field of the frame. The most up-to-date values of the Protocol field are specified in the most recent Assigned Numbers Request For Comments (RFC).

The Data field is zero or more bytes which contain the datagram for the protocol specified in the Protocol field. The end of the Data field is found by locating the closing flag sequence and allowing two bytes for the FCS field. The default maximum length of the Data field is 1,500 bytes. By prior agreement, consenting PPP implementations can use other values for the maximum Data field length.

The Frame Check Sequence (FCS) field is normally 16 bits (two bytes). By prior agreement, consenting PPP implementations can use a 32-bit (four-byte) FCS for improved error detection. The PPP LCP can negotiate modifications to the standard PPP frame structure. However, modified frames will be clearly distinguishable from standard frames.

Multilink PPP

This section describes how Multilink PPP operates. We will examine Multilink PPP, describe how to configure Multilink PPP on an ISDN interface, and configure Multilink PPP on an ISDN interface.

Introduction to Multilink PPP

Multilink PPP provides load balancing over dialer interfaces, including ISDN, synchronous, and asynchronous interfaces. It improves throughput and reduces latency between systems, by splitting packets and sending the fragments simultaneously over multiple point-to-point links to the same remote address.

Multilink PPP solves several problems relating to load balancing over multiple WAN links. These problems include: multi-vendor interpretability as specified by RFC 1717, packet fragmentation to improve latency of each packet, packet sequence, and load calculation. Multilink PPP supports RFC 1717 fragmentation and packet sequencing specifications.

Use Multilink PPP with applications in which bandwidth requirements are dynamic, as in remote LAN access applications for telecommuters or small office/home office (SOHO) environments.

Multilink PPP works over single or multiple Basic Rate Interfaces (BRIs) and Primary Rate Interfaces (PRIs) that support both dial-on-demand rotary groups and PPP encapsulation.

When a single interface is used with dialer maps, contention for the interface can occur. This starts a fast-idle timer that causes lines to remain connected for a shorter idle time than usual, allowing other destinations to use the interface.

Rotary groups prevent contention by creating a set of interfaces that can be used to dial out. Rather than statically assigning an interface to a destination, rotary groups dynamically allocate interfaces to telephone numbers. Before a call is placed, the rotary group is searched for an interface not in use to place the call. It is not until all of the interfaces in the rotary group are in use that the fast-idle timer starts.

During PPP's LCP option negotiation, a system indicates to its peer that it can combine multiple physical links into a "bundle" by sending the Maximum Received Reconstructed Unit (MRRU) option. Multilink systems must be able to do the following: combine multiple physical links into one logical link (bundle), receive and reassemble upper layer protocol data units (PDU), and receive PDUs of a negotiated size.

After the LCP negotiation is completed, the remote destination must be authenticated. The authenticated username or CallerID is used to determine which bundle to add the link to. By default, a BRI is a two-link rotary group. PRI can have up to 23 links per rotary group for T1, or 30 links for E1.

There are two types of Multilink PPP authentication: Challenge Handshake Authentication Protocol (CHAP) and Password Authentication Protocol (PAP). CHAP does not itself prevent unauthorized access. It identifies the remote connection and the router or access server determines if that user is allowed access. PAP allows peers to authenticate one another. The remote router attempting to connect to the local router is required to send an authentication request. PAP passes the password and hostname or username unencrypted. It identifies the remote connection and the router or access server determines if that user is allowed access.

Multilink PPP Configuration

When configuring Multilink PPP over ISDN, you need to specify an ISDN interface: interface bri *number*. The *number* is the interface number.

```
Vermont(config)#interface bri 0
Vermont(config-if)#ip address 10.10.10.7 255.255.255.0
Vermont(config-if)#encapsulation ppp
Vermont(config-if)#no ip route-cache
Vermont(config-if)#dialer idle-timeout 30
Vermont(config-if)#dialer map ip 10.10.10.8 name Maine
81012345678901
Vermont(config-if)#dialer group 1
Vermont(config-if)#ppp authenication pap
Vermont(config-if)#ppp multilink
Vermont(config-if)#dialer load-threshold 160 either
```

The interface is then provided with an appropriate protocol address using the IP Address command:

```
ip address ip-address mask
```

The Encapsulation PPP command enables PPP encapsulation on the interface:

```
encapsulation ppp
```

The Dialer Idle-Timeout command specifies the idle time before the line is disconnected:

```
dialer idle-timeout seconds
```

The *seconds* parameter is the time in seconds the line may remain idle before it is disconnected.

The ISDN interface must be configured to call the remote site using the `Dialer Map` command:

```
dialer map ip next-hop-address [name hostname] [dial-string]
```

The *next-hop-address* is the protocol address used to match against addresses to which packets are destined. The *hostname* is the name or ID of the remote device; this string is case sensitive. The *dial-string* is the telephone number sent to the dialing device when it recognizes packets with the specified next hop address.

Add the interface to a dialer rotary group using the `Dialer Group` command:

```
dialer group group-number
```

The *group-number* is the number of the dialer access group to which the interface belongs. You enable authentication on the ISDN interface using the `PPP Authentication` command:

```
ppp authentication {chap  pap}
```

To enable Multilink PPP on a rotary group, use the `PPP Multilink` command:

```
ppp multilink
```

The rotary group must use PPP encapsulation. The maximum number of links in a bundle is the number of interfaces in the dialer/ISDN interface.

The `Dialer Load-Threshold` command enables a rotary group to bring up links and adds the links to a Multilink bundle:

```
dialer load-threshold load [outbound  inbound  either]
```

The *load* measures bandwidth and is the interface load beyond which the dialer will initiate another call to the destination (in the range 1–255). The keyword `Outbound` is the default and indicates that the load is calculated using outbound data only.

The keyword `Inbound` indicates that the load is calculated using inbound data only. The keyword `Either` indicates that the calculated load is the maximum of either outbound or inbound traffic.

The configuration example below enables Multilink on the BRI 0 interface rotary group.

The `Dialer Load-Threshold` command sets the load value to 160 for bidirectional traffic. At that threshold value, the dialer places another call to the PPP peer. Configure dialer load threshold on only one PPP peer.

In small offices, use the `Either` option to ensure that the maximum of the inbound and outbound traffic is calculated as the load threshold. If multiple rotary groups on a router are configured for Multilink, and each rotary group dials the same destination, multiple bundles are created between the two routers.

When single multilink BRIs are calling a PRI or a rotary group with multiple BRIs, do not put a dialer load threshold on the PRI or multiple BRI rotary group. Use the `Dialer Load-Threshold` command on the single BRI interfaces to prevent attempts to bring up a third B-channel to a single BRI destination. Standard DDR configuration should be in place before configuring Multilink.

The `Show Dialer` command displays bundle information on a rotary group in the packet muxing section, including the number of members in a bundle and the bundle to which a link belongs.

```
Vermont#show dialer
BRI0 - dialer type = ISDN
Dial String      Successes      Failures      Last called    Last status
81012345678902        2            0           0:03:02        Successful
0 incoming call(s) have been screened.
BRI0: B-Channel 1
Idle timer (30 secs), Fast idle timer (20 secs)
Wait for carrier (30 secs), Re-enable (15 secs)
Time until disconnect 9 secs
Current call connected 0:03:03
Connected to 81012345678902
BRI0: B-Channel 2
Idle timer (30 secs), Fast idle timer (20 secs)
Wait for carrier (30 secs), Re-enable (15 secs)
Current call connected 0:03:04
Connected to 81012345678902
Packet Muxing
Group = 81012345678902 : No. members = 2 : Rec. seq = A : Send seq = A
Group = 81012345678902 : lost packets = 0 : Out of order = 3
Group = 81012345678902 : Unassigned = 0 : First link = BRI0: B-Channel 1
```

The `Show Interfaces` command displays Multilink status. The Multilink field shows the status as "Open" if Multilink is enabled.

```
Vermont#show interfaces b0 b1
BRI0: B-Channel 1 is up, line protocol is up
  Hardware is BRI
  MTU 1500 bytes, BW 64 Kbit, DLY 20000 usec, rely 255/255, load 1/255
  Encapsulation PPP, loopback not set, keepalive not set
  lcp      = OPEN      multilink = OPEN
  ipcp     = OPEN
  Last input 0:05:51, output 0:05:52, output hang never
  Last clearing of "show interface" counters never
  Input queue: 0/75/0 (size/max/drops); Total output drops: 0
  Output queue: 0/64/0 (size/threshold/drops)
    Conversations 0/1 (active/max active)
    Reserved Conversations 0/0 (allocated/max allocated)
    5 minute input rate 0 bits/sec, 0 packets/sec
    5 minute output rate 0 bits/sec, 0 packets/sec
    15 packets input, 804 bytes, 0 no buffer
    Received 0 broadcasts, 0 runts, 0 giants
    0 input errors, 0 CRC, 0 frame, 0 overrun, 0 ignored, 0 abort
    14 packets output, 806 bytes, 0 underruns
    0 output errors, 0 collisions, 19 interface resets, 0 restarts
    0 output buffer failures, 0 output buffers swapped out
    1 carrier transitions
```

The Debug Dialer command indicates whether the Multilink is up after authentication. The Debug PPP Multilink command displays packet sequence numbers. The Debug PPP Negotiation command displays the MRRU option negotiation.

```
Vermont#debug dialer
Vermont#ping 7.1.1.7
Type escape sequence to abort.
Sending 5, 100-byte ICMP Echos to 7.1.1.7, timeout is 2 seconds:

1:59:03: BRI0: Dialing cause: BRI0: ip PERMIT
1:59:03: BRI0: Attempting to dial 81-2345678902
%LINK-3-UPDOWN: Interface BRI0: B-Channel 1, changed state to up.!
1:59:03: BRI0: B-Channel 1: 81012345678902, multilink up, first link!!!
Success rate is 80 percent (4/5), round-trip min/avg/max = 84/112/128 ms
Vermont#
1:59:06: BRI0: rotary group to 81012345678902 overloaded (1)
1:59:06: BRI0: Attempting to dial 81012345678902
%LINK-3-UPDOWN: Interface BRI0: B-Channel 2, changed state to up
1:59:06: BRI0: B-Channel 2: 81012345678902, multilink up
!
!
Vermont#debug ppp multilink
Vermont#ping 7.1.1.7
Type escape sequence to abort.
Sending 5, 100-byte ICMP Echos to 7.1.1.7, timeout is 2 seconds:
!!!!!
Success rate is 100 percent (5/5), round-trip min/avg/max = 32/34/36 ms
Vermont#
```

```
2:00:28: MLP BRIO: B-Channel 1: 0 seq 80000000 : size 58
2:00:28: MLP BRIO: B-Channel 2: 0 seq 40000001 : size 59
2:00:28: MLP BRIO: B-Channel 2: I seq 40000001 : size 59
!
!
Vermont#debug ppp negotiation
Vermont#ping 7.1.1.7
Type escape sequence to abort.
Sending 5, 100-byte ICMP Echos to 7.1.1.7, timeout is 2 seconds:
%LINK-3-UPDOWN: Interface BRIO: B-Channel 1, changed state to up
2:02:36 ppp: sending CONFREQ, type = 11 (CI_MULTILINK_MRRU), value = 640
2:02:36 ppp: sending CONFREQ, type = 3 (CI_AUTHTYPE), value = C223/5
2:02:36 ppp: sending CONFREQ, type = 5 (CI_MAGICNUMBER), value = AC90092
2:02:36 PPP BRIO: B-Channel 1: received config for type = 0x11 (MULTILINK_MRRU)
valued = 0x640 acked
2:02:36 PPP BRIO: B-Channel 1: received config for type = 0x3 (AUTHTYPE) value =
0xC223 value = 0x5 acked
2:02:36 PPP BRIO: B-Channel 1: received config for type = 0x5 (MAGICNUMBER) value =
0x263299 acked
!
!
```

The Show PPP Multilink command displays the PPP Multilink configuration. To display specific information relating to calls on the router, use the Show Dialer command.

Let's configure the Maine router to handle Multilink PPP so it can call the Vermont router. You are logged onto the Maine router and need to enter Global Configuration mode. You do this by typing config term or configure terminal, and pressing **Enter**.

```
Maine>enable
Password:
Maine#config term
Enter configuration commands, one per line. End with CNTL/Z.
```

First, establish a username-based authentication system to be used by CHAP. Using the Username command, enter username Vermont password ver4cup. This command specifies a password for the local router or the remote device. The password can be a string up to 11 printable ASCII characters.

```
Maine(config)#username Vermont password ver4cup
```

To define the ISDN switch on the network, use the ISDN Switch-Type command. This defines the ISDN central office switch using the standard NorTel DMS-100 switch.

```
Maine(config)#isdn switch-type basic-dms100
```

Type `interface ethernet 0` to configure Ethernet 0. Next, use the `IP Address` command to provide the appropriate protocol address for the interface.

```
Maine(config)#interface ethernet 0
Maine(config-if)#ip address 172.16.1.1 255.255.255.0
```

Now enter Interface Configuration mode for the ISDN basic rate interface. Type `encapsulation ppp` to set the encapsulation method to PPP. A protocol address is then set for the BRI 0 interface.

```
Maine(config-if)#interface bri 0
Maine(config-if)#encapsulation ppp
Maine(config-if)#ip address 172.16.46.1 255.255.255.0
```

To configure the ISDN lines, use the `ISDN Spid1` and `ISDN Spid2` commands. These will define at the router the service profile identifier (SPID) number assigned by the ISDN service provider for the B1 and B2 channels. The `ISDN Spid1` and `ISDN Spid2` commands are not always necessary, depending on the switch type.

```
Maine(config-if)#isdn spid1 8064223
Maine(config-if)#isdn spid2 8064324
```

To enable a rotary group to bring up links and add the links to a Multilink bundle, use the `Dialer Load-Threshold` command.

Here you can see the command to set the load value to 128 for bidirectional traffic.

```
Maine(config-if)#dialer load-threshold 128 either
```

To specify a period of time (in seconds) during which the line can remain idle before disconnection, use the `Dialer Idle-Timeout` command. Here, the time is set to 60 seconds.

```
Maine(config-if)#dialer idle-timeout
```

The `ISDN Caller` command configures ISDN caller screening on specified numbers.

```
Maine(config-if)#isdn caller 8064325
Maine(config-if)#isdn caller 8064326
```

Type ppp multilink to enable Multilink PPP on the ISDN interface. The PPP Authentication command enables CHAP authentication on the interface.

```
Maine(config-if)#ppp multilink
Maine(config-if)#ppp authentication chap
```

To configure the Maine ISDN interface to a particular site, use the Dialer Map command. This command will configure the interface to call the Vermont router.

```
Maine(config-if)#dialer map ip 172.16.46.2 name Vermont 8064325
```

The Dialer Group command controls access to the dialer access group to which the interface belongs. Type exit to return to Global Configuration mode.

```
Maine(config-if)#dialer group 1
Maine(config-if)#exit
```

The Dialer-List command defines the access group to control dialing by protocol or by a combination of protocol and access list. Typing dialer-list 1 protocol ip permit, controls dialing by means of the IP protocol in dialer group 1.

```
Maine(config)#dialer-list protocol ip permit
```

The IP Route command establishes static routes on the router. Press **Ctrl+Z** to exit Global Configuration mode.

```
Maine(config)#ip route 172.16.0.0 255.255.0.0 172.16.46.2
Maine(config)#ip route 0.0.0.0 0.0.0.0 172.16.46.2
Maine(config)#^Z
Ldonon#
```

The Copy Running-Config command specifies the currently running configuration as the destination of the copy operation.

```
Maine#copy running-config startup-config
Building configuration...
[OK]
Maine#
```

You can now check your Multilink configuration by typing show ppp multilink.

```
Maine#show ppp multilink
Bundle Vermont, 1 member, first link is BRI0: B-Channel 1
   0 lost fragments, 0 reordered, 0 unassigned, sequence 0x0/0x0
recvd/sent
Maine#
```

To display specific information relating to calls on the router, use the Show Dialer command. One incoming call was made to the Maine router. This call originated in Vermont.

```
Maine#show dialer
BRI0 - dialer type = ISDN
Dial String      Successes        Failures        Last called      Last status
8064325              0                0             never
1 incoming call(s) has been screened.
BRI0: B-Channel 1
Idle timer (60 secs), Fast idle timer (20 secs)
Wait for carrier (30 secs), Re-enable (15 secs)
Time until disconnect 59 secs
Connected to 8064325 (Vermont)
BRI0: B-Channel 2
Idle timer (60 secs), Fast idle timer (20 secs)
Wait for carrier (30 secs), Re-enable (15 secs)
Maine#
```

 ## PPP Callback

This section describes how PPP Callback operates. We will examine PPP Callback, describe how to configure PPP Callback on an ISDN interface, and configure PPP Callback on an ISDN interface.

Introduction to PPP Callback

PPP Callback is initiated by the PPP LCP Callback request option (RFC 1570) and is implemented over dial-up interfaces with PPP encapsulation. PPP Callback permits a Cisco router to operate as either a Callback server that answers the initial call and makes the return call if properly configured or as a Callback client that makes the initial call and requests to be called back. A router acting as a Callback server must be able to recognize that a callback is desired, terminate the current connection, and initiate a connection back to the caller.

Using PPP Callback at a remote site, a Callback client calls a Callback server to initiate the callback sequence. The Callback client requests callback and waits for the server to disconnect. The Callback server acknowledges the callback request and checks its configuration to verify that Callback is enabled. If the Callback server accepts the option and authentication is successful, the server decides whether to maintain the initial call, disconnect the initial call, or disconnect and callback.

The Callback client and server can authenticate using either CHAP or PAP authentication. The username is used to identify the dial string for the return call. After successful initial authentication, the Callback server identifies the callback dial string and compares the username of the authentication to the hostname in a dialer map table.

The dial string can be identified by a mapping table or by the Callback OptionMessage field during the PPP LCP negotiations. The Callback Option-Message field is defined in RFC 1570. The PPP Callback client does not support callback via dial string.

If Dialer Callback-Secure, PPP Callback Accept, and CHAP/PAP authentication are enabled on an interface, all calls answered on that interface are disconnected after authentication.

If Callback is enabled on the Callback server, a series of steps are carried out. The Callback server disconnects the initiating call. It then uses the dial string to initiate the callback; if the return call fails, no additional calls are attempted (Callback is not negotiated on the return call). After the call is authenticated, the Callback server then calls the Callback client.

If Dialer Callback-Secure, PPP Callback Accept, and CHAP/PAP authentication are not enabled, the Callback server maintains the initial call if the authenticated username is not configured for callback.

PPP Callback provides the following important benefits: improved network security, remote connections made to preconfigured call client numbers, managed telephone expenses, making the call and paying for the connection time, and enhanced telecommuting connectivity. When added security is necessary and telephone expenses are billed directly to the company, you can configure PPP Callback to call predetermined telephone numbers.

PPP Callback Configuration

The configuration for either a Callback server or a Callback client involves entering several commands in Interface Configuration mode. Assume an ISDN central office switch is defined on the basic rate interface using the ISDN Switch-Type command.

```
Vermont(config)# interface bri 0
```

An appropriate protocol address for the interface is then provided using the IP Address command. PPP Encapsulation is enabled on the interface using the Encapsulation PPP command.

```
Vermont(config-if)# ip address 10.1.1.7 255.255.255.0
Vermont(config-if)# encapsulation ppp
```

Whether the router is a Callback server or a Callback client, it must be able to place calls to another site. The Dialer Map command configures the router to make calls: dialer map *protocol next-hop-address* [name *hostname*] [*dial-string*].

```
Vermont(config-if)# dialer map ip 10.1.1.8 name Maine class dial1
5678
```

The *protocol* can be any one of the following protocol keywords: appletalk, bridge, clns, clns_es, clns_is, decnet, decnet_router-L1, decnet_router-L2, decnet_node, ip, ipx, vines, or xns.

The *next-hop-address* is the protocol address used to match against addresses to which packets are destined. The next-hop-address parameter is not used with the Bridge protocol keyword.

The keyword Name indicates the remote system that the local router is communicating with. The *hostname* is a case-sensitive name or ID of the remote system.

The *dial-string* is the telephone number sent to the dialing device when packets are recognized with the specified next hop address that matches the access lists defined.

To control access to the interface, use the Dialer Group command: dialer-group *group-number*. The *group-number* is the number of the dialer access group to which the interface belongs.

```
Vermont(config-if)# dialer group 1
```

A router interface operating as a Callback server must be able to accept calls from a particular site. Likewise, a Callback client has to be able to request calls from a particular site.

The PPP Callback command defines whether the router operates as a Callback server or as a Callback client: ppp callback {accept   request}.

```
Vermont(config-if)# ppp callback accept
```

The keyword `Accept` enables the interface to accept callback requests (and function as a Callback server).

The keyword `Request` enables the interface to request callback (and function as a Callback client). In this example, the interface operates as a Callback server.

There are two methods of authentication that can be used when configuring PPP Callback: CHAP and PAP.

```
Vermont(config-if)# ppp authentication chap
```

The `PPP Authentication` command enables authentication on the interface:

```
ppp authentication {chap pap}
```

There are two extra `Interface Configuration` commands used when configuring a Callback server: `Dialer Callback-Secure` and `Dialer Callback-Server`.

```
Vermont(config-if)# dialer callback-secure
Vermont(config-if)# dialer callback-server username
Vermont(config-if)# exit
```

The `Dialer Callback-Secure` disconnects the initial call by the Callback server after authentication is successful. This command also disconnects calls which are not properly configured for callback.

The interface must be able to return calls when callback is successfully negotiated. This is done using the `Dialer Callback-Server` command:

```
dialer callback-server [username  dialstring]
```

The keyword `Username` identifies the return call by looking up the authenticated hostname in a `Dialer Map` command. The keyword `Dialstring` identifies the return call during callback negotiation.

The `Map-Class` command is an additional `Global Configuration` command used when configuring the Callback server.

```
Vermont(config)# map-class dialer dial1
```

To define a class of shared configuration parameters associated with the `Dialer Map` command, use the `Map-Class Dialer` command:

```
map-class dialer classname
```

The *classname* is the unique class identifier.

The Dialer-List command defines the access group to control dialing by protocol or a combination of protocol and access list for the Callback server or client: dialer-list *dialer-group* protocol *protocol-name* {permit deny}.

```
Vermont(config)#dialer-list 1 protocol ip permit
```

The *dialer-group* is the number of a dialer access group identified in any Dialer-Group command.

The *protocol-name* can be any one of the following protocol keywords: appletalk, bridge, clns, clns_es, clns_is, decnet, decnet_router-L1, decnet_router-L2, decnet_node, ip, ipx, vines, or xns.

The keyword Permit allows access to an entire protocol. The keyword Deny blocks access to an entire protocol.

Static routes can be established on the interface using the IP Route command.

The Hold-Queue Timeout on the Callback server is the number of seconds that the router holds packets waiting for the return callback connection. If the Callback client's hold queue is configured, all packets destined for the Callback server are queued until the callback from the server is made.

When the client router dials the initial call, the router's hold-queue timer is started. No calls to this destination will be made again until the hold-queue timer expires.

The server must make the return call before the client hold-queue timer expires to prevent the client from trying again. Another attempted call from the client could prevent the return call from being connected. The timer is stopped if PPP NCP negotiation is successful or if the call fails. The client hold queue should be approximately four times longer than the callback server's callback timer.

The Enable Timeout on the Callback server is the number of seconds between the disconnection of the initial call and the server's making the callback. This interval must be long enough to guarantee that the initial call has been completely disconnected.

For rotary groups, including ISDN, if the enable time is long and another user dials into the last interface before the enable timer expires, the return call will never be made. If an interesting packet arrives at the server during the enable time the dialer may use the last interface for the interesting packet and the return call will never be made.

The Debug Dialer and the Debug PPP Negotiation commands are used to monitor PPP Callback.

Let's configure the basic rate interface on the Maine router to handle PPP Callback. Maine will be the PPP Callback server and Vermont the Callback client.

You are logged onto the Maine router and need to enter Global Configuration mode. Do this by typing `config term` or `configure terminal`, and pressing **Enter**.

```
Maine>enable
Password:
Maine#config term
Enter configuration commands, one per line. End with CNTL/Z.
Maine(config)#
```

To define the ISDN switch on the network, use the `ISDN Switch-Type` command. This defines the ISDN central office switch using the standard NorTel DMS-100 switch.

```
Maine(config)#isdn switch-type basic-dms100
```

Type `interface bri 0` to configure the basic rate interface. Next, provide the appropriate protocol address for the interface using the `IP Address` command.

```
Maine(config)#interface bri 0
Maine(config-if)#ip address 172.16.46.1 255.255.255.0
```

Type `encapsulation ppp` to set the encapsulation method to PPP.

```
Maine(config-if)#encapsulation ppp
```

The `Dialer Callback-Secure` command ensures the initial call is disconnected by the Callback server after authentication.

```
Maine(config-if)#dialer callback-secure
```

Now you need to configure the interface to accept calls from a particular site (in this case, Vermont). To do this, use the `Dialer Map` command.

```
Maine(config-if)#dialer map ip 172.16.46.2 name Vermont class
dial1 8064325
```

The `Dialer Group` command controls access to the dialer access group to which the specific interface belongs.

```
Maine(config-if)#dialer group 1
```

Now configure the interface on the Maine router to function as a Callback server by typing `ppp callback accept`. Type `ppp authentication chap` to specify CHAP authentication on the interface.

```
Maine(config-if)#ppp callback accept
Maine(config-if)#ppp authentication chap
```

Before exiting Interface Configuration mode, you need to enable the interface to return calls when callback is successfully negotiated.

To do this, use the `Dialer Callback-Server` command. Type `exit` to return to Global Configuration mode.

```
Maine(config-if)#dialer callback-server username
Maine(config-if)#exit
```

To define a class of shared configuration parameters associated with the `Dialer Map` command, use the `Map-Class` command.

```
Maine(config)#map-class dialer dial1
```

The `Dialer-List` command defines the access group to control dialing by protocol or a combination of protocol and access list. Typing `dialer-list 1 protocol ip permit` causes dialing to be controlled by the IP protocol in dialer group 1.

```
Maine(config)#dialer-list 1 protocol ip permit
```

The `IP Route` command establishes static routes on the router. Press **Ctrl+Z** to exit Global Configuration mode.

```
Maine(config)#ip route 172.16.0.0 255.255.0.0 172.16.46.2
Maine(config)#ip route 0.0.0.0 0.0.0.0 172.16.46.2
Maine(config)#^Z
Maine#
```

To monitor the PPP Callback sequence, use the `Debug Dialer` command.

```
Maine#debug dialer
%LINK-3-UPDOWN: Interface BRI0: B-Channel 1, changed state to up
3:24:02: BRI0: B-Channel 1: disconnecting call
%LINK-3-UPDOWN: Interface BRI0: B-Channel 1, changed state to
down
3:24:02: BRI0: B-Channel 1: disconnecting call
3:24:18: Callback timer expired
3:24:18: BRI0: Attempting to call 8064323
```

```
$LINK-3-UPDOWN: Interface BRI0: B-Channel 1, changed state to up
3:24:18: BRI0: B-Channel 1: No callback negotiated
3:24:18: BRI0: B-Channel 1: 8064323, multilink up, first link
%LINKPROTO-5-UPDOWN: Line protocol on Interface BRI0:
B-Channel 1, changed state to up
%ISDN-6-CONNECT: Interface BRI0: B-Channel 1 is now
connected to 8064325
```

As you can see, Maine (the Callback server) has received a call from Vermont (the Callback client). The Callback server then disconnects the call. The Callback server's timer (the number of seconds the server waits before making the callback) expires. By default, the callback timer on the server is set to 15 seconds. For ISDN interfaces, the default setting is 5 seconds. The Callback server now calls the Callback client.

Finally, we see a connection has been established between the Callback server and the Callback client.

The "No" version of the Debug Dialer command will disable debugging on the interface.

```
Maine#no debug dialer
```

Configuring PPP Callback

Now we will configure the basic rate interface on the Vermont router to handle PPP Callback. Vermont will be the PPP Callback client and Maine the Callback server.

You are logged onto the Vermont router and need to enter Global Configuration mode. Do this by typing config term or configure terminal, and pressing **Enter**.

```
Vermont>enable
Password:
Vermont#config term
Enter configuration commands, one per line. End with CNTL/Z.
Vermont(config)#
```

The ISDN Switch-Type command defines the ISDN switch on the network. The ISDN central office switch is defined using the standard NorTel DMS-100 switch.

```
Vermont(config)#isdn switch-type basic-dms100
```

Type interface bri 0 to configure the basic rate interface on the Vermont router.

```
Vermont(config)#interface bri 0
```

Now configure the interface to call a particular site (in this case, Maine). To do this, use the `Dialer Map` command.

```
Vermont(config-if)#dialer map ip 172.16.46.1 name Maine 8064323
```

Type `encapsulation ppp` to set the encapsulation method to PPP. Next, provide the appropriate protocol address for the interface using the `IP Address` command.

```
Vermont(config-if)#encapsulation ppp
Vermont(config-if)#ip address 172.16.42.2 255.255.255.0
```

The interface is configured on the Vermont router to function as a Callback client by typing `ppp callback request`.

```
Vermont(config-if)#ppp callback request
```

To specify CHAP authentication on the interface, type `ppp authentication chap`.

```
Vermont(config-if)#ppp authentication chap
```

The `Dialer Group` command controls access to the dialer access group to which the specific interface belongs. Type `exit` to return to Global Configuration mode.

```
Vermont(config-if)#dialer group 1
Vermont(config-if)#exit
Vermont(config)#
```

Typing `dialer-list 1 protocol ip permit` causes dialing to be controlled by the IP protocol in dialer group 1.

```
Vermont(config)#dialer-list 1 protocol ip permit
```

The `IP Route` command establishes static routes on the router. Press **Ctrl+Z** to exit Global Configuration mode.

```
Vermont(config)#ip route 172.16.1.0 255.255.255.0 172.16.46.1
Vermont(config)#^Z
```

The `Copy Running-Config` command copies the currently running configuration into `startup-config`. The next time the router is brought up, this configuration will be loaded in `startup-config`.

```
Vermont#copy running-config startup-config
Building configuration...
[OK]
Vermont#
```

To monitor the PPP Callback sequence, use the `Debug Dialer` command.

```
Vermont#debug dialer
%LINK-3-UPDOWN: Interface BRI0: B-Channel 1, changed state to up
3:24:02: BRI0: B-Channel 1 :disconnecting call
%LINK-3-UPDOWN: Interface BRI0: B-Channel 1, changed state to
down
3:24:02: BRI0: B-Channel 1: disconnecting call
3:24:18: Callback timer expired
3:24:18: BRI0: Attempting to call 8064323
$LINK-3-UPDOWN Interface BRI0: B-Channel 1, changed state to up
3:24:38: BRI0: B-Channel 1: No callback negotiated
3:24:38: BRI0: B-Channel 1: 8064323, multilink up, first link
%LINEPROTO-5-UPDOWN: Line protocol on Interface BRI0:
B-Channel 1, changed state to up
%ISDN-6-CONNECT: Interface BRI0: B-Channel 1 is now
connected to 8064323
Vermont#
```

By typing `no debug dialer`, you disable debugging on the interface.

```
Vermont#no debug dialer
```

NetBEUI over PPP

This section describes how the Network Basic Extended User Interface (NetBEUI) over PPP operates. We will discuss the configuration commands necessary to enable NetBEUI over PPP and describe the commands used to monitor NetBEUI over PPP operation.

Introduction to NetBEUI over PPP

NetBEUI is a networking protocol developed by IBM for use by PCs in a LAN environment. It is an extension of the IBM original Network Basic Input/Output System (NetBIOS).

NetBEUI resolves NetBIOS names to physical (hardware) 802.x addresses using a broadcast mechanism. A physical 802.3 address is an Ethernet address and a physical 802.5 address is a token ring address. NetBIOS communicates using names. However, these names have to be resolved to physical 802.x addresses because machines only communicate using these addresses.

NetBEUI uses broadcasts in order to find out 802.x addresses. For example, if Machine 1 wanted to send data to Machine 2, it would broadcast a request for Machine 2 to send its 802.x address.

NetBEUI is a nonroutable protocol, because it has no network layer. The traditional approach to networking with NetBEUI is to bridge it or to encapsulate it in IP or IPX. To negotiate NetBEUI specifics over the PPP link, Microsoft has developed the NetBIOS Frames Control Protocol (NBFCP) PPP Control Protocol.

NetBEUI over PPP allows remote NetBEUI users to access LAN-based NetBEUI services without protocol conversion. The PPP link becomes the ramp for the remote node to access NetBIOS services on the LAN.

An LLC2 connection is set up on the PPP link and a second LLC2 connection is set up between the Cisco router and the NetBEUI server. NetBEUI over PPP enables a Cisco access server to be a native NetBEUI dial-in access server for remote NetBEUI clients. Before Cisco supported NetBEUI over PPP, Cisco access servers provided remote access to NetBIOS networks using IP or IPX.

As telecommuting and remote access become more popular, customers offer remote access to their NetBEUI network by means of dial-in telephone lines or ISDN connections. The Microsoft response to the increased need for remote access is Remote Access Client (RAS client) with Windows NT, Windows for Workgroups, and Windows 95.

RAS clients connect to RAS servers that are usually running Windows NT Advanced Server with multiple async or ISDN ports connected to modems. RAS clients and servers support the following protocol stack variations: NetBEUI/PPP, IPX PPP, NetBIOS/IPX/PPP, and TCP/IP PPP.

NetBEUI over PPP Configuration

When you are configuring NetBEUI over PPP, the NetBIOS NBF command enables NetBIOS Frame Protocol on each NetBEUI interface. Let's say, for example, that one interface is named "async 6". In this case you would enter the code shown below. For the second interface, you would enter the code shown. The "No" version of the NetBIOS NBF command will disable NetBIOS Frame support.

```
(config)#interface async 6
(config-if)#netbios nbf
(config-if)#interface ethernet 0
(config-if)#netbios nbf
```

There are a number of related Global Configuration commands for Net-
BEUI over PPP. You can define the offset and hexadecimal patterns with
which to match byte offset in NetBIOS packets. To do this, use the
NetBIOS Access-List Bytes command:

```
netbios access-list bytes name {deny  permit} offset pattern
```

The *name* is the name of the access list being defined. The keywords Deny
or Permit determine whether access is blocked or allowed.

The *offset* is a decimal number indicating the number of bytes into the
packet where the byte comparison should begin. The *pattern* is a hexadecimal string of digits representing a byte pattern.

You can also assign the name of the access list to a station or set of stations using the NetBIOS Access-List Host command:

```
netbios access-list host name {deny  permit} pattern
```

The *pattern* is a set of characters which can be the name of the station,
or a combination of characters and pattern-matching symbols identifying a
set of NetBIOS station names.

You can set a timer on the router which will drop any duplicate
Add_Name_Query, Add_Group_Name, or Status_Query frames. The time
specified is called the "dead" time. It starts when a host sends any
Add_Name_Query, Add_Group_Name, or Status_Query frames. To set the
"dead" timer, use the NetBIOS Name-Cache Query-Timeout command:

```
netbios name-cache recognized-timeout seconds
```

The *seconds* parameter is the "dead" time period in seconds (the default
is 6 seconds).

Use the NetBIOS Name-Cache Timeout command to enable NetBIOS
name caching. This command also sets the time that entries can remain in
the NetBIOS name cache:

```
netbios name-cache timeout minutes
```

The *minutes* parameter is the time period in minutes that entries can
remain in the NetBIOS name cache; when the time expires, the entry will be
deleted from the cache.

There are three commands you can use to monitor NetBEUI over PPP functionality: Show NBF Sessions, Show NetBIOS-Cache, and Show LLC2.

The Show NBF Sessions command displays the Async NetBIOS Session Table.

```
Vermont#show nbf sessions
Async6 NetBIOS Sessions Table:
Srcnum     Destnum    Dest-Interface DestMAC
8          6          Ethernet0 00aa.005b.c17b
3          4          Ethernet0 00aa.005b.c17b
Async7 NetBIOS Session Table:
Srcnum     Destnum    Dest-Interface DestMAC
7          5          Ethernet0 00aa.005b.c05f
9          10         Ethernet0 00aa.005b.c05f
!
!
```

The Async NetBIOS Session Table contains the following NetBIOS connection information: the source and destination NetBIOS connection numbers, the connection's interface, and the connection's MAC address.

In this example, the Async6 interface has two pairs of connections. Packets that come in on Async6 port are sent out the Ethernet0 interface.

The NetBIOS Global LAN Session Table summarizes all NetBIOS connection information.

```
NetBIOS LAN Session Table:
Srcnum     Destnum    Dest-Interface DestMAC     Src-Interface SrcMac(I)
6          8          Async6 0000.0000.0000      Ethernet0 00aa.005b.c17b(95)
4          3          Async6 0000.0000.0000      Ethernet0 00aa.005b.c17b(95)
5          7          Async7 0000.0000.0000      Ethernet0 00aa.005b.c05f(95)
10         9          Async7 0000.0000.0000      Ethernet0 00aa.005b.c05f(95)
ADD_[GROUP]NAME_QUERY queuesize=0
STATUS_QUERY queuesize=0
STATUS_RESPONSE queuesize=0
NAME_QUERY queuesize=0
NAME_RECOGNIZED queuesize=0
SESSION_INITIALIZE queuesize=0
SESSION_INITIALIZE (pending) queuesize=0
```

A summary of the NetBIOS datagram queues follows the NetBIOS Global LAN Session Table.

To display a list of NetBIOS cache entries, use the Show NetBIOS-Cache command. HW Addr is the MAC address mapped to the NetBIOS name in this entry. Name is the NetBIOS name mapped to the MAC address in this entry.

```
Vermont#show netbios-cache
HW Addr          Name      How      Idle     NetBIOS Packet Savings
1000.5a89.449a   IKBA      E0       6        0
0000.0000.0000   NANOO     async1   21       0
!
!
```

How is the interface through which this information was learned.

Idle is the period of time (in seconds) since this entry was last accessed; a hyphen indicates a static entry in the NetBIOS name cache. NetBIOS Packet Savings is the number of packets to which local replies were made (thus preventing transmission of these packets over the network).

The Show LLC2 command displays the LLC2 connections active in the router.

```
Vermont#show llc2
LLC2 Connections:
Ethernet0 DTE: 00aa.005b.c05f 0000.0000.0000.0000 F0 F0 state NORMAL
   V(S)=101, V(R)=94, Last N(R)=101, Local Window=8, Remote Window=127
   akmax=3, n2=8, Next timer in 2048
    xid-retry timer  57828/60000    ack timer       0/1000
    p timer              0/1000     idle timer   2048/10000
    rej timer            0/3200     busy timer      0/9600
    akdelay timer         0/100     txQ count        0/200
Async7 DTE: 0000.0000.0000.0000.0000.0000 FO FO state NORMAL
   V(S)=94, V(R)=101, Last N(R)=94, Local Window=7, Remote Window=127
   akmax=3, n2=8, Next timer in 1424
    xid-retry timer  57808/60000    ack timer       0/1000
    p timer              0/1000     idle timer  10432/10000
    rej timer            0/3200     busy timer      0/9600
    akdelay timer         0/100     txQ count        0/200
```

Use various LLC2 Interface command options to configure NBFCP negotiable parameters. n2 is the number of times the router should retry various operations.

There are additional LLC2 Interface command options you can use to configure NBFCP negotiable parameters. *dynwind* is a congestion control with a dynamic window. *t1-time* is the amount of time the router waits for an acknowledgment to transmitted I-frames. *tpf-time* is the amount of time the router waits for a final response to a poll frame before re-sending the original poll frame. *xid-neg-val-time* is the frequency of exchange of identification (XID).

akdelay timer is the maximum time the router allows incoming I-frames to stay unacknowledged. Akmax is the maximum number of I-frames received before an acknowledgment must be sent.

idle timer is the frequency of polls during periods of idle traffic. *Local Window* is the maximum number of I-frames to send before waiting for an acknowledgment.

busy timer is the amount of time the router waits while the other LLC2 station is in busy state before attempting to poll the remote station.

rej timer is the amount of time the router waits for a re-send of a rejected frame before sending the reject command.

txQ count is the queue for holding LLC2 information frames. *xid-retry timer* is the amount of time the router waits for a reply to an exchange of identification (XID).

The Clear Line command will clear a transmission line on an interface or shut down an interface: clear line *line-number*. The *line-number* is the asynchronous interface number.

```
Vermont#clear line 7
%LINEPROTO-5-UPDOWN: Line protocol on Interface Async7, changed state to down
%LINK-5-CHANGED: Interface Async7, changed state to reset
nbf nbf_cleanup_11c idb=Async7
nbf Hash table entry freed: srcnum=5 dstnum=7 srcidb=Ethernet0 dstidb=Async7
srcmac=00aa.005b.c05f dstmac-0000.0000.0000
Async7 nbf session entry freed: srcnum=7 dstnum=5 dstidb=Ethernet0
dstmac=00aa.005b.c05f
nbf Hash table entry freed: srcnum=8 dstnum=10 srcidb=Ethernet0 dstidb=Async7
srcmac=00aa.005b.c05f dstmac=0000.0000.0000
Async7 nbf session entry freed: srcnum=10 dstnum=8 dstidb=Ethernet0
dstmac=00aa.005b.c05f
%LINK-3-UPDOWN: Interface Async7, changed state to down
```

When an interface resets, a NetBIOS session end is sent to the corresponding session in the Async, Ethernet, or Token Ring interface. The session information in the session tables is removed, informing the end-to-end NetBIOS session of the session termination.

The Debug NetBIOS Packet command is used to troubleshoot NetBEUI over PPP. It displays NetBEUI over PPP debugging information.

```
Vermont#debug netbios packet
NETBIOS: NetBIOS packet display debugging is on
Async1 (i) U-format UI C_R=0x0
(i) NETBIOS_ADD_NAME_QUERY
Resp_correlator= 0x6F 0x0
Src name=CS-NT-1
Async1 (i) U-format UI C_R=0x0
(i) NETBIOS_ADD_GROUP_QUERY
Resp_correlator= 0x6F 0x0
Src name=COMMSERVER-WG
Async1 (i) U-format UI C_R=0x0
(i) NETBIOS_ADD_NAME_QUERY
```

```
Resp_correlator= 0x6F 0x0
Src name=CS-NT-1
Ethernet0 (i) U-format UI C_R=0x0
(i) NETBIOS_DATAGRAM
Length= 0x2C 0x0
Dest name=COMMSERVER-WG
Src name=CS-NT-3
```

In the above example, the following NetBIOS packet types are displayed:
`NETBIOS_ADD_NAME_QUERY`, `NETBIOS_ADD_GROUP_QUERY`, and
`NETBIOS_DATAGRAM`.

CHAPTER 22

ISDN
Configuration

Introduction to ISDN

This section gives an overview of ISDN services, operation, and capabilities. We will describe ISDN devices, functions, and reference points, explain how ISDN operates, and describe the ISDN facilities available when Cisco routers are used.

ISDN Services

Integrated Services Digital Network (ISDN) is a circuit-switched WAN technology that involves the digitization of the telephone network through the use of a set of communication protocols. It allows the communication of data, voice, text, graphics, music, and video. ISDN was developed by the Consultative Committee for International Telegraph and Telephone (CCITT)—the precursor to the International Telecommunication Union Telecommunication Standardization Sector (ITU-T)—and Bell Laboratories.

Developers proposed a set of integrated services using a limited, defined set of standardized user-to-network interfaces and network and internetwork capabilities. Despite standardization of ISDN services, ISDN providers such as national Postal Telephones and Telegraphs authorities (PTTs) use a variety of switch types across different regions. A switch is an electronic or mechanical device that establishes and terminates session connections. In the US and Canada the switch types commonly used are *AT&T 5ESS* and *4ESS* and *Northern Telecom DMS-100*. In the United Kingdom the switch types are *Net3* and *Net5*. In France switch types are *VN2* and *VN3*, in Australia *TS-013*, and in Japan *NTT*. You need to know what switch type is used at your network's central office (CO) so that your router can place ISDN network-level calls and send data.

Many carriers are now offering ISDN services under tariff. ISDN is considered a useful alternative to frame relay and T1 wide-area telephone services (WATS).

The ISDN bearer (B) channel sends user data at 64 Kbps and is known as a *full-duplex channel*. The term "full duplex" means that the channel is capable of the simultaneous transmission of data between sending and receiving stations. By running multiple B channels, ISDN offers its users a large amount of telecommuting bandwidth.

ISDN has become one of the leading technologies for facilitating telecommuting. Its applications include high-speed image transmission; file transfer; video conferencing; internetworking for small, remote offices; and multiple home links for telecommuters.

ISDN is helping to promote worldwide connectivity through standardization and continuously declining prices. It is now particularly popular for applications using remote connectivity, Internet access, and the World Wide Web.

ISDN operates services over two main interface types: Basic Rate and Primary Rate. The *Basic Rate Interface (BRI)* offers two bearer (B) channels (2B) and one data (D) channel (+D). With BRI the B channel is a full-duplex, 64-Kbps ISDN channel that carries user data. The D channel is a full-duplex 16-Kbps channel that carries control and signaling information. With some service providers it can also be used to carry packet-switched user data. The D channel signaling protocol comprises the physical, data-link, and network layers of the OSI model. BRI also provides for framing control and other overheads. This brings its total bit rate to 192 Kbps.

The *Primary Rate Interface (PRI)* service is different depending on the region in which it is operating. In North America and Japan it consists of 23 B channels for voice or data and a single 64-Kbps D channel, known as a *T1/DS1 facility*. In Europe and elsewhere in the world the PRI consists of a single 64-Kbps D channel and 30 B channels for voice or data (an E1 facility). PRI uses a data service unit/channel service unit (DSU/CSU) for T1/E1 connection. A CSU is a digital interface device connecting data terminal equipment (DTE) to the local digital telephone loop. A DSU is used in digital transmission that adapts the physical interface on a DTE device to a transmission facility such as T1 or E1.

There are regional differences in who provides key ISDN functions and where ISDN equipment is located. In North America and Japan, the PRI interfaces to a DSU/CSU are provided by the end-user. In Europe and many other parts of the world, the DSU/CSU is part of the ISDN service provider's equipment.

ITU-T standardization has organized the ISDN protocols into groups according to different topics. The *E-series protocols* deal with telephone network standards for ISDN. For example E.163 describes the international telephone numbering plan. E.164 describes international ISDN addressing.

The *I-series protocols* deal with concepts, terminology, and interfaces: for example, the I.100 series deals with general concepts, I.200 deals with services aspects, I.300 describes network aspects, and I.400 deals with User-Network interfaces. The BRI physical-layer specification is I.430 and the PRI physical layer specification is I.431.

The *Q-series protocols* cover switching and call set processes. For example, Q.931 specifies functions that occur at the OSI network layer. Q.931 recommends a network layer between the terminal endpoint and the local ISDN switch. Different ISDN providers and switch types use different implementations of Q.931.

Functions and Reference Points

There are several different devices with associated functions that you may use as part of your ISDN network. There are two basic terminal equipment types: *Type 1 (TE1)* and *Type 2 (TE2)*.

TE1 is a specialized or "native" ISDN terminal, including equipment or telephones used to connect to ISDN through a four-wire, twisted-pair cable digital link. *TE2* is a non-ISDN terminal, such as a DTE that predates the ISDN standard and needs a terminal adapter (TA) to connect it to ISDN.

A TA can be either a standalone device or a board inside the TE2. The terminal adapter has the function of converting EIA/TIA-232-C, V.24, and V.35 physical interface signals into BRI signals.

After the TE1 and TE2 devices, the next connection point in the ISDN network is the *network termination (NT) device*. This converts BRI signals into a form that can be used by the ISDN digital line. NT devices connect the four-wire subscriber wiring to the conventional two-wire local loop. The NT device takes three forms: Type 1 (NT1), Type 2 (NT2), and NT Type 1/2 (NT1/2).

An NT1 device is customer-premises equipment in North America but is carrier-provided equipment elsewhere. An NT2 is a more complex device used on digital private branch exchanges (PBXs) that provides both data-link and network-layer functions as well as concentration services. *Concentration* refers to the process by which a network device repeats signals sent through it. An NT1/2 device combines the features of NT1 and NT2 devices and is compatible with both.

Other devices and their functions include local termination (LT) where a portion of the local exchange that terminates the local loop and exchange termination (ET) communicates with other ISDN components.

The ITU-T defines the local loop of an ISDN network by specifying five reference points that refer to the interfaces between different ISDN devices.

Each of the reference points has a letter: *R* defines the interface between non-ISDN equipment and a TA, *S* defines the interface between users' terminals and network terminating equipment (NT1/NT2), *T* defines the interface between NT1 and NT2 devices, *U* defines the interface between NT1 devices and line-termination equipment in a carrier network (only in North America), and *V* defines the interface between LT and ET devices.

As network administrator, you have to be aware of the devices your router requires to access ISDN. You need to look at the back of your router to see if your router needs a TA. If you see a connector labeled BRI, your router is a native ISDN TE1 that already contains the ISDN TA function. If there is no BRI connector, your router has a non-native ISDN interface and is a TE2. Usually this router will have a serial interface labeled S0. You will need to attach an external TA to the serial interface to provide a BRI interface. Whether your router is a TE1 or a TE2, you will need an external NT1 which will terminate the local loop of wires to the central office of your ISDN provider.

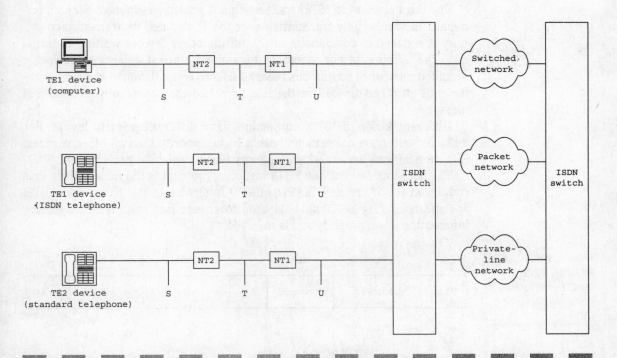

FIGURE 22.1   *Sample ISDN configuration illustrates relationships between devices and reference points.*

ISDN Operation

At the physical layer, ISDN transmission has three basic operational stages. The first is the *contention* process through which end devices can check when other devices are transmitting. When an NT device receives a bit over the D channel from a TE, it echoes E bits along the D channel. The TE listens to determine whether its own transmission is echoed. By the contention process, multiple ISDN user devices can be physically attached to a single ISDN link. The contention process allows them to check when the channel is free for transmission.

The second part of the transmission process, *D channel transmission*, begins once a terminal has determined that no other signals are being transmitted. By checking the E channel, the terminal transmits through the D channel when other terminals are not transmitting. As soon as the TE device detects a bit in the E channel that is different from its own D bits, it stops transmitting.

The third element in ISDN transmission is *priority negotiation*. When a terminal has successfully transmitted over the D channel, its transmission priority is reduced in comparison to that of the other devices waiting to transmit. The terminal is not permitted to transmit until it detects a previously specified number of continuous binary 1s. The terminal cannot raise its priority until all other devices on the line have had the opportunity to send a D message.

Different kinds of ISDN equipment have different priority levels. For instance, telephone connections have a higher priority than all other services. Signaling information has a higher priority than non-signaling information.

The data-link layer of the ISDN signaling protocol is the Link Access Procedure on the D channel (LAPD). LAPD is similar to the HDLC and LAPB specifications (Figure 22.2). It is used to ensure that control and signaling information flows properly and is received.

FIGURE 22.2
LAPD frame format is similar to HDLC and LAPB.

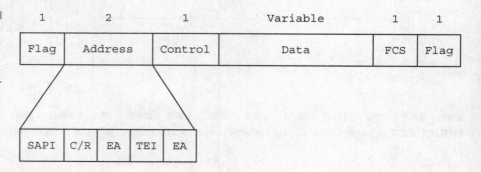

The ISDN data-link frame consists of four fields set between a start flag field and end flag field: Address, Control, Data, and Frame check sequence (FCS). The Address field, which immediately follows the start flag field, consists of several elements. The first of these is the Service Access Point Identifier (SAPI). This identifies the entry point at which LAPD services are provided to the network layer. Next follows a command/response bit to indicate whether the frame carries a command or response.

The next elements in the Address field are the extended addressing bits. These are used to determine whether an address is 1 or 2 bytes in length. If the extended addressing bit is set, the address is 2 bytes, if not, it is 1 byte. Finally, the Terminal End-Point Identifier (TEI) identifies whether the frame is going to single or multiple terminals. When this portion of the field contains only binary 1s, the message is broadcast.

The next field in the LAPD data-link frame format is the Control field. The LAPD frame can be supervisory, information, or unnumbered. It is in the Control field that the type of frame is specified.

If the frame is an information (I) frame, the Control field carries upper-layer and control information. In particular, it contains send and receive sequence numbers, and a poll final (P/F) bit. These elements perform flow and error control.

The send sequence number gives the number of the next frame to be sent. The receive sequence number shows the number of the next frame to be received. The P/F bit is used by a primary station to tell the secondary station when it requires an immediate response. The secondary station uses the P/F bit to tell the primary station whether the current frame is the last in its current response.

If the LAPD frame is a supervisory (S) one, then the Control field contains control information. A supervisory frame can request transmission, suspend transmission, report on status, and acknowledge receipt of I frames. There is no additional information field in a supervisory frame.

When the LAPD frame is an unnumbered frame it is not sequenced. The Control field in the supervisory frame contains information used to initialize secondary stations. Some unnumbered frames also contain an information field.

In an LAPD I frame format, the Control field is followed by a Data field, which contains the information being transported. The Frame Check Sequence (FCS) field is before the end flag field. This field checks the integrity of transmitted data.

There are two network-layer specifications used for ISDN signaling: ITU-T I.450 and ITU-T I.451. These specified protocols support user-to-user, circuit-switched, and packet-switched connections.

ISDN network-layer operation involves a series of call stages (Figure 22.3): call establishment, call termination, information, and miscellaneous messages. The OSI model's definition of ISDN describes the specifics of ISDN call stages.

The different call stage characteristics and components define how an ISDN call is initiated, acknowledged, and completed. Call stage components include set up, connect, release, user information, cancel, status, and disconnect.

Cisco ISDN Features

Cisco routers include models that contain native ISDN interfaces (TE1s). They can transmit over multiple ISDN channels at the standard 64-Kbps, B channel rate. Alternatively, you can configure for 56 Kbps.

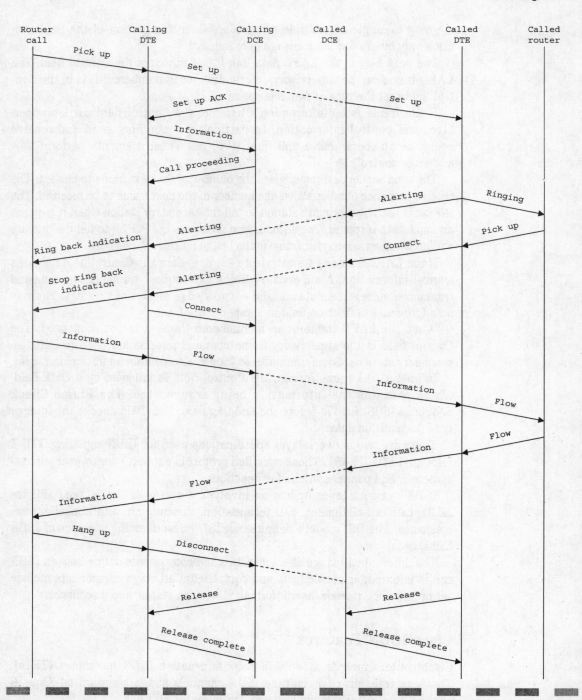

FIGURE 22.3 An ISDN circuit-switched call moves through various stages to its destination.

As network administrator you can use a Simple Network Management Protocol (SNMP)-based management application to control your ISDN interfaces. SNMP allows you to manage configurations, statistics collection, performance, and security.

SNMP will also monitor and control network devices and will manage a Management Information Base (MIB) for routers. In addition, routers themselves can act as managed objects.

Cisco routers offer the facility of call screening for incoming ISDN calls. The destination router can be configured with entries which specify which calls from a calling router it will accept. You can configure Cisco ISDN routers with PPP encapsulation.

PPP uses its own Link Control Protocol (LCP) to organize link access permissions and compression methods. Access control follows from an authentication process whereby the calling side of the link must enter information to show that the network administrator has given permission to call. The PPP compression option increases effective throughput by reducing the amount of data in a frame that will travel across the link.

Cisco routers support the ISDN bandwidth-on-demand option, which is implemented through the use of dial-on-demand routing (DDR). DDR refers to a technique by which a Cisco router can automatically initiate and close a circuit-switched session as transmitting stations demand.

DDR is mainly supported over ISDN using BRI. When a router is running Cisco IOS software (version 10.2 or above) and has a T1 channelized interface, PRI also supports DDR. You need to identify a BRI in a DDR access list group. Then you specify which traffic is to be considering "interesting."

DDR will only initiate call setup for interesting traffic. This process involves the router's mapping a host ID and a dialer string for that particular traffic. The router then dials the call from the BRI through the ISDN NT1 or DSU/CSU using dialer commands. If the router is using an external TA, it needs to be able to support V.25bis dialing. V.25bis is a ITU-T specification for call setup.

You should specify static routes on links used by DDR to remote sites. Static routes prevent you from being charged by service providers for all routing updates from remote sites. Once the call has been dialed, end-stations use the static route to transmit packet traffic. By using an idle timer, DDR disconnects the call sometime after traffic ceases.

If the bandwidth required for calls exceeds a pre-established load threshold, DDR makes a specified type of channel active. For example, a 64-Kbps B channel may be provided for just as long as is required.

The DDR feature of dropping the ISDN call once the link is no longer needed makes ISDN more cost effective.

The Basic Rate Interface

This section enables you to understand and configure Basic Rate Interface (BRI). We will examine basic configuration commands, outline the advanced configuration tasks on the BRI interface, see how BRI is configured and monitored, and configure and monitor a BRI interface.

BRI Basic Configuration Tasks

The Basic Rate Interface (BRI) channel is used globally for ISDN services. The Cisco ISDN BRI provides two B channels and one D channel. The B channels send and receive data at 64 Kbps. The D channel signals and communicates with the ISDN switch at 16 Kbps. Table 22.1 shows Cisco certifications for ISDN compliance.

<table>
<tr><td rowspan="6">**TABLE 22.1**
Certification from regional PTTs for ISDN compliance</td><td>Australia</td><td>Germany</td><td>Spain</td></tr>
<tr><td>Austria</td><td>Ireland</td><td>Sweden</td></tr>
<tr><td>Belgium</td><td>Japan</td><td>Switzerland</td></tr>
<tr><td>Canada</td><td>New Zealand</td><td>The Netherlands</td></tr>
<tr><td>Denmark</td><td>Norway</td><td>United Kingdom</td></tr>
<tr><td>Finland</td><td>Portugal</td><td>United States</td></tr>
</table>

When setting up ISDN connections, you must consider the central office switches through which your ISDN connections will be made. Depending on the central office switch used by your telephone company, you need to configure different options on your router equipment.

First, you must specify a particular switch type on your router. This is because signaling specifics and associated switch types differ depending on the regions or countries involved. Use the ISDN Switch-Type Global Configuration command to select a particular switch.

The AT&T 5ESS and the NorTel DMS-100 are the two main switch types used in North America. When entering the Switch-Type command, specify a keyword that represents the particular switch type required. For example, the keyword for the AT&T basic rate switch is basic-5ESS. The keyword for the Nortel DMS-100 basic rate switch is basic-dms100. Your telephone company can tell you the type of switch located in the central office that will connect with your router. Table 22.2 shows various ISDN switch types around the world.

TABLE 22.2

ISDN switches around the world

ISDN switches in Australia, Europe, Japan, and New Zealand

Country	Switch Type	Keyword
Australia	TS013 BRI switch	`basic-ts013`
	TS014 PRI switch	`primary-ts014`
France	VN2 ISDN switch	`vn2, vn3`
Germany	1TR6 ISDN switch	`basic-1tr6`
Japan	NTT ISDN switch	`ntt`
	ISDN PRI switch	`primary-ntt`
New Zealand	NET3 ISDN switch	`basic-nznet3`
Norway	NET3 ISDN switch	`basic-nznet3`
United Kingdom	NET3 BRI switch	`basic-net3`
	NET5 PRI switch	`primary-net5`

ISDN switches in Canada and the United States

Switch Type	Keyword
AT&T basic rate switch	`basic-5ess`
NorTel DMS-100 basic rate switch	`basic-dms100`
National ISDN-1 switch	`basic-ni1`
AT&T 4ESS (ISDN PRI only)	`primary-4ess`
AT&T 5ESS (ISDN PRI only)	`primary-5ess`
NorTel DMS-100 (ISDN PRI only)	`primary-dms100`

Depending on the switch type used, another configuration task may be to specify a *Service Profile Identifier (SPID)*. This is a number used by some service providers to identify the line configuration of the BRI service that an ISDN device uses. SPIDs are required by DMS-100 and National ISDN-1 switches. Depending on which software version is running, AT&T 5ESS might also require SPIDs.

The ISDN device uses the SPID when accessing the switch that initializes the connection to a service provider. The device first attempts a D-channel data-link layer initialization process that causes a TEI to be assigned to the device. Next the device attempts a D-channel network-layer initialization. When SPIDs are necessary but not configured, the network layer initialization fails and the call is not completed.

SPIDs allow multiple ISDN devices, such as voice and data, to share the local loop. However, you cannot run data and voice traffic over the same B channel simultaneously.

The AT&T 5ESS switch supports up to eight SPIDs per BRI. In this case, multiple SPIDs can be applied to any single B channel, so multiple services can be supported simultaneously. For example, you can configure the first B channel for data only and the second for both data and voice. DMS-100 and National ISDN-1 switches support only two SPIDs per BRI—one for each B channel.

Use the ISDN Spid1 and ISDN Spid2 interface configuration commands to assign SPID values for a given BRI. These commands also allow you to specify a local directory number (LDN). This is a seven-digit number, assigned by the service provider, that is part of the incoming set up message. The LDN is necessary only when two SPIDs are configured, as it allows incoming calls to the second B channel to be answered correctly.

If you configure static routes for a routing protocol, you eliminate the need for the protocol to broadcast routing updates and thereby you lower your ISDN tariffs. Assign static routes by using the IP Route command and specifying the network address.

To configure an interface to use bandwidth-on-demand, use the Dialer Load-Threshold command in Interface Configuration mode. This command specifies a load value between 1 and 255 (representing 0 to 100% of bandwidth capacity), beyond which another call to a destination is to be initiated. The load value varies from 1 to 255, where 255 represents 100% of bandwidth capacity.

When the Dialer Load-Threshold command is applied to BRIs, it brings up the second B channel for use once the load on the first B channel reaches a specified value. The Dialer Load-Threshold command can only be used with dialer rotary groups. A rotary group consists of several physical interfaces that act as a single serial interface when operating DDR calls. By default, each ISDN interface is a dialer rotary group. The syntax of the Dialer Load-Threshold command is:

```
dialer load-threshold load [outbound/inbound/either]
```

The load is a specified volume of traffic between 1 and 255 Kbps. The optional parameters are assigned according to whether you want the load to be calculated by reference to outbound, inbound, or combined outbound and inbound traffic.

If you want to use the bandwidth-on-demand DDR ISDN facility, you must define what are to be considered interesting packets to ring up a specific link. The Dialer-List global configuration command defines interesting packets.

A dialer list can permit or deny network-layer protocol traffic at a general level. For example, typing `dialer-list 5 protocol ip permit` creates a dialer list for access group 5 and permits all IP traffic.

You need to associate a dialer list with a specific ISDN interface. To do this, use the `Dialer-Group` command in Interface Configuration mode.

As part of your interface configuration you issue the `Dialer Map` command. This associates the IP address of the destination router with the ISDN number to be dialed. An example of a `Dialer Map` command is:

```
dialer map ip 172.16.66.2 name Router A 12345
```

Here the IP address 172.16.66.2 is associated with the router name Router A and dial string 12345. The router name used in the command must also exist as a user name with a password on the router that is being dialed.

Optional configuration parameters in the `Dialer Map` command include the `Broadcast` keyword. If you use the `Broadcast` keyword, broadcast traffic is permitted to cross the ISDN link in addition to the usual unicast traffic. If static routes are used, you do not specify the `Broadcast` keyword since you do not need information on routing updates. However, if RIP or IGRP routing is used, and you want routing updates to cross the link, you must specify the `Broadcast` keyword.

Useful optional features you may want to configure are time to wait for the ISDN carrier to respond to a call and seconds of idle time before the router times out and drops the call.

The `Dialer Wait-For-Carrier-Time` command specifies the maximum number of seconds allowed for the provider to respond once a call is initiated. The `Dialer Idle-Timeout` command specifies how many seconds of idle time are to be allowed before the router drops the ISDN call.

ISDN interfaces can be configured for the following types of encapsulation: High-Level Data Link Control (HDLC), frame relay, Link Access Procedure Balanced (LAPB), Point-to-Point Protocol (PPP), and X.22.

The PPP encapsulation feature offers useful LCP options such as data compression and call authentication. Specify PPP encapsulation with the `Encapsulation PPP` command.

The PPP compression option increases effective throughput by reducing the volume of data in a frame that will travel across the link. Use the `Compress Interface` command at both ends of the link to enable compression. You can specify either the `stac` or `predictor` keyword to enable the Stacker (LZS) compression algorithm or the RAND predictor algorithm respectively. The Stacker algorithm is appropriate for LAPB and PPP encapsulation and is the preferred option for PPP encapsulation.

For call authentication you can specify the use of either the Password Authentication Protocol (PAP) or the Challenge Handshake Authentication Protocol (CHAP). Both PAP and CHAP send a password to the remote end node. The router or access server then determines whether the remote device is allowed access. CHAP is recommended instead of PAP since it sends an encrypted form of the password, whereas PAP sends the password in clear text. The syntax of the `PPP authentication` command is:

```
ppp authentication [chap pap]
```

PPP Multilink (MP) is an Internet Engineering Task Force (IETF) standard that allows equipment sold by a large number of vendors to interoperate. MP defines a way of sequencing and transmitting packets over multiple physical interfaces. It also defines a method of fragmenting and reassembling large packets for protocols such as AppleTalk and IPX that do not tolerate out-of-order packets.

MP does not define how connections should be initiated or terminated. However, like the `Dialer Load-Threshold` command, Cisco's implementation of MP allows users to define a load factor at which a second B channel call should be initiated.

MP's load factor can be defined for incoming or outgoing data or for both. MP is therefore useful if you need to download a large amount of information from the World Wide Web since another channel for additional traffic will become available. It is also effective if you have a large amount of outgoing traffic such as files being sent to colleagues.

In the graphic, MP has already brought a second channel into operation. Incoming packets A and B are fragmented into smaller packets and given sequence numbers, A1, A2, B1, and B2. The fragmented packets are shared over the two B channels. When the fragments arrive at the receiving router, MP reassembles the original packets and sequences them correctly in the data stream. To configure MP, use the `PPP Multilink` command.

Advanced Configuration Tasks

Advanced ISDN configuration tasks include applying extended access lists for DDR call triggering, filtering inbound call setups with caller ID screening, enabling rate adaptation for calls been placed at lower speeds than 64 Kbps, and verifying subaddresses.

A basic configuration task is to assign a dialer list that permits or denies network layer-protocol traffic at a general level. A more advanced configuration task is to enable a dialer list to call a specific data-link or network-layer access list. For example, typing `dialer-list protocol ip 3 list 99` creates dialer list 3 and calls all access lists numbered 99.

The `Access-List` Global Configuration command establishes access lists. These use network layer filtering to control traffic. The `Dialer-List` command is used to call access and extended access lists. Standard IP access lists are numbered from 1 to 99, and extended access lists from 100 to 199.

You apply a more specific set of conditions for the DDR call trigger using extended access list conditions. In this example you want to allow all IP traffic on Cisco A, except TELNET and IGRP, to trigger an ISDN call to network 172.16.49.0 through Cisco B. DDR will be configured on Cisco A with the specified interesting traffic defined in an access list.

First deny the traffic that should not initiate DDR routing to Cisco B.

```
access list 101 deny tcp 172.16.49.0 0.0.0.255 172.16.59.0
0.0.0.255 eq 23
```

To deny Telnet traffic, type the `Access-List` command and number (101), the `Deny` subcommand, the protocol type traffic to be denied (TCP), the address range from which the traffic is coming (through Router A), and the address range to which traffic is to be denied (through Router B). `eq 23` denies traffic from IP port 23 which is the TELNET port.

Deny IGRP traffic using the same steps as for TCP. Then permit all other IP traffic not denied by prior statements. Other protocol packets are implicitly denied and will not trigger DDR calls.

```
access list 101 deny igrp 172.16.49.0 0.0.0.255 172.16.59.0
0.0.0.255
access list 101 permit ip 172.16.49.0 0.0.0.255
```

You can set up caller identification screening during ISDN configuration. Caller ID allows the router to verify that an incoming call comes from an expected and authorized source. When caller ID screening is configured, the called number supplied in the call message setup request is verified against a table of allowed numbers. The call is not set up unless the number is found to be an authorized one. This prevents calls from unauthorized numbers.

Configure Caller ID screening with the `ISDN Caller Interface` command. For example, if you type `isdn caller 41555512xx`, your BRI will accept a call with a delivered caller ID of 41555512 and any number in the last two positions. If you configure caller ID screening but your CO switch does not support it, the router will reject all calls.

Caller ID screening is a less useful alternative to PPP encapsulation with PAP or CHAP. PPP encapsulation allows an administrator to control access

to ISDN where the caller ID or called number value is not specified. Some
providers do not supply called number values in the setup request.

You may want to adjust your ISDN channel to a speed lower than the usual
64 Kbps if it is requested by the call destination in the call-setup request.
Many ISDN destinations in North America use 56 Kbps.

You configure the speed of a call to a remote host as part of the `Dialer
Map Speed` version of the `Dialer Map` interface configuration command. The
syntax of the command is:

```
dialer map protocol next hop address [speed speed]
```

You must define a network-layer protocol and then specify the network-
layer address of the next-hop router. You then have the option of specifying
whether you want the channel speed at 56 or 64 Kbps

If you have multiple devices and a router sharing the same ISDN local
loop, you can specify which device is to answer particular calls. You configure
the device to compare its own configured number and subaddress with the
called-party number and subaddress that are delivered in the switch's setup
message. The subaddress is an address used to select multipoint devices.

You can configure your router to verify the called-party number and subaddress in the incoming setup message by using the `ISDN Answer1` or `ISDN
Answer2` commands. You can specify the called-party number, its subaddress,
or both. The syntax for specifying these variables is:

```
isdn [called party number] [:subaddress]
```

With DDR, you use the `Dialer Map Protocol` version of the `Dialer Map`
command with an ISDN subaddress to specify which specific multipoint destination is the target of your call.

The ISDN SBus (or S reference) allows the connection of multiple ISDN
devices. You can have a multipoint connection of up to eight devices using the
same main ISDN dial string. Each multipoint connection has a unique subaddress.

The `Dialer Map protocol` command ensures that each multipoint device
only responds to calls specifically directed to its particular subaddress. The
subaddress to which a call is destined is specified during the call setup
request over the D channel.

The syntax for specifying a subaddress in the `Dialer Map Protocol`
command is:

```
dialer map protocol next-hop-address name hostname
dial-string [:isdn-subaddress]
```

The `Dialer Map Protocol` command consists of the protocol to be used (IP, IPX, or Appletalk) the address of the next-hop router destination, the name of the remote host used for authentication in the hostname table, the dialer string number used to reach the remote host, and the subaddress of the multipoint device.

BRI Configuration on Cisco Routers

You want to configure an ISDN network so that you can transmit a variety of types of digitized data between users on networks in Maine and Vermont (Figure 22.4). You want to configure a BRI for each of the routers, beginning with Maine. The Maine router has an Ethernet interface with the IP address 172.16.1.1. The Maine router's BRI0 basic rate interface 172.16.46.1 will be configured as an ISDN BRI.

FIGURE 22.4
Configuring an ISDN network so a variety of types of digitized data can transmit between users on networks in Maine and Vermont.

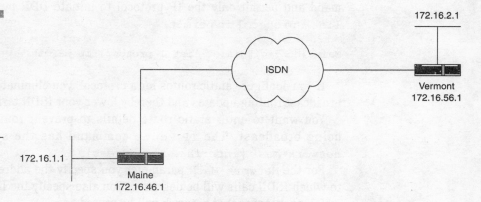

In ISDN configuration, you perform global tasks such as specifying switch type and the traffic that is to trigger DDR calls. You also perform interface configuration tasks to configure addressing, interface specifications, and optional features.

In this instance assume you want to configure a BRI port for IP routing. Assume also that you want to specify PPP and CHAP encapsulation. The Maine router is the remote router. The Vermont router is located at the central site which offers routes to other networks.

You prepare to configure the Maine router by entering the `Configure Terminal` command to put the router in Configuration mode. Your first task is to enter the appropriate username and password for the central site router at Vermont. The username is Vermont and the password is ver4cup. Enter these details in Global Configuration mode by typing `username Vermont password ver4cup`.

```
Maine>enable
Password:
Maine#configure terminal
Enter configuration commands, one per line. End with CNTL/Z.
Maine(config)#username Vermont password ver4cup
```

Now you need to specify a switch type in order to connect the router to the central office switch. In this case, the central office is using the Nortel DMS-100 basic rate switch. The keyword for this switch type is basic-dms100. The command to specify the DMS 100 switch type is isdn switch-type basic-dms100.

```
Maine(config)#isdn switch-type basic-dms100
```

You want dial-on-demand routing to be initiated only by IP routing. Specify a dialer access group number, (in this case 1), with the Dialer-List command and permit only the IP protocol to initiate DDR by typing dialer-list 1 protocol ip permit.

```
Maine(config)#dialer-list 1 protocol ip permit
```

If you configure static routes for a protocol, you eliminate the need for it to broadcast routing updates and thereby lower your ISDN tariffs.

You want to enter static route details to prevent routing updates from being broadcast. The IP Route command has the syntax ip route *network-mask* {*interface ip-address*}.

For the Network-Mask parameter you specify the address of the network to which ISDN calls will be delivered. You also specify the IP address through which packets for that network will be routed.

You want to specify routing for the 172.16.192.0 network. The address of the remote interface through which packets for that network will be routed is 172.16.46.2. Enter ip route 172.16.192.0 255.255.255.0 172.16.46.2.

```
Maine(config)#ip route 172.16.192.0 255.255.255.0 172.16.46.2
```

The 0.0.0.0 route is a default route in the IP routing table. It stands for any other route besides that specified in the first IP static route command.

By typing ip route 0.0.0.0 172.16.46.2 you ensure that packets for all networks connected to the Vermont router will be routed through 172.16.46.2. Maine has two static routes configured, one to route to network 172.16.192.0 and the other for the rest of the Internet.

```
Maine(config)#ip route 0.0.0.0 172.16.46.2
```

Next you move on to configuring the interfaces. The Maine router's Ethernet 0 interface is configured with the IP address 172.16.1.1. The mask (255.255.255.0) signifies a Class B address that has been subnetted with 8 bits of subnetting.

```
Maine(config)#interface ethernet 0
Maine(config-if)#ip address 172.16.1.1 255.255.255.0
```

Next you must configure the BRI interface, so you type `interface bri 0`.

```
Maine(config-if)#interface bri 0
```

You want to specify that the encapsulation type is PPP. Enter `encapsulation ppp`.

```
Maine(config-if)#encapsulation ppp
```

You assign the IP address 172.16.46.1 to the BRI interface.

```
Maine(config-if)#ip address 172.16.46.1 255.255.255.0
```

Since the switch type is DMS-100, you need to configure SPIDs. In this case, the SPID number for the first B channel is given as 515898333442 8064323. The SPID number for the second B channel is 515898333530 8064324. You specify these SPID numbers on the BRI interface using the `Spid1` and `Spid2` commands.

```
Maine(config-if)#isdn spid1 515898333442 8064323
Maine(config-if)#isdn spid2 515898333530 8064324
```

You want to configure bandwidth on demand for DDR routing. You want the maximum load allowed before the dialer places an additional call to be set at 128 (representing 50% of bandwidth capacity), calculated by reference to inbound and outbound loads. The load value varies from 1 to 255, where 255 represents 100% of bandwidth capacity.

Where bandwidth on demand is configured to initiate at 128 (or 50%) load calculated by reference to the inbound and outbound loads combined, you enter `dialer load-threshold 128 either`.

```
Maine(config-if)#dialer load-threshold 128 either
```

For DDR routing, you also want to specify how many seconds of idle time are to be allowed before the Maine router drops the ISDN call. You have decided that to reduce costs you will configure the idle timeout at 60 seconds. Enter `dialer idle-timeout 60`.

```
Maine(config-if)#dialer idle-timeout 60
```

You want to configure Caller ID screening. Calls will be accepted only if the delivered caller ID is either 8064325 or 8064326. Enter `isdn caller 8064325` and then `isdn caller 8064326`.

```
Maine(config-if)#isdn caller 8064325
Maine(config-if)#isdn caller 8064326
```

Another option you can configure in order to save costs is B channel aggregation multivendor interoperability. This will allow you to spread the transmission of your data over multiple physical interfaces. The command that allows B channel aggregation and the transmitting of data over multiple physical channels is `ppp multilink`. This is normally used as an alternative to the `Load-Threshold` command to activate a second ISDN line. In order for it to work both routers must support Multilink PPP.

```
Maine(config-if)#ppp multilink
```

Some of the information in your business is highly confidential so you need to configure a security feature. You decide on authentication of remote users using the CHAP protocol, which sends an encrypted password. Enter `ppp authentication chap`.

```
Maine(config-if)#ppp authentication chap
```

For routing purposes, you need to use the `Dialer Map` command. This associates the IP address of the destination router that you specified in the static route with the ISDN number to be dialed.

As part of the `Dialer Map` command you also enter the IP address, router name, and dial string. In this case, type `dialer map ip 172.16.46.2 name Vermont 8064322`.

```
Maine(config-if)#dialer map ip 172.16.46.2 name Vermont 8064325
```

As part of global configuration earlier, a general dialer list, referencing dialer group 1, specified that all IP traffic could generate ISDN calls. During interface configuration it is important to remember to associate the group number from your dialer list with your ISDN interface. The `Dialer-Group` command associates the dialer group number with the interface that is being configured. Here you type `dialer-group 1`.

```
Maine(config-if)#dialer-group 1
```

You have specified all the options that you require for the BRI interface and are now ready to save the configuration changes. Enter **Ctrl+Z** and type `copy running-config startup-config` to exit Configuration mode and save the changes.

```
Maine(config-if)#^Z
Maine#copy running-config startup-config
Building configuration...
[OK]
Maine#
```

To check on the status of ISDN and the various parameters configured on it, type `show isdn status`.

```
Maine#show isdn status
The current ISDN Switchtype = basic-dms100
ISDN BRI0 interface
    Layer 1 Status:
        ACTIVE
    Layer 2 Status:
        TEI = 64, State = MULTIPLE_FRAME_ESTABLISHED
    Layer 3 Status:
        1 Active Layer 3 Call(s)

    Activated dsl 0 CCBs = 1
        CCB:callid=3, sapi=0, ces=1, B-chan=1
    Total Allocated ISDN CCBs = 1
Maine#
```

The output shows that the switch type has been configured as basic-dms100. Layers 1, 2, and 3 are active.

To look at details of the BRI channel, type `show interface bri0`.

```
Maine#show interface bri0
BRI0 is up, line protocol is up (spoofing)
  Hardware is BRI
  Internet address is 172.16.46.1/24
  MTU 1500 bytes, BW 64 Kbit, DLY 20000 usec, rely
  Encapsulation PPP, lookback not set
  Last input 00:00:03, output 00:00:03, output hang never
  Last clearing of "show interface" counters never
  Output queue 0/40, 0 drops; input queue 0/75, 0 drops
```

```
    5 minutes input rate 0 bits/sec, 0 packets/sec
    5 minutes output rate 0 bits/sec, 0 packets/sec
        198 packets input, 892 bytes, 0 no buffer
        Received 0 broadcasts, 0 runts, 0 giants
        1 input errors, 0 CRC, 0 frame, 0 overrun, 0 ignored, 1
abort
        201 packets output, 950 bytes, 0 underruns
        0 output errors, 0 collisions, 8 interface resets
        0 output buffer failures, 0 output buffers swapped out
        5 carrier transitions
Maine#
```

If you specify the interface number only, you can see details of the D channel. The value of the interface number is 0 through 7 if the router has one BRI NIM, or 0 through 15 if the router has two BRI NIMs. To view details of the first or second B channel you enter 0 or 1 respectively, after the interface number.

The output of the Show Interface BRI command shows that the BRI D channel is active, the network address is 172.16.46.1, the encapsulation is PPP, and there have been 198 packets input on the D channel.

The Primary Rate Interface

This section enables you to understand and configure Primary Rate Interface (PRI). We will examine the configuration tasks and outline the commands used in PRI configuration.

PRI Configuration Tasks

The Primary Rate Interface (PRI) is a physical interface with a specified data rate and channel number over which users can access services from other networks. It is implemented using a CSU digital interface device.

There are two main classes of PRI—T1 and E1. In North America and Japan, the T1 facility consists of 23 B channels for voice or data and a single 64-Kbps D channel, which is described as 23B+D. These channels yield a combined rate of 1.544 Mbps.

In Europe, PRI's E1 facility consists of a single 64-Kbps D channel and 30 B channels for voice or data, described as 30B+D. The E1 facility channels yield a combined rate of 2.048 Mbps.

Both the T1 and E1 facilities use a CSU digital interface device that connects data terminal equipment (DTE) to the local digital telephone loop. The CSU is used in combination with a data service unit (DSU) located in the router. The DSU adapts the DTE physical interface for digital transmission.

As part of ISDN configuration, you need to configure the PRI interface. As with the BRI interface, you need to specify the correct PRI switch type with which the router will interface at the provider's central office (CO). See Table 22.3.

TABLE 22.3
ISDN switches

Country	Switch type	Keyword
Australia	TS014 PRI switch	`primary-ts014`
Japan	ISDN PRIswitch	`primary-ntt`
Europe	NET5 PRI switch	`primary-net5`

ISDN switches in Canada and the United States

Switch type	Keyword
AT&T 4ESS (ISDN PRI only)	`primary-4ess`
AT&T 5ESS (ISDN PRI only)	`primary-5ess`
NorTel DMS-100 (ISDN PRI only)	`primary-dms100`

There is a keyword for each PRI switch type. For example, commonly used switch types in North America are AT&T 4ESS-Primary switches (keyword `pri-4ess`), AT&T 5ESS-Primary switches (keyword `pri-5ess`), and NT DMS-100 PRI switches (keyword `pri-dms100`).

Use the `ISDN Switch-Type` command in the following format to specify a switch type for the PRI interface: `isdn switch-type primary-rate-switch-type`.

A MultiChannel Interface Processor (MIP) card provides PRIs on Cisco 4000 and Cisco 7000 series routers. It provides either two channelized T1 or two E1 connections through serial cables to a CSU. The two controllers on the MIP can each provide up to 24 T1 or 30 E1 channel groups. Each channel group is represented as a serial interface which can be configured individually.

There are several commands to use for configuring MIPs and MIP-related connections: the `Controller` command, the `Framing` command, the `Linecode` command, and the `PRI-Group` command.

Use the `Controller` command to configure an MIP card and specify the interface as T1 or E1. On Cisco 7000 and 7500 series routers you also specify the slot in which the MIP card is installed and the port to be configured. On Cisco 4000 routers you specify the Network Interface Module (NIM) number. On Cisco 7000 routers the syntax of the `Controller` command is `controller {t1/e1} slot/port`. See Table 22.4.

TABLE 22.4
Cisco router slot
numbers.

Cisco router series	Slot number
Cisco 7000	0, 1, 2, 3, or 4 from left to right
Cisco 7010	0, 1, 2 from bottom to top
Cisco 7505	0, 1, 2, or 3 from bottom to top
Cisco 7507	0 and 1 (CyBus0) and 4 through 6 (CyBus1) from left to right
Cisco 7513	0 through 5 (CyBus0) and 8 through 12 (CyBus1) from left to right

The slot numbers on the Cisco 7000 series go from 0 to 4 from left to right. The port number of the interface can be 0 or 1 for the MIP and are numbered from the top down. On Cisco 4000 routers the syntax for the Controller command is:

```
controller {t1/e1} number
```

The number to be entered is the Network Interface Module (NIM) number in the range 0 to 2.

Following on from the Controller command, you must also specify the framing type and line code type required for T1 and E1 connections. Do this in Controller Configuration mode. Depending on whether you have a T1 or E1 connection the syntax in the Framing command is different. For T1 lines the syntax is:

```
framing {sf esf}
```

SF specifies super frame as the T1 frame type. ESF specifies extended super frame as the T1 frame type. The ESF and SF frame types provide timing and error checking functions respectively. ESF is an enhanced version of SF.

For E1 lines the syntax of the Framing command is:

```
framing {crc4  no-crc4} [australia]
```

You can specify either a Cyclic Redundancy Check 4 (CRC4) frame type or no CRC4 frame as the E1 frame type. CRC is an error-checking technique. For lines in Australia you add the optional parameter [australia].

As well as specifying the frame type, you also need to specify a linecode type. This is a coding scheme used on serial lines to maintain data integrity and reliability. The linecode type used is determined by the carrier service provider.

For T1 connections use the command `linecode b8zs` to select the binary 8-zero substitution (B8ZS) linecode type. With binary 8-zero substitution a special code is substituted whenever eight consecutive zeros are sent through the link. This code is interpreted at the remote end of the connection. For E1 connections use the command `linecode hdb3` to select the high density bipolar 3-linecode type.

After configuring the MIP card, you must also specify that the card is to be used as an ISDN PRI. To do this, use the `PRI-Group` command in Controller Configuration mode. Use the `timeslots` parameter to specify a range of channels if you want only a portion of all channels to be used for ISDN. For timeslots, use a number in the range 1 to 23 for T1 and 1 to 30 for E1.

Digital signal level 0 (DS0) is a framing specification used in transmitting digital signals over a single channel on a T1 or E1 at 64 Kbps. The DS0 channels numbering 0 to 22 are configured as B channels. The last channel, channel 23, is configured as the D channel. On the E1, the 15th DS0 is designated as the D channel, and the remaining 30 DS0s as B channels.

You need to specify an interface for PRI operation. On Cisco 7x00 series routers, use the syntax `interface serial slot port: {23 15}`. The slot port is specified in the same way as it was for the `Controller` command. Specify the D channel as the 23rd channel on a T1 connection and the 15th on a E1 connection.

The Series 4x00 version of the `Interface Serial` command takes the form `interface serial unit: {23 15}`. The unit number is designated on the router. As with the 7x00 routers, you specify the D channels as the 23rd channel on a T1 and the 15th channel on an E1.

As well as configuring the MIP card and T1/E1 connections on the PRI interface, you also configure the same type of static mappings and DDR commands as on BRI interfaces.

PRI Configuration

You enter several different types of commands to configure a PRI interface. As with BRIs, you use static mapping, DDR, and provider specification commands. However, you also need to enter commands to configure the MIP card and physical interface details.

Here you can see the commands to use with PRI interfaces to configure the MIP card and physical interfaces. Once these are configured, you then start to configure static routes, networks, dialer, and provider-related commands.

```
isdn switch-type primary-4ess
```

```
controller t1 2/0
pri-group timeslot 1-23 speed 64
framing esf
linecode b8zs
!
int s 2/0:23
!
ip address 172.16.11.2 255.255.0.0
```

The switch type has been specified as an AT&T 4ESS-Primary switch with the PRI keyword `primary-4ess`.

The `Controller` command is specified in Global Configuration mode to configure the MIP card for either a T1 or E1 interface. In the command `controller t1 2/0` the number 2 stands for the slot number, and 0 for the port number of the T1 interface.

The `Controller` command puts the router in Controller Configuration mode. Here the `PRI-Group` command has been specified. The `PRI-Group` command `pri-group timeslot 1-23 speed 64` specifies that the interface port is to function as a PRI, there are 23 timeslots on the PRI, and each timeslot has a speed of 64 Kbps.

The ESF frame type has been specified for the PRI interface. ESF is one of the framing types used for T1 circuits.

As well as the frame type, the linecode integrity check type B8ZS must be specified. Enter `linecode b8zs` in Controller Configuration mode.

You must specify the physical or hardware interface that will be used for PRI operation. Here the `Interface Serial` command was specified by typing `int s 2/0: 23`. We can tell that the router belongs to the Cisco 7x00 series because the slot and port number are specified. On a Series 4x00 router you would specify a serial unit number.

Because the channel is T1, 23 channels are specified. Channel 23 is the D channel. When there is an E1 connection, the 15th (D channel) is specified in the `Interface Serial` command.

Once you have entered the commands to configure the MIP and physical interfaces, you then move on to the static routes, networks, dialer, and provider-related commands. These are the same as those you configured on the BRI interface.

SMDS and ATM Configuration

SMDS Overview

This section gives an overview of SMDS operation, describes SMDS addressing, and outlines the features of the SMDS Interface Protocol.

SMDS Networking

Switched Multimegabit Data Service (SMDS) is a cell-relay WAN technology. As a cell-relay technology, SMDS uses small, fixed-size packets that can be processed and switched at high speeds. SMDS uses a packet-switching networking method where nodes share bandwidth with each other by sending packets.

SMDS is a connectionless service. The SMDS datagram-based service does not require data-link acknowledgments. However, this service is usually implemented over a fiber-based *full mesh* topology (this exists where each network node has either a physical or virtual circuit connecting it to every other network node).

SMDS is used for communication over public data networks (PDNs). Its development reflects trends in WAN technology such as extensive use of distributed processing and greater efficiency of fiber-based media. *Distributed processing* or client/server computing requires high performance networking. *Fiber-based media* are becoming more economical and have high-bandwidth capabilities. SMDS was developed in response to these trends. Its features are detailed in a series of specifications produced by Bell Communications Research (Bellcore).

Although presently used mainly over fiber-based media, SMDS can also run over copper-based media. SMDS supports speeds of 1.544 Mbps over Digital Signal level 1 (DS-1) transmission facilities and 44.736 Mbps over Digital Signal Level 3 (DS-3) transmission facilities.

The SMDS protocol is based on the three SMDS Interface Protocol layers. These do not correspond to the layers of the OSI model but the basic functionality of the bottom three layers of the OSI model is used. Layer 3 has variable-sized SMDS SDUS (SMDS data units) capable of containing up to 9,188 bytes of user data. The data units are large enough to encapsulate entire IEEE 802.3, IEEE 802.5, and Fiber Distributed Data Interface (FDDI) frames.

Access to an SMDS network is provided through a SMDS-specific CSU/DSU, known as SDSU. It is the SMDS-specific data service unit transmission device over the data-link and physical layers (Figure 23.1). It is used for access to SMDS through High Speed Serial Interfaces and other serial interfaces.

OSI Reference Model

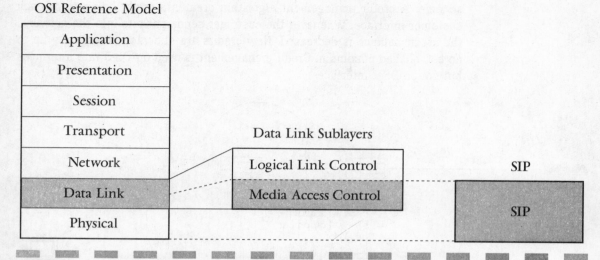

FIGURE 23.1 *SIP provides services associated with the physical and data-link layers of the OSI model.*

SMDS networks consist of three main elements: customer premises equipment, carrier equipment, and subscriber network interface.

Customer premises equipment (CPE) is terminal equipment owned and maintained by the customer. It includes end devices (terminals and personal computers) and intermediate nodes (routers, modems, and multiplexers). Intermediate nodes are sometimes provided by the SMDS carrier.

Carrier equipment consists of high-speed WAN switches that conform to network equipment specifications. As well as defining network operations, the specifications also define the interfaces between a local and a long-distance carrier network and the two switches inside a single carrier network.

The *Subscriber Network Interface (SNI)* is the interface between CPE and carrier equipment (Figure 23.2). The SNI is the point at which the customer network ends and the carrier network begins. Its function is to make the technology and operation of the carrier SMDS network transparent to the user.

SMDS implements a set of access classes. These constrain different CPE devices to a specified sustained or average rate of data transfer. Access classes make it possible for SMDS to accommodate a wide range of traffic requirements and equipment capabilities.

Each access class defines a maximum sustained information transfer rate and a maximum allowed volume of traffic sent in bursts. For instance the five access classes for DS-3 rate access are 4 Mbps, 10 Mbps, 16 Mbps, 25 Mbps, and 34 Mbps. Access classes are implemented using a credit management scheme. A credit management algorithm creates a credit balance for each customer interface. Whenever the customer sends packets into the network, the credit balance is decreased. New credits are allocated periodically up to an established maximum. Credit management is used on DS-3 rate interfaces but not on DS-1 interfaces.

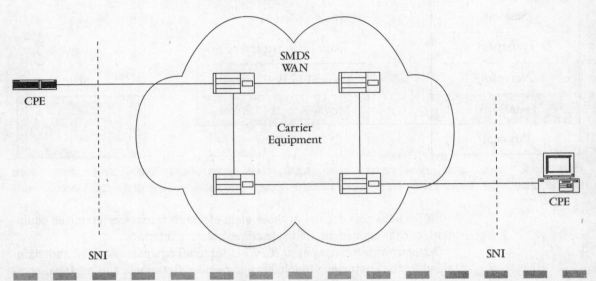

FIGURE 23.2   The SNI provides an interface between the CPE and the carrier equipment in SMDS.

SMDS Addressing

SMDS addresses are assigned by the service provider. SMDS uses 64-bit addresses specified in E.164 format. The address type constitutes 4 bits and the telephone number, 60 bits. The *address type* is either unicast, denoted by a C; or multicast, denoted by an E. Unicast addresses are individual CPE addresses. Multicast addresses are group addresses.

SMDS protocol data units (PDUs) carry both a source and a destination address. The source address can be used by the recipient of a data unit to return data to the sender. The source address can also be used for address resolution to discover the mapping between higher-layer addresses and SMDS addresses.

SMDS group addresses allow a single address to refer to multiple CPE stations. A CPE station specifies the group address in the Destination Address field of the PDU. The network makes multiple copies of the PDU for delivery to all the members of the address group.

SMDS group addressing is similar to multicasting on LANs. The group addressing facility has the advantage of reducing the amount of network resources required for distributing route information, resolving addresses, and dynamically discovering network resources.

SMDS implements two addressing security features: source address validation and address screening. *Source address validation* is a method of ensuring that the PDU source address given is the legitimate address of the SNI from which the PDU was sent. Users are protected against *address spoofing*, where illegal traffic uses the source address of a legitimate device.

SMDS can also carry out source and destination *address screening*. Source address screening acts on addresses as data units are leaving the network. Destination address screening acts on addresses as data units are entering the network. If the address is not an authorized one, the data unit is not delivered. Address screening allows a subscriber to establish a private virtual network that excludes unwanted traffic. The subscriber is provided with an initial security screen. Address screening also allows for greater networking efficiency since it prevents SMDS devices wasting resources on handling unwanted traffic.

SMDS Interface Protocol

The SMDS Interface Protocol (SIP) is used for communications between CPE and SMDS carrier equipment. SIP provides a connectionless service across the SNI that allows the CPE to access the SMDS network.

SIP is the SMDS implementation of the IEEE 802.6 Distributed Queue Dual Bus (DQDB) data-link communication protocol for metropolitan area networks (MANs). The DQDB defines a Media Access Control (MAC) protocol that allows many systems to interconnect through two unidirectional logical buses.

DQDB is also aligned with emerging standards for Broadband ISDN (BISDN). This enables it to interoperate with broadband video and voice services. However, to interface with SMDS networks, only the connectionless data portion of the IEEE 802.6 protocol is required. This means that SIP cannot define voice or video application support.

The DQDB protocol was designed to support many different data and non-data applications. As a shared-medium access control protocol, it is quite complex, consisting of the protocol syntax and a distributed queuing algorithm that constitutes the shared-medium access control.

The term *access DQDB* refers specifically to the operation of DQDB *across an SNI* for access to an SMDS network, as opposed to operation *inside* the SMDS network (Figure 23.3). A switch in the SMDS network operates as one station on an access DQDB. Customer equipment operates as one or more stations on the access DQDB. An SMDS access DQDB can be arranged in either a single- or multi-CPE configuration.

FIGURE 23.3
A basic access DQDB
may consist of an
end node, router,
and a switch.

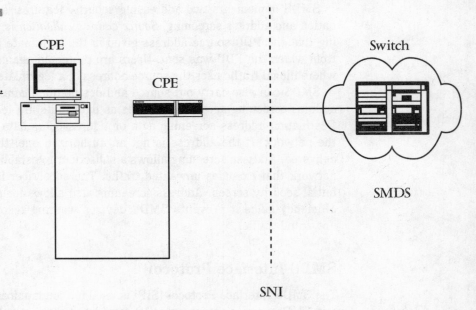

A single-CPE access DQDB configuration consists of one switch in the carrier SMDS network and one CPE station at the subscriber site. This combination results in a two-node DQDB subnetwork where communication occurs only between the switch and the one CPE device across the SNI. There is no contention on the bus because there are no other CPE devices attempting to access it.

A multi-CPE configuration consists of one switch in the carrier SMDS network and a number of interconnected CPE devices at the subscriber site. In this situation, local communication between CPE devices is possible. Some of the local communication is visible to the switch serving the SNI. Multiple devices' contention for the bus is managed by the DQDB distributed queuing algorithm.

SIP maps onto the physical and data-link layers of the OSI model. It consists of three layers. Level 3 maps with the Media Access Control (MAC) sublayer of the data-link layer. Level 2 also operates at the MAC sublayer of the data-link layer. Level 1 operates at the physical layer of the OSI model.

SIP level 3 functionality is provided in the router. User information takes the form of SMDS service data units (SDUs) that are passed to SIP level 3 where they are encapsulated in a SIP level 3 header and trailer. The frame that results is called a *level 3 protocol data unit (PDU)*. As well as generating PDUs, the router is also responsible for mapping network protocol addresses to SMDS addresses.

Level 3 PDUs are passed to SIP level 2. SIP level 2 and 1 functionality is provided in the SDSU, which segments PDUs into fixed-size cells of 53 bytes each. The cells are then passed to SIP level 1 for placement on the physical medium.

SIP level 1 operates at the physical layer. It provides the physical-link protocol that operates at DS-1 or DS-3 rates between CPE devices and the network. There are two sublayers in Level 1. The *transmission system sublayer* defines the characteristics and method of attachment to a DS-1 or DS-3 transmission link. The *physical layer convergence protocol (PLCP)* specifies how SIP level 2 cells are to be arranged relative to the DS-1 or DS-3 frame. It also defines management information.

SMDS Configuration

This section enables configuration of SMDS. We will examine configuration tasks and commands and configure SMDS.

SMDS Configuration Tasks

To configure your router to route traffic through an SMDS networking environment, you need to enable SMDS encapsulation, assign a specific SMDS address, map upper layer addresses to SMDS ones, and map SMDS addresses to multicast addresses.

In Figure 23.4 the Vermont and Maine routers wish to transmit over an SMDS Network. We shall see how the Maine router is configured.

FIGURE 23.4
An illustration of the SMDS Network that connects the Vermont and Maine routers.

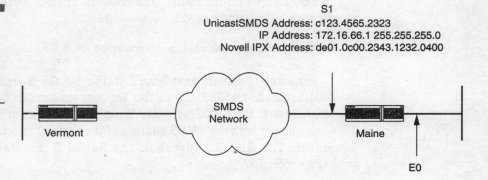

S1
UnicastSMDS Address: c123.4565.2323
IP Address: 172.16.66.1 255.255.255.0
Novell IPX Address: de01.0c00.2343.1232.0400

The Maine router's Serial interface is the link to the SMDS network, via the SDSU. A service provider has assigned the unicast SMDS address c123.4565.2323 to the Serial interface.

The IP address of the interface is 172.16.66.1 255.255.255.0. The full Novell IPX address is de01.0c00.2343.1232.0400. There is also an Ethernet interface connected to the Maine router.

Once the router is in Configuration mode, your first configuration task is to assign the IP address for the Ethernet link. Here we see that the address 172.16.1.1 255.255.255.0 has been assigned to it.

```
Maine>enable
Password:
Maine#configure terminal
Enter configuration commands, one per line. End with CNTL/Z.
Maine(config)#interface ethernet 0
Maine(config-if)#ip address 172.16.1.1 255.255.255.0
```

As usual, you prepare to configure the Serial 1 interface by entering interface serial 1. Next you need to specify SMDS encapsulation on the interface so that it will be configured as an SMDS service interface. Enter encapsulation smds.

```
Maine(config-if)#interface serial 1
Maine(config-if)#encapsulation smds
```

The SMDS address c123.4565.2323, assigned by the service provider, is configured on the interface. This address is protocol independent. The IP address 172.16.66.1 255.255.255.0 is also configured.

```
Maine(config-if)#smds address c123.4565.2323
Maine(config-if)#ip address 172.16.66.1 255.255.255.0
```

In this case a Novell network, over which Novell protocol traffic runs, is also configured on the router. The network number de01 is assigned to the network by entering novell network de01.

```
Maine(config-if)#novell network de01
```

You want to ensure that Novell traffic for the Novell network address de01.0c00.1234.4532.0411 at the Vermont router can be transmitted successfully over the SMDS network. To do this you need to map the Novell network number with the SMDS address of the Serial 0 interface on the Vermont router. The SMDS address of the Serial 0 interface in Vermont is c123.4565.6767.

To map the Novell network address to this address, use the `Static-Map` command. The syntax of the command is:

```
smds static-map protocol protocol-address smds-address
```

In this case, enter `smds static-map novell de01.0c00.1234.`
`4532.0411` and the SMDS address `c123.4565.6767`.

```
Maine(config-if)#smds static-map novell de01.0c00.1234.4532.0411
c123.4565.6767
```

You can allow broadcasts to be sent on the SMDS interface by linking the SMDS E.164 multicast address with the broadcast address of a higher-level routed protocol. This facility ensures that the router does not have to replicate broadcast messages to every remote host. To link addresses for multicast traffic, use the SMDS Multicast command with the syntax:

```
smds multicast protocol smds-address
```

The SMDS E.164 group address has been specified as e180.0999.9999. To assign this address to Novell traffic, enter the command shown.

```
Maine(config-if)#smds multicast novell e180.0999.9999
```

If you have an Address Resolution Protocol (ARP) server on your network ou need to configure the SMDS Multicast ARP command on the router. This command maps an SMDS group address to an ARP multicast address.

Whether you specify the multicast ARP address or not is optional. When broadcast ARPs are sent, SMDS first attempts to send the packet to all multicast ARP SMDS addresses. If you have not specified one in the configuration, broadcast ARPs are sent instead to all multicast IP SMDS multicast addresses. If you do not specify the optional ARP multicast address, you must specify an IP multicast command to be used for broadcasting.

In this case the SMDS Multicast ARP command has been entered with the SMDS address but without the ARP multicast address. You also enter the SMDS Multicast IP command which maps the SMDS address to a multicast IP address.

```
Maine(config-if)#smds multicast arp e180.0999.9999
```

When there is no IP address specified in the SMDS Multicast IP command, the default value is the IP address specified on the interface. Here the default form of the command is entered as `smds multicast ip` e180.0999.9999. Broadcasts for Novell, ARP, and IP will now use the SMDS group address.

```
Maine(config-if)#smds multicast ip e180.0999.9999
```

You can enable dynamic address learning using the Address Resolution Protocol by typing smds enable-arp. The multicast address for ARP *must* be set before this command is issued.

```
Maine(config-if)#smds enable-arp
```

Type exit to put the router in Configuration mode. Then exit out of Configuration mode and save the changes. The Maine router is now configured for data transmission across the SMDS network. The router's Serial 1 interface has been configured with an SMDS address and higher-level protocols are mapped with an SMDS address for broadcasts.

```
Maine(config-if)#exit
Maine(config)#^Z
Maine#copy running-config startup-config
Building configuration...
[OK]
Maine#
```

Introduction to ATM

This section examines ATM features and operation. We will describe the ATM layers and explain how LAN emulation works.

ATM Overview

Asynchronous Transfer Mode (ATM) is an evolving cell-based technology. It is based on work done by the ITU-T to develop the Broadband Integrated Services Digital Network (BISDN) for the high-speed transfer of voice, video, and data through public networks.

The ATM forum was jointly founded in 1991 by Cisco Systems, NET/ADAPTIVE, Northern Telecom, and Sprint. Its aim is to extend ATM to private networks and to guarantee interoperability between public and private networks.

ATM uses very large-scale integration (VLSI) technology to segment data, such as frames, at high speeds into units called *cells*. ATM cells consist of 5 bytes of header information and 48 bytes of payload data. A *payload* is a portion of a frame that contains upper layer information.

Cells transit ATM networks by passing through devices called ATM switches. Information in the cell header is analyzed so that the cell can be switched to the output interface connecting the cells switch with the next switch on its path to a destination.

ATM combines the constant transmission delay and guaranteed capacity of *circuit switching* with the flexibility and efficiency of *packet switching*. ATM also builds on the strengths of time-division multiplexing (TDM) by using time slots. However, unlike TDM's fixed time slot transmission, ATM time slots are made available on demand and a station can send cells whenever necessary.

ATM uses a star topology. The ATM switch acts as a hub in the ATM network where all devices are directly attached. A star topology network offers easier troubleshooting and support for network configuration changes and additions.

ATM's switching fabric provides *additive* bandwidth. As long as the switch can handle the aggregate cell transfer rate, additional connections to the switch can be made and bandwidth increases accordingly.

ATM supports point-to-point and point-to-multipoint connection types. Multipoint-to-multipoint connections have to be provided by a multicast server.

There are two types of connection service with ATM: switched virtual connections (SVC) and permanent virtual connections (PVC). An SVC is a virtual connection that is dynamically established on demand and is torn down when transmission is complete. SVCs are used when data transmission is sporadic.

A PVC is a permanently established virtual circuit. PVCs save bandwidth associated with circuit establishment. A PVC operates like frame relay in that a virtual connection mesh, partial mesh, or star is administratively established through the ATM network between the routers. The advantages of ATM PVC are direct ATM connection between routers and simplicity of specification and implementation. The disadvantages of ATM PVC include static connectivity and the administrative overhead of manually providing virtual connections.

Some of the transmission links over which ATM can communicate are: European Digital Signal 3 (DS3/E3) at 34 Mbps, Transparent Asynchronous Xmitter/receiver Interface (TAXI) at 100 Mbps, Synchronous Optical NETwork (SONET) at 155 Mbps, Synchronous Digital Hierarchy (SDH), and Data eXchange Interface (DXI).

The ATM Forum specifies the subnetwork model of addressing. This means that ATM's ATM layer must map network layer addresses to ATM addresses.

One ATM address format is used in public networks and three different formats are for use in private networks. Public ATM networks use *E.164 numbers*, which are also used by Narrowband Integrated Services Digital Network (N-ISDN) networks. E.164 numbers consist of 1 byte of authority and format identifier, 8 bytes of ISDN telephone number, 2 bytes of routing domain, 2 bytes of area identifier, 6 bytes of end system identifier (an IEEE 802 MAC address), and 1 byte of Network Service Access Point (NSAP) selector.

The three private network formats are Data Country Code (DCC), International Code Designator (ICD), and NSAP encapsulated E.164. The DCC and the ICD have formats similar to the E.164 except that in place of the ISDN telephone number they contain 2 bytes of DCC or ICD, 1 byte of domain specific part (DSP) format identifier, and 3 bytes of administrative authority (AA).

ATM address formats are modeled on ISO NSAP addresses but identify SubNetwork Point of Attachment (SNPA) addresses. An SNPA is a data-link layer MAC address. Incorporating such MAC addresses into the ATM address facilitates mapping of ATM addresses into existing LANs.

ATM Layers

The ATM consists of three functional layers: ATM physical layer, ATM layer, and ATM adaptation layer (AAL). The ATM layers roughly correspond with the physical layer and the error control and framing portions of the data-link layer of the OSI reference model (Figure 23.5).

The ATM physical layer controls transmission and receipt of bits on the physical medium. It keeps track of ATM cell boundaries and also packages cells into the appropriate type of frame for the physical medium being used. The ATM physical layer consists of the physical medium sublayer and transmission convergence sublayer.

The *physical medium sublayer* is responsible for sending and receiving a continuous flow of bits. The bits are transmitted with timing information to synchronize transmission and reception. The exact specification of the physical medium sublayer depends on the physical medium used. There are several physical media capable of carrying ATM cells: SONET, Synchronous Digital Hierarchy (SDH), European Digital Signal Level 3 (DS3/E3), FDDI physical layer, 100 Mbps local fiber, and Fiber Channel physical layer, 155 Mbps local fiber.

The *transmission convergence sublayer* of the ATM physical layer is responsible for cell delineation and header error control sequence generation and verification. It also provides cell-rate decoupling, in which unassigned ATM cells are inserted or suppressed to adapt the rate of valid ATM cells to the payload capacity of the transmission system.

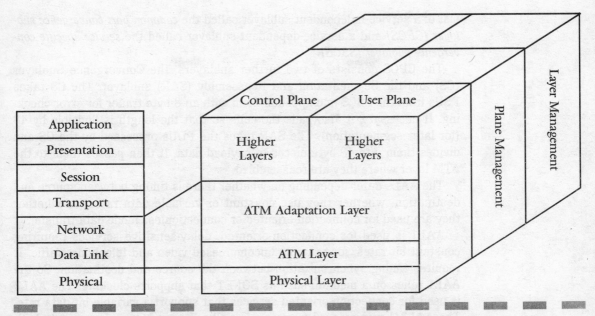

| Application |
| Presentation |
| Session |
| Transport |
| Network |
| Data Link |
| Physical |

Control Plane | User Plane | Plane Management | Layer Management

Higher Layers | Higher Layers

ATM Adaptation Layer

ATM Layer

Physical Layer

FIGURE 23.5 The ATM reference model relates to the lowest two layers of the OSI reference model.

In the transmission convergence sublayer ATM cells are adapted into appropriate frames for physical-layer implementation. The appropriate physical-layer frame structure is also generated and maintained.

The next layer is the ATM layer, which is responsible for establishing connections and passing cells through the ATM network. The ATM layer is where switching takes place. ATM switches use the *virtual channel information (VCI)* and *virtual path information (VPI)* fields of a cell header to identify the next network segment that the cell needs to transit on its route. A *virtual channel* is equivalent to a virtual circuit and describes a logical connection between the two ends of a communication connection. A *virtual path* is a logical grouping of virtual circuits. The main function of the ATM switch is to receive cells on a port and switch those cells to the proper output port based on the VPI and VCI values of the cell. A switching table maps input ports to output ports based on the value of the VPI and VCI fields.

The next ATM layer is the ATM adaptation layer (AAL). This translates between the larger *service data units (SDUs)* of upper layer processes (such as video streams and data packets), and ATM cells. The ATM adaptation layer (AAL) receives packets from upper level protocols and breaks them into 48-byte ATM payload segments.

The ITU-T has specified four types of AAL according to the different services they support. These are AAL1, AAL2, AAL3/4, and AAL5. All AALs consist of a service-independent sublayer called the *common part convergence sub-layer (CPCS)* and a service-dependent sublayer called the *service specific convergence sublayer (SSCS)*.

The CPCS consists of two further sublayers, the Convergence Sublayer (CS) and the Segmentation and Reassembly (SAR) sublayer. The CS takes PSUs from the SSCS and appends them with an 8-byte trailer for error checking. If necessary, it also pads the cells so that the length is divisible by 48 (for later segmentation). The SAR takes the PDUs processed by the CS and divides them into 48-byte pieces of payload data. It then passes them to the ATM layer where they are reassembled.

The AALs differ depending on whether there is timing between source and destination, whether they use constant or variable data rates, or whether they are used for connection-oriented or connectionless mode data transfer.

AAL1 is used for connection-oriented, delay-sensitive services requiring constant bit rates, for example uncompressed video and telephone traffic. It requires timing synchronization between the source and destination. So the AAL1 relies on a medium such as SONET that supports clocking. The AAL2 is used for connection-oriented services that support a variable bit data rate. The AAL3/4 was merged from two initially distinct layers. It supports both connectionless and connection-oriented links. It is primarily used for the transmission of SMDS packets over ATM networks.

The AAL5 supports connection-oriented, variable bit rate services and is used to transfer most non-SMDS data such as classical IP over ATM and LAN emulation (LANE) traffic. AAL5 uses the Simple and Efficient AAL (SEAL) scheme where the SAR sublayer segments CS PDUs without adding additional fields. AAL5 offers low-bandwidth overhead and simple processing requirements. Consequently there is reduced bandwidth capacity and error-recovery capability.

LAN Emulation

If you have existing legacy LAN technology you can use *LAN emulation (LANE)* to provide interoperability between this technology and ATM-based workstations and devices. The ATM LANE standard provides that workstations attached through ATM have the same capabilities as legacy LAN equipment (Figure 23.6).

LANE uses a MAC data-link layer encapsulation method so that a large number of network-layer protocols can be supported. Since communication is at the data-link layer, all devices attached to an emulated LAN act as a bridged segment. Bridges function at the data-link layer to connect and pass packets between two network segments that use the same communications

protocol. Traffic from network-layer protocols such as AppleTalk and IPX can
be forwarded rapidly between networks as in any bridged environment.

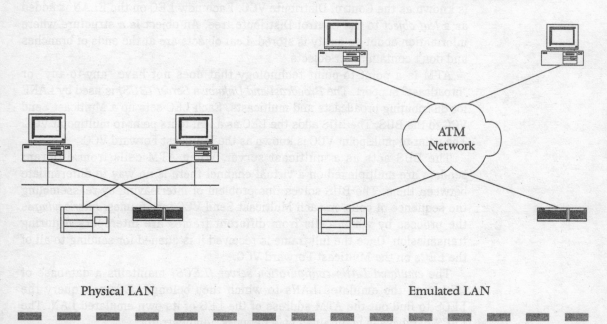

Physical LAN   **Emulated LAN**

FIGURE 23.6   *ATM networks can emulate a physical LAN.*

In ATM LANE environments, ATM switches handle traffic within a particular emulated LAN (ELAN) and routers handle inter-ELAN traffic. LANE
components include: LAN emulation client (LEC), LAN emulation server
(LES), Broadcast and Unknown Server (BUS), and LAN emulation configuration server (LECS).

A *LAN emulation client (LEC)* is an entity in an end system. It performs
data forwarding, address resolution, and registration of MAC addresses with
the LANE server. A LEC also provides a LAN service interface to any higher
layer entity that interfaces to the LEC.

Each LEC is identified by a unique ATM address and is associated with
one or more MAC addresses reachable through that ATM address. End systems that support LANE, such as network interface card (NIC)-connected
workstations, Catalyst 5000 switches, and Cisco 7000 routers, require LEC
implementation. LECs communicate with each other via ATM virtual channel
connections (VCCs).

Another element in a LANE is a *LAN emulation server (LES)*. This provides
a central control point for all LECs. LECs forward registration and control

information to the LES through a Control Direct VCC. In turn the LES forwards control information to LECs through its point-to-multipoint VCC which is known as the Control Distribute VCC. Each new LEC on the ELAN is added as a *leaf object* to the Control Distribute tree. An object is a structure where information about an entity is stored. Leaf objects are at the ends of branches and don't contain other objects.

ATM is a point-to-point technology that does not have "any-to-any" or "broadcast" support. The *Broadcast and Unknown Server (BUS)* is used by LANE for distributing broadcasts and multicasts. Each LEC sets up a Multicast Send VCC to the BUS. The BUS adds the LEC as a leaf to its point-to-multipoint VCC. The point-to-multipoint VCC is known as the Multicast Forward VCC.

The BUS acts as a multicast server. When ATM cells from different senders are multiplexed on a virtual channel there is no way to differentiate between them. The BUS solves this problem of interleaving by reassembling the sequence of cells on each Multicast Send VCC into frames. *Interleaving* is the process by which cells from different frames are interspersed during transmission. Once the full frame is received it is queued for sending to all of the LECs on the Multicast Forward VCC.

The *emulated LANs configuration server (LECS)* maintains a database of LECs and the emulated LANs to which they belong. LECs can query the LECS to find out the ATM address of the LES of its own emulated LAN. The LECS database is maintained by a network administrator.

FIGURE 23.7
An ELAN consists of clients, servers, and various intermediate nodes.

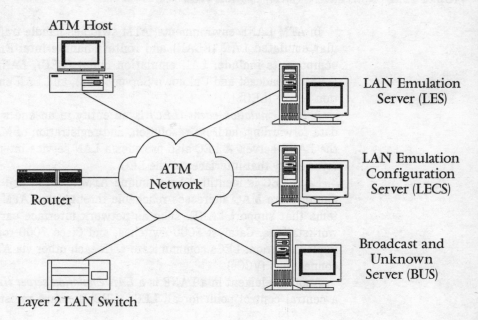

ATM Host

LAN Emulation
Server (LES)

LAN Emulation
Configuration
Server (LECS)

ATM
Network

Router

Broadcast and
Unknown
Server (BUS)

Layer 2 LAN Switch

In LAN emulation operation, the LEC must first find the LECS in order to discover which emulated LAN it should join. First the LEC queries the ATM switch through the Interim Local Management Interface (ILMI). The switch has a Management Information Base variable set up with the ATM address of the LEC.

The LEC uses unicast signaling to contact the LECS. It searches for a fixed ATM address. This address is specified by the ATM forum as the LECS ATM address.

The LEC creates a signaling packet containing the ATM address of the LECS. It then signals a Configure Direct VCC, and issues an LE_CONFIG-URE_REQUEST on that VCC. The LECS compares the information in this request with the data in the database. It assigns the LEC to an emulated LAN on the basis of the LEC's source ATM address.

If a matching entry is found for the LEC then the LECS returns an LE_CONFIGURE_RESPONSE. This contains the address of the LES that serves the desired emulated LAN. If no matching entry is found the LEC may be assigned to a default LES.

Once the LEC has discovered the ATM address of the desired LES, it drops the connection to the LECS. It then creates a signaling packet with the ATM address of the LES and signals a Control Direct VCC.

Once there is successful VCC setup, the LEC sends an LE_JOIN REQUEST. This contains the LEC ATM address and the MAC address that the LEC wants to register with the ELAN. This information is maintained so that no two LECs can register the same MAC or ATM addresses.

When the LES receives the LE_JOIN_REQUEST it verifies the request with the LECS. Once the client's membership is confirmed, the LES adds the LEC as a leaf of its point-to-multipoint Control Distribute VCC. Finally the LES issues the LEC a successful LE_JOIN_RESPONSE containing a LANE client ID (LECID). This is the client's unique identifier and is used by the LEC to filter its own broadcasts from the BUS.

Once the LEC has successfully joined the LES, its first task is to find the ATM address of the BUS and join the broadcast group. To do this, the LEC creates an LE_ARP_REQUEST packet with the MAC address 0xFFFFFFFF. The LE_ARP packet is sent on the Control Direct VCC to the LES. The LES then forwards the ATM address of the BUS to the LEC over the Control Distribute VCC.

Once the LEC has the ATM address of the BUS, it creates a signaling packet containing the address and signals a Multicast Send VCC. When the BUS receives the signaling request it adds the LEC as a leaf on its point-to-multipoint Multicast Forward VCC. The LEC is now a member of the emulated LAN.

LANE has the valuable capability of providing an ATM forwarding path for unicast traffic between LECs. To send a data packet to a destination with an unknown ATM address, the LEC initially utilizes two separate but simultaneous methods. The LEC issues an LE_ARP_REQUEST on the Control Direct VCC to the LES. The ARP will map the destination's MAC address with its ATM address. The LES sends the request over the Control Distribute VCC so that it is received by all LECs. At the same time the unicast data packets are sent to the BUS to be forwarded to all endpoints (Figure 23.8).

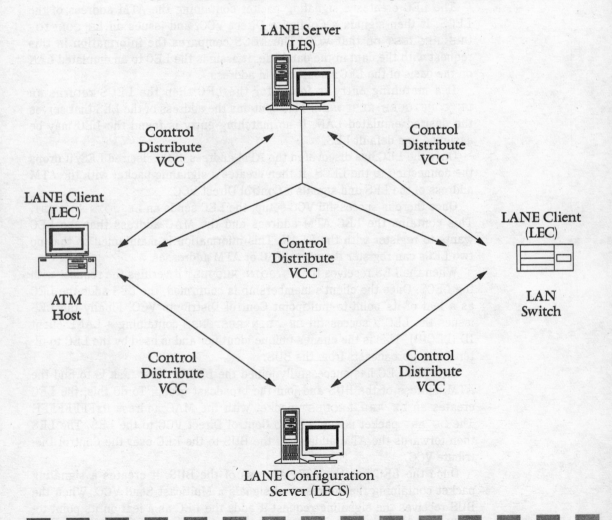

FIGURE 23.8   LANE control connections link the LES, LECS, LAN switch, and ATM host.

Flooding data packets through the BUS is not a bandwidth-efficient transmission method. In response to this, the LANE standard allows a transmission rate on this path of just 10 packets per second. Unicast packets only continue to use the BUS until the LE_ARP_REQUEST has been resolved.

Bridging or switching devices with LEC software on the emulated LAN translate and forward the ARP on their LAN interfaces. The appropriate LEC issues an LE_ARP_RESPONSE and sends it to the LES. The LES sends the response over the Control Distribute VCC so that all LECs can learn the new MAC-to-ATM address binding.

Once the requesting LEC receives the LE_ARP_RESPONSE with the required ATM address, it begins to signal the other LECs and sets up a Data Direct VCC for unicast transmission. The Data Direct VCC path is an optimal path compared to BUS unicasting. The LEC cannot switch immediately to the new path because sent packets may then arrive out of order.

To prevent ordering difficulties, the LEC generates a flush packet and sends it to the BUS. When the LEC receives its own flush packet on the Multicast Forward VCC, it knows that all other unicast packets have finished transmitting on the BUS. The Data Direct VCC can now be used.

Cisco IOS Software Release 11.0 implements LECS, LEC, LES, and BUS functionality in the ATM interface processor (AIP) card. LECS, LEC, LES, and BUS functions are defined on ATM subinterfaces. One physical interface, for example OC-3 fiber, may be logically divided into as many as 255 interfaces.

Design considerations to bear in mind are that VCCs can be either SVCs or PVCs but PVCs are so administratively complex as to allow only small networks to be manageable; if an LEC on a router is assigned an IP, IPX, or AppleTalk address, that protocol is routable over that LEC; and when multiple LECs on a router have protocol addresses, routing only occurs between emulated LANs (ELANs).

What follows are various LANE design considerations to keep in mind. The AIP is limited to 60K packets per second bidirectionally. One LECS supports all ELANs. In each ELAN, there is one LES/BUS pair and some number of LECs. The LES and BUS functionality must be defined on the same interface and cannot be separated. There can only be one LES/BUS pair per ELAN. The current LANE Phase 1 standard does not provide for any LES/BUS redundancy. The LECS and LES/BUS can be different routers, bridges, or workstations. When you are defining VLANS with the Catalyst 5000 switch, each VLAN color should be assigned to a different ELAN. The LES/BUS pair for each ELAN can reside on different subinterfaces on the same AIP, different AIPs in the same router, or different AIPs in different routers. There can be only one LEC per subinterface. For routing between ELANs to function correctly, an ELAN should only be in one subnet for a particular protocol.

The ATM Forum has developed a standard called the ATM Data Exchange Interface (DXI). This is an interim specification to provide ATM functionality as soon as possible to network designers. DXI can be used to provide User-Network Interface (UNI) support between Cisco routers and ATM networks. The ATM data service unit (ADSU) receives data from the router in ATM DXI format over a High-Speed Serial Interface (HSSI). The DSU converts the data into ATM cells and transfers them to the ATM network over a DS-3/E3 line.

ATM DXI addressing consists of a DXI Frame Address (DFA) which is equivalent to a frame relay data-link connection identifier (DLCI). A DLCI is a virtual circuit address on a UNI that allows a frame to be identified as coming from a particular PVC. The DSU maps the DFA into appropriate VPI and VCI values in the ATM cell.

ATM DXI is available in three frame modes: 1a, 1b, and 2. These differ according to the ATM adaptation layers they support, the number of virtual circuits provided, and the maximum number of octets of data carried.

Cisco Software Release 9.21 and above supports only Mode 1a, which has the following features: it supports AAL5 only, it has a 9,232 octet maximum, it has a 16-bit Frame Check Sequence field, and it provides 1,023 virtual circuits. Here the router is configured as a DTE device and is connected to an ADSU. The ADSU is configured as a data communications equipment (DCE) device.

The router encapsulates data from upper-layer protocols into ATM DXI frame format. It then sends the ATM DXI frames to the ADSU. Here the frames are converted into ATM cells by being processed through the AAL5 CS and the SAR. The ATM layer attaches the header and the cells are sent out the ATM UNI interface.

ATM Configuration

This section explains how an ATM AIP is configured. We will outline the ATM configuration tasks and the commands used for AIP configuration.

ATM Configuration Tasks

To configure your router for access to ATM networks you need to configure the ATM Interface Processor (AIP). This is the network interface to ATM used on Cisco 7000 and 7010 router series running software later than Cisco IOS Release 10.0.

Higher-level protocols running over LANs can connect to an ATM network through the AIP interface (Figure 23.9). In this case an ATM network connects Routers A, B, and C, each of which has LANs connected. An IP packet is being sent through Router A from network 172.16.46.0 to 172.16.45.0.

FIGURE 23.9
An illustration of an ATM network with an AIP interface.

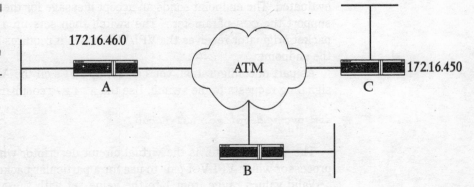

Router A's routing table determines the next hop. It does this by mapping the destination network number with the address of the router (Router C) connected to the desired network. Next, an address resolution table maps the next-hop IP address to an ATM NSAP. Finally the source router (Router A) signals the destination router (Router C) over the ATM network to establish a virtual connection. The packet is then forwarded.

ATM has a system for regulating traffic flow which is similar to the SMDS access classes. When an end station connects to an ATM network, it is considered to have entered a *contract* with the network. The contract specifies an *envelope* which describes the manner in which traffic is intended to flow. The envelope specifies values for peak bandwidth, average sustained bandwidth, and maximum burst size. These parameters are known as *Quality of Service (QoS)* parameters and form an important part of the switching process.

An ATM device (Router A) attempts to establish a connection with another ATM device (Router B) by sending a signaling request packet to its directly connected ATM switch. The signaling request contains the ATM address of the desired ATM destination and the QOS parameters required for the connection.

The signaling packet is reassembled by the switch. Once it has found the switch table entry for Router B's ATM address, the switch also checks whether it can support the specified QOS parameters.

If the QOS parameters cannot be supported, the signaling request is rejected and a rejection message is returned to the end station. If the QOS parameters are supported, the switch then sets up a virtual connection on the input link and forwards the signaling request out over the appropriate interface. The correct interface is specified in the switching table for the ATM NSAP of

Router B. This process occurs over a series of switches as far as the switch directly connected to the destination router.

When the signaling packet reaches the endpoint it is reassembled and evaluated. The endpoint sends an accept message for the packet only if it can support the QOS parameters. The switch then sets up a virtual circuit. The packet originator receives the VPI/VCI values it requires for cell switching to the endpoint.

As part of configuration, you can set up PVCs on the AIP interface to carry signaling requests to the switch. Use the ATM PVC command, whose syntax is:

```
atm pvc vcd vpi vci aal-encap
```

The VCD parameter is the virtual circuit descriptor which identifies to the processor which VPI-VCI pair to use for a particular packet.

Valid values range from 1 to the value set with the ATM MAXC command, which can establish a ceiling value for the VCD of 256, 512, 1024, 2048, or 4096. The VPI parameter is the network virtual path identifier of this PVC in the range 0 through 255. The VPI value must match that of the switch. The VCI parameter is the network virtual channel identifier of the PVC in the range 0 through 65535. You can specify either the VPI or VCI parameters as 0 but not both as 0 simultaneously.

You need to specify a value for the Aal-Encap parameter. Values differ depending on the type of PVC, the AAL layer used, and the encapsulation type. For instance the value qsaal is specified for a signaling-type PVC that is used for setting up or tearing down SVCs. The value ilmi is used to set up communication with the ILMI.

The AIP card uses multiprotocol encapsulation over AAL5 to transport data through an ATM network. Multiprotocol encapsulation is specified in RFC 1483. AIP supports AppleTalk, Banyan Virtual Network System (VINES), Connectionless Network Service (CLNS), DECnet, Internet Protocol (IP), and Novell Internetwork Packet Exchange (IPX).

RFC 1483 specifies null encapsulation, known as *VC Mux*. This creates a separate virtual circuit for each protocol. Where VC Mux is used you specify the Aal-Encap value as aal5mux *protocol name*, for example aal5mux ip. RFC 1483 also specifies the use of an LLC/SNAP 8-byte header to identify the encapsulated protocol. The value specified in this instance is aal5snap.

The switch can use traffic policing to check that the end station complies with the QOS parameters. It compares the actual traffic flow with those criteria. If the agreed parameters have been violated, the switch sets the Cell Loss Priority (CLP) bit of the illegal cells. This makes the cells *discard eligible*, so that they will be dropped during periods of congestion.

The end station uses *traffic shaping* in order to comply with the QOS parameters. One important configuration task is to configure queues on the AIP in order to constrain data bursts, limit peak data rate, and set sustainable rates.

In AIP configuration you can assign a virtual circuit to one of eight *rate queues*. Each rate queue represents a portion of the overall bandwidth available on an ATM link. You can program each rate queue with a different peak rate at which the circuit will transmit data by using the ATM Rate-Queue command.

In the ATM Rate-Queue command, you specify a queue number of zero to three for high-priority queues and four to seven for low-priority queues. You also specify the maximum speed or peak rate according to the Physical Layer Interface Module (PLIM) type used.

You can also assign the peak and average rate and a specific burst size to each virtual circuit. To do this, use the Peak, Average, and Burst optional parameters in the ATM PVC command. The peak value should match the value specified by the ATM Rate-Queue command.

If some of your data transmission over the ATM network occurs only on a sporadic basis, your AIP will use SVC mode. In this case you need to set a network service access point (NSAP) address. This is a network-layer address that marks the junction with the OSI transport layer and is required for signaling.

The Map-List command used with an IP address sets up the static mapping of an IP network number to an ATM NSAP address. If required, this static mapping can also specify that QoS parameters will be used. The Map-Group command associates the map list to the ATM interface being configured for a PVC or SVC.

Use the Map-Class command to put the router in Map-Class Configuration mode. This is so that the QOS parameters that are associated with the static map for an SVC can be defined. The Map-Class configuration commands for SVCs have a function similar to that of Peak, Average, and Burst optional parameters of the ATM PVC command.

Examples of Map-Class configuration commands are ATM Forward-Max-Burst-Size, ATM Forward-Peak-Cell-Rate, and ATM Forward-Sustainable-Cell-Rate. These commands set the maximum number, the peak rate (in Kbps), and the sustainable rate (in Kbps) respectively of cells going from the source router to the destination router on the SVC. To set values for cells from the destination to the source router, replace the syntax Forward and Backward.

ATM AIP Configuration

Here are the commands that are used to configure an AIP. The ATM interface has been configured with the IP address 192.168.2.1.

```
interface atm 4/0
ip address 192.168.2.1 255.255.255.0
```

The interface is using an SVC, and its NSAP address has to be configured so it can be identified by routers. The NSAP address is the 40-digit hexadecimal address of the interface (source address).

```
atm nsap-address ab.cef.01.234567.bcde.f012.3456.7890.1234.12
```

A PVC is required on the interface. The ATM PVC command is used to assign a PVC to the ATM interface. In this case the PVC is used for establishing and tearing down SVCs, so the AAL encapsulation value is qsaal.

When the QSAAL option is used in the ATM PVC command, the VPI must be 0 and the VCI, 5. The VCD value for this AIP is 1. The syntax for the command is:

```
atm pvc vcd vpi vci aal-encap
```

The complete command to enter is:

```
atm pvc 1 0 5 qsaal
```

The Map-Group command associates a map list to the ATM interface. The map list is configured at a later stage. In this case the map list has been given the name shasta.

```
map-group shasta
```

Here two rate queues have been configured. Queue 0 specifies a speed of 155 Mbps for use of the PLIM SONET. Queue 1 specifies a speed of 45 Mbps, used for the DS-3. These rate queues are numbered within the range 0 through 3, so they are high priority queues.

```
atm rate-queue 0 155
atm rate-queue 1 45
```

The Map-List command sets up the static mapping of a specified network number and an ATM NSAP address and the Map-Class command sets up QOS parameters.

Here the map list shasta sets up the static mapping of IP addresses 172.17.3.5 and 172.18.1.2 with the NSAP address of the interface. There are no QOS parameters associated with the static mapping of 172.17.3.5. However er the mapping of IP address 172.18.1.2 will be confined by the QOS parameters specified as part of Map-Class configuration.

```
map-list shasta
ip 172.17.3.5 atm-nsap
bb.cdef.01.234567.890a.bcde.f012.3456.7890.1234.12
ip 172.18.1.2 atm-nsap
bb.cdef.01.234567.890a.bcde.f012.3456.7890.1234.12 class qos
```

The Map-Class command puts the router in Map-Class Configuration
mode. Then the QOS parameters can be specified. In this case there is a forward-peak-cell-rate and a backward-max-burst-size specified.

```
map-class qosclass
atm forward-peak-cell-rate-clp0 15000
atm backward-max-burst-size-clp0 96 interface atm 4/0
```

In the ATM Forward-Peak-Cell-Rate-Clp0 command, the Cell Loss
priority 0 (Clp0) element indicates that the command relates to high priority
cells or *insured traffic*. In the ATM Forward-Peak-Cell-Rate-Clp1 command, Clp1 indicates *best-effort traffic* which may be dropped in congested
conditions. The Forward element of the command indicates that the peak
rate is specified for traffic flowing from the source to the destination router.
In this case, the peak rate at which the SVC can send the high priority cells
have been specified as 15000 Kbps.

In the ATM Backward-Max-Burst-Size-Clp0 command, the number of
high priority (Clp0) cells, traveling from the destination to the source router
at the burst level on the SVC has been specified. This maximum number or
cell count has been set at 96.

On the AIP, an ATM interface has been configured with a PVC and SVC.
Rate queues have been specified for the PVC. An NSAP address for the SVC
has been configured and the SVC's QoS parameters have been specified.
There is static mapping of two IP addresses with the interface's NSAP
address. The router is now ready for ATM transmission.

Bandwidth
on Demand

Dial-on-demand Routing (DDR)

This section describes how to configure dial-on-demand routing (DDR). We will examine how to configure DDR on a Cisco router and describe how to configure DDR traffic filters and authentication. We will then configure DDR traffic filters and monitor authentication on a Cisco router.

Overview

Bandwidth refers to the available traffic capacity of a link. Cisco routers support the following types of bandwidth on demand: dial-on-demand routing (DDR), advanced DDR (DDR with access lists, rotary group DDR, DDR for IPX), dial backup, and dial backup using Integrated Services Digital Network (ISDN) DDR.

DDR is used for low-volume, periodic network connections. For this dial-up environment, you specify static routes so that routing updates are not exchanged across the ISDN or the Public Switched Telephone Network (PSTN).

DDR in-band calls start when the router receives packet traffic marked as *interesting*. Interesting traffic consists of packets that pass the restrictions of access lists. You identify a serial interface for a DDR access group and specify protocol list (or access list) statements to check for interesting traffic. You can use different list settings to designate interesting traffic mapped for other DDR destination routers.

The routers attach to Data Circuit-terminating Equipment (DCE), such as ISDN Terminal Adaptors (TAs) or modems that support V.25bis dialing. Some routers don't need an ISDN TA because they have an ISDN interface. You set up calling details for these devices in scripts and dialer commands.

When an interesting packet arrives at the router, this traffic dictates a need for DDR. The router sends call setup information to the DCE device on the specified serial line. The call connects the local device to the remote device attached to the destination router.

DDR can now use this static route to transmit packet traffic. An idle timer starts as soon as no more traffic is transmitted over the DDR call. After the idle timeout occurs, the call is disconnected.

FIGURE 24.1 An illustration of the Maine router connecting to Vermont via DDR.

Let's look now at a DDR configuration example. Here, DDR is being configured to connect a router called Maine to another router called Vermont.

```
1   Maine>enable
2   Password:
3   Maine#configure terminal
4   Enter configuration commands, one per line. End with CNTL/Z.
5   Maine(config)#isdn switch-type basic-net3
6   Maine(config)#interface ethernet0
7   Maine(config-if)#ip address 172.16.1.1 255.255.255.0
8   Maine(config-if)#interface bri0
9   Maine(config-if)#encapsulation ppp
10  Maine(config-if)#ip address 172.16.46.1 255.255.255.0
11  Maine(config-if)#dialer idle-timeout 60
12  Maine(config-if)#dialer map ip 172.16.46.2 8064325
13  Maine(config-if)#dialer-group 1
14  Maine(config-if)#exit
15  Maine(config)#dialer-list 1 protocol ip permit
16  Maine(config)#ip route 172.16.192.0 255.255.255.0 172.16.46.2
17  Maine(config)#^Z
18  Maine#copy running-config startup-config
19  Building configuration...
20  [OK]
21  Maine#
```

There are two main configuration tasks in global configuration, switch type and traffic to specify the trigger for a DDR call are entered. In interface configuration, addressing, interface specifications, and optional features are configured.

All the networks shown have subnet masks of 255.255.255.0. Static route statements define the IP route to the Vermont router over 172.16.46.0 (line 16).

IP packets, but not IPX packets or IGRP routing updates, will trigger a call (line 12). An access list must define the details on what is interesting to DDR (line 15). The service provider's switch is a model basic-net3 (line 5). The number to be dialed (8064325) is the number of the DCE device (line 12).

The Dialer-List Protocol command is used to associate the interface dialer group number with a list of protocols permitted for DDR. The command is:

```
dialer-list dialer-group protocol protocol-name {permit  deny}
```

The Dialer-Group argument specifies the number of the dialer group. The Protocol-Name keyword specifies the protocol for packets to be considered for DDR. Choices for the Protocol-Name keyword include IP and IPX. In line 15, the dialer group is 1 and the protocol name is IP.

The `Permit/Deny` argument is an optional entry to specifically permit or deny a protocol for DDR. Permit is the default.

The `Dialer-Group` command is used to assign an interface to a dialer access group. This command connects the interface you are configuring to access list statements that identify interesting protocol traffic. You may need additional resources to filter interesting traffic for DDR—for example, you must use access lists to select specific packets types in IP and IPX. The command is:

```
dialer-group group-number
```

The `Group-Number` argument specifies the number of the dialer group to which the interface belongs. The group number can be any integer between 1 and 10. In line 13, the Basic Rate 0 interface is associated with dialing access group 1.

The `Dialer Map` command is used to define one or several dial-on-demand numbers for a particular interface. It must be used with the `Dialer-Group` command and its associated access list to initiate dialing. The command is:

```
dialer map protocol next-hop-address dialer-string
```

The `Protocol` keyword can be `ip`, `ipx`, or `appletalk`. The `Next-Hop-Address` argument means the address of the next-hop router. The `Dialer-String` argument means the string sent to the DCE device when packets with the specified next-hop address are received. In line 12, 8064325 is the number of the DCE device to be called.

The `Dialer Load-Threshold` command is used to configure bandwidth on demand by setting the maximum load before the dialer places another call to a destination. The command is:

```
dialer load-threshold load
```

The `Load` argument means the interface load beyond which the dialer will initiate another call to the destination.

The `Dialer Fast-Idle` command establishes the amount of time to wait before disconnecting the currently active call. Active calls will be disconnected when another call needs to use this interface. The command is:

```
dialer fast-idle seconds
```

The `Seconds` argument means the amount of time to wait (in seconds) before an idle link is disconnected when another call is pending on this interface.

The `Dialer Idle-Timeout` command is used to specify the number of idle seconds before a call is disconnected. The command is:

```
dialer idle-timeout seconds
```

The `Seconds` argument means the amount of time to wait (in seconds) before an idle link is disconnected. In line 11, 60 seconds is established as the idle time before the call is disconnected.

DDR Traffic Filters and Authentication

Identifying interesting traffic is essential to the operation of DDR. You can define interesting traffic within a protocol using access lists because filtering offers greater precision for specifying what is interesting.

Let's look now at a DDR traffic filter example. In this example, extended IP access lists are used to identify interesting traffic for DDR and only FTP traffic is allowed to trigger a call to activate to the link.

```
1   Maine>enable
2   Password:
3   Maine# configure terminal
4   Enter configuration commands, one per line. End with CNTL/Z.
5   Maine(config)# isdn switch-type basic-net3
6   Maine(config)# interface ethernet0
7   Maine(config-if)# ip address 172.16.1.1 255.255.255.0
8   Maine(config-if)# interface bri0
9   Maine(config-if)# encapsulation ppp
10  Maine(config-if)# ppp authentication chap
11  Maine(config-if)# ip address 172.16.46.1 255.255.255.0
12  Maine(config-if)# dialer idle-timeout 60
13  Maine(config-if)# dialer map ip 172.16.46.2 8064325
14  Maine(config-if)# dialer-group 1
15  Maine(config-if)# exit
16  Maine(config)# username Vermont password secret
17  Maine(config)# access-list 101 deny igrp any any
18  Maine(config)# access-list 101 deny icmp any 172.16.192.0
    0.0.0.255 echo
19  Maine(config)# access-list 101 permit ip any 172.16.182.0
    0.0.0.255 eq ftp
20  Maine(config)# dialer-list 1 list 101
21  Maine(config)# ip route 172.16.192.0 255.255.255.0
    172.16.46.2
22  Maine(config)# ^Z
23  Maine# copy running-config startup-config
24  Building configuration...
25  [OK]
26  Maine#
```

Using access lists allows you to specify interesting packets for DDR. Access lists also specify traffic within a single protocol (see lines 17 through 19). The access lists in this example deny IGRP routing updates and the ICMP operation. However, they allow FTP to trigger the call.

The `Dialer-List List` command is the variation for DDR filtering that associates the dialer group number with the access lists of permit and deny statements. In line 20, dialer group 1 is associated with access list 101.

An echo request cannot initiate the link. An FTP session can be successfully tried to machine 172.16.192.23. As soon as the link is up and the file transfer is in progress, you can ping the devices in the network.

```
Vermont# ping 172.16.192.23

Type escape sequence to abort.
Sending 5, 100-byte ICMP Echoes to 172.16.192.23, timeout is 2
seconds:
.....
Success rate is 0 percent (0/5)
Vermont#

Vermont# ping 172.16.192.23

Type escape sequence to abort.
Sending 5, 100-byte ICMP Echoes to 172.16.192.23, timeout is 2
seconds:
!!!!!
Success rate is 100 percent (5/5)
Vermont#
```

Let's look now at using authentication to verify incoming calls. There are two protocols commonly used for authentication on PPP interfaces: challenge handshake authentication protocol (CHAP) and password authentication protocol (PAP). CHAP is preferred over PAP.

CHAP provides a three-way handshake: a station sends a password challenge message to a remote connection, the remote connection replies with a value using the one-way hash function, and if the reply matches the station's own calculation, authentication is acknowledged. A variable-password challenge message is used for security reasons.

Let's look at authentication using the Maine router example.

```
1    Maine>enable
2    Password:
3    Maine#configure terminal
4    Enter configuration commands, one per line. End with CNTL/Z.
5    Maine(config)#isdn switch-type basic-net3
6    Maine(config)#interface ethernet0
```

```
 7    Maine(config-if)#ip address 172.16.1.1 255.255.255.0
 8    Maine(config-if)#interface bri0
 9    Maine(config-if)#encapsulation ppp
10    Maine(config-if)#ppp authentication chap
11    Maine(config-if)#ip address 172.16.46.1 255.255.255.0
12    Maine(config-if)#dialer idle-timeout 60
13    Maine(config-if)#dialer map ip 172.16.46.2 name Vermont
      8064325
14    Maine(config-if)#dialer-group 1
15    Maine(config-if)#exit
16    Maine(config)#username Vermont password secret
17    Maine(config)#access-list 101 deny igrp any any
18    Maine(config)#access-list 101 deny icmp any 172.16.192.0
      0.0.0.255 echo
19    Maine(config)#access-list 101 permit ip any 172.16.182.0
      0.0.0.255 eq ftp
20    Maine(config)#dialer-list 1 list 101
21    Maine(config)#ip route 172.16.192.0 255.255.255.0 172.16.46.2
22    Maine(config)#^Z
23    Maine#copy running-config startup-config
24    Building configuration...
25    [OK]
26    Maine#
```

The PPP Authentication CHAP command is used to enable CHAP on a PPP enabled interface (line 10). The command requires incoming calls to answer password challenges. CHAP is enabled as the authentication method for the Vermont and Maine routers.

The PPP Authentication PAP command is used to enable PAP on a PPP. The command sets password checking for incoming calls.

The Username Password command is used to specify the password to be used in CHAP and PAP caller identification (line 16).

The Name keyword can be the host name, server name, user ID, or command name. For CHAP authentication, the Secret-Pwd keyword specifies the code for the local router or the device and is encrypted when it is stored on the local router. In the Maine router example, secret is defined as the password to be used in authentication with the Maine router.

The Dialer Map Name command is used to define dial-on-demand connections based on hostnames used during the authentication process (line 13). This comand is:

```
dialer map protocol next-hop-address name hostname
dialer-string
```

This command must be used with the Dialer-Group command and its associated protocol or access list to initiate dialing (line 14).

The Protocol keyword can be ip, ipx, appletalk, and so on. See Table 24.1.

The Next-Hop-Address argument means the address of the next-hop router. The Name keyword is used to indicate that a hostname is being associated with a protocol and a next-hop forwarding device. The Hostname keyword means the name of a host previously established in the incoming call verification name table. The Dialer-String argument means the number of the DCE device connected to that host. In the Maine router example, IP address 172.16.46.2 is linked as the next-hop device to reach the Vermont router.

TABLE 24.1
Keyword and protocol.

Keyword	Protocol
appletalk	AppleTalk
bridge	Bridging
clns	ISO CLNS
decnet	DECnet
ip	IP
ipx	Novell IPX
novell	Novell IPX
snapshot	Snapshot Routing
vinesBanyan	VINES
xns	Xerox Network Services

Let's look now at monitoring a Basic Rate interface.

To display information about the Basic Rate 0 interface which was config-ured for DDR in the example, type show interface bri0.

```
Maine# show interface bri0
BRI0 is up, line protocol is up (spoofing)
  Hardware is BRI
  Internet address is 172.16.46.1/24
  MTU 1500 bytes, BW 64 Kbit, DLY 20000 usec, re
  Encapsulation PPP, loopback not set
  Last input 00:00:02, output 00:00:02, output
  Last clearing of "show interface" counters never
  Output queue 0/40, 0 drops; input queue 0/75, 0 drops
  5 minute input rate 0 bits/sec, 0 packets/sec
  5 minute output rate 0 bits/sec, 0 packets/sec
     184 packets input, 938 bytes, 0 no buffer
     Received 0 broadcasts, 0 runts, 0 giants
     1 input errors, 0 CRC, 0 frame, 0 overrun, 0 ignored, 1 abort
     172 packets output, 873 bytes, 0 underruns
     0 output errors, 0 collisions, 7 interface resets
```

```
        0 output buffer failures, 0 output buffers swapped out
        5 carrier transitions
Maine#
```

To display the information about memory, Layer 2, and Layer 3 timers, as well as information about the status of PRI channels, use the Show ISDN Global Configuration command.

```
Maine# show isdn status
The current ISDN Switchtype = basic-net3
ISDN BRI0 interface
    Layer 1 Status:
        ACTIVE
    Layer 2 Status:
        TEI = 68, State = MULTIPLE_FRAME_
    Layer 3 Status:
        1 Active Layer 3 Call(s)
    Activated dsl 0 CCBs = 1
        CCB:callid=3, sapi=0, ces=1, B-chan=1
    Total Allocated ISDN CCBs = 1
Maine#
```

DDR and Dial Backup

This section describes DDR using a rotary group and dial backup. We will examine DDR using a rotary group, describe how to configure dial backup, and configure dial backup using ISDN DDR.

DDR Using a Rotary Group

A rotary group is a set of physical interfaces that acts as a single serial interface when placing and receiving DDR calls. Rotary groups are common in situations where multiple destinations must be reached at the same time using dial-on-demand routing.

Once a physical interface has been included in a rotary group, it assumes the parameters that have been configured for the rotary group. A special, software-only, "dialer interface" is used to apply the configuration parameters to a rotary group.

Let's look now at configuring a DDR rotary group. The Interface Dialer command is used to define a dialer rotary group: interface dialer *number*. The Number keyword refers to the number of the dialer rotary group.

The Dialer Rotary-Group command is used to include an interface in a dialer rotary group: dialer rotary-group *number*. The Number keyword refers to the number of the dialer interface in whose rotary group you want to include this interface.

The `Encapsulation PPP` command is used to configure Point-to-Point Protocol (PPP) encapsulation. The command defines the encapsulation type as PPP and is needed by rotary group DDR.

Let's look now at a DDR rotary example that involves three routers—Vermont, Maine, and Sherman.

```
1    Sherman#enable
2    Password:
3    Sherman#configure terminal
4    Enter configuration commands, one per line. End with CNTL/Z.
5    Sherman(config)#isdn switch-type basic-net3
6    Sherman(config)#interface ethernet0
7    Sherman(config-if)#ip address 172.16.124.1 255.255.255.0
8    Sherman(config-if)#interface dialer 0
9    Sherman(config-if)#ip address 172.16.126.1 255.255.255.0
10   Sherman(config-if)#encapsulation ppp
11   Sherman(config-if)#ppp authentication chap
12   Sherman(config-if)#dialer idle-timeout 60
13   Sherman(config-if)#dialer load-threshold 160
14   Sherman(config-if)#dialer map ip 172.16.126.2 name Maine
     8064323
15   Sherman(config-if)#dialer map ip 172.16.126.3 name
     Vermont 8064325
16   Sherman(config-if)#dialer-group 1
17   Sherman(config-if)#exit
18   Sherman(config)#username Maine password secret
19   Sherman(config)#username Vermont password secret
20   Sherman(config)#dialer-list 1 protocol ip permit
21   Sherman(config)#ip route 192.168.5.0 255.255.255.0
     172.16.126.2
22   Sherman(config)#ip route 192.168.10.0 255.255.255.0
     172.16.126.3
23   Sherman(config)#interface bri0
24   Sherman(config)#dialer rotary-group 1
25   Sherman(config)#interface bri1
26   Sherman(config)#dialer rotary-group 1
27   Sherman(config)#interface bri2
28   Sherman(config)#dialer rotary-group 1
29   Sherman(config)#interface bri3
30   Sherman(config)#dialer rotary-group 1
31   Sherman(config)#^Z
32   Sherman#copy running-config startup-config
33   Building configuraton...
34   [OK]
35   Sherman#
```

In line 8, `interface dialer 0` creates dialer interface 0.

The code `ppp authentication chap` specifies that password authentication for remote access will use the CHAP protocol (line 11).

The code `dialer-group 1` places the interface into dialer group 1 and links back to a previously defined access list (line 16).

The code `dialer load-threshold 160` specifies that additional calls will be placed by the rotary group when the load on one line reaches approximately 63 percent (160/255) (line 13). The Load argument is the calculated weighted average load value for the interface—1 is unloaded and 255 is fully loaded. The load is calculated by the system dynamically, based on bandwidth.

The code `dialer rotary-group 1` places physical interfaces BR0, BR1, BR2, and BR3 into rotary group 1 (lines 24, 26, 28, 30).

Let's look now at the configuration of the Maine router.

```
1    Maine>enable
2    Password:
3    Maine#configure terminal
4    Enter configuration commands, one per line. End with CNTL/Z.
5    Maine(config)#isdn switch-type basic-net3
6    Maine(config)#interface ethernet0
7    Maine(config-if)#ip address 192.169.5.1 255.255.255.0
8    Maine(config-if)#interface bri0
9    Maine(config-if)#encapsulation ppp
10   Maine(config-if)#ppp authentication chap
11   Maine(config-if)#ip address 172.16.126.2 255.255.255.0
12   Maine(config-if)#dialer idle-timeout 60
13   Maine(config-if)#dialer load-threshold 160
14   Maine(config-if)#dialer map ip 172.16.126.1 name sherman
     8043030
15   Maine(config-if)#dialer map ip 172.16.126.3 name Vermont
     8064325
16   Maine(config-if)#dialer-group 1
17   Maine(config-if)#exit
18   Maine(config)#username sherman password secret
19   Maine(config)#username Vermont password secret
20   Maine(config)#dialer-list 1 protocol ip permit
21   Maine(config)#ip route 172.16.124.0 255.255.255.0
     172.16.126.1
22   Maine(config)#ip route 192.168.10.0 255.255.255.0
     172.16.126.3
23   Maine(config)#^Z
24   Maine#copy running-config startup-config
25   Building configuraton...
26   [OK]
27   Maine#
```

In line 21, `ip route 172.16.124.0 255.255.255.0   172.16.126.1` establishes a static route to subnet 172.16.124.0 using the router at IP address 172.16.126.1 as the next-hop device.

The code `ip route 192.168.10.0 255.255.255.0 172.16.126.3` in line 23 establishes a static route to subnet 192.168.10.0 using the router at IP address 172.16.126.3 as the next-hop device.

The code `dialer-list 1 protocol ip permit` in line 20 defines IP as interesting traffic linked to interfaces that are part of dialer group 1.

The code `dialer load-threshold 160` in line 13 specifies that the second B channel will activate when the load on the first line reaches approximately 63 percent (160/255).

The code `dialer map ip 172.16.126.1 name sherman 8043030` in line 14 defines 8043030 as the number to be dialed when trying to reach the router at IP address 172.16.126.1.

The code `dialer map ip 172.16.126.3 name Vermont 804325` in line 15 defines 804325 as the number to be dialed when trying to reach the router at IP address 172.16.126.3.

The code `dialer idle-timeout 60` in line 12 disconnects the call after 60 seconds of idle time.

Let's look at the configuration of the Vermont router.

```
1    Vermont#configure terminal
2    Enter configuration commands, one per line. End with CNTL/Z.
3    Vermont(config)#isdn switch-type basic-net3
4    Vermont(config)#interface ethernet0
5    Vermont(config-if)#ip address 192.169.10.1 255.255.255.0
6    Vermont(config-if)#interface bri0
7    Vermont(config-if)#encapsulation ppp
8    Vermont(config-if)#ppp authentication chap
9    Vermont(config-if)#ip address 172.16.126.3 255.255.255.0
10   Vermont(config-if)#dialer idle-timeout 60
11   Vermont(config-if)#dialer load-threshold 160
12   Vermont(config-if)#dialer map ip 172.16.126.1 name sherman
     8043030
13   Vermont(config-if)#dialer map ip 172.16.126.2 name Maine
     8064323
14   Vermont(config-if)#dialer-group 1
15   Vermont(config-if)#exit
16   Vermont(config)#username sherman password secret
17   Vermont(config)#username Maine password secret
18   Vermont(config)#dialer-list 1 protocol ip permit
19   Vermont(config)#ip route 172.16.124.0 255.255.255.0
     172.16.126.1
20   Vermont(config)#ip route 192.168.10.0 255.255.255.0
     172.16.126.2
21   Vermont(config)#^Z
22   Vermont#copy running-config startup-config
23   Building configuraton...
24   [OK]
25   Vermont#
```

In line 16, `username sherman password secret` defines "secret" as the password to be used in authentication with the Sherman router.

The code `username Maine password secret` in line 17 defines "secret" as the password to be used in authentication with the Maine router.

Dial Backup

When a WAN link goes down, a dial backup configuration will raise the Data Terminal Ready (DTR) signal on a backup serial port. A preconfigured auto-dial modem or data service unit (DSU), or an ISDN Terminal Adapter (TA), will then make a circuit-switched connection to the remote site. As an additional feature, high usage on the primary link that exceeds a pre-established load percentage threshold can trigger use of the secondary link.

Let's look now at an example of dial backup using ISDN DDR.

```
1   Maine>enable
2   Password:
3   Maine#configure terminal
4   Enter configuration commands, one per line. End with CNTL/Z.
5   Maine(config)#isdn switch-type basic-net3
6   Maine(config)#interface ethernet0
7   Maine(config-if)#ip address 172.16.1.1 255.255.255.0
8   Maine(config-if)#interface bri0
9   Maine(config-if)#encapsulation ppp
10  Maine(config-if)#ppp authentication chap
11  Maine(config-if)#ip address 172.16.46.1 255.255.255.0
12  Maine(config-if)#dialer idle-timeout 60
13  Maine(config-if)#dialer map ip 172.16.46.2 name Vermont
    8064325
14  Maine(config-if)#dialer load-threshold 200
15  Maine(config-if)#dialer-group 1
16  Maine(config-if)#interface serial1
17  Maine(config-if)#ip address 172.16.66.1
18  Maine(config-if)#backup interface bri0
19  Maine(config-if)#backup delay 30 30
20  Maine(config-if)#exit
21  Maine(config)#username Vermont password secret
22  Maine(config)#dialer-list 1 protocol ip permit
23  Maine(config)#ip route 172.16.192.0 255.255.255.0 172.16.46.2
    170
24  Maine(config)#^Z
25  Maine#copy running-config startup-config
26  Building configuration...
27  [OK]
28  Maine#
```

In lines 9 and 10, the `Encapsulation PPP` and `Authentication CHAP` commands set up authentication.

The `Dialer Map` command in line 13 sets up details for the router and the dialing device.

The `Dialer Load-Threshold` in line 14 is approximately 78 percent (200/255).

The `Dialer-List Protocol` command in line 22 associates dialer group 1 with the IP protocol.

The `IP route` command in line 23 sets up a floating static route with a large administrative distance.

The `Backup Interface` command is used to assign a secondary interface to be used in the event of a primary link failure. The `Interface-Name` keyword means the serial port that is to be set as the secondary interface line.

In line 18, the Basic Rate 0 interface is set as the backup line to the Serial1 interface. The backup link will be activated only if the primary link fails.

The `Backup Load` command is used to set the traffic load thresholds for dial backup service. The command is:

```
backup load {enable-threshold  never} {disable-load  never}
```

The `Enable-Threshold` argument and the `Disable-Load` argument both refer to the percentage of the primary line's available bandwidth. The `Never` keyword prevents the secondary line from being activated by traffic load. In general, when the transmitted or received load on the primary line is greater than the value assigned to the `Enable-Threshold` argument, the secondary line is enabled.

The secondary line is disabled if the transmitted load on the primary line plus the transmitted load on the secondary line is less than the value entered for the `Disable-Load` argument or the received load on the primary line plus the received load on the secondary line is less than the value entered for the `Disable-Load` argument. If the `Never` keyword is used instead of an `Enable-Threshold` value or a `Disable-Load` argument, the secondary line is never activated because of traffic load.

The `Backup Delay` command in line 19 is used to define how much time should elapse before a secondary line is set up or taken down when a primary line fails or comes back up. The command is:

```
backup delay {enable-delay  never} {disable-delay  never}
```

The `Enable-Delay` argument defines the number of seconds that elapse after the primary line goes down before the secondary line is activated. The `Disable-Delay` argument defines the number of seconds that elapse before the secondary line is deactivated. The `Never` keyword prevents the secondary line from being activated or deactivated.

A dial backup connection can be triggered by losing the primary line or by setting a traffic threshold that applies to the primary line. The backup delay inserts some flexibility into the process so that the dial backup link doesn't connect or drop whenever the primary link goes down or up. Cisco recommends enabling some delay before activating and deactivating a secondary line if spurious signal disruptions are appearing as intermittent lost carrier signals.

In line 19, the secondary line will wait 30 seconds before initiating a connection and be disconnected after 30 seconds.

Configuring Dial Backup

As a network administrator, you need to be able to configure dial backup. In this exercise you are going to configure dial backup using ISDN DDR on the Vermont router. First, you will define the service provider's switch as a model Basic-Net3. Assume that you have logged into the Vermont router, entered Privileged Exec mode, and started the configuration process from a terminal.

```
Vermont>enable
Password:
Vermont#configure terminal
Enter configuration commands, one per line. End with CNTL/Z.
```

Type `isdn switch-type basic-net3` to define the service provider's switch as a model Basic-Net3.

```
Vermont(config)#isdn switch-type basic-net3
```

Next type `interface ethernet0` to enable Interface Configuration mode so that you can assign an IP address to the Ethernet0 interface.

```
Vermont(config)#interface ethernet0
```

Next type `ip address 172.16.192.1 255.255.255.0` to assign an IP address to the Ethernet0 interface.

```
Vermont(config-if)#ip address 172.16.192.1 255.255.255.0
```

Now type `interface bri0` to enable Interface Configuration mode to configure the Basic Rate 0 interface for DDR.

```
Vermont(config-if)#interface bri0
```

Next type `encapsulation ppp` to configure Point-to-Point Protocol encapsulation.

```
Vermont(config-if)#encapsulation ppp
```

Type `ppp authentication chap` to enable CHAP on the Basic Rate 0 interface.

```
Vermont(config-if)#ppp authentication chap
```

Now type `ip address 172.16.46.2 255.255.255.0` to assign an IP address to the Basic Rate 0 interface.

```
Vermont(config-if)#ip address 172.16.46.2 255.255.255.0
```

Type `dialer idle-timeout 60` to specify 60 seconds as the idle time to wait before a call is disconnected.

```
Vermont(config-if)#dialer idle-timeout 60
```

Now you are going define the telephone number to be dialed when attempting to reach the Maine router. Type `dialer map ip 172.16.46.1 name Maine 8064323` to link IP address 172.16.46.1 as the next-hop device to the Maine router, associate the Maine router with the mapping information, and define 8064323 as the telephone number to be dialed when attempting to reach the Maine router.

```
Vermont(config-if)#dialer map ip 172.16.46.1 name Maine 8064323
```

Now you are going to configure bandwidth on demand by setting the maximum load before the dialer places another call to a destination. Type `dialer load-threshold 200` to set the maximum load at approximately 78 percent, beyond which the dialer will initiate another call to the destination.

```
Vermont(config-if)#dialer load-threshold 200
```

Next type `dialer-group 1` to assign the Basic Rate 0 interface to dialer access group 1.

```
Vermont(config-if)#dialer-group 1
```

Now type `interface serial0` to enable Interface Configuration mode so that you can assign an IP address to the Serial0 interface.

```
Vermont(config-if)#interface serial0
```

Type `ip address 172.16.66.2` to assign an IP address to the Serial0 interface.

```
Vermont(config-if)#ip address 172.16.66.2
```

Now you are going to assign a secondary interface to be used in the event of a primary link failure. Type `backup interface bri0` to set the Basic Rate 0 interface as the secondary interface to be used in the event of a primary link failure.

```
Vermont(config-if)#backup interface bri0
```

Now you are going to define how much time should elapse before a secondary line is set up or taken down when a primary line fails or comes back up. Type `backup delay 30 30` to define 30 seconds as the amount of time that should elapse before a secondary line is set up or taken down when a primary line fails or comes back up.

```
Vermont(config-if)#backup delay 30 30
```

Next type `exit` to leave Interface Configuration mode.

```
Vermont(config-if)#exit
```

Next type `username Maine password secret` to define "secret" as the password to be used in authentication with the Maine router.

```
Vermont(config)#username Maine password secret
```

Now you are going to associate a dialer group with a protocol permitted for DDR. Type `dialer-list 1 protocol ip permit` to associate dialer group 1 with the IP protocol.

```
Vermont(config)#dialer-list 1 protocol ip permit
```

Now you are going to set up a static route with a longer administrative distance. Type `ip route 172.16.1.0 255.255.255.0 172.16.46.1 170` to set up a static route with a longer administrative distance. RIP routing is already enabled and is operating over the interface.

```
Vermont(config)#ip route 172.16.1.0 255.255.255.0 172.16.46.1 170
```

To end the configuration of the Vermont router, press **Ctrl+Z**.

```
Vermont(config)#^Z
```

Next type `copy running-config startup-config` to copy the configuration to the Vermont router's startup configuration file.

```
Vermont#copy running-config startup-config
Building configuration...
[OK]
Vermont#
```

Configuring DDR Protocol Support

This section describes how to configure DDR for routed protocols and transparent bridging. We will configure DDR for IP over Frame Relay, and DDR for IPX.

Protocols and Transparent Bridge Routing with DDR

Routed protocols supported by DDR include AppleTalk, Banyan VINES, DECnet, IP, and Novell IPX. To configure DDR for AppleTalk, specify AppleTalk access lists and then define DDR dialer lists. The command is:

```
dialer-list dialer-group protocol protocol-name {permit | deny}
```

To define `Permit` or `Deny` conditions for the entire protocol, use the `Dialer-List Protocol` command. For a more specific configuration, use the `Dialer-List Protocol` command with the `List` keyword. This command is:

```
dialer-list list protocol protocol-name {permit | deny}
```

To configure DDR for IP, specify an IP standard access list or an IP extended access list in Global Configuration mode. The command is:

```
access-list access-list-number {permit | deny} source [source-mask] [destination] [destination-mask]
```

You can also employ simplified IP access lists that use the abbreviation `any` instead of the numeric forms of source and destination addresses and masks.

Let's look at an example of DDR configuration for IP. This example uses two routers (Vermont and Maine) configured for IP over frame relay using in-band dialing (Figure 24.2). A frame relay static map is used to associate the next-hop protocol address to the data link connection identifier (DLCI). The dialer string allows dialing to only one destination.

FIGURE 24.2

An illustration of two routers configured for IP over Frame Relay using in-band dialing.

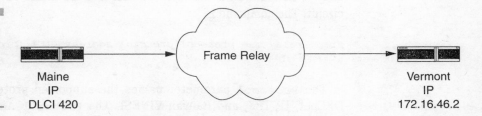

Maine
IP
DLCI 420

Frame Relay

Vermont
IP
172.16.46.2

Let's focus on the configuration of the Maine router.

```
1    Maine>enable
2    Password:
3    Maine#configure terminal
4    Enter configuration commands, one per line. End with CNTL/Z.
5    Maine(config)#interface ethernet0
6    Maine(config-if)#ip address 172.16.1.1 255.255.255.0
7    Maine(config-if)#interface serial1
8    Maine(config-if)#ip address 172.16.46.1 255.255.255.0
9    Maine(config-if)#encapsulation frame-relay
10   Maine(config-if)#frame-relay map ip 172.16.46.2 420 broadcast
11   Maine(config-if)#dialer-string 32435555
12   Maine(config-if)#dialer-group 1
13   Maine(config-if)#exit
14   Maine(config)#dialer-list 1 protocol ip permit
15   Maine(config)#ip route 172.16.192.0 255.255.255.0 172.16.46.2
16   Maine(config)#^Z
17   Maine#copy running-config startup-config
18   Building configuration...
19   [OK]
20   Maine#
```

The `Encapsulation Frame-Relay` command in line 9 is used to specify the data-link encapsulation type to be used on the serial interface communicating with the frame relay network. Two different data-link encapsulations are supported: the default Cisco encapsulation developed by the "gang of four" (Cisco, Digital, Northern Telecom, and Stratacom) which operates only with other Cisco routers; and the Internet Engineering Task Force (IETF) encapsulation (specified in RFC 1294/1490) that allows interoperation with other vendor routers. The encapsulation can be specified globally or on a circuit-by-circuit basis. The standard frame relay encapsulation, as defined by the IETF, is derived from the PPP. The default encapsulation on a Cisco router is proprietary.

The `Frame-Relay Map` command in line 10 is used to map destination network protocol addresses statically to a designated DLCI. This command is used in configurations where the Inverse ARP protocol is not used dynamically to determine the network protocol address at the other end of a virtual circuit. The command is:

```
frame-relay map protocol protocol-address DLCI [broadcast] [ietf]
[cisco]
```

The `Protocol` parameter names the supported protocols (AppleTalk, DECnet, IP, IPX, and Banyan VINES). The `Protocol-Address` parameter defines the address for the protocol. The `DLCI` argument means the DLCI number of the virtual circuit.

The `Broadcast` keyword means that broadcasts should be forwarded when multicast is not enabled. The `IETF` keyword is used to enable the IETF form of encapsulation. The `Cisco` keyword is used to enable Cisco encapsulation. This is the default.

In line 10, the destination network IP address 172.16.46.2 is statically mapped to DLCI 420 and broadcasts are to be forwarded when multicast isn't enabled.

The `Dialer String` command in line 11 is an `Interface Configuration` command used to specify the string (telephone number) to be called for interfaces calling a single site. If a `Dialer-String` command is specified without a `Dialer-Group` command with access lists defined, dialing will not be initiated.

In line 11, 32435555 is the telephone number that is to be called.

Let's look now at configuring DDR for Novell IPX. On DDR links for IPX, the link may come up often even when all client sessions are idle because the server sends watchdog or keepalive packets to all the clients approximately every five seconds.

You can configure a local router or access server with the DDR link to idle out the link and still make the server believe the clients are active. It can do this by responding to the server's watchdog packets on behalf of the clients. To do this, perform the following tasks in Interface Configuration mode: enable DDR, disable IPX fast switching, and enable either IPX watchdog spoofing or SPX keepalive spoofing.

Let's look at an example of configuring DDR for IPX. This example involves the Vermont and Maine routers and illustrates DDR over dialup lines. The link between the two routers will only be brought up with IPX.

```
1    Vermont>enable
2    Password:
3    Vermont#configure terminal
4    Enter configuration commands, one per line. End with CNTL/Z.
5    Vermont(config)#ipx routing
6    Vermont(config)#interface serial0
7    Vermont(config-if)#ipx network 10
8    Vermont(config-if)#dialer in-band
9    Vermont(config-if)#no ipx route-cache
10   Vermont(config-if)#ipx watchdog-spoof
11   Vermont(config-if)#dialer map ipx 20 457180
12   Vermont(config-if)#dialer-group 1
13   Vermont(config-if)#exit
14   Vermont(config)#dialer-list 1 protocol ip deny
15   Vermont(config)#dialer-list 1 protocol ipx permit
16   Vermont(config)#ipx route 20 10.0000.0c92.9048
17   Vermont(config)#^Z
18   Vermont#copy running-config startup-config
19   Building configuration...
20   [OK]
21   Vermont#
```

Let's focus on the configuration of the Vermont router. The IPX Routing command in line 5 is a Global Configuration command that enables IPX routing on a router.

The IPX Network command in line 7 is an Interface Configuration command that is used to enable IPX routing on a particular interface. You can choose to use it to select the type of encapsulation.

The Network parameter defines the number of the network. This is an eight-digit hexadecimal number that uniquely identifies a network cable segment. It can be any hexadecimal number in the range 1 to FFFFFFFD. You need not specify leading zeros in the network number. For example, for the network number 000000AA, you can enter AA.

In line 6, IPX routing is configured on the Serial0 interface.

The Dialer In-Band command in line 8 is used to enable DDR. Dialers specified by this command use chat scripts on asynchronous interfaces and V.25bis on synchronous interfaces. If you are using V.25bis, you can choose to specify parity. The 1984 version of the V.25bis specification states that characters must have odd parity. However, the default is no parity.

The No IPX Route-Cache command in line 9 is used to disable fast switching on the interface. This command is necessary because the router needs to look inside packets to determine their contents.

The IPX Watchdog-Spoof command in line 10 is used to enable spoofing of the idle DDR link. This prevents the link and route from being dropped from the routing table. An IPX server sends a watchdog (keepalive) packet to its clients every five seconds. Spoofing allows a local router to respond to watchdog packets on behalf of its clients while the DDR interface is idle.

Alternatively, you can use the IPX SPX-Spoof command to enable SPX watchdog spoofing. The command is:

```
ipx spx-spoof ipx spx-idle-time delay-in-seconds
```

The IPX SPX-Idle-Time command sets the idle time after which spoofing begins.

The Dialer Map command in line 11 is an Interface Configuration command used to configure a serial interface or an ISDN interface to call one or multiple sites. The command is:

```
dialer-map protocol next-hop-address [dial string]
```

The Protocol parameter names the protocols supported for DDR. The Next-Hop-Address parameter defines the protocol address used to match against addresses to which packets are destined.

The optional Dial-String parameter defines the telephone number sent to the dialing device when it recognizes packets with the specified next-hop address that matches the access lists defined.

In line 11 IPX is the protocol, the destination network address is 20, and 457180 is the dial string.

The IPX Route command in line 16 is a Global Configuration command used to add a static route to a routing table. The command is:

```
ipx route {network [network-mask] | default} {network.node |
interface} [floating static]
```

The Network argument identifies the network to which you want to establish a static route. The optional Network-Mask argument identifies a portion of the network address common to all addresses in an NLSP route summary. When used with the Network argument, it specifies the static route summary.

The Default keyword creates a static entry for the "default route." The router forwards all non-local packets for which no explicit route is known via the specified next-hop address (Network.Node) or interface.

The Network.Node argument identifies the router to which to forward packets destined for the specified network. The Network argument is an eight-digit hexadecimal number that uniquely identifies a network cable segment. The Node argument is the node number of the target router. This is a 48-bit value represented by a dotted triplet of four-digit hexadecimal numbers (xxxx.xxxx.xxxx).

The Interface argument identifies the network interface to which to forward packets destined for the specified network. Specifying an interface instead of a network node is intended for use on IPXWAN unnumbered interfaces. The specified interface can be a null interface. The optional Floating-Static argument specifies that this route is a floating-static route. This is a static route that can be overridden by a dynamically learned route.

In the Vermont router configuration, line 16, 20 is the network to which a static route is to be established and 10.0000.0c92.9048 is the network.node address of the router to which to forward packets destined for the specified network.

Let's look now at configuring DDR for transparent bridging. To do this, you must complete the following tasks: define the protocols to bridge, specify the bridging protocol, control access for bridging, and configure an interface for bridging.

IP packets are routed by default unless they are explicitly bridged. By default all other packets are bridged unless they are explicitly routed. To bridge IP packets, use the No IP Routing command in Global Configuration mode. If you choose not to bridge another protocol, use the relevant command to enable routing of that protocol.

You must specify the type of spanning-tree bridging protocol to use and also identify a bridge group. Use the Bridge Protocol command in Global Configuration mode to specify the spanning-tree protocol and a bridge group number. The Bridge Group Number is used when you configure the interface and assign it to a bridge group. Packets are bridged only among members of the same bridge group.

To control access for DDR bridging, you must complete one of the following tasks in Global Configuration mode: permit all bridge packets or control bridging access by Ethernet type codes. Spanning-tree bridge protocol data units (BPDUs) are always treated as uninteresting.

The Dialer-List Protocol Bridge command is used to define a dialer list that treats all transparent bridge packets as interesting.

To control access by Ethernet type codes, you must use two commands. The Access-List Type-Code command identifies interesting packets by Ethernet type codes (access list numbers must be in the range 200–299). The Dialer-List Protocol Bridge List command defines a dialer list for the specified access list.

You can configure serial or ISDN interfaces for DDR bridging by completing the following tasks in Interface Configuration mode: specify the interface, configure the destination, and assign the interface to a bridge group.

The Interface Type Number command is used to specify the serial or ISDN interface.

You can configure the destination by specifying a dial string for unauthenticated calls to a single site or by specifying a dialer bridge map when you want to use authentication. The `Dialer String Dialer Map Bridge` command is used to configure the destination for bridging over a specified interface. You can define only one dialer bridge map for the interface. If you enter a different bridge map, the previous one is replaced immediately.

Packets are bridged only among interfaces that belong to the same group. The `Bridge Group` parameter is used to assign an interface to a bridge group.

Transparent and Source-Router Bridging

Bridging Techniques

This section describes the basic functions of bridging and identifies the various bridge types supported by Cisco. We will compare bridges and routers and describe the advantages associated with each device, identify the challenges associated with bridging between transparent bridging domains and source-route bridging (SRB) domains, and describe the techniques implemented to meet these challenges.

Bridging Overview

Bridges became commercially available in the early 1980s. At the time of their introduction, bridges connected and enabled packet forwarding between homogeneous networks. More recently, bridging between different networks has also been defined and standardized.

Although an intense debate about the comparative benefits of bridging versus routing raged in the late 1980s, most people now agree that each has its place. Both are often necessary in any comprehensive internetworking scheme. A bridge retransmits packets from one segment of a network to another. A router relays packets from one network to another.

Cisco routers support the following: transparent bridging (TB), concurrent routing and bridging (CRB), source-route bridging (SRB), and translational bridging (TLB). Cisco also supports advanced bridging options including encapsulated bridging, source-route transparent bridging (SRT), source-route translational bridging (SR/TLB), and remote source-route bridging (RSRB).

Several kinds of bridging have emerged as important. Transparent bridging defines the connection of two Ethernet domains. Source-route bridging defines the connection of two token rings. Path information is carried in a routing information field (RIF) and gathered by an explorer packet. Source-route bridging uses RIFs to define path to destination. Translational bridging provides translation between the formats and transit principles of different media types (usually Ethernet and token ring). Encapsulated bridging provides for the encapsulation of transparently bridged frames over WAN and LAN links, such as Fiber Distributed Interface (FDDI). Encapsulated bridge frames use serial links or FDDI media.

Source-route translational bridging provides mixed-media bridging between a RIF and a RIF-less environment. Remote source-route bridging provides a means to transport bridge traffic over arbitrary media combinations. Source-route transparent bridging combines the algorithms of transparent bridging and source-route bridging. It allows communication in mixed Ethernet/token ring environments.

Diminishing price and the inclusion of bridging capability in many routers has taken substantial market share away from pure bridges. Those bridges that have survived include features such as sophisticated filtering, pseudo-intelligent path selection, and high throughput rates.

Some protocols have no network-layer address and must be bridged. Routable protocols can be bridged, but this is not recommended. Examples of non-routed protocols include Digital Equipment Corporation's Local Area Transport (DECLAT) and some forms of NetBIOS.

Bridging connects LANs at the data-link layer (layer 2). This layer controls data flow, handles transmission errors, provides physical (as opposed to logical) addressing, and manages access to the physical medium. Bridges provide these functions by using various link-layer protocols which dictate specific flow control, error handling, addressing, and media-access algorithms. Examples of popular link-layer protocols include Ethernet, token ring, and FDDI.

Bridges analyze incoming frames, make forwarding decisions based on information contained in the frames, and forward the frames toward their destination. In some cases (for example, source-route bridging), frames are forwarded the entire path to the destination, which is contained in each frame. In other cases (for example, transparent bridging), frames are forwarded one hop at a time toward the destination.

Upper-layer protocol transparency is an important advantage of bridging. Because bridges operate at the data-link layer, they are not required to examine upper-layer information. This means that they can rapidly forward traffic representing any network layer protocol. It is not uncommon for a bridge to move AppleTalk, DECnet, TCP/IP, XNS, and other traffic between two or more networks.

Bridges are capable of filtering frames based on any layer 2 fields. For example, a bridge can be programmed to reject (not forward) all frames sourced from a particular network. Since link-layer information often includes a reference to an upper-layer protocol, bridges can usually filter on this parameter. Further, filters can be helpful in dealing with unnecessary broadcast and multicast packets.

By dividing large networks into self-contained units, bridges provide several advantages. They reduce traffic experienced by devices on all connected segments because only a percentage of traffic is forwarded. They act as firewalls for some potentially damaging network errors.

Bridges allow for communication between a larger number of devices than would be supported on any single LAN connected to the bridge. They extend the effective length of a LAN, permitting attachment of distant stations that were not previously connected.

Bridges can be grouped into categories based on various product characteristics. Using one popular scheme, bridges are classified as either local or remote. Local bridges provide direct connections between multiple LAN segments in the same area. Remote bridges connect multiple LAN segments in different areas, usually over telecommunications lines, known as *WAN links*.

Remote bridging presents several unique internetworking challenges. One of these is the difference between LAN and WAN speeds. LAN speeds are often very much faster than WAN speeds. Vastly different LAN and WAN speeds sometimes prevent users from running delay-sensitive LAN applications over the WAN.

Remote bridges cannot improve WAN speeds, but can compensate for speed discrepancies through sufficient buffering capability. If a LAN device capable of transmitting at 3 Mbps wishes to communicate with a device on a remote LAN, the local bridge must regulate the 3-Mbps data stream so that it does not overwhelm the 64-kbps serial link.

This is done by storing the incoming data in on-board buffers and sending it over the serial link at a rate the serial link can accommodate. This speed compensation can be achieved only for short bursts of data that do not overwhelm the bridge's buffering capability.

The Institute of Electrical and Electronic Engineers (IEEE) has divided the OSI link layer into two distinct sublayers: the media access control (MAC) sublayer and the logical link control (LLC) sublayer. The MAC sublayer permits and orchestrates media access (for example, contention and token passing). The LLC sublayer is concerned with framing, flow control, error control, and MAC sublayer addressing.

Some bridges are MAC-layer bridges. These devices bridge between homogeneous networks (for example, IEEE 802.3 and IEEE 802.3). Other bridges can translate between different link-layer protocols (for example, IEEE 802.3 and IEEE 802.5). After being processed, the packet is passed back to an IEEE 802.5 implementation which encapsulates the packet in an IEEE 802.5 header for transmission on the IEEE 802.5 network to the IEEE 802.5 host (Host B).

A bridge's translation between networks of different types is never perfect. This is because it is likely that one network will support certain frame fields and protocol functions not supported by the other network. For example, the bit sequence for token ring addresses is an order which is the reverse of that for Ethernet addresses. This is because token ring considers the first bit encountered in the bit sequence to be the high-order bit. Ethernet, on the other hand, considers the first bit encountered to be the low-order bit.

Router/Bridge Operation

Before bridging and routing capabilities can be contrasted, you must understand where each falls within a common framework of internetworking terminology. For this comparison, we will focus on transparent bridging.

The primary difference between routing and bridging is that bridging occurs at the data-link layer of the OSI model, while routing occurs at the network layer (layer 3). This distinction provides routers and bridges with different information to use in the process of moving information from source to destination. As a result, they accomplish their tasks in different ways (Figure 25.1).

In general, link-layer devices assume a common logical network in which information traverses a single hop to reach a destination. Network layer devices are designed to handle multiple hops and multiple networks. These distinctions lead to constraints for bridging that result in four important differences between routing and bridging.

The header associated with data-link packets lacks information fields that are present in network-layer packets. Examples of fields in network-layer packets include final destination address, hop count, and fragmentation and reassembly information.

Bridges do not support handshaking protocols, such as the Internet Control Message Protocol (ICMP) associated with the Internet Protocol (IP). These protocols are used by end nodes and routers to learn about each other.

Bridges cannot reorder packets from the same source. Network-layer protocols expect some degree of reordering caused by fragmentation.

Bridges use the MAC addresses defined at the time of equipment manufacture to identify an end node. Therefore, the address has no topological meaning. With routers, a network address is associated with the LAN to which a particular node is attached.

Despite the constraints associated with bridging, there are often situations that require bridging technology. Similarly, routing might be necessary to ensure proper segmentation of traffic or to support a specific topology that does not permit a single logical internetwork.

Routing offers the following advantages over bridging: routers can choose the best path between source and destination and bridges are limited to a specific path (referred to as a *spanning-tree*) through an internetwork. Bridges must learn the location of stations from the direction from which traffic is received. They are "transparent" and therefore are not permitted to modify a packet in any way. These characteristics do not apply to source-route bridges.

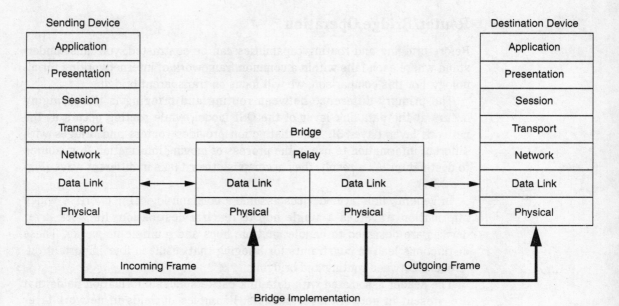

Bridge Implementation

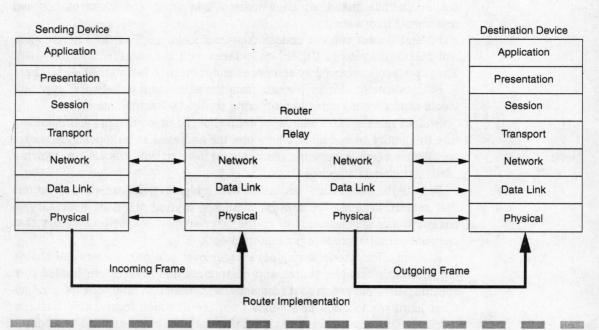

Router Implementation

FIGURE 25.1   Bridge versus routing implementation.

Unlike transparent bridges, source-route bridges do not maintain a station location table. In addition, loops are not possible in a source-route bridge environment. The source-route bridging standard states that a source-route bridge must verify that the output network segment was not traversed before transmitting packets.

Routers reconfigure topology changes much more quickly than bridges do, so that there is reduced service loss. Loops pose a substantially greater risk to a bridged internetwork than to a routed internetwork because bridges are transparent. Thus, new bridge paths are recognized gradually, while new routing paths are recognized as soon as routing information is received.

The total number of stations that can be supported in a routed internetwork is virtually unlimited. However, the maximum number of stations in a bridged internetwork is constrained to several thousands of stations.

Routers can accommodate a much larger address space because network-layer addresses include information that groups nodes into areas or domains. Bridges have no hierarchical addressing component and cannot direct traffic in a hierarchical manner.

Routers can provide a barrier against broadcast storms; bridges cannot. By design, when bridges join a series of LAN segments, those segments form a single LAN from the perspective of upper-layer protocols. A broadcast storm disables the entire bridged internetwork because all the bridges forward the broadcast traffic throughout the internetwork and are unable to intervene. Routers block broadcasts by default.

For some protocols, the network-layer header includes fragmentation and reassembly information; the data-link-layer header does not. As a result, routers fragment and reassemble large packets, while bridges drop packets that are too big to forward. In addition, bridges are unable to inform the source that the packet was dropped.

Routers provide congestion feedback to end stations when traffic is heavy; bridges do not. In the International Standards Organization for Connectionless Network Service (ISO CLNS), mechanisms in the network-layer protocols provide congestion-based information. This information can be relayed to source nodes, forcing them to reduce transmission rates. The data-link layer provides no analogous capability. These advantages of routers are not in relation to source-route bridging. However, one weakness of SRB is that it does not provide any form of dynamic rerouting. This is left to the end stations.

Network designers aim to solve multiple internetworking problems without creating multiple networks or writing off existing data communications investments. A network designer might employ bridges in a remote site for their ease of implementation, simple topology, and low traffic requirements.

Routers might be relied upon to provide a reliable, self-healing backbone, as well as a barrier against inadvertent broadcast storms in local networks.

A dedicated bridging implementation for simple internetworks (often remote sites) can be used in a number of circumstances. For example, an IGS can be implemented for local bridging at a remote site, while providing the option of routing as the remote network evolves.

If you are interconnecting the remote site to a corporate backbone, it is best to implement routing at the point of access from the local internetwork to the backbone. If you have a very large, meshed local internetwork, routers provide superior segmentation and more efficient traffic handling than bridges. An example of this is a campus consisting of several buildings and running protocols that derive significant benefits from routing.

When you are choosing between routing and bridging, the following issues should be considered carefully: bridges require minimal configuration and routers require maximum configuration. For example, IP routers require the configuration of separate addresses for each interface, and substantial configuration of end nodes, addresses, and masks.

In some situations, basic learning bridges require virtually no configuration. To begin operation, you can simply take the bridge out of the box, power it up, and attach it to a network.

Bridges have a better price-to-performance ratio than routers. With less overhead to handle, bridges have enjoyed an advantage over routers in terms of pure packet traffic handling. This advantage is diminishing due to improved router performance and the reduced price difference between routers and bridges.

Bridges are protocol independent while routers are protocol dependent. As routers have become capable of handling multiple protocols in either integrated or ships-in-the-night environments, this perceived advantage is also diminishing. Nonetheless, bridges can handle multiple protocols with almost no configuration.

Nonroutable protocols, such as DECLAT, are bridged and cannot be routed. Some protocols that provide upper-layer functionality are not routable. This remains a compelling reason for implementing bridging capabilities for supporting end-to-end connectivity.

Concurrent routing and bridging (CRB) enables a specific protocol to be both routed and bridged within a single router on separate groups of interfaces. A network designer planning for future growth might like to replace the two devices with a single large router.

The migration is straightforward if the intention is to eliminate bridging altogether and to route all protocols. If the intention is to route a given protocol on two interfaces and to bridge the same protocol on two other interfaces, it becomes more complex. This situation occurs if the current topology was maintained for a period of time before migrating to an all-routed environment. This can be resolved only by using CRB.

With CRB, the decision to bridge or route a packet is determined by transparent bridge group configuration. CRB introduces a two-step decision process that identifies bridging and routing options for each protocol being passed within a bridge group. The most important result of this change is that it is now possible for protocol traffic associated with a running network-layer protocol to reach the bridging software.

Bridging Different Media

Mixed-media bridging involves moving frames from one LAN medium to another, typically from Ethernet to token ring and vice versa. This can also apply for Ethernet to FDDI, and token ring to FDDI. Transparent bridges are found predominantly in Ethernet networks, and source-route bridges (SRBs) are found almost exclusively in token ring networks. Successful communication between these two domains requires that many issues be resolved.

Both transparent bridges and SRBs are popular, so it is reasonable to ask whether a method exists to bridge between them. Ultimately, the goal of connecting transparent bridging and SRB domains is to allow communication between transparent bridges and SRB end stations. There are two possible solutions to mixed-media bridging: source-route/translational bridging (SR/TLB) and source-route transparent bridging (SRT).

Transparent and source-route configurations must share information in order to translate. A more sophisticated translation requires the transparent bridge and SRB configurations to share information. This is achieved using translational bridging.

Translational bridging provides a relatively inexpensive solution to mixed-media bridging. It first appeared in the mid- to late-1980s, but has not been championed by any standards organization. As a result, many aspects of translational bridging are left to the administrator who implements them.

Translational bridging is a bridging scheme whereby source-route stations can communicate with transparent bridge stations via an intermediate bridge. It translates between the two bridging protocols.

There are a number of challenges associated with translational bridging: incompatible bit ordering, embedded MAC addresses, incompatible MTU sizes, handling exclusive token ring functions, handling the route discovery process, and incompatible spanning-tree algorithms.

There has been no real standardization in how communication between the two types of medium should occur. Although several popular methods exist, there is no single translational bridging implementation that can be called correct.

Translational bridges can create a software gateway between the SRB and transparent bridging domains. To the SRB end stations, the translational bridge has a ring number and an associated bridge number and looks like a standard SRB. The ring number, in this case, reflects the entire transparent bridging domain. To the transparent bridging domain, the translational bridge is simply another transparent bridge.

In bridging between Ethernet and token ring, it is necessary to convert between frame formats. Common examples of frame conversions in translational bridging are between the following: IEEE 802.3 Ethernet and token ring, Ethernet Type II and token ring Subnetwork Access Protocol (SNAP), and Ethernet Type II 0x80D5 and token ring.

In the frame conversion between IEEE 802.3 Ethernet and token ring, the following fields are passed to the corresponding destination frame: Destination Address and Source Address (DASA)—the bits are reordered, Service Access Point (SAP), Logical Link Control (LLC), Data.

In bridging from IEEE 802.3 Ethernet to token ring, the Length field is removed in the frame conversion. In bridging from token ring to IEEE 802.3 Ethernet, the following fields are removed: Access Control (AC) byte and Routing Information Field (RIF)—the RIF can be cached in the translational bridge for use by return traffic.

In the frame conversion between Ethernet Type II and token ring SNAP, the following fields are placed by SNAP in the Data field of the token ring frame: Vendor Code and Type. In bridging from token ring SNAP to Ethernet Type II, the following fields are removed: AC byte, RIF (the RIF can be cached in the translational bridge for use by return traffic), SAP, LLC information (Control portion), and Vendor Code. In bridging from Ethernet Type II to token ring SNAP, no fields are removed.

In the frame conversion between Ethernet Type II 0x80D5 format and token ring, the following fields are passed to the corresponding destination frame: DASA (bits are re-ordered), SAP, LLC, and Data. In bridging from Ethernet Type II 0x80D5 to token ring, the following fields are removed: Type and 80D5 header. In bridging from token ring to Ethernet Type II 0x80D5, the following fields are removed: AC byte and RIF. The RIF can be cached in the translational bridge for use by return traffic.

In 1990, IBM addressed some of the weaknesses of translational bridging by introducing source-route transparent (SRT) bridging. This combines implementations of the transparent bridging and SRB algorithms. SRT bridges employ both technologies in one device and do not translate between bridging protocols.

SRT bridges can forward traffic from both transparent and source-route end nodes. They form a common spanning tree with transparent bridges. This allows end stations of each type to communicate with end stations of the same type in a network of arbitrary topology.

SRT bridges use the Routing Information Indicator (RII) bit to distinguish between frames employing SRB and transparent bridging. If the RII bit is 1, a RIF is present in the frame, and the bridge performs source routing. If the RII is 0, a RIF is not present in the frame, and the bridge performs transparent bridging.

Like translational bridges, SRT bridges are not perfect solutions to the problems of mixed-media bridging. SRT bridging might require hardware upgrades to SRBs to allow them to handle the increased burden of analyzing every packet. Software upgrades might also be required.

In environments consisting of a combination of SRT bridges, transparent bridges, or SRBs, source routes chosen are based on whatever SRT or SRB routes are available. This could result in a potentially inferior path to a destination created by the transparent bridging spanning tree.

Finally, mixed SRT/SRB bridging networks lose the benefits of SRT bridging. Users will feel compelled to execute a complete switch to SRT bridging at considerable expense.

Transparent Bridging

This section describes transparent bridging and its operation. We will identify and describe how transparent bridges learn about network topology and build bridging tables, describe filtering, forwarding, and flooding, define the operational problems associated with bridging loops, describe the spanning-tree algorithm and its operation, describe how to configure transparent bridging, and configure transparent bridging.

Transparent Bridging Overview

Transparent bridges were developed at the Digital Equipment Corporation in the early 1980s. Digital submitted its work to the IEEE, which incorporated it into the IEEE 802.1d standard. Transparent bridges are very popular in Ethernet and IEEE 802.3 networks.

Transparent bridges are so named because their presence and operation are transparent to network hosts. They pass frames along one hop at a time based on tables that associate end nodes with bridge ports. Transparent bridges perform operations based on the MAC address. When transparent bridges are powered on, they learn the network's topology by analyzing the source address of incoming frames from all attached networks.

Let's look at how transparent bridging operates. If a bridge sees a frame arrive on Ethernet 0 from Host A, the bridge concludes that Host A can be reached through the network connected to ethernet 0. Through this process, transparent bridges build a table. This table is used as the basis for traffic forwarding.

Transparent bridges successfully isolate intrasegment traffic, thereby reducing the traffic seen on each individual segment. This usually improves network response times as seen by the user. The extent to which transparent bridging reduces traffic and response times depends on the volume of intersegment traffic relative to the total traffic and the volume of broadcast and multicast traffic.

Encapsulated bridging is a form of transparent bridging used to connect remote LANs. It is sometimes referred to as *remote transparent bridging*.

The bridges on either side of the WAN link are called *half bridges* because, when taken together, they appear to be a single bridge between the two LANs. Half bridges are connected by a serial line and use data-link encapsulation to carry Ethernet frames from one bridge/router to another. Packets being sent across the network are encapsulated into FDDI or HDLC packets before transmission.

Encapsulation is the wrapping of data in a particular protocol header. For example, Ethernet data are wrapped in a specific Ethernet header before transmission. Also, when bridging dissimilar networks, the entire frame from one network is placed in the header used by the data-link layer protocol of the other network.

Learning, Forwarding, and Filtering

When a transparent bridge is first powered on, it knows nothing of the network topology. It learns which stations can be reached on each of its ports (or interfaces) by monitoring the source MAC addresses of all incoming frames. For this reason, a transparent bridge is sometimes also called a *learning bridge*.

A transparent bridge maintains a database of learned MAC addresses and their associated interfaces. The bridging table containing the learned MAC addresses and associated interfaces.

When a station sends a frame, the bridge updates the table. It also flushes entries of stations if they have not been heard from within a specified time.

When a frame arrives, the transparent bridge searches the table for an association between the destination address and any of the bridge's interfaces other than the one on which the frame was received. If an association is found, the frame is forwarded out the indicated interface.

A transparent bridge forwards broadcast and multicast frames, and frames to unknown stations out through all interfaces (except the one from which the frame was received). (A station is unknown if it is not in the bridging table). This action is known as *flooding*.

If the source and destination addresses are located on different bridged segments, and neither address is known to the bridge, the bridge does the following: notes the source address and updates its table and floods the frame out through all interfaces (except the inbound interface). If a reply comes back, the source address (which was the original target destination) is examined and added to its table. The bridge forwards subsequent communications between the devices.

Filtering controls congestion using the bridge table information. Transparent bridges do not forward packets unnecessarily. If the source and destination addresses are located on the same segment, a transparent bridge filters (or discards) the frames.

If the source and destination addresses are located on the same segment, and the location of the destination address is unknown, the bridge floods the frame out through all interfaces (except the inbound interface). If a reply comes back, the source address (which was the original target destination) is examined and added to its table. The bridge can also filter subsequent frames between the devices.

Spanning-tree and Loop Avoidance

A bridging loop occurs where there is more than one path between any two bridged LANs in a network. Although loops are potentially harmful, they can be useful in some topologies. Without loops, a topology has no redundancy. Without redundancy, if a bridge or LAN segment fails, connectivity is lost. A network with multiple paths from source to destination can increase overall network fault tolerance through improved topological flexibility.

Without a bridge-to-bridge protocol, the transparent bridging algorithm fails when there are multiple paths of bridges and LANs between any two stations in the network.

Suppose Host A sends a frame to Host B. Both bridges receive the frame and correctly conclude that Host A is on Network 2. Unfortunately, after Host B receives two copies of Host A's frame, both bridges will again receive the frame on their Network 1 interfaces because all hosts receive all messages on broadcast LANs.

In some cases, the bridges will then change their internal tables to indicate that Host A is on Network 1. If so, when Host B replies to Host A's frame, both bridges will receive and subsequently drop the replies. This occurs because their tables now indicate that the destination (Host A) is on the same network segment as the frame's source.

In addition to creating basic connectivity problems, the proliferation of broadcast messages in networks with loops represents a potentially serious network problem. Now assume that Host A's initial frame is a broadcast. Both bridges will forward the frames endlessly, using all available network bandwidth and blocking the transmission of other packets on both segments.

There are two types of frames that cause problems in a network containing a loop: frames sent to an unknown station, and broadcast (or multicast) frames. These frames cause problems because, by default, all bridges must flood these types of frame. Frames sent to an unknown station cause transparent bridges to inaccurately and continuously update their tables.

Suppose Station X sends a frame to Station Y. If Station Y has not yet transmitted any of its own frames, neither bridge will have any record of Station Y's location. Both bridges receive the frame and correctly flood it. Now there are two identical frames on Network 1. Both bridges see the other's frames on Network 1. They reach the incorrect conclusion that Station X is now on Network 1, and will modify their tables to reflect this change. When Y replies to X on Network 2, the bridges forward the frame to Network 1, where they believe X is located. The loop continues indefinitely.

Broadcast frames cause *broadcast storms*, an undesirable network event. A broadcast storm occurs when multiple broadcasts are sent simultaneously across all network segments, consuming all available network bandwidth and resources. Ultimately, this leads to a disruption in network service to users. Station X sends a broadcast frame looking for a server. By default, each bridge must forward the broadcast frame onto all connected segments. Now there are two broadcast frames on Network 1. Both bridges see the broadcast frames again, and again forward the frames. A broadcast storm ensues.

Both bridges forward the frames indefinitely, using all available network bandwidth and block the transmission of other frames on both segments. Because a bridge forwards traffic, a bridge loop would create a flood of packets, or a storm that could disable a network. A transparent bridge must deal with this situation by detecting loops and breaking them. It achieves this through the use of the *spanning-tree protocol*.

The spanning-tree algorithm was developed by Digital to preserve the benefits of loops, while eliminating their problems. Digital's spanning-tree implementation was revised by the IEEE and came to be known as IEEE's 802.1d spanning-tree algorithm. The IEEE 802.1d and Digital's spanning-tree implementations are not compatible with one another. Both types of transparent spanning-tree protocols are supported by Cisco.

The spanning-tree algorithm prevents bridging loops by creating a spanning tree of bridges such that there is only one path between any pair of LANs on the network. The spanning-tree protocol elects a root bridge. Each bridge selects the lowest cost path to the root bridge.

Interfaces with alternate paths will block traffic to prevent loops. The spanning-tree algorithm places bridge ports that, if active, would create bridging loops into standby or "blocking" condition. It activates these blocking bridge ports if the primary link fails, providing a new path through the network.

A single frame from an end node spawns two frames on the other segment because both bridges forward the frame.

Once the spanning-tree protocol has disabled interfaces that could cause rooting loops, the traffic will take the only available path to the root bridge. Here, you can see how the spanning-tree algorithm prevents the bridge loop so that only one bridge forwards the frame.

Let's look at the steps involved in the spanning-tree algorithm operation to eliminate loops. Each bridge is assigned an 8-byte unique bridge identifier. The first two bytes are a priority field, and the last six bytes contain one of the bridge's MAC addresses. The bridge with the lowest bridge identifier among all bridges on all LAN segments is elected to be the root bridge.

The network administrator can assign a lower bridge priority to a selected bridge to control which bridge becomes the root. Alternatively, the administrator can use default bridge priorities and allow the spanning-tree algorithm alone to determine the root.

Each bridge port is associated with a path cost. This represents the cost of transmitting a frame onto a bridged segment through that port. The administrator typically configures a cost for each port based on the speed of link. For example, the cost of a serial WAN port could be assigned a higher path cost than a faster Ethernet port would have.

Each bridge determines its root port and root path cost. The root port is the port that represents the shortest path from itself to the root bridge. The root path cost is the total cost to the root. All ports on the root bridge have a zero cost.

All participating bridges elect a designated bridge from among the bridges on that LAN segment. A designated bridge is the bridge on each LAN segment that provides the minimum root path cost. Only the designated bridge is allowed to forward frames to and from that LAN segment toward the root.

All participating bridges select ports for inclusion in the spanning tree. The selected ports will be the root port plus the designated ports for the designated bridge. Designated ports are those where the designated bridge has the best path to reach the root. If two or more bridges have the same root path cost, the bridge with the lowest bridge identifier becomes the designated bridge. Now, all but one of the bridges directly connected to each LAN segment are eliminated, thereby removing all multi-LAN loops.

Now, we can compare the logical view of a transparent bridge network before and after running the spanning-tree algorithm.

The spanning-tree calculation occurs whenever a bridge is powered up or whenever a topology change is detected. The calculation requires communication between spanning-tree bridges. This is accomplished through configuration messages, which are also known as *bridge protocol data units (BPDUs)*.

Configuration messages are exchanged between neighboring bridges at regular intervals (typically one to four seconds). These messages contain the following information: the bridge presumed to be the main bridge or root (the root identifier), the distance from the sending bridge to the root bridge (the root path cost), the bridge and port identifier of the sending bridge, and the age of the information contained in the configuration message.

Configuration messages allow bridges to detect failures. If a bridge fails, causing a topology change, neighboring bridges will soon detect the lack of configuration messages and initiate a spanning-tree recalculation.

Transparent bridges exchange both configuration and topology-change BPDUs. Configuration BPDUs are sent between bridges to establish a network topology. Topology-change BPDUs are sent after a topology change has been detected to indicate that the spanning-tree algorithm should be initiated.

Let's look at the frame format of a spanning-tree BPDU (Figure 25.2). The Protocol Identifier, Version, and Message Type fields contain the value zero. The Flag field is a single byte, of which only the first two bits are used: the topology-change (TC) bit signals a topology change and the topology-change acknowledgment (TCA) bit is set to acknowledge receipt of a configuration message with the TC bit set.

The Root ID field identifies the root bridge by listing its 2-byte priority followed by its 6-byte ID. The Root Path Cost field contains the cost of the path from the bridge sending the configuration message to the root bridge.

The Bridge ID field identifies the priority and ID of the bridge sending the message. The Port ID field identifies the port from which the configuration message was sent. This field allows loops created by multiple attached bridges to be detected and handled.

The Message Age field specifies the amount of time elapsed since the root sent the configuration message on which the current configuration message is based. The Maximum Age field indicates when the current configuration message should be deleted.

PI	V	MT	F	RID	RPC	BID	PI	MA	MX	HT	FD

PI	Protocol Identifier		BID	Bridge ID
V	Version		PI	Port ID
MT	Message Type		MA	Message Age
F	Flag		MX	Maximum Age
RID	Root ID		HT	Hello Time
RPC	Root Path Cost		FD	Forward Delay

The Hello Time field provides the time period between root bridge configuration messages. The Forward Delay field provides the length of time that bridges should wait before transitioning to a new state after a topology change. If a bridge transitions too soon, not all network links might be ready to change their state, and loops can result.

Topology-change messages (four bytes) consist of three fields. The Protocol Identifier and Version fields contain the value 0 and the Message Type field contains the value 128.

Transparent Bridging Configuration

When you are configuring transparent bridging, there are several commands to enter both in Global Configuration mode and Interface Configuration mode. In Global Configuration mode, you need to select a spanning-tree protocol and create a bridge group. In Interface Configuration mode, you need to assign the interface to a spanning-tree group and define filters.

The Bridge Protocol command is used to define a specific spanning-tree algorithm for a bridge group: bridge *group-number* protocol *protocol-type*. The *group-number* is a decimal number in the range 1 to 9 that identifies a particular set of bridged interfaces. The *protocol-type* is either DEC or IEEE, as only DEC and IEEE are used for transparent bridging.

The Bridge-Group command assigns an interface to a particular bridge group: bridge-group *bridge-number*. The *bridge-number* is a decimal number from 1 to 9. Interfaces not participating in a bridge group will not forward bridged traffic.

A specific priority can be assigned to a bridge, assisting in the spanning-tree root definition. The lower the priority, the more likely the bridge will be selected as the root.

The `Bridge Priority` command assigns the bridge priority: `bridge` *group* `priority` *number*. The *group* is a number from 1 to 9. The *number* assigns the priority level and is in the range 0 to 255 (default value is 128).

Let's look at an example of how a bridge becomes a root on a segment. The Cisco A router will become the root because it has a lower bridge priority than Cisco B.

```
Cisco A                          Cisco B
bridge 1 protocol dec            bridge 1 protocol dec
bridge 1 priority 1              bridge 1 priority 100
```

`Bridge-Group Path-Cost` assigns the path cost to an interface for use in the spanning-tree algorithm: `bridge-group` *group* `path-cost` *cost*. The default is 1000 Mbps divided by the data rate of the attached LAN.

The *group* is a number from 1 to 9. The *cost* is a number from 0 to 65535. The Digital and IEEE spanning-tree protocols have different values.

The `FDDI Encapsulate` command disables translational bridging and enables encapsulated bridging: `fddi encapsulate`. To monitor transparent bridging, use the `Show Bridge` and `Show Spanning-Tree` commands.

Let's configure transparent bridging on the Vermont router which has an Ethernet and a Serial interface. Assume you have already logged onto the Vermont router and need to enter Global Configuration mode. Do this by typing `config term` or `configure terminal`.

```
Vermont>enable
Password:
Vermont#config term
Enter configuration commands, one per line. End with CNTL/Z.
Vermont(config)#
```

Now you need to select a spanning-tree protocol for the bridge group. To do this, use the `Bridge Protocol` command.

```
Vermont(config)#bridge 1 protocol dec
```

Now, you need to configure each of Vermont's interfaces. First, we will configure Ethernet 0 by typing `interface ethernet 0`.

```
Vermont(config)#interface ethernet 0
```

The interface now needs to be assigned to a particular bridge group. Using the `Bridge-Group` command with the `Bridge-Number` parameter in the range 1 to 9, assign Ethernet 0 to a bridge group by typing `bridge-group 1`. Remember, interfaces not participating in a bridge group will not forward bridged traffic.

```
Vermont(config-if)#bridge-group 1
```

To enter configuration mode for Vermont's Serial mode, type `interface serial 0`. To assign Serial 0 to the same bridge group as the Ethernet 0 interface (in this case, bridge group 1), use the `Bridge-Group` command and type `bridge-group 1`.

```
Vermont(config-if)#interface serial 0
Vermont(config-if)#bridge-group 1
```

Press **CTRL+Z** to return to Privileged mode. By typing `exit`, you return to the previous mode, in this case, Global Configuration mode.

```
Vermont(config-if)#^Z
```

The `Copy Running-Config` command copies the currently running configuration to NVRAM, which is used when the router is rebooted.

```
Vermont#copy running-config startup-config
Building configuration...
[OK]
Vermont#
```

The `Show Bridge` command displays fields that give information about the system. `Total of 300 station blocks` means the total number of forwarding database elements in the system. The memory to hold bridge entries is allocated in blocks, each of which can hold 300 individual entries.

```
Vermont#show bridge
Total of 300 station blocks, 295 free
BG   Hash   Address          Action    Interface   Age   RX count   TX count
1    00/0   FFFF.FFFF.FFFF   discard   -           P     0          0
1    09/0   0000.0000.0009   forward   Ethernet0   0     2          0
1    49/0   0000.0C00.4009   forward   Ethernet0   0     1          0
1    CA/0   AA00.0400.06CC   forward   Ethernet0   0     25         0
```

When the number of free entries falls below 25, another block of memory sufficient to hold another 300 entries is allocated. Therefore, the size of the bridge-forwarding database is limited by the amount of free memory in the router.

295 free means the number in the free list of forwarding database elements in the system. The total number of forwarding elements is expanded dynamically, as needed. BG means the bridging group to which the address belongs. Hash is the relative position in the keyed list. Address is the Ethernet-ordered MAC address.

Action means the action to be taken when that address is looked up; choices are to discard or forward the datagram. Interface indicates the interface, if any, on which that address was seen. Age is the number of minutes since a frame was received from or sent to that address. The letter P indicates a permanent entry. The letter S indicates the system as recorded by the router. RX count is the number of frames received from that address.

To monitor transparent bridging on the Vermont router, assuming that bridging is configured on the Maine router, type show spanning-tree.

```
Vermont#show spanning-tree
Bridge Group 1 is executing the DEC compatible Spanning Tree protocol
  Bridge Identifier has priority 128, address 0000.0c92.9048
  Configured hello time 1, max age 15, forward delay 30
  We are the root of the spanning tree
  Topology change flag not, detected flag not set
  Times:  hold 1, topology change 30, notification 30
          hello 1, max age 15, forward delay 30, aging 300
  Timers: hello 1, topology change 0, notification 0
Port 2 (Ethernet0) of bridge group 1 is forwarding
   Port path cost 10, Port priority 128
   Designated root has priority 128, address 0000.0c92.9048
   Designated bridge has priority 128, address 0000.0c92.9048
   Designated port is 2, path cost 0
   Timers: message age 0, forward delay 0, hold 0
Port 6 (Serial0) of bridge group 1 is forwarding
   Port path cost 1562, Port priority 128
   Designated root has priority 128, address 0000.0c92.9048
   Designated bridge has priority 128, address 0000.0c92.9048
   Designated port is 6, path cost 0
   Timers: message age 0, forward delay 0, hold 1
```

As you can see, the first line of output indicates which type of spanning-tree protocol (IEEE or DEC) the bridge group is executing. In this case, the DEC spanning-tree protocol is being used. The next three lines show the current operating parameters of the spanning tree.

The remaining lines display related information that is useful when examining the spanning-tree parameters. Port 2 is the port number associated with the interface. Ethernet0 is the interface on which translational bridging has been configured. Bridge group 1 is the bridge group to which the interface has been assigned.

`Forwarding` is the state of the interface. Other possible values include `Down`, `Listening`, `Learning`, and `Blocking`. Port path cost 10 is the cost associated with this interface. Port priority 128 is the port priority.

Source-route Bridging

This section describes source-route bridging (SRB) and its operation. We will discuss how to configure Multiport SRB.

Overview

SRB is a method of bridging developed by IBM for use in token ring networks. With SRB, the entire route to a destination is predetermined in real time before the data is sent. This is in contrast to transparent bridging, where bridging occurs on a hop-by-hop basis. Once all paths to the destination are known, the source host chooses the route to use, hence the term *source-route bridging*.

IBM proposed SRB to the IEEE 802.5 committee as a means to interconnect LANs. The IEEE 802.5 committee subsequently adopted SRB into the IEEE 802.5 Token Ring LAN specification.

Since its initial proposal, IBM has offered a new bridging standard to the IEEE 802 committee—the source-route transparent (SRT) bridging solution. SRT bridging eliminates pure SRBs entirely, proposing that the two types of LAN bridge be transparent bridges and SRT bridges. Although SRT bridging has achieved support, SRBs are still widely deployed.

Although the name connotes routing, SRB is really a bridging implementation because path determination is performed at the data link layer (layer 2) of the OSI reference model. With SRB, the source places the complete source-to-destination route in the frame header of all inter-LAN frames. To discover a route to the destination, end stations transmit an explorer frame to determine where the destination is located.

There are three types of explorer: *local ring test frame*, which checks the local ring for the destination host; *spanning explorer*, which allows the algorithm to find the best (spanning) route to the destination host after checking all rings; and *all-routes explorer*, which finds all routes to the destination host by checking all rings. The spanning explorer has the advantage of minimizing explorer traffic as it only searches for the best route to the destination host.

Specifications for IBM Token Ring define a maximum of eight rings and seven bridges. Specifications for 802.5 token ring define a maximum of 14 rings and 13 bridges.

Let's look at the SRB route discovery process. Assume that the source end station (Host X) wishes to send a frame to the destination end station (Host Y).

For Host X to know the route to Host Y, it must first go through a route discovery process to locate the destination. Initially, Host X does not know whether Host Y resides on the same or a different LAN. To determine this, Host X sends out a local-ring test frame. SNA devices send a test frame, Net-BIOS devices do not.

If the local-ring test frame returns to Host X with a positive indication that Host Y has seen it, Host X sends the data frame onto the local ring. If it returns without a positive indication that Host Y has seen it, Host X must assume that Host Y is on a remote segment. To determine the exact remote location of Host Y, Host X sends an all-routes explorer frame.

Each bridge receiving the all-routes explorer frame (Bridges 1 and 4 in this example) copies the frame onto all its outbound ports. Route information is added to the routing information fields (RIFs) of the all-routes explorer frames as they travel through the internetwork. Routing information consists of the bridge number and the attached ring number.

Host Y receives as many copies as there are routes. In this case, there are two routes: Ring 500 to Bridge 4 to Ring 503 to Bridge 3 to Ring 502, and Ring 500 to Bridge 1 to Ring 501 to Bridge 2 to Ring 502. Host Y replies to each individually, using the accumulated route information. It changes the direction bit in the routing control field of the RIF, causing the packet to traverse back along the same path to the source end station.

Reversing the direction causes the bridge to read the route information in reverse order. For example: Ring 502 to Bridge 3 to Ring 503 to Bridge 4 to Ring 500, and Ring 502 to Bridge 2 to Ring 501 to Bridge 1 to Ring 500.

Upon receipt of all response frames, Host X chooses a path based on some predetermined criteria. The IEEE 802.5 specification does not mandate the criteria Host X should use in choosing a route, but it does make several suggestions: first frame received, response with the minimum number of hops, response with the largest allowed frame size, and various combinations of the above criteria.

In most cases, the route contained in the first frame received will be used and the others discarded. This is because it is most likely that the first frame received contains the fastest path. Both Host X and Host Y will use that route for the duration of their session.

After a route is selected, it is inserted into frames destined for Host Y in the form of a RIF. The RIF is included only in those frames destined for other

LANs. The presence of routing information within the frame is indicated by the setting of the most-significant bit within the source address field, called the routing information indicator (RII) bit.

Basic SRB configuration is used when no more than two Token Ring interfaces are connected to a router. Multiport SRB is a form of SRB used when more than two token ring interfaces are connected to a router. The fundamental difference between SRB and Multiport SRB is that Multiport SRB defines a virtual ring group within the router.

Multiport SRB Configuration

When you are configuring Multiport SRB, there are several commands to enter both in Global Configuration mode and Interface Configuration mode. In Global Configuration mode, you need to define a virtual ring group. In Interface Configuration mode, you need to assign each interface to the ring group, manually enable or disable spanning-tree support, and set up filters (optional).

When more than two token ring interfaces are connected to a router, a virtual ring is required. To create this software-generated virtual ring group within the router, use the Source-Bridge Ring-Group command:

```
source-bridge ring-group ring-group
```

The *ring-group* is the number of the virtual ring. It replaces the target ring number.

Each interface must be assigned to the ring group, specifying the local bridge connection. To specify the ring and bridge number to which the interface is attached, use the Source-Bridge Active command:

```
source-bridge active local-ring bridge-number target-ring
```

The *local-ring* is the number of the interface's ring. It must be a number between 1 and 4095 that uniquely identifies a network segment or ring within the bridged token ring network. The *bridge-number* is a number between 1 and 15 that uniquely identifies the bridge connecting the two rings. The *target-ring* is the number of the target ring. It must be unique within the bridged token ring network and it can also be a ring group.

You can use the Source-Bridge Spanning command to enable the passing of spanning or single-route explorers: source-bridge spanning *group*. The *group* is a number between 1 and 9 that uniquely identifies all interfaces which will be part of the bridge group.

The `Source-Bridge Spanning` command specifies that the interface is capable of forwarding a spanning explorer. If spanning tree is not automatically run, the tree must be manually configured on each forwarding interface.

The `Bridge Protocol IBM` command enables IBM's dynamic spanning-tree algorithm for bridging: `bridge group protocol ibm`. The group is a number between 1 and 9 that uniquely identifies all interfaces that participate in the automatic spanning algorithm.

The `Source-Bridge Proxy-Explorer` command enables an interface to respond to explorer packets. The contents of the RIF cache are used to describe the path to the destination end host.

When two routed networks are connected through a source-route bridged network the multiring command enables routed frames to pass through the SRB bridge, by inserting RIF fields into the routed frames.

The `All` keyword enables multiring for all frames. The `Other` keyword enables multiring for any routed frame not among the supported protocols listed under the `Keyword` parameter. The `Keyword` parameter specifies a routed protocol that will have RIF information inserted in its frame. Options include `apollo`, `appletalk`, `clns`, `decnet`, `ip`, `ipx`, `vines`, and `xns`.

In the example below, two routed domains are separated by an SRB domain. In order for the routed frames to traverse the SRB network, the routed frames must have RIF fields inserted.

To monitor Multiport SRB, use the `Show Source-Bridge` command. `max hp` is the maximum routing descriptor length in hops. `receive cnt` is the number of bytes received on interface for SRB. `transmit cnt` is the number of bytes transmitted on interface for SRB.

```
Vermont#show source-bridge
Local Interfaces    max receive   transmit
    srn  bn  trn r p s n hp cnt:bytes cnt:bytes      drops
TR0 5    1   10  * *    7  39:1002  23:62923
Rings:
 bn: 1 rn: 5    local ma: 4000.3080.844b TokenRing0              fwd: 10
 bn: 1 rn: 2    remote ma: 4000.3080.8473 TCP 150.136.93.93      fwd: 18
Explorers: ------- input -------    ------ output -------
        spanning all-rings  total      spanning all-rings  total
   TR0    0         3         3             3         5       8
```

`srn` is the ring number of the Token Ring. `bn` is the bridge number of the router, for the ring. `trn` is the group in which the interface is configured (the target ring number or virtual ring group).

`Rings` describes the ring groups, including the bridge groups, ring groups, whether the group is local or remote, the MAC address, the network address or interface type, and the number of packets forwarded. `Explorers` describes the explorer packets that the router has transmitted and received.

TR0 is the interface on which explorers were received. spanning indicates the number of spanning-tree explorers. all-rings is the number of all-routes explored. total is the total number of spanning and all-routes explorers.

The Show RIF command is also used to monitor Multiport SRB. How indicates the means through which the RIF was learned; possible values include a ring group (rg) or interface (TR). Idle (min) is the number of minutes since the last response was received directly from this node. Routing Information Field lists the RIF.

```
Vermont#show rif

Codes: * interface, - static, + remote
Hardware Addr    How    Idle (min)    Routing Information Field
5C02.0001.4322   rg5       -          0630.0053.00B0
5A00.0000.2333   TR0       3          08B0.0101.2201.0FF0
5B01.0000.4444   -         -          -
0000.1403.4800   TR1       0          -
0000.2805.4C00   TR0       *          -
0000.2807.4C00   TR1       *          -
0000.28A9.4800   TR0       0          -
0077.2201.0001   rg5       10         0830.0052.2201.0FF0
```

Let's configure Multiport SRB on the Vermont router which has three token ring interfaces. Assume you have already logged onto the Vermont router and need to enter Global Configuration mode. Do this by typing config term or configure terminal.

```
Vermont>enable
Password:
Vermont#config term
Enter configuration commands, one per line. End with CNTL/Z.
Vermont(config)#
```

First, you need to create a software-generated virtual ring group within the router. To do this, use the Source-Bridge Ring-Group command.

```
Vermont(config)#source-bridge ring-group 10
```

Now, you need to configure each of Vermont's token ring interfaces. First, we will configure Tokenring 0 by typing interface tokenring 0.

```
Vermont(config)#interface tokenring 0
```

The interface now needs to be assigned to the ring group. The Source-Bridge Active command specifies local ring 500, bridge number 1 as the bridge connecting the two rings, and target ring 10.

```
Vermont(config-if)#source-bridge active 500 1 10
```

The `Source-Bridge Spanning` command manually enables the interface belonging to bridge group 7 to pass spanning or single-route explorers.

```
Vermont(config-if)#source-bridge spanning 7
```

Vermont's Tokenring 1 interface is configured in the exact same way. Using the `Source-Bridge Active` command, type `source-bridge active 501 1 10` to specify the local ring, the bridge number connecting the two rings, and the target ring.

```
Vermont(config-if)#interface tokenring 1
Vermont(config-if)#source-bridge active 501 1 10
```

The `Source-Bridge Spanning` command manually enables the interface to pass spanning or single-route explorers.

```
Vermont(config-if)#source-bridge spanning 7
```

Finally, we will configure Vermont's Tokenring 2 interface. To specify the ring and bridge number to which the interface is attached, type `source-bridge active 502 1 10` to specify the local ring, the bridge number connecting the two rings, and the target ring.

```
Vermont(config-if)#interface tokenring 2
Vermont(config-if)#source-bridge active 502 1 10
```

Again, manually enable the interface to pass spanning or single-route explorers by typing `source-bridge spanning 7`.

```
Vermont(config-if)#source-bridge spanning 7
```

Type `exit` to return to Global Configuration mode. Remember, **Ctrl+Z** returns you to Privileged mode.

```
Vermont(config-if)#exit
```

Now that all three token ring interfaces have been configured, you want to enable IBM's dynamic spanning-tree algorithm for bridging. To do this, use the `Bridge Protocol IBM` command.

```
Vermont(config)#bridge 7 protocol ibm
```

Multiport SRB has now been configured, press **Ctrl+Z** to return to Privileged mode.

```
Vermont(config)#^Z
```

26

Concurrent Routing and Bridging and Advanced Bridging Options

Concurrent Routing and Bridging

This section describes concurrent routing and bridging as implemented on Cisco routers. We will examine the key features of transparent bridging, demonstrate the implementation of CRB on Cisco routers, and configure CRB on a Cisco router.

Transparent Bridging with CRB

Transparent bridging is used to interconnect like-media LANs, such as Ethernet and IEEE 802.3, to give the appearance of a single larger network. It is so named because it is transparent to network hosts. It operates at the data-link layer of the OSI reference model. All operations are based on the MAC address.

Transparent bridges pass frames along one hop at a time, based on tables associating end node MAC addresses with bridge ports. When transparent bridges are powered on, they learn the network's topology by analyzing the source address of incoming frames from all attached networks. Transparent bridges are often called learning bridges for this reason. A transparent bridge performs two basic operations: forwarding and filtering.

When the destination address is known to exist on an attached segment, frames are forwarded from the inbound interface to the correct outbound interface for the destination. A transparent bridge will forward a broadcast or multicast frame on all interfaces except the one on which the frame is received. Similarly, frames received for stations not listed in the bridging table are flooded on all interfaces except the interfaces on which they are received.

A transparent bridge filters (or discards) frames whose source and destination addresses are known to exist on the same network segment. Therefore, the knowledge accumulated in the bridging table provides the basis for congestion control.

A transparent bridge ensures a loop-free topology. A bridging loop occurs where there is more than one path between any two bridged LANs in a network. Because a bridge forwards traffic, a bridge loop can create a flood of packets that could disable a network.

Transparent bridges detect and break loops using a spanning-tree algorithm. This prevents bridging loops by creating a spanning tree of bridges so that there is only one path between any pair of LANs. Duplicate paths between network segments are blocked. The spanning-tree algorithm does allow redundant paths (loops), which can be used as backup in the event of link segment or bridge failure.

Transparent spanning-tree protocols include DEC (Digital Equipment Corp.) and IEEE 802.1d. These implementations are not compatible with each other. Both spanning-tree protocols function by electing a root bridge which is then used to determine lowest-cost paths. Once the spanning-tree algorithm has disabled interfaces that could cause routing loops, the traffic takes the only available path to the root bridge.

Cisco's transparent bridging software provides a concurrent routing and bridging (CRB) feature that enables a specific protocol to be both routed and bridged within a single router, but on separate interfaces. For example, consider an existing network that contains a two-port router and a two-port bridge. A network designer planning for future growth might want to replace the two devices with a single large router.

The migration is straightforward if the intention is to route all protocols and eliminate bridging altogether. If the intention is to route a given protocol on two interfaces and to bridge the same protocol on two other interfaces, then concurrent routing and bridging is the solution. This situation might arise if the current topology is to be maintained for a period of time before migrating to an all-routed environment.

Without CRB, the decision to bridge or route a packet is determined globally. If the appropriate network-layer protocol is running on the router, then the packet is passed to the routing software. If the network-layer protocol is not running, then the packet needs to be bridged.

With CRB, the decision to bridge or route a packet is determined by transparent bridge group configuration. CRB introduces a two-step decision process that identifies bridging and routing options for each protocol being passed within a bridge group.

First, a check is made to see if the interface receiving the packet is a member of a transparent bridge group. If it is not a member, then the packet is routed. If it is a member, then a second check is made to see if the protocol is explicitly configured for routing. Protocols so configured are sent to the bridging software.

CRB applies only to transparent bridging. It is not supported for source-route bridging. It has a number of distinguishing features: interfaces are collected in a bridge group, all protocols are bridged by default, and specific protocols are chosen for routing.

A bridge group should be defined for each separately bridged (topologically distinct) network connected to the router. Each bridge group is distinct, in that bridged traffic and configuration messages cannot be exchanged between different bridge groups on the same router. Network interfaces are placed into a bridge group for two reasons: to bridge all nonrouted traffic among the network interfaces making up the bridge group and to participate in the spanning-tree algorithm by receiving and transmitting configuration messages (BPDUs) on the LANs to which they are attached. Bridge protocol data units are configuration messages exchanged regularly between the spanning-tree bridges. They are used in spanning-tree calculations.

CRB does have some well-defined limitations. It does not switch packets between the routed and the bridged domain. This feature is called *Integrated Routing and Bridging (IRB)*. Interfaces in a bridge group cannot both route and bridge the same protocol. An interface can be a member of only one bridge group.

CRB Configuration

Let's look at an example of how to configure CRB on a Cisco router. Referring to the topology shown in the diagram, the objective is to route IP on the Ethernet 0 and Ethernet 1 interfaces, and to bridge it on the Ethernet 2 and Ethernet 3 interfaces. IP is routed using the RIP routing protocol.

Assume that this implementation refers to the Vermont router, where you are currently logged on in Privileged Exec mode. Before enabling CRB, you first need to enter Global Configuration mode using the `Configure Terminal` command.

```
Vermont>enable
Password:
Vermont#configure terminal
Enter configuration commands, one per line. End with CNTL/Z.
Vermont(config)#
```

CRB is disabled by default. Enable it using the `Bridge CRB` command, which has no arguments. When CRB is first enabled in the presence of existing bridge groups, it will generate a `Bridge Route` configuration command for any protocol configured for routing on any interface in the bridge group. This is done to maintain backward compatibility with previous versions of Cisco IOS.

```
Vermont(config)#bridge crb
```

Next, you need to select a spanning-tree protocol and identify a bridge group. This is achieved using the `Bridge Protocol` command. In this example, DEC is chosen as the spanning-tree protocol for bridge group 1. The full syntax of the `Bridge Protocol` command is `bridge bridge-group protocol {ieee | dec}`.

```
Vermont(config)#bridge 1 protocol dec
```

It is at this point in the configuration process that you include explicit `Bridge Route` commands for the bridge group. The `Bridge Route` command is used to identify a protocol for a bridge group that will be excepted from bridging and will instead be routed. The full syntax is `bridge group-number route protocol`. No explicit `Bridge Route` command is required for the simple example presented here.

As RIP is used to route IP, the next step is to enable the RIP routing process on the Vermont router. Do this by entering `router rip` in Global Configuration mode. In this example, it is assumed that IP routing has already been enabled on the router. If IP routing was not enabled before entering `router rip`, the system informs you of this with the message "IP routing not enabled". You can enable IP routing by entering `ip routing` in Global Configuration mode.

```
Vermont(config)#router rip
```

Next, you need to specify the network on which you want RIP routing to operate. Here, the `Network` command specifies IP network 172.16.0.0 as the network on which RIP will operate.

```
Vermont(config-router)#network 172.16.0.0
```

Type `exit` to return to Global Configuration mode.

```
Vermont(config-router)#exit
```

You now need to configure each of the Ethernet interfaces. Here, IP is to be routed on Ethernet 0 and Ethernet 1, and bridged on Ethernet 2 and Ethernet 3.

Begin configuring the Ethernet 0 interface by typing `interface ethernet 0` in Global Configuration mode. In this example, the interface is configured for IP traffic by assigning it IP address 172.16.1.1 255.255.255.0. IP packets are routed by default unless they are explicitly bridged. All other types of packet are bridged by default unless explicitly routed. Therefore, the configuration of Ethernet is now complete.

```
Vermont(config)#interface ethernet 0
Vermont(config-if)#ip address 172.16.1.1 255.255.255.0
```

The Ethernet 1 interface is configured in similar fashion. Here, it is given IP address 172.16.2.1.

```
Vermont(config-if)#interface ethernet 1
Vermont(config-if)#ip address 172.16.2.1 255.255.255.0
```

IP is to be bridged on the Ethernet 2 interface. When configuring Ethernet 2, you first assign the interface an IP address using the IP Address command. You get an interface to bridge traffic by assigning the interface to a bridge group. This is done using the Bridge-Group command, which takes the bridge group number (1 in this case) as its only argument.

```
Vermont(config-if)#interface ethernet 2
Vermont(config-if)#ip address 172.16.3.1 255.255.255.0
Vermont(config-if)#bridge-group 1
```

As IP traffic is to be bridged between Ethernet 2 and Ethernet 3, they must be made members of the same bridge group. The configuration of the Ethernet 3 interface is similar to that of Ethernet 2.

```
Vermont(config-if)#interface ethernet 3
Vermont(config-if)#ip address 172.16.4.1 255.255.255.0
Vermont(config-if)#bridge-group 1
```

This completes the configuration of CRB on the Vermont router. Return to Privileged Exec mode by pressing **Ctrl+Z**. Finally, you can save the new running configuration to the backup configuration file in NVRAM by typing copy runn start.

```
Vermont(config-if)#^Z
Vermont#copy runn start
Building configuration...
[OK]
```

You can now check the configuration of CRB on the Vermont router.

Cisco IOS provides the command Show Interfaces CRB to help monitor CRB on a router. This command only displays the configuration of those interfaces that have been configured for routing or bridging.

```
Vermont#show interface crb
Ethernet0
 Routed protocols on Ethernet0:
  ip
Ethernet1
 Routed protocols on Ethernet1:
  ip
Ethernet2
 Bridged protocols on Ethernet2:
  appletalk    clns       decnet      ip
```

```
 vines         apollo    ipx      xns
Software MAC address filter on Ethernet2
 Hash Len    Address        Matches  Act     Type
 0x00    0 ffff.ffff.ffff      0  RCV Physical broadcast
 0x04    0 0900.0700.0003      0  RCV Appletalk zone
 0x2A    0 0900.2b01.0001      0  RCV DEC spanning tree
 0x35    0 0900.0700.0032      0  RCV Appletalk zone
-- More --
```

You can see from the display that Ethernet 0 and Ethernet 1 both list IP as the only routed protocol. The display confirms that there are no bridged protocols on either of these two interfaces.

Ethernet 2 lists IP among its bridged protocols. This excludes it from appearing as a routed protocol on the interface. In fact, there are no routed protocols configured on the Ethernet 2 interface.

The display includes a section detailing the contents of the software MAC address filter. This consists of a table of important traffic destined for the router itself.

The appearance of "--More--" in the last line of the display indicates that there is another screen of information to follow. This can be viewed by pressing **Return**. The resulting display shows that IP is a bridged protocol on Ethernet 3. No protocols have been configured for routing on this interface.

```
 0x42    0 0000.0c92.904e      0  RCV Interface MAC address
 0x57    0 0100.5e00.0009      0  RCV IP multicast
 0xA8    0 0900.0700.00af      0  RCV Appletalk zone
 0xC0    0 0100.0ccc.cccc      0  RCV CDP
 0xC2    0 0180.c200.0000      0  RCV IEEE spanning tree
 0xEA    0 0900.0700.00ed      0  RCV Appletalk zone
 0xEC    0 0900.0700.00eb      0  RCV Appletalk zone
 0xF8    0 0900.07ff.ffff      0  RCV Appletalk broadcast
Ethernet3
Bridged protocols on Ethernet3:
 appletalk     clns      decnet   ip
 vines         apollo    ipx      xns
Software MAC address filter on Ethernet2
 Hash Len    Address        Matches  Act     Type
 0x00    0 ffff.ffff.ffff      0  RCV Physical broadcast
 0x04    0 0900.0700.0003      0  RCV Appletalk zone
 0x2A    0 0900.2b01.0001      0  RCV DEC spanning tree
 0x35    0 0900.0700.0032      0  RCV Appletalk zone
 0x42    0 0000.0c92.904e      0  RCV Interface MAC address
 0x57    0 0100.5e00.0009      0  RCV IP multicast
 0xA8    0 0900.0700.00af      0  RCV Appletalk zone
--More--
```

The Ethernet 3 interface has the same software MAC address filter as Ethernet 2.

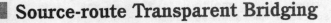

Source-route Transparent Bridging

This section describes the operation and implementation of source-route transparent bridging. We will examine its key elements, describe its features and operation, demonstrate the configuration of SRT on Cisco routers, and configure SRT bridging on a Cisco router.

Source-route and SRT Bridging

Source-route bridging (SRB) is a method whereby an end host locates another end host by discovering available paths. In SRB, the entire route to a destination is predetermined, in real time, prior to the sending of data. Once all paths to the destination are known, the source host chooses the route to use. Contrast this with transparent bridging, in which bridging occurs on a hop-by-hop basis.

In SRB, paths are determined by sending explorer frames. There are three types: local ring test frames, spanning-tree explorers, and all-routes explorers. A *local ring test frame* checks the local ring for the destination host. This is the first explorer sent by the source. A *spanning explorer frame* allows the algorithm to find the best (that is, loop-free) route to the destination host after checking all rings. Finally, the *all-routes explorer* finds all routes to the destination host by checking all rings.

The destination host replies to all explorers it receives. The source host uses the Routing Information Field (RIF) contained in the reply to learn and select a route through the network.

SRBs are so named because they assume that the complete source-to-destination route is placed in all inter-LAN frames sent by the source. As source-route bridging maintains multiple paths, it offers fast selection of alternate routes in the event of failure.

Let's consider the example of source-route bridging shown in the diagram. Host X transmits a local ring explorer looking for Host Y on the local ring. If this fails, Host X transmits a spanning explorer. This follows the spanning tree.

Inside the spanning explorer is the RIF field. This contains a map that lists each bridge and ring in the path taken by the explorer packet. The path to the destination uses a combination of token rings and source-route bridges.

The target destination receives as many copies as there are routes. In this example, there are two routes: ring 500 to bridge 4 to ring 503 to bridge 3 to ring 502, and ring 500 to bridge 2 to ring 501 to bridge 2 to ring 502.

The destination end station, Host Y, replies to each frame individually. It changes the direction bit in the Routing Control subfield of the RIF, sending the packet back as an all-routes explorer. It reverses the path used by the explorer to reach this destination.

Host X, therefore, receives maps identifying alternate routes to Host Y. Host X, as the source, selects which route to use, hence the name source-route bridging.

Usually, the source end station selects the first route received and disregards the others. Selection can also be based on the minimum number of hops, the response with the largest allowed frame size, or a combination of these criteria.

Specifications for IBM Token Ring define a maximum of eight rings and seven bridges. Specifications for 802.5 Token Ring define a maximum of 14 rings and 13 bridges.

Source-route transparent bridging (SRT) is defined as an optional protocol on top of transparent bridging and is specified in IEEE 802.1d. It combines implementations of both transparent bridging and SRB.

SRT bridges employ both technologies in one device. They do not translate between bridging protocols. They can forward traffic from both transparent and source-route end nodes at the same time, one packet per transfer. They can form a common spanning tree with transparent bridges. This allows end stations of each type to communicate with end stations of the same type in a network of arbitrary topology.

SRT is used when token ring networks, some using RIFs and others not using RIFs, need to communicate. In general, Token Ring-to-Ethernet communication is not provided by SRT. The two domains are kept separate, with a few exceptions.

SRT bridges use the Routing Information Indicator (RII) bit to distinguish between frames employing SRB and transparent bridging. If the RII bit is 1, then an RIF is present in the frame, and the bridge performs source-route bridging. If no RIF is present, the bridge performs transparent bridging.

Cisco SRT can use either the IEEE or DEC spanning-tree algorithms. Interoperability with non-Cisco SRT bridges requires the IEEE spanning-tree algorithm to be configured on the Cisco router.

Mixed-media bridging involves moving frames from one LAN media to another, such as Ethernet to token ring or token ring to FDDI. While transparent bridging is found predominantly in Ethernet networks, it can also exist in token ring and FDDI LANs. By comparison, SRB is exclusive to token ring LANs.

SRT bridges are not perfect solutions to the problems of mixed-media bridging. SRT bridging might require hardware and software upgrades to SRBs to allow them to handle the increased burden of analyzing every packet.

In environments consisting of SRT bridges, transparent bridges, and SRBs, source routes chosen are based on whatever SRT and SRB routes are available. This could result in a potentially inferior path to a destination created by the transparent bridging spanning tree.

Mixed SRT/SRB bridging networks lose the benefits of SRT bridging. However, a complete change to SRT bridging can be prohibitively expensive.

Bridges that run only SRT never add or remove RIFs from frames, so they do not integrate SRB with transparent bridging. A host connected to a source-route bridge that expects RIFs can never communicate with a device across a bridge that does not understand RIFs.

To tie in existing source-route bridges to a transparent bridged network, you must use source-route translational bridging (SR/TLB) instead. SR/TLB creates a software gateway between the SRB and transparent bridging domains.

Despite its shortcomings, SRT bridging permits the coexistence of two incompatible environments. It allows communication between end stations of the same type in a network of arbitrary topology.

SRT Configuration

Let's now look at how you might configure SRT on a Cisco router. A mixed-media topology will form the basis of the discussion. The router is to be configured as an SRT bridge connecting Ethernet and token ring data links.

Let's carry out this configuration on the Vermont router. Assume that you are currently logged on in Privileged Exec mode. To begin the configuration process, first enter Global Configuration mode using the `Configure Terminal` command.

```
Vermont>enable
Password:
Vermont#configure terminal
Enter configuration commands, one per line. End with CNTL/Z.
Vermont(config)#
```

Next, you need to select a transparent bridge group and a spanning-tree protocol. Here, bridge group 1 and the IEEE spanning-tree protocol are specified with the `Bridge Protocol` command. The full syntax of the `Bridge Protocol` command is `bridge bridge-group protocol {ieee | dec}`.

```
Vermont(config)#bridge 1 protocol tree
```

Where token rings are connected to a router, you need to decide if a software-generated virtual ring is required inside the router. In general, a virtual ring is only needed when more than two token ring interfaces are connected to the router.

In the network shown, there are two token rings connected to the router. Although this does not strictly require the generation of a virtual ring, let's define one to demonstrate the process.

To create a virtual ring group within the router, use the `Source-Bridge Ring-Group` command, whose syntax is `source-bridge ring-group` *ring-group*. The *ring-group* is the number of the virtual ring and is used in place of the target-ring number.

```
Vermont(config)#source-bridge ring-group 10
```

The next step is to configure each of the router's interfaces for SRT bridging. Let's begin with the Ethernet 0 and Ethernet 1 interfaces. Implement transparent bridging between the two Ethernet networks attached to the router by making the Ethernet 0 and Ethernet 1 interfaces members of the same bridge group. Having entered Interface Configuration mode by typing `interface ethernet 0`, you then use the `Bridge-Group` command to assign the interface to bridge group 1. The syntax of the `Bridge-Group` command is `bridge-group` *bridge-group* where *bridge-group* can have a value in the range 1 to 63.

```
Vermont(config)#interface ethernet 0
Vermont(config-if)#bridge-group 1
```

Ethernet 1 is configured in the same way as Ethernet 0, and is also assigned to bridge group 1. Begin configuring the Tokenring 0 interface by typing `interface tokenring 0`.

```
Vermont(config-if)#interface tokenring 0
```

To implement SRT bridging, you need to assign the two token ring interfaces to the same bridge group as the Ethernet interfaces. Therefore, the configuration of Tokenring 0 continues by assigning it to bridge group 1 using the command `bridge-group 1`.

```
Vermont(config-if)#bridge-group 1
```

Next, you need to specify the SRB bridge number assigned to the router and the local ring to which the Tokenring 0 interface is attached. Do this using the `Source-Bridge Active` command, whose syntax is `source-bridge active` *local-ring bridge-number target-ring*. The *local-ring* is the number of the interface's ring (range 1–4095). The *bridge-number* uniquely identifies the SRB bridge connecting the two rings (range

1–15). The `target-ring` is the number of the target ring or virtual ring group.

For Tokenring 0, enter `source-bridge active 500 1 10`, where the local ring is 500 and the SRB bridge number is 1. Virtual ring number 10 takes the place of the target-ring number in the command.

```
Vermont(config-if)#source-bridge active 500 1 10
```

Next, you need to define the type of explorer packets to be generated on the interface—all-routes explorers or spanning-tree explorers. A spanning-tree explorer packet is sent to a defined group of nodes that comprise a statically configured spanning tree in the network. In contrast, an all-routes explorer packet is sent to every node in the network on every path.

Forwarding all-routes explorer packets is the default. This default can, however, generate an exponentially large number of explorers in networks with complex topologies. The number of explorer packets traversing the network can be reduced by sending spanning-tree explorer packets.

Let's enable forwarding of spanning-tree explorer packets out of the Tokenring 0 interface. You can do this using the `Source-Bridge Spanning` command. This command has no arguments.

```
Vermont(config-if)#source-bridge spanning
```

The configuration of the Tokenring 1 interface is similar to Tokenring 0. Begin by entering `interface tokenring 1`. You then assign Tokenring 1 to bridge group 1.

```
Vermont(config-if)#interface tokenring 1
Vermont(config-if)#bridge-group 1
```

Type `source-bridge active 501 1 10` to indicate that the interface is attached to local ring 501 and bridge group 1. The target ring is the virtual ring group 10.

```
Vermont(config-if)#source-bridge active 501 1 10
```

The `Source-Bridge Spanning` command enables the interface to pass spanning-tree explorers.

```
Vermont(config-if)#source-bridge spanning
```

Press **Ctrl+Z** to return to Privileged Exec mode.

```
Vermont(config-if)#^Z
```

Finally, you can save the new running configuration to the backup configuration file in NVRAM by typing copy runn start.

```
Vermont#copy runn start
Building configuration...
[OK]
Vermont#
```

Source-route Translational Bridging

This section describes the operation and implementation of source-route translational bridging (SR/TLB). We will describe the problems when translating between SRB and transparent bridging domains, describe how to configure SR/TLB, and implement SR/TLB on a Cisco router.

SR/TLB Overview

SR/TLB is a Cisco IOS software feature that allows you to combine SRB and transparent bridging domains. This is done without the need to convert all your existing source-route bridges to source-route transparent (SRT) bridges. SR/TLB forms an intermediate software "bridge" that translates between the two bridging domains.

To the source-route end station, this bridge looks like a standard SRB. To the transparent bridging station, the translational bridge represents just another transparent bridge or port in the bridge group. SR/TLB uses a ring (called a *pseudo-ring*) to represent the entire transparent bridging domain.

Transparent bridges do not inherently understand what to do with SRB explorer frames. They learn about the network's topology through analysis of the source address of incoming frames. They have no knowledge of the RIF field or SRB route discovery process.

When bridging occurs from the SRB domain to the transparent bridging domain, SRB information is removed. RIFs are usually cached for use by subsequent return traffic. When bridging happens between domains, the router checks the packet to see if it has a multicast (or broadcast) destination or a unicast (single-host) destination. If it is multicast, the packet is sent as a spanning-tree explorer. If the packet has a unicast destination, the router looks up the path to the destination in the RIF cache. If a path is found, it will be used. Otherwise, the router will send the packet as a spanning-tree explorer. As the spanning-tree implementations for each domain are not compatible, multiple paths between the SRB and the transparent bridging domains are not allowed.

Translating between Ethernet (transparent bridging) and token ring (SRB) domains presents several problems, any of which may prevent successful communication. The main challenges that need to be addressed include incompatible bit ordering, embedded MAC addresses, incompatible MTU sizes, and handling exclusive token ring functions.

Both Ethernet and token ring support 48-bit MAC addresses, but the internal hardware representation of these addresses differs. Token ring and FDDI transmit the most significant bit first, while Ethernet transmits the least significant bit first. SR/TLB reorders the source and destination address bits when translating between Ethernet and token ring frame formats.

MAC addresses are sometimes carried in the data portion of a frame. These are termed *embedded addresses*. For example, TCP/IP's Address Resolution Protocol (ARP) places a hardware address in the data portion of a link layer frame. Conversion of embedded addresses is difficult as they need to be handled on a case-by-case basis. The problem is solved by programming the bridge to check for various types of MAC addresses. However, the solution must be adapted for each new type of embedded MAC address. If the translational bridging software runs in a multiprotocol router, then the router can successfully route these protocols and avoid the problem entirely.

Token ting and Ethernet support different maximum transmission unit (MTU) sizes. Ethernet's MTU is approximately 1,500 bytes, whereas token ring frames can be 4 to 18 KB. Bridges are not capable of frame fragmentation and reassembly, so frames that exceed the MTU of a given network must be dropped. The RIF field has a subfield that indicates the largest frame size that can be accepted by a particular SRB implementation.

Translational bridges that send frames from the transparent bridging domain to the SRB domain set the MTU to 1500 bytes. This limits the size of token ring frames entering the transparent bridging domain. If the network includes hosts that cannot correctly process this field, then translational bridges are forced to drop frames that exceed Ethernet's MTU size. They typically discard bits representing token ring functions that have no Ethernet equivalent. The question of how to deal with exclusive Token Ring functions is left to the Ethernet/token ring manufacturer.

Take the example of a token ring's frame status bits. The Address Recognized (A) bit tells the source whether the destination recognized its address in the frame. The Frame Copied (C) bit tells the source whether the destination was able to copy the frame into its buffers. These bits are duplicated as a basic form of error checking because the Frame Status is not CRC-protected. Some translational bridge manufacturers completely ignore these bits, preventing the token ring source from tracking lost frames. Others set the C bit to allow the tracking of lost frames, but do not set the A bit, as the bridge is not the final destination.

Because of the way end nodes implement token ring, problems are most prevalent when bridging between token rings and Ethernets or between token ring and FDDI LANs. There is currently no real standarization in how communication between SRB and transparent bridging domains should be effected. Hence, there is no single correct translational bridging implementation.

Transparent bridging over serial lines and FDDI uses data link encapsulation. Sometimes bridges on either side of a WAN link are called *half-bridges* because, when taken together, they appear to be a single bridge between the two LANs.

On FDDI, translational bridging can be disabled in favor of encapsulated bridging. In the example shown, encapsulated bridging is configured on the two routers connecting Host A and Host B to the FDDI Dual Ring. This, however, will prevent Host A from communicating with Host C or any other hosts attached to the FDDI Dual Ring.

Some mixed-media networks may be too complex and difficult to bridge. As an alternative to SR/TLB, you could use TCP/IP and encapsulate the SRB frames inside the higher-level protocols available. The encapsulated frames can then be routed across the complex network and de-encapsulated at the destination. This technique is known as *remote source-route bridging (RSRB)*.

Not all interfaces will support translational bridging. Routers with interfaces that do include Cisco 7000 series and Cisco 4000 series.

SR/TLB Configuration

Let's now look at how to implement SR/TLB on a Cisco router. SR/TLB can only be enabled after source-route and transparent bridging have both been configured on the router. Cisco provides the `Source-Bridge Transparent` command to establish communication between the transparent and source-route configurations. It creates two virtual environments and activates media translation features.

The syntax of the `Source-Route Transparent` command is:

```
source-bridge transparent ring-group pseudo-ring
bridge-number tb-group [oui]
```

The *ring-group* refers to the virtual ring group that the Source-Bridge Ring-Group command creates inside the router. The Pseudo-Ring parameter assigns a ring number for the entire transparent bridging domain The *pseudo-ring* number must be a unique SRB domain.

The *bridge-number* is the SRB number assigned to the router. The *tb-group* is the transparent bridge group number assigned to the "virtual Ethernet" that contains the SRB domain. The optional *OUI* parameter is an organizationally unique identifier that holds the vendor code of the interface that sourced the frame.

Let's illustrate SR/TLB configuration using the Vermont router. Imagine a network attached to the Vermont router has the topology of both Ethernet and token ring. Vermont's transparent bridging domain is to be assigned pseudo-ring number 15. Remember, the pseudo-ring refers to Cisco's technique of representing the entire transparent bridging domain as just another token ring. The source-route domain is to be configured by generating virtual ring group 10 in the router.

Assume you are currently in Privileged Exec mode on the Vermont router. To begin the configuration process, first enter Global Configuration mode by typing configure terminal at the prompt.

```
Vermont>enable
Password:
Vermont#configure terminal
Enter configuration commands, one per line. End with CNTL/Z.
Vermont(config)#
```

Next, you need to select a transparent bridge group and a spanning-tree protocol. To specify transparent bridge group 4 and the IEEE spanning-tree protocol, enter bridge 4 protocol ieee. The full syntax of the Bridge Protocol command is as follows: bridge *bridge-group* protocol {ieee | dec}.

```
Vermont(config)#bridge 4 protocol ieee
```

To implement SR/TLB, you need to have the two token rings communicate through a virtual ring. Create virtual ring group 10 by entering source-bridge ring-group 10. The syntax of the Source-Bridge Ring-group command is source-bridge ring-group *ring-group*. The *ring-group* is the number of the virtual ring, and is used in place of the target-ring number.

```
Vermont(config)#source-bridge ring-group 10
```

Now that SRB and transparent bridging have been globally configured, you can enable SR/TLB on the router by entering `source-bridge transparent 10 15 1 4`, where `10` is the virtual ring created for SRB and `15` is the pseudo-ring number it assigns to the transparent bridging domain. `1` is the SRB bridge number assigned to the router, while `4` is the transparent bridge group number specified in the `Bridge Protocol` command.

```
Vermont(config)#source-bridge transparent 10 15 1 4
```

The next step is to configure each of the router's interfaces for SRB or transparent bridging as appropriate. As traffic is bridged only between members of the same bridge group and not between bridge groups, you need to assign the Ethernet and token ring interfaces to the same bridge group (bridge group 4).

Let's begin with the Ethernet 0 and Ethernet 1 interfaces. Start configuring the Ethernet 0 interface by entering `interface ethernet 0`. Then use the `Bridge-Group` command to assign the interface to bridge group 4. The syntax of the `Bridge-Group` command is `bridge-group` *bridge-group* where *bridge-group* can have a value 1 to 63.

```
Vermont(config)#interface ethernet 0
Vermont(config-if)#bridge-group 4
```

Ethernet 1 is configured in the same way as Ethernet 0, and it too is assigned to bridge group 4.

```
Vermont(config-if)#interface ethernet 1
Vermont(config-if)#bridge-group 4
```

Begin configuring the Tokenring 0 interface by typing `interface tokenring 0`.

```
Vermont(config-if)#interface tokenring 0
```

Next, you need to assign the two Tokenring interfaces to the same bridge group as the Ethernet interfaces, which is bridge group 4. Do this by entering the command `bridge-group 4`.

```
Vermont(config-if)#bridge-group 4
```

Then, you need to identify the local ring to which the Tokenring 0 interface is attached, the SRB bridge number assigned to the router, and the target ring for traffic sourced from the local ring. Do this using the `Source-`

Bridge Active command. The syntax is source-bridge active *local-ring bridge-number target-ring*. Here, Tokenring 0 is attached to local ring 500, the SRB bridge number assigned to the router is 1, and the target ring is virtual ring 10.

```
Vermont(config-if)#source-bridge active 500 1 10
```

Next, you need to define the type of explorer packets generated on the interface—all-routes explorers or spanning-tree explorers. Forwarding all-routes explorer packets is the default. The number of explorer packets traversing the network can be reduced by sending spanning-tree explorer packets.

Let's enable forwarding of spanning-tree explorer packets out of the Tokenring 0 interface by entering source-bridge spanning. This command has no arguments.

```
Vermont(config-if)#source-bridge spanning
```

The configuration of the Tokenring 1 interface is similar to Tokenring 0. Begin by entering the command interface tokenring 1. Then assign the interface to bridge group 4 by entering bridge-group 4.

```
Vermont(config-if)#interface tokenring 1
Vermont(config-if)#bridge-group 4
```

Type source-bridge active 501 1 10 to indicate that the interface is attached to local ring 501 and bridge group 1, and the target ring is virtual ring 10.

```
Vermont(config-if)#source-bridge active 501 1 10
```

The Source-Bridge Spanning command forces Tokenring 1 to forward spanning-tree explorers, rather than all-routes explorers. Press **Ctrl+Z** to return to Privileged Exec mode.

```
Vermont(config-if)#^Z
```

Finally, you can save the new running configuration to the backup configuration file in NVRAM by typing copy running-config startup-config or, more simply, copy runn start.

```
Vermont#copy runn start
Building configuration...
[OK]
Vermont#
```

 ## Remote Source-route Bridging

This section describes remote source-route bridging (RSRB) and its operation. We will describe how to configure RSRB, and configure RSRB.

Remote Source-route Bridging Overview

Source-route bridging involves bridging between token ring media only. In contrast, remote source-route bridging (RSRB) involves bridging between multiple token rings connected by non-token ring network segments. When you are bridging across token ring media, we recommend that you do not use RSRB; use SRB instead.

RSRB connects bridged networks using an IP network. It is used in complicated heterogeneous networks that are difficult to bridge. RSRB is token ring *frame tunneling* where the frames are tunneled through TCP, IP, or HDLC. An RSRB tunnel is treated as a virtual token ring by assigning it to a ring group.

Every router with which you want to exchange token ring traffic must be a member of the ring group. These routers are known as remote peers.

The virtual ring can extend across any non-token ring media supported by RSRB, such as serial, Ethernet, FDDI, and WANs. The type of media you select determines the way you set up RSRB.

The main functions of RSRB are: using TCP/IP and encapsulating SRB (token ring) frames inside higher-layer protocols; routing SRB frames across an IP network, and de-encapsulating SRB frames and placing them on the target ring.

In order to identify the destination for encapsulated SRB frames, the routers that are participating in the virtual ring must be identified as remote peers. The IP address of a remote peer is used in forming the datagram that carries the SRB frame.

IP encapsulation is sometimes referred to as Fast Sequenced Transport (FST), a minimal protocol that enables the destination router to determine whether SRB frames are arriving out of sequence. Reliability and resequencing limitations are inherent in FST encapsulation. FST is therefore best implemented in a reliable network with few alternative paths. For FST to be effective, media frames must contain a logical link control (LLC) field.

TCP and FST encapsulation allow for arbitrary topologies. There are no hop count limitations, and traffic is routable. Software overhead for TCP and FST varies: TCP has a high overhead, and is very reliable because of its connection-oriented design. FST has a medium overhead, and is a connectionless datagram service.

Direct encapsulation restricts traffic to a single topology. There is a single-hop count limit, and traffic is not routable. Software overhead is minimal because error-checking is done at the hardware level.

RSRB Configuration

When you are configuring RSRB, commands are entered both in Global Configuration mode and Interface Configuration mode. In Global Configuration mode, you need to define a virtual ring group and establish a peer relationship with a station on the virtual ring. In Interface Configuration mode, you need to configure an interface for RSRB.

When more than two token ring interfaces are connected to a router, a virtual ring is required. To create this software-generated virtual ring group within the router, use the `Source-Bridge Ring-Group` command:

```
source-bridge ring-group ring-group
```

The `Ring-Group` parameter is the number of the virtual ring. It replaces the target ring number and is in the range 1 to 4095.

A peer relationship must be established between routers. The `Source-Bridge Remote-Peer` command identifies the IP address of a peer station connected to the virtual ring and selects the encapsulation style:

```
source-bridge remote-peer ring-group [tcp | fst] ip-address
```

The `Ring-Group-Number` parameter must match the number you have specified with the `Source-Bridge Ring-Group` command. `tcp` is an encapsulation style providing reliable delivery with a high software overhead. `fst` is an encapsulation style providing datagram delivery with a medium software overhead. The `IP-Address` parameter is the IP address of a remote peer with which the router will communicate.

The `Source-Bridge Remote-Peer` and `Source-Bridge Ring-Group` commands are identical for all routers using TCP encapsulation. Only the interface configuration is unique to each router. Use the `Source-Bridge` command to configure an interface for RSRB:

```
source-bridge local-ring bridge-number target-ring
```

The `Local-Ring` parameter is the ring number for the interface's token ring. It must be a decimal number between 1 and 4,095 that uniquely identifies a network segment or ring within the bridged token ring network. The

`Bridge-Number` parameter is a number that uniquely identifies the bridge connecting the local and target rings. It must be a decimal number between 1 and 15. The `Target-Ring` parameter is the ring number of the destination ring on the router. It is a decimal number and must be unique within the bridged token ring network. The target ring can also be a ring group.

Let's configure RSRB over a TCP connection on the Vermont router which has a token ring and a Serial interface. Assume you have already logged onto the Vermont router and need to enter Global Configuration mode. Do this by typing `configure terminal` or `config term`.

```
Vermont>enable
Password:
Vermont#configure terminal
Enter configuration commands, one per line. End with CNTL/Z.
Vermont(config)#
```

First, you need to create a software-generated virtual ring group within the router. To do this, use the `Source-Bridge Ring-Group` command.

```
Vermont(config)#source-bridge ring-grou 5
```

You need to identify the IP address of a peer in the ring group with which to exchange source-bridge traffic using TCP. Using the `Source-Bridge Remote-Peer` command, type `source-bridge remote-peer 5 tcp 172.16.1.1`.

```
Vermont(config)#source-bridge remote-peer 5 tcp 172.16.1.1
```

Now, you need to configure both of Vermont's interfaces. First, to configure the Tokenring 0 interface, type `interface tokenring 0`.

```
Vermont(config)#interface tokenring 0
```

In Interface Configuration mode, you need to set an IP address for Tokenring 0 to enable IP routing. To do this, use the `IP Address` command.

```
Vermont(config-if)#ip address 172.16.192.1 255.255.255.0
```

Now configure Tokenring 0 for RSRB using the `Source-Bridge` command.

```
Vermont(config-if)#source-bridge 501 1 5
```

Vermont's Serial 0 interface is now configured for IP routing.

```
Vermont(config-if)#interface serial 0
```

Do this by using the IP Address command with its IP-Address and Mask parameters. To return to Privileged mode, press **Ctrl+Z**.

```
Vermont(config-if)#ip address 172.16.1.2 255.255.255.0
Vermont(config-if)#^Z
```

The Copy Running-Config command copies the currently running configuration to NVRAM, which is used when the router is rebooted.

```
Vermont#copy runn start
Building configuration...
[OK]
Vermont#
```

Data-Link Switching

This section describes data-link switching (DLSw+) and its operation and how to configure DLSw+.

DLSw+ Overview

DLSw+ is Cisco's implementation of DLSw. DLSw+ transports nonroutable SNA and NetBIOS protocol traffic over an IP network using encapsulation. The "+" stands for extended and enhanced features to the DLSw standard.

DLSw+ is an alternative to SRB and addresses the following limitations of SRB: SRB's hop-count limit of 7, broadcast traffic from SRB explorer frames or NetBIOS name queries, unnecessary traffic caused by acknowledgments, data link control timeouts, and lack of flow control and prioritization.

SRB limitations occur when SRB is extended across a WAN. Therefore, DLSw+ is typically used to transport SNA and NetBIOS across a WAN.

The DLSw standard, documented in RFC 1795, defines the switch-to-switch protocol between DLSw routers. The standard calls for the transport protocol to be TCP. It requires that data link control connections be locally terminated.

The standard requires that the SRB RIF be terminated at the DLSw router. It describes a means for establishing priorities and flow control. Error-recovery procedures assure data link control connections are appropriately disabled if any part of their associated circuits breaks. The DLSw standard does not specify when to establish TCP connections. The capabilities exchange allows compliance to the standard, but at different levels of support.

The standard does not specify how to cache learned information about MAC addresses, RIFs, or NetBIOS names. It also does not describe how to track both capable or preferred DLSw partners for either backup or load-balancing purposes.

The standard does not prescribe the specifics of media conversion, but leaves the details up to the implementation. It does not define how to map switch congestion to data link control flow control.

DLSw+ includes enhancements of DLSw in the following areas: modes of operation, scalability, performance, and availability. It operates in three modes: *Backward Compatibility mode*, *Standards Compliance mode*, and *Enhanced mode*.

DLSw+ operation in Backward Compatibility mode can be used in parallel with RSRB. It communicates with older releases of Cisco IOS running RSRB and SDLC-to-LLC2 conversion (SDLLC).

DLSw+ can automatically detect through the DLSw+ capabilities exchange whether the participating router is manufactured by another vendor. DLSw+ then operates in DLSw Standards Compliance mode.

Even when operating in Standards Compliance mode, some DLSw+ enhancements are available. In particular, enhancements that are locally controlled options on a router can be accessed even though the remote router is not running DLSw+ active. These include location learning (the ability to determine if a destination is on a local LAN before sending "canureach" frames across a WAN), explorer firewalls, and media conversion.

DLSw+ can automatically detect whether the participating router is another DLSw+ router. DLSw+ then operates in Enhanced mode, making the additional features of DLSw+ available to the SNA and NetBIOS end systems. Cisco routers will detect this Enhanced mode automatically when packets are exchanged during the "capabilities exchange" part of the session. The mode is determined by the configuration of the other peer. DLSw+ does not interoperate with pre-standard implementations of DLSw, such as RFC 1434.

One significant factor that limits the size of token ring internetworks is the amount of explorer traffic that traverses the WAN. DLSw+ includes the following features to reduce the number of explorers: peer groups, border peers, on-demand peers, and explorer firewalls.

The large token ring internetworks that Cisco has helped build over the last several years all follow a similar structure—a hierarchical grouping of routers based upon the usual flow of broadcasts through the network.

A cluster of routers in a region or a division of a company is combined into a peer group. Within a peer group, one or more routers are designated as *border peers*. When a DLSw+ router receives a test frame or NetBIOS name query, it sends a single explorer frame to its border peer.

The border peer takes complete responsibility for forwarding the explorer on behalf of the peer group member. This arrangement eliminates duplicate explorers on access links and minimizes the processing required in access routers.

On-demand peers greatly reduce the number of peers that must be configured. As you can see in the graphic, you can use on-demand peers to establish an end-to-end circuit. This can be done even though the DLSw+ routers servicing the end systems have no specific configuration information about the peers.

This configuration permits casual, any-to-any connection without the burden of configuring the connection in advance. It also allows any-to-any routing in large internetworks where persistent TCP connections would not otherwise be possible.

An *explorer firewall* permits only a single explorer for a particular destination MAC address to be sent across the WAN. While an explorer is outstanding and awaiting a response from the destination, subsequent explorers for that MAC address are merely stored.

When the explorer response is received at the originating DLSw+, all explorers receive an immediate local response. This eliminates the start-of-day explorer storm that many networks experience.

The transport connection between DLSw+ routers can vary according to the needs of the network. DLSw+ is not necessarily tied to TCP/IP as required by the DLSw standard. Cisco supports three different transport protocols between DLSw+ devices: TCP/IP, FST/IP, and direct. These transport options enhance performance when line speeds and traffic conditions do not require local acknowledgment (LACK).

TCP/IP transports SNA and NetBIOS traffic across WANs where bandwidth is limited and termination of data-link control sessions is required. This transport option is required when DLSw+ is operating in DLSw+ standards compliance mode. TCP/IP requires FST and LACK.

DLSw+ allows media conversion between local or remote LANs and Synchronous Data Link Control (SDLC) or Ethernet. It also converts between LAN/SDLC and Qualified Logical Link Control (QLLC) for PU 2.0 and PU 2.1 devices. FST and direct encapsulation support no media conversion.

FST/IP transports across WANs that have an arbitrary topology and sufficient bandwidth to accommodate SNA and NetBIOS. FST is used for token ring-to-token ring environments only and provides transport over serial, FDDI, and Ethernet.

Direct encapsulation transports across a point-to-point connection where the benefits of an arbitrary topology are not important. Like FST, it is used for token ring-to-token ring environments only and provides transport over serial, FDDI and Ethernet. Direct encapsulation uses HDLC or frame relay. FST and direct support no media translation.

DLSw+ offers enhanced availability by maintaining a peer table of multiple paths to a given MAC address or NetBIOS name, where a path is either a remote peer or a local port. The Cisco IOS software maintains a preferred path and one or more capable paths to each destination. The *preferred peer* is either the peer that responds first to an explorer frame or the peer with the least cost.

The *preferred port* is always the port over which the first positive response to an explorer was received. If the preferred peer to a given destination is unavailable, the next available capable peer is promoted to the new preferred peer.

No additional broadcasts are required, and recovery through an alternate peer is immediate. Maintaining multiple paths to each destination is especially attractive in SNA networks.

A common technique used in the hierarchical SNA environment is assigning the same MAC address to different token ring interface couplers (TICs) on the IBM front-end processors (FEPs). DLSw+ ensures that duplicate TIC addresses are found, and if multiple DLSw+ peers can be used to reach the FEPs, they are all cached. The way that multiple capable peers are handled with DLSw+ can be biased to meet either of the following network needs: fault tolerance and load balancing. DLSw+ recovers rapidly from failures by caching multiple peers that can be used to reach a given destination.

Whenever a new circuit is established between a pair of end systems, usually the end-to-end path for the circuit is already known (that is, cached). If this is so, the originating DLSw+ router sends a circuit-establishment message directly to the preferred partner. If the preferred partner is no longer available, a circuit-establishment message is sent to the next capable router in the cache. Maintaining multiple cache entries facilitates a timely reconnection after session outages.

Load balancing distributes network traffic over multiple DLSw+ peers in the network. The Cisco IOS software can be configured to perform load balancing, in which case circuits are established in round-robin fashion using the list of capable routers. When used for load balancing, this technique improves overall SNA performance.

RIF passthrough involves end-to-end RIF visibility, with a hop total of seven. RIF termination involves two RIFs, with seven hops maximum on each side. RSRB supports RIF passthrough, where the entire router cloud appears as one ring in the RIF. Therefore, the complete RIF is visible from a SNIFFER-like tool that captures packets from the network and can be used to examine the contents of the RIF field. Depending on whether RIF passthrough or RIF termination is used, the RIF information will be different. This technique, however, supports only six additional SRB hops along the entire path.

In DLSw+, the RIF terminates in the virtual ring. This technique scales better than RSRB, allowing six additional SRB hops on each end of the router network. However, it does not allow the entire ring path to be viewed from a SNIFFER-like tool. With DLSw+, the RIF is terminated, even if the DLC is not terminated (as in FST or Direct mode).

You can compare the functionality offered by RSRB, RFC 1434, DLSw, and DLSw+. RFC 1434 was the original specification replaced by the DLSw standard version 1.0 RFC. This new RFC had not been assigned a number at the time this was written, although one is expected in the near future.

DLSw+ Configuration

When configuring DLSw+, there are several commands you must enter both in Global Configuration mode and Interface Configuration mode. In Global Configuration mode, you need to define a virtual ring group and the parameters of the DLSw+ local peer, and specify the remote peer with which the router will connect.

In Interface Configuration mode, you need to set the ring speed for the token ring interfaces, assign the interface to the ring group, and enable the use of spanning explorers. When more than two token ring interfaces are connected to a router, a virtual ring is required.

To create this software-generated virtual ring group within the router, use the Source-Bridge Ring-Group command: source-bridge ring-group *ring-group*. The *Ring-Group* parameter is the number of the virtual ring. It replaces the target ring number.

```
Vermont(config)#source-bridge ring-group 100
```

The DLSw Local-Peer command defines the parameters of the DLSw+ local peer: dlsw local-peer peer-id ip-address. The IP-Address parameter is the local peer IP address required for FST and TCP.

```
Vermont(config)#dlsw local-peer peer-id 10.2.17.1
```

The DLSw Remote-Peer TCP command identifies the IP address of a remote peer with which to exchange traffic using TCP: dlsw remote-peer *list-number* tcp *ip-address*.

```
Vermont(config)#dlsw remote-peer 0 tcp 10.2.17.2
```

The `List-Number` parameter is the remote peer ring group list number. The ring group list number default is 0. If the ring group list number is not 0, the value must match the number you specify with the `DLSW Ring-List`, `DLSW Port-List`, or `DLSW Bgroup-List` command. The `IP-Address` parameter is the TCP/IP address of the remote peer with which the router is to communicate.

Now set the ring speed for the token ring interface by using the `Ring-Speed` command: `ring-speed` *speed*.

```
Vermont(config)#interface tokenring 0
Vermont(config-if)#ring-speed 16
```

The `Speed` parameter is an integer that specifies the ring speed, either 4 for 4 Mbps or 16 for 16 Mbps operation.

The token ring interface must be assigned to the ring group, specifying the local bridge connection. To specify the ring and bridge number to which the interface is attached, use the `Source-Bridge Active` command: `source-bridge active` *local-ring bridge-number target-ring*.

```
Vermont(config-if)#source-bridge active 25 1 100
```

The `Local-Ring` parameter is the number of the interface's ring. It must be a number between 1 and 4,095 that uniquely identifies a network segment or ring within the bridged token ring network. The `Bridge-Number` parameter is a number between 1 and 15 that uniquely identifies the bridge connecting the two rings. The `Target-Ring` parameter is the number of the target ring. It must be unique within the bridge token ring network, and it can also be a ring group.

You can use the `Source-Bridge Spanning` command to enable the use of spanning explorers: `source-bridge spanning`.

```
Vermont(config-if)#source-bridge spanning
```

If spanning tree is not automatically run, the tree must be manually configured on each forwarding interface. This is a simple configuration with no border peers or peer groups specified. Because no peer groups and border peers are specified, explorer frames are sent to all peers. This configuration is very similar to RSRB configurations.

With DLSw+, the ring group number can be different in each router. Keeping it consistent in all routers can help with problem diagnosis. DLSw+

includes a ring list concept which provides a means of controlling to which local rings explorers are forwarded. Since no ring lists were configured, explorers are forwarded on all rings for which DLSw is enabled.

Index

Note: Boldface numbers indicate illustrations.

1000BaseLx (*See* Gigabit Ethernet)
1000BaseSx (*See* Gigabit Ethernet)
1000BaseT (*See* Gigabit Ethernet)
100BaseFx (*See* Fast Ethernet)
100BaseT4 (*See* Fast Ethernet)
100BaseTx (*See* Fast Ethernet)
100VG-AnyLAN, 34
10Base5/10Base2 (*See* coaxial cable for Ethernet)
10BaseF (*See* fiber optic for Ethernet)
10BaseT (*See* UTP category 3 cables)
802.1d protocol, concurrent routing and bridging (CRB), 731
802.2, IPX, 330
802.3 (*See* Ethernet)
802.5 (*See* token ring)
802.6, 34
802.x addressing in NetBEUI over PPP, 619

A

abstract syntax notation one (ASN.1), 24
access servers, 13
access classes, switched multimegabit data service (SMDS),
    653–65
access DQDB, switched multimegabit data service (SMDS), 655
access lists, 290, 291–305, **293, 296,** 380–385
    AppleTalk, 478, 485–491, 494–500, **494, 495, 496,**
        500–504, **500, 501,** 502
    border gateway protocol (BGP), 260, 262–264
    dial-on-demand routing (DDR), 678, 679, 682, 694
    enhanced IGRP (EIGRP), 244
    ISDN, 639
    NetBEUI over PPP, 620
    redistribution of routes, 271–272
access rate, in frame relay, 64
acknowledgment/acknowledgment packets, 27, 38
    NetBEUI over PPP, 622
    enhanced IGRP (EIGRP), 235
active vs. passive (silent) mode, routing information protocol
    (RIP), 185
adaptive cut-through mode switching, 85
additive bandwidth, 661
address management, 167–168
address mapping (*See* mapping addresses)
address mapping table (AMT), AppleTalk, 416
address resolution protocol (ARP), 42, 44
    ARP broadcast, 44
    ARP cache, 44
    asynchronous transfer mode (ATM), 74–75
    broadcast storms, 44
    frame relay, 62, 66–67, 572–573
    IPX, 329
    LAN emulation (LANE), 668
    MAC addresses, 45
    proxy ARP, 44–45
    reverse ARP (RARP), 45
    switched multimegabit data service (SMDS), 659, 660
address screening, switched multimegabit data service
    (SMDS), 655

address spoofing
    dial-on-demand routing (DDR), 698
    switched multimegabit data service (SMDS), 655
addressing, 2, 167–168, 643, 661
    AppleTalk, 423–432
    asynchronous transfer mode (ATM), 662, 673, 674
    data link switching (DLSw+), 751
    dial-on-demand routing (DDR), 679, 680, 684, 691, 693
    frame relay, 568, 569–570, 572–574, 577
    IP protocol, 173
    IPX, 328–334
    ISDN, 637
    LAN emulation (LANE), 665, 666, 667, 669
    NetBEUI over PPP, 619
    point-to-point protocol (PPP), 598, 600, 602, 607, 611, 614
    point-to-point protocol (PPP) Callback, 611, 614
    routers, 122, **122**
    routing information protocol version 2 (RIP-2), 188
    source route translational bridging (SR/TLB), 742
    switched multimegabit data service (SMDS), 654, 655,
        658, 659
    X.25, 533, 547
adjacency, 560
    NetWare link services protocol (NLSP), 344, 345
    open shortest path first (OSPF), 195, 204–206
adjacency database, NetWare link services protocol (NLSP), 344
adjacent layer communication, 28–29, 29
adjacent router, open shortest path first (OSPF), 195–196
adjacent-layer communications, 25
administrative distance, border gateway protocol (BGP),
    258–259
advanced peer-to-peer networking (APPN), 2
advanced program-to-program communications (APPC), 2
aggregation of routes, 87, 476
    border gateway protocol-4 (BGP-4), 226
    ISDN, 644
    NetWare link services protocol (NLSP), 359–373, 359
all routes explorer
    source route bridging, 722
    source route transparent bridging, 736, 740
All-SPFRouters address, open shortest path first (OSPF), 200
Apollo
    LAPB, 522
    X.25, 538
AppleTalk, 288, 377, 411–432, **413,** 433–453
    802.3, 414
    802.5, 414
    access lists, 478, 485–491, 494–500, **494, 495, 496,**
        500–504, **500, 501, 502**
    address acquisition, 424
    address mapping table (AMT), 416
    addressing, 423–432
    AppleTalk Address Resolution Protocol (AARP), 415, 416,
        424, 478
    AppleTalk Data Stream protocol (ADSP), 418
    AppleTalk Echo Protocol (AEP), 416
    AppleTalk Filing Protocol (AFP), 419

AppleTalk Printer Access Protocol (PAP), 418
AppleTalk Session Protocol (ASP), 418
AppleTalk Transaction protocol (ATP), 417
AppleTalk Update-based Routing protocol (AURP), 417,
    438–440, **438**, 478
asynchronous transfer mode (ATM), 672
AURP tunneling, 406, 417, 443–453
bridging, 703
broadcasting, 478
cable-range filters, 500–504
cable-ranges, 420, 434
carrier sense multiple access/collision detect (CSMA/CD),
    414, 415
Chooser facility, 421–422, 493
configuration, 440–443
congestion, 477–478
data-link layer, 414–415
datagram delivery protocol (DDP), 415, 416, 434–436, 435
dial-on-demand routing (DDR), 485, 511, 694, 696
Discovery mode, 429–431, **431, 432**
dynamic configuration, 429–431, **431, 432**
encapsulation, 417, 438–439
enhanced IGRP (EIGRP), 233, 234, 240, 455–473
Ethernet, 414
EtherTalk, 414
EtherTalk Link Access Protocol (ELAP), 415
extended access lists, 478, 487–491
extended networks, 420
FDDI, 414
FDDITalk, 414
FDDITalk Link Access Protocol (FLAP), 415
filtering, 478, 485, 491–503
flow control, 418
GZL filters, 493
IPX, 324
ISDN, 638
LAN emulation (LANE), 665
LAPB, 522
link access protocol (LAP), 415
LocalTalk Link Access Protocol (LLAP), 415
LocalTalk, 414–415
logical link control (LLC), 415
manually configured interfaces, 424–429
multicasting, 422
multipoint AURP tunnels, 440
multiprotocol networks, 478
Name Binding Protocol (NBP), 417, 478, 485, 488–489
network addresses, 423
network entities, 419–420
network layer, 415–417
network-visible entities (NVE), 420
nodes, 419–420
nonextended networks, 420
OSI model and, 413
physical layer, 414–415
point-to-point AURP tunnels, 440
queuing, 479–485
routers and routing, 424–429, 433–453
routing table maintenance protocol (RTMP), 417, 419,
    434, 436–437, **436**
routing tables, 478
seed routers, 429–431, **431, 432**
session layer, 418
sockets, 419–420

TCP/IP, 438–439
token ring, 414
TokenTalk, 414
TokenTalk Link Access Protocol (TLAP), 415
traffic management, 475–504
transition routing, 429
transport layer, 415–417
tunneling, 417, 438–440, **438,** 443–453
upper layers, 418–419
user datagram protocol (UDP), 438–439
versions, phase 1 and phase 2, 412
WAN links, 478
X.25, 538
ZIP filters, 494
zone information protocol (ZIP), 418–419, 477–478
zone information table (ZIT), 419
zones, 419–422
AppleTalk Address Resolution Protocol (AARP), 415, 416, 478
AppleTalk Control Protocol (ATCP), 72
AppleTalk Data Stream protocol (ADSP), 418
AppleTalk Echo Protocol (AEP), 416
AppleTalk Filing Protocol (AFP), 419
AppleTalk Printer Access Protocol (PAP), 418
AppleTalk Session Protocol (ASP), 39, 418
AppleTalk Transaction protocol (ATP), 417
AppleTalk Update-based routing protocol (AURP), 406, 417,
    478, 438–440, **438**
Application layer, 24, 40
applications for networks, 92
APPN High Performance Routing Control Protocol (APPN
    HPRCP), 72
APPN Intermediate Session Routing Control Protocol (APPN
    ISRCP), 72
arbitration in local area networks (LAN), 8
ARCnet and IPX, 325, 327
area address/area address database, NetWare link services
    protocol (NLSP), 360, 362
area border routers, open shortest path first (OSPF), 192,
    193, 194
area count fields, NetWare link services protocol (NLSP), 362
area ID, open shortest path first (OSPF), 198
areas, open shortest path first (OSPF), 192
ARPANET, 174, 219
AS border/boundary routers (ASBR)
    border gateway protocol-4 (BGP-4), 192, 193, 217
    open shortest path first (OSPF), 192, 193
AS connections, border gateway protocol-4 (BGP-4), 218
AS consistency, border gateway protocol-4 (BGP-4), 221
AS external links, open shortest path first (OSPF), 199, **200**,
    208, 209
AS numbers, border gateway protocol-4 (BGP-4), 218
AS path, border gateway protocol-4 (BGP-4), 219
AS path access lists, border gateway protocol (BGP),
    264–266
AS types, border gateway protocol-4 (BGP-4), 218
ASCII, 40
asynchronous balanced mode (ABM), HDLC, 521
asynchronous transfer mode (ATM), 28, 44, 74–78, 287,
    660–675
    additive bandwidth, 661
    address resolution protocol (ARP), 74–75
    addressing, 661, 662, 673, 674
    AppleTalk, 672
    ATM adaptation layer (AAL), 663–664

ATM data exchange interface (DXI), 670
ATM Forum, 661, 670
ATM interface processor (AIP), 670–671, **671**, 673–675
ATM layer, 663
bandwidth, 661, 673
best-effort traffic, 675
bridges, 664
broadband ISDN (BISDN), 660
broadcasting, 76
cell count, 675
cell loss priority (CLP), 672, 675
cells, 74, 660–661
circuit switching, 661
classical IP (CIP), 74–76
classical IP over PVC (CIP over PVC), 75
common part convergence sublayer (CPCS), 664
comparison with CIP and LANE, 77
compression, 523
configuration, 670–674
connectionless network service (CLNS), 672
contracts, 671
convergence sublayer (CS), 664
data country code (DCC), 662
data exchange interface (DXI), 661
DECnet, 672
digital signal 3 (DS-3), 661, 662
discard eligibility, 672
encapsulation, 662, 672, 674
end system identifier (ESI), 75
Ethernet vs., 74, 76
FDDI, 662
frame relay, 661
frames, 74
insured traffic, 675
international code designator (ICD), 662
IP addressing, 673, 674
IP, 672
IPX, 672
jitter, 520
LAN emulation (LANE), 76–78, 664–670, **665**
layers, 662–664, **663**
locally administered address (LSA), 75
logical IP subnets (LIS), 74–75
mapping addresses, 673–675
multiplexing, 661
multiprotocol encapsulation, 672
narrowband ISDN (N-ISDN), 662
network service access points (NSAP), 662, 673, 674, 675
packet switching, 661
permanent virtual circuits (PVC), 75
permanent virtual connections (PVC), 661, 675
physical layer interface module (PLIM), 673
physical medium sublayer, 662
point-to-multipoint connections, 661
point-to-point connections, 661
private networks, 662
public networks, 662
quality of service (QoS), 74, 671–672, 674, 675
rate queues, 673, 674
routers and routing, 97, 671
segmentation and reassembly sublayer (SAR), 664
service data unit (SDU), 663
service specific convergence sublayer (SSCS), 664
simple and efficient AAL (SEAL) scheme, 664

SONET, 661, 662, 664, 674
subnets, 74–75
subnetwork point of attachment (SNPA), 662
switched high-speed LAN vs., 90–91
switched multimegabit data service (SMDS), 664
switched virtual connections (SVC), 661, 674, 675
switches, 76, 661, 663, 671–672
switches, ATM switches, 88
synchronous digital hierarchy (SDH), 661, 662
time division multiplexing (TDM), 661
token ring vs., 74, 76
topologies, 661
traffic policing, 520
traffic shaping, 520, 673
transmission convergence sublayer, 662
transparent asynchronous Xmitter/receiver interface (TAXI), 661
VC Mux, 672
VINEs, 672
virtual channel identifier (VCI), 75, 663, 672
virtual channels, 76
virtual circuits, 75
virtual connections, 661
virtual LAN (VLAN), 74
virtual path identifier (VPI), 75, 663, 672, 674
virtual paths, 663
wide area networks (WAN), 11, 15, 514, 518, 519
AT&T 5ESS/4ESS switches, ISDN, 626
ATM (*See* asynchronous transfer mode)
ATM adaptation layer (AAL), 663–664
ATM data exchange interface (DXI), LAN emulation (LANE), 670
ATM Forum, 661
   LAN emulation (LANE), 670
ATM interface processor (AIP), 670–671, **671**, 673–675
   LAN emulation (LANE), 669
ATM layer, 663
ATM switches, 13, 88
   local area networks (LAN), 11
Attachment Unit Interface (AUI), 31
AURP tunneling, 417, 443–453
authentication
   dial-on-demand routing (DDR), 681–685, 687, 692, 693
   ISDN, 638, 639, 644
   point-to-point protocol (PPP), 71–72, 510, 602, 606, 608, 610, 612, 614
   point-to-point protocol (PPP) Callback, 610, 612, 614
   routing information protocol version 2 (RIP-2), 188
AutoInstall for routers, 120–122, **121**
automatic repeat request (ARQ), 2
autonomous networks, 36
autonomous system (AS), 161, 174, 174, **176**
   border gateway protocol (BGP), 271–219, 250, 251, 254, 258
   enhanced IGRP (EIGRP), 241
auxiliary port, routers, 96, 97
availability of data, 7

B

B (bearer) channel, ISDN, 59, 626, 636
backbone networks, 11, 88, 287
   open shortest path first (OSPF), 192
backup designated router
   frame relay, 595
   open shortest path first (OSPF), 196, 203–204

backup interfaces, dial-on-demand routing (DDR), 693
backup of IOS image, routers, 131
backward compatibility mode, data link switching (DLSw+), 751
backward explicit congestion notification (BECN), frame relay, 63–64, 568
bandwidth, 6, 377, 661
  asynchronous transfer mode (ATM), 673
  border gateway protocol (BGP), 252
  dial-on-demand routing (DDR), 680, 690, 692
  enhanced IGRP (EIGRP), 237, 240
  Ethernet, 48, 49–50
  frame relay, 67–69
  ISDN, 633
  local area networks (LAN), 10
  NetWare link services protocol (NLSP), 346
  point-to-point protocol (PPP), 603
  redistribution of routes, 271
  wide area networks (WAN), 506, 514
  X.25, 547, 552, 555–556
bandwidth allocation protocol (BAP), 73
bandwidth-on-demand (See also dial-on-demand routing), 6, 73, 633, 636, 677–700
bandwidth allocation control protocol (BACP), 73
Banyan VINES Control Protocol (BVCP), 72
basic rate interface (BRI)
  dial-on-demand routing (DDR), 684–685, 690
  ISDN, 59, 627, 633, 634–646
  point-to-point protocol (PPP), 601, 602, 604, 607, 610, 616
  point-to-point protocol (PPP) Callback, 610, 616
  routers, 97
BCP, 72
Berkeley Software Distribution (BSD), 185
best-effort traffic, asynchronous transfer mode (ATM), 675
binary 8-zerosubstitution (B8ZS) line code, ISDN, 649
binary synchronous communications, 39
blocking, 23
Bootstrap protocol (BOOTP), 121, 320
border gateway protocol/border gateway protocol 4 (BGP/BGP-4), 174, 175, 216–228, 250–269
  access lists, 260, 262–264
  administrative distance, 258–259
  aggregation of routes, 226
  AS border routers (ASBR), 217
  AS connections, 218
  AS consistency, 221
  AS numbers, 218
  AS path access lists, 264–266
  AS path, 219
  AS types, 218
  autonomous system (AS), 217–219, 250, 251, 254, 258
  bandwidth, 252
  border gateway, 217
  border routers, 217
  classless interdomain routing (CIDR), 165, 216
  configuration, 252–258
  confirming a BGP connection, 222
  default networks, 258–260
  distribute lists, 262–264
  enhanced IGRP (EIGRP), 234
  error notification, 227, **228**
  exterior gateway protocol (EGP), 250
  external BGP (EBGP), 250, 253
  filtering, 260–269

floating static routes, 259
hop count, 226, 252
inter-AS routers, 221
interior gateway protocols (IGP), 251
internal BGP (IBGP), 250, 253
intra-AS routers, 221
KEEPALIVE message, 223, 252
keepalive messages, 216
link type, 252
loops, 250
maintaining a BGP connection, 223
messages, 222–223, **222, 223**
metrics, 251, 252
monitoring, 252–258
multi-homed, 219, 261–262
neighbors, 216, 253, 254–255
network layer reachability information (NLRI), 224, **225**
next hop, 226
NOTIFCATION message, 223, 227, **228**, 251
OPEN message, 223, **224**, 251
opening a BGP connection, 222
origin codes, 255
path attributes, 226, **227**
path cost, 252
path selection, 219
peers, 253
reachability information, 224
route maps, 265–268
routing information exchange, 221
routing policy, 219, 220–221, **221**
routing tables, 251
sessions, 216, 253
show ip bgp command, 255
single-homed, 261–262
speakers, 216, **217**
static routing, 258–260
topology, 219
traffic types, 218
transit policies, 261–262, **262**
transport control protocol (TCP), 251
UPDATE message, 221, 223, 224, **225**
weighting of routes, 220, 264–266
withdrawn routes, 226–227, **228**
border peers, data link switching (DLSw+), 751–752
border routers, border gateway protocol-4 (BGP-4), 217
bridge groups, concurrent routing and bridging (CRB), 731–732
bridge protocol data unit (BPDU), transparent bridging, 716–717, **717**
bridges and bridging, **9**, 35, 80–82, **80.** 289, 371–318, 378, 477, 702–727
  asynchronous transfer mode (ATM), 664
  dial-on-demand routing (DDR), 699
  LAN emulation (LANE), 664, 669
  local area networks (LAN), 10
  routers vs., 84., 705–709, **706,** 705
bridging spanning tree protocol, 317–318
broadband ISDN (BISDN)
  asynchronous transfer mode (ATM), 660
  switched multimegabit data service (SMDS), 655
broadband switches, 88
broadcast addresses/broadcasting, 44, 151, 153, 290, 315–321, 380
  address resolution protocol (ARP), 44
  AppleTalk, 478

asynchronous transfer mode (ATM), 76
BOOTP, 320
bridging spanning tree protocol, 317–318
bridging, 317–318
broadcast storms, 317
dial-on-demand routing (DDR), 696
directed broadcasting, 316
dynamic host configuration protocol (DHCP), 320
Ethernet, 320
flooding, 316–319, **318**
frame relay, 573, 575, 592–595
helper addresses, 319–321
open shortest path first (OSPF), 196
packets, 315
spanning tree protocol, 317–318
switched multimegabit data service (SMDS), 659
time-to-live, 319
turboflooding, 319
UDP, 319
wide area networks (WAN), 518
Broadcast and Unknown Server (BUS), 76, 665, 666–670, **666**
broadcast groups, LAN emulation (LANE), 667
broadcast storms, 44, 153, 317, 707, 714
browsers, 40
Btrieve, IPX, 338, 339
bundled links/packets, point-to-point protocol (PPP), 73, 601, 603, 604
burst committed (BC), frame relay, 64
burst exceeded (BE), frame relay, 64
bursty traffic, 6
bus configuration of local area networks (LAN), 8, **9**
byte offset, NetBEUI over PPP, 620

cable-range filters, 500–504
cable-ranges, AppleTalk, 420, 434
cache
    ARP, 44
    NetBEUI over PPP, 620, 621–622
call user data (CUD) packets, X.25, 545–546, 559
callback control protocol (CCP), 72
Callback, PPP (*See* PPP Callback)
caller ID
    ISDN, 639, 640
    point-to-point protocol (PPP), 602, 607
campus area networks (CAN), 11
campus switches, 88
carrier detect signal, routers, 146
carrier equipment, switched multimegabit data service (SMDS), 653
carrier protocol in tunneling, 404
carrier sense multiple access with collision detection (CSMA/CD), 34, 46, **46**, 46
    AppleTalk, 414, 415
    IPX, 327
Cayman TunnelTalk AppleTalk encapsulation, 406
CDDI, 287
cell count asynchronous transfer mode (ATM), 675
cell loss priority (CLP), asynchronous transfer mode (ATM), 672, 675
cell relay, 11, 13, 15, 518–519, 652
cells, asynchronous transfer mode (ATM), 74, 660–661
central office (CO), wide area networks (WAN), 507
centralized processing, 2

challenge handshake authentication protocol (CHAP), 71, 510
    dial-on-demand routing (DDR), 682, 683, 687, 692
    ISDN, 638, 639, 641, 644
    point-to-point protocol (PPP), 602, 606, 608, 610, 617
    point-to-point protocol (PPP) Callback, 610, 617
channel interface protocol (CIP), 97
channel service unit (CSU), 13, 57, 652
    frame relay, 566
    ISDN, 627, 633, 646
    wide area networks (WAN), 507, 515, 516
channelized T1/E1, 524–525
chat, 40
Chooser facility, AppleTalk, 421–422, 493
circuit-switching, 661, 631, **632**
Cisco Discovery Protocol (CDP), 138–141, **139**
classes of IP addresses, 150–152, **152**
classical IP (CIP), asynchronous transfer mode (ATM), 74–76
classical IP over PVC (CIP over PVC), asynchronous transfer mode (ATM), 75
classless inter-domain routing (CIDR), 163–166, **164**
    border gateway protocol-4 (BGP-4), 216
    routing information protocol version 2 (RIP-2), 187
client/server, 6, 290, 652
    point-to-point protocol (PPP) Callback, 609–612, 615, 617
closed user group (CUG), X.25, 556
coaxial cable for Ethernet, 47
collision detection, 5
collisions, 46
command lists, 105–106
command modes, routers, 98–103
Commerce, Department of, U.S., 30
committed information rate (CIR), frame relay, 64, 586
common object request broker architecture (CORBA), 18
common part convergence sublayer (CPCS), asynchronous transfer mode (ATM), 664
complete sequence number packet (CSNP), NetWare link services protocol (NLSP), 345
complex networks and traffic management, 287–289, 376–378, 476–477
compressed TCP, X.25, 538
compression, 289, 377, 477
    asynchronous transfer mode (ATM), 523
    frame relay, 523
    header compression, 523
    lossless compression, 523
    payload compression, 523
    serial compression, 522–524
    SLIP, 70
    switched multimegabit data service (SMDS), 523
    Van Jacobsen algorithm, 523
    X.25, 523
concentration, ISDN, 628
concurrent database access, 39
concurrent routing and bridging (CRB), 289, 378, 477, 702, 708–709, 729–735
    802.1d protocol, 731
    802.3, 730
    bridge groups, 731–732
    configuration of, 732–735
    DEC protocol, 731
    Ethernet, 730, 733–735
    filtering, 730
    forwarding, 730
    integrated routing and bridging (IRB), 732

LAN, 730
loops, loop avoidance, 730
MAC address, 730
OSI reference model, 730
spanning tree algorithm/protocol, 730, 732–733
transparent bridging, 730
configuration files, 127–133
congestion control, 38, 290, 707
AppleTalk, 477–478
frame relay, 63–64, **63**, 568
IPX, 378–380
NetBEUI over PPP, 622
X.25, 555
connection-oriented networks, 26, **26**, 27
connectionless network service (CLNS)
asynchronous transfer mode (ATM), 672
LAPB, 522
X.25, 538
connectionless networks, 26, 27–28
connectionless protocols, 326
connections for workstations
Ethernet, 49
token ring, 50
console port, routers, 96
contention, ISDN, 629
context-sensitive help, routers, 106–108
contracts, asynchronous transfer mode (ATM), 671
controller, ISDN, 650
controller configuration, routers, 129
convergence, 177–178
enhanced IGRP (EIGRP), 232, 456
NetWare link services protocol (NLSP), 343
convergence sublayer (CS)
asynchronous transfer mode (ATM)
conversations, 312, 484, 576
copy flash tftp command, 132
copy running-config startup-config command, 134, 137–138
copy startup-config running-config command, 134–135
copying IOS, routers, 131
cost, root and path cost, 7–8, 93, 346, 715
count-to-infinity problem, 179–181, **179**, 180
cursor movement, routers, 109
custom queuing, 290, 306–307, 309–312, 379, 479, 481–484, 481
customer premises equipment (CPE)
switched multimegabit data service (SMDS), 653, 654
wide area networks (WAN), 507
cut-through mode switching, 85
cyclic redundancy check (CRC)
frame relay, 576
ISDN, 648
wide area networks (WAN), 506–507, 518
X.25, 551

D

D (data) channel, ISDN, 59, 627, 629–630, 635, 650
daemon, 174
data carrier detect (DCD), X.25, 551
data circuit terminating equipment (DCE), 57
dial-on-demand routing (DDR), 678
frame relay, 564, **565**
point-to-point protocol (PPP), 598
wide area networks (WAN), 507–508
X.25, 528, **529**, 530, 531, 534, 535, 536, 540–542

data country code (DCC), asynchronous transfer mode
(ATM), 662
data exchange interface (DXI), 661
data integrity, 40
data link connection (DLC), frame relay, 66
data link connection identifier (DLCI), frame relay, 61, 68,
566–569, **567**, 579, 583–584, 586–590, **589**
data link layer, 31, 42, 703
data link switching (DLSw+), 84, 750–756
addressing, 751
backward compatibility mode, 751
border peers, 751–752
configuration, 754–756
encapsulation, 753
enhanced mode, 751
Ethernet, 752, 753
explorer firewalls, 752
FDDI, 753
frame relay, 753
HDLC, 753
LAN, 752
MAC addresses, 751, 753
NetBIOS, 750, 751, 752
on-demand peers, 752
preferred peer, 753
preferred port, 753
qualified logical link control (QLLC), 752
routers, 750
SNA, 750, 752
standards compliance mode, 751
synchronous data link control (SDLC), 752
TCP, 752
TCP/IP, 752
token ring, 751, 752, 753–756
WAN, 750, 752
data service unit (DSU), 57, 652
dial-on-demand routing (DDR), 689
frame relay, 566
ISDN, 627, 646
wide area networks (WAN), 507, 515, 516
data terminal equipment (DTE), 57
frame relay, 66, 564, 565, 568
ISDN, 627, 646
point-to-point protocol (PPP), 598
wide area networks (WAN), 507–508
X.25, 528, **529**, 531, 532, 534, 535, 536, 540–542
data terminal ready (DTR), dial-on-demand routing (DDR),
689
Data-link layer, 22
AppleTalk, 414–415
database description packet, open shortest path first (OSPF),
205–206, **205**
database exchange, open shortest path first (OSPF), 204–206
datagram delivery protocol (DDP), AppleTalk, 415, 416,
434–436, 435
datagrams, 26, 27, 38, 326
frame relay, 65
local area networks (LAN), 10
open shortest path first (OSPF), 200
X.25, 58, 530
debug commands
NetBEUI over PPP, 624
point-to-point protocol (PPP), 605
routers, 146, 147

Index

DEC protocol, 3, 731
DECnet
asynchronous transfer mode (ATM), 672
bridging, 703
dial-on-demand routing (DDR), 694, 696
IPX, 324
LAPB, 522
X.25, 538
DECnet Control Protocol (DNCP), 72
dedicated lines/links
point-to-point protocol (PPP), 73
wide area networks (WAN), 515
dedicated services, wide area networks (WAN), 14
default networks, border gateway protocol (BGP), 258–260
delay, 6, 42, 289
dial-on-demand routing (DDR), 690, 693
enhanced IGRP (EIGRP), 237, 460
X.25, 557
demarcation, wide area networks (WAN), 507
design of networks (See also traffic management), 91–93, 286–287, **287**
designated routers
frame relay, 595
open shortest path first (OSPF), 195, 196, 202
destination address broadcasts, 153
destination unreachable errors, IP protocol, 173
destinations, active vs. passive, enhanced IGRP (EIGRP), 237–238
dial backup, dial-on-demand routing (DDR), 685–694
dial map, dial-on-demand routing (DDR), 680
dial strings, point-to-point protocol (PPP), 611
dial up lines for wide area networks (WAN), 14
dial up private networks, 13
dial-on-demand routing (DDR), 289, 377, 476, 510–511, 678–700, **678**
access lists, 678, 679, 682, 694
address spoofing, 698
addressing, 679, 680, 684, 691, 693
AppleTalk, 485, 694, 696
authentication, 681–685, 687, 692, 693
backup interfaces, 693
bandwidth, 680, 690, 692
basic rate interface (BRI), 684–685, 690
bridges, 699
broadcasting, 696
challenge handshake authentication protocol (CHAP), 682, 683, 687, 692
configuration, 679, 691–694
data circuit-terminating equipment (DCE), 678
data service unit (DSU), 689
data terminal ready (DTR), 689
DECnet, 694, 696
delay, 690, 693
dial backup, 685–694
dial map, 680, 688
dialer groups, 680, 692, 693
encapsulation, 686, 692, 695
Ethernet, 699
filters, 681–685
frame relay, 695–696
idle timer, 678, 680–681, 688, 692, 698
IGRP, 679
interesting packets, 678
IP, 680, 694, 695, 696

IP addressing, 679, 691, 693
IPX, 678, 679, 680, 694, 696–699
ISDN, 633, 636, 640, 642, 649, 678, 689–694, 699
load, 690
monitoring, 684–685
password authentication protocol (PAP), 682, 683
passwords, 682, 683, 693
point-to-point protocol (PPP), 686, 692
protocol support, 684, 694–700
public switched telephone networks (PSTN), 678
rotary groups, 678, 685–689
routers and routing, 678, 680, 684, 688, 690, 693
spanning-tree protocol, 699
spoofing, 698
switches, 679
terminal adapters (TA), 678, 689
traffic filters, 681–685
transparent bridge routing, 694
transparent bridging, 699
trigger for DDR calls, 679
V.25bis dialing, 678
VINEs, 694, 696
wide area networks (WAN), 116–117, 515, 516
dial-on-demand service, ISDN, 59
dial-up connections, wide area networks (WAN), 515
dialer groups
dial-on-demand routing (DDR), 680, 692, 693
ISDN, 644–645
point-to-point protocol (PPP), 613, 614, 617
point-to-point protocol (PPP) Callback, 613, 614, 617
dialer lists
ISDN, 636–637, 639
point-to-point protocol (PPP), 608
dialer map
dial-on-demand routing (DDR), 688
ISDN, 640, 641, 644
point-to-point protocol (PPP) Callback, 611, 615, 617
point-to-point protocol (PPP), 601, 608, 611, 615, 617
diffusing computation, enhanced IGRP (EIGRP), 457
diffusing update algorithm (DUAL), enhanced IGRP (EIGRP), 232, 234, 236, 237, 456–458, 461
Digital Equipment Corporation Local Area Transport (DECLAT), bridging, 703, 708
Digital Network Architecture Session Control Protocol (DNA SCP), 39
digital service units (DSU), 13, 633
digital signal 1 (DS-1), 519, 652
digital signal 3 (DS-3), 652, 661, 662
digital signal level, ISDN, 649
digital subscriber line (DSL), 14–15
Dijkstra's algorithm, 346
directed broadcasting, 316
directed graph database, open shortest path first (OSPF), 198
discard eligibility
asynchronous transfer mode (ATM), 672
frame relay, 63, 64
discovering neighbors
open shortest path first (OSPF), 202
enhanced IGRP (EIGRP), 236–238, 460
Discovery mode, AppleTalk, 429–431, **431, 432**
distance and size limits to local area networks (LAN), 10–11
distance vector routing, 177–182, **178**
convergence time, 177–178
count-to-infinity problem, 179–181, **179, 180**

poison reverse, with split horizon, 181
split horizon, 181, **181**
triggered updates, 182
distilled configuration, routers, 118
distribute lists, border gateway protocol (BGP), 262–264
Distributed Computing Environment (DCE) (Open Group), 18
distributed processing, 652
distributed queue dual bus (DQDB), 11, 34, 655, **656**
distributed relational database architecture (DRDA), 18
domain name server (DNS), 121
DOS file names, 134
dotted decimal notation, 151
draft standard protocols, 187
dual attachment station ring, FDDI, 52
duplex communication, 39, 48–49
dynamic configuration, AppleTalk, 429–431, **431, 432**
dynamic host configuration protocol (DHCP), 320

E

E channel, ISDN, 629–630
E-series protocols, ISDN, 627
E1
ISDN, 646, 648, 649, 650
wide area networks (WAN), 507, 524–525
EBCDIC, 40
editing commands for routers, 108–109
electing designated routers, open shortest path first (OSPF), 202
elective status of protocols, 187
e–mail, 40
embedded addresses in source route translational bridging (SR/TLB), 742
emulated LAN (ELAN) (*See also* LAN emulation), 665, 669
enabled links, point-to-point protocol (PPP), 73
encapsulated bridging, 702
encapsulation, 42, 377, 520–522
AppleTalk, 417, 438–439
asynchronous transfer mode (ATM), 662, 672, 674
data link switching (DLSw+), 753
dial-on-demand routing (DDR), 686, 692, 695
frame relay, 65, 571, 577–578
IPX, 329–331, 337
IPXWAN, 355
ISDN, 637, 639, 641
point-to-point protocol (PPP), 510, 617
point-to-point protocol (PPP) Callback, 617
remote source route bridging (RSRB), 747–750
routers, 102, 120, 123
serial encapsulation protocols, 520–522
source route translational bridging (SR/TLB), 743
transparent bridging, 712
X.25, 58, 532, 534–538, **534**, 547, 552
X.25, 537–538, 537
encoding/decoding, 24, 37
end system identifier (ESI), asynchronous transfer mode (ATM), 75
end-to-end flow control, IPX, 336
end-to-end transport services, 38
enhanced editing commands, 108–109
enhanced IGRP (EIGRP), 231–247, 288, 376, 377
access lists, 244
acknowledgment packets, 235
advertising routes, 237, 461
AppleTalk, 233, 234, 240, 455–473

autonomous systems (AS), 241
bandwidth, 237, 240
border gateway protocol (BGP), 234
configuration, 239–242
convergence, 232, 456
delay, 237, 460
destinations, active vs. passive, 237–238
diffusing computation, 457
diffusing update algorithm (DUAL), 232, 234, 236, 237, 456–458, 461
discovery methods, 236–238, 460
Ethernet, 234–235, 457
exterior gateway protocol (EGP), 234
feasible successors, 235, 237, 457, 459
filtering, 244, 245
hello packets, 234–235, 457
hold time, 236, 460
IGRP, 241
intermediate system-to-intermediate system (IS-IS), 234
IP integration, 241–242
IPX, 233, 234, 240, 458
load, 237
metrics, 237
minimizing routing updates, 242–246
multicasting, 457
neighbor discovery, 456, 457, 459
neighbor tables, 236
NetWare link services protocol (NLSP), 367–373, **369**
network layer protocols, 233
network numbers, 245
network routing table updates, 238–239
open shortest path first (OSPF), 234
packets, 235–236, 457–459
protocol-dependent modules, 234
redistribution of routes, 270, 272–278
reliability, 237, 457
reliable transport protocol (RTP), 234
reply packets, 236
request packets, 236
route recomputation, 457
routing information protocol (RIP), 234, 240
routing table maintenance protocol (RTMP), 458
routing table protocol (RTP), 460
routing tables, 233, 234, 237–239, 460–465
service advertisement protocol (SAP), 234, 240
states, active vs. passive, 461
static routing, 245–246
subnet masks, 232, 240
subnetting, 233, 240, 456
summarization of routes, 233, 246–247, 456
TCP/IP, 233, 458
topology tables, 236, 460–461
topology, 233, 236
unicasting, 459
update packets, 235, 238–239, 456, 459, 462–465, **462, 463, 464**
variable-length subnet masks (VLSM), 240
WAN, 240
wildcard masks, 245
enhanced mode in data link switching (DLSw+), 751
entering commands for routers, 129
enterprise networks, 16–19, **17**
common object request broker architecture (CORBA), 18
computing strategy/model for, 18

Distributed Computing Environment (DCE) (Open Group), 18
Distributed relational database architecture (DRDA), 18
Internet, 19
Internetworking packet exchange (IPX), 18
intranet, 19
multitiered approach, 19
object management architecture (OMA), 18
Object Management Group, 18
SQL Access Group (SAG), 18
systems network architecture (SNA), 18
TCP/IP, 18
Web development, 19
Windows Open Services Architecture (WOSA) (Microsoft), 18
X/Open Group, 18
EON-compatible Connectionless Network Service (CLNS), 406
erase startup-config command, 135
error control, 2, 3, 23, 27, 31, 40
border gateway protocol-4 (BGP-4), 227, **228**
frame relay, 576
frame relay, 61
IP protocol, 173
ISDN, 648
routers, 146, 147
SLIP, 70
X.25, 551
Ethernet, 9, 32, 44–50, **46**, 54–55, 287, 378
AppleTalk, 414
asynchronous transfer mode (ATM) vs., 74, 76
bandwidth, 48, 49–50
bridging, 702, 703, 704, 709–711
broadcast management, 320
cabling, 47
carrier sense multiple access with collision detection
(CSMA/CD), 46, **46**
coaxial cable, 47
collisions, 46
comparison of technologies for, 48
concurrent routing and bridging (CRB), 730, 733–735
connections for workstations, 49
data link switching (DLSw+), 752, 753
dial-on-demand routing (DDR), 699
duplex mode, 48–49
enhanced IGRP (EIGRP), 234–235, 457
Fast Ethernet, 47, 48, 49
FDDI vs., 52–53
fiber optic, 47
flooding, turboflooding, 319
frames, 46–47, **47**
Gigabit Ethernet, 47, 48, 49
hubs, 78–79
IPX, 325, 327, 329, 330, 332–334
local area networks (LAN), 10
maximum transmission unit (MTU), 46
Media Access Control (MAC), 33–34, **33**
NetWare link services protocol (NLSP), 348–359
open shortest path first (OSPF), 196
remote source route bridging (RSRB), 747–750
routers, 97, 120, 122, 123
scalability, 47
SoHo use, 50
source route translational bridging (SR/TLB), 741–746
transparent bridging, 712, 713, 717–721
UPT category 3 cables, 47
EtherTalk, 414

EtherTalk Link Access Protocol (ELAP), AppleTalk, 415
exchange identification (XID), frame relay, 66
EXEC mode, routers, 98, 99, 100
exhaustion of IP addresses, 161–163
explorer firewalls, data link switching (DLSw+), 752
explorers
source route bridging, 721–722, 724
source route translational bridging (SR/TLB), 741–742
source route transparent bridging, 736, 740
extended access lists, 298–305
AppleTalk, 478, 487–491
IPX, 382–385
extended address (EA), frame relay, 568
extended networks, AppleTalk, 420
extended packet sequence numbering, 543
exterior gateway protocol (EGP)
border gateway protocol (BGP), 250
enhanced IGRP (EIGRP), 234
RFCs, 228–229
exterior routing protocols (EGP), 215–228
external link advertisement, open shortest path first (OSPF),
214–215, **214**
extranets, 6

F

fair queuing (*See* weighted fair queuing)
Fast Ethernet, 45, 47, 49
fast sequenced transport (FST), remote source route bridging
(RSRB), 747–750
Fast Serial Interface Processor (FSIP), 524
fault detection, 37
fault tolerance, 92
FDDI (*See* fiber distributed data interface)
FDDITalk, 414
FDDITalk Link Access Protocol (FLAP), 415
feasible successors, enhanced IGRP (EIGRP), 235, 237, 457,
459
FEIP, routers, 97
fiber distributed data interface (FDDI), 34, 44, 52–54, **53,
54**, 287, 652
AppleTalk, 414
asynchronous transfer mode (ATM), 662
bridging, 702, 703, 709–711
data link switching (DLSw+), 753
Ethernet vs., 52–53
flooding, turboflooding, 319
IPX, 325, 327, 328, 329, 330
remote source route bridging (RSRB), 747–750
routers, 97, 120, 122
source route translational bridging (SR/TLB), 742, 743
transparent bridging, 712
fiber optic Ethernet, 47
fiber-based media, 652
filtering, 81, 83, 289–305, 380
access list configuration, 292–298, **293, 296**
access lists, 291–305, **293, 296,**
AppleTalk, 478, 485, 491–503
border gateway protocol (BGP), 260–269
bridging, 703
concurrent routing and bridging (CRB), 730
dial-on-demand routing (DDR), 681–685
enhanced IGRP (EIGRP), 244, 245
extended access lists, 298–305
IP access lists, 291–292

IPX, 379, 385–404, **391, 393, 395**
NLSP, 381
transparent bridging, 712–713
first in first out (FIFO) queuing, frame relay, 564
flash memory, routers, 97, 131
floating static routes, 259
flooding, 183, 316–319, **318**
LAN emulation (LANE), 669
NetWare link services protocol (NLSP), 345
open shortest path first (OSPF), 192, 207
transparent bridging, 713
flow control, 23, 37
AppleTalk, 418
frame relay, 570
X.25, 547, 555–556
flush packets, LAN emulation (LANE), 669
forward error correction (FEC), 3
forward explicit congestion notification (FECN), 63–64, 568
forwarding, 172
concurrent routing and bridging (CRB), 730
IP protocol, 172
NetWare link services protocol (NLSP), 344, 346
transparent bridging, 712–713, 720–721
forwarding database, NetWare link services protocol (NLSP), 344, 346
fragmentation, 43, 707
point-to-point protocol (PPP), 73
X.25, 58
frame check sequence (FCS)
frame relay, 567, 571
ISDN, 631
point-to-point protocol (PPP), 600
X.25, 537
frame relay, 13, 28, 44, 61–69, **62**, 289, 377, 477, 520, 563–595, 661
access rate, 64
address resolution protocol (ARP), 66–67, 572–573
addressing, 568–577
address resolution protocol (ARP), 62
backup designated routers (BDR), 595
backward explicit congestion notification (BECN), 63–64, 568
bandwidth, 67–69
broadcasting, 573, 575, 592–595
burst committed (BC), 64
burst exceeded (BE), 64
channel service unit (CSU), 566
committed information rate (CIR), 64, 586
compression, 523
configuration, 571–579, **577**
congestion management, 63–64, **63**, 568
conversations, 576
cyclic redundancy check (CRC), 576
data circuit-terminating equipment (DCE), 564, **565**
data link connection (DLC), 66
data link connection identifier (DLCI), 61, 68, 566–569, **567**, 579, 583–584, 586–590, **589**
data link switching (DLSw+), 753
data service unit (DSU), 566
data terminal equipment (DTE), 66, 564, 565, 568
datagrams, 65
designated routers (DR), 595
dial-on-demand routing (DDR), 695–696
discard eligibility (DE), 63, 64
encapsulation, 65, 571, 577–578

error checking, 61, 576
exchange identification (XID), 66
extended address (EA), 568
first in first out (FIFO) queuing, 564
flow control, 570
forward explicit congestion notification (FECN), 63–64, 568
frame check sequence (FCS), 567, 571
frames, 66, 566–569, **566, 568**
generic route encapsulation (GRE), 590
Get Nearest Server (GNS), 592
global addressing, 569
hub-and-spoke topology, 67
information elements (IE), 570
inverse ARP, 66–67, 572–573
IP, 65, 67
IP addressing, 573–574, 577
IPXWAN, 354
ISDN, 626, 637
keepalive intervals, 572, 575
LAN, 565
local management interface (LMI), 64–65, 566, 569–572, 575, 578
mapping addresses, 572–574, 578
maximum transmission unit (MTU), 66
minimum acceptable throughput, 64
monitoring, 573–579
multicasting, 569
multiplexing, 65, 564
network level protocol ID (NLPID), 65
network-to-network interface (NNI), 61, 590–591
nonbroadcast multi-access (NBMA), 573, 579–581, **581**, 594
open shortest path first (OSPF), 67, 593–595
options for, 579–592
OSI reference model, 564
packet switching, 564
packets, 575
permanent virtual circuits (PVC), 61, 67, 565–568, 569, 590
point-to-point protocol (PPP), 70–74
prioritizing traffic, 579, 586–590, **589**
queues, 576
routers, 61, 67, 120, 564, 572, 579
routing information protocol (RIP), 592
SAP advertising, 592
Serial Line IP (SLIP), 69–70
service advertisement protocol (SAP), 592–593
simple flow control, 570
speed of transmission, 565
split horizon, 580–581
star topology, 67, **68**
static mapping, 572–574
status messages, 570
subinterfaces, 579, 581–586, **583**
Subnetwork Access Protocol (SNAP), 65
switched virtual circuits (SVC), 62, 67–69, **69**
switching, 564, 590–592, **591**
TCP/IP, 62
Telnet, 70
topology, 67, **68**
traffic management, 64–65
traffic shaping, 64
tunneling, 590
unreliable links, 565
user-to-network interface (UNI), 61

virtual circuit status messages, 569
virtual circuits, 61, 62, 67–69, **69**, 564–569, 572, 573, 590
wide area networks (WAN), 11, 15, 506, 508, 516, 518, 564–566
X.25 vs., 65, 564
frames
asynchronous transfer mode (ATM), 74
Ethernet, 46–47, **47**
frame relay, 66, 566–569, **566, 568**
ISDN, 630–631, **630**, 648, 650
local area networks (LAN), 10
logical link control (LLC), 32–33, **32**
NetBEUI over PPP, 619
point-to-point protocol (PPP), 600, **600**
switched multimegabit data service (SMDS), 657
token ring, 50–52, **51**
X.25, 535, 537
FTAM, 31
FTP, 83, 290
full mesh topology, 652
full-duplex communication, 39, 626

G

gateD, 174, 189
gateways, 161, 172
general format identifier (GFI), X.25, 535
generic filters, IPX, 388
generic route encapsulation (GRE), 406, 590
generic routing encapsulation protocol over IP (GRE IP), 404
geographical locations of networks, 92
get nearest server (GNS)
frame relay, 592
IPX, 335–336, 379
NetWare link services protocol (NLSP), 363
Gigabit Ethernet, 45, 47, 49
global addressing, frame relay, 569–570
global configuration mode, 101, 128–130
global internetworking, 6–7
global parameters, routers, 125
global topology, 288–289, 376, 377, 476
GNS filters, IPX, 396, 397–404
Government Centre for Information Systems, U.K., 30
Government OSI Profile (GOSIP), 30
GZL filters, AppleTalk, 493

H

half bridges
source route translational bridging (SR/TLB), 743
transparent bridging, 712
half-duplex communication, 39
hardware addresses, 43
HDLC (See high level data-link control)
header, 25, 27
open shortest path first (OSPF), 200, **201, 209**
header compression, 523
Hello interval, NetWare link services protocol (NLSP), 358
hello packets, 182–183
enhanced IGRP (EIGRP), 234–235, 457
NetWare link services protocol (NLSP), 344
Hello protocol, open shortest path first (OSPF), 195, 202, **203**
help for routers, 105, 106–108
helper addresses, 319–321
hierarchical design, 286–287, **287**

high level data link control (HDLC), 32, 520–522, 599
asynchronous balanced mode (ABM), 521
data link switching (DLSw+), 753
flooding, turboflooding, 319
IPX, 330–331
ISDN, 59, 637
normal response mode (NRM), 521
point-to-point protocol (PPP), 598
routers, 120
transparent bridging, 712
wide area networks (WAN), 508, 525
high speed serial interface (HPPI), 652
High Speed Token Ring, 50
historic protocols, 215
history of commands entered, routers, 107–108
hold time, enhanced IGRP (EIGRP), 236, 460
hold-queue timers, PPP, 613
hop count, 35, 172, 326
border gateway protocol-4 (BGP-4), 226, 252
IP protocol, 172
NetWare link services protocol (NLSP), 343, 346
routing information protocol version 2 (RIP-2), 188
host number, 82, 151
HSSI, routers, 97
hub-and-spoke topology, frame relay, 67
hubs, 10, 78–79, **79**
hybrid topology of, **9**

I

I-series protocols, ISDN, 627
idle timer, 642–644
dial-on-demand routing (DDR), 678, 680–681, 688, 692, 698
ISDN, 633, 637
NetBEUI over PPP, 622, 624
point-to-point protocol (PPP), 602–603, 607
X.25, 548, 553
IGMP, 88
IGRP (See also enhanced IGRP)
dial-on-demand routing (DDR), 679
enhanced IGRP (EIGRP), 241
ISDN, 639
redistribution of routes, 270, 272–278
information elements (IE), frame relay, 570
information frames, ISDN, 631
information highway, 5
initialization of routers, 98–193
insured traffic, asynchronous transfer mode (ATM), 675
integrated routing and bridging (IRB), concurrent routing and bridging (CRB), 732
integrated services digital network (ISDN), 13, 23, 59–61, 88, 625–650
access lists, 639
addressing, 637, 643
advanced configuration, 638–641
aggregation, B channel, 644
AppleTalk, 638
AT&T 5ESS/4ESS switches, 626
authentication, 638, 639, 644
B (bearer) channel, 59, 626, 636
bandwidth, 633
bandwidth-on-demand, 633, 636
basic rate interface (BRI), 59, 627, 633, 634–646
binary 8-zerosubstitution (B8ZS) line code, 649
caller ID, 639, 640

challenge handshake authentication protocol (CHAP), 638, 639, 641, 644
channel service unit (CSU), 627, 633, 646
circuit-switching, 631, **632**
concentration, 628
contention, 629
controller, 650
cyclic redundancy check (CRC), 648
D (data) channel, 59, 627, 629–630, 635, 650
data service unit (DSU), 627, 646
data terminal equipment (DTE), 627, 646
dial-on-demand routing (DDR), 59, 511, 633, 636, 640, 642, 649, 678, 589–694, 699
dialer groups, 644–645
dialer lists, 636–637, 639
dialer map, 640, 641, 644
digital service units (DSU), 633
digital signal level, 649
E channel, 629–630
E-series protocols, 627
E1, 646, 648, 649, 650
encapsulation, 637, 639, 641
error checking, 648
frame check sequence (FCS), 631
frame relay, 626, 637
frames, 630–631, **630**, 648, 650
full-duplex communications, 626
functions, 628–629
high level data link control (HDLC), 59, 637
I-series protocols, 627
idle timer, 633, 637, 642–644
IGRP, 639
information frames, 631
IP addressing, 637, 643
IP, 641
IPX, 638
leased lines, 60
linecodes, 648, 649, 650
link access procedure, balanced (LAPB), 637
link access procedure, D channel (LAPD), 630, 631
link control protocol (LCP), 633
management information base (MIB), 633
monitoring, 645–646
multichannel interface processor (MIP), 647, 649–650
Net3/Net5 switches, 626
NetBEUI over PPP, 619
network interface module (NIM), 647, 648
network termination device (NT), 628
Northern Telecom DMS-100 switch, 626
NT1/NT2/NT Type1/2 (NT1/2), 628
NTT switch, 626
password authentication protocol (PAP), 638
passwords, 641, 644
point-to-point protocol (PPP) Callback, 610, 614, 616
point-to-point protocol (PPP) Multilink (MP), 638
point-to-point protocol (PPP), 602, 606, 607, 610, 614, 616, 633, 637, 639, 641
primary rate interface (PRI), 59, 627, 646–650
priority negotiation, 630
protocols, 640
Q-series protocols, 627
reference points, 628–629, **629**
rotary groups, 636
routers, 628–629, 631, 636, 641, 642, 648, 649

S reference/S bus, 640
send sequence numbers, 631
service profile identifiers (SPIDs), 635, 636, 643
simple network management protocol (SNMP), 633
slot numbers, 648
standards, 626
subaddressing, 640
super frame, 648
supervisory frames, 631
switches, 626, 634, 635, 642, 643, 645, 647, 650
T1, 626, 633, 646, 648, 649, 650
T1/DS1 facility, 627
TE1 (Type 1 Terminal Equipment), 628
TE2 (Type 2 Terminal Equipment), 628
TELNET, 639
terminal adapter (TA), 628
terminal equipment (TE), 628
timeslots, 649
TS-013 switch, 626
unnumbered frames, 631
V.25bis dialing, 633
VN2/VN3 switches, 626
wide area networks (WAN), 15, 506, 507, 508, 515
wide area telephone services (WATS), 626
X.22, 637
X.25, 61
X.31 for X.25 packets, 61
integration data/voice/video, 6
inter-area routers, open shortest path first (OSPF), 210
inter-AS routers, border gateway protocol-4 (BGP-4), 221
interesting packets, 476
dial-on-demand routing (DDR), 511, 678
interface command, 123
interface configuration mode, 101
interfacing with service providers, wide area networks (WAN), 507–508
interior gateway protocol (IGP), 175, 184–215
border gateway protocol (BGP), 251
open shortest path first (OSPF), 191–215
RFCs, 228–229
RIPng for IPv6, 189–191, **190**
routing information protocol version 2 (RIP-2), 187–190, **188**
routing information protocol (RIP), 184–187, **186**
interleaving, LAN emulation (LANE), 666
intermediate system-to-intermediate system (IS-IS), 326
enhanced IGRP (EIGRP), 234
NetWare link services protocol (NLSP), 342
internal BGP (IBGP), border gateway protocol (BGP), 250, 253
international code designator (ICD), asynchronous transfer mode (ATM), 662
International Organization for Standardization (ISO), 5
International Telecommunication Union Telecommunication Standardization (ITU-T), 5
Internet, 6, 14–16, 19, 28, 36
Internet Assigned Number Authority (IANA), 151, 160
Internet control message protocol (ICMP)
bridging, 705
IP protocol, 173
Internet Protocol (*See* IP)
Internet Protocol next gen (IPng), 166–167
Internet Protocol version 6 (IPv6), 166–167
Internet service providers (ISP), 11, 160, 258
internets, 6
Internetworking Operating System (IOS), 175

Internetworking packet exchange (*See* IPX)
internetworks, 4–7, **6**
InterNIC, 160
intra-area routers, open shortest path first (OSPF), 192–193
intra-AS routers, border gateway protocol-4 (BGP-4), 221
intranets, 6, 16, 19
inverse address resolution protocol (ARP), frame relay, 66–67, 572–573
inverse multiplexing over asynchronous transfer mode (ATM), 88
IP, 28, 36, 42, 56, 288, 377
  asynchronous transfer mode (ATM), 672
  bridging, 705
  dial-on-demand routing (DDR), 680, 694, 695, 696
  enhanced IGRP (EIGRP), 241–242
  frame relay, 65, 67
  IPX, 337
  ISDN, 641
  NetBEUI over PPP, 619
  X.25, 538
IP access lists, 291–292, 291
IP addressing, 27, 36, 43, 82, 150–163, 643
  asynchronous transfer mode (ATM), 673, 674
  autonomous systems (AS), 161
  broadcast addressing, 151, 153
  broadcast storms, 153
  classes of IP addresses, 150–152, **152**
  classless inter-domain routing (CIDR), 163–166, **164**
  destination address broadcasts, 153
  dial-on-demand routing (DDR), 679, 691, 693
  dotted decimal notation, 151
  exhaustion of IP addresses, 161–163
  frame relay, 573–574, 577
  gateways, 161
  helper addresses, 319–321
  host number, 151
  Internet Assigned Number Authority (IANA), 151, 160
  Internet service providers (ISP), 160
  InterNIC, 160
  ISDN, 637
  loopback addresses, 153–154
  multicast addressing, 151, 152
  multihoming, 161
  NetBEUI over PPP, 619
  network number, 151
  open shortest path first (OSPF), 197, 213
  point-to-point protocol (PPP), 598, 600, 602, 607, 611, 614
  point-to-point protocol (PPP) Callback, 611, 614
  private IP addresses, 154, 168–169
  registration of IP addresses, 151, 160–161
  routers, 122–123, **122**, 134
  routing information protocol (RIP), 159
  switched multimegabit data service (SMDS), 658, 659
  source address broadcasts, 153
  special case (reserved) addresses, 151, 152–154
  static subnetting, 159
  subnet masks, 155–157, **156, 157,** 158, **158**
  subnetting, 153, 154–155, 157–160, **159**
  unicast addressing, 151
  variable-length subnetting, 160
  X.25, 547, 548, 552, 553
IP control protocol (IPCP), 71, 72
IP datagrams, open shortest path first (OSPF), 200

IP protocol, 172–175, **173**
  addressing, 173
  autonomous systems (AS), 174
  destination unreachable errors, 173
  error control, 173
  forwarding, 172
  hop count, 172
  Internet control message protocol (ICMP), 173
  redirect messages, 173
  router information protocol (RIP), 174
  routing information, 172–173
  routing tables, 173
  source quench messages, 173
  time exceeded messages, 173
  time-to-live, 173
IP subnets, 82
IP-enhanced IGRP (*See* enhanced IGRP), 231
IPv6, routing information protocol (RIP)ng for, 189–191, **190,** 189
IPV6 Control Protocol (IPv6CP), 72
IPX, 56, 288, 323–339, 376, 377
  802.2, 330
  802.3, 325, 327, 330
  802.5, 325, 327, 328, 330
  access lists, 380–385
  address resolution protocol (ARP), 329
  addressing, 328–334
  advertising routes, 326
  AppleTalk, 324
  ARCnet, 325, 327
  assigning IPX network addresses, 332–334
  asynchronous transfer mode (ATM), 672
  broadcasting, 380
  Btrieve, 338, 339
  carrier-sense multiple access/collision detection (CSMA/CD), 327
  congestion, 378–380
  connectionless protocols, 326
  custom queuing, 379
  datagrams, 326
  DECnet, 324
  dial-on-demand routing (DDR), 511, 678, 679, 680, 694, 696–699
  encapsulation, 329–331, 337
  end-to-end flow control, 336
  enhanced IGRP (EIGRP), 233, 234, 240, 458
  Ethernet, 325, 327, 329, 330, 332–334
  extended access lists, 382–385
  FDDI, 325, 327, 328, 329, 330
  filtering, 379, 385–396, **391, 393, 395,** 396, 397–404
  generic filters, 388
  get nearest server (GNS), 335–336, 379
  GNS filters, 396, 397–404
  HDLC, 330–331
  hop count, 326
  intermediate system-to-intermediate system (IS-IS), 326
  IP, 337
  IPXWAN, 354
  ISDN, 638
  keepalive packets, 336–337
  LAN emulation (LANE), 665
  LAPB, 522
  layers of, 324, **324**
  link-state routing, 326

logical link control (LLC), 327, 330
logical unit (LU), 339
MAC address, 329
maximum transmission unit (MTU), 331
media access control (MAC) protocols, 325, 326–329
message handling services (MHS), 338–339
NetBEUI over PPP, 619
NetBIOS filters, 387
NetWare, 324
NetWare Core Protocol (NCP), 325, 327, 338
NetWare link services protocol (NLSP), 326, 342, 350–354, 360
NetWare Loadable modules (NLM), 338, 339
NetWare message handling service (NetWare MHS), 338
NetWare Remote Procedure Call (NetWare RPC), 337
NetWare transport and upper layers, 334–339
NetWare transport layer, 336–337
network addressable units (NAU), 339
Network basic input/output (NetBIOS), 325, 327, 339
network number, 329
Novell Link Services protocol (NLSP), 325
Novell/IPX protocol stack, 324
packets, 326, 331–332
physical layer, 328
physical media dependent (PMD) sublayer, 328
point-to-point protocol (PPP), 325, 327–331
priority policies, 379
priority queuing, 379
queuing, 379, 380
redirector, 337
redistribution of routes, 379
round-robin routing, 335
routers, 326
routing information protocol (RIP), 325, 326, 379
routing table filters, 386
SAP filters, 387, 396, 397–404, **398**
segment sequencing, 336
semaphores, 338
sequenced packet exchange (SPX), 325, 326–327
sequenced packet protocol (SPP), 336
serial interfaces, 330
server-centric architecture of NetWare, 334
service access points (SAP), 330
service advertisement protocol (SAP), 325, 326, 334–336, 378, 379
shell, NetWare, 337
sockets, 331
spoofing, 336–337
subinterfaces, 333
subnetwork access protocol (SNAP), 330
TCP, 337
TCP/IP, 324, 329
tick values, 326, 335–336
token ring, 325, 327, 328, 329, 330
traffic management, 375–409
tunneling, 396, 404–409, **406**
upper layer protocols and services, 337–339
user datagram protocol (UDP), 337
virtual file system, 337
virtual loadable modules (VLM), 337
watchdog keepalive packets, 336–337
weighted fair queuing, 379
wide area networks (WAN), 517
X.25, 538

Xerox Network systems (XNS), 324
XNS, 336
IPX Control Protocol (IPXCP), 72
IPX router configuration, routers, 130
IPXWAN, 354–359
    configuration, 354–359
    encapsulation, 355
    frame relay, 354
    Hello interval, 358
    IPX, 354
    NetWare link services protocol (NLSP), 346–348
    NetWare multiprotocol router (MPR), 348
    network addresses, 356
    network numbers, 357
    NLSP, 347, 358
    point-to-point protocol (PPP), 354, 355
    requester or master, 347
    responder or slave, 347
    routing information protocol (RIP), 347
    SAP, 347
    X.25, 354
ISDN (*See* integrated services digital network (ISDN))

J

jitter, asynchronous transfer mode (ATM), 520

K

KA9Q/NOS, 406
keepalive frames, routers, 146
keepalive interval, frame relay, 572, 575
KEEPALIVE message, border gateway protocol (BGP), 216, 223, 252
keepalive packets, IPX, 336–337

L

LAN, 5, 23
LAN access, NetBEUI over PPP, 619
LAN emulation (LANE), 76–78
    address resolution protocol (ARP), 668
    addressing, 665, 666, 667, 669
    AppleTalk, 665
    ATM data exchange interface (DXI), 670
    ATM Forum, 670
    ATM interface processor (AIP), 669
    asynchronous transfer mode (ATM), 664–670, **665**
    bridges, 664, 669
    Broadcast and Unknown Server (BUS), 76, 665, 666–670, **666**
    broadcast groups, 667
    design considerations, 669
    emulated LAN (ELAN), 665, 669
    flooding, 669
    flush packets, 669
    interleaving, 666
    IPX, 665
    LAN Emulation Client (LEC), 76, 665, 666–670, **666**
    LAN emulation configuration server (LECS), 76, 665, 666–670, **666**
    LAN emulation server (LES), 76, 665–666
    LANE client ID (LECID), 667
    leaf objects, 666
    multicast addressing, 666, 667
    Next Hop Resolution Protocol (NHRP), 77
    switches, 669

unicast addressing, 667, 668
virtual channel connections (VCC), 665, 666, 667
LAN Emulation Client (LEC), 76, 665, 666–670, **666**
LAN emulation configuration server (LECS), 76, 665,
    666–670, **666**
LAN emulation server (LES), 76, 665–670, **666**
LANE client ID (LECID), LAN emulation (LANE), 667
LAT, 377
layer 2 switching, 85, 87
layer 3 switching, 85, 87
layering of networks, 5, 22
layers in asynchronous transfer mode (ATM), **662–664**
leaf objects, LAN emulation (LANE), 666
leaking of route information, NetWare link services protocol
    (NLSP), 362
learning bridges, transparent bridging, 712–713
leased lines, 56–57
    ISDN, 60
    wide area networks (WAN), 515
leased-line private networks, 13
level 1/2/3 routing, NetWare link services protocol (NLSP),
    343–344
line configuration, routers, 130
linecodes, ISDN, 648, 649, 650
link access procedure, balanced (LAPB), 520–522
    ISDN, 637
    wide area networks (WAN), 508
    X.25, 530, 534, 536–537, **536**
link access procedure, D channel (LAPD), ISDN, 630, 631
link access protocol (LAP), AppleTalk, 415
link advertisement, open shortest path first (OSPF), 210–215,
    211, 212
link aggregation, 87
link control protocol (LCP), 509–510, 599–600, 633
link establishment, point-to-point protocol (PPP), 71
link quality, point-to-point protocol (PPP), 71
link state advertisement, open shortest path first (OSPF),
    199, **200**, 208
link type, border gateway protocol (BGP), 252
link-state acknowledge packet, open shortest path first
    (OSPF), 198
link-state database
    NetWare link services protocol (NLSP), 344, 345, 352
    open shortest path first (OSPF), 198
link-state header, open shortest path first (OSPF), **209**
link-state packets (LSP), 183, 345
link-state propagation, open shortest path first (OSPF), 206–210
link-state request packet, open shortest path first (OSPF),
    206, **206**
link-state routing protocols, 182–184, 326
    flooding, 183
    hello packets, 182–183
    link state packets (LSPs), 183
    open shortest path first (OSPF), 182, 199
    shortest path first (SPF) algorithm, 183–184, **184**
link-state update packet, open shortest path first (OSPF),
    207, 207
load/load balancing
    dial-on-demand routing (DDR), 690
    enhanced IGRP (EIGRP), 237
    NetWare link services protocol (NLSP), 343
    point-to-point protocol (PPP), 603–604
local area network (LAN), 3–5, **4,** 8–11, **9,** 45–55
    arbitration, 8

ATM switches, 11, 88
ATM vs. switched high-speed LAN, 90–91
bandwidth, 10
bridges, 10, 702, 703–704
bus topology of, 8, **9**
cabling, 47
campus switches, 88
carrier sense multiple access with collision detection
    (CSMA/CD), 46, **46**
collisions, 46
comparing technologies for, 53–55, **54**
concurrent routing and bridging (CRB), 730
connectionless service in, 28
data link switching (DLSw+), 752
datagrams, 10
devices on, **9,** 10
distance and size limits to, 10–11
Ethernet, **9,** 10, 45–50, **46,** 54–55
fiber distributed digital interface (FDDI), 52–55, **53, 54**
frame relay, 565
frames, 10, 46–47, **47**
hubs, 10
hybrid topology of, **9**
logical link control (LLC), 32
MAC addresses, 10
maximum transmission unit (MTU), 46
Media Access Control (MAC), 8, 33–34, **33**
multicast addressing, 10
open shortest path first (OSPF), 196
repeaters, 10
ring topology of, **9**
routers, 11
star topology of, 8, **9**
switches, 10, 11, 87–90
token ring (IEEE 802.5), 10, 50–52, **51,** 54–55
topologies of, 8–11, **9**
transparent bridging, 713
tree topology of, **9**
virtual LAN (VLAN) (*See* virtual LAN)
wide area network (WAN) vs., 56
local bridges, 82
local loop, wide area networks (WAN), 507
local management interface (LMI)
    frame relay, 64–65, 566, 569–572, 575, 578
    wide area networks (WAN), 518
local ring test frame, source route transparent bridging, 736
local ring test frame explorer, source route bridging, 721–722
locally administered address (LSA), asynchronous transfer
    mode (ATM), 75
LocalTalk, 414–415
LocalTalk Link Access Protocol (LLAP), 415
logging in to/out of routers, 103–104
logical addresses, 43
logical channel identifier (LCI), X.25, 535, 540–542
logical channel number (LCN), X.25, 531
logical IP subnets (LIS), asynchronous transfer mode (ATM),
    74–75
Logical Link Control (LLC), 31, 32–33, **32**
    AppleTalk, 415
    bridging, 704
    IPX, 327, 330
    point-to-point protocol (PPP), 600
    remote source route bridging (RSRB), 747–750
logical link control 2 (LLC2), NetBEUI over PPP, 622

logical unit (LU), IPX, 339
loopback addresses, 153–154
loopback interface, open shortest path first (OSPF), 197
loops, loop avoidance, 707
    border gateway protocol (BGP), 250
    concurrent routing and bridging (CRB), 730
    transparent bridging, 713–717, **717**
lossless compression, 523

M

MAC address
    address resolution protocol (ARP), 45
    bridging, 705, 709
    concurrent routing and bridging (CRB), 730
    data link switching (DLSw+), 751, 753
    IPX, 329
    local area networks (LAN), 10
    routing information protocol (RIP), 185
    source route translational bridging (SR/TLB), 742
    transparent bridging, 712
MAC filters, 81
management (*See* network management)
management information base (MIB), ISDN, 633
managing traffic (*See* traffic management)
manufacturing automation protocol (MAP), 34
map-list configuration, routers, 129–130
mapping addresses, 42
    asynchronous transfer mode (ATM), 673, 674, 675
    frame relay, 572–573, 574, 578
    X.25, 553, 558
masks, NetWare link services protocol (NLSP), 360
master/slave, IPXWAN, 347
MaxAge value, open shortest path first (OSPF), 210
maximum received reconstructed unit (MRRU), point-to-point
    protocol (PPP), 601
maximum transmission unit (MTU), 43
    Ethernet, 46
    frame relay, 66
    IPX, 331
mean time between failure (MTBF), 7
mean time to repair (MTTR), 7
Media Access Control (MAC) protocols, 31, 33–34, **33** 326
    bridging, 704
    IPX, 325–329
    local area networks (LAN), 8
    switched multimegabit data service (SMDS), 655
Medium Dependent Interface (MDI), 31
merging configuration information, routers, 134–135
message handling services (MHS), IPX, 338–339
messages, border gateway protocol-4 (BGP-4), 222–223,
    222, 223
metrics
    border gateway protocol (BGP), 251, 252
    enhanced IGRP (EIGRP), 237
    NetWare link services protocol (NLSP), 343, 346
    open shortest path first (OSPF), 212
    redistribution of routes, 270, 271
metropolitan area networks (MAN), 11, 34, 655
microsegmentation, 85, **86**
Microsoft PPP CHAP (MS-CHAP), 71
minimum acceptable throughput, frame relay, 64
mixed-area route aggregation, NetWare link services protocol
    (NLSP), 367–373
modems, 13

wide area networks (WAN), 14, 507, 515
X.25, 528
monitoring
    border gateway protocol (BGP), 252–258
    dial-on-demand routing (DDR), 684–685
    frame relay, 573–579
    ISDN, 645–646
    NetBEUI over PPP, 621
    point-to-point protocol (PPP), 606, 608–609, 615
    point-to-point protocol (PPP) Callback, 615
    transparent bridging, 720
    X.25, 547–551, 554
multi-access networks, open shortest path first (OSPF), 196
multicasting/multicast addressing, 88, 151, 152, 290
    AppleTalk, 422
    enhanced IGRP (EIGRP), 457
    frame relay, 569
    LAN emulation (LANE), 666, 667
    local area networks (LAN), 10
    NetWare link services protocol (NLSP), 342–343
    open shortest path first (OSPF), 200
    switched multimegabit data service (SMDS), 654, 655, 659
Multichannel Interface Processor (MIP), 97, 524, 647, 649–650
multihoming, 161
    border gateway protocol-4 (BGP-4), 219, 261–262
multilink PPP (MP), 72–74, 601–609
multiplexers/multiplexing, 13, 23, 37, 88, 661
    frame relay, 65, 564
    X.25, 531–532
multipoint AURP tunnels, AppleTalk, 440
Multiport SRB configuration, 723–727
multiprotocol encapsulation, asynchronous transfer mode
    (ATM), 672
multiprotocol traffic, 290, 478
multitiered approach, 19

N

nailed-up circuits, 476
Name Binding Protocol (NBP), AppleTalk, 417, 478, 485,
    488–489
names, NetBEUI over PPP, 620
naming files, routers, 134
naming the router, 136–137
narrowband ISDN (N-ISDN), asynchronous transfer mode
    (ATM), 662
National Institute of Standards and Technology (NIST), 30
NBCP, 72
NBFCP, 72
neighbors/neighbor discovery
    border gateway protocol (BGP), 216, 253, 254–255
    enhanced IGRP (EIGRP), 456, 457, 459
    open shortest path first (OSPF), 195
neighbor tables, enhanced IGRP (EIGRP), 236
Net3/Net5 switches, ISDN, 626
NetBEUI over PPP, 618–624
    802.x addressing, 619
    access lists, 620
    acknowledgment, 622
    addressing, 619
    byte offset, 620
    cache, 620, 621–622
    clearing transmission lines, 624
    configuration, 619–624
    congestion control, 622

debugging, 624
frames, 619
idle timer, 622, 624
IP, 619
IP addressing, 619
IPX, 619
ISDN, 619
LAN access, 619
logical link control 2 (LLC2), 622
monitoring, 621
names, 620
NetBIOS Frame Control Protocol (NBFCP), 619, 622
point-to-point protocol (PPP), 619
remote access client (RAS client), 619
routers, 622
session tables, 621, 624
NetBIOS
bridging, 703
data link switching (DLSw+), 750, 751, 752
NetBIOS filters, IPX, 387
NetBIOS Frame Control Protocol (NBFCP), NetBEUI over PPP, 619, 622
NetWare (*See also* IPX; NetWare link services protocol), NetWare, 334–336
NetWare Core Protocol (NCP), IPX, 325, 327, 338
NetWare link services protocol (NLSP), 326, 342–373, 376, 377
adjacency, 344, 345
adjacency database, 344
aggregation of routes, 359–373, 359
area address database, 362
area addresses, 360
area count fields, 362
bandwidth, 346
complete sequence number packet (CSNP), 345
configuration, 348–359
convergence, 343
cost, 346
enhanced IGRP, 367–373, **369**
Ethernet, 348–359
filtering, 381
flooding, 345
forwarding, 344, 346
forwarding database, 344, 346
get nearest server (GNS), 363
Hello interval, 358
hello packets, 344
hop count, 343, 346
intermediate system-to-intermediate system (IS-IS), 342
IPX, 325, 342, 350–354, 360
IPXWAN, 346–348, 354–359
leaking of route information, 362
level 1/2/3 routing, 343–344
link-state database, 344, 345, 352
link-state packets (LSP), 345
load balancing, 343
masks, 360
metrics, 343, 346
mixed-area route aggregation, 367–373
multicasting, 342–343
network numbers, 348–349, 365
partial sequence number packet (PSNP), 345
prefix for addresses, 361
pseudonodes, 346
receipt confirmation, 345

redistribution of routes, 362
routers, 343–344
routing areas, 343, 344, 360–361
routing information protocol (RIP), 342, 343, 350–351, 360, 367–373
SAP, 342, 343, 363
shortest path first (SPF), 346, 352, 361
single process routers, 361–367
SPX, 342
summarization of routes, 361, 366
WAN links, 343, 363
NetWare Loadable modules (NLM), IPX, 338, 339
NetWare message handling service (NetWare MHS), IPX, 338
NetWare multiprotocol router (MPR), IPXWAN, 348
NetWare Remote Procedure Call (NetWare RPC), IPX, 337
network addressable units (NAU), IPX, 339
network addresses, IPXWAN, 356
Network Basic Extended User Interface (NetBEUI), 618
network basic input/output (NetBIOS), 618, IPX, 325, 327, 339
network command, 130
network configuration file, routers, 134
network control protocol (NCP), 70–72, 509–510, 599
network design, 167
network evolution, 2–8
Network File System (NFS), 39
network interface cards (NIC), 43
network interface module (NIM), ISDN, 647, 648
Network layer, 23, 34–36
AppleTalk, 415–417
network layer reachability information (NLRI), border gateway protocol-4 (BGP-4), 224, **225**
network level protocol ID (NLPID), frame relay, 65
network links, open shortest path first (OSPF), 199, **200,** 208
network management, 7, 89–90, 97
network mask, open shortest path first (OSPF), 213
network number, 82, 151
enhanced IGRP (EIGRP), 245
IPX, 329
IPXWAN, 357
NetWare link services protocol (NLSP), 348–349, 365
network segments, 78
network service access points (NSAP), asynchronous transfer mode (ATM), 662, 673, 674, 675
network terminal number (NTN), X.25, 533
network termination 1 (NT1), wide area networks (WAN), 507
network termination device (NT), 13, 628
network user identification, X.25, 558
network-to-network interface (NNI), frame relay, 61, 590–591
network-visible entities (NVE), AppleTalk, 420
newsgroups, 40
next hop, 35, 172
border gateway protocol-4 (BGP-4), 226
point-to-point protocol (PPP), 603
routing information protocol version 2 (RIP-2), 188
next-hop route table entry, routing information protocol (RIP)ng, 190, **191**
nodes, AppleTalk, 419–420
non-blocking switches, 85
non-routable traffic, 289, 377–378, 477
nonbroadcast multi-access (NBMA)
frame relay, 573, 579–581, **581,** 594
open shortest path first (OSPF), 196, 197
wide area networks (WAN), 517
nonextended networks, AppleTalk, 420

normal response mode (NRM), HDLC, 521
Northern Telecom DMS-100 switch, ISDN, 626
NOTIFCATION message, BGP, 223, 227, **228,** 251
Novell/IPX protocol stack, IPX, 324
NT1/NT2/NT Type1/2 (NT1/2), ISDN, 628
NTT switch, ISDN, 626
NVRAM, routers, 97, 98, 126

O

object management architecture (OMA), 18
Object Management Group, 18
on-demand peers, data link switching (DLSw+), 752
on-line help, routers, 105
OPEN message, border gateway protocol (BGP), 223, **224,** 251
open shortest path first (OSPF), 174, 175, 182, 191–215, 288
    adjacency, 195, 204–206, 560
    adjacent router, 195–196
    All-SPFRouters address, 200
    area border routers, 192–194
    area borders, 192
    area ID, 198
    areas in, 192
    AS external links, 199, **200,** 208, 209
    backbones, 192
    backup designated router, 196, 203–204
    broadcasting, 196
    database description packet, 205–206, **205**
    database exchange, 204–206
    datagrams, 200
    designated routers, 195, 196, 202
    directed graph database, 198
    discovering neighbors, 202
    electing designated routers, 202
    enhanced IGRP (EIGRP), 234
    Ethernet, 196
    external link advertisement, 214–215, **214**
    flooding, 192, 207
    frame relay, 67, 593–595
    header, 200, **201, 209**
    Hello protocol, 195, 202, **203**
    inter-area routers, 210
    interfaces, 197
    intra-area routers, 192–193
    IP addressing, 197, 213
    IP datagrams, 200
    LAN, 196
    link advertisement, 199, **200,** 210–215, **211, 212**
    link-state acknowledge packet, **207**
    link-state database, 198
    link-state header, **209**
    link-state propagation, 206–210
    link-state request packet, 206, **206**
    link-state routing protocols, 199
    link-state update packet, **207**
    loopback interface, 197
    MaxAge value, 210
    metrics, 212
    multi-access networks, 196
    multicasting, 200
    neighbor routers, 195
    network links, 199, **200,** 208
    network mask, 213
    network, **193**
    non-broadcast multi–access (NBMA), 197

    non-broadcast networks, 196
    packets, 200, 202
    physical network types, 196
    point-to-multipoint networks, 196
    point-to-point interface, 196, 197
    protocol identifiers, 200
    redistribution of routes, 270, 278–284, **279**
    request packet, 206, **206**
    router ID, 199, 213
    router links, 199, **200,** 208
    router priority, 199
    routing tables, 198, 210–215
    shortest path first (SPF) algorithm, 198
    shortest path tree, 198, 210
    stages of routing in, 201–202
    states, 195
    stub areas, 194
    summary links, 199, **200,** 208, 213, **213**
    token ring, 196
    topological database, 198
    transit areas, 194
    type of service (ToS) metrics, 197–198, 212
    virtual links, 192, 193–194, **194**
    X.25, 560–561
open standards, 6–7, 17
open systems interconnection (OSI) layered model, 21–40, **23**
    adjacent layer communication, 25, 28–29, **29**
    AppleTalk, 413
    Application layer, 24, 40
    Attachment Unit Interface (AUI), 31
    concurrent routing and bridging (CRB), 730
    connection-oriented networks, 26, **26,** 27
    connectionless networks, 26, 27–28
    Data-link layer, 22, 31
    frame relay, 564
    headers, 25
    IPX, 324, **324**
    layering of networks, 22
    Logical Link Control (LLC), 31, 32–33, **32**
    Media Access Control (MAC), 31, 33–34, **33**
    Medium Dependent Interface (MDI), 31
    Network layer, 23, 34–36
    peer-to-peer communications, 24–25, **25**
    Physical Layer Signaling (PLS), 31
    Physical layer, 22, 31
    Physical Medium Attachment (PMA), 31
    Presentation layer, 24, 40
    presentation services access point (PSAP), 29
    profiles, 30
    protocols, 25, 30
    service access point identifier (SAP-ID), 29
    service access points (SAP), 28–29
    service providers, 25
    service users, 25
    services, 22, 25
    Session layer, 24, 39
    source route bridging, 721
    standards, 30
    sublayers in, 31–34
    switched multimegabit data service (SMDS), **653**
    Transport layer, 23–24, 36–39, **37**
    X.25, 530
operating system image for routers, 131
origin codes, border gateway protocol (BGP), 255

OSI Control Protocol (OSICP), 72
overhead, 42, 290

P

pacing, 3
packet assembler/disassembler (PAD), 57
    X.25, 528, **529**, 530, 538
packet network carriers, X.25, 558
packet switching, 11, 13, 27, 35, 289, 377, 477, 652, 661
    frame relay, 564
    wide area networks (WAN), 11, 15, 515–520
    X.25, 58, 528
packet switching exchange (PSE), 57
    X.25, 528, **529**, 532–533
    wide area networks (WAN), 517
packet type identifier (PTI), X.25, 535
packet-layer protocol (PLP), X.25, 530, 531, 535
packet-switched networks (PSN)
    wide area networks (WAN), 516–520
    X.25, 528, **529**
packets, 27, 43, 326
    broadcast, 315
    enhanced IGRP (EIGRP), 235–236, 457–459
    frame relay, 575
    IPX, 331–332
    open shortest path first (OSPF), 200, 202
    routing information protocol (RIP), 186, **186**
    transparent bridging, 712
    wide area networks (WAN), 517
parameters, global, routers, 125
parity, 5
partial sequence number packet (PSNP), NetWare link servic-
    es protocol (NLSP), 345
partitioning of network, 92
passenger protocol in tunneling, 404
password authentication protocol (PAP), 71, 510
    dial-on-demand routing (DDR), 682, 683
    ISDN, 638
    point-to-point protocol (PPP), 602, 610
passwords
    dial-on-demand routing (DDR), 682, 683, 693
    ISDN, 641, 644
    routers, 103–104, 135
path attributes, border gateway protocol-4 (BGP-4), 226, **227**
path cost
    border gateway protocol (BGP), 252
    transparent bridging, 715
path determination, 35
path selection, border gateway protocol-4 (BGP-4), 219
pattern matching, X.25, 559–560
payload compression, 523
peer-to-peer communications, 24–25, **25**
peers, border gateway protocol (BGP), 253
performance, 7
permanent virtual circuits (PVC), 57
    asynchronous transfer mode (ATM), 75
    frame relay, 61, 67, 565–569, 590
    routers, 102
    wide area networks (WAN), 506, 518
    X.25, 532, 540–542, 557
permanent virtual connections (PVC), 28, 661
    asynchronous transfer mode (ATM), 675
personal computers (PCs), 3, **4**
Physical layer, 22, 31

AppleTalk, 414–415
    IPX, 328
physical layer convergence protocol (PLCP), switched multi-
    megabit data service (SMDS), 657
physical layer interface module (PLIM), asynchronous trans-
    fer mode (ATM), 673
Physical Layer Signaling (PLS), 31
physical media dependent (PMD) sublayer, IPX, 328
Physical Medium Attachment (PMA), 31, 328
physical medium sublayer, asynchronous transfer mode
    (ATM), 662
physical network types, open shortest path first (OSPF), 196
ping utility, 144–145
plain old telephone service (PTOS), 506
plug and play, 17
point-to-multipoint connections, 196, 661
point-to-point AURP tunnels, AppleTalk, 440
point-to-point connections, 196–197, 661
point-to-point protocol (PPP), 56, 70–74, 509–510, 520–522,
    597–624
    addressing, 598, 600, 602, 607, 611, 614
    AppleTalk Control Protocol (ATCP), 72
    APPN High Performance Routing Control Protocol (APPN
        HPRCP), 72
    APPN Intermediate Session Routing Control Protocol
        (APPN ISRCP), 72
    authentication, 71–72, 510, 602, 606, 608, 610, 612, 614
    bandwidth allocation protocol (BAP), 73
    bandwidth on demand (POD), 73
    bandwidth, 603
    bandwidth allocation control protocol (BACP), 73
    Banyan VINES Control Protocol (BVCP), 72
    basic rate interface (BRI), 601, 602, 604, 607, 610, 616
    BCP, 72
    bundled links, 73
    bundling of packets, 601, 603, 604
    callback control protocol (CCP(), 72
    caller ID, 602, 607
    challenge/handshake authentication protocol (CHAP), 71,
        510, 602, 606, 608, 610, 617
    configuring multilink PPP, 602–609
    data circuit-terminating equipment (DCE), 598
    data terminal equipment (DTE), 598
    debugging, 605
    DECnet Control Protocol (DNCP), 72
    dedicated links, 73
    dial strings, 611
    dial-on-demand routing (DDR), 686, 692
    dialer groups, 613, 614, 617
    dialer lists, 608
    dialer maps, 601, 608, 611, 615, 617
    enabled links, 73
    encapsulation, 510, 617
    fragmentation, 73
    frame check sequence (FCS), 600
    frames, 600, **600**
    high level data link control (HDLC), 598–599
    hold-queue timers, 613
    idle timer, 602–603, 607
    IP addressing, 598, 600, 602, 607, 611, 614
    IP control protocol (IPCP), 71, 72
    IPV6 Control Protocol (IPv6CP), 72
    IPX Control Protocol (IPXCP), 72
    IPX, 325–331

IPXWAN, 354, 355
ISDN, 602, 606, 607, 610, 614, 616, 633, 637, 639, 641
link control protocol (LCP), 70, 509–510, 599–600
link establishment, 71
link quality, 71
load, 603–604
logical link control (LLC), 600
maximum received reconstructed unit (MRRU), 601
Microsoft PPP CHAP (MS-CHAP, 71
monitoring, 606, 608–609, 615
multilink PPP (MP), 72–74, 601–609
NBCP, 72
NBFCP, 72
NetBEUI over PPP, 618–624
network control protocol (NCP), 70, 71, 72, 509–510, 599
next hop, 603
OSI Control Protocol (OSICP), 72
password authentication protocol (PAP), 71, 510, 602, 610
point-to-point protocol (PPP) Callback, 609–618
primary rate interface (PRI), 601, 604
protocol data units (PDU), 601
protocol negotiation, 71
protocols supported, 603, 611, 617
rotary groups, 601, 603, 604, 607, 613
routers and routing, 608, 611, 615, 617
service profile identifiers (SPIDs), 607
Shiva Password Authentication Protocol (SPAP), 72
switching, 606, 614
virtual connections, 73
poison reverse, with split horizon, 181
political issues in network design, 92
port-based VLAN, 85
positive acknowledgment, 38
PPP Callback, 609–618
    addressing, 611, 614
    authentication, 610, 612, 614
    basic rate interface (BRI), 610, 616
    CHAP, 610, 617
    client and server for, 609–612, 615, 617
    configuration, 610–618, 61
    copy configuration, 618
    debugging, 613
    dial strings, 611
    dialer groups, 613, 614, 617
    dialer maps, 611, 615, 617
    encapsulation, 617
    hold-queue timers, 613
    IP addressing, 611, 614
    ISDN, 610, 614, 616
    monitoring, 615
    PAP, 610
    protocols, 611, 617
    rotary groups, 613
    routers, 611, 615, 617
    switching, 614
PPP Multilink (MP), ISDN, 638
preferred peer, data link switching (DLSw+), 753
preferred port, data link switching (DLSw+), 753
prefix for addresses, NetWare link services protocol (NLSP), 361
Presentation layer, 24, 40
presentation services access point (PSAP), 29
primary rate interface (PRI)
    ISDN, 59, 627, 646–650
    point-to-point protocol (PPP), 601, 604

prioritizing traffic, frame relay, 579, 586–590, **589**
priority negotiation, ISDN, 630
priority policies, IPX, 379
priority queuing, 290, 306–309, 379, 479–481
private IP addresses, 154, 168–169
private leased lines, wide area networks (WAN), 14
private networks
    asynchronous transfer mode (ATM), 662
    wide area networks (WAN), 14
privileged EXEC mode, 98, 100–101
privileged mode command list, 105–106
profiles, OSI, 30
prompts to setup dialog for routers, 125
protocol assemblers (PAD), 13
protocol data unit (PDU)
    point-to-point protocol (PPP), 601
    switched multimegabit data service (SMDS), 654, 657
    X.25, 58
protocol identifiers, open shortest path first (OSPF), 200
protocol negotiation, point-to-point protocol (PPP), 71
protocol VLAN (PVLAN), 85
protocol-dependent modules, enhanced IGRP (EIGRP), 234
protocols, 17–18
proxy ARP, 44–45
pseudo-ring, source route translational bridging (SR/TLB), 741
pseudonodes, NetWare link services protocol (NLSP), 346
public data networks (PDN), 652
public networks, asynchronous transfer mode (ATM), 662
public switched telephone networks (PSTN), 515, 678

Q

Q-series protocols, ISDN, 627
qualified logical link control (QLLC), 538, 752
quality of service (QoS), 23
    asynchronous transfer mode (ATM), 74, 671–672, 674, 675
    LAN switches, 89
    wide area networks (WAN), 15, 519
question mark at system prompt, 98
queued packet synchronous exchange (QPSX), 11
queuing, 289–291, 305–315, 379, 380, 479–485, 576

R

RAM/DRAM, routers, 97
rate queues, asynchronous transfer mode (ATM), 673, 674
RDA, 31
reachability information, border gateway protocol-4 (BGP-4), 224
receipt confirmation, NetWare link services protocol (NLSP), 345
recognized private operations agencies (RPOA), X.25, 558
redirect messages, IP protocol, 173
redirector, IPX, 337
redistribution of routes, 269–284
    access lists, 271–272
    bandwidth, 271
    enhanced IGRP, 270, 272–278
    IGRP, 270, 272–278
    IPX, 379
    metrics, 270, 271
    NetWare link services protocol (NLSP), 362
    open shortest path first (OSPF), 270, 278–284, **279**
    routing information protocol (RIP), 270, 278–284, **279**
redundancy in LAN switches, 89
reference points, ISDN, 628–629, **629**
registration of IP addresses, 151, 160–161
regular expressions, X.25, 559–560

reliability, 7, 26, 167, 237, 457
reliable transport protocol (RTP), enhanced IGRP (EIGRP), 234
remote access, wide area networks (WAN), 16
remote access client (RAS client), NetBEUI over PPP, 619
remote bridges, 82, 704
remote source route bridging (RSRB), 702, 747–750
    source route translational bridging (SR/TLB), 743
remote switching, X.25, 544–546, 544
remote transparent bridging, 712
repeater, 9, 10, 78
reply packets, enhanced IGRP (EIGRP), 236
request packet,
    enhanced IGRP (EIGRP), 236
    open shortest path first (OSPF), 206, 206
    routing information protocol (RIP), 185
request priority, 34
resource management, 2
response packets, routing information protocol (RIP), 185
response time, 7
reverse address resolution protocol (RARP), 45, 121
reverse charging, X.25, 557
RFC1027 (See proxy ARP)
ring topology of, 9
RIP (See routing information protocol (RIP)
RIPng for IPv6, 189–191, 190
ROM in routers, 97, 98
ROM monitor configuration, routers, 130
ROM monitor mode, routers, 102
root cost, transparent bridging, 715
rotary groups
    dial-on-demand routing (DDR), 678, 685–689
    ISDN, 636
    point-to-point protocol (PPP), 601, 603, 604, 607, 613
    point-to-point protocol (PPP) Callback, 613
round-robin routing, NetWare link services protocol (NLSP), 335
route maps, 130, 265–268
route recomputation, enhanced IGRP (EIGRP), 457
route table entry (RTE), routing information protocol
    (RIP)ng, 190, 190
route tag, routing information protocol version 2 (RIP-2), 188
routeD, 174
router ID, open shortest path first (OSPF), 199, 213
router links, open shortest path first (OSPF), 199, 200, 208
router priority, open shortest path first (OSPF), 199
routers and routing, 13, 27, 42, 43, 35–36, 36, 55, 82–84,
    83, 95–147, 326
    accessing configuration,138–147
    address management, 122, 122, 167–168
    advertising routes, 174
    AppleTalk, 424–429, 433–453, 440–443
    asynchronous transfer mode (ATM), 97, 671
    AutoInstall, 120–122, 121,
    autonomous systems (AS), 161, 174, 175, 176
    auxiliary port, 96, 97
    backup of IOS image, 131
    basic rate interface (BRI), 97
    Bootstrap protocol (BOOTP), 121
    bridges vs., 84., 705–709, 706
    broadcast storms, 153
    carrier detect signal, 146
    channel interface protocol (CIP), 97
    Cisco Discovery Protocol (CDP), 138–141, 139
    classless inter-domain routing (CIDR), 163–166, 164
    command lists, 105–106

command modes, 98–103
configuration control flowchart, 133
configuration files, 127–133
configuration, 96–97, 96, 120–138, 120
console port, 96
context-sensitive help, 106–108
controller configuration, 129
convergence time, 177–178
copy flash tftp command, 132
copy running-config startup-config command, 137–138
copy running-config tftp command, 134
copy startup-config running-config command, 134–135
copying IOS, 131
count-to-infinity problem, 179–181, 179, 180
cursor movement, 109
data link switching (DLSw+), 750
debug commands, 146, 147
dial-on-demand routing (DDR), 678, 680, 684, 688, 690,
    693, 510–511
distance vector routing, 177–182, 178
distilled configuration, 118
domain name server (DNS), 121
DOS file names, 134
editing commands, 108–109
encapsulation, 102, 120, 123
enhanced editing commands, 108–109
entering commands, 129
erase startup-config command, 135
error control, 146, 147
Ethernet, 97, 120, 122, 123
examining status of router, 110–120
EXEC mode, 98, 99, 100
FDDI, 97, 122
FEIP, 97
fiber distributed data interface (FDDI), 120
filtering, 83
flash memory, 97, 131
flooding, 183
frame relay, 61, 67, 120, 564, 572, 579
global configuration mode, 101, 128–130
global parameters, 125
hello packets, 182–183
help, 105, 106–108
high level data link control (HDLC), 120
history of commands entered, 107–108
HSSI, 97
initial configuration, 120
initialization, 98–193
interface command, 123
interface configuration, 129
interface configuration mode, 101
interfaces, 97
internal configuration components, 98
Internet Protocol next gen (IPng), 166–167
Internet Protocol version 6 (IPv6), 166–167
IP addressing, 122, 122, 123, 134
IPX router configuration, 130
ISDN, 628–629, 631, 636, 641, 642, 648, 649
keepalive frames, 146
line configuration, 130
link state routing, 182–184
local area networks (LAN), 11
logging in/out, 103–104
management, 167

map-list configuration, 129–130
merging configuration information, 134–135
MIP, 97
multihoming, 161
naming files, 134
naming the router, 136–137
NetBEUI over PPP, 622
NetWare link services protocol (NLSP), 343–344
network command, 130
network configuration file, 134
network design, 167
network management stations, 97
NVRAM, 97, 98, 126
on-line help, 105
operating system image, 131
parameters, global, 125
passwords, 103–104, 135
permanent virtual circuits (PVC), 102
ping utility, 144–145
point-to-point protocol (PPP), 608, 611, 615, 617
point-to-point protocol (PPP) Callback, 611, 615, 617
poison reverse, with split horizon, 181
private IP addresses, 154, 168–169
privileged EXEC mode, 98, 100–101
privileged mode command list, 105–106
prompts to setup dialog, 125
question mark at system prompt, 98
RAM/DRAM, 97
reliability, 167
reverse address resolution protocol (RARP), 121
ROM, 97, 98
ROM monitor configuration, 130
ROM monitor mode, 102
route-map configuration, 130
routing information protocol (RIP), 159, 174
running configuration, 127, 128
scalability of network, 167
security, 167
serial interfaces, 97, 120
setup dialog, 124
Setup mode, 98
shortest path first (SPF) algorithm, 183–184, **184**
show buffers command, 110, 114–115
show cdp entry command, 140–141
show cdp neighbors command, 141
show flash command, 111, 115–116, 132
show interface command, 111, 116, 145–146
show ip command, 110
show ip protocol command, 117
show ip route command, 111, 119–120, 145
show memory command, 111, 114
show processes command, 110, 113
show protocols command, 110, 116–117
show running-config command, 111, 117–119, 128, 133
show start-up command, 117–119
show startup-config command, 111, 127–128, 135
show version command, 110, 111–112
SLARP, 121
SNA, 97
split horizon, 181, **181**, 580–581
startup configuration files, 127
startup sequence, **99**
static routing, 175–177
static subnetting, 159

subinterface configuration, 129
subinterface configuration mode, 101–102
subinterfaces, 101–102
subnet masks, 155–157, **156, 157,** 158, **158**
subnetting, 153, 154–155, 157–160, **159**
TELNET, 97, 138, 141–143
testing connectivity, 144–147
TFTP server, 97, 98, 121, 122, 123
token ring, 97, 120, 121, 122, 125
trace command, 145
triggered updates, 182
UNIX file names, 134
user datagram protocol (UDP), 133
user mode command list, 105
variable-length subnetting, 160
virtual circuits, 102
virtual terminals, 97, 141–143
wide area networks (WAN), 508–509, 515
word help, 106
working storage, 97
X.25, 59, 539, 544–546, 559
routing algorithms, 35
routing areas, NetWare link services protocol (NLSP), 343, 344, 360–361
routing information protocol (RIP), 159, 174, 175, 184–187, **186,** 326
   active vs. passive (silent) mode, 185
   AppleTalk, 437
   Berkeley Software Distribution (BSD), 185
   enhanced IGRP (EIGRP), 234, 240
   frame relay, 592
   IPX, 325, 379
   IPXWAN, 347
   MAC addresses, 185
   NetWare link services protocol (NLSP), 342, 343, 350–351, 360, 367–373
   packets, 186, **186**
   redistribution of routes, 270, 278–284, **279**
   request packets, 185
   response packet, 185
   routing information protocol version 2 (RIP-2) and, 189
   subnet masks, 186
   user datagram protocol (UDP), 185
   versions of, 185
routing information protocol version 2 (RIP-2), 187–190, **188**
   addressing, 188
   authentication, 188
   classless interdomain routing (CIDR), 187
   elective status of, 187
   gateD, 189
   hop count, 188
   message format, 187–188, **188**
   next hop, 188
   route tag, 188
   routing information protocol (RIP) with, 189
   routing information protocol (RIP)ng for IPv6, 189–191
   subnet masks, 188
   versions of, 187
routing policy, border gateway protocol-4 (BGP-4), 219
routing table filters, IPX, 386
routing table maintenance protocol (RTMP)
   AppleTalk, 417, 419, 434, 436–437, **436**
   enhanced IGRP (EIGRP), 458
routing table protocol (RTP), enhanced IGRP (EIGRP), 460

routing tables, 35
 AppleTalk, 478
 border gateway protocol (BGP), 251
 enhanced IGRP (EIGRP), 233, 234, 237, 238–239, 460–465
 IP protocol, 173
 open shortest path first (OSPF), 198, 210–215
running configuration, routers, 127, 128

S

S reference/S bus, ISDN, 640
SAP advertising, frame relay, 592
SAP filters, IPX, 387, 396–404, **398**
scalability, 6, 167
 Ethernet, 47
 wide area networks (WAN), 513–525,
 X.25, 555–561
screening addresses, switched multimegabit data service
 (SMDS), 655
SDLC, 377
security, 7, 35, 81, 167, 376, 377, 655
seed routers, AppleTalk, 429–431, **431, 432**
segment sequencing, IPX, 336
segmentation and reassembly sublayer (SAR), asynchronous
 transfer mode (ATM), 664
segmenting/network segments, 23, 78, 85, **86,** 287
semaphores, IPX, 338
send sequence numbers, ISDN, 631
sequence, 23, 27
sequenced packet exchange (SPX), 325–327
sequenced packet protocol (SPP), 336
serial compression, 522–524
serial encapsulation protocols, 520–522
serial interface, 97, 120, 330
Serial Line IP (SLIP), frame relay, 69–70
server-centric architecture of NetWare, 334
service access point identifier (SAP-ID), 29
service access points (SAP), 28–29, 288, 376
 IPX, 330
 IPXWAN, 347
 NetWare link services protocol (NLSP), 342, 343, 363
service advertisement protocol (SAP), 326
 enhanced IGRP (EIGRP), 234, 240
 frame relay, 592–593
 IPX, 325, 378, 379
 NetWare link services protocol (NLSP), 334–336
service data unit (SDU)
 asynchronous transfer mode (ATM), 663
 switched multimegabit data service (SMDS), 656
service profile identifiers (SPIDs), 643
 ISDN, 635, 636
 point-to-point protocol (PPP), 607
service providers, 25, 506–507
service specific convergence sublayer (SSCS), asynchronous
 transfer mode (ATM), 664
service users, 25
services, 22, 25
 connection-oriented network, 27
 connectionless networks, 27
Session layer, 24, 39
 AppleTalk, 418
session tables, NetBEUI over PPP, 621, 624
sessions, border gateway protocol (BGP), 216, 253
setup dialog, 124
Setup mode for routers, 98

shell, NetWare, IPX, 337
Shiva Password Authentication Protocol (SPAP), 72
shortest path first (SPF) algorithm, 183–184, **184**
 NetWare link services protocol (NLSP), 346, 352, 361
 open shortest path first (OSPF), 198
shortest-path tree, 198, 210
show buffers command, 110, 114–115
show cdp entry command, 140–141
show cdp neighbors command, 141
show flash command, 111, 115–116, 132
show interface command, 111, 116, 145–146
show ip command, 110
show ip protocol command, 117
show ip route command, 111, 119–120, 145
show memory command, 111, 114
show processes command, 110, 113
show protocols command, 110, 116–117
show running-config command, 111, 117–119, 128, 133
show start-up command, 117–119
show startup-config command, 111, 127–128, 135
show version command, 110, 111–112
signaling system 7 (SS7), wide area networks (WAN), 506
simple and efficient AAL (SEAL) scheme, asynchronous
 transfer mode (ATM), 664
simple flow control, frame relay, 570
simple network management protocol (SNMP), ISDN, 633
simplex communication, 39
single process routers, NetWare link services protocol
 (NLSP), 361–367
single-homed border gateway protocol (BGP), 261–262
size of networks, 91
SLARP, routers, 121
slot numbers, ISDN, 648
SMDS data units (SDUS), 652
SMDS Interface Protocol (SIP)
 switched multimegabit data service (SMDS), 655–657
 wide area networks (WAN), 519
snooping, 88
sockets
 AppleTalk, 419–420
 IPX, 331
SoHo and Ethernet, 50
SONET, 661, 662, 664, 674
source address broadcasts, 153
source address validation, switched multimegabit data service (SMDS), 655
source quench messages, IP protocol, 173
source route bridges (SRB), 81, 702, 707, 709–711, 721–727
 802.5, 721
 all routes explorer, 722
 explorers, 721–722, 724
 local ring test frame explorer, 721–722
 Multiport SRB configuration, 723–727
 OSI reference model, 721
 spanning explorer, 721–722, 724
 spanning tree algorithm, 724
 token ring, 721–727
source route translational bridging (SR/TLB), 702, 709–711,
 741–746
 addressing, 742
 configuration, 743–746
 embedded addresses, 742
 encapsulation, 743
 Ethernet, 742–746

explorers, 741–742
FDDI, 742, 743
half bridges, 743
MAC addresses, 742
pseudo-ring, 741
remote source route bridging (RSRB), 743
token ring, 742–746
WAN, 743
source route transparent (SRT) bridges, 81–82, 702, 709–711, 736–741
all routes explorer, 736, 740
configuration, 738–741
explorers, 736, 740
local ring test frame, 736
spanning explorer, 736, 740
token ring, 736–741
spanning explorer
source route bridging, 721–722, 724
source route transparent bridging, 736, 740
spanning tree algorithm/protocol, 317–318, 705
bridging, 709
concurrent routing and bridging (CRB), 730, 732–733
dial-on-demand routing (DDR), 699
source route bridging, 724
transparent bridging, 713–717, **717**, 717
speakers, border gateway protocol-4 (BGP-4), 216, **217**
special case (reserved) addresses, 151, 152–154
split horizon, 181, **181**, 580–581
spoofing
dial-on-demand routing (DDR), 698
IPX, 336–337
switched multimegabit data service (SMDS), 655
SPX, NetWare link services protocol (NLSP), 342
SQL Access Group (SAG), 18
standards, 6–7, 30, 89, 93, 626
standards compliance mode, data link switching (DLSw+), 751
star topology, 8, **9**, 67, **68**
startup configuration files, routers, 127
states,
enhanced IGRP (EIGRP), 461
open shortest path first (OSPF), 195
static mapping, frame relay, 572–574
static routing, 175–177
border gateway protocol (BGP), 258–260
enhanced IGRP (EIGRP), 245–246
static subnetting, 159
status messages, frame relay, 570
status of router, 110–120
store-and-forward, 27
strategy of network design, 93
stub areas, open shortest path first (OSPF), 194
subaddressing
ISDN, 640
X.25, 533
subinterface configuration, 101–102, 129
frame relay, 579, 581–586, **583**
IPX, 333
sublayers in OSI model, 31–34
subnet masks, 155–158, **156, 157, 158**
enhanced IGRP (EIGRP), 232, 240
routing information protocol (RIP), 186
routing information protocol version 2 (RIP-2), 188
subnetting, 23, 82, 153–155, 157–160, **159**
asynchronous transfer mode (ATM), 74–75

enhanced IGRP (EIGRP), 233, 240, 456
Subnetwork Access Protocol (SNAP)
bridging, 710
frame relay, 65
IPX, 330
subnetwork point of attachment (SNPA), asynchronous transfer mode (ATM), 662
subscriber network interface (SNI), switched multimegabit data service (SMDS), 653, **654**
summarization of routes, 288, 376, 476
enhanced IGRP (EIGRP), 233, 246–247, 456
NetWare link services protocol (NLSP), 361, 366
summary link advertisement, OSPF, 199, **200**, 208, 213, **213**
super frame, ISDN, 648
supervisory frames, ISDN, 631
switched digital services, 13, 15
switched multimegabit data service (SMDS), 520, 652–660, 652
802.3, 652
802.5, 652
access classes, 653–65, 653
access DQDB, 655
address resolution protocol (ARP), 659, 660
address screening, 655
address spoofing, 655
addressing, 654, 655, 658, 659
asynchronous transfer mode (ATM), 664
broadband ISDN (BISDN), 655
broadcasting, 659
carrier equipment, 653
cell relay, 652
channel service unit (CSU), 652
client and server, 652
compression, 523
configuration, 657–660
customer premises equipment (CPE), 653, 654
data service unit (DSU), 652
digital signal 1 (DS-1), 652
digital signal 3 (DS-3), 652
distributed processing, 652
distributed queue dual bus (DQDB), 655, **656**
fiber distributed data interface (FDDI), 652
fiber-based media, 652
frames, 657
full mesh topology, 652
high speed serial interface (HPPI), 652
IP addressing, 658, 659
MANs, 655
media access control (MAC), 655
multicast addressing, 654, 655, 659
OSI reference model, **653**
packet switching, 652
physical layer convergence protocol (PLCP), 657
protocol data unit (PDU), 654, 657
public data networks (PDN), 652
screening addresses, 655
security, 655
service data units (SDU), 656
SMDS data units (SDUS), 652
SMDS interface protocol (SIP), 655, 656–657
source address validation, 655
spoofing addresses, 655
subscriber network interface (SNI), 653, **654**
switches, 655–657
topologies, 652

transmission system sublayer, 657
unicast addressing, 654, 658
wide area networks (WAN), 14, 15, 516, 518, 519, 652
switched virtual circuit (SVC), 28, 57
X.25, 540–542
frame relay, 62, 67–69, **69**
wide area networks (WAN), 506, 518
X.25, 532, 535, 548, 553, 556
switched virtual connections (SVC), 661
asynchronous transfer mode (ATM), 674, 675
switches and switching, 13, 42, 55, 84–85, 92–93, 643, 661
asynchronous transfer mode (ATM), 76, 663, 671–672
ATM vs. switched high-speed LAN, 90–91
campus switches, 88
dial-on-demand routing (DDR), 679
frame relay, 564, 590–592, **591**
ISDN, 626, 634, 635, 642, 645, 647, 650
LAN emulation (LANE), 669
LAN switches, 87–90
local area networks (LAN), 10, 11
point-to-point protocol (PPP) Callback, 614
point-to-point protocol (PPP), 606, 614
switched multimegabit data service (SMDS), 655–657
wide area networks (WAN), 507, 517
X.25, 58, 544–546, 555
synchronous digital hierarchy (SDH), asynchronous transfer
mode (ATM), 662
synchronization, 3, 38
synchronous data link control (SDLC)
data link switching (DLSw+), 752
wide area networks (WAN), 508
synchronous digital hierarchy (SDH), 661
syntax, 40
Systems Network Architecture (SNA), 2, **3**, 5, 18
data link switching (DLSw+), 750, 752
routers, 97

T

T1, 34
ISDN, 626, 633, 646, 648, 649, 650
wide area networks (WAN), 507, 518, 524–525
T1/DS1 facility, ISDN, 627
tagging, VLAN tagging, 88
TCP, 28, 37, 38
data link switching (DLSw+), 752
IPX, 337
TCP/IP, 16, 18, 35, 36, 37, 42, 84, 149–169
address management, 150
AppleTalk, 438–439
bridging, 703
data link switching (DLSw+), 752
enhanced IGRP (EIGRP), 233, 458
frame relay, 62
IP addressing (See IP addressing)
IPX, 324, 329
loopback addresses, 153–154
routing protocols (See entries for individual protocols),
171–247
X.25, 59, 544
TE1 (Type 1 Terminal Equipment), ISDN, 628
TE2 (Type 2 Terminal Equipment), ISDN, 628
Telnet, 13, 83
ISDN, 639
routers, 97, 138, 141–143

terminal access controller access control system (TACACS),
wide area networks (WAN), 516
terminal adapter (TA), 13
dial-on-demand routing (DDR), 678, 689
ISDN, 628
wide area networks (WAN), 507, 508
terminal equipment (TE), ISDN, 628
testing connectivity in routers, 144–147
text, 40
TFTP server, 97, 98, 121–123, 290
throughput, 7, 38–39
X.25, 555–557
tick values, 326, 335–336
time division multiplexing (TDM), 13, 506, 661
time exceeded messages, IP protocol, 173
time-to-live, 173, 319
timers, X.25, 550–551
timeslots, ISDN, 649
token bus, 34
token passing, 50–52, **51**
token ring, 34, 44, 50–52, **51**, 54–55, 378
AppleTalk, 414
asynchronous transfer mode (ATM)vs., 74, 76
bridging, 702, 703, 704, 709–711
data link switching (DLSw+), 751, 752, 753, 754–756
IPX, 325, 327, 328, 329, 330
local area networks (LAN), 10
Media Access Control (MAC), 33–34, **33**
Multiport SRB configuration, 723–727
open shortest path first (OSPF), 196
remote source route bridging (RSRB), 747–750
routers, 97, 120, 121, 122, 125
source route bridging, 721–727
source route translational bridging (SR/TLB), 741–746
source route transparent bridging, 736–741
TokenTalk, 414
TokenTalk Link Access Protocol (TLAP), 415
toll network, wide area networks (WAN), 507
topological database, open shortest path first (OSPF), 198
topologies, 288, 376, 652, 661
local area networks (LAN), 8–11, **9**
border gateway protocol-4 (BGP-4), 219
enhanced IGRP (EIGRP), 233, 236
frame relay, 67, **68**
topology table, enhanced IGRP (EIGRP), 236, 460–461
trace command, 145
traffic filters, dial-on-demand routing (DDR), 681–685
traffic management (See also filters; queuing), 285–321
aggregation of routes, 476
AppleTalk, 475–504
bridging, 289, 477
broadcast management, 315–321
complex internetworks, 287–289, 376–378, 476–477
compression, 477
concurrent routing and bridging (CRB), 477
congestion control, 290, 378–380, 477–478
dial-on-demand routing (DDR), 476
filtering, 289–305
frame relay, 64–65, 477
global topology, 288–289, 376, 476
interesting traffic, 476
internetworking growth and hierarchical design, 286–287,
287
IPX, 375–409

multiprotocol traffic, 290
nailed-up circuits, 476
non-routable traffic, 289, 477
overhead traffic, 290
packet switching, 477
queuing, 289–291, 479–485
security, 376
service access points (SAP), 376
summarization of routes, 376, 476
usage tracking, 288–289
X.25, 477
traffic policing, asynchronous transfer mode (ATM), 520
traffic shaping
 asynchronous transfer mode (ATM), 520, 673
 frame relay, 64
traffic types, border gateway protocol-4 (BGP-4), 218
transceiver, **9**, 31
transparent bridging, concurrent routing and bridging (CRB), 730
transit areas, open shortest path first (OSPF), 194
transit policies, border gateway protocol (BGP), 261–262, **262**
transit routing domains (TRDs), CIDR, 164–165
transition routing, AppleTalk, 429
translational bridging (TLB), 702
Transmission Control Protocol (TCP), 26, 251, 544–546
transmission convergence sublayer, asynchronous transfer
 mode (ATM), 662
transmission coordination, 3
transmission system sublayer, switched multimegabit data
 service (SMDS), 657
transparency, bridging, 703
transparent asynchronous Xmitter/receiver interface (TAXI), 661
transparent bridge routing, dial-on-demand routing (DDR), 694
transparent bridges (TB), 81, 702, 709–721
 802.3, 711
 bridge protocol data unit (BPDU), 716–717, **717**
 broadcast storms, 714
 configuration, 716, 717–721
 cost, root and path cost, 715
 dial-on-demand routing (DDR), 699
 encapsulation, 712
 Ethernet, 712, 713, 717–721
 FDDI, 712
 filtering, 712–713
 flooding, 713
 forwarding, 712–713, 720–721
 half bridges, 712
 HDLC, 712
 LAN, 713
 learning bridges, 712–713
 loops, loop avoidance, 713–717, **717**
 MAC addresses, 712
 monitoring, 720
 packets, 712
 remote transparent bridging, 712
 spanning-tree algorithm, 713–717, **717**
 WAN, 712
transport layer, 23–24, 36–39, **37**
 AppleTalk, 415–417
tree topology of, **9**
trigger for DDR calls, dial-on-demand routing (DDR), 679
triggered updates, 182
TS-013 switch, ISDN, 626
tunneling
 AppleTalk, 417, 438–440, **438**, 443–453

frame relay, 590
IPX, 396, 404–409, **406**
wide area networks (WAN), 16
X.25, 530
turboflooding, 319
type of service (ToS), open shortest path first (OSPF),
 197–198, 212

U

unicast addressing, 151
 enhanced IGRP (EIGRP), 459
 LAN emulation (LANE), 667, 668
 switched multimegabit data service (SMDS), 654, 658
UNIX, 134, 174
unnumbered frames, ISDN, 631
unreliable links, frame relay, 565
UPDATE message, border gateway protocol-4 (BGP-4), 221,
 223, 224, **225**
update packets, enhanced IGRP (EIGRP), 235
uplinks, 88
usage tracking, 288–289
user datagram protocol (UDP), 133
 AppleTalk, 438–439
 broadcast management, 319–320
 flooding, turboflooding, 319
 IPX, 337
 routing information protocol (RIP), 185
user facilities, calling, X.25, 556–559
user mode command list, 105
user-to-network interface (UNI), 61
UTP category 3 cables, Ethernet, 47

V

V.25bis dialing
 dial-on-demand routing (DDR), 678
 ISDN, 633
Van Jacobsen algorithm for compression, 523
variable-length subnet masks (VLSM), enhanced IGRP
 (EIGRP), 240
variable-length subnetting, 160
VAX systems, 3–4
VC Mux, asynchronous transfer mode (ATM), 672
video, 6
videoconferencing, 40
VINEs
 asynchronous transfer mode (ATM), 672
 dial-on-demand routing (DDR), 694, 696
 LAPB, 522
 X.25, 538
virtual channel connections (VCC), 665–667
virtual channel identifier (VCI), asynchronous transfer mode
 (ATM), 75, 663, 672
virtual channels
 asynchronous transfer mode (ATM), 76
 X.25, 59
virtual circuit identifier (VCI), X.25, 531
virtual circuit number (VCN), X.25, 531, 540–542
virtual circuit status messages, frame relay, 569
virtual circuits, 27, 57
 asynchronous transfer mode (ATM), 75
 frame relay, 61, 62, 67–69, **69**, 564–569, 572, 573, 590
 routers, 102
 wide area networks (WAN), 15, 506, 518
 X.25, 58, 530–532, **531**, 535, 540–542, 548, 551, 553, 556

virtual connections, 661
  point-to-point protocol (PPP), 73
virtual file system, IPX, 337
virtual LAN (VLAN), 85, 87, 91
  asynchronous transfer mode (ATM), 74
  tagging, 88
virtual links, open shortest path first (OSPF), 192–194, **194**
virtual loadable modules (VLM), IPX, 337
virtual path identifier (VPI), asynchronous transfer mode
  (ATM), 75, 663, 672, 674
virtual paths, 27, 663
virtual private networks (VPN), 16
virtual terminals, 97, 141–143
VN2/VN3 switches, ISDN, 626
voice, 6

W

WAN links, 290
  AppleTalk, 478
  bridging, 704
  NetWare link services protocol (NLSP), 343, 363
watchdog keepalive packets, IPX, 336–337,
Web development, 19, 40
weighted fair queuing, 290, 306–307, 312–315, 379, 479,
  484–485
weighting of routes, border gateway protocol (BGP), 220,
  264–266
wide area network (WAN), 3–5, 11–16, **12,** 55–78, 505–525, 652
  access servers, 13
  asynchronous transfer mode (ATM), 11, 15, 74–78, 514,
    518, 519
  ATM switches, 13
  bandwidth, 506, 514
  bridging, 702, 704
  broadcasting, 518
  cell relay, 11, 13, 15, 518–519
  central office (CO), 507
  channel service unit (CSU), 13, 57, 507, 515, 516
  channelized T1/E1, 524–525
  connection services, 515
  connection-oriented services in, 28
  customer premises equipment (CPE), 507
  cyclic redundancy check (CRC), 506–507, 518
  data circuit terminating equipment (DCE), 57, 507–508
  data link switching (DLSw+), 750, 752
  data service unit (DSU), 57, 507, 515, 516
  data terminal equipment (DTE), 57, 507–508
  dedicated lines, 515
  dedicated services, 14
  demarcation, 507
  dial up lines, 14
  dial up private networks, 13
  dial-on-demand routing (DDR), 116–117, 510–511, 515, 516
  dial-up connections, 515
  digital service units (DSU), 13
  digital signal 1 (DS-1), 519
  digital subscriber line (DSL), 14–15
  E1, 507, 524–525
  encapsulation, 520–522
  enhanced IGRP (EIGRP), 240
  Fast Serial Interface Processor (FSIP), 524
  frame relay, 11, 13, 15, 61–69, **62,** 506, 508, 516, 518,
    520, 564, 565, 566
  high level data link control (HDLC), 508, 520–522, 525

integrated services digital network (ISDN), 13, 15, 59–61, 506
interfacing with service providers, 507–508
Internet, 14, 15, 16
IPX, 517
ISDN, 507, 508, 515
LAN emulation (LANE), 76–78
LAN vs., 56
leased lines, 56–57, 515
leased–line private networks, 13
link access procedure, balanced (LAPB), 508, 520–522
local loop, 507
local management interface (LMI), 518
modems, 13, 14, 507, 515
Multichannel Interface Processor (MIP), 524
multiplexers, 13
network termination 1 (NT1), 507
network terminators (NT), 13
nonbroadcast multi-access environments (NBMA), 517
packet assembler/disassembler (PAD), 57
packet switching, 11, 13, 15
packet switching exchange (PSE), 57, 517
packet-switched networks (PSN), 516–520
packet-switching, 515, 516–520
packets, 517
permanent virtual circuits (PVC), 57, 506, 518
plain old telephone service (PTOS), 506
point-to-point protocol (PPP), 56, 509–510, 520–522
private leased lines, 14
private networks, 14
protocol assemblers (PAD), 13
protocols, 56
PSTN, 515
quality of service (QoS), 15, 519
remote access, 16
remote source route bridging (RSRB), 747–750
routers, 13, 55, 508–509, 515
scalability, 513–525
serial compression, 522–524
serial encapsulation protocols, 520–522
service providers for, 506–507
signaling system 7 (SS7), 506
switched multimegabit data service (SMDS), 14, 15, 516,
  518–520
SMDS Interface Protocol (SIP), 519
source route translational bridging (SR/TLB), 743
switched digital services, 13, 15
switched virtual circuits (SVC), 57, 506, 518
switches, 13, 55, 507, 517
synchronous data link control (SDLC), 508
T1, 507, 518, 524–525
Telnet, 13
terminal access controller access control system
  (TACACS), 516
terminal adapters (TA), 13, 507–508
time division multiplexing (TDM), 13, 506
toll network, 507
transparent bridging, 712
tunneling, 16
virtual circuits, 15, 57, 506, 518
virtual private networks (VPN), 16
wireless, 16
X.25, 13, 15, 57–59, 506, 507, 508, 516, 518, 520, 555
wide area telephone services (WATS), ISDN, 626
wildcard masks, enhanced IGRP (EIGRP), 245

window size (packets), in X.25, 543, 548, 553, 555–556
windowing, 38–39
Windows Open Services Architecture (WOSA) (Microsoft), 18
wireless wide area networks (WAN), 16
withdrawn routes in border gateway protocol-4 (BGP-4), 226–227, **228**
word help for routers, 106
working storage in routers, 97

X

X Windows Systems, 39
X.121 addressing, in X.25, 533, **533,** 535, 539, 550, 553, 545–546, 555
X.22, ISDN, 637
X.25, 13, 23, 27, 35, 57–59, 289, 377, 477, 520, 527–561
  addressing, 533, 547
  adjacency, 560
  Apollo, 538
  AppleTalk, 538
  bandwidth, 547, 552, 555–556
  Bridge, 538
  call user data (CUD) packets, 545–546, 559
  CLNS, 538
  closed user group (CUG), 556
  compressed TCP, 538
  compression, 523
  configuration of, 537–554
  congestion, 555
  cyclic redundancy check (CRC), 551
  data carrier detect (DCD), 551
  data circuit-terminating equipment (DCE), 528, **529,** 530, 531, 534, 535, 536, 540–541
  data terminal equipment (DTE), 528, **529,** 531, 532, 534, 535, 536, 540–541
  datagrams, 58, 530
  DECnet, 538
  delay, 557
  encapsulation, 58, 532, 534–538, **534,** 547, 552
  error control, 551
  extended packet sequence numbering, 543
  flow control, 547, 555–556
  fragmentation, 58
  frame check sequence (FCS), 537
  frame relay vs., 65, 564
  frames, 535, 537
  general format identifier (GFI), 535
  idle periods, 548
  idle time, 553
  IP, 538
  IP addressing, 547, 548, 552, 553
  IPX, 538
  IPXWAN, 354
  ISDN, 61
  link access procedure, balanced (LAPB), 530, 534, 536–537, **536**
  logical channel identifier (LCI), 535, 540–542
  logical channel number (LCN), 531
  mapping addresses, 553, 558
  modems, 528
  monitoring, 547–551, 554
  multiplexing, 531–532
  network terminal number (NTN), 533
  network user identification, 558
  open shortest path first (OSPF), 560–561

  OSI reference model and, 530
  packet assembler/disassembler (PAD), 528, **529,** 530, 538
  packet network carriers, 558
  packet size, 542–543, 552, 555–557
  packet switched network (PSN), 528, **529**
  packet switching, 58, 528
  packet switching exchange (PSE), 528, **529,** 532–533
  packet type identifier (PTI), 535
  packet-layer protocol (PLP), 530, 531, 535
  pattern matching, 559–560
  permanent virtual circuits (PVC), 532, 540–542, 557
  protocol data units (PDU), 58
  protocol suite for, 530, **530**
  protocols, 538, 540
  QLLC, 538
  recognized private operations agencies (RPOA), 558
  regular expressions, 559–560
  remote switching, 544–546
  reverse charging, 557
  routers, 59, 539, 544–546, 559
  scalability, 555–561
  session initiation, 528
  subaddressing, 533
  switched virtual circuits (SVC), 532, 535, 540–542, 548, 553, 556
  switching, 58, 544–546, 555
  TCP/IP, 59, 544
  throughput, 555–557
  timers, 550–551
  transmission control protocol (TCP), 544–546
  tunneling, 530
  user facilities, calling, 556–559
  VINES, 538
  virtual channels, 59
  virtual circuit identifier (VCI), 531
  virtual circuit number (VCN), 531, 540–542
  virtual circuits, 58, 530–532, **531,** 535, 540–542, 548, 551, 553, 556, 557
  wide area networks (WAN), 15, 506, 507, 508, 516, 518, 555
  window size, 543, 548, 553, 555–556
  X.121 addresses, 533, **533,** 535, 539, 545–546, 550, 553, 555
  X.25 Transport Protocol (XTP), 59, **60**
  X.25-over-TCP (XOT), 544–546
  X.2bis, 531
  XNS, 538
X.25 Transport Protocol (XTP), X.25, 59, **60**
X.25-over-TCP (XOT), X.25, 544–546
X.2bis, X.25, 531
X.31 for X.25 packets, ISDN, 61
X.400, 31
X/Open Group, 18, 31
Xerox Network systems (XNS)
  IPX, 324, 336
  LAPB, 522
  X.25, 538
XN bridging, 703

Z

ZIP filters, AppleTalk, 494
zone information protocol (ZIP), AppleTalk, 418–419, 477–478
zone information table (ZIT), AppleTalk, 419
zones, AppleTalk, **419–422**